THE PARAMEDIC MANUAL

JONATHAN GREENWALD

Morton Publishing Company
925 West Kenyon Avenue, Unit 12
Englewood, Colorado 80110

10 9 8 7 6 5 4 3 2

Printed in the United States of America

ISBN: 0-89582-167-2

Contents

NOTICE

The author and publisher have taken great care to ensure that all drug dosages, indications, contraindications (other drug information), guidelines for treating patients, and all other information in this book are accurate and in accord with the Department of Transportation's Paramedic guidelines, American Heart Association's Advanced Cardiac Life Support recommendations, and Prehospital Trauma and Advanced Trauma Life Support guidelines at the time of publication. Users of this book are, however, advised to always check the manufacturer's product information sheet that is packaged with the respective products to be fully informed of changes in recommended dosages, contraindications, and other information prior to administration of medications. In addition, it is the user's responsibility to know and follow local care protocols as provided by the medical advisor of the emergency care system by which the EMT or paramedic is employed or volunteers for; and to stay informed of changes that take place in emergency care procedures.

Acknowledgements

I would like to express my appreciation to the following individuals who contributed significantly to this book:

Scott Bourn and Earl Hall for their critical review of the manuscript; Kathy Cohn for her review of both the OB/GYN and Geriatric chapters; Dr. Stewart Greisman for his evaluation of the manuscript and suggestions; Debra Scherger for her review of the Toxicology chapter; R. L. Cline for his medical support throughout this project; Dianne Borneman and Robert Lansky for their editing of the manuscript; Shadow Canyon Graphics for the book design and typography; Leslie Thorpe, Clare Barela, and all the sundry people and students who have helped in one way or another to make this a successful project.

This book is dedicated to my mother
and to the memory of my father,
and to all those who worked with me
at A-1 Ambulance Company in Boulder, Colorado

Preface

This textbook is a clear and precise presentation of the clinical aspects of today's paramedicine. It follows the latest Department of Transportation's (DOT) paramedic curriculum (1985). *The Paramedic Manual* is a comprehensive book that includes the 1987 American Heart Association (AHA) Advanced Cardiac Life Support (ACLS) protocols, and the most up-to-date information on medications, toxicology, and trauma management. This book contains pertinent information necessary for the training of paramedics. In addition, it may be used for study and review, and as a reference book.

This book contains twenty-one chapters and seven appendices. The appendices may be used as a quick reference guide. One of the latest advances in field care is the increased use of intraosseous infusions. The reader will find complete information on this topic in Appendix 7.

This manual was written primarily for the Emergency Medical Technician-Paramedic (EMT-P) in training or in preparation for recertification (either individually or in a refresher class). It may also be used by any Emergency Medical personnel involved with the treatment of the traumatically injured and acutely ill regardless of the level of training.

This book has many uses:

1. As a **textbook** for those who are in training to be Emergency Medical Technician-Paramedics, Emergency Medical Technician-Intermediates, or recertifying as either.
2. As a **reference** for the field paramedic.
3. As a **resource** for the EMT who wants additional information.
4. As a **useful aid** for the nursing staff of Emergency Departments and Intensive Care Units (ICUs) to familiarize themselves with EMT-P procedures.

The field paramedic has a demanding job — one that requires rapid and correct action. With constant study and practice, the paramedic will be able to maintain his/her knowledge and skill level.

Two cautions need to be heeded:

1. Changes occur rapidly in prehospital field care.
2. Treatment protocols around the country vary.

With this in mind, the paramedic must read current literature to keep updated on the changes that take place in the field and follow local protocols when differences in the treatment protocols are noted between the text and what is suggested "locally."

It is the intent of the author to aid the paramedic in gaining a greater understanding of the human body in health and in illness, and to teach the paramedic the best procedures for evaluating and treating the sick and injured patient. In this way, the paramedic will become a better practitioner of field medicine. This textbook can make the paramedic's education in the classroom and street and easier and more enjoyable experience.

Division One

Prehospital Environment

1

Medical and Legal Considerations

Legal issues are of increasing concern to the paramedic as the trend toward frequent litigation increases. Prehospital care providers are at as much risk as any other health care providers. Historically, only the physician carried the risk along with high insurance premiums. Now, the risk of litigation is more widespread. The paramedic is, and will continue to be, under more scrutiny than ever before. He/she must protect him/herself from liability. It is the responsibility of the paramedic to be familiar with local laws and regulations as well as legislation at the state level.

Naturally, the best way for the paramedic to protect him/herself is to provide appropriate assessment and medical treatment and to maintain accurate medical records.

MEDICAL LEGISLATION

The paramedic should be familiar with the following information in order to function within the limits of the law.

The Good Samaritan Act

Every state has some form of legislation that protects the ''Good Samaritan'' from liability when rendering first aid. Essentially, the Good Samaritan

Act encourages people to help those in need of aid. Each state has different definitions of first aid, where it may be rendered, and who may be considered a "Good Samaritan." In general, a person who provides first aid in a manner that any other prudent person with similar training would provide is covered by the Good Samaritan Act. Again, it should be noted that every state is different. In some states, EMS personnel are well protected by this type of legislation, and in other states they are not. The paramedic must be familiar with the statutes in his/her state.

The Medical Practice Act and State EMS Legislation

Each state legislates the specific procedures that EMS providers may perform, beginning at the first aid level and including paramedic activity. The EMT-P must be familiar with the practices allowed in his/her state.

Standard of Care

This is the level of practice identified as common and acceptable by law. The provider is generally held to the standard of care that others with similar training and experience must maintain.

Negligence/Omission

If the provider's treatment fails to meet the standards of care, four elements must be proven in order to show a paramedic liable for a lawsuit:

1. That there was a duty to perform.
2. That there was a breach of duty.
3. That there was damage (injury) done to the patient.
4. That there was proximate cause. (A casual relationship between the actions of the paramedic and the injury sustained by the patient.)

PATIENT CONSENT

Informed Consent

In order to receive informed consent, the paramedic must explain to a patient:

1. The nature of the illness or injury.
2. The recommended treatment and associated risks.

3. The alternative treatment and risks.
4. The dangers of refusing treatment.

In prehospital treatment, it is usually not necessary to give extensive explanation for informed consent. The paramedic should explain to the patient in simple terms the nature of the injury or illness and the treatment. In most cases, the patient will either verbally agree to the intended treatment or nonverbally agree to treatment by allowing the paramedic to provide care (e.g., extend an arm to allow the starting of an intravenous line [IV]).

Implied Consent

When a patient is unable to give conscious consent to treatment due to unconsciousness, mental alterations from drugs, intoxication from alcohol, trauma, shock, or mental disorder, it is assumed that if the patient is in need of emergency treatment, he/she **would agree to being treated** if he/she were conscious.

If the patient is a minor or is mentally incompetent, consent from a guardian is necessary. In an emergency situation, treatment may be rendered without a guardian's consent.

Patient Refusal

An alert, mentally competent adult has the right to refuse treatment. It is in the best interests of both the patient and the paramedic to encourage the patient to accept treatment. Communications with medical control can sometimes help. If all attempts to have a patient accept treatment fail, ask the injured person to sign a release form, or have a witness who observed the patient's refusal sign the form. Be sure to follow local protocol.

AREAS OF POTENTIAL LIABILITY

Abandonment

This means that a paramedic terminates care to a patient prematurely or does not provide for the orderly transfer of a patient by releasing him/her to a provider who can perform care of equal or better quality.

To avoid this accusation, do not begin providing care and then discontinue it prematurely, or do not release the patient to a provider who is not capable of caring properly for the patient.

Assault

Assault occurs when a paramedic creates apprehension by an unauthorized handling and treatment of the patient. This is most easily avoided by informing a patient of suggested treatment and by obtaining consent.

Battery

Battery is the touching and treating of the patient without consent. This may be avoided by obtaining consent.

False Imprisonment

This refers to intentional and unjustifiable detention and transport. It most commonly occurs with psychiatric cases. It may be prevented by showing evidence of medical necessity, by obtaining consent, and by following local protocols.

Libel

Libel is injury to a person's character, name, or reputation by false and malicious written accusations. This is easily prevented through **accurate** and **confidential** written reports.

Slander

Slander is injury of a person's character, name, or reputation by false and malicious spoken words. To avoid this accusation, limit oral reporting to the appropriate personnel.

THE MEDICAL REPORT

The medical report is a legal document. It is essential for the paramedic to maintain a thorough and accurate record for each and every patient treated (or released at the scene after treatment or because of patient refusal of treatment) in the field. There may come a time when a paramedic will be called to testify in court regarding the treatment of a patient. The paramedic's best protection is a carefully detailed and **legible** report. The information on the report should include:

1. The date and all appropriate times (time call received, response time, etc.).
2. Scene observations.

3. Physical findings.
4. History.
5. Treatment.

One of the most commonly used formats for writing the medical report is "S.O.A.P.". It is a simple way to accurately record a patient's case history.

S = subjective — this includes the patient's description of his/her chief complaint, the associated symptoms, the onset, the medications, the pertinent past medical history, and the patient's allergies. In addition, it includes any information taken from bystanders or relatives.

O = objective — this includes observations of the mechanism of injury and the condition of the patient. The condition consists of the level of consciousness, a description of the illness or injury(ies), vital signs, pertinent physical findings (both negative and positive) obtained from a head-to-toe examination, and electrocardiogram (ECG) findings.

A = assessment — what the paramedic believes is the cause of the patient's chief complaint or distress. Remember, the paramedic is not making a diagnosis but is suggesting the possible cause of the problem. In some cases, the cause is obvious (i.e., deformity of femur), so use of the word "possible" would not be necessary.

P = plan — what the paramedic intends to do, and what actually is done. This should include the complete treatment provided to the patient in detail: IV size, site, and fluid administered; all medications given in the order administered; procedures performed — splinting, spinal precautions, dressing/bandaging of wounds, oral or nasal endotrachial intubation, etc.; if electrocardiogram (ECG) is done, report findings. Describe any changes in patient's condition after treatment. Be specific.

MEDICAL LIABILITY PROTECTION

It is prudent for a paramedic to learn what kind of liability protection is provided by his/her employer. It is possible that the coverage is inadequate or does not cover the paramedic at all.

The best precaution is for the paramedic to take out an individual medical liability-protection policy. This policy will generally cover the emergency medical technician-paramedic's specific needs, and the underwriter will be an advocate for the policy holder (the paramedic). It is essential that the EMT-P understand the coverage provided and that he/she know how to report a potential liability case to the insurance company.

SUMMARY

This chapter is to educate the paramedic about his/her medical/legal obligations to the patient, thereby reducing the threat of litigation (i.e., being sued by the patient or his/her family). The paramedic should be familiar with his/her state's medical legislation, as well as with the role of patient consent when treating the sick and injured.

The EMT-P should be knowledgeable about the areas of greatest liability (i.e., abandonment, assault, slander, etc.). In addition, the paramedic should recognize the importance of the written report and its classifiction as a legal document.

If rescue personnel regard the rights of the patient, assess and treat him/her appropriately, and protect the patient's privacy, the chances of a court action will be reduced significantly. Naturally, the paramedic may still be sued (though not necessarily successfully). In order to best protect him/herself, the paramedic should know the extent of liability coverage provided by his/her employer and consider carrying additional personal liability insurance.

2

Scene Survey

A paramedic should protect him/herself from injury and death, since it is well known that an injured or dead paramedic is useless to a patient. In order to prevent mishap, the paramedic must observe the scene to determine if danger is present and if additional help (i.e., police, fire) is needed. The EMT-P should then see to the safety and welfare of the patient.

The paramedic must be observant of the many possible hazards that are present on the scene. He/she should evaluate the situation carefully to make correct decisions. Several factors must be taken into consideration

ENVIRONMENT

First, identify the presence of hazards. Then identify (if possible) the cause of the emergency and the immediate environmental dangers. Is the paramedic trained to handle the particular hazard that is found on the scene? If not, he/she must call for the agency that has trained personnel to deal with the problem. The paramedic should not endanger him/herself. The following are possible hazards that may be encountered in the field:

1. Fire or the potential for fire.
2. Hazardous materials — chemicals, gases, and/or radioactive material.
3. Traffic.
4. Weather — temperature and precipitation.

5. Water — lakes, rivers, streams, and floods.
6. Ice rescue — frozen bodies of water.

HOSTILE SITUATION

This can sometimes be anticipated by information received from dispatch. In these cases, wait for police cover. The EMT-P should make sure that the police have secured the scene before entering.

Domestic disputes are common and are one of the most volatile situations that both EMT-Ps and police face in the field.

The following are possible situations for the paramedic to beware of:

1. In an assault or other possible crime scene, be sure that the perpetrator's location is known or that he/she is captured.
2. Is the patient cooperative or hostile?
3. If there are bystanders, what is their mood? Are they hostile or supportive?

TYPES OF CASES

The paramedic may find him/herself in a variety of situations in the field. The paramedic should consider answers to the following questions when evaluating the scene.

1. Where is the patient located?
2. Is the situation an **acute** emergency?
3. Is the situation an **urgent** emergency?
4. Is the situation **nonurgent**?
5. Is backup needed and available?
6. Are additional personnel needed?
7. Is additional transport needed?
8. Is extrication equipment needed?
9. Does the EMT-P need protection?
10. Does the patient need protection?

CLASSIFICATION OF THE CASE

1. Medical.

2. Traumatic.
3. Behavioral.
4. Obstetrical/gynecological (OB/GYN).
5. Mass-casualty incident (MCI).

TRIAGE

Triage is a French word that means "to sort." To the paramedic, it means sorting of medical problems (either in the multiple-patient situation or the multiple-trauma patient) according to the treatment priorities. In addition, triage can also be a prioritizing of injured, wounded, or sick persons in order to **ensure the efficient use of** rescue manpower, EMS personnel, medical and nursing staff, and equipment and facilities. The goal of triaging is to do the greatest good for the greatest number of patients. Triage is used when there are more patients than the medical personnel can handle immediately.

Various systems are used to prioritize patients for both treatment and evacuation. One premise to keep in mind is that the survival of life takes precedence over the survival of limb. Another point to remember is that the most common threats to life are asphyxia and hemorrhage.

A common method of prioritizing patients is to attach color-coded triage tags to the patients. The following is one method that categorizes the injuries for each color — be familiar with local protocol when triaging patients.

Red Tag

Red-tag injuries are priority 1 (most urgent). These include:

1. Thoracic injuries — flail chest, a condition that is caused by multiple fractures of the rib cage resulting in paradoxical movement of the injured area during inspiration and expiration.
2. Tension pneumothorax — air that enters the chest cavity but cannot escape, leading to an increase in pressure and resulting in a collapsed lung or worse.
3. Sucking chest wounds — a wound to the chest wall that allows air to enter and exit the chest cavity.
4. Shock, severe hemorrhage, acute respiratory difficulty, burns to the airway, third-degree burns to more than 30 percent of the body, acute myocardial infarction (AMI), and coma.

Yellow Tag

Yellow-tag injuries are priority 2. These include chest pain, decreased level of consciousness, active bleeding, severe pain, dyspnea (shortness of breath), spinal injuries, evisceration (protrusion of abdominal viscera), and third-degree burns to less than 30 percent of the body surface.

Green Tag

Green-tag injuries are priority 3. These include (the walking wounded) minor fractures, minor lacerations, and minor burns.

Black Tag

A black tag indicates priority 4 and means that the patient is dead or has little possibility of survival with the resources available.

Other Triage Systems

Another system that is used categorizes patients with triage tags that label them as **now, later,** or **presumed dead**.

Treatment of Patients in Triage

In general, treatment of patients in a triage situation follows this order:

1. Airway patency (an open airway), with control of cervical spine.
2. Breathing to ensure adequate ventilation.
3. Circulation support, including assessment of the patient, control of bleeding, providing for volume replacement, and providing cardiopulmonary resuscitation (CPR) when adequate manpower is available.
4. Wound management.
5. Fracture management.

MASS-CASUALTY INCIDENT (MCI)

An MCI most commonly takes place at a single location, has many patients, and taxes the EMS system in both the prehospital and hospital settings. The teams that seem most successful in handling a disaster are the ones that do preplanning, are prepared, have practiced, and have coordinated their management plans with other appropriate agencies in the area. The following is one description of preparation and management for the mass-casualty incident.

Preparation

The preplanning process for a response to an MCI should include the following:

1. A disaster plan for each EMS agency.
2. All EMS agencies should coordinate with nearby EMS services (i.e., rescue, fire, hospitals, etc.) to ensure that there is a workable integrity to MCI plans.
3. MCI drills must be held periodically to maintain effectiveness and ensure familiarization with the disaster plans.
4. Special resources must be identified and included in emergency plans:
   - Air evacuation and rescue: Including both helicopter and fixed-wing aircraft.
   - Search-and-rescue from cave, mine, water, avalanche, and mountaineering/climbing emergency incidents.
   - Hazardous materials emergency response: Including chemical spill teams, state and local environmental health department resources, radioactive material spill teams, hazardous gas teams, and other appropriate manpower groups.
   - Heavy equipment resources, including location of: cranes, front-end loaders, tractors, etc. for possible emergency use.
   - Disaster services: Including the American Red Cross.

The MCI Scene

Most people who work as paramedics will not serve at a major disaster during their lifetime. Yet, it is important for EMS personnel to be familiar with the setup and functioning of an MCI plan. There are several ways to manage a disaster. The method presented in this text is recommended by the Department of Transportation (DOT).

Field EMS Commander

The first arriving paramedic is the initial field EMS commander. (It is important to note that in some MCI scenes, an emergency department physician may come to the scene to take charge.) He/she activates the disaster plan, sets up a command post (which may include the communications center), and coordinates all medical communications and medical aspects of the scene. When necessary, the field EMS commander, together with the chief law enforcement agent, sets up the staging area for arriving ambulances. The field EMS commander is in charge of all medical aspects of the scene and must coordinate closely with the overall scene commander — usually a law enforcement agent or the fire chief. The field EMS commander should request ambulances and special EMS resources, and must convey or designate someone to communicate patient information to the receiving hospitals.

Field Triage Officer

The triage officer must have strong clinical experience and be able to communicate well. He/she must:

1. Make rapid assessment of the situation, since detailed information on each patient (i.e., vital signs, injuries) may not be immediately obtainable.
2. Be obviously identifiable as the triage officer.
3. Tag patients according to the severity of their injuries.
4. Count the number of patients and identify the types of injuries.
5. Set up triage and treatment areas along with the EMS commander.

The paramedic faces a difficult task when handling a mass-casualty incident. The paramedic, regardless of what level he/she is working at, must keep his/her wits, use caution, and be skillful. By learning the setup procedures of on-site emergency care delivery at an MCI, the paramedic with practice can be successful in handling most situations.

SUMMARY

The scene survey is the actual assessment of what is going on at the incident, whether it is a medical problem at the patient's home or a traumatic injury on the street. The paramedic is given information by dispatch prior to arrival, and this is the first opportunity for the paramedic to actually confirm this information for him/herself.

The first criteria in scene management is for the paramedic to protect him/herself by evaluating any dangers present. After this, the paramedic can proceed with assessing the need for additional emergency services (e.g., a second ambulance for a multi-patient situation; fire service for a fire hazard; police for a hostile situation or traffic control; and/or personnel from the power company for downed power lines). Finally, the paramedic must appropriately treat and transport the patient.

Division Two

Preparatory

3

General Patient Assessment

Patient assessment is one of the most critical skills that the paramedic should develop and use in the field. Through proper evaluation of the patient, appropriate care can be provided. This section will discuss rapid assessment (primary survey) and the secondary examination.

In general, the information received from dispatch allows the paramedic to initiate the evaluation process prior to arriving on the scene. Occasionally, the information from dispatch is inaccurate and the assessment must change correspondingly.

The paramedic actually starts the ''real'' assessment when he/she arrives on the scene. The situation provides information (mechanism of injury: Auto accident — speed, steering wheel bent, windshield starred; fall — how far, patient position; etc.). The rescuer then surveys the patient for further information. What is the general appearance of the patient? Is there pain or discomfort? What is the patient's facial expression?

Correct treatment of the patient depends on an accurate assessment. There are times when a thorough assessment will be impossible to perform prior to treatment. What this means is that there is a life-threatening condition that needs immediate care, and recognition and management must occur simultaneously.

PRIMARY SURVEY

The primary survey, or rapid assessment, is the recognition of immediate life-threatening situations and the attempt to correct them. In these cases, transport to definitive care must not be delayed. This premise is important particularly when dealing with significant trauma cases.

The primary survey consists of the following:

Responsiveness

Is the patient conscious or unconscious? For quick evaluation, the EMT-P may use the mnemonic AVPU:

A = Is the patient alert?
V = Does the patient respond to verbal stimuli?
P = Does the patient respond only to painful stimuli?
U = Is the patient unresponsive?

Spine

In all unconscious trauma patients, the paramedic must assume spinal column/cord injury. In all conscious trauma patients, the paramedic should consider the possibility of spinal column/cord injury.

Airway

Is the airway open? Observe for occlusion and partial occlusion. Correct when necessary. Consider neck injury with trauma (i.e., use modified jaw thrust [see Chapter 4], keep head and neck in neutral position).

Consider the use of adjunctive airways:

1. Nasal airway.
2. Oral airway.
3. Esophageal intubation.
4. Endotracheal intubation.

Breathing

When evaluating respiration, the paramedic should answer the following questions about the patient:

1. Is the patient breathing?

2. Respiratory rate: Rapid or slow?
3. Rhythm: Regular or irregular?
4. Depth: Shallow, normal, or deep?
5. Noisy respirations: Wheezing, stridor (high-pitched seal bark), rhonchi, (rattling sound in the throat during inspiration or expiration), or snoring?
6. Respiratory effort: Easy or difficult?
7. Retractions (a pulling back): Intercostal, above and/or below the clavicles?
8. Skin color: Pale, cyanotic (a blue or purple color of the skin caused by a deficiency of oxygen in the blood), or red?

If the patient is apneic, ventilate and check for a pulse. If the respiratory rate is below 10 per minute or above 28 per minute, assist ventilations by:

1. Mouth-to-mouth.
2. Mouth-to-mask.
3. Bag-valve-mask.
4. Demand valve.
5. Esophageal intubation device.
6. Endotracheal intubation.
7. Transtracheal ventilation: jet insufflation; cricothyrotomy.

To evaluate the effectiveness of the patient's ventilatory efforts and artificial ventilation, the paramedic should:

1. Observe the movement of the chest.
2. Auscultate both the left and right lung fields as well as the epigastrium.
3. Observe changes in skin color, pupillary response, and LOC.

Circulation

The paramedic must evaluate the following when assessing the patient's circulatory system:

1. Is there a pulse?
2. Heart rate: tachycardia (heart rate over 100 beats per minute), normal, or cardia (heart rate under sixty beats per minute)?
3. Rhythm: regular or irregular?
4. Strength: weak, strong, or thready?
5. Capillary refill: under two seconds?
6. Location of a palpable pulse?

7. Skin color: Pink, pale, cyanotic, or mottled?
8. Hemorrhage: Major or minor?

If there is no pulse, start CPR unless the patient is in profound shock, in which case the paramedic must treat for shock. If the pulse is very rapid, start fluid resuscitation. If there is massive external hemorrhage, control it. In all cases, treat for shock.

Expose (Physical Inspection)

The areas of the body in which death is most likely to occur during or after injury are the **head, neck, chest,** and **abdomen.** The paramedic should inspect those areas when significant trauma has occurred. Consider the mechanism of injury. The limitations for exposing a patient's body are the environment, bystanders, and the specific situation.

SECONDARY SURVEY

The secondary survey consists of the assessment of the patient for non-life-threatening emergencies. The survey consists of the following:

1. Vital signs.
2. Physical examination (head-to-toe survey).
3. History.

Vital Signs

The vital signs consist of:

1. Pulse.
2. Blood pressure.
3. Respiration.
4. Skin temperature and color.
5. Pupils.

The paramedic must make a full evaluation and should be able to readily interpret the observations. The normal values of each vital sign must be known in order to understand what abnormal vitals are and what they represent. (See Appendix 4 for pediatric vitals.)

Pulse

A normal rate is generally considered sixty to eighty beats per minute. The paramedic assessment consists of rate, rhythm (regularity), and strength (weak, thready, or strong). If the patient has a radial pulse, there should be a blood pressure of at least 80 mmHg; if the patient has a femoral pulse, there should be a blood pressure of at least 70 mmHg; and if the patient has a carotid pulse, there should be a blood pressure of at least 60 mmHg.

When the patient's pulse is **tachycardic**, it may indicate any of the following: Physical exertion, anxiety, fright, blood loss, hypoxia (inadequate tissue oxygenation), cardiac dysrhythmias (irregular heart rhythm), or other problems.

When the patient is **bradycardic**, it may indicate any of the following: a well-conditioned athlete, increasing intracranial pressure, hypoxia, profound shock, cardiac dysrhythmias, or other problems.

Blood Pressure

This is the measurement in millimeters of mercury of the pressure being exerted against the arterial walls during contraction of the heart (**systolic blood pressure**) and during relaxation of the heart (**diastolic blood pressure**). In general, normal blood pressures for men are: 100 plus age in mmHg for systolic pressure up to the age of fifty and between 70 and 90 mmHg for diastolic pressure. For women, the normal blood pressure is 90 plus age in mmHg for systolic up to the age of fifty. Systolic pressures above 180 mmHg and below 90 mmHg are cause for concern (there are exceptions). Diastolic pressures should remain above 60 mmHg and below 95 mmHg.

When a patient's **systolic** blood pressure falls below 90 mmHg, it may indicate any of the following: hypotension due to blood loss, hypoxia, cardiac dysrhythmias, pulmonary embolism, or other problems.

When the patient's **systolic** blood pressure rises above180 mmHg, it may indicate increasing intracranial pressure or hypertension.

Respirations

The normal rate of respirations in adults at rest is between 12 to 20 breaths per minute. The paramedic assessment consists of rate, rhythm, and depth. Listen to breath sounds in the cardiac patient, trauma patient, and the patient experiencing dyspnea.

Skin

The skin color and temperature give additional pertinent information.

Possible skin colors are:

1. Normal.
2. Red — carbon monoxide poisoning (not common), heat-related problems.
3. Pale — shock, fright, hypothermia.
4. Cyanotic (bluish tint to the skin) — inadequate oxygenation.
5. Mottled — allergic reaction, death.

Pupils

The pupils are windows into the brain. By observing the pupils and their reactions, important neurologic information may be gained. There are two parameters in pupillary evaluation:

1. Equality — are both pupils the same size?
2. Reactivity — do both pupils react appropriately to light (constrict)?

Other indications that may be looked for are:

1. Pinpoint pupils: Possible narcotic use.
2. Dilated pupils: Possible hallucinogen use, head injury, or death.
3. Unequal pupils: Serious head injury (stroke, tumor, trauma); it should be noted that a small portion of people have unequal pupils normally.
4. Bilaterally dilated and fixed pupils: Severe brain stem damage (terminal).

Be sure to document all changes that are noted.

PHYSICAL EXAMINATION (HEAD-TO-TOE)

The head-to-toe examination is to assess the whole body of the sick or injured patient in an organized fashion. The paramedic will:

1. Inspect (to look).
2. Palpate (to feel).
3. Auscultate (to listen).
4. Smell.

This is done to locate any abnormalities. The paramedic is specifically checking for:

1. Tenderness.
2. Contusions.
3. Deformities.
4. Hemorrhage.
5. Swelling.
6. Other obvious pathological findings.

Most frequently, the paramedic will start at the head and work down to the feet. The head-to-toe examination ideally should take no more than two minutes.

In each of the following areas, the paramedic will examine by inspection, palpation, and auscultation when appropriate.

Head

The paramedic should note deformities, swelling, discoloration, soft tissue injury, etc. in the following areas:

1. Skin and scalp.
2. Eyes — pupils, are they equal and reactive to light?
3. Ears — CSF in the external auditory canal.
4. Nose.
5. Mouth — can the patient speak ok?
6. Bones — skull and facial.

The technique involves inspection, palpation, and smell.

Neck

The paramedic must note soft tissue injury, subcutaneous emphysema, swelling, discoloration, etc. in the following areas:

1. Skin.
2. Trachea — deviation?
3. Vessels — jugular venous distention?
4. Cervical spine — potential for injury (in trauma, the cervical spine should be stabilized during the primary survey).

The technique involves inspection, palpation, and auscultation for bruises over the carotid arteries.

Thorax

The paramedic should check for soft tissue injury, deformities, swelling, discoloration, and unequal chest expansion by examining the:

1. Skin.
2. Chest wall — bones and muscles.
3. Lungs — auscultate all fields.
4. Heart — electrocardiogram (if necessary).

The technique involves inspection, palpation, and auscultation.

Abdomen

The paramedic should check for soft tissue injury, evisceration, distention, and rigidity of the abdomen in the:

1. Skin.
2. Muscles.
3. Retroperitoneal space (kidneys, pancreas).
4. Lumbar spine.
5. Pelvis — for deformity.
6. Genitalia.

The technique involves inspection and palpation.

Extremities

The paramedic must check for soft tissue injury, deformities, swelling, discoloration, sensation, movement, and distal pulses of both lower and upper extremities (when assessing the lower extremities, check for incontinence [loss of control over bowel movement and urination]) by examining the:

1. Skin.
2. Soft tissues.
3. Vessels.
4. Bones.

The technique involves inspection and palpation.

Neurologic Examination ("Neuros")

The following should be checked:

1. Level of consciousness (AVPU). Alert and oriented to **person, time,** and **place.**
2. Seizure activity (clues: elevated pulse, possible incontinence, and possibly a cut lip or tongue).
3. Motor — movement of all four extremities.
4. Sensory — sensation in all four extremities.
5. Pupils — equal and reactive to light.

HISTORY

The case history may be gathered from different sources, the primary source being the patient. Additional sources of information are:

1. Relatives.
2. Bystanders.
3. Other EMS personnel on the scene prior to the paramedic's arrival.
4. Law enforcement personnel.

The information received from the patient is most important. The paramedic will do well if he/she develops a comfortable and consistent approach to taking histories.

The paramedic must establish a good rapport with the patient and with anyone else who offers material relevant to history taking. The paramedic will be most successful if he/she behaves in a professional, friendly, and businesslike fashion.

The following format for obtaining patient histories can be effective:

1. Mechanism of injury or illness.
2. Chief complaint: It may be a verbal or nonverbal complaint. The most common chief complaint is pain. Note its nature, location, and severity.
3. Present illness or trauma: Symptoms related to the patient's chief complaint and associated symptoms. Note the onset, precipitating factors, and what factors aggravate or alleviate the symptoms.

4. A history mnemonic is AMPLE:
   A = allergies.
   M = medications.
   P = past medical history.
   L = last oral intake.
   E = events leading up to the emergency.

Another format for history taking is using the mnemonic PQRST for describing the chief complaint:
   P = provoking factors.
   Q = quality of pain/problem.
   R = region/radiation of pain/referred pain.
   S = severity.
   T = time of onset.

Additional information needed would be allergies, pertinent past medical history, and medications taken.

RE-EVALUATION OF THE PATIENT

It is necessary for the paramedic to continue evaluation until the patient is admitted to the emergency department. The need for re-evaluating the patient is based on the following:

1. Normal monitoring of all vital signs to keep a timely assessment while transporting the patient.
2. Missed injuries due to poor initial conditions for evaluation.
3. Improved status of patient allows for further identification of areas of injury.
4. A rapid change in condition due to **continuing blood loss, airway compromise** (decreased ventilation), and/or drop in **cardiac output.**
5. Areas to continue to monitor:
   - Airway.
   - Ventilation.
   - Pulse.
   - Skin color.
   - Blood pressure.
   - EKG.
   - Neurological status.

- Circulation distal to a fracture site.
- Intravenous rate.
- Oxygenation.
- Breath sounds.

SUMMARY

Patient assessment is the foundation upon which all medical personnel build their medical skills. In the prehospital setting, the paramedic's assessment skills must be impeccable. He/she has only a short period of time in which to thoroughly evaluate the patient and then make the appropriate treatment decisions.

The paramedic has been presented with the generally accepted format for performing the primary and secondary surveys, as well as history taking. These skills must be developed and practiced continually in order to maintain a high degree of expertise. In addition, the paramedic must be flexible when performing the assessment. He/she must know when to cut short the history taking, complete the physical examination en route to the hospital, or omit parts of the examination altogether.

The basis for excellent medical care in the field develops with a broad base of knowledge, strong skills, and the ability to make sound judgments. Each paramedic develops these skills and abilities over time — some faster than others. It is important for the paramedic to recognize his/her weaknesses and work on improving those areas.

4

Airway and Ventilation

Patients in respiratory distress are commonly seen in the prehospital setting and are given high priority. Airway management is a major key to successful patient care. If the airway is not maintained adequately, the patient's outcome is dubious.

In order for the paramedic to do the best possible job in monitoring and maintaining the airway, he/she must be familiar with the anatomy and physiology of the respiratory system and the pathological processes that alter normal respiratory function. In the following sections, the anatomy and physiology of the upper and lower airways will be reviewed, followed by airway management and ventilation procedures.

ANATOMY OF THE UPPER AIRWAY

The paramedic should be familiar with the following structures and their general functions.

Nasopharynx

This is where air enters into the upper airway and is warmed, cleaned, and humidified. It is comprised of:

1. Nares (nostrils).

2. Cartilage.
3. Turbinates.
4. Maxilla (upper jaw).

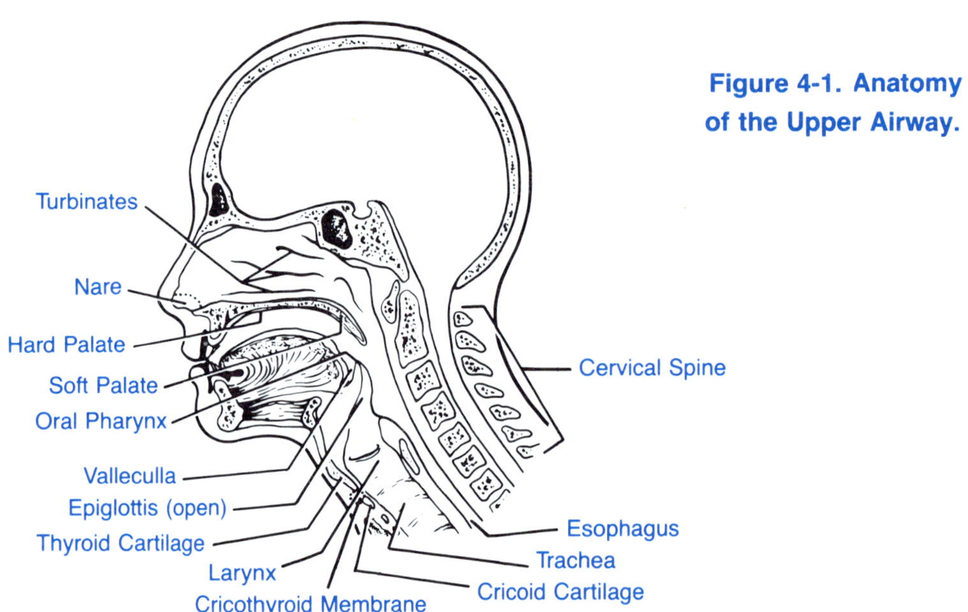

Figure 4-1. Anatomy of the Upper Airway.

Oropharynx

The oropharynx is used for the entrance of both air and food. Words are formed here, and the mechanical/chemical breakdown of food begins here. The oropharynx is comprised of:

1. Lips.
2. Cheeks.
3. Tongue.
4. Hard palate.

5. Soft palate.
6. Tonsils.
7. Teeth.
8. Mandible (lower jaw).
9. Mandible/tongue relationship — the tongue may be moved from the back of the throat by pulling forward (anteriorly) on the mandible. When a patient has a broken jaw, the airway cannot be controlled easily because the tongue attaches to the mandible. Thus, it may occlude the oral pharynx.

Figure 4-2. Anatomy of the Lower Airway.

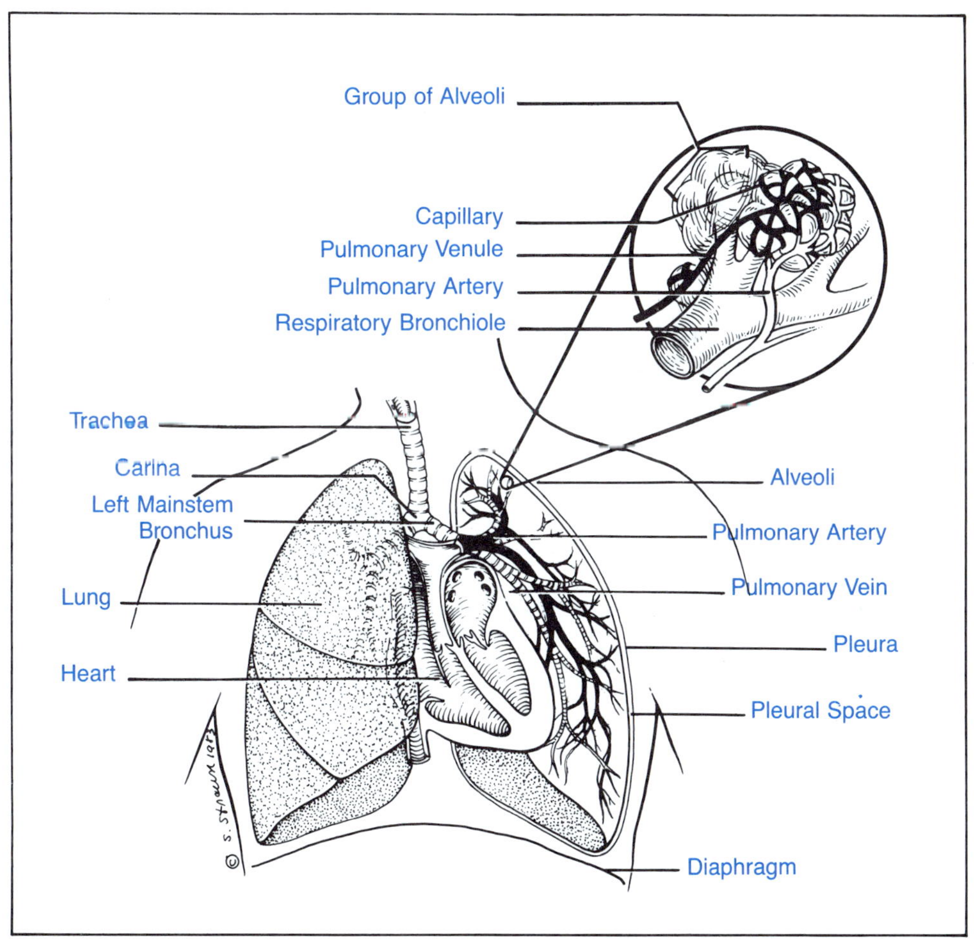

Valleculla

This is the area between the epiglottis and tongue where a curved endotracheal blade is placed during oral intubation.

Epiglottis

The epiglottis is a soft, cartigenous flap of tissue that prevents food or liquids from entering the larynx and lungs.

Larynx

The larynx, also known as the voice box, is where sound is created by air passing over the vocal cords. It is comprised of:

1. Thyroid cartilage.
2. Cricothyroid cartilage.
3. Vocal cords — these need to be visualized when performing tracheal intubation.

Functions of the Upper Respiratory Tract

1. Warms the air prior to reaching the lungs.
2. Humidifies the air on its way to the lungs by the release of moisture from the mucous membranes covering the respiratory tract.
3. Cleans the air and airway by:
   - Turbinates creating a turbulent air flow and providing more surface area.
   - Foreign matter adhering to the mucous membranes of the nose and nasopharynx.
   - Cilia moving foreign particles toward the pharynx and out of the airway.

ANATOMY OF THE LOWER AIRWAY

The paramedic should be familiar with the following structures and their general functions.

Trachea

The trachea is the part of the airway that conducts air into the lungs. The endotracheal tube is inserted here.

1. It is made up of C-shaped, incomplete rings, allowing for easier passage of

food through the esophagus.
2. It is four to five inches in length.
3. Its walls are lined with cilia and mucous-producing cells.
4. The paramedic must avoid placing the endotracheal tube in the esophagus rather than the trachea when performing intubation.

Right and Left Mainstem Bronchi

1. The carina is a ridge between the right and left mainstem bronchi.
2. The right mainstem bronchus branches at a wide angle, thus making it easy for the paramedic to place an endotracheal tube into it while performing an intubation. When this occurs, the left lung is left unoxygenated.
3. Secondary bronchi.
4. Bronchioles.
5. Respiratory bronchioles.
6. Alveolar ducts/sacs.
7. Alveoli
   - This is the most important functional unit of the system.
   - Oxygen (O_2) and carbon dioxide (CO_2) gas exchange takes place here.
   - These are hollow, thin-walled sacs.
   - Their outer surface is covered with capillaries that originate from the terminal branches of the pulmonary artery.

Lungs

The lungs are the inflatable structures that are comprised of the bronchi, bronchioles, respiratory bronchioles, and alveoli.

1. The lungs are covered with a membrane called the visceral pleura. The interior chest wall is covered with the parietal pleura. This creates a near-frictionless environment for lungs in which to expand and contract.
2. The area between the visceral pleura and the parietal pleura is called the pleural space. This is a potential space because at times of injury, the pleural space may fill with air or blood. If enough air or blood fills this space, it will compress lung tissue, reducing the surface area available for the exchange of oxygen and carbon dioxide.
3. The right lung has three lobes, and the left lung has two.
4. The blood supply of the lungs is made up of the pulmonary artery and veins and the bronchial artery and veins.

MECHANICS OF RESPIRATION

Respiration is the exchange of gases between a living organism and its environment. In humans, it is the movement of air into the lungs, where oxygen is exchanged for carbon dioxide at the site of the alveoli. The freshly oxygenated blood is transported to the rest of the body, where cellular respiration takes place (i.e., the cells exchange carbon dioxide for oxygen).

The respiratory cycle, or the movement of air into and out of the lungs, involves the respiratory system, the central nervous system, and the musculoskeletal system.

The movement of air into and out of the lungs is a result of variations in air pressure within the thoracic cavity. These changes occur when the size of the chest expands or contracts due to the action of the diaphragm and intercostal muscles. Just after a normal expiration, the pressure within the thorax is equal to the atmospheric pressure. When the chest enlarges, the intrathoracic pressure drops and air rushes into the lungs. When the muscles relax, the chest cavity reduces in size and the air in the lungs moves out.

Inspiration is initiated by the contraction of the diaphragm and the intercostal muscles. The action of the diaphragm causes the flattening of the diaphragm muscle toward the abdomen, resulting in an increase in the vertical dimension of the thoracic cavity. The actions of the intercostal muscles cause the elevation of the ribs upward and outward to increase the horizontal and transverse dimensions of the chest. The highly elastic lungs fill the greater space, resulting in larger lung dimensions. As a result, air pressure in the lungs decreases rapidly. Then, air moves into the lungs, where oxygen and carbon dioxide are exchanged at the alveoli.

Expiration occurs when the inspiratory muscles relax, thus decreasing thoracic volume. This causes an increase of thoracic pressure, thereby forcing air out of the lungs with an elastic recoil. The normal expiratory process is passive.

In respiratory inadequacy, the accessory muscles aid in inspiration and expiration (i.e., the intercostal and neck muscles assist in breathing).

PULMONARY CIRCULATION

Pulmonary circulation refers to the movement of unoxygenated blood (carbon dioxide–rich, oxygen-poor) through the right atrium and ventricle, where it is then pumped via the pulmonary artery to the lungs. At the site of the lungs, the pulmonary artery bifurcates to the right and left lungs.

Arteries branch into microscopic capillaries surrounding the alveoli. At this point, carbon dioxide is released and oxygen is absorbed into the red blood cells (RBCs). The now-oxygenated blood is transported through the pulmonary vein to the left atrium and ventricle, where it is pumped and circulated through the systemic arterial system.

GAS EXCHANGE IN THE LUNGS

The exchange of oxygen and carbon dioxide occurs in the alveoli. In the healthy person, the alveoli have a high concentration of oxygen and a low concentration of carbon dioxide.

The concentration of gases (or the number of molecules of gas) in the blood is measured in terms of **partial pressure** in torrs (millimeters of mercury) — Torr — written as either Pa mmHg or P mmHg. For oxygen, it is written PO_2 or PaO_2. Gases move from areas of higher concentrations (Pa) to areas of lower concentrations. This movement of gases is called diffusion.

The PO_2 in the alveoli is approximately 140 mmHg (torr), and the PCO_2 in the alveoli is close to zero. Thus, the oxygen-poor blood that enters the lungs releases carbon dioxide in exchange for oxygen. The venous blood coming to the lungs from the right heart has a PCO_2 of about 40 torr and a PO_2 of about 46 torr. The freshly oxygenated blood returning to the left heart (arterial blood) has a normal PCO_2 of 35 to 40 torr and a normal PO_2 of 80 to 100 torr, at sea level.

REGULATION OF RESPIRATION

People have both voluntary and involuntary control of their respirations. Breathing is primarily an involuntary action that is regulated by chemical, physical, and nervous reflexes which control the oxygen and carbon dioxide levels in the body.

The primary control of respirations is located in the brainstem (pneumotaxic center). Nerve impulses are sent to the diaphragm and intercostal muscles from the respiratory center in the brainstem, where signals for the initiation of inspiration are given.

Microscopic "stretch receptors," located in the lungs and pleura, help regulate inspiration. During inspiration, the expansion of the lungs activates the stretch receptors, causing nerve impulses to go to the brainstem. The brainstem interprets these messages and curtails inspiration, allowing the lungs to "recoil." When the lungs revert to pre-inspiration shape, the stretch receptors stop sending messages to the brainstem. The cycle begins again with inspiratory impulses originating in the brainstem.

Respiration is also regulated by "chemoreceptors," located centrally in the medulla of the brain and peripherally in the aortic arch and the carotid bodies. These chemoreceptors are stimulated by the balance of gases and by acidity/alkalinity (pH) of the blood and cerebrospinal fluid. Specifically, the receptors respond to a decrease of PO_2, an increase in PCO_2, or a decrease in pH.

It is the carbon dioxide level in the blood that determines the respiratory rate of normal people by causing either a decrease or an increase in respiratory activity. A high concentration of carbon dioxide in the blood increases respiratory activity by stimulating the chemoreceptors. Low levels of carbon dioxide decrease respiratory activity. Chemoreceptors also monitor inadequate levels of oxygen in the blood, as well as carbon dioxide levels. However, a low level of oxygen in the blood is a powerful stimulus to respirations.

Many people have respirations that are determined by what is called hypoxic drive, or low levels of oxygen in their blood. These individuals with chronic obstructive pulmonary disease (COPD) have a decreased ability to eliminate carbon dioxide; thus, their respiratory centers learn to accommodate high levels of carbon dioxide (PCO_2) in the blood. The respiratory rate and depth of COPD patients are responsive to PO_2 levels of below 60 mmHg (this is hypoxic drive) — normal PO_2 at sea level is 80 to 100 mmHg. The primary determinant of respiration rate in these patients is the change in the PO_2 levels of their blood. If the paramedic increases the COPD patient's PO_2, the patient may develop hypoventilation or respiratory arrest. These patients must be monitored continually when high dosages of oxygen are administered.

NORMAL RESPIRATORY FUNCTIONS

Knowing the normal functions of the respiratory system will enable the paramedic to recognize abnormal functions. Normal respiratory rates are as follows:

1. Adults — approximately ten to fourteen breaths per minute.
2. Children — approximately twenty-four breaths per minute.
3. Infants — approximately forty to sixty breaths per minute.

The factors that most commonly affect the respiratory rate are:

1. Fever — increases the rate.
2. Anxiety — increases the rate.
3. Insufficient oxygen — increases the rate.
4. Drugs cause varied responses — may increase, decrease, or arrest respirations.
5. Sleep — decreases the rate.
6. Hemorrhage — increases the rate.

The normal lung capacity in an adult male is six liters. The following are terms that will help the paramedic understand more about lung capacity.

1. **Tidal volume** is the volume of air that is inhaled or exhaled during a single respiratory cycle. This is normally 500 cubic centimeters of air.

2. **Dead air space** is the air remaining in the conducting passageways that is unavailable for gas exchange. This is normally 150 cubic centimeters of air.

3. **Alveolar air** is the actual air reaching the alveoli for gas exchange. This is normally 350 cubic centimeters of air.

4. **Minute volume** is the amount of gas moved in and out of the respiratory system in a minute. It is determined by multiplying the tidal volume by the respiratory rate.

5. **Vital capacity** is the volume of air that can be forcefully exhaled out of the respiratory tract.

FACTORS ALTERING CARBON DIOXIDE AND OXYGEN LEVELS IN THE BLOOD

Arterial carbon dioxide represents a balance between carbon dioxide produced during metabolism and carbon dioxide eliminated through respiration. There are many causes for increased carbon dioxide production. The most common are:

1. Fever.

2. Muscular exertion.
3. Shivering.
4. Metabolic processes resulting in the formation of acids.
5. Anaerobic metabolism (chemical changes that occur without oxygen).

Decreased elimination of carbon dioxide results primarily from hypoventilation. This can be caused by:

1. Respiratory suppression by drugs.
2. Airway obstruction.
3. COPD.
4. Trauma to the chest wall.

The basic cause of decreased PCO_2 is hyperventilation. This may result from any of the following:

1. Anxiety.
2. Pulmonary embolism — obstruction of the pulmonary artery (or one of its branches) by a clot of foreign material.
3. Pain.
4. Pulmonary edema — an accumulation of fluid in the tissues and air spaces of the lung that prevents the normal exchange of gases at the alveoli.
5. Trauma.

Some causes of decreased oxygen levels in the blood are:

1. Pulmonary edema.
2. Atelectasis (a collapsed or airless condition of the lung). This may be caused by pneumonia or splinting of the chest wall.
3. Pulmonary embolism.
4. Respiratory suppression by drugs.
5. Airway obstruction.
6. COPD.
7. Trauma.

PATHOLOGY OF THE RESPIRATORY SYSTEM

The following are the most common airway problems encountered in the prehospital setting.

Obstruction

1. Tongue — the most common cause of obstruction by occluding the posterior pharynx (back of the throat).
2. Foreign body:
   - Most commonly in the form of food aspirated while eating, though it may occur in children from loose teeth or from "eating" inanimate objects.

     During trauma from fractured facial bones, broken teeth, fractured nasal bones, vomitus, and clotted blood.
3. Laryngeal spasm due to cord edema and/or cord spasm.
4. Fractured larynx resulting in nonsupport of cords and/or collapse into the tracheal/laryngeal lumen (opening).

Aspiration (Inhalation) of Foreign Material

1. Vomitus.
2. Blood.
3. Liquid.
4. Food.

Inadequate Ventilation

This may be due to:

1. Rate:
   - Hyperventilation.
   - Hypoventilation.
2. Depth:
   - Shallow.
   - Deep.
3. Trauma:
   - Flail chest (fracture of two or more ribs in two or more places).
   - Pneumothorax (presence of air in the pleural cavity).
   - Pulmonary contusion (bruise).
   - Tension pneumothorax.
4. Disease:
   - COPD.
   - Asthma.
   - Pulmonary embolus.
   - Pulmonary edema.

- Infections.
- Pneumonia.
- Cardiac.

5. Environmental factors:
   - Burns.
   - Noxious gases.

ASSESSMENT

Inspection of the Chest

1. Watch the rise and fall of the chest.
2. Note the symmetry of the chest.
3. Note the color of the skin.
4. Look for obvious trauma.
5. Look for retraction (drawing in of the accessory muscles during respirations.
   - Intercostal.
   - Suprasternal notch.
   - Supraclavicular.
   - Subcostal (beneath the ribs).

Auscultation of the Chest

1. Listen for movement of air at the nose and mouth.
2. Check bilateral lung fields:
   - The most accurate method is to use a stethoscope.
   - Place the stethoscope on the anterior and lateral chest wall, specifically mid-clavicular in the intercostal space below the clavicle and at the anterior axillary line at the eighth or ninth intercostal space. Be sure to compare left to right sides, and, if possible, the posterior chest wall.

Palpation of the Chest

1. Feel for movement of air at the nose and mouth by using the back of the hand or cheek.
2. Chest wall — check for:
   - Abnormalities.
   - Deformity.
   - Open wounds.
   - Symmetry of chest wall movement.

3. When using a bag-valve-mask/tube, check:
   - Compliance of lungs.
   - Rate of emptying.

AIRWAY MANAGEMENT

Proper management of the patient's airway is critical and of top priority in patient care. There are many ways in which the airway can be managed. How it is handled depends on the specific problem and the skill level of the paramedic. The following is a presentation of most of the possible ways the airway can be managed in the field.

One point must be remembered constantly. When dealing with a trauma patient, the paramedic should consider the possibility of cervical spine injury. An open airway, however, has the highest priority. When possible, a technique for opening the airway should be selected which minimizes movement of the spine.

Manual Methods

Head Tilt-Chin Lift

1. Head hyperextended.
2. Hand on the forehead.
3. Hand on the cervical spine.
4. Should be avoided with the trauma patient.

Jaw-Lift

1. Thumb on the lower incisors.
2. Index finger on the inferior mandible.
3. Pull jaw anteriorly.

Jaw-Thrust

1. Two hands.
2. Thumbs on the zygoma bilaterally.
3. Fingers beneath the symphysis of the mandible.
4. Thrust the jaw anteriorly.

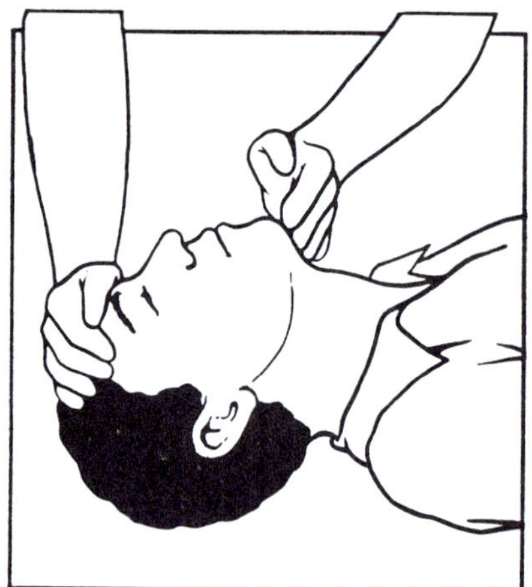

Figure 4-3. Head Tilt-Chin Lift.

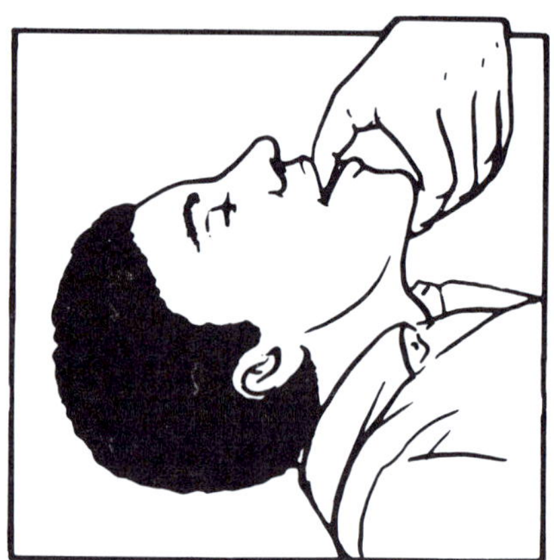

Figure 4-4. Jaw Lift.

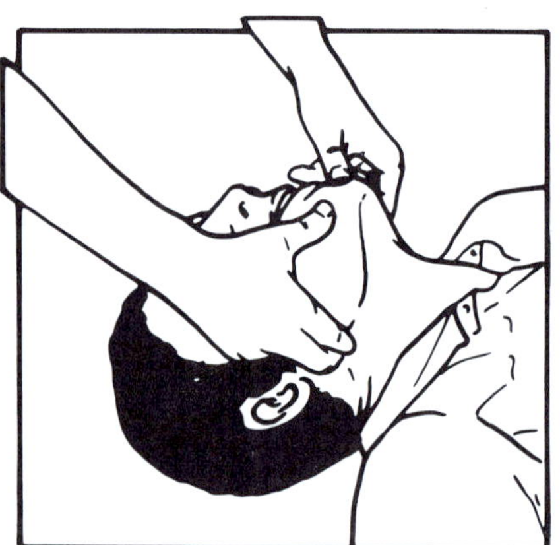

Figure 4-5. Jaw Thrust.

Mechanical Methods

Nasal Airway

The length is between seventeen and twenty centimeters and the diameter is between twenty and thirty-six french. The nasal airway has a gentle curve and the distal end is flanged.

Advantages of Use

1. Rapid insertion.
2. Bypasses the tongue.
3. May be used when a gag reflex is present.

Disadvantages of Use

1. Small size.
2. May not extend beyond the tongue.
3. May be difficult to insert if nasal damage is present.
4. Does not isolate trachea.
5. Difficult to suction through.
6. Should be used with extreme caution if a basal skull fracture is suspected.

Method of Insertion

1. Lubricate with a water-soluble lubricant.
2. Insert into a nare.
3. Follow the natural curvature of the nasal passage.
4. Use only gentle pressure.
5. If obstructed, try other nare.
6. Do not force.

Oral Airway

This airway may be three to fourteen centimeters in length (there are six different lengths). It may be shaped as a hollow, oblong cylinder or like the letter ''H.'' The oral airway has a gentle curve with a flange on the distal end.

Advantages of Use

1. If applied properly, it will hold the tongue forward and down.
2. Airway suction is easy to perform.
3. Effective as a bite block to protect the endotracheal tube (ET-tube); and during convulsions.

Disadvantages of Use

1. Does not isolate the trachea.
2. May obstruct the airway with the tongue if not properly inserted.
3. It cannot be inserted when a gag reflex is present or if the teeth are tightly clenched.

Method of Insertion

1. For proper sizing: measure the patient from the corner of the mouth to the tip of the earlobe.
2. For straight insertion, use a tongue blade to push the tongue down and forward. Then insert the airway with the tip following the roof of the mouth into the back of the throat (hypopharynx).
3. For reverse insertion, point the tip toward the hard palate, insert gently to the soft palate, then rotate 180 degrees into the hypopharynx.

Esophageal Obturator (EOA)

This is approximately a fifteen-inch flexible tube with a mask adapter at the proximal end; it is closed at the distal end. The top third of the tube has perforations to allow the flow of oxygen in the airway. The following equipment is necessary for proper use and insertion:

1. 35-cubic-centimeter syringe.
2. Lubricant.
3. Bag-valve or demand valve.
4. Oxygen with connecting tube.
5. Suction equipment.
6. Stethoscope.
7. Oral airway.

Advantages of Use

1. Rapid insertion.
2. Prevents regurgitation and aspiration.
3. Provides for delivery of high concentrations of oxygen.
4. Blind insertion is possible.
5. Allows for ET-tube placement.
6. Requires less training than ET-tube intubation.
7. Insertion is possible without neck flexion or hyperextension.

Disadvantages of Use

1. Requires the patient to be unresponsive without a gag reflex.

2. Must be removed when the patient becomes responsive or agitated.
3. Can possibly lacerate the esophagus.
4. May intubate trachea, which would prevent oxygenation of the patient.
5. May be used for short periods of time only.
6. Requires a tight seal (of the mask) to adequately oxygenate the patient.

Contraindications (Inadvisable Circumstances)

1. Known or suspected esophageal disease of the patient.
2. Caustic poisoning ingestion.
3. Gag reflex is present.
4. The patient is under five feet tall or over seven feet tall.
5. Should not be used with patients younger than sixteen years of age.

Method of Insertion

1. Suction equipment available.
2. Test balloon cuff (used to secure the tube in the esophagus) and inlet port integrity.
3. Assemble mask and tube.
4. Lubricate tube.
5. Place the patient's head in a neutral position.

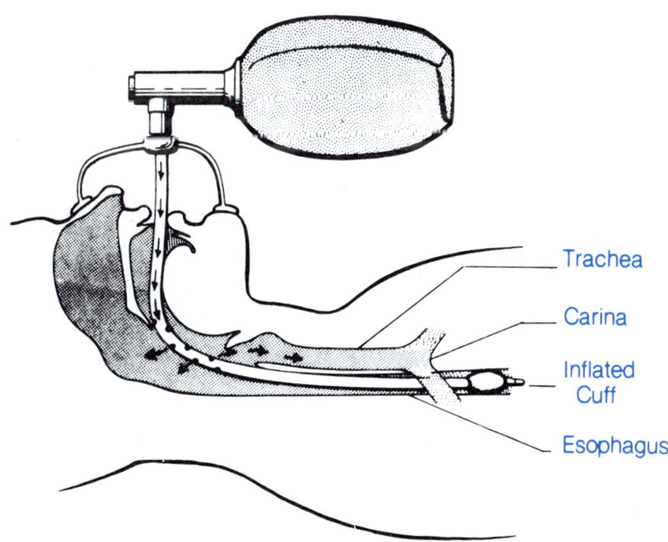

Figure 4-6. Esophageal Obturator in the Correct Position.

Courtesy Department of Transportation.

6. Oxygenate the patient sufficiently prior to attempting the procedure.
7. Advance the tube into the esophagus until the mask is flush with the face.
8. Make a tight seal.
9. Auscultate the lung fields bilaterally while ventilating the patient.
10. Auscultate the epigastrium (stomach).
11. Inflate the cuff to thirty-five cubic centimeters after positioned correctly.
12. Ventilate and check for chest movement.
13. Reauscultate.
14. Oxygenate.

Method of Removal

Remove the EOA only if the patient is intubated, regains consciousness, or has a gag reflex. The procedure is as follows:

1. Have suction available.
2. Turn the patient on his/her side if not intubated.
3. Detach the mask from the tube.
4. Deflate the cuff.
5. Gently and quickly remove the tube.
6. Be prepared for vomiting.
7. Assess the respiratory status.
8. Oxygenate.

Esophageal Gastric Tube

1. Essentially, this is the same as the EOA. The esophageal gastric tube allows for the passage of a nasogastric (NG) tube for the decompression of the stomach, which reduces the chance of regurgitation.
2. Insertion is the same as with the EOA except for the measurement and placement of the NG-tube. To measure the NG-tube, extend the tubing from the tip of the nose, then to the earlobe, and then to the xiphoid process.

Pharyngeo-Tracheal Lumen Airway (PtL)

The PtL airway is a tube within a tube. A long, endotracheal-type tube is located within a short tube with a larger diameter. The distal end of the long tube opens into either the trachea or esophagus, while the short tube opens into the retropharynx above the epiglottis. Both tubes have low-pressure balloons at their distal ends. On the long tube, the balloon provides a seal for either the trachea or esophagus, depending on placement. On the short tube, the larger-volume balloon seals off the oropharynx when the balloon is fully inflated.

When the PtL airway is placed in the esophageal position, the large cuff diverts air delivered through the short tube into the trachea. Both tubes are fitted with fifteen-millimeter adapters to allow universal connection to ventilatory devices. Inflation lines are provided in order that each cuff may be inflated simultaneously or separately. A stylet facilitates insertion, and a plastic bite block prevents the teeth from occluding the airway. The following equipment is necessary for insertion:

1. A water-soluble lubricant.
2. Bag-valve mask or demand valve.
3. Oxygen and connecting tube.
4. Suction equipment.
5. Stethoscope.

Advantages of Use

1. The PtL airway cannot be improperly placed.
2. When it acts as an EOA, it does not need a face-mask seal.
3. It requires little skill training or skill maintenance.
4. It requires minimal C-spine movement for insertion.
5. In patients with a short neck where endotracheal tube placement is impossible, the PtL airway can be inserted.
6. Ease of suctioning.

Disadvantages of Use

1. Requires the patient to be unresponsive without a gag reflex.
2. Must be removed when the patient becomes responsive or agitated.
3. Should be replaced with an endotracheal tube as soon as possible in cases of facial burns, inhalation of heat, air, or facial trauma with the possibility of the development of upper airway edema.
4. May lose its effectiveness with cuff malfunction.

Contraindications

1. A patient who is under five feet tall or younger than fourteen years of age.
2. Caustic ingestions.
3. Esophageal disease.
4. The patient has a gag reflex.

Method of Insertion

1. Except in cases of C-spine injury, hyperextend the patient's head.

2. The paramedic should insert his/her thumb deep into the supine patient's mouth, grasping the tongue and lower jaw between the thumb and index finger, and pull the jaw forward.
3. While holding the jaw in one hand, take the PtL airway so that it curves in the same direction as the natural curvature of the oral pharynx.
4. Insert the tip into the patient's mouth and advance it carefully behind the tongue until the teeth strap touches the patient's teeth. There will be modest resistance in passing the tube when making the right-angle bend at the oral pharynx. **Do not use force.** If the tube does not advance, either redirect it or withdraw, and start over.
5. When the flange meets the teeth, the tube is in proper position.
6. Flip the neck strap over the patient's head and tighten it with the hook tape closures on both sides.
7. Inflate both cuffs simultaneously by blowing into the main inflation valve with a sustained breath. By using cheek pressure, the seal may be improved.
8. Ventilate the lungs by first blowing forcefully into the number 2 short green tube. If the chest rises, the long, clear tube number 3 is in the esophagus and the paramedic may continue to ventilate through the number 2 tube (use a bag-valve with a reservoir to achieve approximately 100 percent concentration of oxygen).
9. If the chest does not rise, the number 3 tube may be in the trachea. In this case, remove the stylet from tube number 3 and ventilate through it. During lung inflation, listen for breath sounds bilaterally and over the stomach with a stethoscope.

Method of Removal

Removal is indicated if the patient regains consciousness, if the protective airway reflexes return, or if endotracheal intubation is to be attempted (in some cases, the paramedic may be able to intubate while the PtL airway is in place).

1. If there is no spinal injury, turn the patient on his/her side.
2. Evaluate for stomach decompression to reduce the possibility of emesis.
3. Open the white port on the number 1 inflation valve to deflate both cuffs and remove.

Endotracheal (ET) Intubation

The ET-tube comes in varying lengths and widths. It is a flexible tube that has an inflatable balloon cuff on the tracheal end to keep the ET-tube in place. There is a fifteen-millimeter adapter on the distal end for placement of a bag-valve device.

The purpose of the ET-tube is to assure the maintenance of an open airway and to protect the patient from aspiration.

Advantages of Use

1. Complete control of airway.
2. Prevents aspiration.
3. Can provide positive pressure ventilation.
4. Tracheal suctioning is possible.
5. Prevents gastric distention.
6. May provide high-volume, high-concentration of oxygen and ventilation.
7. It is an available route for some medications.
8. It may be placed around an EOA.

Disadvantages of Use

1. Requires direct visualization of the vocal cords for proper placement.
2. It may damage tissue.
3. There is a possibility of esophageal intubation.
4. Laryngospasm (an involuntary constriction) may occur during an intubation attempt, causing the airway to close.
5. May delay oxygenation of patient prior to a successful intubation.
6. May lose effectiveness with cuff puncture.

Cautions

1. Avoid extending or flexing the neck of the trauma patient.
2. Prolonged attempts increase hypoxia.

Method of Placement for Oral Intubation

Remember — the actual intubation should take fifteen to twenty seconds.

1. First establish ventilation with exposure to high oxygen concentration.
2. Estimate correct size of ET-tube.
3. Be sure that the cuff will inflate.
4. Hyperventilate the patient with bag-valve-mask (BVM).
5. In the **nontrauma** patient, the position of the head should be the "sniff" position (head/neck slightly extended). In the **trauma** patient, have partner maintain inline stabilization by holding the patient's head in a neutral position. Only the mandible and tongue should be moved during oral intubation. The EMT-P may lie prone or straddle the patient's head,

superiorly, during the intubation.

6. Remove the bag-valve-mask.
7. Insert the laryngoscope from the right side of the oral cavity, sweeping the tongue to the left (see the section "Laryngoscope/Blade").
8. Visualize the epiglottis, larynx, and the vocal cords.
9. Do not touch (lever) the teeth with the laryngoscope or blade (the paramedic may break a patient's teeth by doing this).
10. Slight pressure on the larynx may allow the paramedic to visualize the cords more easily (have partner apply pressure with fingertips to the thyroid cartilage).
11. Lift the tongue and mandible with the laryngoscope/blade.
12. Insert the ET-tube between the cords. Be sure that you see the tube slip by the cords. (See Figures 4-7 and 4-8.)
13. Remove the laryngoscope/blade.
14. Connect bag-valve to ET-tube adapter.
15. Ventilate the lungs.
16. Assure adequate ventilations by watching the chest rise, and auscultate the lungs fields and the epigastrium.
17. Inflate the cuff to not greater than ten cubic centimeters.
18. Secure the ET-tube.
19. Reassess breath sounds in the epigastrium.
20. If:
    - ET-tube is in the esophagus,
    - no breath sounds are auscultated during ventilations,
    - air is auscultated in the stomach during ventilation,
    - the paramedic is unable to properly place the ET-tube, the paramedic should return to BVM ventilation. After the patient is well-ventilated, the paramedic should make a second attempt to intubate.

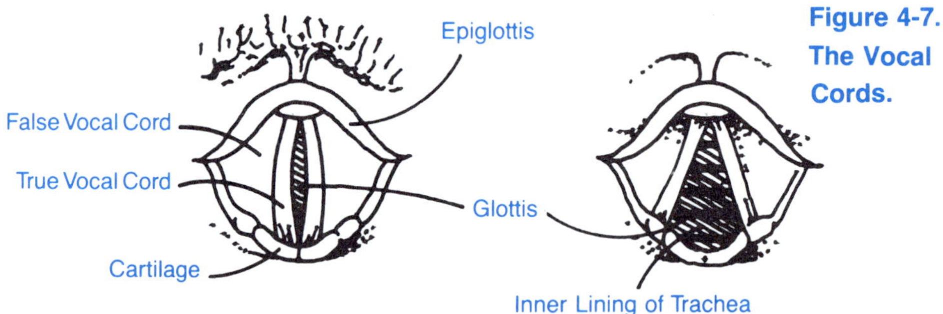

Figure 4-7. The Vocal Cords.

21. If breath sounds are auscultated on the right side only: while auscultating the left chest, withdraw the tube slowly until breath sounds are heard in the left lung field.

Removal of the ET-Tube

Removal of the ET-tube is not indicated in the field unless the patient develops intolerance to the tube and/or has a gag reflex.

To remove the ET-tube:

1. Have suction available.
2. Deflate the cuff completely.
3. Withdraw on inspiration.
4. Assess respiratory status.
5. Oxygenate.

Nasal Intubation

When attempting to secure the airway by nasal intubation, the paramedic needs to take a different approach than when orally intubating. The paramedic does **not** need:

1. A scope/blade.
2. The stylet in the ET-tube.

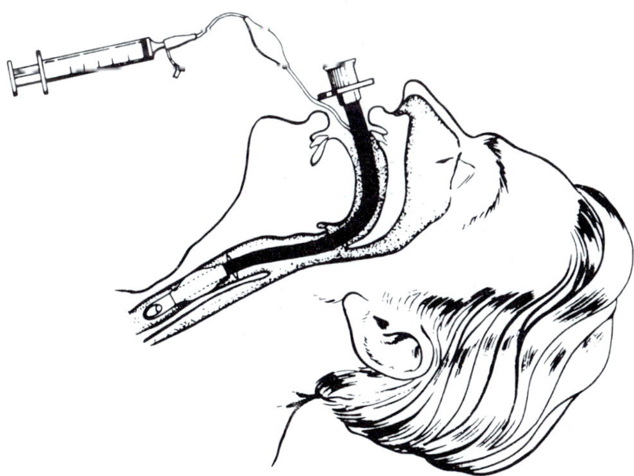

Figure 4-8. Inflated Endotracheal Tube in the Correct Position.
Courtesy Department of Transportation.

Nasal intubation is easiest when the patient is breathing. The tube is "slipped in" during inspiration.

1. The paramedic must lubricate (with a water-soluble jelly — preferably a xylocaine formula) both the tube and the nostril where insertion is to take place.
2. Keep the head and neck in the neutral position.
3. Light pressure to the thyroid cartilage may be helpful.
4. When inserting the tube, use gentle pressure.
5. If unsuccessful in one nostril, use the other.

As with oral intubation, be sure that all the equipment is in readiness and that the patient is well ventilated prior to the first attempt and in between any other attempts.

Laryngoscope/Blade

The laryngoscope/blade is an integral part of oral intubation. It has a battery-containing handle with removable blades that have small light bulbs on their ends. The laryngoscope/blade is used to expose the glottic opening in order for the paramedic to visualize the vocal cords for proper placement of the ET-tube. There are two types of blades — curved and straight. The curved blade is placed in the vallecula (crevice) of the throat in order to visualize the vocal cords. The curved blade is usually easier to use than the straight one. The straight blade is placed under the epiglottis to expose the vocal cords. Each type of blade comes in three or four sizes.

Stylet

The stylet is usually a soft metal wire that fits within the ET-tube. It is used to shape the ET-tube to allow for easy insertion during oral intubation. The stylet should stop two centimeters from the tracheal end of the tube to prevent injury to the throat and/or larynx. A right-angle, hook-over adapter is necessary to prevent the stylet from slipping out of the tube down the patient's throat. The stylet is generally **not** used in tubes that are size 3 or smaller.

Other Important Equipment for Mechanical Airway Management

In addition to the equipment mentioned above, the paramedic should have:

1. A suction unit.

2. A bag-valve device to be used with a face mask for ventilation prior to intubation and to be used with an ET-tube adapter to ventilate the patient after successful intubation.
3. A water-soluble lubricant to make the insertion of the ET-tube easier.
4. A stethoscope.
5. An oral airway.
6. A ten-cubic-centimeter syringe to inflate the cuff.
7. An oxygen source and tubing.

Transtracheal Ventilation (Transtracheal Jet Insufflation)

(This is **not** a DOT-required skill.)

This is an emergency technique used for temporarily oxygenating a patient when he/she has an airway obstruction (due to edema of the glottis, fracture of the larynx, severe oropharyngeal hemorrhage that prevents intubation) that cannot be relieved by endotracheal intubation. It is used until tracheal intubation, cricothyrotomy, or a tracheostomy is accomplished. It is ventilation by the insertion of an over-the-needle catheter through the cricothyroid membrane and intermittent jet oxygenation. The following equipment is necessary for this procedure:

1. A twelve- or fourteen-gauge, over-the-needle catheter with a ten-milliliter syringe.
2. Alcohol or povidone-iodine swabs.
3. Adhesive tape or ties.
4. Adequate length of oxygen tubing (five feet).
5. A "Y" or "T" connector (if available).
6. Oxygen cylinder that can provide fifty psi (most oxygen tanks and regulators can provide that at fifteen liters per minute or opened to flush).

Advantages of Use

1. Simple, inexpensive, and effective when applied properly.
2. No neck motion.
3. Least invasive of surgical procedures.
4. A quick procedure to perform.

Disadvantages of Use

1. An invasive procedure.
2. Requires **constant** attention.
3. Does not allow for efficient elimination of carbon dioxide. The patient may

only be adequately ventilated for thirty to forty-five minutes using this technique.[1]

4. May produce a pneumothorax.
5. May produce hemorrhage.
6. May produce subcutaneous or mediastinal emphysema.

Contraindications

This method is contraindicated when other less invasive airways (EOA, PtL, endotracheal tubes) can be safely and efficiently used.

Method of Insertion

1. The paramedic needs to identify the trachea, the cricoid cartilage, the cricothyroid membrane, and the thyroid cartilage. The small depression below the thyroid cartilage is the location of the cricothyroid membrane.
2. Prep the area with an antiseptic solution.

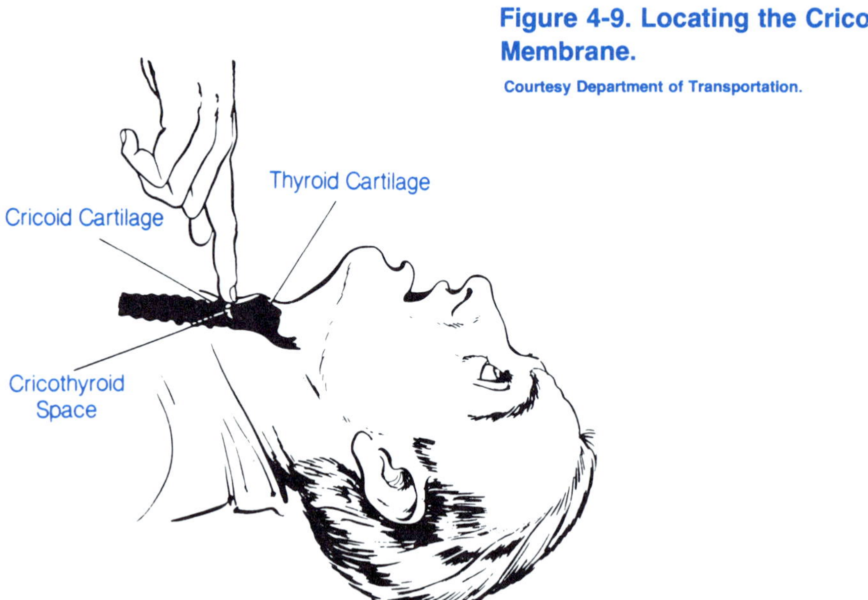

Figure 4-9. Locating the Cricothyroid Membrane.

Courtesy Department of Transportation.

[1]American College of Surgeons Committee on Trauma, *Advanced Life Support Course Student Manual*, ACSCT, 1985, p. 26.

3. ''The catheter-needle combination attached to the syringe is directed in the midline downward and caudally at a forty-five-degree angle.''[2] To confirm the needle's placement in the trachea, the paramedic pulls back on the syringe. If free air is returned, the needle is in the trachea.
4. The catheter should be advanced over the needle until the hub is against the skin. While holding the catheter, remove the needle.
5. Reconfirm proper placement by aspirating air out of the trachea.
6. Secure the catheter to the skin.
7. Connect the oxygen tubing directly to the catheter of the ''Y'' or ''T'' connector. If there are no connectors, cut a hole in the oxygen tubing. When the lungs are being inflated, the paramedic should put his/her finger over the hole; when exhalation occurs, the finger should be removed from the hole and the oxygen turned off. Then start the cycle again.
8. Turn on the oxygen regulator and follow directions directly above.
9. The American College of Surgeons' Committee on Trauma recommends that inflation should be one second and deflation four seconds.

Method of Removal

This device is designed to allow time to perform airway management procedures on an urgent rather than an emergent basis. Removal should be done after these other management techniques have been successfully accomplished.

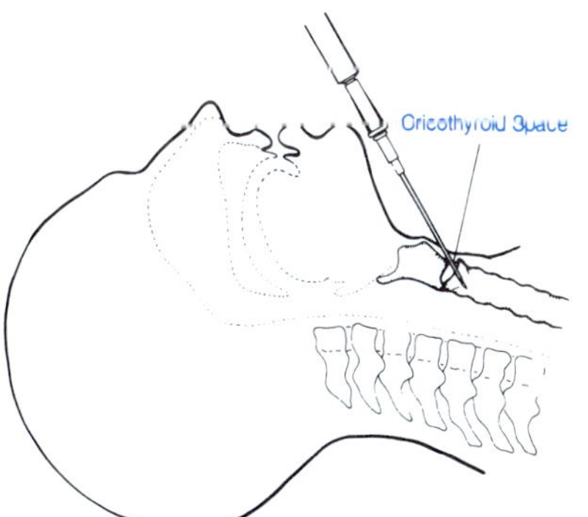

Figure 4-10a. Fourteen-Gauge Catheter Insertion.

Courtesy Department of Transportation.

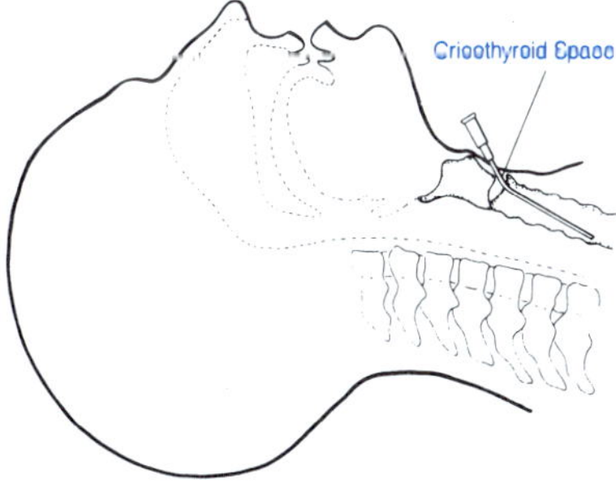

Figure 4-10b. Transtracheal Insufflation.

Courtesy Department of Transportation.

[2]American Heart Association, *Textbook of Advanced Cardiac Life Support,* American Heart Association, 1987, p. 33.

1. Remove by pulling out the needle and dressing the wound properly.

Cricothyrotomy

(This is **not** a DOT-required skill.)

This is a surgical procedure used to secure the airway when other less invasive procedures are not possible. It is performed by making a vertical incision in the cricothyroid membrane with a scalpel blade. The following equipment is necessary for this procedure:

1. Scalpel blade.
2. Pediatric-size ET-tube.
3. Antiseptic solution.
4. (A commercially prepared cricothyrotomy kit.)

Advantages of Use

1. Provides definitive airway control.
2. Provides minimal airway dissection.
3. Useful in upper airway injury and obstruction.

Disadvantages of Use

1. It is an invasive procedure.
2. Hemorrhage is possible.
3. Subcutaneous or mediastinal emphysema may occur.
4. Possibility of misplacement.
5. Possibility of injury to the larynx or other surrounding structures.

Contraindications

1. Do not perform with people under fourteen years of age.

Method of Insertion

1. Identify the cricothyroid membrane.
2. Make a vertical incision (less likely to cause hemorrhage than a horizontal incision[3]) through the skin.
3. A horizontal stab wound is made through the membrane.
4. Twist the scalpel blade to allow the insertion of the largest possible pediatric ET-tube.

[3]Joseph E. Clinton, M.D., and Ernest Ruiz, "Emergency Airway Management: Methods To Meet the Challenge," *Topics in Emergency Medicine*, Vol. 10, No. 1, p. 38.

5. Insert the tube and inflate the cuff (if appropriate).
6. Connect the bag-valve with the reservoir to provide the highest possible concentration of oxygen.
7. Auscultate breath sounds bilaterally and the stomach.

Method of Removal

This should not be removed in the field.

VENTILATION

Mouth-to-Mouth

Immediate ventilation occurs because no special equipment is necessary. There is a risk of exposure to communicable disease. It is difficult to provide increased oxygen concentrations.

Mouth-to-Pocket Mask

This device is easy to use, can provide oxygen concentrations up to 50 percent, and protects the user from contamination.

Bag-Valve-Mask

The benefits of this device are many. Oxygen concentrations of between 21 percent (room air concentrations) to nearly 100 percent (using supplemental oxygen and a reservoir) may be achieved. Positive-pressure ventilation can assist the patient whose breathing is shallow, and can also assist slow respiratory rates. However, the bag-valve-mask may be difficult to use, and an adequate seal between the mask and the face may not be attained easily.

Method of Use

1. Position the patient appropriately (hyperextend the neck in a nontraumatic patient and keep the head in the neutral position if traumatic).
2. Open and clear the airway.
3. Insert an oral airway.
4. Connect to an oxygen source with a reservoir.
5. Place the mask on the patient's face, making a tight seal by placing a thumb on the nose area, an index finger by the chin, and the rest of the fingers spread along the mandible.
6. Squeeze the bag.

Demand Valve

This device is easily connected to a mask, EOA, or ET-tube. It can ventilate past minor airway obstructions and delivers 100 percent oxygen concentrations. It is used primarily to assist respirations in the conscious patient who is experiencing difficulty in breathing. When a patient starts his/her inhalation, negative pressure occurs, which triggers the demand valve to move air until the negative pressure ceases. It may also be triggered manually when used on the apneic patient.

The paramedic should be aware of certain limitations and cautions when using this device:

1. On the nonbreathing patient with a face mask, pay close attention to the abdomen, because gastric distention (the stomach filling with oxygen or air) is apt to occur even during short periods of use.
2. There is danger of injury to the lungs when the demand valve is used with an ET-tube. Extreme caution must be maintained in this setting.
3. Do not use with persons younger than sixteen years of age.
4. Compliance of the lungs is not easily detectable, so the paramedic will not be able to gauge the ease or difficulty with which the oxygen is being delivered. The effectiveness may only be gauged by chest expansion.
5. The device is dependent on an oxygen source to power it.

Method of Use

1. Explain the procedure to the conscious patient.
2. Choose the proper size face mask.
3. Make a tight seal or explain to the patient how to use.
4. Trigger the device (either patient or paramedic).
5. Assess the rise of the chest.
6. Remember that expiration is passive.

Suction Devices

Suction devices can be used to clear fluids and small solid particles from the airway. An airway must be cleared because material is obstructing it from the paramedic's view or making it difficult for the patient to breathe.

The items most commonly suctioned out of the airway are:

1. Vomitus.
2. Saliva.
3. Food.

4. Blood.
5. Oxygen.

When a patient is being suctioned, oxygen is also being removed. Make sure that the patient is well oxygenated prior to suctioning. When performing tracheal suction, **do not apply suction for more than ten seconds.** Prolonged suctioning can reduce the oxygen available to the blood, causing cardiac arrest.

Assessment

1. Inspect the airway.
2. Auscultate the lung fields and trachea.

Management

Whistle Tip Suction Catheter

This is a narrow, flexible tube that is used primarily for tracheal suctioning and suctioning down an ET-tube. It has a thumb hold at the distal end for controlling the application of suction.

It is not possible to move large volumes of fluid rapidly or to remove small particles of food with whistle tip catheters. Remember — when suctioning the trachea, prolonged suctioning may cause hypoxemia (inadequate oxygenation of the blood in the arteries).

The whistle tip catheter is used in the following manner:

1. It may be inserted into a nasal airway or an ET-tube.
2. Close side hole with the thumb.
3. Aspirate for a maximum of ten seconds while removing the catheter slowly.

Tonsil Tip Suction Catheter

This is a rigid, large-tipped catheter that can be used to suction the mouth and throat. Because of the catheter's relatively large size, fluids may be rapidly suctioned. It can remove food particles that are sucked onto the tip of the catheter.

The paramedic must visualize the area being suctioned and should not vigorously insert the catheter; lacerations or other injuries to the oropharynx may occur.

The tonsil tip catheter is used in the following manner:

1. Insert the tonsil tip along the side of the oral airway into the mouth and back into the hypopharynx. It may also be guided by the hard and soft palates. (Be careful not to trigger the gag reflex.)
2. Slowly remove while suction is activated to remove large particles.

SUMMARY

Airway management is the number-one priority in patient care. The primary survey is the assessment and treatment of emergent airway difficulties (ABCs: airway, breathing, circulation). As all paramedics are aware of, the human brain may survive only four to six minutes without adequate oxygenation. Therefore, it is imperative for the paramedic to act rapidly, efficiently, and effectively when managing the patient with an airway problem.

The paramedic has the tools to successfully maintain most patients with airway problems. Sometimes, simply providing oxygen is all that is necessary; at other times an oral or nasal intubation or a cricothyrotomy may be necessary to keep a patient alive. With continued study of the management techniques and adequate practice (airway manikins can be of great help), the well-trained paramedic should be able to handle most airway management cases.

In addition to skill management, the paramedic should study the anatomical features that are important (both internal [e.g., vocal cords] and external [e.g., cricoid membrane]) for landmarking when performing certain skills. For some, managing the airway is the most difficult task that a paramedic may face.

This chapter has included the most up-to-date and commonly used airway control and maintenance devices. The field practice continues to change. At present, oral and nasal intubation is still the state-of-the-art method of airway control.

5

Shock:

Fluids, Electrolytes, and Acid-Base Balance

Shock is inadequate perfusion of bodily tissues. It is not a disease in itself but occurs secondary to trauma or illness. Shock may develop when serious injury causes significant blood loss, pump (heart) damage, spinal cord injury, or pulmonary injury, or when serious illness causes peripheral vasodilatation or severe dehydration. Remember — in order for blood to circulate properly there must be adequate blood volume, a good working pump, and an intact vascular system.

When the cells of the body are not adequately oxygenated and/or nourished, a sequence of events may occur that, if left uncorrected, will result in death. The body will set in motion a series of complex mechanisms in an attempt to achieve homeostasis and compensate for shock. If the state of shock is severe or prolonged, it may become irreversible. If this occurs, no intervention will save the patient.

This chapter will discuss shock as it relates to the whole organism as well as what occurs at the cellular level. This will entail a brief discussion of acid-base balance, the buffer systems, fluids, electrolytes, and the assessment and management of the patient in shock.

AEROBIC AND ANAEROBIC METABOLISM

Aerobic metabolism is the production of energy with adequate oxygen in the cells and is dependent upon:

1. Diffusion of oxygen across the alveolar capillary membranes.
2. Red blood cell (RBC) transportation, which requires an intact pump and vascular system.
3. Tissue oxygenation, which requires an adequate number of red blood cells, adequate tissue perfusion, and adequate off-loading (movement of oxygen from the red blood cells) to the tissue cells.

When any of these three requirements are not met, inadequate cellular oxygenation may occur, resulting in **anaerobic metabolism** (i.e., chemical breakdown of substances in the cell without oxygen). When anaerobic metabolism takes place, acids are produced. In the shock state, this acid buildup occurs faster than it can be removed (or neutralized), leading to a lowering of the blood pH (acid-base balance). Normal pH is between 7.35 and 7.45. As the pH drops below 7.35, the more acidotic the patient becomes, and as the pH increases above 7.45, the more alkalotic the patient becomes.

ACID-BASE BALANCE

Acid-base balance refers to the regulation of acidity and alkalinity in bodily fluids. The acidity or alkalinity of blood is a direct result of the number of hydrogen ions present. An increase of hydrogen ions in blood increases acidity, and a decrease of hydrogen ions in blood increases alkalinity.

The term "pH" is used to express the concentration of hydrogen ions in bodily fluids. As mentioned previously, the normal pH in bodily fluids is 7.35 to 7.45, which is slightly alkaline. When the pH is below 7.35, the patient is considered acidotic (a high concentration of hydrogen ions), and when the pH is above 7.45, the patient is considered alkalotic (a low concentration of hydrogen ions). The limits of pH that support life are approximately 6.9 at the low end (acidotic) and 7.8 at the high end (alkalotic). When the body is functioning properly, the normal pH is maintained. If a problem occurs that prevents adequate respiration or circulation of blood, the pH may drop, leading to acidosis. As the pH drops, bodily dysfunction increases. The body has mechanisms to attempt maintenance of normal acid-base balance even under "stress."

pH Compensation Systems

Under normal conditions, the body produces acids that need to be balanced so that homeostasis will be maintained. The body has three mechanisms to achieve this acid-base balance:

1. The buffer system.
2. The respiratory system.
3. The renal system.

These systems play an important role in the shocky patient who becomes acidotic (increased hydrogen ions) by trying to keep acid and base in balance.

The Buffer System

This system reacts immediately to changes in pH. The buffer system modifies any systemic changes in pH in order to maintain equilibrium (i.e., a pH between 7.35 and 7.45). Buffers absorb hydrogen ions when in excess and release hydrogen ions when in deficit.

Carbonate is the most important component of the buffer system. It consists of carbonic acid (H_2CO_3) and bicarbonate (HCO_3). These are found in the ratio 20-H_2CO_3 to 1-HCO_3. Carbonic acid is a weak acid and may break down in one of two ways, depending on whether a system is acidic or basic. The following shows how this may work:

$$H_2O + CO_2 \leftrightarrow H_2CO_3 \leftrightarrow H^+ + HCO_3$$

When there are too many hydrogen ions, the direction of the reaction goes to the left. When there are too few hydrogen ions, the direction is to the right. This system immediately goes into action when the patient experiences inadequate perfusion due to shock.

The Respiratory Compensation System

When there is an increase of either carbon dioxide or hydrogen ions in the system, the brain receives a stimulus to increase the rate of respirations. This generally takes one to three minutes. By reducing the carbon dioxide in the extracellular fluid (fluid outside the cells), the amount of carbonic acid is also reduced. When the system starts to normalize (reduced carbon dioxide and hydrogen ions), the respiratory rate returns to normal.

The Renal Compensation System

This is the slowest of the body's mechanisms for combating acidosis or alkalosis. It starts to operate hours to days after it is first stimulated. Simply put, excess hydrogen ions are eliminated if the body is too acidic, and excess bicarbonate ions are eliminated if the body is too basic.

Causes of Acidosis/Alkalosis

Respiratory Causes

When the lungs retain carbon dioxide, there is an increase of hydrogen ions and carbonic acid. The pH falls, leading to a respiratory acidosis. This might be caused in a person experiencing inadequate pulmonary ventilation, such as in chronic obstructive pulmonary disease (COPD) or respiratory insufficiency due to trauma. Since the respiratory system is the origin of the problem, it cannot participate in compensation. The renal system, on the other hand, compensates by keeping bicarbonate in the body and releasing more hydrogen ions in order to normalize the pH.

When the lungs release too much carbon dioxide, there is a decrease in carbon dioxide (hydrogen ions), leading to an increase in bicarbonate. The pH then rises, leading to respiratory alkalosis (e.g., hyperventilation).

Metabolic Causes

When there is an increase in the acids produced (anaerobic metabolism) by the cells, the extracellular fluid becomes acidotic. The pH then falls, leading to metabolic acidosis. Immediate compensation occurs from the respiratory system by increasing the rate and depth of breathing.

When there is an increase in a basic (alkaline) in the body through ingestion or injection of sodium bicarbonate, or through excessive loss of hydrogen ions from the kidneys or GI tract, the pH rises, leading to metabolic alkalosis. Compensation occurs by the body slowing its respirations and the kidneys excreting bicarbonate ions and retaining hydrogen ions.

CARDIOVASCULAR AND CELLULAR FUNCTION

When discussing tissue perfusion and shock, the paramedic must have a basic understanding of the cardiovascular system, electrolytes, and the fluids that make up the body.

Cardiovascular System

The cardiovascular system is made up of the following parts:

1. The pump (heart). Cardiac output and effectiveness are dependent on three components:
   - The heart rate.
   - The force of the heart's contractions.
   - Preload — the volume (this is the amount of blood in the heart after relaxation-diastole or filling of the heart) and force of contractions available for cardiac pumping.
2. The contents (blood) — most important, the volume of blood available for circulation.
3. The container (vessels). For optimum performance of the cardiovascular system, the container must be filled adequately for maintenance of an adequate blood pressure. This means that the vessels must be intact (no injuries) and appropriately constricted for blood pressure control.
   - Afterload — the resistance to the ventricles when pumping blood throughout the system; this measure is called systemic vascular resistance (SVR) or peripheral vascular resistance (PVR).
   - The effect of fluid volume in relationship to the container size and the effect of the container size in relationship to the amount of fluid. In other words, if the container is "larger" than the fluid volume available, the blood pressure will drop. This may occur in two ways: either the volume is reduced (i.e., hemorrhage, dehydration, etc.), or the container enlarges (vasculature dilation from spinal cord injury or sepsis).

Bodily Fluids and Electrolytes

The fluids and electrolytes of the body provide an internal environment that supplies necessary substances for cellular activity and removes the waste products of these activities. Maintenance of homeostasis within these fluids is vital to the survival of the cell and the entire organism.

Total Body Water

Total body water (TBW) is between 55 and 60 percent of an adult's body weight and is divided into the following compartments:

1. Extracellular fluid (ECF). This is composed of all the fluids that are found outside the cell, making up 20 percent of body weight. Extracellular fluid may be further divided into interstitial fluid (fluid bathing the cells) and intravascular fluid (the plasma portion of blood).
2. Intracellular fluid (ICF). This is the fluid found inside the cell membrane, making up 40 percent of body weight.

Electrolyte (Salt) Ions

An electrolyte is a substance that, when dissolved in water, will dissociate (separate) into electrically charged particles (ions). The two types of ions are cations (positively charged ions) and anions (negatively charged ions).

Cations

The principal cations are:

1. Sodium (Na^+). This is the most abundant ion in extracellular fluid. This cation has an effect on the water volume in the body. Water follows sodium. When the body excretes sodium, water is lost. When the body retains sodium (ingestion), water is also retained.
2. Potassium (K^+). This is the most important cation in the intracellular fluid. It plays an important role in mediating electrical impulses in muscles and nerves.
3. Calcium (Ca^{++}). This is the most abundant cation. It is essential for bone development, blood clotting, normal heartbeat, and initiation of neuromuscular and metabolic activity.
4. Magnesium (Mg^+). This is necessary for the metabolism of carbohydrates and proteins. Magnesium, along with calcium, prevents neuromuscular irritability.

Changes in these ion concentrations, particularly those of potassium, calcium, and magnesium, affect skeletal and cardiac muscle cell function.

Anions

The principal anions are:

1. Chloride (Cl^-). This ion follows sodium and is primarily found in extracellular fluid.
2. Bicarbonate (HCO_3^-). This is the principal buffer in the body. It plays an important role in maintaining acid-base balance.

Nonelectrolytes

Nonelectrolytes include:

1. Glucose. This is a sugar that is the most important carbohydrate in metabolism.
2. Urea. This is the chief nitrogenous endproduct of protein metabolism and the main component of urine. It is formed in the liver.

Proteins

Proteins include:

1. Albumin — a simple protein found in plant and animal tissue.
2. Plasma — the fluid portion of blood.
3. Lymph — an alkaline fluid found in the lymphatic system; similar to plasma.

How Materials Move at a Cellular Level

Osmosis

Osmosis is the movement of a solvent (water) through a semipermeable membrane from a solution of lower concentration to that of a higher concentration in an attempt to equalize the concentration on both sides of the membrane.

Semipermeable Membrane

This is a membrane through which water is freely interchangeable on both sides, and through which electrolytes cannot actively cross to the other side. When water crosses the semipermeable membrane to equalize the concentration of ions, the higher concentration pulls fluid from the lower concentrations.

Osmotic Pressure

This is the pressure that develops when two solutions of varying concentrations are separated by a semipermeable membrane. It is this force that causes the movement of water from a lesser concentration of solution to a greater one.

Isotonic Fluids

The osmotic pressure is equal to normal bodily fluid. The concentration of the solute is the same as that within the cells. This is a neutral solution. Normal saline is an isotonic fluid and will stay in the vascular space for a longer time than hypotonic or hypertonic solutions.

Hypotonic

The osmotic pressure is less than that of normal bodily fluids. The concentration of the solute is less than within the cells. Water will move from the vascular space into the cells. One-half normal saline is a hypotonic solution.

Hypertonic

The osmotic pressure is greater than that of normal bodily fluids. The concentration of the solute is greater than within the cells. Water will move from the cells into the vascular space. Fifty percent dextrose is a hypertonic solution.

Diffusion

Diffusion is the tendency of molecules in solution to move from a greater concentration to a lesser concentration. Molecules move more slowly than water. Small molecules cross semipermeable membranes faster than larger molecules. Glucose rapidly moves across membranes to create equal concentrations on both sides of a membrane.

Active Transport

This is the process of moving molecules across a cell membrane by the use of energy. Molecules generally move in the direction of higher concentration. Active transport is faster than diffusion.

PATHOLOGY

Types of Shock

Hypovolemic Shock

Hypovolemic shock occurs when there is inadequate tissue perfusion and oxygenation due to low volume. This may be a result of blood loss, fluid loss, or water loss from hemorrhage, burns, severe diarrhea, and multiple trauma. It is commonly associated with a 25 percent or greater blood volume loss. These patients usually present with an increased heart rate, increased diastolic pressure, decreasing pulse pressure (pulse pressure is the difference between the systolic and diastolic blood pressure), low cardiac output, pale, clammy skin, and anxiety.

Cardiogenic Shock

Cardiogenic shock occurs when there is inadequate tissue perfusion and oxygenation secondary to pump failure. This form of shock is usually a result of acute myocardial infarction, dysrhythmias, cardiac tamponade, cardiac contusion, pulmonary embolism, severe congestive heart failure, and dissecting aortic aneurysm. Most patients in cardiogenic shock present with increased heart rate, low cardiac output, pale and clammy skin, and anxiety. The mortality rate is about 80 percent.

Septic Shock

Septic shock is usually the result of a widespread infection affecting almost all the physiologic systems of the body. The spread of urinary tract infections, peritonitis, staphylococcal/streptococcal skin infections, pneumonia, and endocarditis are some of the primary infections that may lead to sepsis. This form of shock is not often seen in the prehospital setting. Between 40,000 and 120,000 people each year develop septic shock. It most commonly occurs among the elderly, alcoholics, and neonates. Generally, there are two stages — early and late. Early signs and symptoms are warm, flushed skin; tachycardia; and elevated respirations. Late-stage is the typical presentation of shock.

Neurogenic Shock

In neurogenic shock, a brainstem or spinal cord injury may lead to loss of sympathetic nervous control over vascular tone. This loss causes vasodilation, venous and arterial pooling of blood, and a resultant fall in blood pressure. The patient usually presents with hypotension without tachycardia or peripheral vasoconstriction. Volume replacement is still the appropriate treatment.

Anaphylactic Shock

This is an acute event caused by a severe allergic reaction that may result in circulatory and/or respiratory failure and death, usually from one minute to one hour after exposure. The signs and symptoms are dependent on the severity of the reaction. Common manifestations are hives, flushing, and edema. The more serious ones are laryngeal edema, constriction of the bronchial tree, and hypotension. (See Chapter 14 for a detailed discussion.)

Mechanism of Shock

Baroreceptors

Baroreceptors, found in the carotid arteries and aortic arch, detect changes in blood pressure. When low pressure is detected, transmissions are sent to the brain.

In response to the baroreceptor transmissions, the sympathetic nervous system causes the secretion of norepinephrine and epinephrine into the bloodstream. This leads to an increased force of cardiac contractions and increased cardiac rate, resulting in greater cardiac output. The peripheral effects are arteriolar constriction of the musculoskeletal and digestive systems, resulting in a decreased container size and increased peripheral resistance (this increases blood pressure and tissue perfusion).

Compensated Shock

This occurs when the body is able to compensate for blood loss or inadequate perfusion by the following changes:

1. Increased force of cardiac contractions.
2. Increased cardiac rate.
3. Increased cardiac output.
4. Increased systemic peripheral resistance (for maintenance of systolic blood pressure). The vessels to the skin, skeletal muscles, and digestive system are constricted.
5. Increased diastolic pressure.

The body's compensation mechanisms will attempt to maintain blood pressure and perfusion for as long as possible. If the underlying cause of shock is left untreated or prolonged at some point, the compensatory mechanisms will collapse.

Uncompensated Shock

This is the point when the body can no longer compensate for blood loss or other causes of shock and the body begins to fail.

1. The heart (pump) is unable to maintain blood pressure. The systolic and

diastolic pressures begin to fall.

2. Decreased myocardial strength occurs due to the following:
   - Ischemia due to a reduction of circulating red blood cells.
   - Decreased red blood cell oxygenation.
   - Decreased cardiac perfusion, leading to decreased coronary blood flow and decreased diastolic pressure.
   - Necrosis (tissue death) of the myocardium, possibly leading to myocardial infarction or an increase in the size of the infarction secondary to a decrease in perfusion.
   - Dysrhythmias secondary to hypoxia.
3. Peripheral effects of uncompensated shock are peripheral vascular changes, resulting in a relaxation of precapillary sphincters. This causes peripheral pooling and stagnation of the flow of blood.
4. Cellular changes that result from decreased perfusion are: anaerobic metabolism producing increased (hydrogen ions) acidosis and increased extracellular (potassium ions) hyperkalemia.

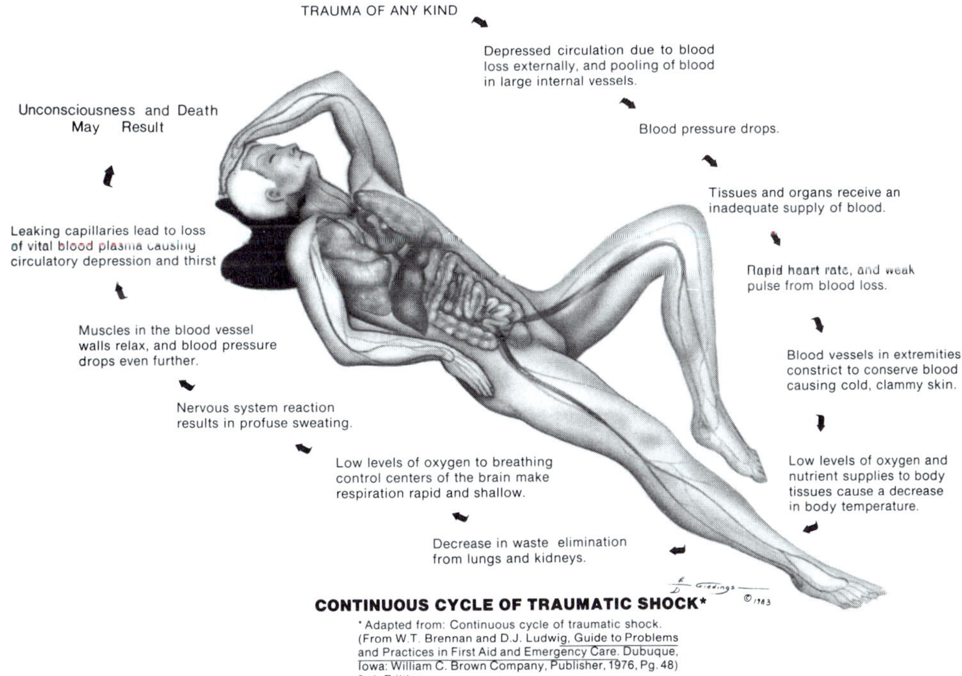

Figure 5-1. Continuous Cycle of Traumatic Shock.

Irreversible Sequelae of Shock

As shock continues, the following develops:

1. Anaerobic cellular metabolism leads to cellular necrosis.
2. Cellular necrosis leads to organ failure.
3. Organ failure leads to organism death, which is a total system failure.

Capillary-Cellular Relationship in Shock

1. The peripheral resistance is increased because there is precapillary sphincter contraction, thereby reducing the area in which blood will circulate.
2. The ischemic phase occurs because the capillaries contain minimal blood due to minimal perfusion. The oxygen supply is then cut off to the cells perfused by these capillaries, resulting in anaerobic metabolism. This creates an increased production of potassium and hydrogen ions (acidosis).
3. The stagnant phase consists of the relaxation of the precapillary sphincter with continued contraction of the postcapillary sphincter, resulting in capillary engorgement. As shock continues, there is still a minimal blood flow with continued anaerobic metabolism and increasing acidosis. Red blood cells cluster together like "rolls of coins," called Rouleaux formation.
4. The washout phase occurs when the postcapillary sphincter relaxes, causing the accumulated waste products to move back to the core body. These products are hydrogen ions, potassium ions, Rouleaux red blood cells, and increased carbon dioxide available for the production of carbonic acid (which increases acidosis). The Rouleaux red blood cells become microemboli to the lungs, blocking some small vessels, and systemic metabolic acidosis develops further.

PATIENT EVALUATION

Primary Survey

1. Evaluate the airway.
2. Evaluate breathing.
3. Evaluate circulation:
   - Pulse.
   - Hemorrhage.
   - Skin.

- Capillary refill. If less than two seconds, good perfusion; if more than two seconds, inadequate perfusion.

4. Disability. Evaluate the patient for:
   - Confusion.
   - Disorientation.
   - Agitation (may result from decreased cerebral perfusion and decreased oxygenation of brain cells).
5. Expose. Inspect the head, neck, chest, and abdomen in the seriously injured trauma patient.

Secondary Survey

1. Take all vital signs.
2. Monitor the ECG when appropriate.
3. Do a complete physical examination in a non-life-threatening situation.
4. Obtain a history.

Monitoring the Patient

Pulse

1. Normal rate may be seen even with a 10 to 15 percent volume deficit.
2. Pulse assessment may be altered due to increased peripheral resistance (difficult to obtain).
3. If a radial pulse is present, systolic pressure is greater than 80.
4. If a femoral pulse is present, systolic pressure is greater than 70.
5. If a carotid pulse is present, systolic pressure is greater than 60.

Diastolic Pressure

Diastolic pressure may stay within normal limits with a blood loss as great as 30 percent.

1. It is increased initially with increased peripheral resistance.
2. Coronary blood flow may remain normal with up to a 30 percent deficit.
3. The paramedic should not be deceived because the patient presents with a normal blood pressure. The patient may still be seriously injured.

Systolic Pressure

Systolic pressure may stay normal with a blood loss as great as 30 percent.

Skin

1. The color reflects the adequacy of red blood cell oxygenation.
   - Pale is decreased perfusion (ischemic).
   - Cyanotic is stagnant pooling of the blood with inadequate oxygenation.
   - Mottled is a combination of both and is a late sign of shock.
2. Temperature of the skin reflects adequacy of perfusion and heat retention to the core body. Skin is usually cool to touch.

Respiration

The respiration rate is usually normal with up to a 15 percent blood loss (twelve to twenty respirations per minute). As blood loss or shock continues, the respirations increase to as many as thirty-five or more per minute.

The body responds to an increase of hydrogen ions by increasing the respiratory rate in order to remove excess carbon dioxide. The removal of carbon dioxide reduces the number of hydrogen ions available to produce carbonic acid. This is an attempt to normalize the pH and reduce the buildup of acids in the bodily fluids.

RESUSCITATION

Tissue Ischemia Sensitivity

1. The heart, brain, and lungs may tolerate four to six minutes of warm ischemia. (This is the length of time these organs may survive without sustaining damage when oxygen is unavailable.)
2. The gastrointestinal tract, liver, and kidneys may tolerate between forty-five and sixty minutes of warm ischemia.
3. The muscles and skin may tolerate between two and three hours of warm ischemia.

Red Blood Cell Oxygenation

The paramedic must:

1. Assure an open airway; intubate if necessary.
2. Assure adequate breathing, providing 100 percent of oxygen concentration with ventilatory assistance as needed.
3. Transport as an emergency.

Pneumatic Antishock Garment (PASG) or Medical Antishock Trousers (MAST)

"For the last fifteen years PASGs have played a lifesaving role in the emergency care of the shocky patient. The use of this garment has grown so presently they are standard equipment on ambulances equipped to the American College of Surgeons recommendations. Recently these devices have come under close scrutiny, and their lifesaving benefits have been questioned. Research is underway in an attempt to scientifically determine the PASG's effectiveness. . . . To date the effects on long-term survival rates are not clear, and there can be little doubt as to the short-term benefits of PASG use. The increase in blood pressure and the decrease in blood loss effected by the garment enable patients to reach definitive care who would otherwise expire in the field. Unless future studies prove otherwise, the use of the PASG should be continued as a lifesaving treatment in the immediate care of the trauma patient."[1]

"The MAST suit represents a common situation: It was released for widespread use before a true understanding of its mechanisms of action could be determined by controlled investigation. Interestingly, despite widespread clinical use and acceptance, it has yet to be demonstrated that the use of the antishock suit decreases patient mortality or morbidity. Critics of antishock garments have recently challenged the universal acceptance of these devices."[2]

As can be seen by the two opposing views on the PASG (MAST), there is much controversy regarding their use. Until the controversy is settled, the following are the presently accepted indications for PASG usage. The paramedic should follow local protocol.

Indications for Use of the PASG

1. For resuscitation of shock.
2. For hemorrhage control.
3. Tamponading soft-tissue and intra-abdominal hemorrhage.

---

[1]Scott B. Frame, M.D. and Norman E. McSwain, "Pneumatic Anti-Shock Garments: Where They Stand Today." *Emergency Care Quarterly,* Volume 3, Number 4, February 1988, pp. 65-72.

[2]Scott M. Davis, "Antishock Trousers: A Collective Review." *The Journal of Emergency Medicine,* Volume 4, January 1986, pp. 145-155.

4. For fracture stabilization of the pelvis, femur, and lower extremities.
5. To provide venous distention in the upper extremity (antecubital) veins (that have collapsed), permitting easier IV route accessibility.
6. In the cardiac arrest patient, PASG may increase cardiac output, may increase carotid blood flow, and may increase cerebral blood flow from 3 to 10 percent.

Possible Contraindications

Always consult with medical control and follow local protocol.

1. Pulmonary edema.
2. Isolated head trauma.
3. Serious thoracic trauma.

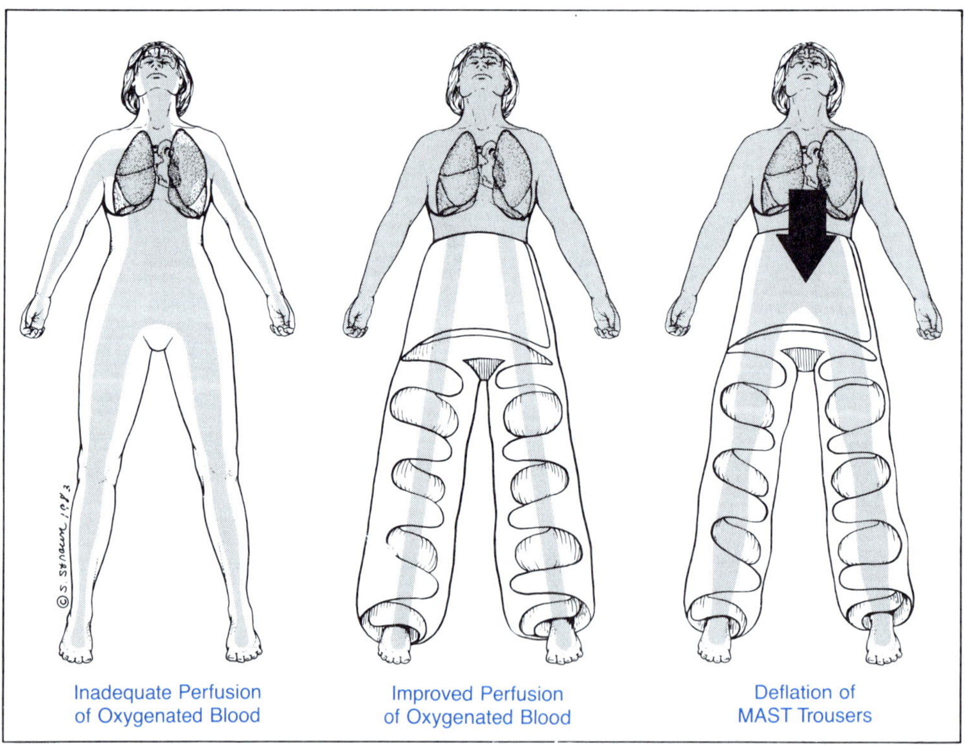

Figure 5-2. MAST Application.

Effects of Use

1. Reduces the container size and/or increases vascular resistance beneath the device.
2. May increase perfusion of very ischemia-sensitive tissues (i.e., brain, heart, and lungs).
3. Increased blood pressure.
4. Increased preload, which may increase cardiac output.
5. Peripheral resistance is increased, which may increase the flow of blood to the upper body.
6. Decreased blood flow to muscles and skin of the legs, which are relatively ischemic-resistant.
7. Diaphragmatic excursion (movement) has a 50 percent reduction with an increase in intrathoracic pressure. Usually there is no change in the PaO_2, pH, or $PaCO_2$. The paramedic must observe for inadequate ventilations.
8. Hemorrhage control through circumferential tissue pressure on the lower extremities and abdomen. This specifically may reduce intra-abdominal, pelvic fracture, retroperitoneal, and lower extremity hemorrhage.
9. Rigid external stabilization of lower extremity fractures.
10. Pelvic fracture stabilization.
11. Femur fracture stabilization (traction splint superior when shock is not present).

Fluid Replacement

Whole Blood

Whole blood is the most desirable because of its oxygen-carrying capacity, but it is not available for use in the field.

Crystalloid-Volume Expanders

Volume expanders are used to increase volume for the patient who is in shock, particularly hypovolemic shock. They immediately expand the volume, but two-thirds of the volume is lost to the intrastitial space within one hour of administration. It is best not to exceed a dosage of two to three liters when treating a patient in the field.

The following are the two most widely used volume expanders in the prehospital setting.

1. Ringer's lactate is an isotonic fluid that acts as a buffer when metabolized,

helping to combat acidosis.
2. Normal saline is an isotonic fluid but does not act as a buffer.

Other volume expanders include the following:

1. Glucose has immediate volume-expansion effects but leaves the intravascular compartment rapidly. Its volume-replacement benefits may last five to fifteen minutes.
2. Plasma acts as a volume expander, but because of storage problems (it must be refrigerated) and cost (it is expensive), it is not used as a prehospital IV fluid.
3. Dextran has similar properties of plasma with the additional problems of possibly causing type and cross-match difficulties as well as causing clotting problems.

Rate of Fluid Replacement

1. The monitoring parameters are the vital signs returning to normal or stabilizing. They are:
   - The pulse rate and strength.
   - Blood pressure (systolic blood pressure above 90 mmHg).
   - Skin color, temperature, and capillary refill time (less than two seconds.
2. Fluid replacement is usually ''wide open'' (i.e., flowing as fast as possible in the patient experiencing shock).

Routes of Fluid Replacement

1. The length of the catheter (an inverse relationship). The longer the catheter, the slower the infusion rate.
2. The internal diameter of the catheter (a direct relationship). The wider the catheter, the faster the infusion rate. Therefore, the area inside of the lumen determines the rate of flow.
3. The most common IV needle sizes are 22-gauge, 20-gauge, 18-gauge, 16-gauge, and 14-gauge.
4. In the adult patient, a 14-gauge needle should be used in starting an IV when treating a patient in serious shock.
5. The size of the vein has no relationship to the flow rate of fluid into that vein.
6. Central IV lines presently have no prehospital use.

Peripheral IV Placement

1. Fourteen-gauge is preferred because of the increased flow rates possible from this size catheter.
2. Advantages:
   - The IV sites are easily located and accessible.
   - Minimal equipment is needed for insertion.
   - A peripheral IV is inserted rapidly.
   - It can be accomplished while other activities are going on.
   - Peripheral IVs are easy to maintain.
3. Disadvantages:
   - In severe volume depletion, it may be difficult to locate venous blood vessels (consider application of PASG) to start an IV.
   - Veins may easily roll and may possibly collapse.
4. Preliminary steps for IV insertion:
   - Apply a venous tourniquet.
   - Identify the vein.
   - Prepare the tape.
   - Prepare the IV setup.
   - Clean the IV site.
   - Insert the largest gauge needle possible.
   - Watch for blood to enter the flashback chamber.
   - Tape the catheter down securely.
   - Adjust the flow rate.

Steps in Shock Resuscitation for the Severely Injured Patient

1. Perform the ABCs.
2. Stabilize the cervical spine and vertebral column as appropriate for the situation.
3. Continue airway management, providing high-flow, high-concentration oxygen and ventilatory support.
4. Apply pneumatic antishock garment.
5. Load the patient in the ambulance for rapid transport.
6. While en route to the hospital:
   - Administer IV fluids using a large-bore needle; consider inserting two "lines." Usually run in no more than three liters of fluid.
   - Monitor the vital signs continually.
   - Continue evaluation and stabilization of wounds and fractures, if possible.

- Monitor the ABCs.
- Continue evaluation of the patient.

SUMMARY

Shock is not a disease but a syndrome that occurs secondary to trauma or illness. To best manage the patient in shock, it is helpful to understand what shock is, how it affects the body, how the body compensates for it, and what interventions the paramedic may perform.

The paramedic must be observant and have a high index of suspicion that shock may be developing or already is progressing when treating the seriously ill or injured patient.

6

General Pharmacology

A drug is any substance intended for use in the diagnosis, cure, treatment, or prevention of disease. It is a chemical that affects the life processes of a living organism.

It is of great importance for the paramedic to be thoroughly familiar with all drugs that may be used in the field. Few drugs can be administered without risk. Therefore, the following information about drugs must be understood thoroughly.

1. The effects of the drug (action).
2. Indications.
3. Contraindications.
4. Appropriate administration:
   - The proper route.
   - The proper dosage (the paramedic must know the usual dosage and should know when to modify this based on a patient's history).
5. Side effects.
6. Incompatibility with other medications.
7. Antidotes.

Most paramedics know that there are both benefits and dangers in using drugs. The benefits are usually apparent. The dangers most often can be avoided if the paramedic is thoroughly familiar with each medication carried in the drug kit.

TERMINOLOGY

1. **Additive.** The combined effects of two or more agents being equal to the sum of their separate effects.
2. **Antagonism.** Mutual opposition in action between drugs.
3. **Cumulative action.** Increasing in effect by successive additions. The action of a drug that may accumulate in the blood over the period of usage.
4. **Depression.** Decreased level of function.
5. **Habituation.** The act of becoming accustomed to anything from frequent use. In drug use, it is the mental dependency that results from frequent use.
6. **Hypersensitivity.** Abnormal sensitivity to a drug.
7. **Idiosyncracy.** An uncommon response to a drug. This can manifest itself as a toxic or inappropriate response to a therapeutic dose of a drug.
8. **Irritation.** A possible reaction to a drug.
9. **Potentiation.** The enhancement of one agent by another (so that the combined effect is greater than the effects of each one alone).
10. **Synergism.** The joint action of agents (drugs) so that their combined effect is greater than the algebraic sum of their individual effects.
11. **Therapeutic.** Having medicinal or healing properties.
12. **Tolerance.** A progressive decrease in effectiveness of a drug.
13. **Untoward reaction.** An adverse effect of drug therapy.

DRUG SOURCES

There are four major sources of drugs:

1. Animal — insulin and oxytocin.
2. Plant — atropine sulfate and morphine sulfate.
3. Mineral — sodium bicarbonate and calcium chloride.
4. Synthetic — lidocaine and bretylium tosylate.

DRUG NAMES

Four different names are given to describe a drug.

1. Official name — the name of the drug that is listed with either the United States Pharmacopeia (USP) or with the National Formulary (NF).

2. Chemical name — this is the actual chemical formula. It is generally complex.
3. Generic name — simplified version of the chemical name. This is usually the same as the official name.
4. Trade name — this is the name devised for a drug by the pharmaceutical company manufacturing it.

Tetracycline is a commonly used antibiotic medication. Its four names are:

Official name: tetracycline USP.
Chemical name: 4-dimethylamino-1, 4, 4a, 5, 5a, 6, 11, 12a-octahydro-3, 6, 10, 12, 12a-pentahydroxyl-6-methyl-1, 11-dioxo-2-naphthacenecarboxamide.
Generic name: tetracycline.
Trade names: Achromycin®, Panmycin®, Polycycline®.

DRUG STANDARDS AND LEGISLATION

In 1906, the Pure Food and Drug act was enacted by Congress, establishing the Food and Drug Administration (FDA). It prohibited the sale of useless drugs and restricted the sale of medications that had potential for abuse. In 1915, the Harrison Narcotic Act was enacted by Congress. This act was designed to control the importation, manufacture, and sale of the opium plant, the coca plant, and their derivatives. Other drugs were added to this list at later dates.

In 1938, the Federal Food, Drug, and Cosmetic Act was enacted, with the "truth in labeling clause" being an important highlight. It required that the names of all the ingredients used in the preparation of a drug be listed on the label together with clear directions for the drug's use. Habit-forming drugs had to be specified as such with their percentage. This act was revised in 1952 and 1962.

In 1970, Congress passed the Controlled Substance Act, which classified drugs into five schedules. This was a major update in the control and classification of drugs. The schedules are as follows:

1. Schedule 1 — drugs that have a high potential for abuse and no accepted medical use; examples are heroin and LSD.
2. Schedule 2 — drugs that have a potential for abuse and also have medical usefulness; examples are morphine sulfate and meperidine.

3. Schedule 3 — drugs that have a lower potential for abuse while remaining medically useful; an example is the codeine preparation acetominophen number 3.
4. Schedule 4 — lists drugs with a low potential for abuse; an example is Diazepam (valium).
5. Schedule 5 — drugs that have the lowest potential for abuse.

The Drug Enforcement Administration (DEA) is responsible for enforcing the 1970 Controlled Substance Act.

DRUG FORMS

Solid Drugs

1. Pills.
2. Capsules.
3. Caplets.
4. Tablets.
5. Powders.
6. Suppositories (are solid at room temperature).

Liquid Drugs

1. Solutions — preparations in which the drug is usually mixed with water.
2. Tinctures — drugs extracted with alcohol.
3. Spirits — volatile solutions.
4. Syrups — drugs combined with water and sugar to make the drugs palatable.
5. Elixirs — contain a drug in an alcohol solvent with flavor to improve its taste.
6. Emulsions — a combination of an oily substance and a solvent in which the oily substance does not dissolve.
7. Suspensions — drugs that do not remain dissolved in a fluid.

DRUG REFERENCES

1. Physician's Desk Reference.
2. Hospital Formulary.
3. American Medical Association Drug Evaluation.

PHARMACOKINETICS

Pharmacokinetics is the study of the action of drugs on metabolism with an emphasis on the time required for absorption, the duration of action, the distribution in the body, and the method of excretion. The paramedic should be thoroughly familiar with the drugs carried on the ambulance.

Factors That Affect the Action of a Drug

1. Age of the patient.
2. Condition of the patient.
3. Dosage of the drug being administered.
   - What is the minimal dosage?
   - What is the maximal dosage?
   - What is the toxic dosage?
   - What is the lethal dosage?
4. Absorption. The following are methods used to administer medications into the body from fastest to slowest rate of absorption:
   - Direct injection into bloodstream (intravenous — IV).
   - Transtracheal — through an endotracheal tube.
   - Rectal insertion of a drug that is absorbed through the mucous membranes.
   - Intramuscular (IM) injection.
   - Intralingual injection; sublingual absorption of medication into the bloodstream.
   - Injection into the subcutaneous tissue or underneath the skin (SQ).
   - Administration of a drug orally. The drug enters the bloodstream through the digestive tract.

Distribution

Distribution refers to:

1. The way in which a drug is transported within the body.
2. Where a drug binds.
3. How much of a drug that is administered is actually free to act on the body.
4. The rapidity of onset of the effect of the drug.
5. How long a drug effect will last.
6. Whether a drug can pass through the ''blood-brain'' barrier (a membrane surrounding the brain that selectively allows drugs to pass through).

Metabolism

Metabolism is the chemical transformation of material in living cells. It usually results in inactivation of drugs. The liver is the most common site for drug metabolism.

1. Liver impairment may cause a cumulative effect of a drug.
2. Liver impairment might be a reason to change a drug dosage.

Other organs that metabolize drugs to a lesser extent than the liver are:

1. The kidneys.
2. The intestinal mucosa.
3. The plasma.

Elimination

Elimination is the process by which drugs are removed from the body. The kidney is the principal organ of elimination.

1. Kidney impairment will cause increased retention of some drugs.
2. Kidney impairment might be a reason to change a drug dosage to be administered.

Other organs of elimination are:

1. The intestinal tract.
2. The skin.
3. The lungs.

EFFECTS OF DRUGS ON THE HUMAN BODY

Drugs can and do affect many organ systems of the body. The system most affected by drugs used in the field by paramedics is the autonomic nervous system.

Autonomic Nervous System

The autonomic nervous system controls involuntary actions (e.g., heart rate, digestion) and is divided into two systems: the parasympathetic or cholinergic, and the sympathetic or adrenergic (see Table 6-1).

The parasympathetic nervous system controls vegetative (involuntary) functions. It is mediated through the vagus nerve by the hormone actecolyine. Vagus nerve stimulation causes a slowing of the heart. Atropine can block vagal stimulation.

The sympathetic nervous system controls responses to stress (the ''fight-or-flight'' response). It is mediated by nerves from the thoracic and lumbar ganglia. The chemical mediators are norepinephrine and epinephrine. These two chemicals (drugs), as well as other medications, affect the sympathetic nervous system by influencing receptors called alpha and beta. Drugs and certain hormones may affect either alpha or beta receptors, or both. Alpha stimulation effects have no direct effect on the heart. There is little or no

Table 6-1

Category	Parasympathetic	Sympathetic
Natural chemical mediator	Acetylcholine	Norepinephrine Epinephrine
Primary nerve innervation	Vagus	Nerves from the thoracic and lumbar ganglia
Effects of stimulation of these nerves:	Slows the heart. Constricts pupils. Increases digestive functions and other vegetative functions.	Constricts blood vessels dealing with vegetative functions. Increases the rate and force of contraction of the heart, dilates the pupils.
Blocking drugs:	Atropine.	Propranolol.
Stimulating drugs:	Reserpine. Neostigmine	Beta-only Isoproterenol Alpha plus beta norepinephrine epinephrine metaraminol dopamine

bronchoconstriction, but a great vasoconstricting effect that increases peripheral vascular resistance. The beta stimulation effects are increased heart rate, increased force of contraction, arterial dilation, and bronchial tree dilation.

WEIGHTS AND MEASURES

There are two systems of weights and measures — the apothecary and metric.

The Apothecary System

This system, used for measuring and weighing drugs and solutions, was brought to the United States from England at the time of colonization. It is not used extensively in prehospital medicine.

Solid Measures

1. Grain.
2. Dram.
3. Ounce.
4. Pound.

Liquid Measures

1. Minim (or fluid dram).
2. Fluid ounce.
3. Pint.
4. Quart.
5. Gallon.

Metric System

This is a system of weights and measures based upon the meter as the unit of measurement; the gram (1,000 milligrams) as the unit of weight; and the liter (1,000 milliliters) as the unit of volume.

Decimals — A Brief Review

1. The metric system uses multiples of ten; this is the decimal system. The paramedic must be familiar with the decimal system in order to use the

metric system properly. Whole numbers are to the left of the decimal point, and decimal fractions are to the right of the decimal point (see Figure 6-1).

Figure 6-1.

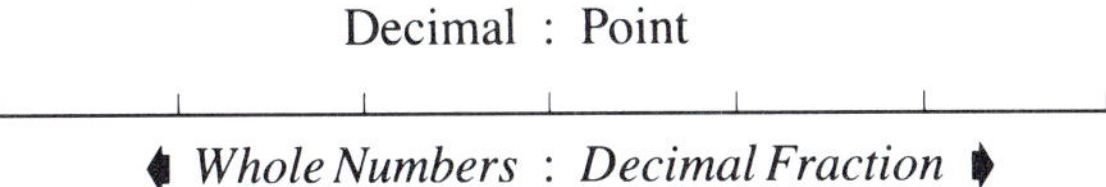

The position of the number in relation to the decimal point gives the number its place name.

Thousands — Hundreds — Tens : Tenths — Hundredths — Thousandths

To eliminate the confusion that might arise from overlooking the decimal point and reading the decimal fraction as a whole number, a zero is placed to the left of the decimal point when there is no whole number (e.g., 0.05, 0.10, 0.75).

2. Addition and subtraction of decimals. Line up the decimals and add zeros to the right of the decimal point as necessary.

   Examples:

   Addition: 2.5 + 31.23

   $$\begin{array}{r} 2.50 \\ +31.23 \\ \hline 33.73 \end{array}$$

   Subtraction: 31.23 - 2.50

   $$\begin{array}{r} 31.23 \\ -2.50 \\ \hline 28.73 \end{array}$$

3. Multiplication of decimals. This is the same as multiplication of whole numbers except that the paramedic must note where the decimal point is placed.

Examples: 123 × 0.2 1.23 × 0.2

$$\begin{array}{r} 123 \\ \times 0.2 \\ \hline 24.6 \end{array}$$

$$\begin{array}{r} 1.23 \\ \times 0.2 \\ \hline .246 \end{array}$$

4. Dividing decimals. This is the same as with whole numbers, but again, the placement of the decimal needs to be watched. Thirty-six divided by six equals six. Thirty-six is the dividend, six is the divisor, and six — the answer — is called the quotient. The divisor must always be a whole number. In 3.6 divided by 0.6, the divisor, 0.6, must be converted into a whole number. The decimal must be moved one place to the right in the divisor and also in the dividend (the decimal in the divisor cannot be moved without moving the decimal in the dividend). Thus, 0.6 becomes 6 and 3.6 becomes 36. Now, the division can continue.

   To divide a decimal by multiples of ten, do the reverse of what is done in multiplying. The decimal is moved to the **left** by the number of zeros in the divisor.

3.6 ÷ 0.6

0.6.) 3.6.

$$\begin{array}{r} 6 \\ 6\overline{)36} \end{array}$$

Solid Measures

1. Milligrams (mgs) — these are secondary units. One milligram is 1/1000th of a gram. There are 1,000 milligrams in a gram.
2. Grams (gms) — primary units consisting of 1,000 milligrams.
3. Kilograms (kgs).
4. Converting milligrams to grams and grams to milligrams:
   - When converting milligrams to grams, the paramedic must move the decimal point three places to the **left**. Example: 500 milligrams equals

0.500 grams. (Remember — there are 1,000 milligrams in a gram.)

- When converting grams to milligrams, the decimal point must be moved three places to the right. Example: 10.0 grams equals 10,000 milligrams.

Liquid Measures

1. Milliliter (ml) and cubic centimeter (cc) are equivalent. They are equal to one one-thousandth (1,1000th) of a liter).
2. Liter (l). Primary unit consisting of 1,000 milliliters.
3. Converting milliliters to liters and liters to milliliters — follow the same format as for converting milligrams to grams and grams to milligrams.

Conversion from Metric to Apothecary and Apothecary to Metric

The following are the most common conversions used by paramedics:

1. Grains to grams, divide by 15. Example: 60 grains: 60 divided by 15 equals 4 grams.
2. Grams to grains, multiply by 15. Example: 4 grams: 4 multiplied by 15

Table 6-2
Comparison of Metric to Apothecary to Household

Metric	Apothecary	Household
4 ml	60 minim/1 fluid dram	60 drops/1 teaspoon
30 ml	1 fluid ounce	2 tablespoonfuls
240 ml	8 fluid ounces	1 cupful
500 ml	1 pint	1 pint
1,000 ml (1 liter)	1 quart	1 quart
4,000 ml (4 liters)	1 gallon	1 gallon
1 mg	1/60 grain	
65 mg	1 grain	
1 gram	15.4 grains	
4 grams	1 dram	
28.3 grams	1 ounce	
1 kilogram	2.2 pounds	

equals 60 grains.

3. Grams to ounces, divide by 30. Example: 60 grams: 60 divided by 30 equals 2 ounces.
4. Ounces to grams, multiply by 30. Example: 2 ounces: 2 multiplied by 30 equals 60 grams.
5. Milligrams to grains, divide by 60. Example: 180 milligrams: 180 divided by 60 equals 3 grains.
6. Grains to milligrams, multiply by 60. Example: 3 grains: 3 multiplied by 60 equals 180 milligrams.
7. Pounds to kilograms, divide the number of pounds by 2.2 pounds. Example: 154 pounds divided by 2.2 equals 70 kilograms.

DRUG CONCENTRATIONS AND CALCULATIONS

In order to administer the correct dosage of a drug, a paramedic must know its concentration: the number of milligrams of the drug mixed in a given volume of solution (milliliters). If the information is not readily available, it can be easily determined by using the following formula:

$$\text{Concentration} = \frac{\text{total milligrams}}{\text{total milliliters}}$$

Example: If a vial contains 100 mg of drug A in 10 ml, the concentration is:

$$\text{Concentration} = \frac{100 \text{ ms}}{10 \text{ ml}} = 10 \text{ mg/ml}$$

To figure out the volume of a drug to be administered (once the concentration is known), use this formula:

$$\text{Volume to be administered (in ml)} = \frac{\text{desired dose (in mgs)}}{\text{concentration on hand (mg/ml)}}$$

Example: A paramedic is asked to administer 50 mg of drug B (desired dose). The concentration of drug B is 5 mg per milliliter (concentration on hand). How many milliliters should the paramedic draw up?

$$\frac{50\text{ mg}}{5\text{ mg/ml}} = \text{Volume to be administered}$$

$$10\text{ ml} = \text{Volume to be administered}$$

IV SETUPS

1. Macro — 15 macro drops equals 1.0 milliliters (or 1.0 cubic centimeters).
2. Macro-blood pump 10 macro drops equals 1.0 milliliters (or 1.0 cubic centimeters.
3. Micro-60 micro drops equals 1.0 milliliters (or 1.0 cubic centimeters).
4. To determine the flow rate:

$$\text{Drops (gtt) per minute} = \frac{\text{volume to be infused} \times \text{drops per milliliter (of the given administration set)}}{\text{total time of infusion in minutes}}$$

Example: How many drops/minute will be needed to infuse 250 ml (volume to be infused) with a micro administration set? 60 drops equals 1 ml over a period of 20 minutes (infusion time).

$$\text{drops/minute} = \frac{250\text{ ml} \times 60}{20}$$

$$\text{drops/minute} = \frac{15{,}000}{20} = 750\text{ drops/minute}$$

DRUG ADMINISTRATION

Safety Considerations and Procedures

1. Concentrate on the task.
2. Be sure that the base physician understands the situation.
3. Be sure that the base physician's orders are clearly understood.
4. Repeat orders back to base to get confirmation on all drug orders.

5. Read labels carefully at least three different times prior to administration of any medication.
6. Double-check all calculations before the dosage is given.
7. Maintain aseptic procedures.
8. Check for incompatibility problems.
9. Monitor the patient continually.
10. Be familiar with local protocols.

Techniques of Administration

Drawing Medication from Ampules and Vials

1. **Ampules.** Lightly shake or tap to release the solution from the ampule's neck. Place an alcohol wipe around the neck and break off. Solution may now be drawn out of the ampule.
2. **Vials.** Wipe off the top of the vial with an alcohol wipe. Pull air into a syringe equal to the amount of solution necessary to be withdrawn from the vial. Insert the needle into the vial, injecting the air into it. Invert the vial and withdraw the required solution.
3. Prevent contamination of the needle during these procedures.

Using Prefilled Syringes

Prefilled syringes are the most convenient form for medications to be supplied for prehospital use. After confirming the drug and the amount to be administered, the paramedic may pop off the ends of the prefills and screw the cartridge into the syringe barrel.

Addition of Medications to An IV Bag

Certain drugs must be mixed with IV fluids. The procedure is as follows:

1. Set up the IV bag (or bottle) and tubing.
2. Carefully check the drug name and concentration to be administered.
3. Figure out the drug volume to be added.
4. Clean the insertion point with an alcohol wipe.
5. Puncture the insertion point and inject the desired amount of the drug.
6. Withdraw the needle and lightly shake to mix medication.
7. Clearly label the IV bag or bottle.
8. Calculate the flow rate.

IV Insertion

IVs are started to provide a route for volume replacement and for the administration of medications. In adults, 14-, 16-, or 18-gauge needles are preferable. The procedure is as follows:

1. Explain to the patient what is being done.
2. Select the IV fluid.
3. Select the correct infusion set.
4. Select the appropriate catheter size. (The larger the needle bore diameter, the greater the flow, and the shorter the length of the catheter, the greater the flow.)
5. Assemble the equipment:
   - Use antiseptic cleaning solution.
   - Open a sterile 4 by 4 dressing.
   - Cut or tear the adhesive tape to secure the catheter and tubing.
   - Use the appropriate size of syringe for collecting a blood sample.
   - Use vacutainer tubes for blood samples.
   - Prepare tourniquet (blood pressure cuff or soft rubber tubing).
6. Select an IV site, avoiding areas of bone joints, where arteries are in close proximity, veins near injured areas, or veins in the lower extremities.
7. Site preparation:
   - Clean the site by wiping in a circular motion away from the center with an antiseptic.
   - Stabilize the vein by applying tension on the skin distal to the point of entry of the needle.
   - Pass the needle through the skin with the bevel of the needle pointing upward. Enter the vein from either the side or the top. A pop should be felt when the needle has entered the vein. Be sure to pass the needle into the vein at least 2 millimeters to be certain that it is secure. There should be a blood return in the flashback chamber.
   - Now, carefully slide the catheter over the needle into the vein.
   - While holding the catheter, insert the syringe for drawing a blood sample.
   - Release the tourniquet and insert the IV tubing, checking for ease of fluid flow.
   - If the flow is adequate, tape down the catheter securely, then clean the site with an antiseptic wipe and cover with a sterile 4 by 4 dressing. Then tape down the IV tubing.

8. **Keep a sterile technique at all times.**

Giving Intramuscular (IM) Injections

Only a few situations call for IM injections. The administration of glucagon is one. This is not a commonly used prehospital technique. The procedure is as follows:

1. Check the name and concentration of the drug to be administered.
2. Prepare the syringe, most often using a 21-gauge needle.
3. Select as a site either the deltoid muscle or the upper, outermost quadrant of the gluteus muscle.
4. Clean the site.
5. Prepare the syringe (be sure to remove all air from the syringe).
6. Pull the skin tight between two fingers.
7. Insert the needle at a 90-degree angle to the skin.
8. Aspirate the area by pulling back on the plunger to be sure that the needle is not in a vein. If there is a blood return, pull back on the needle until it stops. Then, with a slow, steady pressure on the plunger, inject the solution.
9. Remove the needle at the same angle that it was inserted. Then clean the area and dispose of the contaminated equipment.

Giving Subcutaneous (SQ) Injections

These are primarily used to administer epinephrine for mild to moderate asthmatic attacks or allergic reactions in the prehospital setting. The procedure is as follows:

1. Check the name of the drug and the concentration to be administered.
2. Use a 25-gauge needle.
3. Clean the injection site.
4. Prepare the syringe (as stated above).
5. Gently hold the skin, and pull it away from the muscle; quickly insert the needle at a 45-degree angle.
6. Pull back on the plunger to be sure that the needle has not entered an artery or vein. If no blood is drawn back, inject the solution with a slow, steady pressure.
7. Pull out the needle at the same angle that it was inserted. Clean the site, and dispose of the contaminated equipment.

SUMMARY

General pharmacology is an important topic for the paramedic to study. Many of the cases attended by the paramedic may have drug intervention from simply providing oxygen (a drug) or starting an IV (of D_5W, normal saline, or Ringer's lactate) to administering a range of cardiac medications. In order to administer medications safely, the paramedic should know the following information about each drug carried: its action, indications for use, contraindications of use, appropriate administration, its side effects, incompatibility with other medications, and antidotes. This information is found in Appendix 1.

The paramedic should develop a system for him/herself that will allow for a quick and accurate method for determining the correct dosage of a drug to be administered to the patient. For example, some may carry a list of medications with their appropriate dosages written down; others may be capable of memorizing the information. Whatever method the paramedic chooses, the information should be available and should work (be efficient, effective, and accurate).

Division Three

Trauma

7

Trauma

In the United States, approximately 150,000 deaths occur annually from trauma. These deaths account for just a portion of those injured from traumatic injury. Between 10 and 17 million people are injured each year, with 380,000 of them becoming permanently disabled. Trauma is the third leading cause of death in the United States. Auto accidents alone killed over 40,000 people in the United States in 1984.

The majority of people killed as a result of trauma are between the ages of one and forty-four; in fact, trauma is the leading cause of death in this age range. Thirty-eight percent of all deaths in the age group of fifteen to twenty four are caused by motor vehicle accidents. In the age group of one to fourteen, accidents kill four times more children than any other cause.

It is easy to see that severe trauma is a significant problem in the United States. In the past few years, this problem has received increasingly more attention. It is now clearly recognized that with proper assessment and treatment, the trauma patient has an increased chance for survival with reduced disabilities.

With the introduction of Advanced Trauma Life Support (ATLS), Prehospital Trauma Life Support (PHTLS), and Basic Trauma Life Support (BTLS) classes to the EMS community, the awareness of the need to treat the critically injured patient appropriately, consistently, and rapidly has dramatically increased. This new awareness toward the treatment of the trauma patient has reduced mortality and morbidity.

This chapter will present the appropriate assessment and management of the trauma patient (critical and noncritical), and help the paramedic to develop an understanding of the mechanisms (kinematics) of both blunt and penetrating injuries. The single greatest cause of traumatic death in the United States is the motor vehicle accident. The mechanisms involved in automobile accidents will be described at some length.

THE TRAUMA PATIENT

Definition of Trauma

Trauma is a physical wound or injury that is the result of some external force or violence. It may be in the form of a blunt injury (when bodily tissues are compressed or decelerated) or penetrating injury (when an instrument or projectile enters the body, crushing, stretching, and/or forcing tissue out of its normal position).

The Paramedic's Approach

The trauma patient has special needs, some of which may be met by the prehospital health-care provider. As in any medically emergent situation, the paramedic must assure a patent airway, adequate ventilation (oxygenation of the red blood cells), and adequate circulation by controlling hemorrhage and maintaining a pulse (fluid replacement, PASG application, wound management, CPR). Additionally, spinal column immobilization (particularly of the cervical spine), fracture stabilization, and reassurance of the patient are important.

The paramedic's approach to the trauma patient will depend on the extent of the injury. Naturally, minor trauma to a patient will not be treated in the same way as major trauma. In general, the non-life-threatened patient may be treated at the scene (i.e., complete history, physical examination, and stabilization), whereas the severely injured patient might require just the ABCDEs (including cervical spine immobilization and PASG application) on the scene and additional treatment en route to the hospital. It is recommended by PHTLS standards that all multisystem trauma patients should be en route to the hospital in less than ten minutes after the arrival of prehospital care providers under normal circumstances.

Death from Trauma

It is known that death from trauma can occur in one of three different time frames. The first is death that occurs within seconds to minutes after injury. These deaths are often the result of injury to the aorta, other major vessels, the heart, the brain, the brainstem, or the high spinal cord. These patients are difficult to salvage even in the best of circumstances (i.e., in an urban setting with a trauma center in close proximity).

The second time frame is death that occurs within minutes to a few hours after injury. These deaths occur to patients who have sustained lacerated livers or spleens, subdural or epidural hematomas, hemo and/or pneumothoraces, or multisystem trauma associated with significant hemorrhage. This time period is referred to as the "golden hour." It is believed that if the severely injured trauma patient is provided with definitive care (surgery) within one hour after injury, his/her chance for survival is greatly improved. The longer it takes to provide this patient with definitive care, the lower the chance for a full recovery.

The third time frame is death that occurs within days or weeks after the injury and is usually the result of sepsis or organ failure. This complication may be reduced with appropriate prehospital care.

Treating Patients in an Outdoor Environment

When treating a patient in an outdoor environment, the patient should be protected from adverse weather conditions, scene hazards, and bystanders when appropriate. The paramedic should assure his/her own safety at the scene of the emergency.

Transport of the Patient

The patient must be transported to a hospital for definitive care. The choice of hospital (trauma center, etc.) will depend on the severity and type of traumatic injury sustained. The speed of transport (emergent return or nonemergent return) will also depend on the severity of the injury. In serious or life-threatening trauma, the paramedic should not delay transport to take an extended history, to do an extended physical examination, or to make repeated attempts at starting IV lines (IVs should be attempted while the ambulance is en route to the emergency department).

Evaluating the Patient

When the paramedic is evaluating the patient, he/she should prioritize the injuries and patients (triage). Observe for life-threatening versus non-life-threatening injuries, limb-threatening versus non-limb-threatening injuries, and prehospital manageable versus non-prehospitable manageable patients ("scoop and run").

KINEMATICS OF TRAUMA

Kinematics is a look at how the forces and motion of trauma affect a patient (mechanism of injury). This presentation deals primarily with automobile accidents, although other trauma-related accidents may be evaluated in a similar manner.

Laws of Physics

There are certain laws of physics (the study of the interaction between energy and matter) which, when understood by the paramedic, will give him/her a clearer perspective of the types of injuries that are suffered by victims of trauma.

Newton's First Law of Motion

Newton's first law of motion states that a body at rest will remain at rest and a body in motion will remain in motion until acted upon by some outside force. A victim of a gunshot wound, a pedestrian struck by an automobile, or a victim of an explosion are all examples of a body at rest suddenly being put into motion. A climber who has taken a fall or the driver of an automobile involved in a collison are examples of a body in motion coming to a sudden stop.

Second Law of Physics

A second law of physics is that energy cannot be created or destroyed, but can only change form. The energy generated from a sudden stop or start must be transformed to one of the following forms of energy:

1. Thermal.
2. Electrical.
3. Chemical.
4. Radiant.
5. Mechanical.

When a car decelerates slowly, the energy of forward motion is converted to thermal energy by the friction created through the braking action. When a car has a sudden deceleration, the energy is transformed to mechanical energy, resulting in damage to both the car and the occupants.

Relationship between Weight and Speed

Kinetic energy (KE) equals mass (weight) multiplied by velocity (speed) squared, divided by two. The following is the relationship between weight and speed. Example: The kinetic energy of a 150-pound person travelling at twenty miles per hour is as follows:

$$KE = \frac{150 \times (20)^2}{2}, \quad KE = \frac{150 \times 400}{2}, \quad KE = \frac{60,000}{2},$$

$$KE = 30,000 \text{ units of energy}$$

The relationship between weight and speed is critical. If the weight of the person in the example was increased by twenty pounds, the kinetic energy would be (170 pounds at twenty miles per hour) 34,000 units of energy. If the weight was the same but the speed was increased by twenty miles per hour, the kinetic energy would be (150 pounds at forty miles per hour) 120,000 units of energy.

As shown above, speed has a much greater effect on the increase of kinetic energy than does weight.

BLUNT TRAUMA

Three impacts occur in an automobile collison:

1. The automobile striking an object.
2. The occupant colliding with the inside of the car.
3. The internal organs colliding.

Remember—blunt trauma produces injury by both deceleration and compression. A simple rule to follow when assessing damage (injury) to the occupants is to look at the car; the passengers will receive the same types of force that the automobile sustained.

Types of Motor Vehicle Accidents

There are five types of motor vehicle accidents:

1. Head-on or frontal impact.
2. Lateral or side impact.
3. Rear impact.

4. Rotational impact.
5. Rollover.

In the following discussion, the injuries sustained in the various impacts are with occupants who are unrestrained. In 1983, approximately 85 percent of all automobile accident victims in the United States were not wearing restraining devices. As more and more states pass mandatory seat-belt usage laws, the percentage of unrestrained passengers will diminish.

Frontal Impact

The effects on the car of a sudden deceleration accident are front-frame and body damage. The severity will depend on the speed of the vehicle. The following effects may occur to the unrestrained passenger:

1. One path that the passenger may follow is ''down and under.'' In this case, the occupant hits the steering wheel or dash with his/her chest and knees, then ends up underneath the dashboard. The following injuries may occur to these victims:
   - Knee injury.
   - Femur shaft injuries.
   - Posterior fracture or dislocation of the hip.
   - Skull injury.
   - Neck injury.
   - Chest injury, including sternal fracture, rib fracture, and/or flail chest.
2. A second path that the body may follow is ''up and over.'' The body is thrown over the steering column (or dash), and the head impacts the windshield. The following are injuries that this patient may sustain:
   - Rib fractures.
   - Flail chest.
   - Cardiac contusions.
   - Injury to major vessels and/or abdominal viscera.
   - Head, scalp, and/or cervical spine injury.

Lateral or Side Impact

This kind of impact occurs when the car is struck from the side (broad-sided). This results in the car moving from underneath the unrestrained occupant. (Seat belts may reduce the severity of this kind of accident.) Depending on the forces involved, the door and/or support pillar may be pushed into the patient compartment, resulting in injury to the patient. The major areas of injury may be the lateral chest well, the shoulder and pelvic girdle, and the head/neck region. The patient involved in this type of accident is at great risk for cervical spine injury.

Rear Impact

This type of accident occurs when a slower moving or stopped vehicle is struck from behind, resulting in the sudden acceleration of the struck automobile. The passenger's body is forced back into the seat. If the head rest is properly positioned, the possibility of neck injury is greatly reduced. If it is improperly positioned or absent, the passenger may develop injuries to the muscles and ligamentous attachments of the neck. If the car is allowed to stop on its own, the chances of additional injuries will be reduced. If the driver reflexively brakes or strikes another automobile, the occupants may experience additional injuries attributable to a frontal impact.

Rotational Impact

In this type of accident, a portion of the vehicle (usually the front quarter) strikes an immovable object or an automobile moving in the opposite direction. The area of impact loses its forward motion, while the remainder of the vehicle continues in forward motion, pivoting around the point of impact. The effect on the occupants is continued forward motion, which changes to a diagonal direction across the passenger compartment. This results in a combination of lateral and frontal injury patterns.

Rollover

In this type of accident, the automobile may roll side over side or end over end. The unrestrained passenger is at great risk of severe injury and/or ejection from the automobile. These patients need to be evaluated carefully and rapidly.

Seat Belts

In 1983, approximately 85 percent of the population did not wear restraining devices while driving motor vehicles. Many state legislatures are passing laws requiring the wearing of seat belts, thus reducing the numbers of unrestrained drivers/passengers in the United States.

When properly worn, the lap belt and shoulder harness combination has been shown to reduce morbidity and mortality. The occupant who is unrestrained has a great chance of being ejected from a car during an accident, increasing that person's risk of death 300 times. The restrained occupant is less likely to have his/her body collide with the inside of the car, reducing possible injury.

Other Causes of Blunt Trauma

There are many causes of trauma besides automobile accidents. Some of the more common causes are:

1. Automobile/pedestrian accidents.
2. Bicycle accidents.
3. Motorcycle accidents.
4. Falls.
5. Sports-related accidents.
6. Blast accidents from explosions.

In all of these cases, there is the potential for severe injury. The paramedic must identify the mechanism involved in the injury and assume the worse. For example, it is considered significant when a person falls more than three times his/her own height.

PENETRATING TRAUMA

In general, penetrating trauma is the result of gunshot wounds or stab wounds (knife, ice pick). Stab wounds are considered low-energy; hand guns and some rifles are medium-energy; and high-velocity weapons (M-16, 30-30) are high-energy. The more energy involved, the greater the damage to the victim. As mentioned earlier, the more velocity produced by the weapon, the greater the potential for damage.

Low-Velocity (Energy)

In low-velocity penetrating wounds, the damage is primarily caused by the cutting edge of the object. The slow insertion has very little energy to be dissipated, so no secondary damage occurs from a pressure wave. The damage sustained from a knife wound may be very deceiving. The entrance wound into the body may be small, yet the internal injury severe. If the knife was twisted while inside the body, more damage may have been done. When evaluating the victim of a stabbing, be sure to assess the patient for multiple stab wounds, exit wounds, and associated injuries.

Medium-Velocity (Energy)

This group of weapons has a muzzle velocity of less than 1,500 feet per second when leaving the barrel of the weapon. Hand gun and rifle bullets cause injury in two ways:

1. The direct damage from the penetrating missile.
2. Cavitation — in regard to bullet wounds, cavitation is the formation of a temporary cavity caused by the pressure wave of the bullet passing through the body. The greater the energy, the greater the cavitation. What actually occurs is that the pressure wave causes tissue to expand, then return to normal. With high-velocity weapons, this expansion and contraction may occur three to four times before the energy of the wave is dissipated. The energy of the missile is changed into tissue damage. The injury tract is usually two to three times the diameter of the missile.

Bullets are of many different profiles upon impact. They may stay pointed, they may flatten, they may fragment, or they may tumble through the tissue. All bullets can do significant damage to the body, but the greater the surface on impact, the more energy that is transmitted to the tissue.

High-Velocity (Energy)

This group of weapons has a muzzle velocity of greater than 1,500 feet per second when leaving the barrel. These bullets cause a permanent pathway of injury two to three times the diameter of the projectile and produce much larger cavitation than medium-velocity weapons.

Generally, the larger the weapon (caliber), the greater the tissue damage, both externally and internally. If there is an exit wound, it will be larger than the entrance wound. It is difficult to predict the pathway of a bullet. The paramedic must be conservative and assume that the patient is seriously injured, although it may not initially appear that way.

At the Scene of a Gunshot Wound

When on the scene of a gunshot wound, try to determine:

1. The type of weapon used.
2. The size (caliber) of the weapon.
3. The type of bullet.
4. The distance between the assailant and the victim.

However, do not allow the gathering of this information to delay the treatment and transport of the patient.

ASSESSMENT OF THE TRAUMA PATIENT

It is important for the paramedic to recognize that, regardless of the cause of injury (i.e., frontal impact or rollover automobile accident, a fallen person, penetrating or blunt trauma), he/she must use the same systematic approach to all trauma patients. Only the time frame and priorities will vary.

The information provided in the previous section was to give the paramedic a way to gauge the possible extent of a patient's injury. It will strengthen the paramedic's index of suspicion in a given set of circumstances. It is these circumstances that will determine the management priorities for each trauma patient. However, the assessment of all patients will be the same.

Primary Survey

The primary survey or rapid assessment is the brief period during which the paramedic recognizes immediate life threats and attempts to correct them. **In these cases, transport to definitive care must not be delayed. Ten minutes is the maximum amount of time to be on the scene with a severely injured trauma patient in any uncomplicated situation.** Remember the ''golden hour'' for getting critically injured patients to surgical help. In handling the severely injured trauma patient, the paramedic should follow the ABCDEs.

A = Airway with cervical spine control.
B = Breathing.
C = Circulation and bleeding.
D = Disability. This is to determine the patient's level of consciousness and and observe for central nervous system injury.
E = Expose and examine.

Airway with Cervical Spine Control

1. Thoroughly evaluate the patient's airway to make sure that it is open and clear. A quick and simple way of doing this is to talk with the patient, evaluating the ease with which the patient responds.
2. The paramedic should immobilize the cervical spine at this point, if necessary.

3. Quickly evaluate the airway in the unconscious patient. Check the patient for occlusion of the airway by:
   - The tongue (head or jaw position).
   - Hemorrhage.
   - Foreign body.
   - Fractured larynx.
   - Laryngeal edema/spasm.
4. If the airway is closed, take the appropriate steps (see Chapter 4, ''Airway and Ventilation'') to correct the situation immediately.
5. Continue with the primary survey.
6. Whenever there is the potential for cervical spine injury, provide early cervical spine immobilization.

Breathing

1. Observe carefully for spontaneous ventilation. If the patient is not breathing on his/her own, artificial ventilation must be provided immediately.
2. Evaluate the adequacy of respirations. Is the patient moving adequate air? Look at the chest rise and fall, and evaluate any conversation (ease of talking means adequate breathing).
3. If the respiratory rate is less than twelve or over twenty-four per minute, provide high-flow, high-concentration oxygen.
4. If there appears to be a respiratory problem, inspect, palpate, and auscultate the chest at this time. If a problem is discovered, initiate treatment.
5. The following are possible pulmonary/chest injuries that may interfere with adequate ventilation in a patient:
   - Pneumothorax.
   - Tension pneumothorax.
   - Hemothorax.
   - Hemopneumothorax.
   - Flail chest.
   - Pulmonary contusion.
   - Sucking chest wound.

   A detailed discussion on these injuries and others will follow later in this chapter.

Circulation and Hemorrhage Control

1. Assess the circulatory status of the patient. This includes:
   - A quick inspection of the patient to observe for severe bleeding, which must be controlled immediately (usually by direct pressure with a

gloved hand).
- Evaluation for a pulse.
- An estimation of the blood pressure and capillary bed perfusion.

2. Palpate the radial pulse, checking for strength, rate (tachycardia or bradycardia), and regularity.
3. Estimate the blood pressure:
   - If there is a radial pulse, the systolic blood pressure is at least 80 mmHg.
   - If there is a femoral pulse, the systolic pressure is at least 70 mmHg.
   - If there is a carotid pulse, the systolic pressure is at least 60 mmHg.
4. Skin color (pink, pale, cyanotic) may give more information about perfusion.
5. Check capillary refill time. This can be accomplished by pressing the nail bed of a finger and counting the time it takes for the nail bed to "pink up." If capillary refill time is more than two seconds, it is suggestive of decreased capillary perfusion.
6. In cases of hypotension **without** obvious injury, suspect intra-abdominal or pelvic bleeding, along with possible pelvic and/or lower extremity fractures. Suspect abdominopelvic injury and assess these areas. Consider the application of PASG on these patients.

Disability

This is a quick check for the patient's level of consciousness (LOC) and may be accomplished by using the mnemonic AVPU:

A — Alert.
V — Responds to VOCAL stimuli.
P — Responds to PAINFUL stimuli
U — Unresponsive.

If the paramedic recognizes central nervous system injury, particularly increasing intracranial pressure, he/she should hyperventilate the patient with high-flow, high-concentration oxygen.

Expose

In severe trauma, it is imperative for the paramedic to expose, inspect, and palpate the head, neck, chest, and abdomen for injury as soon as possible. These are the areas that, when injured, may cause rapid death. Ideally, it is best done in the privacy of the ambulance, but perform this assessment in whatever location is necessary.

When performing this assessment, the paramedic may expose the front of the chest and abdomen. The posterior portion must be palpated if possible (looking primarily for soft tissue/skeletal injury).

This part of the primary assessment is to locate life-threatening injuries. A more thorough examination may take place en route to the hospital if time permits.

Treatment for the Life-Threatened Trauma Patient

1. Open the airway.
2. Assure adequate ventilation.
3. Assure a pulse.
4. Control hemorrhage.
5. Treat any chest-wall defects (specific treatment will be detailed later in this chapter).
6. Apply the PASG.
7. Institute IV therapy by starting two 14- or 16-gauge peripheral lines with normal saline or Ringer's lactate. Remember — do not delay transport in the attempt to start IVs. These should be started en route to the hospital.

Secondary Survey

The secondary survey consists of taking the vital signs, taking a patient history, and doing the physical examination (head-to-toe). In significant trauma, the secondary survey should be done en route to the hospital. Keeping the patient in the field to accomplish the secondary is not in the patient's best interest. The severely injured trauma patient should be transported from the scene in less than ten minutes whenever possible. The patient needs to receive definitive care within one hour of the injury.

For a detailed description of the secondary survey, see Chapter 3.

History

Depending on the severity of the injury, the paramedic may or may not have an opportunity to question the patient. In the severely injured patient, the history will most likely consist of obtaining information regarding the patient's chief complaint. The paramedic must not spend additonal time on the scene obtaining a history. This should be taken during transport.

History-Taking Format

The following is one history-taking format:

1. What was the mechanism of injury? The paramedic must be observant at the scene. Identifying the mechanism of injury provides important information, giving the paramedic a clear indication of the forces involved in the accident. It is essential for the rescuer to get this information in the trauma setting (if possible). It is not uncommon for a patient to have sustained serious internal injuries that are not visually apparent. In evaluating the scene, the paramedic must have a high index of suspicion that the patient sustained serious injury, even it if it not immediately apparent.
   - For automobile accidents — type of accident (frontal, rollover, etc.)?, extent of damage (external and internal)?, speed of vehicle?, were restraints worn?
   - For fall victims — distance fallen?, kind of surface where impact occurred?
   - For penetrating trauma — what kind of weapon?, caliber of the weapon?, range of the weapon?, type of bullet involved?
   - Is a medical history contributing to the present emergency?
2. What is the patient's chief complaint? (The paramedic may use the acronym AMPLE or the mnemonic PQRST for chief complaint amplification).
3. Are there any additional complaints?

Vital Signs

1. Pulse — increased.
2. Respiration — below ten or above twenty-eight breaths per minute may indicate serious injury.
3. Blood pressure — initially normal, then becomes low (hypotensive).
4. Pupil evaluation — may be equal and reactive; unequal and slow to react to light.
5. Skin — pale or cyanotic and cool and clammy.

The Head-to-Toe

This is a systematic evaluation of the patient from the head to the toe. The paramedic must remember that in the patient with serious (or life-threatening) injuries, the head-to-toe survey must not delay treatment of the serious injury(s) or transport to definitive care (remember — on-scene time should be less than ten minutes).

The following comprises this part of the secondary survey:

1. Inspection (look): observe for contusions, abrasions, lacerations, ecchymosis, edema, hemorrhage, and deformity (angulation, shortening, and/or abnormal position).
2. Palpate (feel): feel for tenderness, deformities, crepitus, masses, edema, and subcutaneous air.
3. Auscultation (listen): listen for breath sounds.

Using the above criteria, the paramedic will proceed with a systematic examination, starting at the patient's head and ending at the patient's toes. In general, it is best to have a systematic approach to assessing a patient. The following is the generally accepted order in performing the head-to-toe examination. There are times when it may be appropriate to deviate from this accepted order. The paramedic may at times prioritize the assessment based on the location and severity of the injuries.

The generally accepted order is the following:

1. The head (scalp, face).
2. The neck (large vessels, larynx, and trachea).
3. The thorax (great vessels, heart, lungs, esophagus, and trachea).
4. The abdominopelvic region (solid/hollow abdominal viscera, female reproductive organs, urinary bladder).
5. The pelvis.
6. The lower extremities.
7. The upper extremities.

Recall that spinal precautions have been taken care of during the primary assessment.

TREATMENT OF SPECIFIC TRAUMATIC INJURIES

Head Trauma

The most significant concern with head injuries is damage to the brain. The brain fits snugly in the skull, and any bleeding or swelling within the cranium will result in pressure being exerted on the brain itself. The brain tissue is soft and may be severely damaged by increased pressure.

How Brain Tissue Is Damaged

Brain tissue may be damaged in several ways:

1. By a direct blow.
2. By deceleration (falls, car accidents).
3. By intracranial bleeding:
   - Epidural (between the dura mater and cranium), which is usually arterial with a mortality rate of 50 percent.

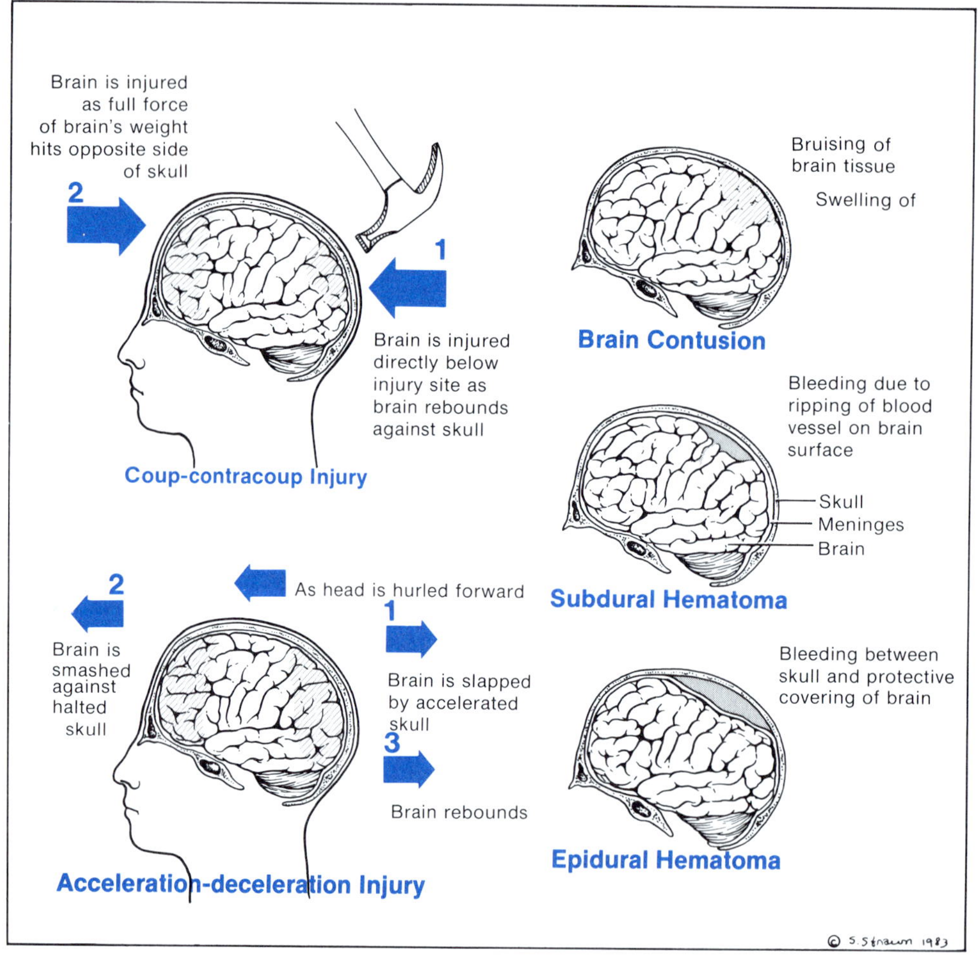

Figure 7-1. Brain Injuries.

- Subdural (between the dura mater and arachnoid), which may be arterial or venous with a mortality rate between 45 and 90 percent.
- Within the brain.

4. By herniation (this refers to the protrusion of brain tissue from its normal anatomical position into an abnormal position).
5. By cerebral edema.

Assume all head-injured patients, particularly those who are unconscious, to have cervical spine injury. PROTECT THE CERVICAL SPINE WITH THESE PATIENTS.

Signs and Symptoms

Early

1. Observe the patient's level of consciousness. If it deteriorates, it is a significant sign of brain injury.
2. There may be obvious soft tissue and skeletal damage.
3. Observe the patient for alcohol or drug intoxication.
4. The patient may complain of headache, dizziness, weakness, or double vision.
5. The patient may complain of nausea with or without vomiting.
6. There may have been a period of unconsciousness.

Intermediate

1. The pupils may be obviously unequal.
2. There may be abnormal posturing with serious injury; abnormal flexion (decorticate rigidity) or abnormal extension (decerebrate rigidity).
3. Respirations may be noisy, with abnormal breathing patterns (Cheyne-Stokes, hyperventilation, or irregular pattern).

Late

1. Increasing blood pressure (hypertension) with a widening pulse pressure and decreasing pulse (bradycardia) are indicative of increasing intracranial pressure.
2. The temperature may be elevated.

Other

1. Hypotension is an unusual occurrence in an isolated head injury. If present, look for additional injury elsewhere and treat for shock.

Treatment — The Conscious Patient

1. Continually assess and treat the ABCs as necessary.
2. Provide complete spinal immobilization.
3. Administer high-flow, high-concentration oxygen.
4. Carefully evaluate and reevaluate the patient's level of consciousness.
5. Continually monitor the vital signs.
6. Start an IV of normal saline at a TKO rate; adjust the flow as indicated.

Treatment — The Unconscious Patient

1. Continually assess and treat the ABCs as necessary.
2. Intubate as necessary — **protect the cervical spine.**
3. Provide high-flow, high-concentration oxygen.
4. All patients with increasing (or increased) intracranial pressure, regardless of the breathing rate, should be moderately hyperventilated at a rate between twenty-five and thirty ventilations per minute with a bag-valve-mask or bag-valve-ET-tube. Hyperventilation reduces the $PaCO_2$, causing cerebral vasoconstriction and resulting in a temporary reduction of cerebral edema. This is a powerful tool that is easily used by the paramedic.
5. Start an IV of normal saline at a TKO rate; adjust the flow as indicated. If shock is present, then treat it. The rate will be based on the overall hemodynamic state.
6. Maintain normal body temperature.
7. Continually monitor the vital signs.
8. Monitor the cardiac rhythm.
9. Assess and reassess the patient's level of consciousness.
10. Cover open wounds with sterile dressings.
11. Consider the administration of dexamethasone (Decadron) by direct physician's order — 12 mg to 100 mg IV push. (See Appendix 1 for further details.) There is controversy over what benefits are derived from the administration of this drug in the head-injured patient.
12. Consider the administration of mannitol by direct physician's order — 1 gm per kilogram of body weight infused over twenty minutes with an in-line filter; 500 ml of a 20 percent solution equals 100 grams (1 gm per 5 ml).
13. Consider the administration of furosemide (Lasix) by direct physician's order — 20 mg to 40 mg IV push.
14. If either mannitol or furosemide is used, consider the insertion of a Foley catheter.

Skull Fractures

Any break in the continuity of the bone is a fracture.

Linear Fractures

Linear fractures (simple cracks) of the skull indicate that a significant force has been applied to the skull. Some linear fractures may result in epidural bleeding.

Depressed Skull Fractures

Depressed skull fractures are caused by loose bone fragments being driven into the cranial cavity. This type of fracture may be accompanied by a scalp laceration. When gently palpating the skull, the paramedic will feel the unstable depressed area.

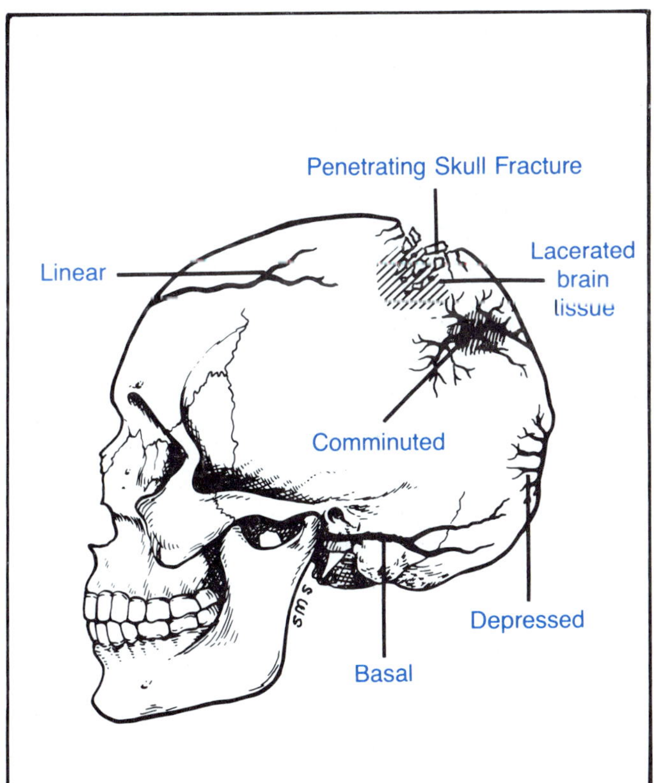

Figure 7-2. Types of Skull Fracture.

Basilar Skull Fractures

Basilar skull fractures occur at the base of the skull in the floor of the cranium. (This part of the skull cannot be palpated.) These fractures may be accompanied by one or more of the following signs:

1. Ecchymosis in the mastoid region (called Battle's sign).
2. Bilateral ecchymosis around the eyes (called raccoon sign).
3. Cerebrospinal fluid leaking from the ears or nose.

Treatment

Treatment of these skull fractures consists of the steps described above (no drug therapy is normally indicated); dressing and bandaging any scalp injury, taking special care not to press on loose bone fragments; and constantly monitoring the patient.

Neck Trauma

The neck houses many vital structures: the cervical spine/cord, major veins and arteries, the larynx, and part of the trachea. Trauma to the neck may result in a number of potentially life-threatening or life-altering injuries.

The patient may experience severe hemorrhage (venous or arterial), airway obstruction (partial or complete), or cervical spine injury that may result in neurologic deficit.

Soft Tissue Injury

The paramedic must control bleeding with direct pressure and, in venous bleeding, prevent the entrance of air into the vein. Air entering a vein may cause a serious air embolism.

Airway Trauma

A compromised airway can lead to rapid deterioration and death. Without an open airway, all other attempts at resuscitation will be useless.

The paramedic needs to suspect cervical spine damage with any injury above the clavicle. The cervical spine may be damaged without any neurologic deficit, and if the patient's neck is moved inappropriately, permanent damage may result.

If the paramedic fails three times to intubate the trauma patient successfully, this may be an indication for transtracheal jet insufflation or cricothyroidotomy (see Chapter 4).

Airway Management Procedures

The paramedic must be familiar with the following airway management procedures:

1. The chin lift and jaw thrust.
2. Proper insertion of oral and nasal airways.
3. Oral intubation with manual in-line cervical spine stabilization.
4. Nasal intubation with in-line cervical spine stabilization.
5. Transtracheal jet insufflation.
6. Cricothyroidotomy.
7. Placement of the esophageal obturator and pharyngeotracheal lumen airway.

Cervical Spine Fractures and Dislocations

Injury to the spinal cord, particularly the cervical spine, may result in one of the most devastating, irreparable injuries — paraplegia or quadriplegia. Cord damage may occur:

1. As a primary result of injury.
2. Secondary to movement of the head/nech.
3. During improper stabilization of the spinal-injured (or suspected) victim.

Injury to the cord may occur from fracture of a vertebra, subluxation (a partial or incomplete dislocation), dislocation, or from spinal cord edema with or without a fracture. The injured area may be stable or unstable. The problem is that the paramedic cannot identify either. It is imperative to treat all suspected spinal-injured patients as if they have sustained unstable spinal fractures.

The paramedic must have a high index of suspicion for spinal injury when dealing with trauma patients. It should be assumed that neck and/or back injury is present in any:

1. Unconscious trauma patient.
2. Significant trauma above the clavicles.
3. Patient whose mechanism of injury (violent forces — falls, ejection from an automobile, etc.) indicates the possibility of spinal injury.

The most common causes of spinal injury are automobile accidents, swimming/diving accidents, motorcycle accidents, fall, and other accidents (e.g., bicycle accidents, gunshot wounds).

Spinal injury results from one of the following movements or combination of movements (see Figure 7-3):

1. Hyperextension.
2. Hyperflexion.
3. Compression.
4. Excessive lateral movement or rotation.

The most common sites of spinal fractures are in the cervical spine (five

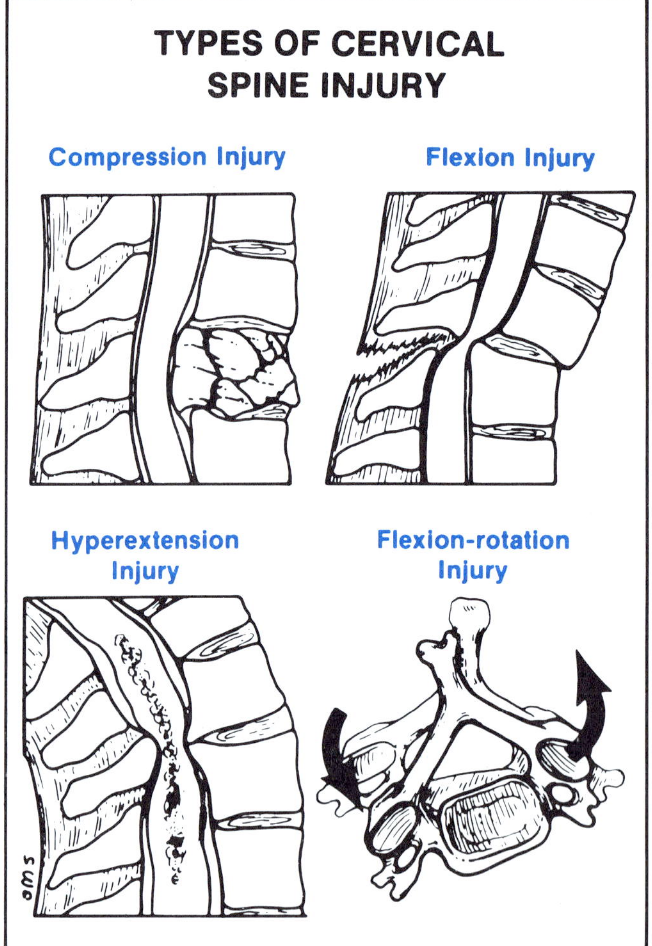

Figure 7-3. Types of Cervical Spine Injury.

and six or one and two) and the lumbar spine. The cervical and lumbar spines are the least protected and are thus most prone to injury.

Signs and Symptoms

The injured individual may present with any variation of signs and symptoms, from no neurologic deficit to loss of sensation and movement in all four extremities. The patient may complain of numbing, tingling, or electricity-like sensations in any or all of the extremities.

Management

The management of cervical spine (and lower vertebral column) injury involves maintaining spinal alignment, particularly of the cervical spine. It should be noted that each situation encountered by the paramedic will be different, so the rescuer must be flexible in managing the spinal-injured patient.

Most frequently, the patient will be placed in the supine position when spinal precautions are being taken. This position is the best for monitoring and managing the patient's airway as well as the entire patient. The supine position is also best for stabilizing the patient's spine.

The general guidelines for spinal immobilization are as follows:

1. The paramedic should stabilize (immobilize) the patient's head by placing the palms of the hands over the patient's ears.
2. Return the patient's head to a neutral, in-line position. Maintenance of the neutral position should occur without traction.
3. The proper-sized rigid cervical collar should be applied to the patient's neck, with extreme care being taken to minimize movement. Remember — a stiff collar is not effective alone. It must be used in conjunction with a backboard and a lateral stabilizing device (towel rolls, blanket, or a commercial device).
4. The patient should be placed on a backboard (the backboard provides stabilization and immobilization for the entire spine if the patient is secured properly to the device), then secured (strapped) to it. First, the body is strapped to the board, followed by immobilization of the head (maintain manual stabilization during this procedure). The patient is successfully secured when he/she cannot move up or down, left or right. Naturally, avoid any flexion or extension of the head during this process.
5. In some situations where extrication from a car is necessary and there are no immediate threats to life, the paramedic may wish to use a short backboard, Kendrick's extrication device, or other equipment used to

stabilize the spine. The paramedic needs to efficiently evaluate the problem, then select the most appropriate equipment for the situation.

6. There are many methods and much equipment available for spinal stabilization. The paramedic must be sure that the spine is secured regardless of the setting. The best way to be assured of success is to practice with the equipment and practice the techniques of spinal immobilization in different settings.

Thoracic Trauma

The thoracic cavity (ribs, spine, and sternum) houses many vital structures: the heart, the lungs, the great veins (e.g., the inferior vena cava) and arteries (e.g., the aorta), the esophagus, the trachea, and the thoracic spine. The structure most commonly injured in trauma is the lung. The external boundaries of the thorax are as follows: the clavicles superiorly, the sternum anteriorly, the diaphragm inferiorly, and the thoracic spine posteriorly.

Chest injuries may be caused by blunt or penetrating trauma. Regardless of the cause, the potential for life-threatening injury is high. The paramedic must do a thorough and rapid assessment of the chest. This is best accomplished by:

1. Inspection.
2. Palpation.
3. Auscultation.

The patient of chest trauma commonly complains of dyspnea and chest pain. The chest pain may occur from movement of the injured chest wall or be due to injury of internal organs.

Depending on the severity and type of injury, the paramedic may see and/or palpate:

1. Bruises.
2. Open wounds.
3. An unstable chest wall.
4. Distended neck veins.
5. Subcutaneous air.
6. Possibly tracheal deviation.

On auscultation, the paramedic may hear:

1. Normal breath sounds bilaterally.

2. Diminished or absent sounds unilaterally, which may indicate air or blood in the pleural space.
3. Rales (crackles) may sometimes be heard.

Rib Fractures

The most commonly injured ribs are three through nine. When isolated rib fractures (simple) occur, the patient may complain of pain on inspiration and breathe shallowly to reduce the pain. The pain will usually be at the site of injury. On assessment, the paramedic may note deformity over the injured rib with pain on palpation. The rescuer should auscultate and observe for a hemothorax or pneumothorax that could result from the fractured rib penetrating the lung or lacerating a vessel.

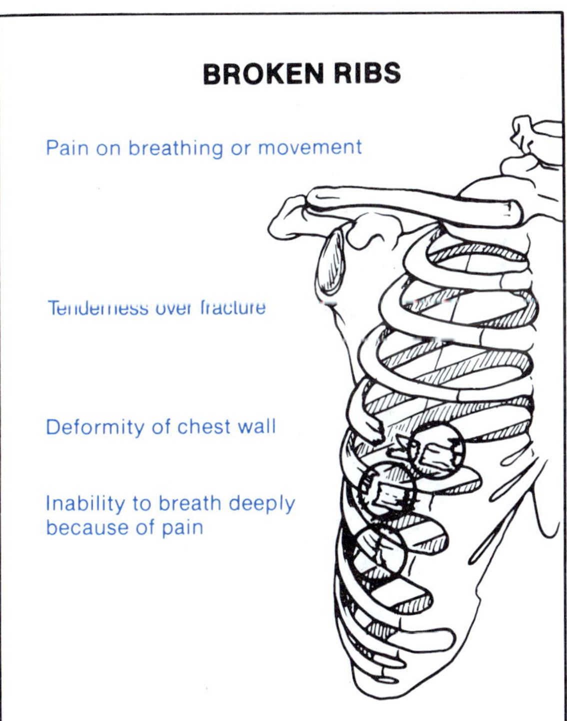

Figure 7-4. Rib Fracture.

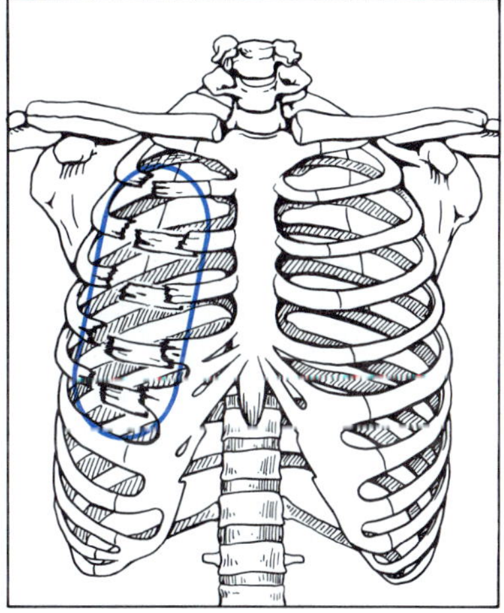

Figure 7-5. Flail Chest.

The treatment is to:

1. Splint the area with a pillow or sling and swathe.
2. If the patient is tachycardic, start an IV with a volume-replacement solution (adjust the rate as needed).
3. Consider application of the PASG in the hypotensive patient.

Flail Chest

Flail chest is an injury to the chest wall that results in the fracture of three or more ribs in two or more places. This creates serious instability of the chest wall and contusions of the underlying lung tissue. This injury is characterized by paradoxical respirations — the inward, rather than outward, movement of the flail segment on inspiration.

The patient experiences decreased respirations with increased work. This, along with underlying lung damage, results in progressive respiratory insufficiency. In addition, the patient experiences pain.

The treatment is to:

1. Stabilize the flail segment. This can be achieved by:
   - Using simple hand pressure.
   - Taping a towel or bulky dressing over the injured area.
2. Provide positive-pressure ventilation, with 100 percent oxygen. A bag-valve-mask may be used to assist ventilation.
3. If necessary, intubate the patient.
4. Start one or two large-bore IVs with a volume replacement solution.
5. Consider application of the PASG.

Pulmonary Contusion

Bruising to the lung may occur from either blunt or penetrating injury. Most commonly, it results from blunt trauma and is accompanied by varying degrees of respiratory distress and pain. A contusion occurs after injury when the alveoli fill with blood and fluid, reducing the area of lung in which gas exchange may occur. The severity of respiratory distress is directly related to the amount of lung tissue damaged.

The treatment is to:

1. Closely monitor the patient (auscultate the lung fields).
2. Provide high-flow, high-concentration oxygen (100 percent).
3. Assist ventilations as necessary.

4. Consider intubation.

Pneumothorax

A simple pneumothorax is the presence of air in the pleural space. Air may enter the pleural space from a laceration or rupture of the lung or from a wound that penetrates the chest wall. Regardless of the cause, as air enters and fills the pleural space, it compresses lung tissue and thus reduces the amount of lung tissue available for the exchange of oxygen and carbon dioxide. This leads to either a partial or total collapse of the lung on the injured side.

Depending on the amount of lung involved, the patient may be stable without respiratory distress or unstable in respiratory distress.

Signs and Symptoms

1. Chest pain in the area of injury.
2. Tachypnea.
3. Respiratory distress (not constant).
4. Possibly tracheal shift to the uninjured side.
5. Diminished or absent breath sounds over the involved area.
6. There may be obvious wounds on the chest.

Treatment

1. Fully evaluate the patient as usual.
2. Provide high-flow, high-concentration (100 percent) oxygen.
3. Constantly monitor the patient for the development of a tension pneumothorax.
4. Start one or two large-bore IVs with a volume expander solution when possible.
5. Be prepared to ventilate.
6. Transport the patient rapidly.

Sucking Chest Wound (Open Pneumothorax)

This is an injury to the chest wall that most commonly occurs from a penetrating wound. It allows the movement of air into the chest cavity, collapsing the underlying lung and possibly compressing the great vessels and the uninjured lung with each inspiration. If the defect in the chest is large enough, it may seriously decrease the patient's ability to breathe through the nose or mouth without respiratory assistance. If air enters the chest without being able to exit, a tension pneumothorax may develop.

The patient will complain of chest pain and dyspnea. The paramedic may hear sucking, bubbling sounds coming from the injury.

Treatment

1. Close the sucking chest wall wound immediately. This may be accomplished with a gloved hand, nonporous material, or a Vaseline gauze.

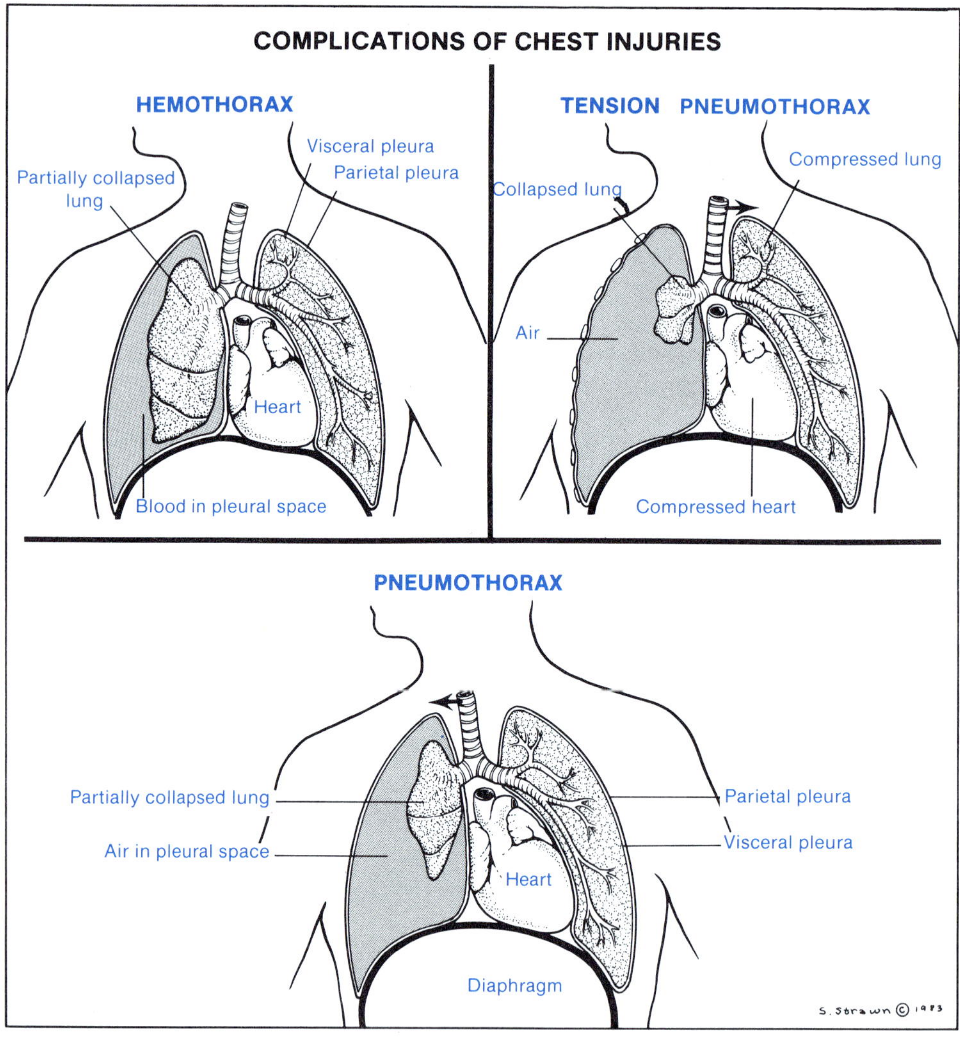

Figure 7-6. Chest Injuries.

2. Prior to dressing the wound, have the patient cough or exhale; this will expel additional trapped air in the thoracic cavity.
3. The dressing may be held in place manually or roller-bandaged in place.
4. Observe for the development of a tension pneumothorax.
5. If signs of increasing respiratory distress develop, lift a corner of the dressing to allow the release of air building up in the chest cavity.
6. Provide high-flow, high-concentration (100 percent) oxygen.
7. With increasing respiratory distress, consider assisting ventilations and intubating the patient.
8. Start one or two IVs with a volume expander when possible.
9. Transport the patient rapidly.
10. Consider application of PASG.

Tension Pneumothorax

A tension pneumothorax develops when air enters the pleural space but cannot leave it (caused by a one-way valve effect). This may occur from an injury to the lung or to a chest wall injury that allows air to enter the cavity but prevents the air from escaping due to blockage. This is a severe life-threatening emergency that requires immediate treatment. A tension pneumothorax will collapse the lung on the injured side, and as it continues to develop, it will cause the mediastinum to be pushed toward the uninjured side.

The following complications may occur:

1. The uninjured lung will be compressed, reducing ventilations and kinking the inferior and superior vena cava (found in the mediastinum).
2. This will reduce venous return to the heart, thus reducing cardiac output. It may also cause compression of lung tissue on the opposite side, resulting in an inability to ventilate the patient.

Signs and Symptoms

The signs and symptoms may vary depending on the degree of tension that the patient is experiencing; some will be mild to moderate, and others severe:

1. The patient may be anxious and restless.
2. The patient may complain of mild to severe dyspnea.
3. The patient may have diminished or absent breath sounds on the affected side.
4. The patient may have tachypnea.

5. The patient may be tachycardic.
6. The patient may appear to be cyanotic.
7. There may be possible jugular venous distention (this will not be present with significant hypovolemia and hypotension).
8. There may be tracheal deviation. However, tracheal deviation is a late sign of a tension pneumothorax and may not always be present. Its absence should not be used to rule out a tension pneumothorax.
9. The patient may have a narrow pulse pressure.
10. The patient may be hypotensive.

It is imperative to remember that tension pneumothorax is an extreme emergency requiring immediate recognition and treatment.

Treatment

The treatment of a tension pneumothorax involves decompressing the affected side of the chest to release the pressure that has developed. This may be done with minimal risk by inserting a 14- or 16-gauge needle into the intercostal space between the second and third or third and fourth ribs at the midclavicular line just superior to the rib. It may also be done by inserting the needle at the midaxillary line between the fifth and sixth ribs (this approach is considered safer by some practitioners). The intercostal artery, vein, and nerve follow the inferior portion of the rib. The following equipment is necessary to perform this procedure:

1. Needle catheter, 10-, 12-, 14-, or 16-gauge (or a McSwain dart).
2. Antiseptic solution to clean the site.
3. One-way valve (Heimlich valve or a finger cut from a sterile surgical glove.
4. A rubber band to secure the valve to the catheter.
5. Tape and sterile dressings.

The procedure is as follows:

1. Prepare the catheter and flutter valve by inserting the catheter through the finger and securing them together. The valve allows air to exit the chest, but not enter it.
2. Locate the second or third intercostal space at the midclavicular line, and prep the area with an antiseptic solution.
3. Insert the catheter just superior to the rib until a rush of air leaves the valve (a ''pop'' may be felt). Advance the catheter over the needle and secure

it in place.
4. Provide high-flow, high-concentration (100 percent) oxygen.
5. Start one or two IVs with a volume expander when possible.
6. Transport the patient rapidly.

Hemothorax

A hemothorax may occur from rib fracture or from any injury that lacerates an artery, vein, or lung tissue. Hemothorax is bleeding into the pleural space. Small accumulations of blood may not interfere with normal respirations, but as the amount of blood in the pleural space increases, more lung tissue is compressed, resulting in dyspnea and reduced oxygenation. In addition, large quantities of blood may be lost into the pleural space, resulting in hypovolemia and shock.

Signs and Symptoms

Depending on the size of the hemothorax, the patient may experience:

1. Difficulty breathing (shortness of breath).
2. Anxiety.
3. Restlessness.
4. Tachycardia.
5. Tachypnea.
6. Hypotension.
7. Breath sounds may be diminished on the injured side.

Treatment

The treatment is to:

1. Provide high-flow, high-concentration oxygen.
2. Assist ventilations as necessary.
3. Start one or two IVs with a volume expander when possible.
4. Transport the patient rapidly.
5. Consider application of PASG.

Cardiac Contusion

In significant blunt trauma — most commonly due to automobile accidents — the heart may be bruised when a patient gets thrown against the steering wheel or dashboard. The heart may forcefully hit the sternum and then be compressed between the sternum and vertebral column. This may result in rupture, bleeding, and/or bruising of the heart. Whenever major forces are involved in chest trauma, the paramedic should assume some heart bruising and monitor the cardiac rhythm.

Signs and Symptoms

The patient may present with the classical signs of a myocardial infarction:

1. Chest pain.
2. Dyspnea.
3. Dysrhythmias.
4. Reduced pumping of blood by the heart.
5. There may be obvious bruising.
6. There may be pain and tenderness of the anterior chest wall.
7. There may be tachycardia, irregular, and/or weak pulse.

Treatment

1. Provide high-flow, high-concentration oxygen.
2. Place the patient on a cardiac monitor.
3. Start one or two IVs with a volume-expander solution.
4. Rapid transport may be required.
5. Be observant for a narrowing pulse pressure and other signs of a cardiac tamponade.
6. Consider application of PASG.

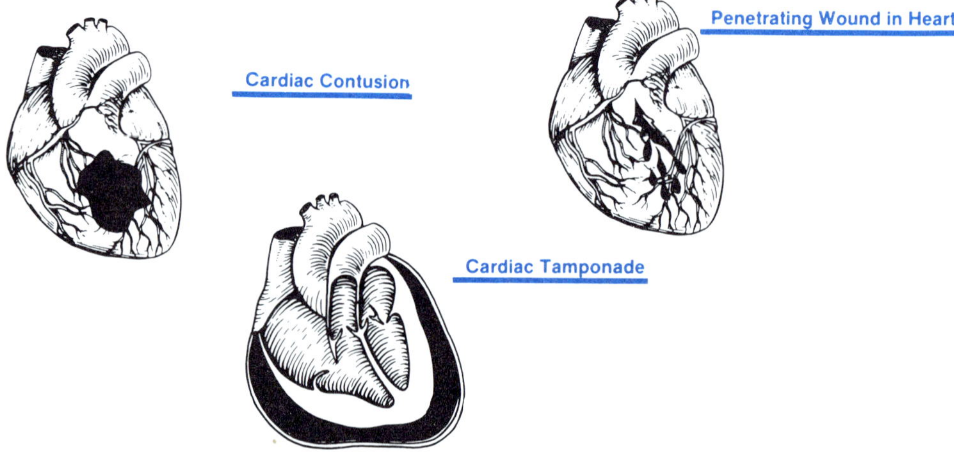

Figure 7-7. Traumatic Cardiac Injuries.

Cardiac Tamponade (Pericardial)

The heart has a tough, fibrous covering called the pericardial sac. This sac cannot be distended easily. A pericardial tamponade occurs when blood fills the sac after blunt or penetrating trauma. This may be caused by the laceration of a coronary blood vessel or chamber of the heart, or by a significant cardiac contusion. As blood fills the pericardial sac, it prevents the heart from filling completely during diastole, and as more pressure is applied to the heart, less filling occurs. This leads to:

1. A reduction in stroke volume.
2. A drop in cardiac output.
3. An increase in venous pressure.
4. Jugular venous distention.
5. Narrowing of the pulse pressure.

It may take as little as 150 milliliters of blood to cause a tamponade.

Signs and Symptoms

Cardiac tamponade is a life-threatening emergency. The patient may initially present with no specific signs and symptoms except those of chest trauma. The following are signs and symptoms that will be noted:

1. Tachycardia.
2. Narrowing (or narrowed) pulse pressure.
3. Jugular venous distention.
4. Quiet or muffled heart sounds.
5. Shock.
6. Hypotension.

Treatment

The definitive treatment is to evacuate the tamponading blood. This is best accomplished in the emergency department setting. The paramedic should:

1. Provide the ABCs.
2. Administer high-flow, high-concentration oxygen.
3. Start one or two IVs with a volume-expansion solution. (Infusing fluid will temporarily increase cardiac output [Starling's Law]).
4. Transport the patient rapidly to the hospital.
5. Consider PASG application.

Traumatic Asphyxia

This is a syndrome that results from severe blunt or crushing injury to the chest. The patient usually presents with chest deformity, cyanosis of the head and neck, bloodshot and possibly protruding eyes, and shock. There will be a rapid pulse and low blood pressure.

The treatment is primarily supportive:

1. Provide the ABCs.
2. Assist ventilations.
3. Start one or two large-bore IVs with volume replacement solution.
4. Transport the patient rapidly.
5. Conside PASG application.

Abdominal Trauma

The boundaries of the abdominopelvic area are the diaphragm superiorly,

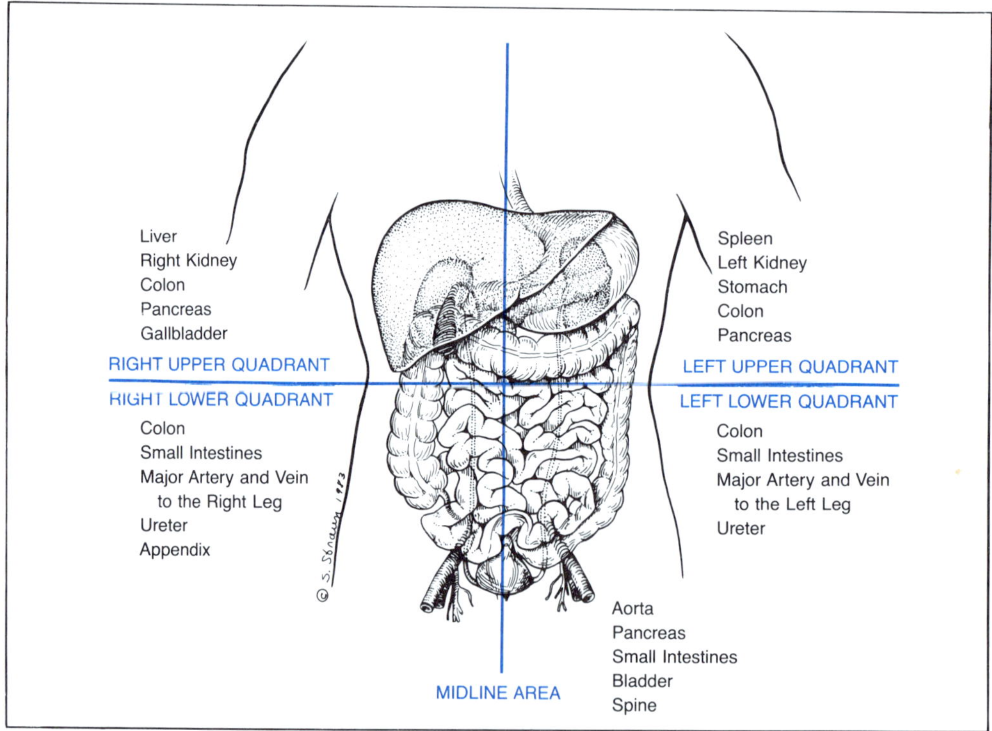

Figure 7-8. The Abdominal Quadrants.

the muscular abdominal wall anteriorly, the pelvis inferiorly, and the vertebral column and low back muscles posteriorly. The abdominopelvic cavity and retroperitoneal space house many structures that may be injured by blunt or penetrating trauma. The solid organs (liver, spleen, pancreas, kidneys, and ovaries) are very vascular and may bleed profusely when injured. The hollow organs (stomach, urinary and gall bladders, small and large intestines) may empty their contents into the surrounding area, causing peritonitis and sepsis. There are many large arteries and veins that may be lacerated, causing serious blood loss.

The paramedic need not attempt to identify the organ(s) injured from trauma. Rather, the paramedic must recognize the potential for serious, possibly life-threatening, injury that may occur from blunt or penetrating injury.

Depending on the severity of the injury, the patient may complain of pain and tenderness and be tachycardic, with signs of shock. The paramedic must have a high index of suspicion for serious injury when an appropriate mechanism is present, when there are obvious signs of abdominal trauma, when shock is present without an obvious cause, or when the patient exhibits abdominal guarding or rigidity. The paramedic should minimize the abdominal assessment.

The treatment involves:

1. Managing the ABCs (consider PASG for reduction of abdominal hemorrhage).
2. Administering high-flow, high-concentration oxygen.
3. Providing ventilatory support as necessary.
4. Starting one or two IVs with volume-expansion solution.
5. Providing rapid transport to the hospital.

Soft-Tissue Injury

The Skin

The skin is composed of two principal layers, the epidermis (outermost layer) and the dermis. The dermis has many important structures, including the nerves, blood vessels, sweat glands, sebaceous glands (secretes an oily substance called sebum, which helps to keep the skin supple and waterproof), and hair follicles.

There is a third, integumentary, layer called subcutaneous tissue. The subcutaneous layer is composed of masses of loose, connective and adipose (fatty) tissues that bind the skin to underlying organs. Skin has many vital functions:

Functions of the Skin

1. It protects the underlying tissue from injury, dehydration, invasion of disease-causing organisms, and temperature extremes.
2. It plays an important role in temperature regulation by vasoconstriction and vasodilation of superficial vasculature.
3. It is a sensory organ recognizing sensations of heat, cold, pressure, pain, and body position.
4. It plays an important role in patient assessment. Information about peripheral perfusion is attained from skin color (which may be red [flushed], pale, blue [cyanosis], or mottled), skin temperature (cool, warm, or hot [febrile]), and texture (moist [clammy] or dry).

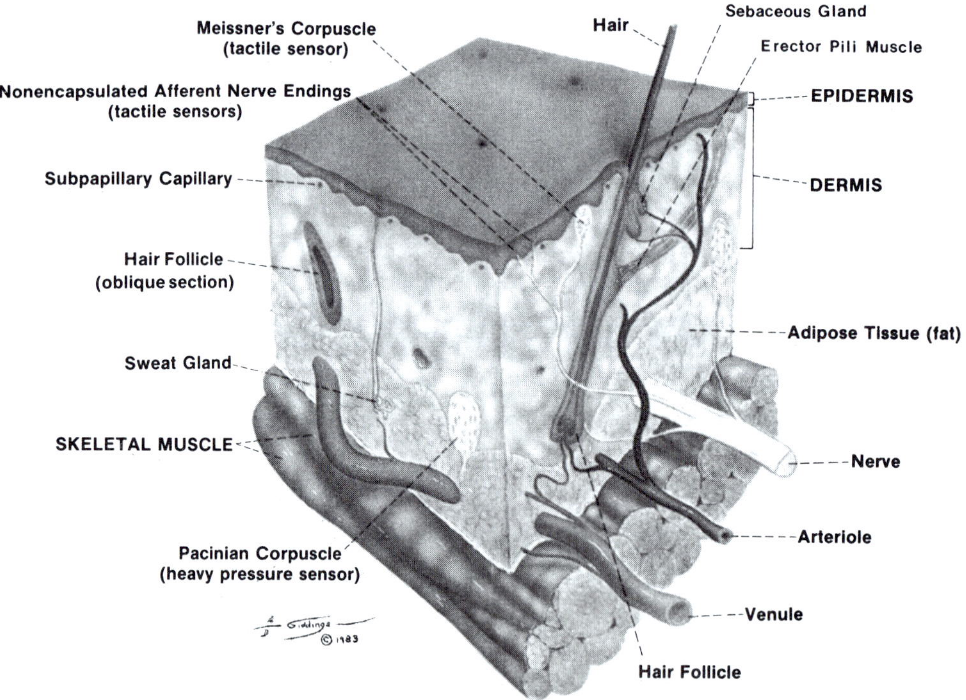

Figure 7-9. The Structure of Normal Skin.

The skin may be damaged easily by trauma. This kind of trauma may be identified as either open or closed. Closed wounds are bruises or contusions that may require pressure and cold applications to reduce discomfort.

Open Wounds

Open wounds require more treatment than closed wounds. They may be identified or typed as follows:

1. Abrasion: a superficial wound caused by rubbing or scraping, resulting in partial loss of the skin.
2. Laceration: a cut made by a sharp instrument (razor, broken glass) that produces a clean (incision) or jagged cut through the skin surface and underlying structures. If a blood vessel is cut, significant bleeding may result.
3. Puncture wound: a stab wound caused by a pointed object. If the penetrating object remains in the wound, it is called an impaled object. Certain guidelines must be followed when treating this type of injury.
4. Avulsion: a ripping or tearing of skin and underlying tissue that may either remain hanging on the body or be completely torn off.
5. Amputation: when a finger, part of an extremity, or all of an extremity is severed from the body.

Treatment of Open Wounds

The treatment of open wounds is directed toward controlling bleeding, preventing further injury, and limiting contamination. It is best for the paramedic to always ''glove-up'' prior to handling a bleeding patient (it may also be necessary to wear goggles and other protective garments). This way, the paramedic may protect him/herself from exposure to infectious organisms that may be found in a patient's bodily fluids. There are several ways in which to control external bleeding:

1. **Direct pressure.** This is generally the most effective way of controlling bleeding. The quickest way is to place a sterile dressing over the wound, then apply manual pressure (with a gloved hand). As soon as it is convenient, secure the dressing in place with a bandage. Direct pressure may be maintained by an air splint, PASG, or a blood pressure cuff when necessary.
2. **Elevation.** If the underlying skeletal structures of an extremity are intact or stabilized, elevation of the injured extremity above the level of the heart may help to reduce bleeding and swelling.

3. **Pressure on the supplying artery.** If the bleeding continues, this technique may help to reduce or stop the flow of blood. Superficial arteries often overlie bone; compressing the artery between the hand and the bone will reduce or stop the flow of blood to the wound. This, in conjunction with direct pressure, is often enough to control bleeding when direct pressure alone proves inadequate. The most common sites for controlling bleeding by this method are:
   - The brachial artery — this lies along the humerus bone in the arm.
   - The femoral artery — this is found overlying the pelvis by the groin.
4. **Tourniquet.** This technique for controlling bleeding should be used as a **last resort.** It should be understood that the portion of the extremity distal to the tourniquet site may be lost. There is also the potential to further damage underlying blood vessels and nerves through improper placement and inadequate tightening of the tourniquet that might result in increased rather than decreased bleeding. If a tourniquet is to be used, the paramedic should employ the following technique:
   - Use wide, flat material only (at least two inches wide). Never use any material that may cut into the skin.
   - Place a pad of 4 by 4s over the artery to be compressed.
   - Apply the tourniquet three to four inches below the axilla or groin, wrapping it twice around the limb and tying a half-knot. Place an oxygen key or similar object on top of the half-knot and tie a square knot over it.
   - Turn the "key" until the bleeding stops.
   - Make sure that the tourniquet will be obvious to other personnel, and clearly mark the time when it was applied.

Impaled Objects and Amputations

The paramedic must pay special attention when treating a patient with an impaled object. Impaled objects should not be removed from the patient **except in one situation** — when the cheek or airway are being obstructed by the object. Other impaled objects are not removed because the object may be penetrating a major vessel or organ. Removal of the impaled object might lead to exsanguination and death of the patient or further injury. The object should be stabilized with bulky dressings and bandaged in place.

In an amputation, both the severed part and the stump need to be managed. The amputated part should be wrapped in sterile, dry gauze, placed in a plastic bag, and kept cool. There may be a chance that the part could be reimplanted. The stump is treated like any soft-tissue injury (dressed and bandaged).

Eye Trauma

The eyes are the photoreceptors that respond to light energy. They are approximately one inch in diameter and are located within the orbits of the skull. They are moved by six muscles. Injury to the eye can be a frightening and serious injury for the patient. Knowledge of its structures will help the paramedic to better assess and treat the eye-injured patient.

Structures of the Eye

The eye consists of the following structures (see Figure 7-10):

1. Sclera — the outer coat of the eyeball; the white of the eye.
2. Conjunctiva — the mucous-membrane lining of the eyelid and eyeball.
3. Cornea — the transparent anterior portion of the eye.
4. Iris — the colored portion of the eye that surrounds the pupil.
5. Pupil — the opening in the center of the iris of the eye.
6. Lens.
7. Aqueous humor — a transparent liquid that fills both the anterior and posterior chambers of the eye.
8. Vitreous humor — gel-like substance found between the lens and the retina that primarily maintains the shape of the eyeball; if this substance

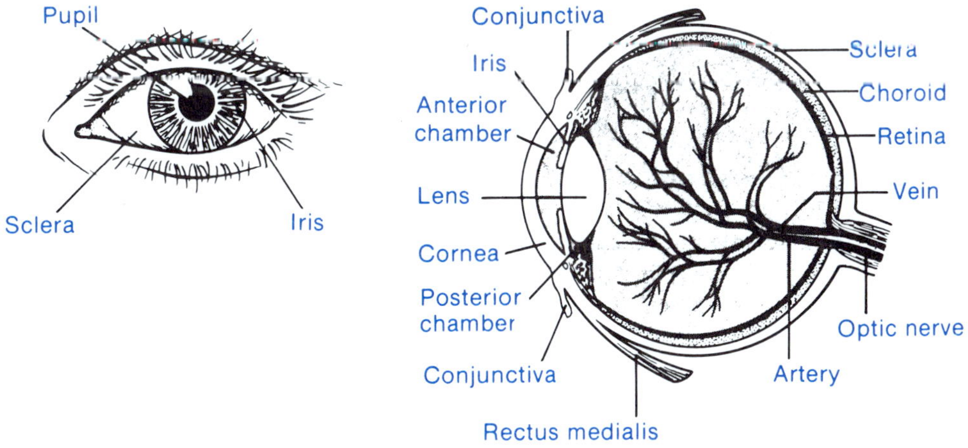

Figure 7-10. Anatomy of the Human Eye.

is lost, it cannot be replaced.

9. Retina — the innermost coat of the eye containing the visual receptors.
10. Optic nerve — the nerve that transmits visual impulses from the retina to the brain; when external pressure (head injury) is applied to this nerve, it causes the pupil to stay dilated.

Causes and Treatment of Eye Injuries

Trauma to the eye may involve only the surrounding soft tissue. In this case, the wound may be treated like any soft-tissue injury.

If the orbit is fractured, the eye may be dropped and the patient may complain of double vision.

Injuries to the globe of the eye may be caused by abrasions, contusions, lacerations, and foreign bodies. These injuries are best treated by an eye specialist. The paramedic should patch both eyes and transport the patient supine or semireclined, whichever is most appropriate.

Ear Injury

The ear is involved with hearing and balance. It is not often injured, although children have a tendency to put objects inside of them. The outer ear may be injured from trauma.

Parts of the Ear

The ear may be divided into three sections:

1. **Outer ear.** This consists of:
   - The auricle or pinna — the fleshy flap attached to the side of the skull. This part of the ear is prone to soft-tissue injury.
   - The external auditory meatus (ear canal), which directs sound to the eardrum.
2. **Middle ear.** This consists of:
   - The eardrum, which forms the lateral wall.
   - The ossicles (three bones) for transmission of sound to the inner ear.
   - The Eustachian tube (auditory tube), which allows equalization of pressure on the two sides of the eardrum.
3. **Inner ear.** This contains:
   - The organ of hearing.
   - Organs concerned with balance and equilibrium.

Treatment of Ear Injuries

Treat ear injuries as soft-tissue injuries. If basilar skull fracture is suspected and cerebrospinal fluid is leaking out of the ear, do not obstruct the flow. Place a loose dressing over the ear. If a child has a foreign body stuck in the ear, it is best left to the emergency department staff.

Nose Trauma

Epistaxis or nosebleed is a common problem caused by trauma, acute infection, or hypertension (most commonly seen in the elderly). Patients with epistaxis are often apprehensive (due to obvious bleeding) and require gentleness and reassurance. Tachycardia and hypotension indicate severe blood loss. When it is secondary to trauma, the bleeding is usually from the anterior part of the nose and is best controlled by manual external compression. The nosebleed is generally not heavy unless associated with a fracture.

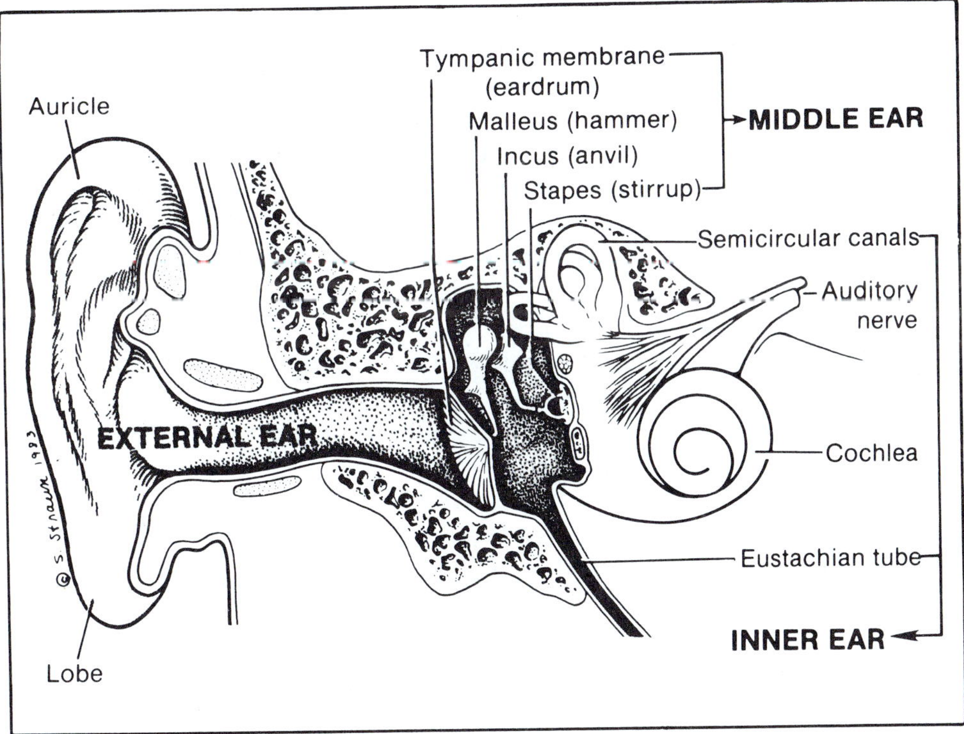

Figure 7-11. Anatomy of the Human Ear.

In any case, this kind of bleeding tends to be self-limiting. There is no need to anteriorly pack the nose, since manual pressure serves the same purpose.

Treatment for Nosebleeds Associated with Hypertension

Nosebleeds are usually more severe when associated with hypertension or coagulation defects. This kind of bleeding is most often posterior, so there is little or no bleeding from the nares — the blood primarily drips down the naso-oropharynx. This posterior bleeding may be life-threatening.

To treat this patient:

1. Start an IV with a volume-replacement solution.
2. If appropriate (vital signs are stable), have the patient sit up with his/her head bent over a bowl; support the mouth to keep it open (use an airway).
3. Tell the patient to breathe only through the mouth and not to swallow any blood (this may lead to nausea and vomiting).

The following is recommended by the Department of Transportation as a paramedic procedure. It is rarely, if ever, performed in the prehospital setting. It is included here for informational purposes only. This procedure is performed in the emergency department setting usually after a vasoconstricting agent is used. Also, in the emergency department, a nasal catheter is used rather than a Foley catheter.

If the procedure listed above does not reduce bleeding, it may be necessary to insert a posterior and anterior nasal pack. The posterior pack will support the anterior pack (see Figures 7-12 and 7-13). The paramedic may use a Foley catheter with a thirty-milliliter balloon for the posterior pack.

1. First, the tip of the catheter distal to the balloon is removed so that it does not stimulate the gag reflex.
2. The catheter should be well lubricated with a water-soluble gel and inserted into the nare until it can be seen at the back of the throat.
3. The balloon should be filled to fifteen milliliters, then pulled forward until slight resistance is met.
4. The balloon may be filled five to seven milliliters more.
5. With the paramedic holding slight traction on the posterior pack, the anterior should be gently packed with the 4-by-4 dressings.
6. When this is complete, an umbilical clamp can be used to hold the Foley tube in place.

Nasal Fractures

Nasal fractures are identified by swelling and deformity. Cold packs are used to help reduce swelling. The paramedic should be observant for head or neck injuries.

The Skeletal System and Fractures

The human skeleton is a dynamic, living structure that serves to protect and support the body. The skull, the vertebral column, the rib cage, and the pelvis protect the underlying organs. Muscles attach (by tendons) to the skeleton to provide skeletal movement; bones are held together by tough, fibrous bands called ligaments. The bones contain calcium and phosphate — essential substances for the body that can be utilized when needed. The bone marrow, a tissue found inside the bones, is a storehouse for nutrients and produces several types of blood cells (red blood cells, white blood cells).

Joints

Bones come together or articulate at the joint. There are two divisions of joints in the body:

1. Cartilagenous — slightly movable joints that are joined by cartilage (e.g., ribs articulating with the sternum).
2. Synovial — freely movable joints that have a cavity, a membrane, synovial

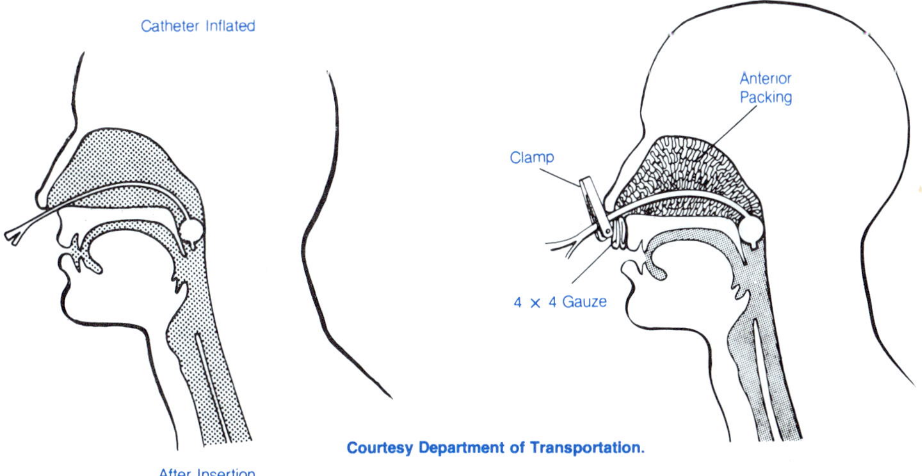

Figure 7-12. How to Use Foley Catheter for Severe Epistaxis.

Figure 7-13. Clamping the Catheter and Applying Traction for Epitaxis.

fluid, and supporting ligaments (e.g., knee, thumb).

There are six types of synovial joints:

1. Hinge joint — permits back-and-forth motion and is a uniaxial joint (e.g., knee, elbow, ankle, finger joint).
2. Pivot joint — permits rotation and is a uniaxial joint (e.g., the "no," back-and-forth motion of the head).
3. Ovoid joint — permits side-to-side and back-and-forth motion; it is a biaxial joint (e.g., the wrist).
4. Saddle joint — a biaxial joint (e.g., the thumb).
5. Gliding joint — a biaxial joint that permits side-to-side and back-and-forth motion (e.g., intercarpal and intertarsal joints).
6. Ball-and-socket joint — a triaxial joint that permits side-to-side, back-and-forth, and rotational motion (e.g., the hip and shoulder).

The motion of all of these joints is a result of the muscles that are attached contracting and relaxing.

Bones

Bones may be classified by their shape: long (femur, radius), short (bones of the wrist, ankle), flat (ribs, scapula), and irregular (vertebrae). Bone is

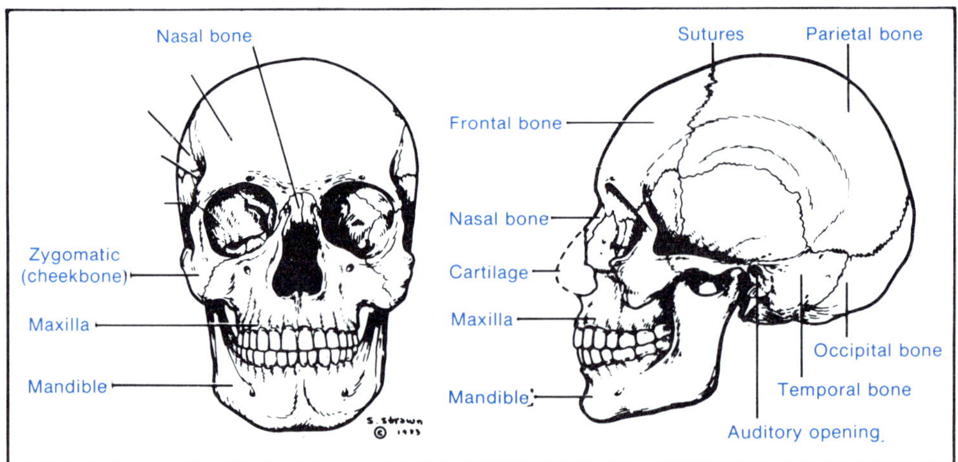

Figure 7-14. Anatomy of the Skull.

covered with a tough, fibrous membrane called the periosteum.

The skeleton is made up of 206 bones and is divided into two parts: the axial skeleton and the appendicular skeleton. The axial skeleton contains eighty bones and is comprised of the skull, the vertebral column, and the thorax (sternum and ribs). The appendicular skeleton contains 126 bones comprised of the upper extremities and the lower extremities, including the pelvis.

The paramedic should know the names of most of the bones that make up the skeleton. Starting with the head, they are as follows:

1. Cranial bones: there are six bones in the skull that paramedics need to know — one frontal, two parietals, one occipital, and two temporals.
2. Facial bones: nasal bones, zygomatics (cheekbone), the orbits, the maxillae, and the mandible.
3. Vertebral column: consists of twenty-four separate bones plus the sacrum and coccyx.
   - The cervical spine consists of seven vertebrae — C-1 through C-7.
   - The thoracic spine consists of twelve vertebrae — T-1 through T-12.

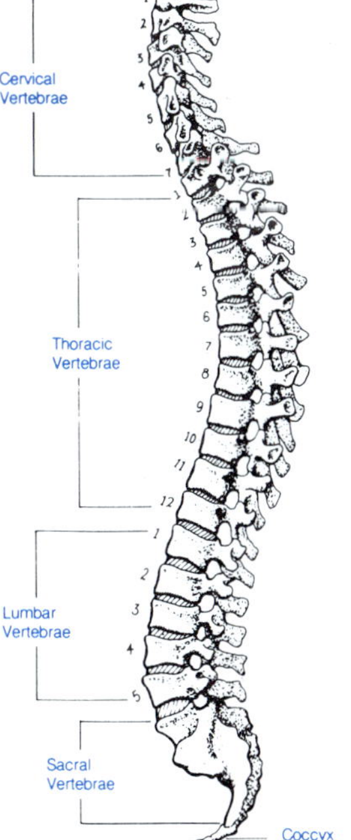

Figure 7-15. The Vertebral Column.

Courtesy Department of Transportation.

- The lumbar spine consists of five vertebrae — L-1 through L-5.
- The sacrum is a single bone composed of five fused vertebrae.
- The coccyx is composed of three to five fused vertebrae.

4. Thoracic bones: a cone-shaped cage formed by the sternum, the thoracic vertebrae, twelve pair of ribs, and the costal cartilage.
5. Upper extremity (arm): consists of thirty-two bones — the clavicle, the scapula, the humerus, the ulna, the radius, the carpals (wrist), the metacarpals (hand), and the phalanges.
6. Lower extremity (pelvis and leg): consists of thirty bones — the pelvis

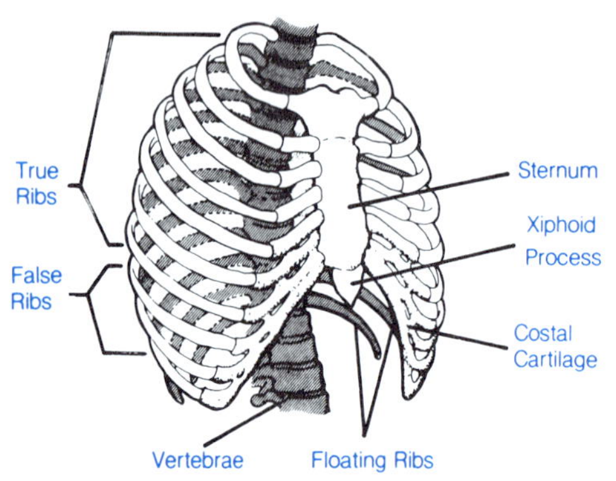

Figure 7-16. Bones of the Thorax.

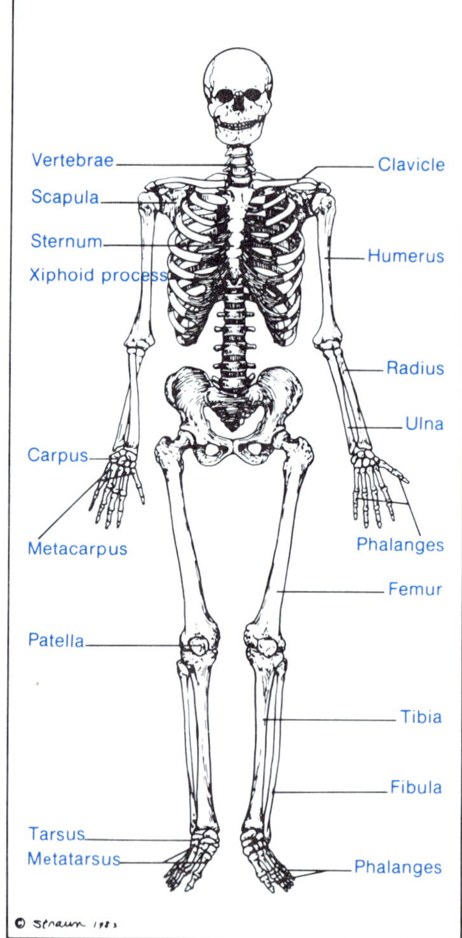

Figure 7-17. The Skeletal System.

(ilium, ischium, and pubis), the femur, the patella, the tibia, the fibula, the tarsals, the metatarsals, and the phalanges.

It is valuable to recognize that many important structures, such as arteries, veins, and nerves, are found running parallel to the bones. These structures may be injured from the fracture itself or secondarily from improper handling and immobilization.

Fractures

A fracture is a common result of trauma and may be defined as a break in the continuity of a bone. Several types of fractures may occur.

1. Greenstick fracture: a break that occurs in children whose bones break similarly to greensticks.
2. Transverse fracture: a break that extends directly across the bone at a ninety-degree angle; usually a result of direct trauma.
3. Oblique fracture: rather than the break being straight across, it is at an angle.
4. Spiral fracture: the fracture line ''spirals'' up or down the bone; usually a

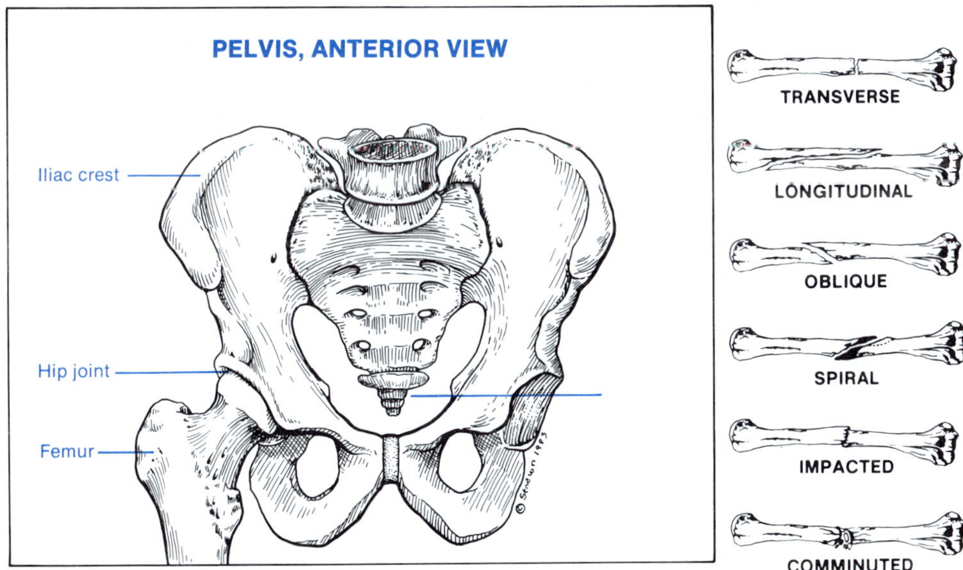

Figure 7-18. The Pelvis.

Figure 7-19. Classification of Fractures.

result of a twisting injury.

5. Comminuted fracture: a fracture that consists of more than two fragments.
6. Impacted fracture: a fracture where the broken bone ends are jammed together.

It is not necessary for the paramedic to identify any of these types of fractures. In all of the above cases, the paramedic will assess and splint the fractures in a similar fashion.

Fractures may also be classified as open or closed. An open fracture is when there is a break in the skin associated with the fracture. It may be in the form of a bone end protruding out of the skin or a wound extending down to the broken bone. A closed fracture occurs when the skin above the fracture is intact.

Dislocations

A dislocation is another injury that may occur to joints of the skeleton. A dislocation is the temporary displacement of a bone out of its normal position in a joint. This injury may occur along with a fracture and results in loss of motion, deformity, and sometimes loss of sensation and distal pulse.

The shoulder is the most commonly injured joint and accounts for approximately 50 percent of all dislocations. A dislocation of the hip is a serious injury requiring surgical reduction. This type of injury usually occurs from the knee striking the dashboard in an automobile accident. Dislocation of the knee usually results from powerful forces like a direct blow, a fall, or a twisting injury involving the knee.

In general, dislocations should be immobilized in the position found. Provide a thorough evaluation of the extremity, distally, for sensation, movement, pulse, and capillary refill before and after immobilization. Additional treatment should be left to the emergency department.

Sprains and Strains

Another injury that may occur to the skeletal system is a sprain, an injury involved with the stretching and/or tearing of ligaments (it may also be associated with fractures). In the field, it is difficult to distinguish sprains from fractures. It is best to splint all suspected sprains as if they were fractures.

Strains are the stretching or tearing of muscle tissue.

General Fracture Assessment

1. Do the ABCs of the primary survey.

2. Do a physical examination. Inspect and palpate the extremities (as well as the skull and chest) for:
   - Pain. This is the most common chief complaint of patients who have experienced a fracture or dislocation.
   - Deformity (abnormal position).
   - Swelling and discoloration (ecchymosis).
   - Pain and tenderness.
   - Loss of movement.
   - Sensation.
   - Distal pulse (a pulse beyond the site of the injury).
   - Capillary refill (should be less than two seconds).
   - Skin temperature and color.
   - Crepitation (the sound and feeling of broken bone ends grating together). Do not check for this sign, but make a note of it if it is felt.
   - The paramedic must be aware that pelvic, hip, and femur fractures may bleed profusely, leading to hypovolemia and shock.
3. History. Question for the mechanism of injury and other injuries, and take a normal history from the patient and bystanders.

General Treatment

1. Do the ABCs. Fractures are rarely an immediate life-threatening problem, so treat the ABCs first.
2. If there are any open wounds, dress and bandage them prior to splinting fractures. If bone ends are exposed, protect them and do not allow them to be returned into the body during dressing/bandaging and splinting.
3. Expose the area of the fracture.
4. General principles of splinting:
   - Check for distal pulse, sensation, movement, and capillary refill before and after splinting.
   - Keep movement of the injured extremity to a minimum.
   - Two paramedics should participate in splinting. One maintains traction and immobilization, while the other applies the splint.
   - Dress and bandage open wounds prior to splinting.
   - Immobilize the joint above and below the site of the fracture.
   - Stabilize the fracture with manual, in-line traction.
   - In severely angulated fractures, attempt to return the limb to the position of normal alignment. Explain to the patient that this may be painful initially. If the 5 ''P''s are present — pallor, pain, pulselessness, paresthesia, and puffiness — the limb may need respositioning (follow local protocols). Repositioning may be done if the area needing to be

straightened does not involve a joint. When repositioning, support the fracture and apply gentle traction and countertraction while moving the limb to the desired position. Maintain traction until splinting has been completed. Reassess circulatory and neurologic status after completion of the move.

- Leave fingers and toes showing when possible so that circulatory status may be assessed after splinting.
- Immobilize dislocations in the position found. If the patient has vascular compromise, follow local protocol for the appropriate treatment.
- Do not attempt to differentiate between fractures and sprains; immobilize both injuries.
- Pad splints well.
- Check airsplints to be sure that they are not overinflated.
- When using a traction splint, check the ankle hitch for comfort.
- Splints should be applied snugly but not overly tight. Assess and reassess the injured extremity for swelling.

Types of Splints

1. Rigid splint. Ladder splints or board splints are typical examples. When these are used, be sure that they are padded adequately. These are commonly used for upper-extremity and tibia/fibula immobilization.
2. Soft splint. Pillows are soft splints sometimes used for ankle fractures.
3. Air splint. This is an inflatable splint commonly used for lower-arm or lower-leg fracture immobilization.
4. Vacuum splint. The vacuum splint is filled with small pellets of styrofoam (or comparable material) that take the position of the extremity when the air in the splint is expelled. The splint is wrapped around the injured extremity.
5. Traction splint. This splint is used primarily for midshaft femur fractures. The muscles in the upper leg are powerful, and when a fracture of the femur occurs, muscular contractions may cause the broken bones to override each other. This leads to additional injury and considerable pain. The traction splint is designed to maintain traction of the upper leg while it is being immobilized.
6. Sling. A sling is made from a triangular bandage to support the upper and lower arm.
7. Sling and swath. The swath can be made from a triangular bandage or a wide roller bandage. The swath is wrapped around the upper body, including the injured arm, and underneath the uninjured arm. This provides greater stabilization of the injured limb. The sling and swath is commonly

used for stabilizing humerus, radius/ulna, and carpal fractures.
8. PASG (MAST). This garment may be used for pelvic, tibia/fibula, and bilateral leg fractures.
9. If the paramedic knows the general principles of splinting, he/she will be able to improvise when commercial splints are not available.

Suggested Specific Treatment of Fractures

1. Vertebral column: backboard.
2. Pelvis: backboard and PASG device.
3. Femur: traction device, PASG device, long backboard, long board, or to the opposite extremity.
4. Tibia/fibula: air splint, rigid splint, PASG, cardboard splint, a traction device, or to the opposite leg.
5. Ankle/foot: air splint, rigid splint, cardboard, or pillow splint.
6. Clavicle: sling and swath.
7. Shoulder: sling and swath.
8. Humerus: rigid splint with sling and swath.
9. Elbow: splint in position found.
10. Radius/ulna: rigid splint, air splint, and sling and swath.
11. Carpals (wrist): consider rigid splint along with sling and swath.
12. Hand: rigid splint or air splint in the position of function, with a sling to support the extremity.
13. Finger: tongue depressor, commercial finger splint, or to the adjacent finger.

MONITORING TECHNIQUES FOR THE TRAUMA PATIENT

Several trauma-scoring systems have been developed over the past few years to enhance the paramedic's ability to assess the critically injured trauma patient and to help determine to which trauma facility the patient should be transported. It is believed that both proper treatment and appropriate triage of the patient are needed to increase the trauma patient's survival rate. The use of trauma scoring serves the following purposes:

1. It indicates the severity of injuries.
2. It determines the need for a Level I Trauma Center (surgery immediately available), if available.
3. It determines the speed (emergent or nonurgent) necessary to get the pa-

tient to a medical facility.

4. It identifies changes in the patient's status.
5. It identifies patients who should not be resuscitated in the field due to trauma.

There is a great deal of controversy over whether trauma scoring is of prehospital use. Studies have been done to evaluate the effectiveness of trauma scoring. Some studies indicate that the individual assessment of the patient without the use of trauma scores is equal to or better than using trauma scoring. The paramedic should follow local protocol. The three systems of trauma scoring are Injury Severity Score (ISS), Trauma Score, and the CRAMS Scale.

Injury Severity Score (ISS)

This system is based on the Abbreviated Injury Scale (AIS), which was

Table 7-1

Trauma Score

Eye Opening		**Capillary Return**	
Spontaneous	3	Normal	2
To Voice	2	Delayed	0
To Pain	1		
None	0	**Motor Responses**	
		Obeys command	4
Verbal Response		Withdraws	3
Oriented	4	Flexion	2
Confused	3	Extension	1
Inappropriate words	2	None	0
Incomprehensible words	1		
None	0		
Respiratory Effort			
Normal	3	***Total Score:***	
Shallow	1		
Retractive	1		
None	0		______________

developed by the American Association of Automotive Medicine. The score is the sum of the squares of the three most severely injured anatomical body regions (ISS — $A^2 + B^2 + C^2$). A is the body region with the most severe injury, B is the body region with the second most severe injury, and C is the body region with the third most severe injury. It is based on clinical findings and is similar to the Apgar Score for newborns. It is the least used trauma-scoring system in prehospital care.

Trauma Score (TS)

This is the most widely used scoring system and helps to identify the severity of the injury. The early scores may be more reliable for blunt trauma than for penetrating trauma.

The paramedic determines the numerical value of each category, then adds all five categories to determine the patient's Trauma Score.

CRAMS Scale

This trauma scoring is less complex than the other systems. The paramedic determines the numerical value of each category, then adds all five categories

Table 7-2

CRAMS Scale

Category	Score	Category	Score
Circulation		**Motor**	
Normal	2	Normal	2
Abnormal	1	Abnormal	1
Severely abnormal	0	Severely abnormal	0
Respiration		**Speech**	
Normal	2	Normal	2
Abnormal	1	Abnormal	1
Severely abnormal	0	Severely abnormal	0
Abdomen		***Total Score:***	
Normal	2		
Abnormal	1		
Severely abnormal	0		________

to determine where the patient is located on the CRAMS Scale.

Patient Evaluation

In general, when the paramedic is evaluating the patient, particularly in regard to what facility the patient should be transported, the following guidelines should be used:

1. Level of consciousness (use the Glascow coma scale).
2. Systolic blood pressure. Is the patient in shock (systolic below 90 mmHg; other clinical signs of shock)?
3. Respiratory rate. Is it over twenty-eight or under twelve?
4. Mechanism of injury. Were powerful forces involved in the accident (fall

Glasgow Coma Scale

Eyes	Open	Spontaneously	4
		To verbal command	3
		To pain	2
	No response		1
Best motor response	To verbal command	Obeys	6
	To painful stimulus*	Localizes pain	5
		Flexion - withdrawal	4
		Flexion - abnormal (decorticate rigidity)	3
		Extension (decerebrate rigidity)	2
		No response	1
Best verbal response**		Oriented and converses	5
		Disoriented and converses	4
		Inappropriate words	3
		Incomprehensible sounds	2
		No response	1
Total			3-15

The Glasgow Coma Scale, based upon eye opening, verbal, and motor responses, is a practical means of monitoring changes in level of consciousness. If response on the scale is given a number, the responsiveness of the patient can be expressed by summation of the figures. *Lowest* score is 3, *highest* is 15.

*Apply knuckles to sternum, observe arms

**Arouse patient with painful stimulus if necessary

Figure 7-20. Glasgow Coma Scale.

of fifteen or more feet, high-speed automobile accident, gunshot wounds, etc.)?
5. Age of the patient. Usually patients under five and over sixty years of age are at greater risk from severe trauma.
6. Underlying medical problems.

One study showed that paramedics did a good job in correctly evaluating patients using criteria similar to the above.

Monitoring and Reassessment of the Patient

The patient's vital signs, neurological status, respiratory efforts, color, temperature, and ECG should be reevaluated and recorded at least every five minutes while on the scene and en route to the hospital.

Particular attention should be paid to any vital sign or assessment area that was abnormal on the initial assessment. These areas should be assessed with greater frequency. Evaluate fluid replacement every five minutes by vital signs and level of consciousness, and by monitoring the IV flow rate.

The paramedic should continually assess the patient's ABCs. Reassessment of injuries for adequate stabilization should occur throughout the paramedic's time with the patient. Finally, repeat the physical exam to look for the possibility of missed injuries and/or complications that might have developed since initial treatment.

Transportation

The patient should be transported to the hospital as rapidly as possible. The generally accepted length of time on the scene of severe trauma is less than ten minutes. The definitive care for the patient is usually surgery. The patient's chances of survival are reduced if he/she does not receive definitive treatment within an hour of injury (the "golden hour"). Unnecessary delay allows for deterioration of the patient.

The severe trauma patient may be "packaged" quickly as a single unit to a backboard. The time required to treat specific non-life-threatening injuries or to start a field IV will delay treatment of the seriously injured patient.

IVs should be started en route to the hospital, if at all possible. Setting up the IV (tearing tape, getting administration set up, tourniquet, prepping skin, etc.) may be done while the ambulance is moving. If the IV is difficult to start, stop the vehicle until the catheter is inserted. Studies have shown that the delay time is zero to two minutes to initiate an IV by this method, and five to ten minutes if the IV is started before the patient is loaded.

The patient should be taken to the closest appropriate hospital as identified by previously established protocols or as identified by the medical command authority while the call is in progress.

SUMMARY

In the critically injured patient, the initial treatment may play a significant role in the final outcome of the patient. The paramedic's knowledge and skill in understanding the kinematics of an accident, rapid patient assessment, airway management, trauma management, and resuscitation of the severely traumatized patient may result in a lowered morbidity and mortality from trauma.[1]

The paramedic is often the first person to treat and evaluate the trauma victim. It is imperative for the paramedic to continue study and practice of those field techniques that may prove invaluable in treating the injured patient.

Maloney, Joseph P., "Foreword," *Emergency Care Quarterly,* Vol. 2, No. 4, February 1987, p. vi.

8

Burns

More than 2 million people suffer thermal injury in the United States each year. Approximately 100,000 persons are hospitalized, and 12,000 persons die yearly from burns. A relatively large number of these burn patients are children and young adults. It is estimated that 80 percent of all burns occur in the home. From these statistics, it is easy to understand the importance of burn care management.

The burn injury is all too often treated as a single-organ injury, with other organs and structures of the body being overlooked during initial care. The morbidity and mortality caused by thermal injury may be reduced by aggressively extinguishing the fire, removing the burning substance from the patient or removing the patient from the heat source, providing life-support measures, and transporting the patient to an appropriate medical facility — a designated burn center.

This chapter will summarize the current manner of treatment for thermal, electrical, and chemical burns by the prehospital care provider. With effective care initiated at the scene by EMTs and paramedics, and through appropriate hospital care, the outcome for burn patients is optimistic.

ANATOMY AND PHYSIOLOGY

Structure of the Integumentary (Body Covering) System

1. Epidermis (most superficial layer).
2. Dermis:
   - Blood vessels.

- Nerve endings.
- Sebaceous glands (oily, fatty).
- Sweat glands.
- Hair follicles.

3. Subcutaneous fat.

Function of the Integumentary System

1. Protection of underlying tissues from bacteria, dehydration, and noxious substances.
2. Body temperature regulation.
3. Maintenance of equilibrium in the chemical composition of fluid and tissues (homeostasis) in:
   - Water.
   - Salts.
   - Organic material.
   - Inorganic material.
4. Organ of sensory perception.
5. Excretion.
6. Produces vitamin D.
7. Determines personal identity.

PATHOLOGY OF BURN SHOCK

1. Normal mechanisms of homeostasis are disrupted.
2. The patient experiences pain.
3. There may be much psychological discomfort, anxiety, and/or fear.
4. Burn shock (hypovolemic shock) occurs with plasma volume reduction and a hematocrit elevation (increase in the ratio of red blood cells to plasma).
5. Vascular bed leakage. Patient loses plasma, causing hypovolemia.
6. Evaporation from damaged surface — may produce hypothermia.
7. Cardiac output may drop 30 to 50 percent — this is a critical initial decrease due to hypovolemia.
8. Development of edema.
9. Depending on the size of the burn, equilibrium may return within twenty-four to forty-eight hours.

MAJOR SOURCES OF BURN INJURY

1. Thermal:
   - Radiation of heat.
   - Conduction of heat from hot liquids, solids, and gases.
   - Flames.
   - The sun.
2. Electrical:
   - Flash or electrical arc.
   - Direct contact.
3. Chemicals.
   - Liquids.
   - Gases.
   - Solids (dry).

CLASSIFICATION OF BURN INJURIES

First Degree

1. Loss of epidermis.
2. Erythema (redness) only.
3. Hyperalgesia (excessive sensitivity to pain).
4. Healing time: three to seven days.

Superficial Second Degree

1. No loss of dermis.
2. Erythema with blisters.
3. Moist (weeping).
4. Hyperalgesia.
5. Healing time: six to fourteen days.

Deep Second Degree

1. Loss of deep dermis.
2. Skin pink, white, or tan.
3. Hyperalgesia to analgesia (absence of normal sense of pain).
4. Healing time: fourteen to twenty-one days; may require grafting.

Third Degree

1. Loss of all epidermis, dermis, and subcutaneous fat.
2. Skin white, charred, tan-colored.
3. Analgesia.
4. Requires grafting.

CATEGORIES OF BURN INJURY BY SEVERITY

Critical Burns

1. Second-degree burns involving more than 30 percent of the body surface area.
2. Second-degree burns involving more than 20 percent of a child's body surface area.
3. Third-degree burns involving more than 10 to 15 percent of the body surface area.

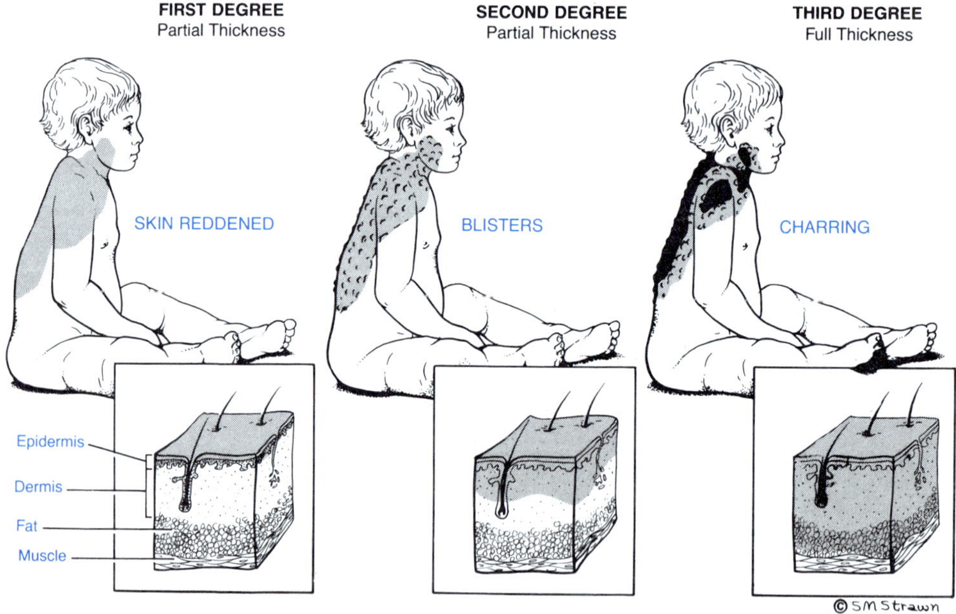

Figure 8-1. Classification of Burns.

4. Burns complicated by respiratory tract injury (inhalation injury).
5. All burns of the face (eyes and ears), hands, feet, or perineum (genital area).
6. Burns complicated by fracture of major soft-tissue injury; burns involving flexion areas, such as elbow, neck, and axilla (armpit).
7. Electrical and deep acid burns.
8. Burns occurring in patients with underlying physical or medical conditions.
9. Burns in patients under two years of age and adults over fifty years of age (these are high-risk patients).

Moderate Burns

1. First-degree burns involving 15 to 30 percent of the body surface area, excluding the hands, feet, or face.
2. Second-degree burns involving 15 to 25 percent of the body surface area in adults and 10 to 20 percent of the body surface area in children.
3. Third-degree burns involving 2 to 10 percent of the body surface area, not

Table 8-1

Survivable Probability for Burn Patients

Age	Body Surface Area Burned (%)	Survival Probability (%)
20	20	95+
	40	85
	60	60
40	20	95+
	40	80
	60	50
60	20	80+
	40	40
	60	7

(Surface Area Burned Producing 50% Survival)

Age	Body Surface Area Burned (%)	Survival Probability (%)
0-14	62	50
15-40	63	50
40	38	50
65	23	50

Auerbach, Paul S., Geehr, Edward C., Management of Wilderness and Environmental Emergencies, 1983, Macmillan.

including eyes, ears, face, hands, feet, and perineum.

Minor Burns

1. First-degree burns involving less than 20 percent of the body surface area, excluding hands, feet, and face.
2. Second-degree burns involving less than 15 percent of the body surface area in adults and less than 10 percent of the body surface area in children.
3. Third-degree burns involving less than 2 percent of the body surface area, except eyes, ears, face, hands, feet, and perineum.

FACTORS AFFECTING SEVERITY OF INJURY

Scene-Related Factors

1. Was the patient confined in the area of the fire?
2. How long was the confinement?
3. Nature of injury.
4. Was there a loss of consciousness during exposure? This would predispose a patient to inhalation injury.

Patient-Related Factors

1. Age — children under two and adults over fifty have a higher mortality and morbidity rate.
2. Percentage of body surface area involved.
3. Degrees of burn.
4. Location of burn.
5. Preexisting diseases (past or present medical problems).
6. General health.
7. Associated injuries.

CALCULATION OF BODY SURFACE AREA

Rule of Nines for Adults

1. Head: 9 percent.
2. Arm: 9 percent.
3. Chest and abdomen: 18 percent.
4. Back and buttocks: 18 percent.

5. Legs: 18 percent each.
6. Genitalia: 1 percent.
7. Estimation is sufficient for emergency situations.
8. The surface of the patient's hand is approximately 1 percent of the body surface area.

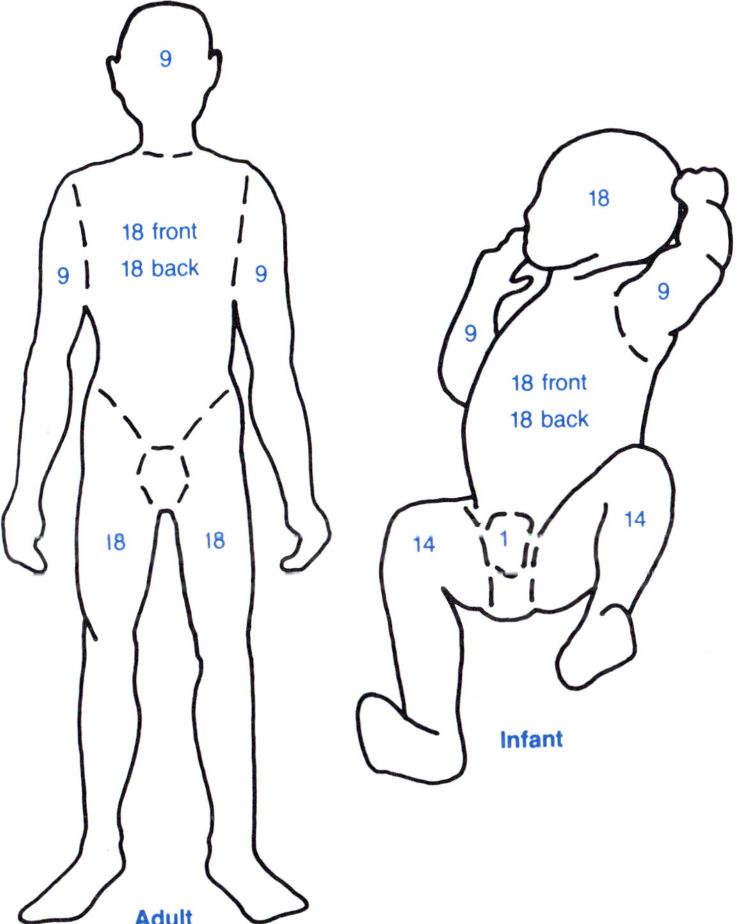

Figure 8-2. Rule of Nines.

Modified Rule of Nines for Infants and Small Children

1. Head: 18 percent.
2. Arm: 9 percent.
3. Chest and abdomen: 18 percent.
4. Back and buttocks: 18 percent.
5. Leg: 14 percent.

THERMAL BURNS

Assessment

History

Note: Before assessment is started, remove the patient from the source of heat. Extinguish the fire and remove burning clothing and jewelry.

1. How long ago did the burn occur?
2. What, if anything, has been done by the patient or bystanders to treat the injury?
3. Was the patient in a closed space?
   - Were steam, smoke, or combustive products involved?
   - For what duration of time was the contact?
   - Was there a loss of consciousness?
4. What was the specific source of the burn?
5. Does the patient's past medical history include:
   - Heart disease that might complicate fluid therapy?
   - Pulmonary problems that may cause a more severe reaction to smoke inhalation?
   - Other serious underlying illness (diabetes, epilepsy)?
6. Does the patient have any allergies?
7. The paramedic must watch for signs of impending upper airway obstruction.
8. Has the patient fallen or jumped, or was he/she thrown to escape fire

Physican Examination

1. Perform a primary survey (ABCs). The paramedic should pay close attention to the airway and breathing. These patients should be provided with oxygen as soon as possible.
2. Perform a head-to-toe examination.

3. Observe for soft tissue and skeletal injury(s) in addition to burns, particularly if the patient had to escape fire (e.g., jumping out of a window).
4. Monitor the patient's vital signs frequently.

Treatment

1. Secure the airway, breathing, and circulation as needed. The paramedic may use an adjunctive airway if necessary. An esophageal obturator or endotracheal intubation may be used.
2. Assess the level of consciousness.
3. Provide oxygen therapy when appropriate with high flow and high concentration. Assist ventilations with a bag-valve-mask if needed.
4. Monitor the ECG and document the cardiac rhythm.
5. Initiate IV therapy. Patients with burns over more than 15 to 20 percent of their total body surface area usually require IV fluid replacement. Ringer's lactate solution is recommended for volume replacement in the field.
   - Choose an IV fluid solution for volume replacement.
   - Select an IV site away from the injured area.
   - IV fluid rate is based on the initial assessment of the patient. Treat for shock as necessary. Use a large-bore needle — 16-gauge.
6. Initiate cooling if within thirty minutes of the burn incident. For first- and second-degree burns on less than 20 percent of the surface area, use cool, wet compresses or immerse the area if appropriate. Be careful not to cause hypothermia by cooling too large an area of the body.
7. Dress the burn injury (follow local protocol). On thermal and chemical burns, apply saline-moistened dressings (to facilitate ease of removal), then cover with a dry, sterile dressing to prevent further contamination. For large areas, use burn sheets. Do not apply any ointments, salves, or sprays. Maintain body temperature.
8. Provide care for associated injuries. The paramedic should suspect other injuries if trauma is involved.
9. The paramedic must be prepared to manage airway difficulties.
10. Analgesics:
    - Administer morphine sulfate intravenously only. Administer 2.0 milligrams to start; then repeat as needed up to a maximum of 10.0 milligrams. This is administered by direct physician's order.
    - Nitronox is a 50:50 ratio of oxygen and nitrous oxide. It is self-administered by the patient intermittently and is supplemented with oxygen.
11. Pneumatic Anti-Shock Garment (see Chapter 5). Follow local protocol regarding use of PASG.

12. Cardiopulmonary resuscitation if needed.

INHALATION INJURIES

Assessment

History

1. Was the patient found in an enclosed space where the fire occurred?
2. Was there an explosion?
3. Was heated air inhaled into the respiratory tract?
4. Fire produces chemically toxic gases and particulate matter as well as heat. Toxic gases are produced by burning of the following:

    - Wood, cotton, paper.
    - Petroleum products.
    - Wool, silk.
    - Polymer plastics.
    - Any synthetic materials produce toxic fumes.

    Any of the toxic gases produced by these materials may cause inhalation injury as well as poisoning.

5. Thermal injury to the respiratory tract may be caused by the inhalation of steam or dry heat. If the history indicates this type of exposure, the paramedic must be prepared for upper airway obstruction due to the development of laryngeal edema.

Physical Examination

1. Perform a primary survey (ABCs). This patient should be provided with high-flow, high-concentration oxygen as soon as possible. Observe for dyspnea or progressive difficulty in breathing.
2. Auscultate the patient's breath sounds periodically.
3. Perform a head-to-toe examination on the patient. Observe for soot around and/or in the mouth, burns on the face, drooling, and other signs that the patient may have inhaled heated air and/or toxic fumes.

Signs and Symptoms of Inhalation Injury

1. Facial burns and/or burns around the mouth (potential for upper air-

way obstruction.
2. Singed nasal hair (potential).
3. Sooty tongue/pharynx/sputum (potential).
4. Restlessness or confusion, indicating inadequate oxygenation (indicative of upper airway obstruction).
5. Dyspnea (indicative).
6. Tachypnea (indicative).
7. Coughing (potential).
8. Hoarseness (indicative).
9. Drooling with an inability to swallow (indicative).
10. Excessive salivation (indicative).
11. Stridor (indicative).
12. Breath sounds may or may not be abnormal. On auscultation, the paramedic may find crackles and/or wheezing.

Possible Complications from Smoke and Heat Inhalation

1. Upper airway injuries: upper airway edema found in the tongue, pharynx, and larynx. This may lead to airway obstruction and laryngospasm.
2. Respiratory lining damage to the cilia and mucosal membranes, leading to the sloughing of tissue and possible bronchospasm.
3. The reduction of surfactant (a fluid secreted in the lung tissue that contributes to the elastic properties of the lungs) in the lungs may lead to atelectasis (collapse of all or part of the lung). This may cause alveolar collapse, decreased lung volume, and inadequate oxygenation.
4. Chemical bronchitis from irritating gases may cause bronchospasm.
5. Chest wall musculature damage with decreased chest wall movement results in poor oxygenation.
6. Physical fatigue may occur from difficulty in inspiration and exhalation.
7. Pulmonary edema can be caused by heat and chemical injury to lung tissue. Inadequate oxygenation results, as well as possible myocardial decompensation.

Patients who inhale steam sustain lung injury from heat. The actual lung damage that occurs most commonly is from the inhalation of toxic gases. Lung damage from toxic gases progressively degenerates in a period of a few days to a few weeks. It is not frequently a problem in the prehospital setting.

Treatment

1. Monitor the ABCs.

2. Administer high-flow, high-concentration oxygen — humidified if possible.
3. Be prepared for upper airway obstruction. Have intubation equipment ready and recognize that intubating a conscious patient, while difficult, may be life-saving.
4. Place the patient in the Fowler's position (semi-reclined).
5. Provide rapid and safe transport to the hospital.

ELECTRICAL BURNS

Electricity may pose many dangers either directly or indirectly to injured patients. It is best to handle electrical hazards with extreme caution.

There are times when motivation may overpower the paramedic's common sense. This could result in injury or death. The paramedic must protect him/herself from contact with the electrical source. If he/she is unable to handle the situation safely, the appropriate support group (i.e., power company, fire department) should be notified.

The surface area damaged by an electrical burn does not give a true indication of the possible injuries that a patient may have received. The entrance and exit wounds may be very slight, yet the current may have produced a core of necrosis well below the skin. Electrical current generates heat and may produce very high temperatures, causing significant tissue damage. It may also interfere with the activity of organs that have a neurological (electrical) conduction system, primarily the heart and lungs. Electrical current may also damage blood vessel tissues. It is also possible for thermal burn injuries to occur as a result of clothing igniting into flames.

The Electrical Current

1. Direct or alternating current may cause ventricular fibrillation (uncoordinated movement of the muscle fibers in the ventricles of the heart) with as little as 100 milliamperes of current.
2. The path may be dependent on the electrical voltage and it may take an unpredictable path from entrance to exit.
3. There is a variation of tissue responses to electrical current:
   - Dry skin is more resistant to electrical current than moist skin.
   - Current flows along blood vessels and nerves at lower voltage (energy) levels than it does through other tissues.
   - At high voltage, electrical current takes the shortest path.
   - Tetanic spasm may occur, preventing a patient from disengaging from

the electrical source. Electrical charges exceeding 22 milliamps can cause this reaction.

Types of Electrical Burn Injury

Contact Burns

1. There may be an entrance wound and a bull's-eye-looking exit wound.
2. May cause a charred zone of third-degree burn.
3. There may be a peripheral gray area.
4. There may be an outer red zone of coagulation necrosis (death of tissue or cells).

Flash Burns

1. They are usually associated with arcing of an electrical current.
2. They produce intense heat.
3. The affected area may have a craterlike appearance.
4. There is usually minimal deep tissue/organ damage.
5. Often, high temperatures are associated with flash burns, and clothing may be ignited.

Assessment

History

1. Document contact with an electrical current.
2. Was the current alternating or direct?
3. Document the duration of exposure.
4. Was the patient thrown or has he/she fallen?

Physical Examination

1. Perform a primary survey (ABCs). The paramedic should be alert to the possibility of the patient experiencing cardiac dysrhythmias.
2. Perform a head-to-toe examination. Observe for both entrance and exit wounds (this may give a clue to the path that the electrical current followed). The damage sustained from electrical burns may not be determined easily by inspection. The paramedic should be conservative and treat the patient as if he/she has a serious injury. In addition to burns, observe and palpate for soft tissue and skeletal injury(s).
3. Monitor and document cardiac rhythm (run a rhythm strip).

4. Monitor vital signs frequently.

Treatment

1. The paramedic should be sure of his/her own safety before making contact with the patient.
2. Remove the patient from the power source.
3. Turn off the power.
4. Have only trained personnel remove a patient from a live power source.
5. Contact the local power company for assistance.
6. Follow general burn care guidelines.
7. Monitor the ECG and document the rhythm.
8. Cardiac dysrhythmias may occur.
9. Be prepared for respiratory arrest.
10. Since the surface area of an electrical burn does not accurately reflect the extent of internal damage, it is best to start an IV with Ringer's lactate solution.

CHEMICAL BURNS

Corrosive chemicals may cause serious burn injury. Contact with strong acids, alkalis, and corrosive materials can result in second- and third-degree burns. Burns from these materials will continue until the wound is thoroughly cleaned of the offending substance.

Assessment

History

1. Document the source of the burn.
2. Document the duration of the exposure.

Physical Examination

1. Perform a primary survey (ABCs).
2. Perform a head-to-toe examination.
3. Auscultate breath sounds.
4. Monitor the vital signs.

Treatment of Chemical Burn Injury

1. The paramedic must protect him/herself from contamination.
2. Immediately flush all water-soluble chemicals with copious amounts of water (note exceptions under special management considerations below). If available, the paramedic should use a shower or hose. After flushing for five minutes, the patient's clothing should be removed. This will facilitate flushing the chemical from the feet and/or other exposed areas. (If the offending chemical is dry, brush it off well, then flush with water.)
3. Monitor the ABCs.
4. Follow general burn management guidelines.

Special Management Considerations

Eye Injury

1. Begin immediate and copious irrigation with any clean solution (i.e., water, normal saline, or Ringer's lactate).
2. Have the patient remove contact lenses.
3. The eyelids should be held open to allow for complete irrigation.
4. Irrigate for a minimum of fifteen minutes (additional irrigation may be done while en route to the hospital).
5. Never use any chemical antidote in the eyes.
6. Cover both the injured and uninjured eyes with sterile dressings.

Sodium Metal

Sodium metal when mixed with water produces high temperatures. When treating this kind of chemical exposure, a hose or shower must be available to wash off the material. If there is only limited access to water, the sodium metal should be covered with oil.

Sulfuric Acid

Concentrated sulfuric acid should be flushed with a hose or flushed in a shower. If only limited amounts of water are available, cover with oil. After flushing, soap or a dilute solution of sodium bicarbonate may be used to neutralize the acid.

Hydrochloric Acid

Hyrochloric acid should be flushed with copious amounts of water, preferably with a hose or in a shower.

Phenol

Phenol is not water-soluble, so, if possible, wash down the area with any alcohol product prior to flushing with water.

Whenever a paramedic is managing a chemical burn case, he/she should not hesitate in calling a base physician or poison center when unclear about treatment protocols.

SUMMARY

Burn patients may be quite difficult cases to manage for the following reasons:

1. The patient is frequently in great pain and discomfort.
2. Occasionally the burns are disfiguring, causing anxiety in both the patient and the paramedic.
3. There may be an unpleasant odor of burnt flesh.
4. IVs may not be started easily.
5. Airway problems may develop rapidly, calling for the intubation of a conscious patient or performing a cricothyrotomy.

The paramedic must be knowledgeable, skilled, and professional when managing the burn patient. He/she should work rapidly and efficiently and treat the seriously burned patient en route to the hospital. (Any patient experiencing dyspnea after exposure to fire should be considered in serious danger of developing an airway obstruction. This patient should not be held at the scene but transported immediately to the emergency department.)

It is best if the paramedic communicates with the conscious patient in a kind, gentle, and empathetic manner. This may reduce patient anxiety and allow for easier treatment.

Even in the face of much difficulty, the paramedic can reduce morbidity and mortality of burn patients by following correct treatment protocols and by keeping up-to-date on treatment modalities for burn patients.

Division Four

Medical

9

Respiratory Illness

It is necessary to know the anatomy and physiology of the respiratory system in order to properly treat a patient in respiratory distress. A review of the anatomy and physiology of the respiratory system is found in Chapter 4, "Airway and Ventilation."

TERMINOLOGY

The paramedic should be familiar with the following terms:

1. Apnea — a temporary cessation of respiration.
2. Cyanosis — bluish discoloration of the skin due to an increase in carbox hemoglobin in the blood.
3. Dyspnea — difficult or labored breathing.
4. FiO_2 — percentage of oxygen in inspired air.
5. Hypercarbia (hypercapnea) — increased PCO_2 in the arterial blood above normal limits.
6. Hyperpnea — deep inhalation.
7. Hyperventilation — an increased rate and depth of breathing resulting in an abnormal decrease in arterial carbon dioxide.
8. Hypoxemia — inadequate oxygen in the blood; reduction of the PO_2 in arterial blood below normal limits.
9. Hypoxia — insufficient oxygen to meet the physiologic needs of body tissues.

10. Hypoventilation — a reduced rate and depth of breathing, resulting in a rise in arterial PCO_2.
11. Nasal flaring — excessive widening of the nostrils on inhalation due to increased respiratory effort.
12. Nocturnal — occurring at night.
13. Orthopnea — labored breathing when lying flat.
14. Respiratory failure — an inability of the respiratory system to maintain an arterial PO_2 greater than 60 torr and PCO_2 less than 50 torr.
15. Tracheal tugging — a downward or sideward pull on the trachea.

ASSESSMENT OF THE RESPIRATORY SYSTEM

History

What is the patient's chief complaint, or what is the patient complaining of? When the chief complaint is dyspnea, the paramedic should determine:

1. How long has dyspnea been present?
2. Was the onset gradual or sudden?
3. Is the dyspnea made better or worse by position?
4. Does the patient have a history of lung disease?
   - How bad is this episode?
   - What happened the last time it was this bad?
5. Does the patient have a history of heart disease and/or hypertension?
6. Has the patient been coughing?
   - If yes, is the cough productive?
   - Describe the sputum.
   - Is there hemoptysis?
7. Past medical history (PMH).
8. Patient's medications.
9. Patient's allergies.

Physical Examination

The paramedic should observe the patient for:

1. Anxiety, discomfort, or distress.
2. Shortness of breath, difficulty in speaking.
3. Coherent response versus a confused response (indicating adequate oxygenation versus inadequate oxygenation).

4. Does the patient show distress while being questioned?
5. What position is most conducive to easy breathing?

Vital Signs

The paramedic should check for:

1. Rate, depth, and character of respirations.
2. Abnormal respirations.
3. Blood pressure.
4. Pulse.
5. Skin color.

Inspection (Visualization)

The paramedic should note:

1. Nasal flaring.
2. Tracheal tugging to the left or right.
3. Retractions — intercostal, supraclavicular, and/or suprasternal.
4. Greater use of accessory muscles during breathing.
5. Cyanosis.

Inspection of the Chest Wall

The paramedic should look for:

1. Symmetrical movement.
2. Deformities.

Auscultation

The paramedic should:

1. Examine all lung fields with a stethoscope.
2. Listen to at least one complete respiratory cycle at each point:
   - Posteriorly (this provides for the best lung sounds):
     —Place stethoscope between the scapulae and spine—right and left.
     —Base of the lungs at the intercostal space between the eighth and ninth ribs.
   - Anteriorly:

— Midclavicular between first and second ribs.
— Midaxillary between the seventh and eighth ribs.
3. Have the patient breathe deeply through his/her mouth.
4. Have the patient sit up if possible.
5. Compare similar fields on opposite sides of both the anterior and posterior chest.
6. Listen for abnormal breath sounds:
   - Snoring — occurs when the upper airway is partially obstructed (most commonly caused by the tongue).
   - Stridor — harsh, high-pitched sound heard on inspiration, characteristic of upper airway obstruction.
   - Wheezing — whistling sound due to the narrowing of the airway by constriction, edema, or a foreign body.
   - Rhonchi (low wheezes) — rattling noises in the throat or bronchi, most commonly associated with congestion.
   - Rales (crackles) — fine, moist sounds associated with fluid in the smaller airways.
   - Friction rub — caused by irritation of the pleura by pleural disease, inflammation, tumor, or the rubbing of the two pleural surfaces together. It is heard as a grating sound.

Palpation

The paramedic should:

1. Palpate for areas of tenderness.
2. Palpate for subcutaneous emphysema.
3. Assess symmetry of chest wall (thumbs on xiphoid, fingers spread over chest wall — hands should move equally on both sides of the chest).
4. Test for tactile fremitus (vibrations felt on the chest wall while the patient is speaking — they should be symmetrical).

AIRWAY EVALUATION

Basic airway management is crucial to the patient's survival. The paramedic must be rapid and accurate in an assessment and expert in the management of upper and lower airway problems. The following are basic principles that must be kept in mind during patient assessment and management:

1. Noisy breathing often means a partial obstruction.
2. Obstructed breathing is not always noisy, particularly a complete airway obstruction.
3. The brain can only survive a few minutes of apnea.
4. Artificial respiration is useless if the patient's airway is blocked.
5. A patent (open) airway by itself is useless. The patient must be breathing or should have artificial ventilation provided for the airway to be of benefit.

General Airway Management Principles

1. The airway always receives first priority. For patients in trauma, consider the possibility of cervical spine injury. Maintain an open airway while keeping the head/neck in a neutral position.
2. Any patient in respiratory distress should receive oxygen.
3. Any patient whose illness or injury suggests the possibility of hypoxia should receive oxygen.
4. Know which patients will respond to oxygen therapy with respiratory depression, and be prepared to assist ventilation.
5. **Never withhold oxygen therapy from a patient suspected of being hypoxic!**

ASSESSMENT AND MANAGEMENT OF RESPIRATORY DISORDERS

Upper Airway Obstruction

The most common source of upper airway obstruction is the tongue. This occurs most frequently during unconsciousness. The next most common cause of obstruction is a foreign body. In adults, this kind of obstruction occurs most commonly while eating and is sometimes referred to as a "cafe coronary." It is usually a middle-aged or elderly person who has his/her hands upon the chest or throat. In addition, they may wear dentures and have had a few alcoholic drinks.

Children have a high incidence of upper airway obstruction due to the habit of putting inappropriate objects into their mouths. Pediatric airway problems are also caused by swellings of the upper airway, leading to possible obstruction (i.e., croup/epiglottitis — see Chapter 19, "Pediatrics," for further discussion).

Laryngeal edema can be caused by burns and allergic reactions. Trauma is another cause of obstruction (see Chapter 7, "Trauma").

Assessment

1. Evaluate the ABCs in both the conscious and unconscious patient.
2. When obstruction is suspected in the conscious patient, ask the patient if he/she is choking.
3. If the patient is unresponsive and has been eating, suspect that a bolus of food is lodged in the airway.
4. Suspect burns as the cause of obstruction (or be prepared for the possibility of obstruction) when the paramedic finds the patient with the following:
   - Burns around the face.
   - Soot around the face.
   - Black, sooty sputum.
   - Patient found in an enclosed area near or in a fire.
5. Suspect laryngeal edema in unconscious patients with obstructed airways until proven otherwise.
6. For patients with food allergies:
   - An itching sensation in the throat, followed by a lump in the back of the throat, may be experienced.
   - Progressive hoarseness may occur.
   - Inspiratory stridor may develop.
   - Urticaria (hives) may be present.
   - The patient may experience increasing dyspnea.
   - Retractions may become evident.

Treatment

Obstruction by the Tongue

1. Open the airway.
2. Insert an oral or nasal airway.
3. Consider endotracheal intubation.

Foreign Body Obstruction

1. For conscious or unconscious patients, administer six to ten abdominal thrusts. (Further instruction can be found in the American Heart Association guidelines for CPR and obstructed airways.)
2. Laryngeal edema secondary to allergy or anaphylaxis:
   - Monitor the ABCs.
   - Administer oxygen with high flow and high concentration, using a face mask and humidified oxygen if possible. Consider early endotracheal intubation.
   - Start an IV line with a crystalloid solution.

- Consider administration of epinephrine (see Appendix 1 for detailed discussion), by physician's order.
  - Adult dosage — 0.3 mg (0.3 ml of 1:1,000 solution) subcutaneously, intramuscularly (IM), or sublingually, or 3 cc of 1:10,000 solution IV.
  - Pediatric dosage — 0.01 mg per kilogram of body weight (0.01 mg per kilogram of body weight in a 1:1,000 solution) subcutaneously, intramuscularly, or sublingually.
- Administer diphenhydramine (Benadryl). Remember, this is a second-line drug in severe reactions used after epinephrine (see Appendix 1).
  - Adult: Usual dosage is 50 mg slow IV push or deep IM.
  - Pediatric up to age twelve: 1 to 2 mg per kilogram of body weight. Should not exceed 50 mg per single dosage.

ASSESSMENT AND MANAGEMENT OF AIRWAY DISEASE

Chronic Obstructive Pulmonary Disease (COPD)

This disease is more common in men than in women and in urban as opposed to rural environments, and the most significant contributing factor is cigarette smoking. The two COPDs discussed here are emphysema and chronic bronchitis.

Emphysema

In emphysema, the following occurs:

1. Destruction of the alveolar walls, causing the following:
   - Increased ratio of air to lung tissue.
   - Weakening of the walls of the small bronchioles.
   - Decreased alveolar membrane area, which lessens the area available for gas exchange.
   - Decreased number of pulmonary capillaries in the lung, which increases the resistance to the pulmonary blood flow.
2. Residual air volume increases.
3. Vital capacity (the volume of air that can be expelled from the lungs from a position of full inspiration) remains near normal.
4. As the disease advances, arterial PO_2 decreases, which may lead to increased red blood cell production.
5. Carbon dioxide retention occurs.

6. Increased resistance to blood flow leads to right heart failure.
7. Other complications include acute respiratory infection and cardiac dysrhythmia.
8. Paramedics are most commonly called to patients who are in an advanced stage of the disease.

Assessment

History

1. May have recent loss of appetite and weight loss.
2. Increasing shortness of breath on exertion.
3. Progressive limitation of physical activity.
4. Coughing — not usually a prominent complaint — can produce small amounts of whitish-gray, mucous-like sputum.

Physical Exam

1. May have decreased chest excursion.
2. Hypertrophied (enlarged) accessory respiratory muscles.
3. Expiration of breath takes place through pursed lips.
4. May have clubbing of the fingers.
5. Decreased breath and heart sounds.
6. Expiration time is lengthened.
7. May have signs of right heart failure: distended neck veins and pedal edema.
8. Cyanosis may be present.
9. Tachycardia is often present.

Treatment

1. Establish an airway (ABCs).
2. Administer oxygen: monitor rate and depth; supplemental oxygen may decrease respiratory drive; be prepared to assist in ventilating the patient.
3. Place the patient in a position of comfort.
4. Start an IV of D_5W at a TKO (to keep open) rate.
5. Administer aminophylline by physician's order (see Appendix 1).
   - Adults — usual dosage, 6 mg per kilogram of body weight added to 100 cc D_5W, titrated to run in over fifteen to twenty minutes or to patient response.
   - Pediatric — same as for adults.
   - Get recent documentation of other medications taken prior to administration of this drug.

6. Do not give sedatives or tranquilizers.
7. Monitor cardiac rhythm.

Chronic Bronchitis

In chronic bronchitis, the following occurs:

1. An increased number of mucous-secreting cells in the respiratory epithelium produce characteristically large amounts of sputum.
2. Alveoli are not seriously affected; diffusion of oxygen remains normal.
3. Alveoli hypoventilation affects respiratory gas exchange.
4. Arterial hypoxemia and carbon dioxide retention occur.
5. Hypoxia may cause increased red blood cell production.
6. Increased PCO_2 levels constrict the pulmonary circulation, possibly leading to right heart failure.
7. Increased PCO_2 levels may lead to irritability, decreased intellectual abilities, headaches, and personality changes.
8. Acute and chronic infections produce scarring in the lungs.
9. Vital capacity is decreased.
10. Residual volume of air is normal or decreased.

Assessment

History

1. History of heavy cigarette smoking.
2. History of frequent respiratory tract infections.
3. Between infections, there is a productive cough that produces at least ten ccs of green or yellow sputum daily.

Physical Examination

1. Frequently, the patient is overweight and cyanotic.
2. Respiratory rate is normal or slightly increased.
3. Dyspnea at rest is uncommon.
4. Signs of right heart failure.

Treatment

Treatment of chronic bronchitis in the decompensating patient is aimed at relieving hypoxia.

1. Establish an airway (ABCs).

2. Administer oxygen: monitor rate and depth; supplemental oxygen may decrease respiratory drive; be prepared to assist in ventilating the patient.
3. Place the patient in a position of comfort.
4. Start an IV of D_5W at a TKO (to keep open) rate.
5. Administer aminophylline by physician's order (see Appendix 1).
   - Adults — usual dosage, 6 mg per kilogram of body weight added to 100 cc D_5W, titrated to run in over fifteen to twenty minutes or to patient response.
   - Pediatric — same as for adults.
   - Get recent documentation of other medications taken **prior** to administration of this drug.
6. Do not give sedatives or tranquilizers.
7. Monitor cardiac rhythm.

Asthma

Asthma affects about 6 million Americans, with 4 to 5 thousand deaths each year. Asthma begins before the age of ten in 50 percent of the cases and begins before age thirty in another 33 percent of the cases. There is a genetic tendency to develop asthma.

Asthma is characterized by increased reactivity of the trachea and bronchi, but primarily in the bronchioles to some stimuli, with widespread reversible narrowing of the airways and increased mucous production. Airway obstruction occurs due to bronchospasm, swelling of the mucous membranes in the bronchial walls, and plugging of the bronchi by thick mucous. Progressive hyperinflation of the chest wall occurs, along with reduced vital capacity, development of hypoxemia, and hypoventilation (hypercarbia occurs only in a very severe attack).

Asthma is precipitated by:

1. Allergies.
2. Reaction to an inhaled irritant.
3. Respiratory infection.
4. Physical activity.
5. Emotional stress.

Assessment

History

1. Have there been previous attacks?

2. Time of onset.
3. Tightness in chest?
4. Commonly a nonproductive cough.
5. Dyspnea — particularly on expiration as the attack continues (dependent on the severity of the attack).

Physical Examination with Signs and Symptoms

1. Evaluate the ABCs.
2. Auscultate breath sounds.
3. Evaluate vital signs.
4. Monitor and record cardiac rhythm.
5. Patient is usually sitting and/or leaning forward.
6. Overuse of accessory respiratory muscles.
7. Audible wheezing.
8. Prolonged expiratory time.
9. Tachycardia.
10. Tachypnea.
11. High-risk patient: hyperinflated chest, central cyanosis, pulsus paradoxus (a pulse that is more or less suppressed at the end of each full inspiration), overuse of accessory respiratory muscles, silent chest on auscultation.
12. Caution — all wheezing is not asthma (may be pulmonary edema due to congestive heart failure or left heart failure).

Treatment

The goals of management are the relief of bronchospasm and improvement of ventilation.

1. Establish an airway (ABCs).
2. Administer oxygen — humidified if available (high-flow, high-concentration).
3. Start an IV crystalloid at at TKO rate (or as ordered for rehydration).
4. Obtain history of recent medication usage prior to administration of any medication.
5. Administer epinephrine by physician's order (see Appendix 1).
   - Adult — 1:1,000 0.3 ml subcutaneously (0.01 ml per kilogram of body weight up to 0.3 ml). May be repeated in thirty minutes if necessary by physician's order.
   - Administer aminophylline by physician's order (see Appendix 1). See

management of emphysema and chronic bronchitis.
6. Status asthmaticus: severe prolonged attack that cannot be broken with epinephrine. It is a serious life-threatening emergency. Management is the same as with asthma but with much greater urgency.

Pneumonia

Pneumonia is an infection of the lower respiratory system that may be caused by any of the following:

1. Bacteria.
2. Virus.
3. Fungus.
4. Parasite.
5. Chemicals.

Assessment

History

Does the patient have:

1. A productive cough?
2. Dyspnea?
3. History of a fever?
4. Chest pain — usually pleuritic?
5. Weakness?

Physical Examination with Signs and Symptoms

Evaluate for:

1. Fever.
2. Possible respiratory distress (auscultate breath sounds).
3. Tachycardia.
4. Possible rales and/or rhonchi. Auscultate lung fields.
5. Evaluate all vital signs.

Treatment

1. ABCs.
2. Oxygen (high-flow, high-concentration as needed).
3. Transport in position of comfort.

4. Start an IV line crystalloid to manage dehydration and possible septic shock (helps loosen mucous).

Pulmonary Embolism (PE)

Pulmonary embolism is a clot or embolus that blocks a pulmonary artery. It is a serious problem accounting for 200,000 deaths per year.

Predisposing factors include the following:

1. Highest risk group: females who take birth control pills and who also smoke cigarettes.
2. Prolonged immobilization.
3. Thrombophlebitis.
4. Use of certain drugs.
5. Congestive heart failure.
6. Recent major surgical procedure.
7. Long-bone fractures.
8. Pregnancy — amniotic fluid emboli.

With a pulmonary embolism, the following complications may occur:

1. A portion of the pulmonary circulation is blocked. The portion blocked is dependent on the size of the pulmonary artery occluded.
2. The right heart pumps against increased resistance.
3. Pulmonary capillary pressure increases.
4. Shunting occurs.

Assessment

There is no single sign or symptom that is specific for pulmonary embolism. The paramedic needs to take a good history, do a thorough physical exam, and maintain a high degree of suspicion.

History

Most pulmonary embolisms occur in patients in the hospital setting, though some may occur at home settings either spontaneously or in the post-operative patient. The patient may complain of sudden onset of dyspnea and/or chest pain, which is the most common.

Physical Examination with Signs and Symptoms

1. ABCs.

2. Evaluate vital signs.
3. Tachycardia.
4. Possible cyanosis.
5. Dyspnea.
6. Tachypnea.
7. Hemoptysis.
8. Blood pressure may be falling.
9. The patient may have signs of right heart failure. Monitor and record cardiac rhythm.

Treatment

1. Establish an airway (ABCs).
2. Assist ventilations as needed.
3. Administer oxygen, high-flow, high concentration.
4. Establish an IV line with D_5W at a TKO rate.
5. Monitor and record cardiac rhythm.
6. Transport early and rapidly.

Pulmonary Edema

For information on pulmonary edema, see Chapter 10 on cardiovascular emergencies.

ASSESSMENT AND MANAGEMENT OF INHALATION INJURIES

See Chapter 8 for further discussion.
Inhalation injuries are caused by:

1. Superheated air.
2. Toxic combustion products.
3. Chemical irritants.
4. Steam inhalation.
5. Poisonous gases.

The effects of inhalation injuries include:

1. Upper airway obstruction due to edema.
2. Bronchospasm.
3. Damage to alveolar capillary membranes.

4. Poisonous gases may do any of the above plus slow down, speed up, or stop vital bodily functions.

Assessment

History

The paramedic should obtain the following information:

1. The nature of the inhalant or the burned material, particularly of synthetic materials because they produce noxious gases that may cause corrosive damage to the air passages and lower respiratory tract.
2. The duration of the exposure.
3. Was the exposure in an enclosed space?
4. Was the patient found unconscious, or did the patient have a history of unconsciousness?

Physical Examination with Signs and Symptoms

1. ABCs.
2. Vital signs.
3. Auscultate breath sounds.
4. Burns around the face and mouth.
5. Singed facial or nasal hair.
6. Soot in the sputum.
7. Hoarseness or cough.
8. Rales, rhonchi, or wheezing on auscultation.

Treatment

1. Remove the patient from the toxic environment (the paramedic should protect him/herself).
2. Establish and maintain an airway (ABCs). Assist ventilations as necessary.
3. Laryngeal edema may require endotracheal intubation, although it may be very difficult.
4. Administer high-flow, high-concentration oxygen.
5. Start an IV line with a crystalloid solution.

Carbon Monoxide (CO)

Carbon monoxide is a colorless, odorless gas that is produced during incomplete combustion of organic fuels. Automobiles, kerosene heaters, and wood-burning stoves are major producers of carbon monoxide.

Carbon monoxide binds to hemoglobin more strongly than oxygen, inhibits oxygen delivery to the cells, and leads to hypoxia at a cellular level.

Carbon monoxide poisoning occurs most commonly from automobiles and from self-contained heaters in the home. Carbon monoxide poisoning is a common method of suicide and is also a common problem for firefighters.

Assessment

History

1. Is there a potential source of exposure?
2. Length of exposure?
3. Suicide note?
4. Accidental poisonings are most common in the winter months.

Physical Examination with Signs and Symptoms

1. Skin color:
   - Pale.
   - Possible cyanosis.
   - Cherry-red coloration of lips rarely seen.
2. Signs and symptoms:
   - Headache.
   - Chest pain.
   - Irritability.
   - Agitation.
   - Confusion.
   - Loss of coordination.
   - Vomiting.
   - Loss of consciousness.
   - Seizures.

Treatment

1. Remove the patient from the exposure site (this should be without threat to the paramedic.
2. Administer high-flow/high-concentration oxygen.
3. Assist respirations as necessary.

HYPERVENTILATION

Hyperventilation causes a fall in arterial PCO_2, which then may cause an electrolyte imbalance resulting in respiratory alkalosis.

Causes of hyperventilation are:

1. Central nervous system disorder.
2. Drug overdose.
3. Anxiety.
4. Trauma.
5. Pulmonary embolism.
6. Electrolyte imbalance.
7. Hypoxemia.
8. Hypocarbia.

Assessment

History

1. Anxiety.
2. Drug overdose.
3. Trauma.

Physical Exam

1. Perform normal primary/secondary examinations as appropriate.
2. Check for tachypnea.
3. Check for numbing and tingling around the mouth and in the hands and feet.
4. The patient may have carpopedal spasm.
5. Observe for signs and symptoms other than anxiety.

Treatment

1. It is important to recognize that hyperventilation is not just an anxiety issue but may be caused by both medical and trauma problems. If the paramedic suspects a cause other than anxiety, treat the underlying problem if possible.
2. If the hyperventilation is anxiety-related: encourage the patient to control respirations and provide calm reassurance.

SUMMARY

Respiratory illness affects a substantial portion of the population in the

United States. Approximately 10 to 20 percent of the adult population has chronic obstructive pulmonary disease (primarily due to smoking) and about 6 million people are afflicted with asthma.

These numbers alone make it apparent that there is a significant need for paramedics to be well trained in the assessment and treatment of the patient who is ill with respiratory disease. The paramedic must be competent in airway management skills as well as in the appropriate drug therapies available.

In addition, it is worth remembering that the patient in respiratory distress from any cause is going to be a frightened and anxious patient. When managing these patients, a kind, reassuring approach is of great benefit.

10

Cardiovascular Illness and ECG (EKG) Interpretation

Approximately 1 million deaths in the United States each year are attributed to cardiovascular disease. More than half of these deaths are due to myocardial infarction, and about 300,000 of the myocardial infarction deaths occur in the prehospital setting. Because of the high number of prehospital deaths, this subject receives great emphasis in the training of paramedics.

This chapter will prepare the paramedic to assess and manage cardiac emergencies, most of which result from coronary atherosclerosis. In addition to primary cardiac problems and EKG interpretation, a number of conditions involving pathology of the peripheral circulation will be discussed. The anatomy of the heart and blood vessels will also be presented.

The use of drugs plays an integral role in the management of the cardiac patient. This chapter will introduce the cardiac drugs as appropriate. A discussion of each medication used in the field is found in Appendix 1.

ANATOMY OF THE HEART

The heart is located in the thoracic cavity posterior to the sternum, with one-third lying to the right of the sternum and two-thirds lying to the left. The heart is approximately the size of the person's fist to whom it belongs. There is a base, which is the superior portion, and an apex, which is the inferior part.

The heart is enclosed by a double-walled protective sac called the pericardium. In this sac are approximately thirty cubic centimeters of fluid that act as a lubricant, allowing the heart to pump in a near-frictionless state. The pericardial sac does not stretch. If the heart is injured and blood fills the pericardium, the heart will not be able to pump (called a pericardial tamponade). It takes approximately 100 cubic centimeters of fluid in the sac to prevent the heart from beating adequately.

The heart muscle is made up of three layers: the epicardium is the outermost layer; the myocardium, the thick middle layer, is the actual work muscle of the heart; and the endocardium is the smooth, innermost layer.

Heart cells are made up of specialized cardiac muscle fibers found only in the heart. These fibers are interconnected in branching networks that spread in all directions throughout the heart. When any portion of this network is stimulated, an impulse moves to all of its parts, causing the whole structure to contract simultaneously. There are two of these networks in the heart. One is found in the walls of the atria, and the other is found in the walls of the ventricles. This property of the heart allows the cardiac muscle to act as if it were one large cell.

The cardiac muscle is extensible; that is, it may be stretched to allow greater filling of the heart chambers. After the chambers are filled, the tension placed on the cardiac muscle by stretching causes the heart to contract with greater force. This property that allows for increased force of contraction is called Starling's Law.

The heart is composed of four chambers — the right and left atria and the right and left ventricles. These chambers really make up two pumps: the right pump is made up of the right atrium and ventricle, and the left pump is made up of the left atrium and ventricle. The right heart pumps unoxygenated blood to the lungs (pulmonary circulation), while the left heart pumps oxygenated blood to the rest of the body (systemic circulation).

There are two sets of valves in the heart: the atrioventricular (AV) valves and the semilunar valves. The atrioventricular valves are found between the atria and the ventricles. The valve in the right heart may also be called the tricuspid valve; the valve on the left may also be called the bicuspid or mitral valve. There are two semilunar valves. The pulmonic valve is found between the right ventricle and the pulmonary artery, and the aortic valve is located between the left ventricle and the aorta.

The "great vessels" is a collective name for the large vessels that attach to the base of the heart. They include:

1. The vena cava — inferior and superior. They deliver unoxygenated blood from the body to the right atrium.
2. The pulmonary artery — this is one main artery with two branches that deliver unoxygenated blood from the right ventricle to the lungs (pulmonary circulation).
3. The pulmonary veins — there are four that deliver freshly oxygenated blood from the lungs to the left atrium of the heart.
4. The aorta — there is one that branches into the ascending and descending portions. Oxygenated blood from the left ventricle is pumped to the body through the aorta.

Coronary arteries provide the exclusive arterial blood supply to the heart muscle and to the electrical conduction system. The coronary arteries originate from the aorta just beyond the aortic valve. This origin permits the heart to receive blood with the highest concentration of oxygen under the highest pressure.

The left coronary artery has two main branches, the anterior descending branch and the circumflex branch, which supply the left ventricle and left atrium. The right coronary artery has two main branches, the posterior descending branch and the marginal branch, which supply the right atrium and ventricle and part of the left ventricle. An interconnection called "anastomoses" occurs between some branches of the coronary arteries. This connection provides for alternate pathways of blood flow (collateral circulation).

The coronary veins drain blood that has passed through the capillaries of the myocardium. They roughly parallel the arterial pathways. These veins join an enlarged vessel called the coronary sinus, which empties blood into the right atrium.

PHYSIOLOGY OF THE HEART

Normal Blood Flow Through the Heart

Blood enters the right atrium by the superior and inferior vena cavum. It passes through the tricuspid valve to the right ventricle, then is ejected through the pulmonic valve into the pulmonary artery. The blood is pumped (pulmonary circulation) to the pulmonary capillaries in the lungs, where it

Figure 10-1. Anatomy of the Heart.

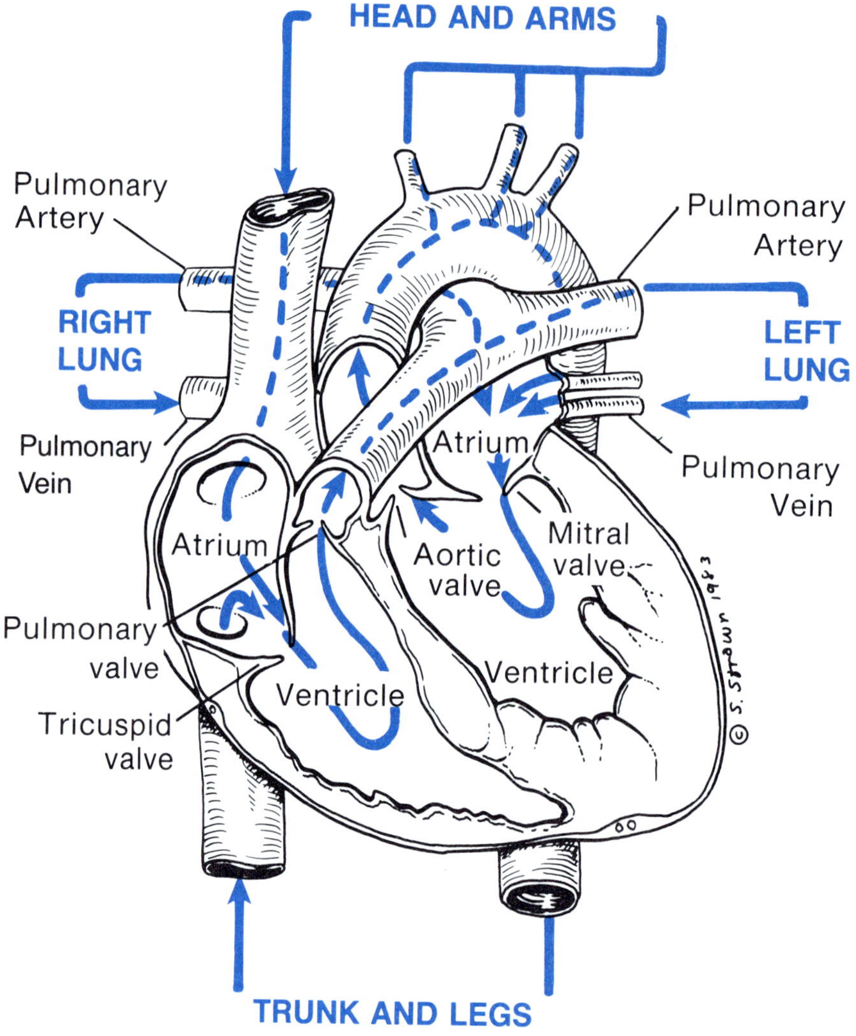

RIGHT HEART:

receives blood from the body and pumps it through the pulmonary artery to the lungs where it picks up fresh oxygen.

LEFT HEART:

Receives oxygen-full blood from the lungs and pumps it through the aorta to the body.

is oxygenated, then passes through the pulmonary veins into the left atrium. The blood passes through the mitral valve to the left ventricle, where it is pumped through the aortic valve to the aorta and the coronary arteries, and then into peripheral circulation (systemic circulation).

The Cardiac Cycle

It is important to note that the individual chambers of the heart do not function independently of each other. Instead, their actions are regulated so that when the atrial walls (right/left) contract, the ventricles (right/left) are relaxed, and when the ventricles contract, the atria are relaxed. A cardiac cycle begins with the contraction of the atrium, followed by the contraction of the ventricles, with a brief moment of relaxation for both. Then the cycle repeats.

Atrial contraction serves to fill the ventricles to their maximum. About 70 percent of the blood that enters the ventricles does so before the atria contract. The atrial contraction forces the last 30 percent of the blood into the ventricles. This is followed by atrial relaxation.

Ventricular contraction pumps blood into pulmonary and systemic circulation. Pressure of the contraction produces closure of the atrioventricular valves and opening of the semilunar valves through which blood is ejected into the arteries.

Systole is the phase of the cardiac cycle during which the ventricular walls are contracting. It lasts approximately 0.28 second. Diastole is the phase of the cardiac cycle during which the ventricular walls are relaxing. It lasts approximately 0.52 second. Refilling of the ventricles and coronary artery filling (about 70 percent) take place at this time.

Pumping Action

The right atrium and ventricle pump blood to the lungs. This is the low-pressure, pulmonary circulation. The left atrium and ventricle pump blood to the rest of the body. This is systemic circulation, where blood is pumped under high pressure.

Stroke volume (SV) is the amount of blood ejected from either ventricle during one contraction. During rest, the amount of blood pumped is 60 to 100 milliliters; in the healthy heart, however, there is a greater capacity for this amount to be increased (Starling's Law).

Heart rate (HR) is the number of cardiac contractions (heartbeats) in one minute. Cardiac output (CO) refers to the amount of blood pumped by one ventricle measured in liters per minute. It should be noted that both ventricles have equivalent output.

1. Cardiac output equals heart rate multiplied by stroke volume.
2. Remember that cardiac output can be increased by either increasing the heart rate or stroke volume or both.
3. There is a point at which cardiac output can no longer be increased by an increasing heart rate.

Systemic blood pressure is equal to cardiac output multiplied by peripheral vascular resistance (the resistance created by the constriction and dilation of the arterioles — a process that is controlled primarily by the sympathetic nervous system). Blood pressure is measured with a sphygmomanometer.

Nervous System and Chemical Control of the Heart

The autonomic nervous system influences the rate, conductivity, and contractility of the heart in varying degrees. The heart is innervated by fibers of both the sympathetic (adrenergic) and parasympathetic (cholinergic) components of the autonomic nervous system.

Parasympathetic Component

This part of the system controls vegetative functions of the body. It is mediated by the vagus nerve through the release of the chemical mediator acethycholine. Parasympathetic stimulation of the heart slows the heart rate by slowing the electrical activity from the pacemaker sites. This component may be stimulated in several ways: the valsalva maneuver (a forced exhalation with the glottis closed, increasing intrathoracic pressure that stimulates the vagus nerve, thus slowing the pulse rate), carotid sinus pressure (applying pressure over the carotid sinus, which may convert certain rapid cardiac rhythms back to a normal sinus rhythm), and straining to have a bowel movement (similar to a valsalva maneuver). The effects of the parasympathetic nervous system may sometimes be blocked by use of the drug atropine.

Sympathetic Component

This part of the system provides the body with a way to handle stress. It is mediated by nerves arising in thoracic and lumbar ganglia (these come off of the vertebral column) through the release of the chemical mediators norepinephrine and epinephrine. The effects of the chemical mediators are classified as alpha, beta, or both.

1. Alpha stimulation — no cardiac effects, constricts the peripheral vasculature (vessels in the extremities), and causes smooth-muscle constriction (bronchoconstriction).
2. Beta stimulation — cardiac effects are increased heart and conduction rates, and increased force of contractions; causes bronchodilation (bronchial tree) and peripheral vasodilation (smooth-muscle vasculature).

Electrolytes

Both electrical and mechanical functions of the heart are influenced by electrolytes. Electrolytes that play a significant role in cardiac function are:

1. Sodium (Na^{+}) — plays an important role in the depolarization phase of myocardial cells.
2. Calcium (Ca^{++}) — plays an important role in the depolarization phase of myocardial pacemaker cells and in myocardial contractility.
   - Hypercalcemia — increased myocardial contractility.
   - Hypocalcemia — decreased myocardial contractility and increased electrical irritability.
3. Potassium (K^{+}) — plays an important role in the repolarization phase.
   - Hyperkalemia — decreased automaticity and conduction.
   - Hypokalemia — increased irritability.

It is important for the paramedic to understand the tremendous role that electrolytes play in the healthy functioning of the heart. If electrolyte imbalances occur in the body, they may dramatically affect the functioning of the heart.

ELECTROPHYSIOLOGY

Electrical Properties of the Heart

1. Automaticity — the ability of cardiac cells to generate an electrical impulse without stimulation from another source; this is a property of the cardiac pacemaker cells.
2. Excitability — the ability of cells to respond to an electrical stimulus; this is a property of all myocardial cells.
3. Conductivity — the ability of an electrical impulse to move rapidly from cell to cell; cardiac cells have this property.

Electrical Conduction System of the Heart

In the heart are specialized tissues whose main function is to initiate and distribute electrical impulses through the myocardium. These specialized tissues conduct electrical impulses through the heart six times faster than through plain cardiac muscle. The electrical conduction system of the heart is made up of the sinoatrial node, the internodal and intra-atrial tracts, the atrioventricular node, the bundle of His, the bundle branches, and the Purkinje fibers.

Functions of the Electrical Conduction Structures

1. **Sinoatrial (SA) node.** This is located in the right atrium near the entrance of the superior vena cava. It is the heart's dominant pacemaker (i.e., it sets the rate of the heart normally at 60 to 100 beats per minute).
2. **Internodal and intra-atrial tracts.** These are the pathways that carry the electrical impulses between the sinoatrial node and atrioventricular node and spread them across the atrial muscle. The impulse travel time is 0.08 second.
3. **Atrioventricular (AV) node.** This makes up part of the area called "atrioventricular junctional tissue." It is responsible for creating a slight delay in conduction before sending the impulses into the ventricles. The impulse travel time is 0.08 to 0.16 second. The atrioventricular node has no pacemaking properties itself, but if a conduction problem with the sinoatrial node arises, the junctional tissue is capable of initiating impulses at a rate of forty to fifty times per minute.
4. **Bundle of His.** This is a bundle of specialized conducting fibers coming off of the atrioventricular node located at the top of the interventricular septum. It is considered part of the atrioventricular junction. The bundle of His makes the electrical connection between atria and ventricles.
5. **Bundle branches.** These are created by the bifurcation of the bundle of His into right and left branches. They carry electrical impulses at high velocity to the interventricular septum and each ventricle simultaneously.
6. **Purkinje fibers.** These are the terminal ends of the bundle branches that spread out through the endocardial surfaces of the ventricles. The impulse conduction through the Purkinje fibers is the most rapid of any tissue in the heart. The impulse travel time is 0.08 to 0.09 second. If a conduction problem arises at the atrioventricular node, the ventricles (bundle branches and Purkinje fibers) are capable of initiating impulses at a rate of twenty to forty times per minute.

Depolarization

Depolarization is the process by which cardiac muscle fibers are stimulated to contract by the alteration of the electrical charge of the cell. It is accomplished by movement of electrolyte concentrations inside and outside the cell.

Repolarization

Repolarization is a process by which cells are recharged and made ready for stimulation. It is the return to a resting or polarized state and is accomplished by the movement of electrolyte concentrations in reverse of depolarization.

Electrocardiogram (ECG or EKG)

An electrocardiogram is the record of the electrical activity (change) that takes place in the myocardium during a cardiac cycle. The EKG provides information only about the heart's electrical activity. See page 223 for a detailed discussion on the EKG.

NERVOUS SYSTEM CONTROL OF CARDIAC ELECTRICAL ACTIVITY

Sympathetic Effects on the Heart (Adrenergic)

1. Effects of alpha stimulation — no direct effect on the heart.
2. Effects of beta stimulation — increased heart rate, increased conduction velocity in atria and ventricles, increased irritability, and increased force of contraction (mechanical effect).

Parasympathetic Effects on the Heart (Cholinergic)

1. Parasympathetic (vagal) stimulation has a depressant effect on the heart. It causes a decreased firing rate of the sinoatrial node and decreased atrioventricular conduction, thus slowing down the heart. The parasympathetic has little direct effect on ventricles.

ANATOMY OF THE PERIPHERAL CIRCULATION

Structures Common to All Blood Vessel Walls

1. Intima — the innermost layer.
2. Media — the middle layer; gives strength and recoil to the vessels; more muscular in arteries than in veins.
3. Adventitia — the outermost layer; provides additional strength to withstand high internal pressures.
4. Lumen — the opening within a blood vessel through which blood flows; the diameter of different vessels varies greatly.

Arteries

1. Arteries carry oxygenated blood away from the heart (except the pulmonary artery).
2. The media muscular layer is predominant.
3. Blood flows through the arteries under high pressure.
4. Arterioles:
   - They are the smallest branch of the arterial tree.
   - They play a significant role in blood distribution and blood pressure maintenance.
5. Major arteries:
   - Aorta (ascending, thoracic, and abdominal).
   - Subclavian.
   - Internal and external carotid arteries.
   - Axillary artery.
   - Brachial artery.
   - Radial artery.
   - Common iliac artery.
   - Femoral artery.

Capillaries

1. They are located where the arterioles terminate and where the arterial and venous system connect (in the capillary bed).
2. The walls of the capillaries are a single cell thick.
3. This is where the exchange of gas, nutrients, metabolic wastes, and fluid occurs.

Veins

1. Veins carry unoxygenated blood back to the heart (except the pulmonary vein).
2. The veins are under low pressure (approximately twenty times lower than arteries), and the blood flow back to the heart is aided by surrounding muscles primarily in the lower extremities (this is called the skeletal pump), and there are valves found within the veins that prevent the backflow of blood.
3. Venules:
   - These are the first vessels of the venous system that leave the capillary bed that direct blood back to the heart.
   - These vessels make up the smallest branch of the venous vascular tree.
4. Major veins:
   - Superior and inferior venae cavum.
   - Internal and external jugular veins.
   - Subclavian vein.
   - Axillary vein.
   - Innominate vein.
   - Iliac veins.
   - Femoral vein.

ASSESSMENT OF THE CARDIAC PATIENT

Common Chief Complaints

Chest Pain/Discomfort

This is the most common (classic) symptom of the myocardial infarction. In addition to substernal chest pain, there may be shoulder, arm, neck, or jaw pain and discomfort. It is often described as moving (radiating) from the chest to the neck and/or jaw, or to the left shoulder and/or arm. Chest pain may be the "cry" of hypoxic or anoxic myocardial cells.

1. History of the chief complaint (present illness): (PQRST — P = Provocation; Q = Quality; R = Region, Radiation, Referred; S = Severity; T = Time Sequence)
   - Onset.
   - Factors that precipitated.
   - Location, radiation of pain.

- Quality of pain.
- Duration.
- Associated signs/symptoms.
- What alleviates or aggravates pain (including medications).
- Previous episodes.

2. Many causes of chest pain are noncardiac. If in doubt, treat as a cardiac problem until proven otherwise.
3. Twenty to 30 percent of myocardial infarctions present with no pain, most commonly in the elderly patient.

Dyspnea

Dyspnea is labored or difficult breathing, or shortness of breath.

1. It is often a symptom of the cardiac patient, particularly one experiencing a myocardial infarction or congestive heart failure.
2. History of dyspnea (PQRST — P = Provocation; Q = Quality; R = Region, Radiation, Referred; S = Severity; T = Time, Sequence). In particular, note the following:
   - Onset may be sudden or gradual. Did the patient experience nocturnal orthopnea?
   - Does any body position alleviate or aggravate?
   - Previous episodes of a similar event.
   - Associated signs/symptoms.
   - Prior cardiac history.
3. Dyspnea has many causes. Take a thorough history prior to ruling out a cardiac origin.

Syncope

Syncope is a faint, temporary loss of consciousness. It is often the result of a drop in cardiac output, causing a reduction in cerebral perfusion.

1. Syncope may be the only symptom of a cardiac problem, particularly in elderly patients.
2. History of syncope:
   - Circumstances of occurrence (position, etc.).
   - Duration.
   - Any symptoms (warnings) prior to the syncopal episode?
   - Previous episodes.
   - Associated signs/symptoms.

Palpitations/Cardiac Irregularities

''Palpitations'' refers to the patient's uncomfortable awareness of his/her own heartbeat. It is usually related to premature ventricular contractions (PVCs) or a sudden onset of a rapid heart rate (paroxysmal tachycardia). History of palpitations:

1. Circumstances of occurrence.
2. Duration.
3. Associated symptoms.
4. Previous episodes/frequency.

Past Medical History in the Cardiac Patient

Do not spend much time trying to illicit the patient's past medical history. The patient's treatment is based on his/her current symptoms regardless of past history.

Attempt to determine the following:

1. Is the patient taking prescription medications regularly, particularly cardiac medications? For example:
   - Nitroglycerine — to relieve pain of angina.
   - Propranolol (Inderal) — for treatment of angina.
   - Digitalis (digoxin, Lanoxin) — for treatment of congestive heart failure, atrial fibrillation or flutter.
   - Diuretics — for treatment of congestive heart failure/hypertension.
   - Antihypertensives.
   - Other antidysrhythmics.
2. Is the patient being treated for any serious illness?
3. Does the patient have a history of:
   - Coronary artery disease (angina)?
   - Myocardial infarction?
   - Congestive heart failure?
   - Hypertension?
   - Diabetes?
   - Chronic obstructive pulmonary disease (COPD)?
4. Does the patient have any allergies?

Physical Examination of the Cardiac Patient

Primary Survey

Check the ABCs.

Vital Signs and Mini-Neuro Exam

1. Blood pressure.
2. Respiratory rate.
3. Rate and regularity of pulse; may be first indication of dysrhythmia.
4. Level of consciousness:
   - Try to determine what is normal for the patient.
   - An alteration in level of consciousness may indicate decreased brain perfusion due to poor cardiac output.

Secondary Survey

1. Visualize:
   - Skin color and capillary refill, which are indicators of adequacy of red-blood-cell oxygenation and of cardiac pump adequacy (peripheral perfusion).
   - Jugular vein distention — may be caused by pump failure, creating back pressure in the systemic venous circulation. This is reflected in neck vein distention. To assess the patient for jugular distention, elevate the patient's head to forty-five degrees (not in the supine position). Then look at the neck veins. This may be difficult to assess in the obese patient.
   - Peripheral/presacral edema — this is caused by chronic back pressure in the systemic venous circulation. It is most obvious in dependent parts (e.g., check the sacral region in bedridden patients, ankles, and sometimes wrists for edema). Recognize mild versus pitting edema.
   - Be observant for items that indicate that the patient is being treated for cardiac problems (e.g., nitropatch on skin, implanted pacemaker, etc.).

2. Auscultate:
   - Lung sounds — assess for equality and for adventitious sounds (rales, wheezes) that may indicate pulmonary congestion/edema.
   - Heart sounds — may be unable to auscultate in field; may discover pulse deficit (this is when the number of pulse beats counted at the wrist is less than the number counted at the heart). S1 is the first heart sound, produced by closure of the atrioventricular valves during ven-

tricular systole. S2 is the second heart sound, produced by closure of the aortic and pulmonic valves during ventricular diastole. S3 refers to the extra heart sounds heard after S2; S3 is compatible with heart failure but is not always present.

- Carotid artery bruit — generally an abnormal sound heard when auscultating the carotid artery. This should be assessed when carotid massage is being considered.

3. Palpate:
   - Peripheral/presacral edema.
   - Pulse — rate, regularity, strength, pulse deficit.
   - Skin — color, temperature, moisture.

PATHOLOGY AND MANAGEMENT OF CARDIAC PROBLEMS

Atherosclerosis

Pathology

Atherosclerosis is a progressive, degenerative disease of medium and larger arteries and is caused primarily by the deposition of fats, lipids, and cholesterol within the intima of the blood vessels. In time, this deposition causes narrowing of the lumen and hardening of the affected arteries. The arteries that are most commonly affected are:

1. Thc aorta and its branches.
2. The cerebral arteries
3. The coronary arteries.

Collateral circulation may develop to compensate for the reduced blood flow created by atherosclerosis.

Atherosclerosis causes the disruption of the intimal surface of the arteries, resulting in reduction in the size of the lumen, loss of vessel elasticity, reduction of blood flow (i.e., oxygen/nutrient supply to the effected tissue is reduced), and a frequent incidence of thrombosis (clot formation) that may result in total obstruction of the artery(s).

Major Risk Factors

Modifiable

The following are risk factors that can be controlled by the patient, thus

Figure 10-2. Atherosclerosis (Coronary Artery Disease).

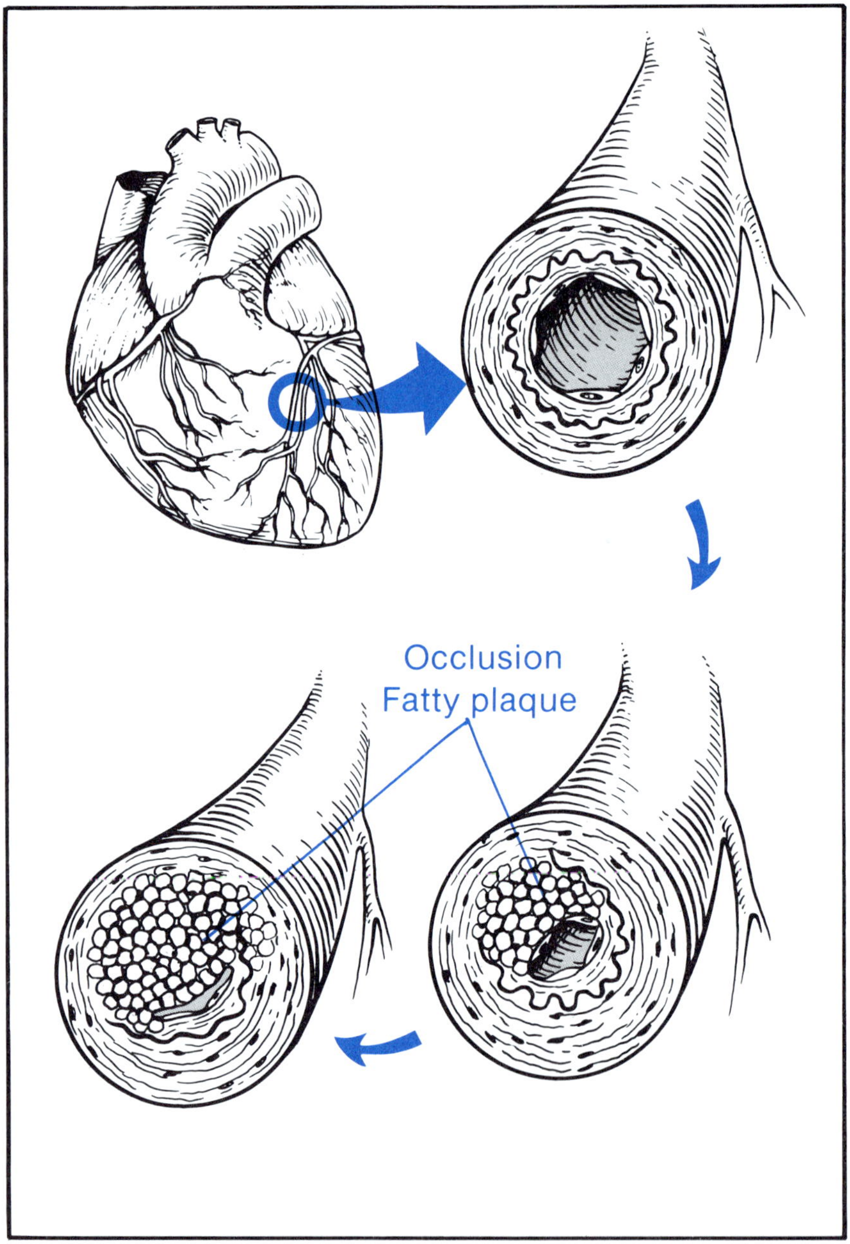

reducing the risk of developing atherosclerosis:

1. Hypertension (high blood pressure).
2. Smoking.
3. Elevated blood lipids — cholesterol.
4. Exercise.
5. Stress.

Nonmodifiable

The following are risk factors that are not controllable by the patient:

1. Diabetes mellitus.
2. Male gender.
3. Advanced age.
4. A family history of early atherosclerosis.

Angina Pectoris (Coronary Artery Disease — CAD)

Pathology

In angina pectoris, the oxygen demands of the myocardium transiently exceed what is able to be delivered through atherosclerotic coronary arteries, causing ischemia (a deficiency of blood due to a constriction of an artery). Angina may also be caused by a spasm of a coronary artery with or without atherosclerosis. There are two categories:

1. Stable angina — is usually precipitated by physical and/or emotional stress; for example, the patient knows that he/she can walk up three flights of steps before the angina symptoms develop.
2. Unstable or preinfarction angina — angina that may occur to the patient under any circumstances or at anytime, even at rest.

Assessment

1. Past medical history (see page 197 in this chapter). What has the patient done to alleviate the pain (nitroglycerine)?
2. Physical examination (see pages 198 to 199 in this chapter).
3. Signs and symptoms are a result of the buildup of lactic acid and carbon dioxide in ischemic myocardium.
   - Substernal chest or epigastric discomfort/pain — may be described as

pressure, squeezing, or tightness in the chest. It is frequently mistaken for indigestion. Approximately one-third of all angina patients experience pain only in the chest.

- Pain may radiate to shoulder(s), arm(s), neck, and jaw, and through to the back.
- Associated symptoms may or may not be present: anxiety, shortness of breath, diaphoresis, nausea, weakness, vertigo, and/or palpitations.
- Stable angina is generally of short duration, lasting three to five minutes and sometimes up to fifteen minutes.
- Dysrhythmias may be precipitated by ischemia.

Management

Angina is relieved by rest and by use of nitroglycerine and/or oxygen. Unstable angina may not respond as readily as stable angina.

1. Place the patient at rest physically and, if possible, emotionally, to decrease the oxygen demand of the myocardium.
2. Administer a high concentration of oxygen to increase oxygen delivery to the myocardium.
3. Administer nitroglycerine, 1/150 or 1/200 grain, sublingually (see Appendix 1). Nitroglycerine dilates peripheral arteries and veins to reduce preload, afterload, and myocardial oxygen demand, and it possibly increases the flow in the collateral vasculature of the heart.
4. Whenever symptoms persist, the paramedic must presume that the patient is having an acute myocardial infarction (AMI).
5. First-time attacks, abnormal attacks, or attacks unresponsive to treatment need hospital evaluation (if in doubt about transport, contact the base physician).

Myocardial Infarction (MI)

Myocardial infarction literally means death of the myocardium. It is commonly referred to as a heart attack.

Pathology

In a myocardial infarction, an area of the heart muscle dies (necrosis), usually as a result of oxygen deprivation most often associated with coronary artery disease caused by an obstruction of part of the heart's blood supply.

Precipitating Events

1. Coronary thrombosis is the most common event.
2. Coronary artery spasm.
3. Microemboli occluding a coronary artery.
4. Acute volume overload.
5. Hypotension from any cause.
6. Acute respiratory failure/acute hypoxia.

Location and Size of Infarct Dependent on Site of the Obstruction

1. A majority of myocardial infarctions involve the left ventricle.
2. Anterior, lateral, and septal wall infarcts are usually the result of a left coronary artery occlusion.
3. Inferior wall infarcts are usually the result of a right coronary artery occlusion.
4. The subendocardial infarct involves only the subendocardial muscle. The transmural infarct involves the full thickness of the ventricular wall.
5. A ring of ischemic myocardium surrounds the necrotic tissue, which is often the origin of many dysrhythmias.
6. Death secondary to myocardial infarction is usually the result of fatal dysrhythmias. These dysrhythmias are the most common cause of sudden death. Pump failure caused by extensive myocardial damage (cardiogenic shock) is a second major cause of death secondary to myocardial infarction.

Assessment

1. Past medical history (see page 197 in this chapter).
2. Physical examination (see pages 198 to 199 in this chapter).
3. Signs and symptoms:
   - Substernal or epigastric discomfort/pain may have the same location and characteristics as anginal pain. It may be severe (crushing) pain but is often mild to moderate. Frequently, the pain radiates to the neck/jaw and/or one or both shoulder/arm(s), primarily the left. Often it occurs at rest; it is not necessarily precipitated by normal or unusual exertion. The pain may persist for long periods of time and is not relieved by nitroglycerine. Pain is generally not affected by anything the patient does (e.g., changing position or taking medication).
   - Acute myocardial infarction without pain is called a ''silent'' myocardial infarction.
   - All patients with chest pain and a compatible history should be pre-

sumed to have a myocardial infarction until proven otherwise. Age is **not** a good discriminator.

- Patients may present with atypical pain; possibly shoulder, arm, neck, or jaw pain **without** chest pain.
- Associated signs and symptoms are common: diaphoresis, anxiety/apprehension, shortness of breath, nausea and/or vomiting, pallor, vertigo, palpitations, and generalized weakness/malaise.
- Patients occasionally present with only general malaise or syncope without pain.
- Patient denial is common. Delays in obtaining medical assistance during the first two hours after onset of signs/symptoms are precarious and may result in death.
- Vital signs vary with the type of cardiac rhythm, the extent of myocardial damage, and the degree of autonomic nervous system response. Blood pressure may be normal, elevated (sympathetic discharge), or low (parasympathetic discharge or pump failure). The pulse is dependent on the presence or absence of dysrhythmias. The rate may be normal, fast, or slow; the rhythm may be regular or irregular. Respirations are normal or increased; breath sounds may be clear or edematous.
- Dysrhythmias are the most common complication in the first few hours after the onset of symptoms. Life-threatening dysrhythmias include ventricular fibrillation (VF), ventricular tachycardia (VT), and some atrioventricular blocks and require immediate intervention. The non-life-threatening dysrhythmias may not require advanced cardiac life support intervention. Warning dysrhythmias such as premature ventricular contractions (PVCs) may be forerunners to life-threatening dysrhythmias and therefore also require immediate treatment.

Management

1. The goals of management are to relieve pain and apprehension, to prevent serious dysrhythmias, and to limit the size of an infarct.
2. Obtain a complete history while conducting the physical examination and initiating treatment. In other words, **do not delay treatment.**
3. Place the patient physically at rest and reassure the patient in an effort to decrease anxiety. This reduces the heart rate and therefore the myocardial oxygen demand. The ideal position of comfort is reclining with the patient's head elevated at least thirty degrees. Do not allow the patient to walk.
4. Administer a high-flow, high-concentration oxygen to increase the oxy-

gen delivery to the myocardium.

5. Take a set of vital signs to identify any abnormalities and to establish a baseline reading for comparison; repeat frequently.
6. Establish an IV as soon as possible with D_5W through a microdrip at a keep open rate.
7. Attach the EKG electrodes and document the initial rhythm; a slow, fast, or irregular pulse may be the first indication of dysrhythmias.
8. Complete the history and physical exam, including lung auscultation; rales may indicate early heart failure.
9. Administer medications according to written protocol or obtain orders from the base physician.
10. Drugs for pain relief (see Appendix 1):
    - Nitroglycerine — dilates peripheral arteries and veins to reduce preload, afterload, and myocardial oxygen demand. It may increase the flow of blood in the collateral vasculature.
    - Morphine sulfate — the drug of choice for pain relief from an acute myocardial infarction. Morphine reduces the myocardial oxygen demand by reducing the cardiac workload (reduced preload and afterload) and is also a central nervous system depressant.
    - Nitrous oxide — also provides analgesia and reduces anxiety.
    - Diazepam — may be appropriate if the patient is extremely agitated or apprehensive with little pain.
11. Drugs for dysrhythmia management and other cardiac problems (see Appendix 1):
    - Lidocaine — suppresses the so-called "warning dysrhythmias" (e.g., PVCs) and may be given in absence of dysrhythmias as a prophylactic measure against the development of life-threatening ventricular dysrhythmias.
    - Procainamide — used for suppressing PVCs and recurrent ventricular tachycardia (VT) that cannot be controlled by lidocaine. **This is not a commonly used field drug.**
    - Bretylium — a second-line drug used when lidocaine and electrical shock fail to convert ventricular fibrillation, when ventricular fibrillation recurs despite the use of lidocaine, or when lidocaine has not controlled ventricular tachycardia accompanied by a pulse.
    - Verapamil — used primarily in the treatment of supraventricular tachycardias that do not require cardioversion.
    - Oxygen — increases the PaO_2 and saturation available in the blood.
    - Epinephrine — produces a favorable redistribution of blood flow during CPR. Makes ventricular fibrillation more susceptible to con-

version by raising the fibrillation threshold.

- Atropine — indicated for the treatment of symptomatic bradycardia.
- Norepinephrine — used for hemodynamically significant hypotension not related to hypovolemia that has not been successfully treated by other drugs.
- Dopamine — used for the treatment of hemodynamically significant hypotension in the absence of hypovolemia.
- Dobutamine — used for treatment of patients with pulmonary congestion and low cardiac output and when vasodilators cannot be used for fear of lowering the blood pressure.
- Isoproternol — used for the immediate and temporary control of hemodynamically significant bradycardia that has not been controlled by atropine in the perfusing patient.
- Propranolol — a beta-blocking drug. The primary indication for beta-blockers is to control recurrent ventricular tachycardia, recurrent ventricular fibrillation, and/or rapid supraventricular dysrhythmias refractory to other treatment.
- Furosemide — used in the treatment of pulmonary edema associated with left heart failure.
- Calcium chloride — no data at present suggest that calcium plays a beneficial role in the treatment of cardiac arrest.
- Sodium bicarbonate — used to treat metabolic acidosis. If it is used in the treatment of cardiac arrest, sodium bicarbonate should be administered after the use of defibrillation, good CPR, endotracheal tube insertion, hyperventilation for at least ten minutes, and administration of first-line drugs (epinephrine/lidocaine).

12. Transport calmly without lights or siren if the patient is stable.

Left Ventricular Failure (LVF or LHF)

Pathology

In left ventricular failure, the left ventricle loses its ability to be an effective forward pump causes back-pressure of blood into the pulmonary circulation, resulting in pulmonary edema (fluid in and around the alveoli). Left ventricular failure is caused by various types of heart disease: myocardial infarction, valvular disease, chronic hypertension, and dysrhythmias.

Failure begins when the left ventricle is unable to eject all the blood that is delivered from the right heart. As the left ventricle fails, left atrial pressure rises and is transmitted to the pulmonary veins and capillaries. As the pulmonary capillary pressure increases, the serum portion of the blood is forced into the alveoli and the surrounding tissue, resulting in pulmonary edema (congestion). The progressive fluid accumulation in alveoli will lead to death from hypoxia unless prompt medical intervention occurs.

All patients in pulmonary edema must be presumed to be having a myocardial infarction or congestive heart failure.

Assessment

1. History (see page 197 in this chapter).
2. Physical examination (see pages 198 to 199 in this chapter).
3. Signs and symptoms:
   - Severe respiratory distress — orthopnea; spasmodic coughing characteristically (in the late stages) produces pink, foamy sputum; patient may have a history of paroxysmal nocturnal orthopnea.
   - Severe apprehension, agitation, or confusion.
   - Cyanosis, if the pulmonary edema is severe.
   - Diaphoresis.
   - Adventitious lung sounds: rales (crackles), caused by fluid in the alveoli — usually found bilaterally. May be in the base of the lungs or up to the scapulae. Rales do not clear with coughing. Rhonchi (low wheezes) are caused by fluid or mucous in the larger airways. Wheezes are caused by reflex bronchospasm and narrowing of the bronchi. Wheezes are sometimes referred to as "cardiac asthma."
   - Jugular vein distention — this may be present if right heart failure is present. Observe the patient with the patient's head elevated at least forty-five degrees for signs of distention.
   - Vital signs — there is an intense sympathetic discharge (epinephrine) to help the body compensate for left heart failure and pulmonary edema. Blood pressure may be highly elevated. The pulse may be rapid to compensate for low stroke volume and may be irregular if dysrhythmias are present. Respirations may be rapid and labored.
   - The patient's level of consciousness varies. He/she may be anxious, agitated, uncooperative, or obtunded due to poor cerebral perfusion.
   - Chest pain may be present.

Management

Left ventricular failure is a dire emergency. The patient may decompensate rapidly and unpredictably. The goals of management are to decrease the venous return to the heart (decrease preload), decrease the myocardial oxygen demand (by reducing the cardiac workload), and improve patient ventilation and oxygenation.

1. Obtain a complete history and physical examination while initiating treatment.
2. Sit the patient up with the feet dangling to enhance venous pooling. **Do not lie the patient flat at any time.**
3. Administer high-flow oxygen. A positive pressure assist is ideal if the patient can cooperate or is very obtunded.
4. Establish an IV of D_5W with a microdrip at a keep open rate. It is crucial to to limit fluid intake.
5. Place EKG electrodes to monitor and document the cardiac rhythm.
6. Administer medications according to written protocols, or obtain physician orders (see Appendix 1):
   - Morphine sulfate — decreases venous return, reduces myocardial workload, and reduces anxiety.
   - Aminophylline — a bronchodilator.
   - Furosemide — a potent diuretic that reduces intravascular volume and dilates the venous system, reducing the blood return to the heart; onset of action within five minutes of administration.
   - Nitroglycerine — relaxes vascular smooth muscle, causing peripheral vasodilation and increasing venous capacitance, thus reducing preload.
7. This patient requires rapid, safe transport to the emergency department.

Right Ventricular Failure (RVF or RHF)

Pathology

In right ventricular failure, the right ventricle loses its ability to function as an effective pump, causing back-pressure of blood into the systemic venous circulation. This results in venous congestion and engorgement with pedal edema, sacral edema, enlargement of the liver, and/or ascites (this refers to an accumulation of fluid in the peritoneal cavity).

The most common cause of right ventricular failure is left ventricular failure. Other causes include chronic hypertension, enlargement of the right ventricle resulting from lung disease, pulmonary embolus, and infarct of the right atrium or right ventricle.

Failure beigins when the right ventricle is unable to keep up with venous return. The stroke volume decreases, and pressure in the right atrium increases. This pressure is transmitted to the vena cava and the entire venous system.

When the systemic venous pressure becomes high, the serum portion of the blood is forced into the interstitial tissues, resulting in edema.

Assessment

1. History (see page 197 in this chapter). There is often a history of a previous myocardial infarction. Most patients are taking medication, such as digitalis and a diuretic (may be called a water pill).
2. Physical examination (see pages 198 to 199 in this chapter).
3. Signs and symptoms:
   - Tachycardia — a compensatory mechanism to make up for inadequate pumping of the heart.
   - Venous congestion — resulting in a tender upper-right quadrant (liver engorgement) and jugular venous distention.
   - Peripheral edema — the lower extremities (pedal edema) and the sacral region (in a bedridden patient) may be mild or severe with pitting edema (when the edematous area retains the indentation produced by pressure). There may be generalized, massive edema called anasarca.
   - Fluid accumulation occurs in the serous cavities of the abdominal cavity (causes ascites), pleural space (causing pleural effusions — the escape of fluid from the blood vessels or lymphatics into the tissues or cavities), and in the pericardium (causing pericardial effusion/rub).

Management

1. ABCs.
2. Right ventricular failure is not usually a medical emergency in itself. It is more important for the paramedic to realize its relationship to left ventricular failure and the potential for acute decompensation.
3. Place the patient at rest with his/her head elevated.
4. Administer oxygen (high-flow, high-concentration).
5. Take vital signs at regular intervals.
6. Start an IV with D_5W through a microdrip at a keep open rate.
7. Place EKG electrodes to monitor and document the cardiac rhythm.
8. Treat any left ventricular failure if present.

Cardiogenic Shock

Pathology

Cardiogenic shock is the most extreme form of pump failure. It occurs when left ventricular function is so compromised that the heart cannot maintain an adequate cardiac output. By definition, cardiogenic shock is shock that persists after correction of existing dysrhythmias, hypovolemia, or altered vascular tone. It is usually due to an extensive myocardial infarction or diffuse ischemia involving approximately 40 percent or more of the left ventricle. The body's compensatory mechanisms can no longer help the sick heart. The mortality rate of cardiogenic shock is 80 percent.

Assessment

1. History (see page 197 in this chapter).
2. Physical examination (see pages 198 to 199 in this chapter).
3. Signs and symptoms:
   - Same signs and symptoms as for acute myocardial infarction.
   - Hypotension with the systolic blood pressure usually less than 80 mmHg.
   - Altered level of consciousness — the patient may be restless, apprehensive, confused, or unconscious.
   - A pulse rate that is tachycardic (compensatory) and thready.
   - The skin is pale, cool, and clammy; may also be cyanotic.
   - Rapid and shallow respiratons.

Management

1. ABCs.
2. Prolonged stabilization in the field not recommended; expedite transport.
3. Maintain an open airway and administer high-flow, high-concentration oxygen.
4. Place the patient in a semireclined position with his/her head elevated fifteen degrees.
5. Start an IV of D_5W through a microdrip at a keep open rate (may be difficult to establish due to cardiovascular collapse). The physician may order a fluid challenge of 100 ml to 250 ml to determine if there is a hypovolemic component to the patient's shock.
6. Apply EKG electrodes to monitor and document the cardiac rhythm.

7. Auscultate the lungs and observe for jugular venous distention.
8. Administer medication according to written protocols, or obtain orders (see Appendix 1).
   - Dopamine infusion — adding 200 mg per 5 ml in a bag of 250 ml D_5W to yield a concentration of 800 micrograms per milliliter. The drip is usually started between 2 to 5 micrograms per kilogram per minute.
   - Norepinephrine infusion — 4 mg added to 250 ml of D_5W, yielding a concentration of 8 micrograms per milliliter. Start the infusion at 4 micrograms per minute.
   - Consider application of the antishock garment; if there is difficulty starting an IV, this may enhance your efforts.
10. Transport rapidly.

Cardiac Arrest/Sudden Death

Sudden death is defined as death within one to two hours after the onset of signs/symptoms of a possible acute myocardial infarction. This is the most serious clinical syndrome of coronary artery disease. Sudden death accounts for approximately 60 percent of all deaths from coronary artery disease. An actual infarction is not always present, but severe atherosclerotic disease is common.

Cardiac arrest may be the first manifestation of coronary artery disease in a significant number of patients. Other causes of cardiac arrest besides coronary artery disease include drowning, congestive heart failure, dysrhythmias, electrocution, electrolyte imbalance, hypothermia, trauma, acid-base imbalance, drug toxicity, hypoxia, etc.

Dysrhythmias Associated with Cardiac Arrest

1. Ventricular fibrillation (V-fib or VF) occurs in the majority of cases (60 to 70 percent). It may be the primary event or secondary to another problem, such as hypovolemia or hypoxemia.
2. Ventricular tachycardia without a pulse.
3. Asystole.
4. Severe bradycardias/heart blocks.
5. Electromechanical dissociation.

Basic Considerations in Management of the Cardiac Arrest Patient

1. Excellent basic life support must be provided; the paramedic must monitor

performance of CPR if delegated to others.

2. Primary ventricular fibrillation is easier to convert than secondary ventricular fibrillation.
3. Defibrillate the patient in ventricular fibrillation as soon as possible; it is the best chance for successful resuscitation.
4. External pacing may be utilized for bradycardias, asystole, or immediately after conversion of ventricular fibrillation.
5. The airway may be managed by a number of methods. The most sophisticated way is not always needed immediately. In other words, do not delay adequate ventilations to intubate.
6. The antishock garment (PASG) may be useful in cardiac arrests, particularly when it is difficult to start an IV.
7. Cardiac arrest in infants and children is rarely a primary event. It is usually secondary to hypoxia.

Management of Unwitnessed Arrest: Ventricular Fibrillation and Pulseless Ventricular Tachycardia

This sequence (see Figure 10-3) was developed to assist in teaching how to treat a broad range of patients with ventricular fibrillation (VF) or pulseless ventricular tachycardia (VT). Some patients may require care not specified herein. This algorithm should not be construed as prohibiting such flexibility. Flow of algorithm presumes that ventricular fibrillation is continuing.

Management of Cardiac Arrest: Asystole

1. Prognosis for resuscitation is poor.
2. May be the end result of ventricular fibrillation or electromechanical dissociation.
3. Presence of asystole may indicate:
   - Extensive myocardial damage.
   - Severe metabolic deficit.
   - High parasympathetic tone.
4. If there is any question of whether the rhythm is asystole or fine ventricular fibrillation, defibrillation is indicated.

The sequence for asystole (see Figure 10-4) was developed to assist in teaching how to treat a broad range of patients with asystole. Some patients may require care not specified in Figure 10-4. This algorithm should not be construed to prohibit such flexibility. Flow of algorithm presumes that asystole is continuing.

Figure 10-3
Ventricular Fibrillation and Pulseless Ventricular Tachycardia[a]

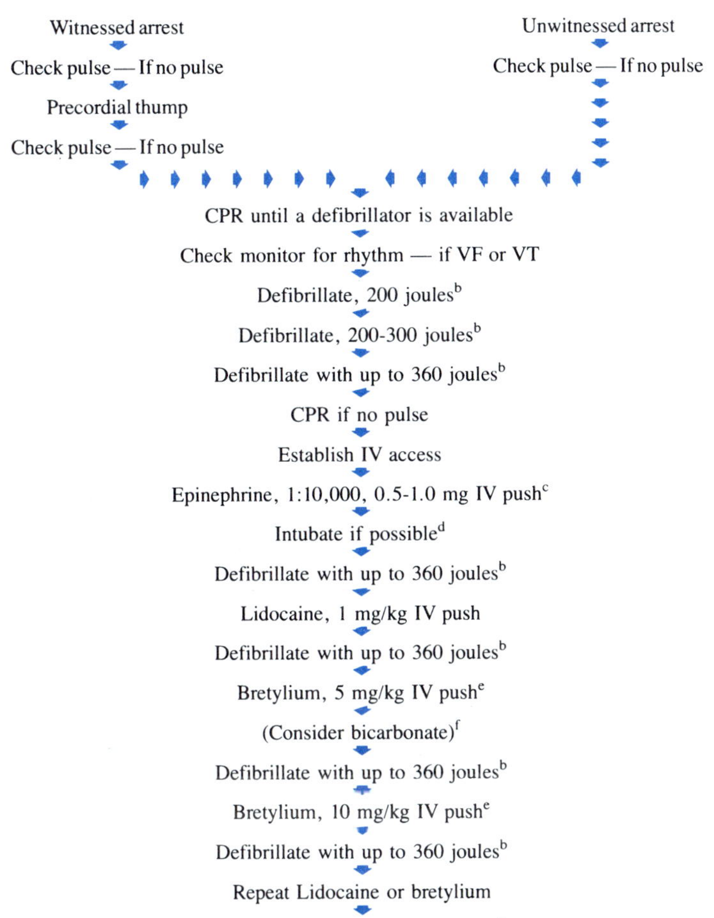

[a] Pulseless VT should be treated identically to VF.

[b] Check pulse and rhythm after each shock. If VF recurs after transiently converting (rather than persists without ever converting), use whatever energy level has previously been successful for defibrillation.

[c] Epinephrine should be repeated every five minutes.

[d] Intubation is preferable. If it can be accompanied simultaneously with other techniques, then the earlier the better. However, defibrillation and epinephrine are more important initially if the patient can be ventilated without intubation.

[e] Some may prefer repeated doses of lidocaine, which may be given in 0.5-mg/kg boluses every eight minutes to a total dose of 3.0 mg/kg.

[f] Value of sodium bicarbonate is questionable during cardiac arrest, and it is not recommended for routine cardiac arrest sequence. Consideration of its use in a dose of 1 mEq/kg is appropriate at this point. Half of original dose may be repeated every ten minutes if it is used.

Figure 10-4

Asystole (Cardiac Standstill)

If rhythm is unclear and possibly ventricular fibrillation, defibrillate as for VF.
If asystole is present[a]:

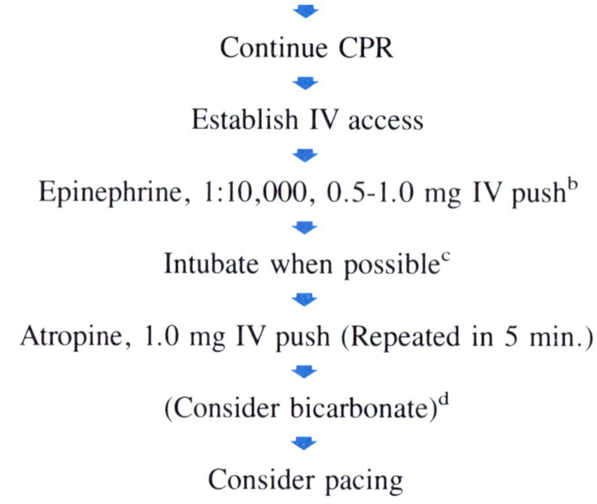

[a] Asystole shoulde be confirmed in two leads.
[b] Epinephrine should be repeated every five minutes.
[c] Intubation is preferable; if it can be accomplished simultaneously with other techniques, then the earlier the better. However, cardiopulmonary resuscitation (CPR) and the use of epinephrine are more important initially if patient can be ventilated without intubation. (Endotracheal epinephrine may be used.)
[d] Value of sodium bicarbonate is questionable during cardiac arrest, and it is not recommended for routine cardiac arrest sequence. Consideration of its use in a dose of 1 mEq/kg is appropriate at this point. Half of original dose may be repeated every ten minutes if it is used.

Management of Cardiac Arrest: Electromechanical Dissociation (EMD)

1. This is defined as any organized rhythm without a pulse.
2. It carries a grave prognosis for resuscitation.

3. There are various etiologies of electromechanical dissociation; some are treatable in the hospital:
   - Massive myocardial damage.
   - Hypovolemia.
   - Cardiac rupture.
   - Cardiac tamponade.
   - Acute pulmonary embolism.

Figure 10-5

Electromechanical Dissociation

Continue CPR
↓
Establish IV access
↓
Epinephrine, 1:10,000, 0.5-1.0 mg IV push[a]
↓
Intubate when possible[b]
↓
(Consider bicarbonate)[c]
↓
Consider:
Hypovolemia,
Cardiac tamponade
Tension pneumothorax
Hypoxemia
Acidosis
Pulmonary embolism

[a] Epinephrine should be repeated every five minutes.
[b] Intubation is preferable; if it can be accomplished simultaneously with other techniques, then the earlier the better. However, epinephrine is more important initially if the patient can be ventilated without intubation.
[c] Value of sodium bicarbonate is questionable during cardiac arrest, and it is not recommended for routine cardiac arrest sequence. Consideration of its use in a dose of 1 mEq/kg is appropriate at this point. Half of original dose may be repeated every ten minutes if it is used.

4. Consider using an antishock garment.
5. Consider using an IV fluid challenge.
6. Consider beginning transport much earlier if there is any suspicion of treatable etiology, such as hypovolemia.

The sequence for electromechanical dissociation (see Figure 10-5) was developed to assist in teaching how to treat a broad range of patients with electromechanical dissociation. Some patients may require care not specified in Figure 10-5. This algorithm should not be construed to prohibit such flexibility. Flow of algorithm presumes that electromechanical dissociation is continuing.

PERIPHERAL VASCULAR AND OTHER CARDIOVASCULAR EMERGENCIES

Abdominal Aortic Aneurysm

Pathology

An aneurysm is a localized abnormal dilation of a blood vessel, primarily in an artery. The most common site for an aneurysm is in the lower portion of the abdominal aorta. This occurs most frequently in men over the age of sixty. The aneurysm develops over a point of weakness — usually the result of atherosclerosis. Most aneurysms develop over a period of time without any patient recognition when they are small. Once the process begins, the aneurysm gradually increases in size. An aneurysm may also develop after trauma occurs to an arterial wall.

The most common site for an abdominal aortic aneurysm is below the renal arteries near their bifurcation. The aneurysm may involve the iliac and renal arteries.

Assessment of the Patient with a Ruptured Abdominal Aortic Aneurysm

1. History: the most common initial symptom is the complaint of sudden onset of moderate to severe abdominal pain, lumbar back pain, or both. The pain tends to increase in severity; there may also be a syncopal episode. Depending on the extent of the aneurysm, the patient may be anxious, confused, or unconscious.

Figure 10-6. Aneurysms: A — Fusiform Aneurysm of Abdominal Aorta; B — Saccular Aneurysm of Abdominal Aorta.

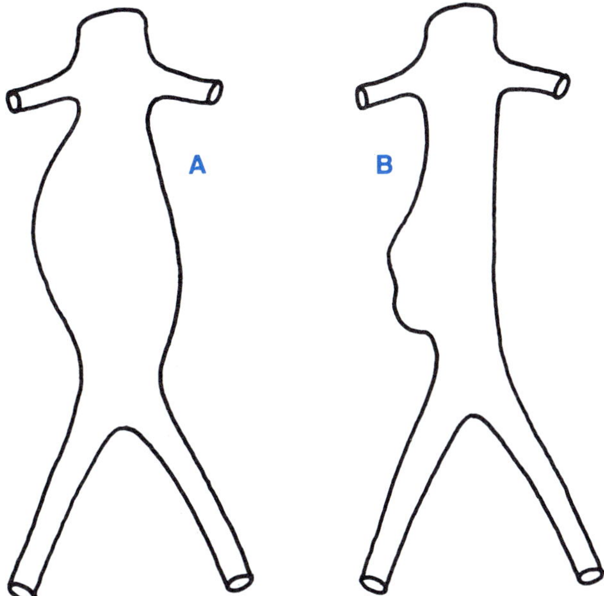

2. Physical examination (signs/symptoms):
   - Lumbar back pain.
   - Pulsatile mass (usually left of midline — can be palpated when greater than five centimeters (palpate gently).
   - Hypotension — severity dependent upon the degree of blood loss that has taken place.
   - Tachycardia.
   - Femoral pulses are usually palpable, and pulses distal to the femoral pulse may be present, diminished, or absent.

Management

1. ABCs.
2. Apply the antishock garment (PASG) to possibly control abdominal bleeding and to help start an IV.
3. Start at least one large-bore IV with normal saline or Ringer's lactate en route to the hospital if possible (to expedite transport), and run at a wide-open rate.
4. Give high-flow, high-concentration oxygen.
5. Monitor vital signs.
6. Provide rapid, safe transport.

Dissecting Aortic Aneurysm

Pathology

A dissecting aortic aneurysm results from a lengthwise splitting of the arterial wall produced by a tear in the inner layer of the artery. This allows blood to travel from the lumen into the newly developed passage. It occurs primarily in the thoracic aorta. The dissecting aorta may rupture at any time and usually results in death.

Causes of a dissecting aortic aneurysm are the following:

1. Atherosclerosis.
2. Seventy-five to 85 percent of the cases are caused by hypertension.
3. Congenital disorders.
4. Usually in patients older than fifty years of age.
5. Most commonly found in blacks.
6. This problem is fatal within one month of onset in approximately 80 percent of all cases.

Assessment

1. History: the most common initial symptom is a sudden onset of pain that may be described as a tearing or ripping sensation. The pain may extend to the neck, shoulders, low back, and abdomen; it rarely radiates to the jaw or arms. Depending on the severity and the exact circumstances, a patient may be anxious, agitated, confused, or unconscious.
2. Physical examination (signs/symptoms):
   - The pain is characteristically ripping, tearing, and substernal and may radiate to the back between the scapulae.
   - Pallor.
   - Diaphoresis.
   - Dyspnea.
   - Tachycardia.
   - Possible cyanosis.
   - Abrupt loss of radial and/or femoral pulses.
   - A wide variation in pulses or blood pressure between arms/legs may be apparent.
   - The patient looks shocky, yet the systolic blood pressure may be normal or significantly elevated.
   - The dissection may cause syncope, stroke heart failure, pericardial tamponade, and an acute myocardial infarction.

Management

1. ABCs.
2. Start at least one large-bore IV with normal saline or Ringer's lactate en route to the hospital.
3. Give high-flow, high-concentration oxygen.
4. Monitor vital signs.
5. Keep the patient quiet.
6. Provide rapid, safe transport.
7. Consider an analgesic (morphine sulfate if the diagnosis is fairly definite).

Acute Arterial Occlusion

Pathology

In its acute form, arterial occlusion is the sudden obstruction of the lumen of any one of the major arteries (carotid, vertebral, innominate, subclavian, mesenteric, and celiac). It most commonly affects the flow of blood to the legs and feet. Arterial occlusive disease is most frequently a complication of atherosclerotic disease. The occlusion may be caused by a thrombosis, emboli, trauma, or fracture.

Predisposing factors include smoking, atherosclerosis, hypertension, diabetes, family history of vascular disease, heart disease (atrial fibrillation/flutter), history of myocardial infarction, and stroke. This problem is more common in men than in women.

Assessment

1. Primary survey (ABCs).
2. History: the patient usually has a history of diabetes, congestive heart failure, cardiac dysrhythmias, COPD, or renal disease. The patient is most commonly over sixty years old.
3. Physical examination (signs and symptoms). Various presentations occur, depending upon where the occlusion takes place.
   - Pain is the frequent common denominator. The pain may have a sudden onset that continues to worsen for several hours.
   - The extremity(ies) may be pale and cool to the touch, with a decreased or absent pulse(s).
   - Over a period of time, the extremity will become mottled and cyanotic.
   - Shock may occur if a major abdominal artery is involved.

Management

1. ABCs.
2. Administer high-concentration oxygen.
3. Treat for shock as necessary with IV volume replacement.
4. Provide pain relief with morphine sulfate.
5. Protect the affected limb. Do not allow the patient to walk.
6. The blood flow to the affected area needs to be reestablished within four to eight hours.

NONCRITICAL PERIPHERAL VASCULAR CONDITIONS

Deep Vein Thrombophlebitis

Pathology

A thrombosis is the development, formation, or existence of a blood clot in the vascular system. A thrombosis can result in a serious or life-threatening situation when the clot reduces or occludes the flow of blood to an organ or extremity, or if it breaks free and becomes an embolist that may occlude the flow of blood to an organ at some other point. Phlebitis is an inflammation of a vein. Venous thrombosis most commonly occurs in the legs or pelvis. Venous thrombophlebitis is an inflammation of the vein, along with a thrombus development. The formation of a thrombus occurs when the flow of blood is reduced and a change in the inner lining of a vessel occurs.

This condition may be caused by trauma, prolonged bed rest, childbirth, surgery, or use of oral contraceptives, or it may be idiopathic.

Signs and Symptoms

1. Pain (may be severe).
2. Swelling and a feeling of heaviness in the affected part.
3. Systematically, the patient may experience chills, fever, and malaise.
4. The patient may be asymptomatic.

Management

1. This is not a medical emergency, but the patient is prone to developing pulmonary emboli.
2. Do not allow the patient to walk.
3. Elevate the patient's leg.
4. Do not massage the affected area.

Varicose Veins

Pathology

Varicose veins are a noncritical condition that results from distended, knotted, swollen veins, most commonly in the subcutaneous tissue of the leg. The condition develops primarily from a stagnated or sluggish flow of blood, in combination with defective valves and weakened walls of the veins.

A patient may be genetically predisposed to varicose veins; they are also caused by pregnancy and obesity, and by engaging in an occupation that requires long periods of standing or sitting motionless.

Signs and Symptoms

1. There is visible distention of the leg veins.
2. Leg discomfort (especially at the end of the day).
3. Feeling of fatigue.
4. Leg cramps at night.
5. Ankle swelling.
6. Because of impaired circulation, ulcers may develop.
7. Severe bleeding from rupture (this is the only associated emergency; the paramedic should control hemorrhage with direct pressure).

Peripheral Arterial Atherosclerotic Disease

Pathology

This is a chronic disease caused by atherosclerosis of the abdominal aorta and its tributaries to lower extremities. It is a gradual, progressive disease that generally is not a medical emergency. It is commonly found in patients who have a history of diabetes, hypertension, and/or high blood cholesterol.

Signs and Symptoms

1. This problem is characterized by intermittent claudication (tension, weakness, pain in the legs during walking), which results in lameness.
2. The patient may develop ulcers or gangrene.
3. The only associated medical emergency is development of an acute arterial occlusion.

Hypertension

Pathology

Hypertension is a consistently high blood pressure. It is generally agreed upon that a systolic pressure above 140 mmHg and/or a diastolic pressure above 90 mmHg is considered hypertension. An estimated 20 percent of adults in the United States have high blood pressure. Of the 20 percent with hypertension, only 15 to 25 percent are being treated. The people who are left untreated have an increased risk of developing congestive heart failure, stroke, acute myocardial infarction, and renal disease. When patients are treated for high blood pressure, the risks can be reduced significantly.

High blood pressure disease can be divided into two categories:

1. Essential hypertension (also known as primary or idiopathic), when the cause is unknown, accounts for approximately 80 to 90 percent.
2. Secondary hypertension, in which the elevated blood pressure is a result of primary illness, accounts for 10 to 20 percent.

Hypertension problems range from mild, borderline (labile), and chronic to a hypertensive crisis (malignant or accelerated hypertension). This section will discuss the hypertensive crisis — a particularly serious form of essential hypertension.

In the hypertensive crisis, diastolic pressures range from 130 mmHg to 170 mmHg. The condition occurs in approximately 2 to 7 percent of patients with hypertension — patients who are usually untreated or poorly controlled. In addition to the above, a hypertensive crisis may occur in a patient who has abruptly discontinued antihypertensive medication, increased salt consumption, or increased stress (including the increased production of renin, epinephrine, and/or norepinephrine).

Assessment

1. History: a history of high blood pressure possibly untreated or poorly controlled, change in medications, change in diet, or stress.
2. Physical examination (signs and symptoms):
   - May be moderate to life-threatening.
   - Hypertensive encephalopathy — a syndrome that consists of a severe/rapid elevation of diastolic blood pressure, blurred vision, severe headache, altered level of consciousness, increased intracranial pressure, seizure, and/or coma.

- There may be nausea and vomiting.
- There may be cardiovascular involvement in the form of an acute myocardial infarction, acute left ventricular failure, pulmonary edema, or stroke.

Management

The care is supportive rather than definitive.

1. ABCs.
2. Administer high-flow, high-concentration oxygen.
3. Keep the patient calm and quiet.
4. Treat the patient symptomatically, especially if pulmonary edema is present.
5. Transport the patient rapidly and gently to the hospital for definitive drug therapy.

ELECTROCARDIOGRAM (ECG OR EKG) MONITORING FOR DYSRHYTHMIA RECOGNITION

Introduction of Electrocardiography

Review the electrical conduction pathway of the normal heart (see the electrophysiology section earlier in this chapter, pages 191 to 193).

The electrocardiogram (ECG or EKG) is a graphic display of the heart's electrical activity (it does not represent mechanical action). The body's surface acts like an electrical conductor, and changes in the electrical activity of the myocardial cells may be detected by applying electrodes at specific body points.

The sequence of events that takes place electrically is recorded on special ECG paper. This paper is standardized to allow comparative analysis of ECG wave patterns. ECG paper is divided into gridlike boxes, like graph paper. Each small box is one millimeter (mm), and horizontally each box represents 0.04 second. There are heavy lines every five millimeters. These five-millimeter horizontal units represent 0.20 second. The horizontal movement of the graph paper represents time, which is used to measure the duration of complexes and intervals. In this way, the time sequence in which cardiac events occur may be accurately recorded. The paper moves past the print stylus at a constant and standard speed of twenty-five millimeters per second. In

Figure 10-7. ECG Paper.

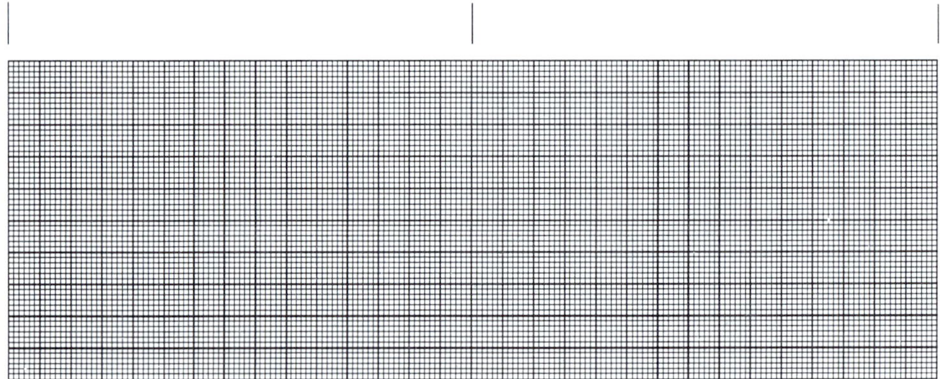

addition, a vertical measurement takes place on this paper. The ECG measures the voltage or amplitude of the positive and negative deflections (waves). The exact voltage can be measured because the ECG is standardized so that one millivolt (mv) produces a ten-millimeter deflection in amplitude (one millivolt equals ten millimeters).

The isoelectric line is a flat line on the ECG indicating the absence of electrical activity. This line is the reference point for positive and negative deflections. Above the line is positive and below is negative.

The electrical activity of the heart enters the ECG machine through a cable of leads, where it is amplified and displayed visually on an oscilloscope and/or graphically on ECG paper. It is recorded as a continuous movement of waves (deflections) and is called the electrocardiogram. The ECG provides a ''view'' of the heart's electrical activity by monitoring the voltage changes between the positive and negative electrodes. Each view is called a lead. The standard leads are called bipolar leads, because they are a combination of two electrodes (one influenced by negative voltages and the other by positive voltages).

The three basic laws of electrocardiography are as follows:

1. Any electrical impulse moving directly toward the positive electrode will create an upward (positive) deflection.
2. Any electrical impulse moving directly toward the negative electrode will create a downward (negative) deflection.
3. If the electrical impulse is moving perpendicular to any electrodes, a bi-

phasic deflection will occur consisting of positive and negative deflections of equal size.

In the field, the most commonly used monitoring leads are Lead II and MCL I. It is important to note that analysis of the monitoring lead can reveal only major dysrhythmias. Information that can be gained from a monitoring lead includes:

1. Heart rate.
2. Regularity; of the heartbeat.
3. Conduction time of the electrical impulse through the heart.

Information that cannot be revealed from the monitoring of a single lead includes:

1. Presence or location of an infarct (requires multilead).
2. Axis deviation (requires multilead) and chamber enlargement.
3. Right to left differences in conduction or impulse formation.
4. Quality of pumping action.

Relationship of the ECG to Electrical Events in the Heart

Isoelectric Line

The isoelectric line is a flat line on the ECG indicating absence of net electrical activity. This line is a reference point for positive and negative deflections. Above the line is positive and below is negative.

P Wave

The P wave is a small, rounded wave (deflection) preceding the QRS complex (see below); it is usually upright (positive). This wave represents atrial depolarization.

P-R Interval

This interval is measured from the beginning of the P wave to the beginning of the QRS complex. It indicates the length of time required for the depolarization wave to go from the atria to the ventricles. Normal valves for the P-R interval vary between 0.12 to 0.20 second.

Figure 10-8. The Electrocardiogram.

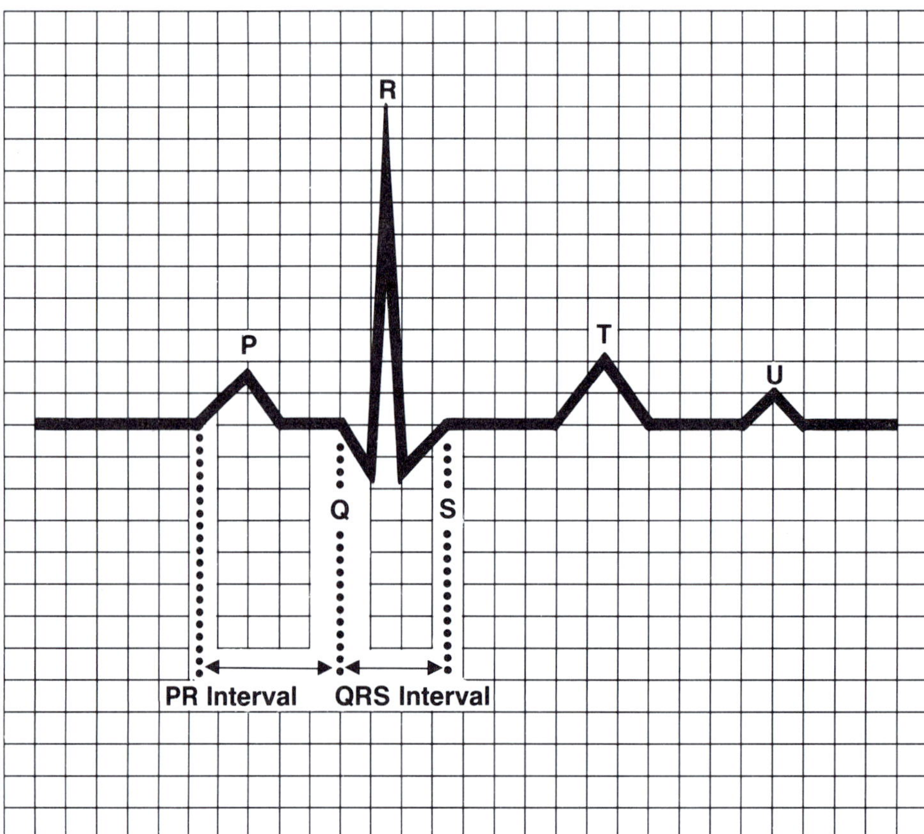

QRS Complex

The QRS complex is a collective term for three deflections normally following the P wave and P-R interval, which represent ventricular depolarization.

1. Q wave — the first negative deflection after the P wave. This represents the conduction of the electrical stimulus through the septum.
2. R wave — the first positive deflection after the P wave. This represents the conduction of the stimulus toward the left ventricle.
3. S wave — the first negative deflection after the R wave. This represents the conduction of the stimulus through both ventricular walls.

All three waves are not always present, and the QRS has many shapes. The normal value for the QRS interval, which is measured from the start of the QRS to the end, is 0.10 second (this can actually vary from 0.08 to 0.12 second).

S-T Segment

The S-T segment is the measurement between the end of the QRS complex and the beginning of the T wave. This represents the beginning of ventricular repolarization. The normal S-T is usually isoelectric — neither positive nor negtive. Changes in the S-T segment may be diagnostic, but they must be noted in many different leads.

T Wave

The T wave is a rounded, asymmetrical wave, with the peak nearer the end than the beginning following the QRS complex. This represents part of ventricular repolarization. In general, the T wave will usually follow the same direction as the net deflection of the QRS wave.

Atrial T Wave

The atrial T wave (atrial repolarization) is usually not visible because it is buried within the QRS complex.

U Wave

The U wave is a small, rounded deflection occasionally appearing after the T wave. It represents part of ventricular repolarization and is smaller than the P wave. Its significance is not known, but a prominent U wave may represent hypokalemia.

R-R Interval

The R-R interval is the measurement from the R wave in the QRS complex to the R wave in the next QRS complex.

P-P Interval

The P-P interval is the measurement from the start of a P wave in a complete cycle to the start of a P wave in the next cycle.

Refractory Period

The refractory period is a segment of time when the cardiac cells have been depolarized and cannot be depolarized a second time until repolarization occurs. The refractory period is divided into two categories:

1. Absolute refractory period — the period of time during which no stimulation will produce depolarization regardless of its strength (beginning of QRS complex to the apex of the T wave).
2. Relative refractory period — the period of time when a sufficiently strong stimulus may produce depolarization (corresponds to the downslope of the T wave).

Artifacts

Artifacts are deflections on the ECG display produced by factors other than the heart's electrical activity. They include:

1. Muscle tremors/shivering.
2. Patient movement.
3. Loose or faulty electrodes.
4. Sixty-cycle interference.
5. Machine malfunction.
6. Standardization (calibration) mark.

Rhythm Strip Analysis

The process of analyzing ECG strips uses simple logic. In order to be successful, the paramedic must be consistent in his/her approach (format). The following is a common format used when doing ECG strip interpretation. Ask these questions:

1. Rate? Normal?
2. Rhythm? Normal?
3. P waves? Normal?
4. P-R interval? Normal?
5. QRS complexes? Normal?

Know the rules for each dysrhythmia and be able to analyze them according to the specific format. Compare the analysis information to the rules for each dysrhythmia. In this way, accurate identification (and treatment if necessary) can be made.

The Analysis Format

Step 1. Analyze Rate.

1. This usually means the ventricular rate, but if the atrial and ventricular rates are different, both rates should be calculated.
2. Normal cardiac rate: 60 to 100 beats per minute.
   - Sixty or less — bradycardia.
   - One hundred or more — tachycardia.
3. The rate is an important element and plays a significant role in identifying regular and irregular cardiac rhythms. There are two ways to calculate the heart rate on an ECG. They are:
   - Counting the number of complete cardiac cycles in six seconds and multiplying by ten. It is easy to determine six seconds because the ECG paper has a bold marking on the top of the paper every three and/or six seconds (see Figure 10-9).
   - 300-150-100-75-60-50. Simply identify an R wave that falls on or near a heavy black line on the ECG paper. The first heavy line to the right is 300, the second heavy line is 150, the third heavy line is 100, and so on until 50. The first heavy line of the next R wave determines the number of heavy lines between the two R waves, thus determining the rate. If there are three heavy lines between the R waves, then the rate is 100. If there are five heavy lines between the R waves, then the rate is sixty. This method becomes less accurate when the rhythm is irregular.

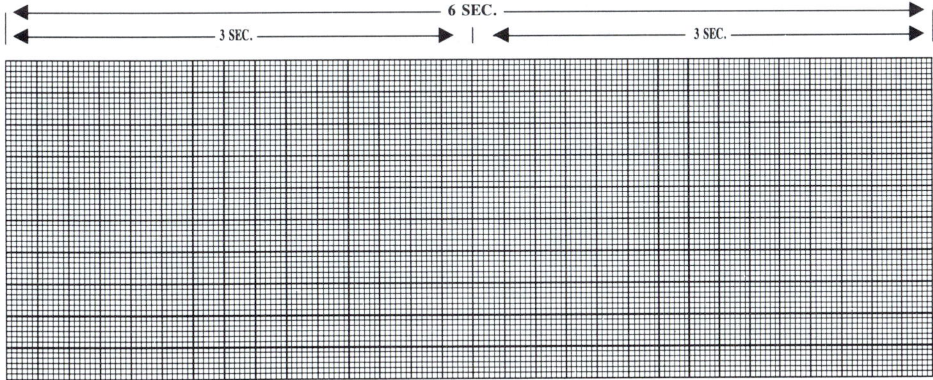

Figure 10-9. Six-Second Count Rate Determination.

Step 2. Analyze the Rhythm for Regularity

1. In general, a strip can be identified as regular or irregular at a glance. To accurately determine the regularity of a rhythm, measure the R-R interval across the entire strip. Is the distance between the R-R constant? If so, it is regular. If the rhythm is not regular, note whether it is:
   - An abnormal pattern due to a premature beat.
   - Regularly irregular — where a clearly observed pattern of irregularity is noted.
   - Occasionally irregular — only one or two R-R intervals are unequal.
   - Totally irregular and chaotic with no obvious pattern.

Step 3. Analyze the P Waves.

1. Are they present?
2. Is there one P wave for each QRS?
3. Does each P wave precede a QRS complex (what is the relationship to the QRS?), and does a QRS complex follow each P wave?
4. Are they upright or inverted?
5. Are they all similar in appearance?

This information gives the interpreter information about the pacemaker site. If there are no P waves, the sinoatrial node is not the pacer site. If there are P waves but they are not followed by a QRS complex, there is probably a block somewhere in the conduction system. If the P waves vary in shape and size, there may be several pacemaker sites in the atria.

Step 4. Analyze the P-R Intervals.

1. They should be constant across the strip.
2. Normal — 0.12 to 0.20 second (three to five small boxes).
3. If the P-R interval is prolonged beyond 0.20 second, it is called a first-degree heart block.

Step 5. Analyze the QRS Complex.

1. Do they all look alike?
2. Normal duration — less than 0.12 second (less than three small boxes).

If the conduction time is longer than 0.12 second, it means that there is abnormal conduction through the ventricles.

Step 6. Examine Other Criteria.

In addition to the above criteria, the paramedic may look at:

1. The S-T segment — normally the S-T is isoelectric; if it is significantly above or below the isoelectric line, it may indicate myocardial ischemia (S-T elevation or depression).
2. The T wave — when a T wave follows a PVC, its position is opposite that of the QRS. In hyperkalemia, it is tall and sharply peaked.

ECG Monitoring

Parts of Portable Monitor/Defibrillator

1. Paddle electrodes.
2. Controls for defibrillator.
3. Synchronizer switch.
4. Oscilloscope.
5. Paper strip recorder.
6. Patient cable and lead wires.
7. Controls for monitoring.

Monitoring Lead Uses Three Electrodes

1. Positive.
2. Negative.
3. Ground.

The Two Most Common Monitoring Leads

1. Lead II — provides the best view of P waves.
2. Lead MCLI — the best for determining the site of origin of the ectopics.

Monitoring Through Paddle Electrodes

1. These are used for a "quick look" in cardiac arrest and the unconscious patient.
2. They may be used when the patient cable is inoperative.
3. The paddle is more apt to pick up artifact than chest electrodes; place chest electrodes at the earliest convenience.
4. Procedure:
   - Turn on oscilloscope power.
   - Apply the conducting medium liberally to paddle surfaces, or position saline or gel pads.
   - Hold the paddles firmly on the chest wall at the right upper chest (negative electrode), and at the left lower chest (positive electrode).

- Observe, monitor, and obtain tracings.

Monitoring Using Chest Electrodes

1. Chest electrode placement for Lead II (see Figure 10-10a):
   - The positive electrode is placed on the left lower chest wall, two centimeters lateral to the midclavicular line at the fifth intercostal space.
   - The negative electrode is placed on the right upper chest wall, midclavicular inferior to the clavicle.
   - The ground electrode is placed on the right lower chest at the fifth intercostal space. (The ground location is not important.)
2. Chest electrode placement for Lead MCLI (see Figure 10-10b):
   - The positive electrode is placed on the right lower chest wall at the third or fourth intercostal space at the right border of the sternum.
   - The negative electrode is placed on the left upper chest wall, two centimeters lateral of the left midclavicular line and inferior to the clavicle.
   - The ground electrode is placed the same as for Lead II.
3. Chest electrode placement for Lead I (see Figure 10-10c):
   - The positive electrode is placed on the left upper chest wall, two centimeters lateral of the left midclavicular line and inferior to the clavicle.
   - The negative electrode is placed on the upper right chest wall on the midclavicular line inferior to the clavicle.
   - The ground electrode is placed the same as for Lead II.
4. Chest electrode placement for Lead III (see Figure 10-10d):
   - The positive electrode is placed on the left lower chest, two centimeters lateral to the midclavicular line at the fifth intercostal space.
   - The negative electrode is placed on the left upper chest wall, two centimeters lateral to the left midclavicular line and inferior to the clavicle.
   - The ground electrode is placed the same as for Lead II.
5. Avoid placing electrodes over large muscle masses, over large quantities of chest hair (shave small areas of chest hair), or any place that prohibits the electrode from lying flat on the skin.
6. Avoid placing electrodes in the same spot that the defibrillation paddles would be placed.
7. Cleanse the patient's skin with an alcohol swab and/or abrasive pad; it removes dirt and body oil for better adhesion and electrode-to-skin contact (for a clearer tracing). Dry the skin well since alcohol breaks down electrode adhesive.
8. Apply electrodes to the skin surface, and attach the ends of the lead wires to the electrodes. Select the desired lead if the monitor has a lead

Figure 10-10. Location for Chest Electrodes: A — Lead 2; B — MCLI; C — Lead 1; D — Lead 3.

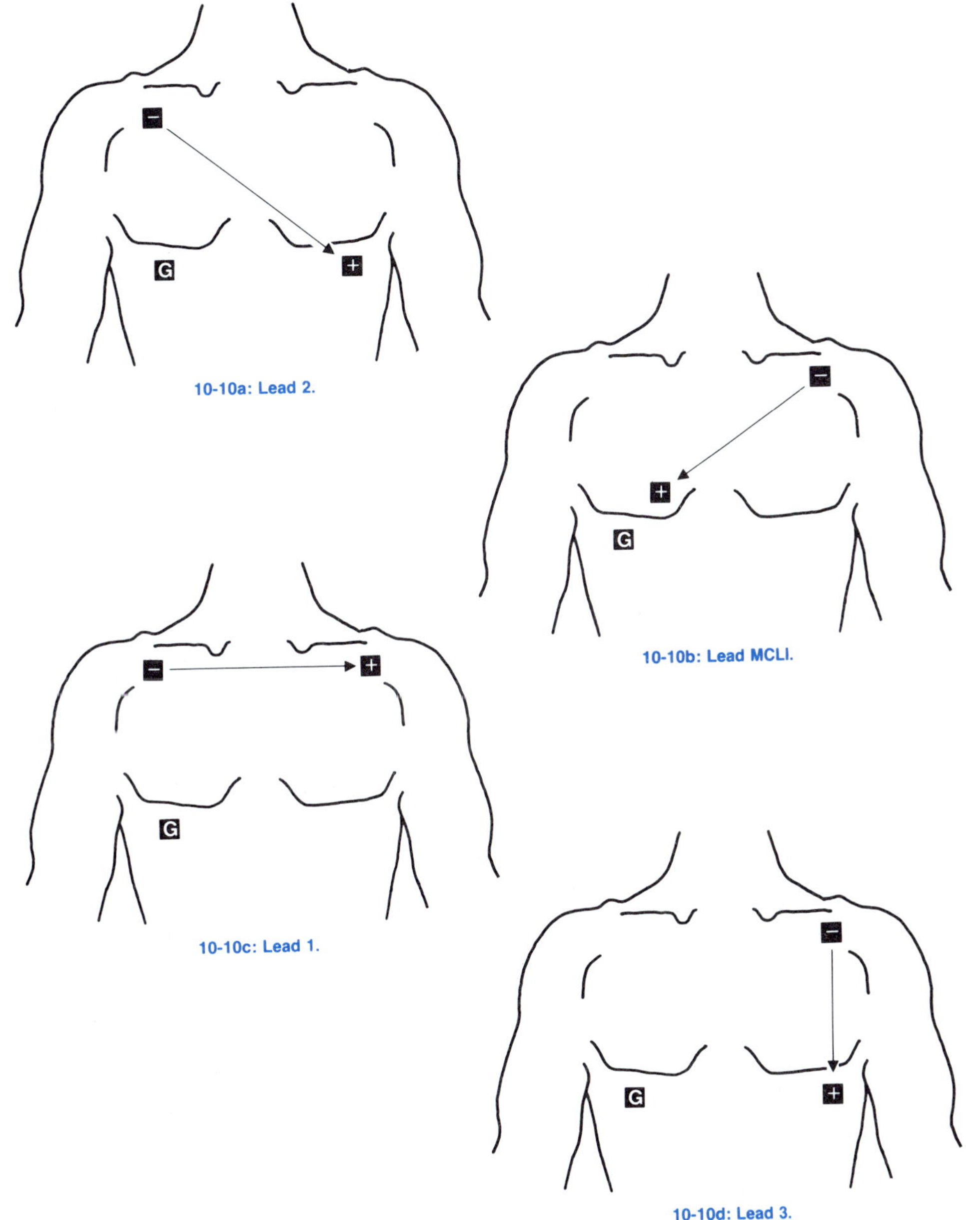

selector. Plug in the patient cable to the monitor.
9. Adjust gain or sensitivity to its proper level (calibrate).
10. The use of the audio control is optional — be sensitive to the patient's response to the QRS "beeper."

Causes of a Poor ECG Signal

1. The most common cause is poor electrode contact with the skin. Check for:
   - Excessive hair, especially in a diaphoretic patient.
   - A loose or dislodged electrode.
   - Dried conductive gel that comes on disposable electrodes.
   - Poor placement of the electrode over bony areas.
2. An initially poor tracing may improve with time as the conductive gel breaks down the skin's resistance.
3. Other causes of a poor tracing:
   - Patient movement or muscle tremor.
   - An inoperative patient cable.
   - A broken lead wire.
   - Faulty grounding.
   - A faulty monitor.

Obtaining a Paper Tracing

1. Adjust the heat of the stylus as necessary.
2. Adjust the calibration (standardization mark); a 1-mv signal; it should produce a 10-mm rise of ECG tracing (two large boxes).
3. It is a good practice to run a short "strip" on all monitored patients.

Analysis of a Normal Sinus Rhythm (NSR) Using a Lead II Rhythm Strip

1. Rate — 60 to 100 per minute.
2. Rhythm — regular (both P-P and R-R).
3. P waves — normal and upright; one P wave before each QRS, and one QRS after every P wave.
4. P-R interval — normal (0.12 to 0.20 second) and constant.
5. QRS — less than 0.12 second.
6. Interpretation — normal sinus rhythm.
7. Treatment — none.

Figure 10-11. Normal Sinus Rhythm.

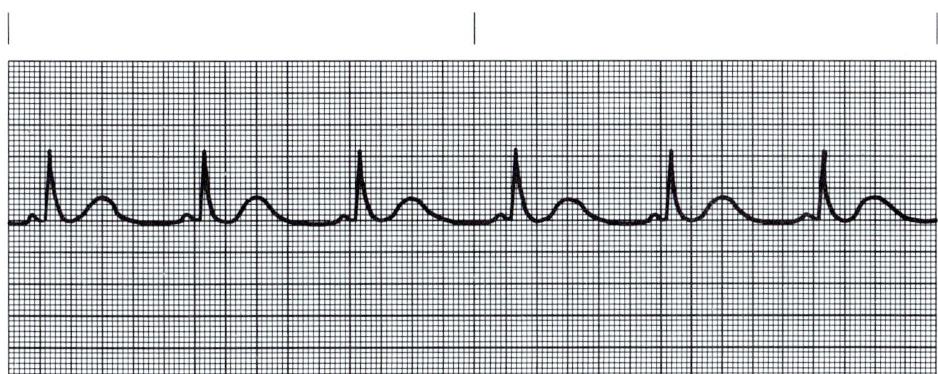

DYSRHYTHMIAS

Etiology

Conditions that may lead to dysrhythmias include:

1. Blood gas abnormalities:
   - Hypoxia.
   - Abnormal pH.
2. Myocardial ischemia or necrosis.
3. Autonomic nervous system imbalance.
4. Distention of the heart chambers.
5. Electrolyte imbalances.
6. Drug effects/toxicity.
7. Electrocution.
8. Hypothermia.
9. Central nervous system damage.
10. Normal occurrence; sinus arrhythmia.

No matter what the etiology or type of dysrhythmia, the patient and symptoms are treated, not merely the dysrhythmia.

Dysrhythmias Originating in the Sinoatrial Node

These include:

1. Sinus bradycardia.
2. Sinus tachycardia.
3. Sinus arrhythmia.
4. Sinus arrest.

ECG features common to all sinus rhythms include:

1. Upright P waves in Lead II, all with a similar appearance.
2. A P-R interval of normal duration.
3. A QRS complex of normal duration.

Sinus Bradycardia

This condition is the result of a slowing of the sinoatrial node.

1. Etiology:
   - Abnormal phenomena.
   - "Sick sinus syndrome."
   - Increased parasympathetic vagal tone.
   - Drug effects, such as those with the use of digitalis or propranolol.
2. Interpretation (using Lead II):
   - Rate — less than sixty per minute.
   - Rhythm — regular.
   - P waves — normal and upright; one P wave before each QRS.
   - P-R interval — normal (0.12 to 0.20 second) and constant.
   - QRS complex — normal, each preceded by a P wave.
3. Clinical significance: in healthy individuals may simply reflect good physical condition; in the elderly or in the setting of a myocardial infarction, a decreased rate may compromise cardiac output and result in hypotension, angina, or central nervous system symptoms.
4. Treatment (see Figure 10-12):
   - Unnecessary if blood pressure is normal and there is no ventricular irritability.
   - If hypotension is present (a systolic blood pressure of less than 90 mmHg), especially with a weak pulse, diaphoresis, a decreased level of consciousness, or if PVCs are present, treat with atropine (see Appendix 1).
   - If atropine is not effective in the symptomatic patient, isoproterenol may be ordered by the physician. Use with caution.
   - The sequence for bradycardia (see Figure 10-12) was developed to

Figure 10-12

Bradycardia

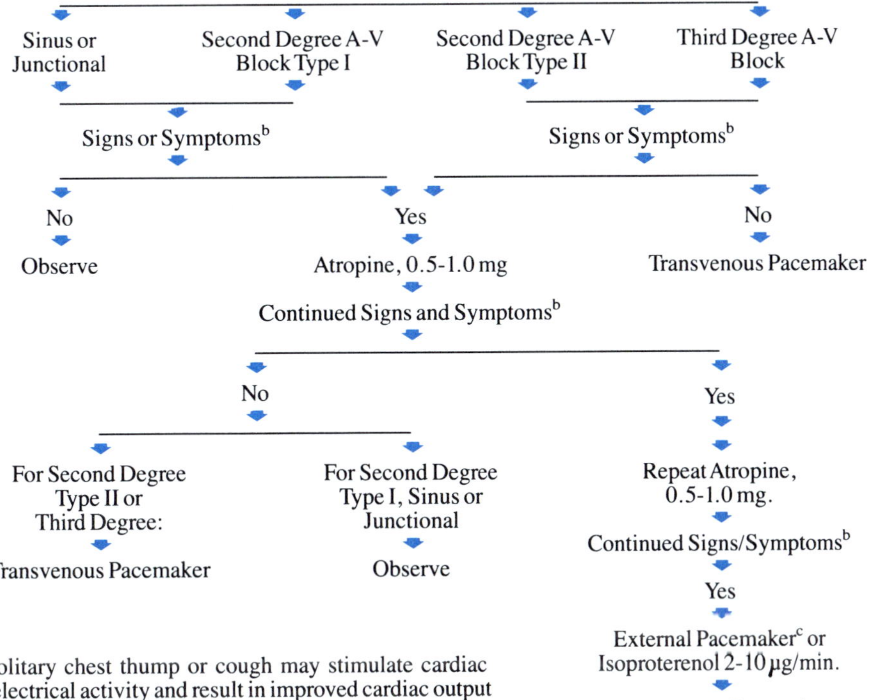

[a] A solitary chest thump or cough may stimulate cardiac electrical activity and result in improved cardiac output and may be used at this point.

[b] Hypotension (blood pressure less than 90 mmHg), premature ventricular contractions, altered mental status or symptoms (e.g., chest pain or dyspnea), ischemia, or infarction.

[c] Temporizing therapy.

Figure 10-13. Sinus Bradycardia.

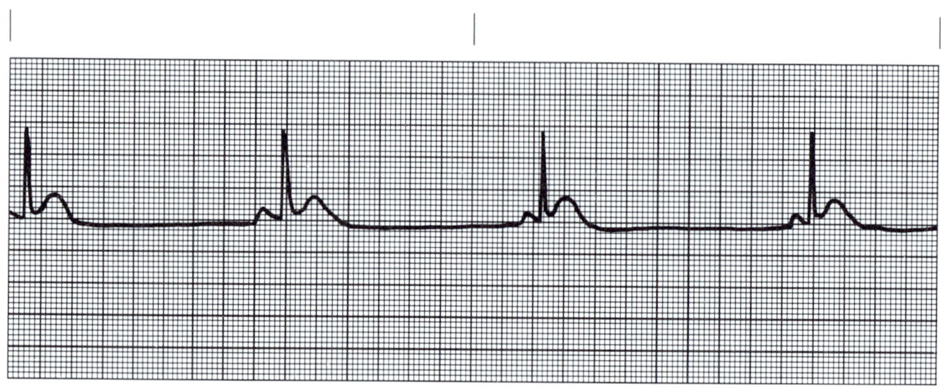

assist in teaching how to treat a broad range of patients with bradycardia. Some patients may require care not specified herein. This algorithm should not be construed to prohibit such flexibility.

Sinus Tachycardia

This is the result of an increase in the rate of sinus node discharge.

1. Etiology — this condition may be due to multiple factors, including:
   - Exercise — a normal occurrence.
   - Fever.
   - Anxiety, pain.
   - Hypovolemia, hypoxia.
   - Congestive heart failure.
   - Certain drugs.
2. Interpretation (using Lead II):
   - Rate — greater than 100 per minute (usually up to 160).
   - Rhythm — regular.
   - P waves — normal and upright; one before each QRS (at this high rate, the P wave may be buried in the T wave so that it will not be seen).
   - P-R interval — normal (0.12 to 0.20 second) and constant.
   - QRS complex — normal (less than 0.12 second).
3. Clinical significance:
   - May be benign.

Figure 10-14. Sinus Tachycardia.

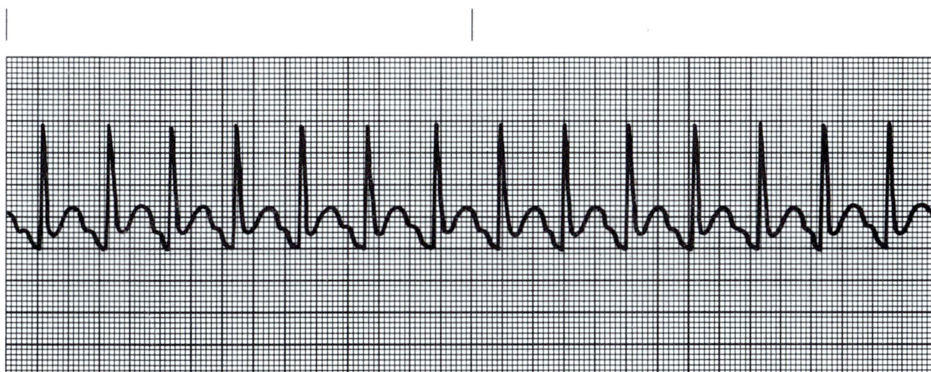

- May be a compensatory mechanism for decreased stroke volume.
- Increases myocardial oxygen consumption.

4. Treatment: treat the underlying cause.

Sinus Arrhythmia

This is a normal phenomenon that causes a slight variation in the sinus rate.

1. Etiology:
   - May be related to the parasympathetic effects of the respiratory cycle (with inspiration, the heart rate normally increases).
   - Nonrespiratory influence is a normal phenomenon.
   - May be a result of enhanced vagal tone.
2. Interpretation (using Lead II):
   - Rate — usually 60 to 100 per minute (in respiratory form, the rate increases with inspiration and decreases with expiration).
   - Rhythm — irregular.
   - P waves — normal and upright; one before each QRS.
   - P-R interval — normal (0.12 to 0.20 second) and constant.
   - QRS complex — normal (less than 0.12 second); each QRS is preceded by a P wave.
3. Clinical significance: normal phenomenon, particularly in young or aged.
4. Treatment: none.

Figure 10-15. Sinus Arrhythmia.

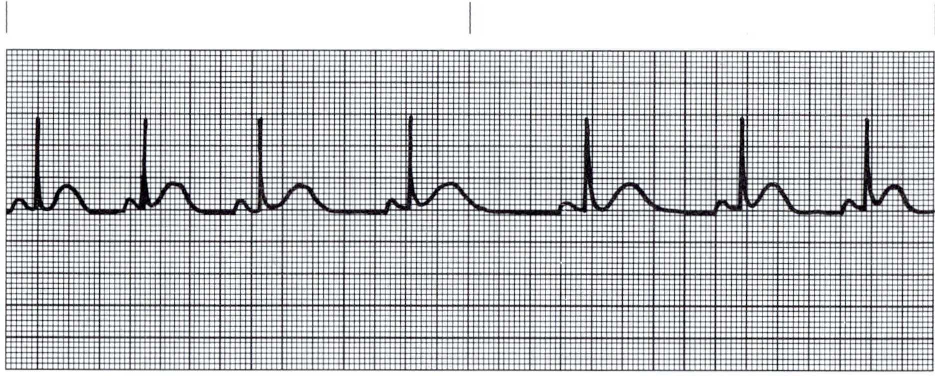

Sinus Arrest

In this case, the sinus node fails to discharge, resulting in missed beats or, at its worst, cardiac standstill. In the more extreme form, a lower pacemaker will often discharge (escape beats) until the sinus node resumes firing.

1. Etiology:
   - Sinus node ischemia.
   - Digitalis toxicity.
   - Excessive vagal tone.
   - Degenerative fibrotic disease.
   - Hypoxia.
2. Interpretation (using Lead II):
   - Rate — normal or slow.
   - Rhythm — irregular.
   - P waves — normal, where present, preceding each QRS; if the sino-atrial node does not discharge, the entire P-QRS-T complex will be absent.
   - P-R interval — normal (0.12 to 0.20 second) and constant when present.
   - QRS complex — normal (less than 0.12 second), each preceded by a P wave.
3. Clinical significance:
   - Frequent or prolonged episodes may reduce cardiac output (rate below

Figure 10-16. Sinoatrial Arrest or Block.

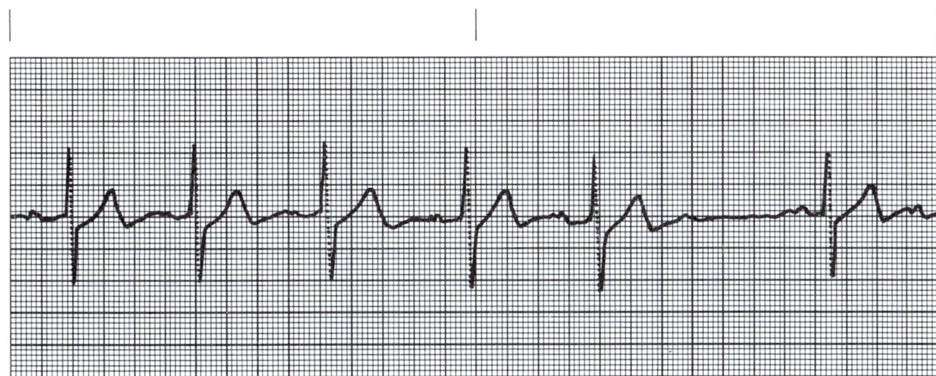

thirty to fifty per minute), causing hypotension.
- Very slow rates enhance electrical instability (e.g., escape ventricular ectopy).
- Danger of complete cessation of sinus node activity.

4. Treatment:
   - If the patient is asymptomatic (patient is normotensive and has no ventricular irregularities), observe only.
   - If the patient is bradycardic and symptomatic (e.g., hypotensive, pale, sweaty, confused, and/or ventricular ectopic), use atropine.

Dysrhythmias Originating in the Atria

These include:

1. Wandering pacemaker.
2. Premature atrial complex.
3. Paroxysmal or atrial tachycardia.
4. Atrial flutter.
5. Atrial fibrillation.

ECG features common to all atrial dysrhythmias include:

1. P waves differ in appearance from sinus P waves.
2. QRS complexes of normal duration are less than 0.12 second.

Wandering Pacemaker

This is the passive transfer of pacemaker sites from the sinus node to other latent pacemaker sites in the atrial and atrioventricular junction.

1. Etiology:
   - A variant of sinus arrhythmia — often a normal phenomenon in the young or aged.
   - May be associated with underlying heart disease.
   - May be due to an overdose of digitalis.
2. Interpretation (using Lead II):
   - Rate — usually 60 to 100 per minute.
   - Rhythm — slightly irregular.
   - P waves — morphology changes from beat to beat; may disappear completely.
   - P-R interval — varies and may become less than 0.12 second.
   - QRS complex — normal (less than 0.12 second), each preceded by a P wave.
3. Clinical significance: generally no detrimental effects.
4. Treatment: none.

Premature Atrial Complex (PAC)

This occurs when a single electrical impulse originates in the atria outside the sinus node, creating a premature complex before the next expected sinus

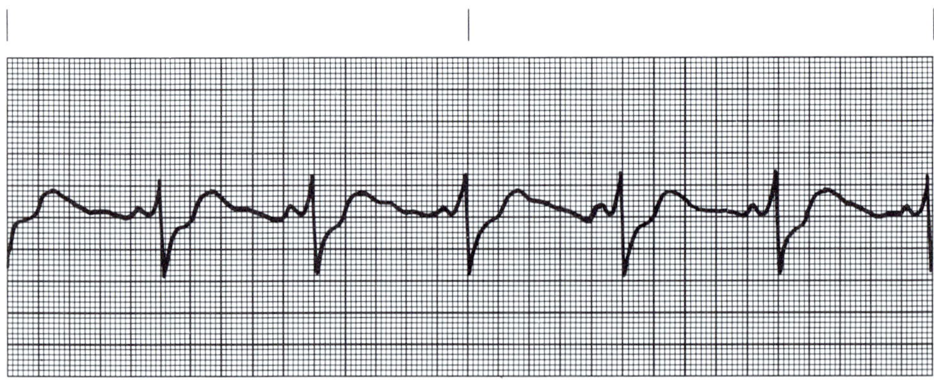

Figure 10-17. Wandering Pacemaker.

beat. It usually depolarizes the sinoatrial node and creates a compensatory pause.

1. Etiology:
   - Use of caffeine, tobacco, alcohol.
   - Sympathomimetic drugs.
   - Hypoxia.
   - Digitalis toxicity.
   - Organic heart disease.
   - Can be a normal phenomenon.
2. Interpretation (using Lead II):
   - Rate — depends on the underlying rhythm.
   - Rhythm — usually regular except for the premature atrial contraction (PAC), described as occasionally irregular. (The rhythm actually depends on the underlying rhythm.)
   - P waves — the P wave of the PAC differs in shape from the sinus P wave and occurs earlier than the next sinus P wave would be expected; it may be hidden in the preceding T wave.
   - P-R interval — usually normal, but may be greater than 0.20 second.
   - QRS complex — usually less than 0.12 second. It may be greater than 0.12 second if the PAC is abnormally conducted through partially refracted ventricles.
3. Clinical significance:
   - Isolated PACs of minimal significance.

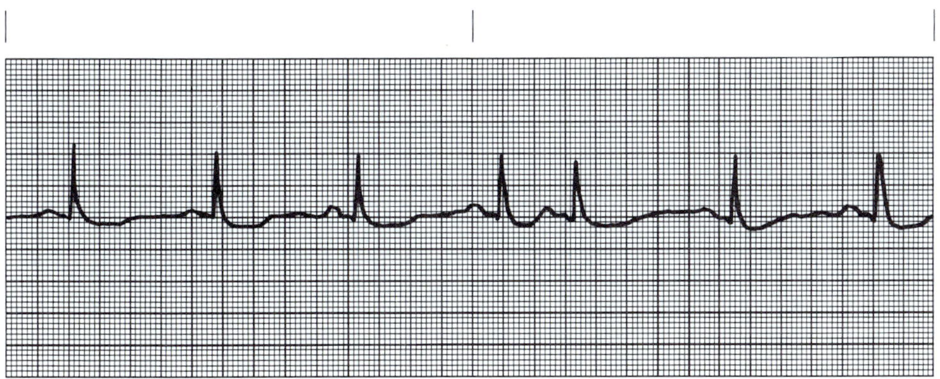

Figure 10-18. Premature Atrial Complex (PAC).

- Frequent PACs may suggest atrial irritability and be the forerunners of other more serious atrial dysrhythmias.

4. Treatment: none.

Paroxysmal Atrial Tachycardia (PAT)

PAT occurs when rapid atrial depolarization overrides the sinoatrial node with a sudden onset (lasting minutes to hours) and abrupt termination. The condition is often termed paroxysmal supraventricular (meaning above the ventricles) tachycardia because it may be indistinguishable from an atrioventricular junctional tachycardia.

1. Etiology:
   - In many cases the cause is unknown.
   - Damage to the sinoatrial or atrioventricular nodes.
   - Digitalis overdose.
   - Stress, overexertion, smoking, drinking coffee.
2. Interpretation (using Lead II):
   - Rate — 150 to 250 per minute.
   - Rhythm — characteristically regular.
   - P waves — abnormal (atrial P wave looks different than sinus P wave) or absent.
   - P-R interval — may be normal or shortened (depends on the distance the ectopic focus is to the atrioventricular node) and constant.
   - QRS complex — normal (less than 0.12 second).
3. Clinical significance:
   - May be tolerated well for a short period of time or in young hearts with good cardiac reserve.
   - Rapid rates may cause significant compromise of cardiac output and coronary artery perfusion.
   - May precipitate angina, hypotension, or congestive heart failure.
4. Treatment (see Figure 10-19):
   - Vagal maneuvers — valsalva maneuver: straining against a closed glottis (bearing down); carotid sinus massage: see page 278, this chapter; do only with direct physician's order.
   - Immersion of the patient's face in ice water (due to the mammalian diving reflex, the heart may slow down); do only with direct physician's order.
   - Verapamil may be ordered if the vagal maneuvers were unsuccessful in converting the patient. Do only with direct physician's order.

Figure 10-19

Paroxysmal Supraventricular Tachycardia (PSVT)

This sequence was developed to assist in teaching how to treat a broad range of patients with sustained PSVT. Some patients may require care not specified herein. This algorithm should not be construed as prohibiting such flexibility. Flow of algorithm presumes PSVT is continuing.

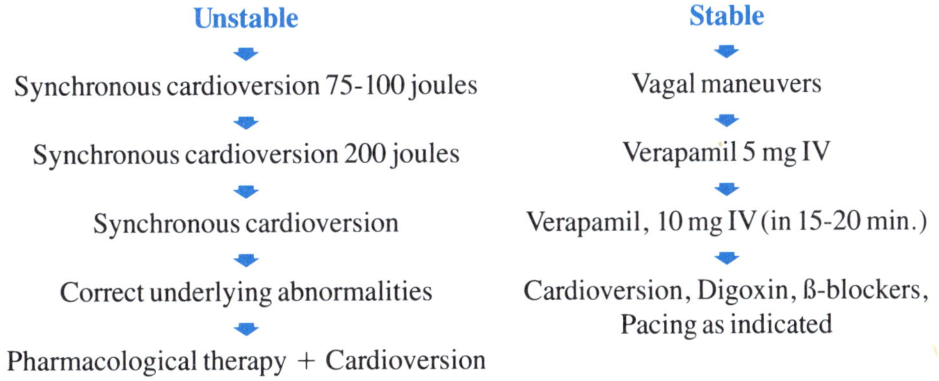

If conversion occurs but PSVT recurs, repeated electrical cardioversion is *not* indicated. Sedation should be used as time permits.

Figure 10-20. Paroxysmal Atrial Tachycardia (PAT).

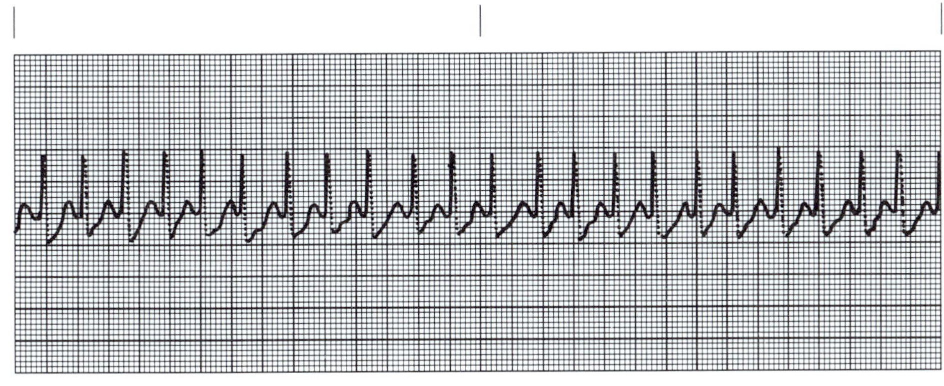

- Cardioversion — indicated in the severely compromised patient (shock, congestive heart failure, stupor, or coma) when transport time may be more than ten minutes; do only with direct physician's order. See page 276 of this chapter.

Atrial Flutter

Atrial flutter is a rhythm resulting from rapid atrial stimulation (between 250 to 350 per minute) and an atrioventricular node that physiologically cannot conduct all of the impulses. The atrioventricular junction conducts impulses in 1:1 (rare), 2:1, 3:1, and 4:1 ratios, resulting in a difference between atrial and ventricular rates. AV block may be constant or variable.

1. Etiology:
   - Usually associated with some underlying heart disease.
   - Damage to the sinoatrial node or atria.
   - Congestive heart failure.
2. Interpretation (using Lead II):
   - Rate — atrial rate of 250 to 350 per minute; ventricular rate varies (may be 140 to 160 in the untreated patient and under 100 in the treated patient).
   - Rhythm — atrial rhythm is regular; ventricular rate is usually regular but may be irregular if there is varying conduction.
   - P waves — no true P waves are present; flutter (F) waves resemble "sawtooth" pattern.
   - P-R interval (really the F-R interval) — usually constant but may vary.
   - QRS complex — usually normal (less than 0.12 second); a QRS may follow every second, third, or fourth F wave. Aberrant conduction can occur.
3. Clinical significance:
   - Normal ventricular rates are usually tolerated well.
   - Rapid ventricular rates may compromise cardiac output with associated symptoms.
4. Treatment:
   - If the patient is asymptomatic (i.e., without hypotension, confusion, or cool and clammy skin), no treatment is indicated.
   - Indicated only for rapid ventricular rates with hemodynamic compromise (i.e., with hypotension, confusion, or cool and clammy skin). Synchronized cardioversion (atrial flutter responds well to low energies) may be indicated. Remember — synchronized cardioversion is

Figure 10-21. Atrial Flutter.

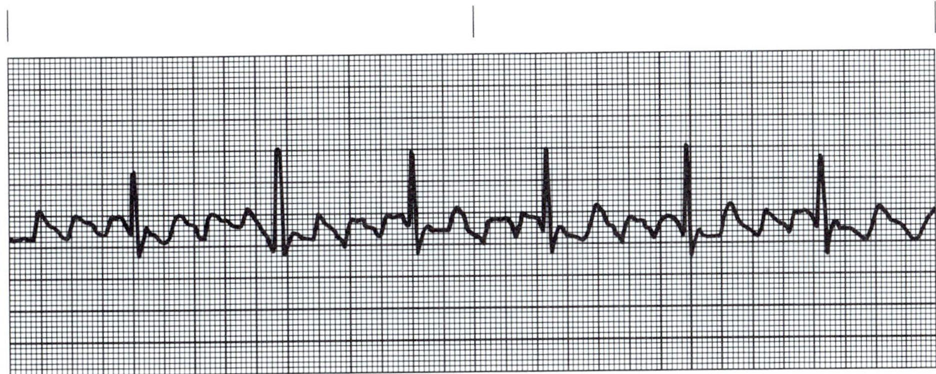

hazardous to the digitalized patient. Use only with direct physician's order.

- Consider verapamil to control the ventricular rate (it may be contraindicated, however). Use only with direct physician's order.

Atrial Fibrillation

Atrial fibrillation is a rhythm resulting from multiple ectopic foci bombarding (400 to 700 per minute) the atrioventricular node, which physiologically cannot handle all of the impulses. The atrioventricular node conduction is random, and ventricular response is highly variable.

1. Etiology — usually associated with underlying heart disease:
   - Valvular heart disease.
   - Hypertensive heart disease.
   - Coronary artery disease (CAD).
2. Interpretation (using Lead II):
   - Rate — atrial rate of 400 to 700 per minute (cannot be counted); in the nondigitalized patient (uncontrolled), the ventricular rate is usually between 160 to 180 per minute. In the digitalized patient (controlled), the ventricular rate is usually under 100.
   - Rhythm — irregularly irregular.
   - P waves — no P waves present; instead, there are fibrillatory waves (f waves), resulting in chaotic atrial activity.

Figure 10-22. Atrial Fibrillation.

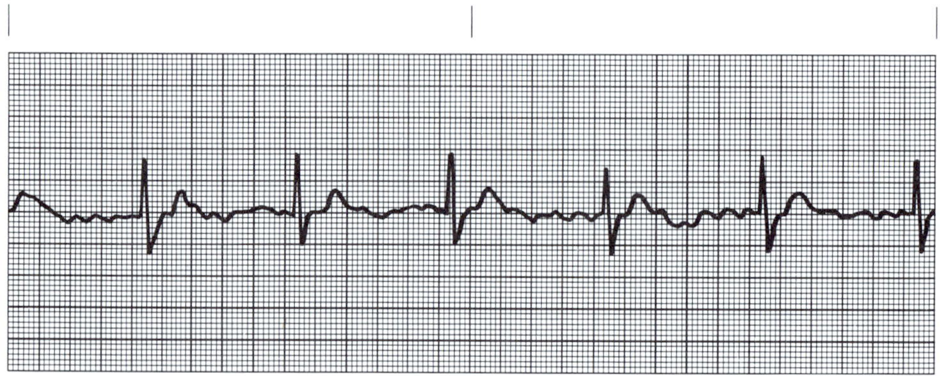

- P-R interval — none.
- QRS complex — normal (less than 0.12 second) unless aberrant conduction occurs.

3. Clinical significance:
   - The atria do not contract, so the normal atrial "kick" is lost. Cardiac output is decreased by 20 to 25 percent.
   - If the rate of ventricular response is normal (often in patients on digitalis), the rhythm is usually well tolerated.
   - A rapid ventricular response, coupled with the loss of the atrial kick, can cause further cardiovascular decompensation (i.e., angina, infarct, congestive heart failure, or shock).
   - A ventricular response of less than sixty may compromise cardiac output; suspect digitalis toxicity.
4. Treatment for rapid ventricular rates with patient decompensation:
   - Synchronized cardioversion by direct physician's order only.
   - Report if the patient is taking digitalis.
   - Consider verapamil (may be contraindicated) by direct physician's order only.

Dysrhythmias Originating in the Atrioventricular Junction

These include:

1. Premature junctional complexes.

2. Junctional escape complexes and rhythm.
3. Accelerated junctional rhythm.
4. Paroxysmal junctional tachycardia.

ECG features common to all junctional rhythms include the following:

1. P waves will be inverted in Lead II because of retrograde depolarization of the atria (impulse moving toward the negative electrode). The relationship of the P wave to the QRS is dependent on the timing of atrial depolarization in relationship to ventricular depolarization. The P wave may occur:
   - Before the QRS — the atria are depolarized first.
   - After the QRS — the ventricles are depolarized first.
   - During the QRS — the atria and ventricles depolarize simultaneously; no P waves are apparent.
   - Some low pacemaker sites (i.e., close to the atrioventricular node) can also create inverted P waves.
2. The QRS complexes are of normal duration (less than 0.12 second).
3. The P-R intervals, if present, are less than 0.12 second.

Premature Junctional (Nodal) Complex (PJC)

This is a single electrical impulse that originates in the atrioventricular junction and occurs before the next expected sinus impulse. This usually results in retrograde depolarization of the atria (P wave will be negative in Leads II and III).

1. Etiology:
   - Use of caffeine, tobacco, or alcohol.
   - Sympathomimetic drugs.
   - Hypoxia.
   - Digitalis toxicity.
   - Organic heart disease.
   - Can be a normal phenomenon.
2. Interpretation (using Lead II):
   - Rate — depends on the rate of the underlying rhythm, along with the number of PJCs.
   - Rhythm — irregular; the PJC is preceded by a shorter-than-normal R-R interval (a noncompensatory pause).
   - P waves — may be absent or present; if present, they differ from the normal sinus P waves in shape, size, and direction. They may be

Figure 10-23. Premature Junctional Contraction.

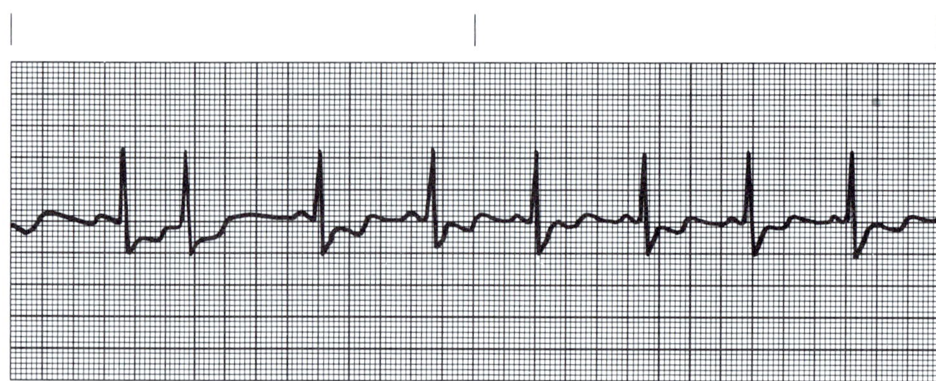

present before, during, or after the QRS complex of the PJC.
- P-R interval — the P-R interval of the PJC, if present, is less than 0.12 second.
- QRS complex — normal (less than 0.12 second).

3. Clinical significance:
   - Isolated PJCs are of no significance.
   - Frequent PJCs may be forerunners of more serious junctional dysrhythmias.
4. Treatment: none.

Junctional Escape Complexes

This is a complex or rhythm (if it is a series of complexes) that results when the impulse from the primary pacemaker, the sinoatrial node, does not reach the atrioventricular node in 1.0 to 1.5 seconds. This occurs if the sinoatrial node is not firing properly or when there is a conduction disturbance. The escape complexes serve as a safety mechanism. The atrioventricular node discharges at an intrinsic rate of forty to sixty per minute.

1. Etiology:
   - Increased vagal tone, causing sinoatrial slowing.
   - Damage to the sinus node or heart block.
   - Digitalis toxicity.
   - Acute myocardial infarction.
   - Hypoxia.

Figure 10-24. Junctional Escape Complexes.

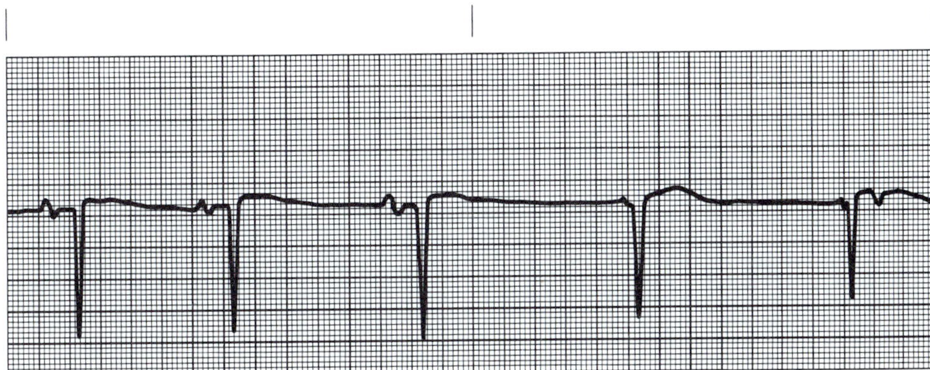

2. Interpretation (using Lead II):
   - Rate — forty to sixty per minute.
   - Rhythm — it is irregular if there is a single junctional escape complex; it is regular if it is a junctional escape rhythm.
   - P waves — negative P waves (seen in Leads II and III) may be seen before, during, or after the QRS complex.
   - P-R interval — it may be variable or constant, and if a P wave precedes QRS, it is less than 0.12 second.
   - QRS complex — usually normal (less than 0.12 second).
3. Clinical significance:
   - A slow rate can cause decreased cardiac output and associated symptoms, or it may be well tolerated.
   - Very slow rates enhance electrical instability of the ventricles.
4. Treatment:
   - If the patient is stable and asymptomatic, no treatment is required.
   - In the symptomatic patient (i.e., hypotension, confusion, etc.), administer atropine by direct physician's order only.
   - If atropine is ineffective, consider using isoproterenol by direct physician's order only.

Accelerated Junctional Rhythm (PSVT)

This is a rhythm that results from increased automaticity of the atrioventricular junction, causing it to discharge faster than its intrinsic rate and overriding the primary pacemaker. This is technically a junctional tachycardia but is not in the rate range for tachycardias.

1. Etiology:
   - Commonly due to ischemia of the atrioventricular junction.
   - Digitalis toxicity.
2. Interpretation (using Lead II):
   - Rate — 60 to 100 per minute.
   - Rhythm — regular.
   - P waves — negative P waves (seen in Leads II and III) may be seen before, during, or after the QRS complex.
   - P-R interval — it is constant when the P wave precedes QRS, and it is usually less than 0.12 second.
   - QRS complex — usually normal (less than 0.12 second).
3. Clinical significance: if a normal rate is present, the rhythm is usually well tolerated.
4. Treatment: none.

Paroxysmal Junctional Tachycardia (A Form of PSVT)

This is a rhythm produced by increased automaticity or a reentry circuit in the atrioventricular junction, resulting in a rapid tachycardia. It often has a sudden onset and termination and is usually indistinguishable from a PAT. Thus, it may be called paroxysmal supraventricular tachycardia (PSVT).

1. Etiology:
   - Digitalis toxicity.
   - Damage to the sinoatrial or atrioventricular nodes.
   - Unknown cause.
2. Interpretation (using Lead II):
   - Rate — 100 to 180 per minute.
   - Rhythm — regular.
   - P waves — if visible, inverted (negative), and may occur before, during, or after the QRS.
   - P-R interval — if P wave precedes QRS, it is less than 0.12 second.
   - QRS complex — usually normal (less than 0.12 second).
3. Clinical significance:
   - May be tolerated well for a short period of time or in young hearts with good cardiac reserve.
   - Rapid rates may cause significant compromise of cardiac output and coronary artery perfusion.

Figure 10-25. Paroxysmal AV Junctional Tachycardia.

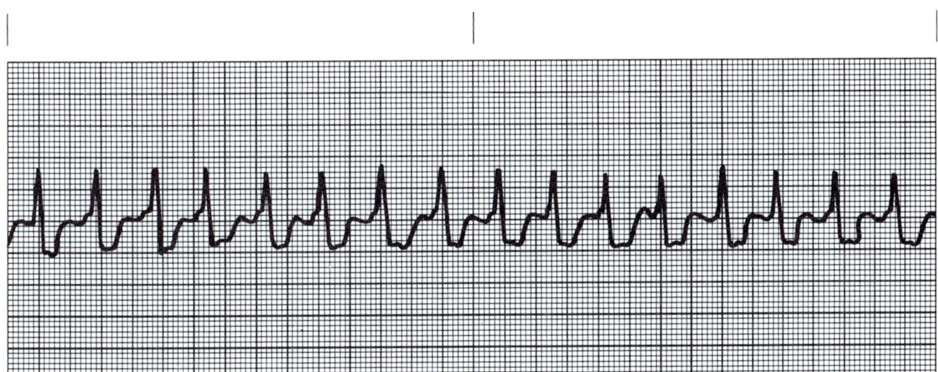

- May precipitate angina, hypotension, or congestive heart failure.

4. Treatment:
   - Vagal maneuvers — valsalva maneuver: straining against a closed glottis (bearing down); carotid sinus massage: see page 278, this chapter; do only with direct physician's order.
   - Immersion of the patient's face in ice water (due to the mammalian diving reflex, the heart may slow down); do only with direct physician's order.
   - Verapamil may be ordered if the vagal maneuvers were unsuccessful in converting the patient. Do only with direct physician's order.
   - Cardioversion — indicated in the severely compromised patient (shock, congestive heart failure, stupor, or coma) when transport time may be more than ten minutes; do only with direct physician's order. See page 276, this chapter.

Dysrhythmias Originating in the Ventricles

These include:

1. Ventricular escape complex.
2. Premature ventricular complex (PVC).
3. Ventricular tachycardia (VT).
4. Ventricular fibrillation (VF).
5. Asystole (cardiac standstill).
6. Artificial pacemaker rhythms.

ECG features common to all ventricular rhythms include the following:

1. QRS complexes will be 0.12 second or greater in duration.
2. P waves will be absent.

Ventricular Escape Complex (or Rhythm)

This is a complex or rhythm that results when impulses from higher pacemakers fail to reach ventricles, or when the rate of discharge of higher pacemakers becomes less than that of the ventricles. It is called a ventricular escape beat or rhythm (if there is a series of complexes), which serves as a safety mechanism. Ventricles discharge at an intrinsic rate of twenty to forty per minute. If the beat is singular, the distance from the last normal beat to the escape beat is greater than the normal R-R interval.

1. Etiology:
   - Slowing of the supraventricular pacemaker sites.
   - High degree of atrioventricular block.
   - Frequently seen as the first organized rhythm following defibrillation.
2. Interpretation (using Lead II):
   - Rate — twenty to forty per minute (occasionally less).
   - Rhythm — if there is a single escape beat, the rhythm is irregular. If there is an escape rhythm, it is usually regular, but the ventricular pacemaker site can be unreliable. The ventricles are capable of developing an increased rate of up to 100 beats per minute — called an accelerated idioventricular rhythm.
   - P waves — none.
   - P-R interval — none.
   - QRS complex — usually wide and bizarre (0.12 second or greater).
3. Clinical significance:
   - Cardiac output can be severely compromised based on the slow rate alone.
   - Serves as a safety mechanism — **do not attempt to suppress.**
   - It may be perfusing or nonperfusing.
4. Treatment:
   - If perfusing, increase the rate by using atropine by direct physician's order only.
   - If unsuccessful, consider isoproterenol by direct physician's order only.
   - Lidocaine is **contraindicated.**
   - If nonperfusing, a sequence has been developed to assist in teaching

Figure 10-26. Ventricular Escape Complex.

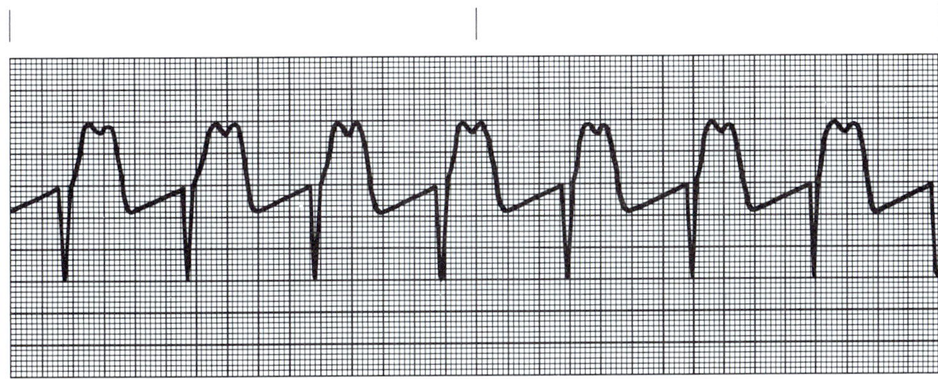

how to treat a broad range of patients with asystole. Some patients may require care not specified herein. This algorithm should not be construed to prohibit such flexibility. Flow of algorithm presumes that asystole is continuing. (See Figure 10-4 on page 214.)

Premature Ventricular Complex (PVC)

This is a single ectopic impulse that arises from one or more irritable foci in either ventricle and that occurs earlier than the next expected sinus beat. It is usually the result of an irritable ventricle. The altered sequence of ventricular depolarization results in a wide, bizarre QRS complex with the T wave pointing in the opposite direction of QRS.

The PVC usually does not depolarize the sinoatrial node or interrupt its rhythm, so the pause following the PVC is fully compensatory. (The distance between R waves of the normal beats flanking the PVC equals two R-R intervals of the underlying rhythm.)

Occasionally, the PVC fails between two sinus beats without interrupting the rhythm. This is called an interpolated PVC.

The PVC may be uniform, originating from a single focus. In this case, all the PVCs will appear the same. The PVCs may also be multiform; that is, originating from more than one irritable focus in the ventricles. This results in PVCs of varying shapes. Multiform (multifocal) PVCs may be a greater danger to the patient than uniform PVCs.

The following frequently occur in patterns of grouped beating:

1. Bigeminy — every other beat is a PVC.

2. Trigeminy — every third beat is a PVC.
3. Quadrigeminy — every fourth beat is a PVC.

(These terms can also describe patterns of PACs and PJCs.)

There are also runs of PVCs in couplets or triples. These may also be called runs of ventricular tachycardia.

1. Etiology:
   - Myocardial ischemia.
   - Acute myocardial infarction.
   - Hypoxia.
   - Acid-base and electrolyte imbalances.
   - Increased sympathetic tone.
   - May be normally occurring.
2. Interpretation (using Lead II):
   - Rate — depends on the underlying rhythm and number of PVCs.
   - Rhythm — irregular rhythm interrupts the regularity of the underlying rhythm (most PVCs are followed by a compensatory pause).
   - P waves — absent before the PVC; normal sinus P waves may be seen near a PVC if they are there in the underlying rhythm.
   - P-R interval — none, because there are no P waves preceding the PVC.
   - QRS complex — the width is 0.12 second or greater; it is bizarre in shape; the S-T segment and T wave are commonly opposite to the QRS.
3. Clinical significance:
   - PVCs in patients without underlying heart disease may be of no significance.
   - In patients with myocardial ischemia (AMI), PVCs indicate ventricular irritability and may trigger lethal ventricular dysrhythmias.
   - Incompletely filled ventricles may produce little or no pulse (pulse deficit). Frequent occurrences of PVCs may result in compromised cardiac output (hypotension).
   - Can trigger lethal ventricular dysrhythmias if they occur during the relative refractory phase of the cardiac cycle (R-on-T phenomenon), causing ventricular fibrillation.
   - Frequent PVCs (six or more per minute) are dangerous.
   - Bigeminy PVCs are dangerous.
   - Multiformed PVCs are dangerous.
   - Salvos of two or more PVCs are dangerous (may lead to ventricular tachycardia or ventricular fibrillation).
   - PVCs may be sensed by the patients as ''skipped beats'' or palpitations.
4. Treatment (see Figure 10-27):

Figure 10-27

Ventricular Ectopy: Acute Suppressive Therapy

Assess for Need for Acute Suppressive Therapy

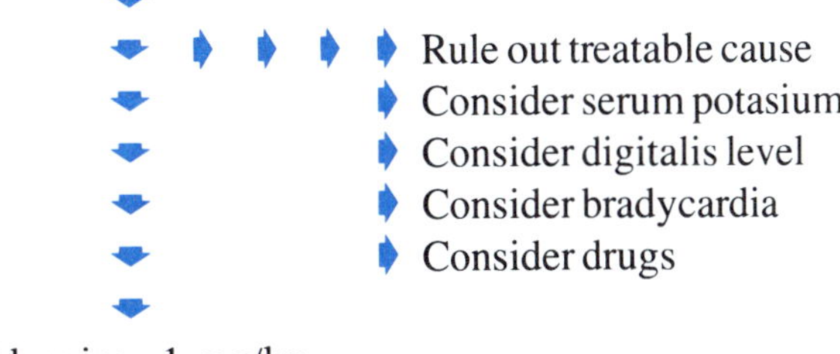

Lidocaine, 1 mg/kg

If not suppressed,
Repeat lidocaine, 0.5 mg/kg every 2-5 min., until no ectopy, or up to 3 mg/kg given

If not suppressed,
Procainamide 20 mg/min. until no ectopy, or up to 1,000 mg given

If not suppressed, and not contraindicated,
bretylium, 5-10 mg;kg over 8-10 min.

If not suppressed, consider overdrive pacing

Once ectopy resolved, maintain as follows:

After lidocaine, 1 mg/kg .... Lidocaine drip, 2 mg/min.
After lidocaine, 1-2 mg/kg .... Lidocaine drip, 3 mg/min.
After lidocaine, 2-3 mg/kg .... Lidocaine drip, 4 mg/min.
After procainamide .... Procainamide drip, 1-4 mg/min. (check blood level)
After bretylium .... Bretylium drip, 2 mg/min.

This sequence was developed to assist in teaching how to treat a broad range of patients with ventricular ectopy. Some patients may require therapy not specified herein. This algorithm should not be construed as prohibiting such flexibility.

Figure 10-28. Premature Ventricular Contractions: Examples.

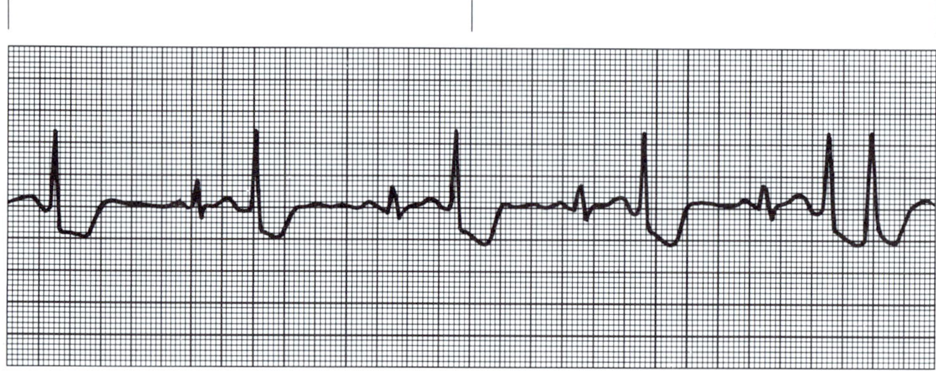

A: Unifocal

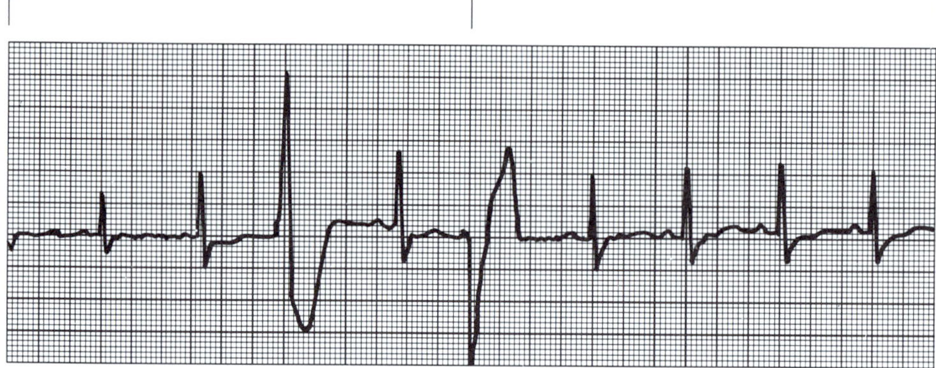

B: Multiformed

- If there are no history or symptoms of cardiac disease, no treatment is required.
- In patients with a cardiac history and/or symptoms, administer a lidocaine bolus, followed by an infusion by direct physician's order only. If unsuccessful at suppressing ectopy after repeated boluses of lidocaine, consider procainamide (if available), or bretylium, by direct physician's order only.

Ventricular Tachycardia

This is a rhythm created by three or more ventricular complexes in succession at a rate of 100 beats per minute or more. The atria and ventricles are functioning independent of each other. Sinus P waves may occasionally be seen but are dissociated from the QRS complexes.

1. Etiology — same as for PVCs.
2. Interpretation (using Lead II):
   - Rate — between 100 to 220 per minute.
   - Rhythm — is usually regular.
   - P waves — none associated with QRS complexes, although some may be visible.
   - P-R interval — none.
   - QRS complex — width is 0.12 second or greater; bizarre in shape; the S-T segment and T wave are commonly opposite to the QRS.
3. Clinical significance:
   - Usually results in poor stroke volume; this, coupled with a rapid rate, may severely compromise cardiac output and coronary artery perfusion.
   - Increases the workload of the heart, including myocardial oxygen consumption, which may lead to serious consequences (acute myocardial infarction, congestive heart failure, shock, myocardial ischemia).
   - May deteriorate to ventricular fibrillation.
   - May be perfusing or nonperfusing.
4. Treatment (see Figure 10-30):

Figure 10-29. Ventricular Tachycardia.

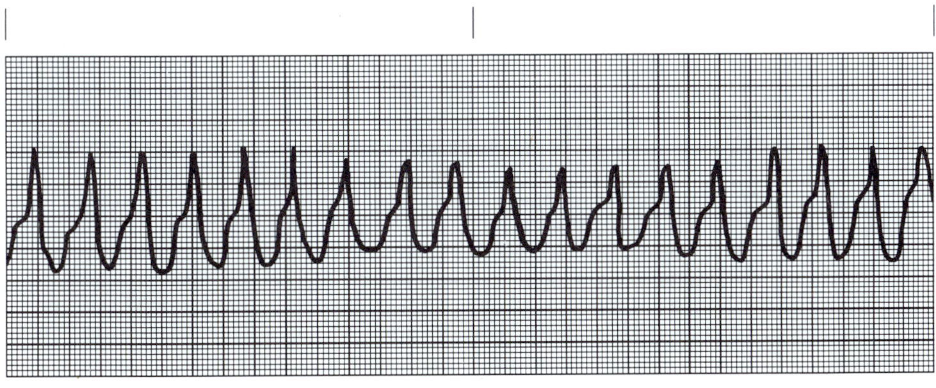

Figure 10-30

Sustained Ventricular Tachycardia (VT)

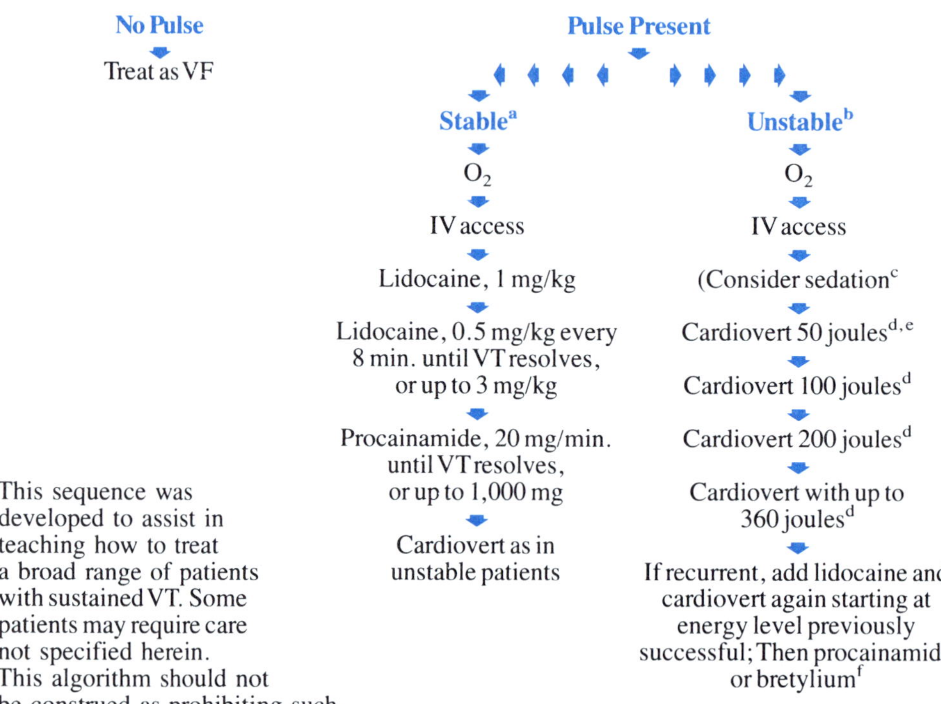

This sequence was developed to assist in teaching how to treat a broad range of patients with sustained VT. Some patients may require care not specified herein. This algorithm should not be construed as prohibiting such flexibility. Flow of algorithm presumes that VT is continuing. VF indicates ventricular fibrillation.

[a] If patient becomes unstable (see footnote b for definition) at any time, move to "Unstable" arm of algorithm.

[b] Unstable indicates symptoms (e.g., chest pain or dyspnea), hypotension (systolic blood pressure less than 90 mmHg), congestive heart failure, ischemia, or infarction.

[c] Sedation should be considered for all patients, including those defined in footnote b as unstable, except those who are hemodynamically unstable (e.g., hypotensive, in pulmonary edema, or unconscious).

[d] If hypotension, pulmonary edema, or unconsciousness is present, unsynchronized cardioversion should be done to avoid delay associated with synchronization.

[e] In the presence of hypotension, pulmonary edema, or unconsciousness, a precordial thump may be employed prior to cardioversion.

[f] Once VT has resolved, begin intravenous (IV) infusion of antirhythmic agent that has aided resolution of VT. If hypotension, pulmonary edema, or unconsciousness is present, use lidocaine if cardioversion alone is unsuccessful, followed by bretylium. In all other patients, recommended order of therapy is lidocaine, procainamide, and then bretylium.

- If the patient is perfusing and conscious: administer a lidocaine IV bolus, followed by a maintenance infusion, by direct physician's order only. If the rhythm fails to respond to lidocaine, consider bretylium tosylate by direct physician's order only. If the above is unsuccessful, consider procainamide (if available), by direct physician's order only. If all drug therapy proves unsuccessful, consider synchronized cardioversion.
- In a monitored patient who is decompensating: synchronized cardioversion at 50, 100, 200, 360 joules (or consider defibrillation), by direct physician's order only. Then lidocaine, cardiovert, then bretylium or procainamide, by direct physician's order only.

Ventricular Fibrillation (VF or V Fib)

Ventricular fibrillation is a chaotic ventricular rhythm, with the absence of any organized ventricular depolarization (contraction) resulting in no cardiac output. This is the most common cause of cardiac arrest from an acute myocardial infarction or myocardial ischemia.

1. Etiology:
   - Wide variety of causes.
   - Most commonly associated wtih coronary artery disease, acute myocardial infarction, and myocardial ischemia.
2. Interpretation:
   - Totally chaotic undulations of varying amplitude and shape with no discernible waves or complexes. There are two categories of ventricular fibrillation — ''coarse'' V fib and ''fine'' V fib. These relate to the amplitude of the waveforms. Coarse V fib is of greater amplitude (greater than or equal to 10 mm) and represents a more recent onset. It therefore has the greatest chance of conversion. Fine V fib (amplitude less than 10 mm) usually means that there has been a significant time delay since collapse, and the chance for conversion and subsequent survival is poor.
   - Rate — 150 to 300 uncoordinated waves per minute.
   - Rhythm — totally irregular.
   - P waves — absent.
   - P-R interval — none.
   - QRS — QRS complexes are absent; in their place are fibrillatory waves.
3. Clinical significance: produces no organized contraction or pulse, resulting in cardiac arrest and clinical death.
4. Treatment (see Figure 10-3 on page 213):

Figure 10-31. Ventricular Fibrillation.

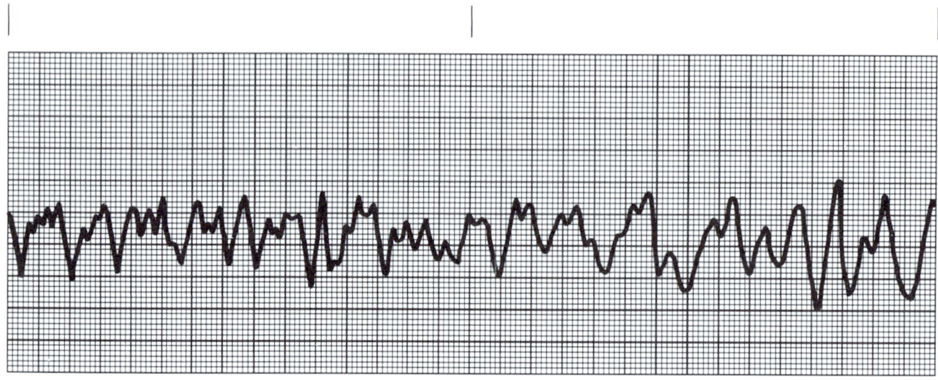

Coarse VF

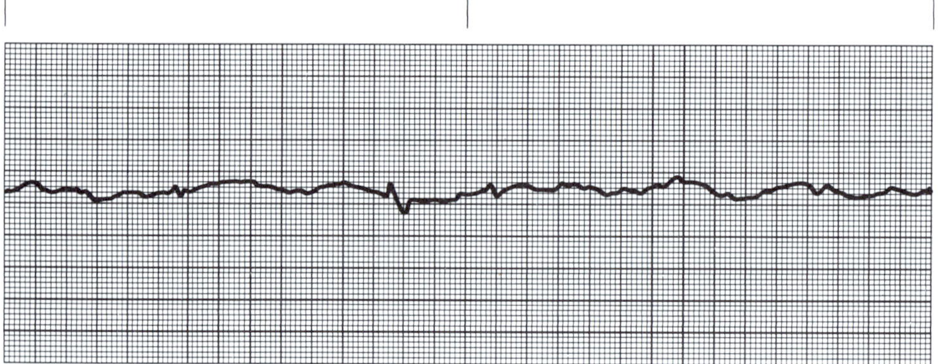

Fine VF

- CPR.
- Immediate defibrillation.
- Airway management.
- Drug therapy.

Asystole (Cardiac Standstill)

Cardiac standstill is the absence of all electrical and mechanical activity in the heart.

1. Etiology:

Figure 10-32. Ventricular Asystole.

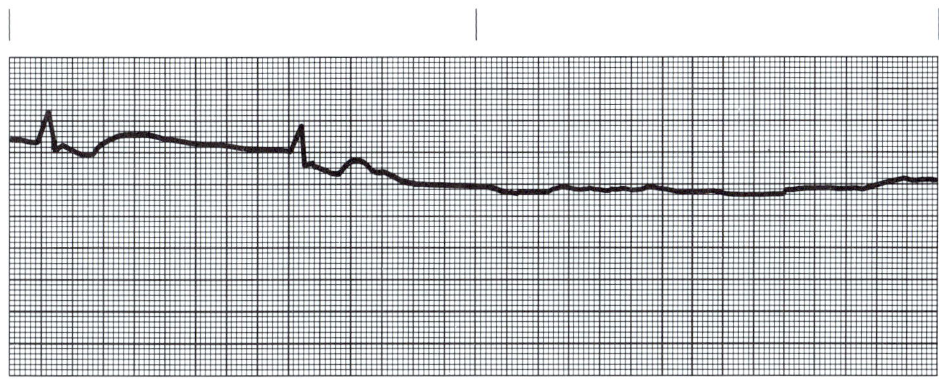

- May be the primary event in cardiac arrest or associated with massive myocardial ischemia and necrosis.
- May be the end result of ventricular fibrillation.
- May occur in the presence of complete heart block when there is no functional escape pacemaker.

2. Interpretation:
   - No discernible waves or complexes; only an isoelectric line.
   - Rate — none.
   - Rhythm — none.
   - P waves — none.
   - P-R interval — none.
   - QRS complex — none.
3. Clinical significance:
   - Produces cardiac arrest.
   - Prognosis for resuscitation is poor.
4. Treatment (see Figure 10-4, page 214):
   - CPR.
   - Airway management.
   - Drug therapy.

Artificial Pacemaker Rhythms

A paced rhythm is generated by regular electrical synthetic stimulation of the heart through an electrode that is implanted in the myocardium and connected to a power source. The pacemaker may be implanted in different locations in the heart. The most common types are the ventricular pacemaker and the dual-chambered pacemaker.

Pacemakers may be preset to fire constantly or variably. The fixed rate (asynchronous) fires continuously at a preset rate without regard to the patient's own electrical activity. The demand pacer (synchronous) contains a sensing device and fires only if the patient's own rate drops below the pacemaker's preset rate (acts as an escape rhythm).

The pacemaker stimulates the ventricles or the atria and ventricles to artificially produce an idioventricular rhythm.

1. Etiology: it is most frequently implanted in a patient with complete heart block or with episodes of severe bradycardia.
2. Interpretation (using Lead II):
   - Rate — varies according to the preset rate of the pacemaker; should not be pacing at a rate less than sixty.
   - Rhythm — regular if pacing constantly; irregular if pacing only on demand.
   - P waves — none are produced by a ventricular pacemaker. Sinus P waves may be seen but are unrelated to the QRS complexes. Dual-chambered pacemakers produce a P wave following each atrial spike.
   - Pacemaker spike — a spike going upward or downward from the baseline; an artifact created each time the pacemaker fires; indicates only that the pacemaker is discharging.
   - P-R interval — normal to prolonged if present.
   - QRS complex — 0.12 second or greater and bizarre; similar to PVCs. Each time the ventricular pacemaker spike is seen, a QRS should follow. The pacemaker is said to be "capturing" when a spike elicits a QRS. With a demand pacemaker, some of the patient's own QRSs may be seen (different shape). No pacemaker spike should be seen with the patient's own QRS.
3. Problems with pacemaker rhythms:
   - Battery failure results in no pacing, and a patient's own rhythm may become bradycardic or asystolic.
   - A runaway pacemaker is the result of low battery power, causing a very rapid discharge rate. This is rarely seen in newer pacemakers. These newer pacers gradually increase in rate as the battery runs low.
   - Failure of the sensing device in demand pacemakers occurs when the pacer fails to shut off when the patient has his/her own adequate rate, and it competes with the natural pacemaker. It also may discharge during the vulnerable period of the cardiac cycle.
   - Failure to capture is identified when the pacemaker spikes are present

Figure 10-33. Pacemaker Rhythm.

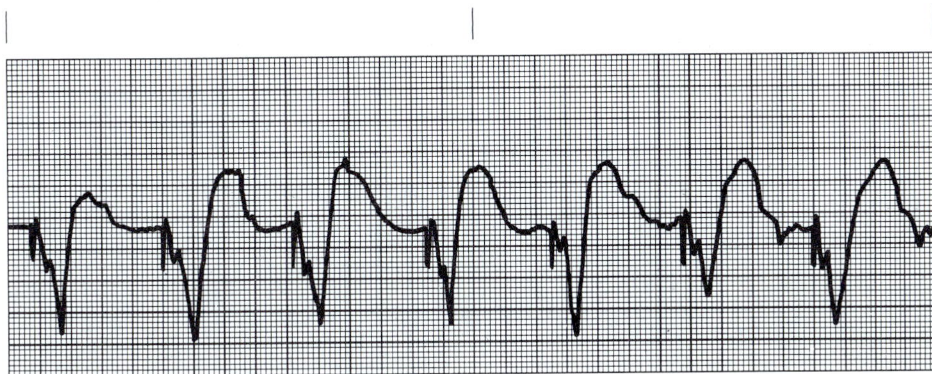

but are not followed by P waves or QRS complexes. This problem may result in a bradycardia.

4. Management of the pacemaker patient:
   - When examining unconscious patients, be alert for battery packs implanted underneath the skin (often in the shoulder or axillary region).
   - Bradydysrhythmias, asystole, and ventricular fibrillation resulting from pacemaker failure are treated as usual.
   - Ventricular irritability may be treated with lidocaine without fear of suppressing the response of the ventricles to the pacemaker.
   - The patient with a pacemaker may be defibrillated as usual, but do not discharge the paddles directly over the battery pack.
   - Expedite the transport of a patient with a pacemaker failure. These patients need a new power pack or pacer implanted, not prolonged field stabilization.

Dysrhythmias That Are Disorders of Conduction

AV Block

An AV block is a delay or interruption in the conduction of impulses through the atrioventricular junction. It is caused by disease of atrioventricular junctional tissue.

1. Etiology:
   - Atrioventricular junctional ischemia.

- Lesions along the conduction pathways (calcium, fibrosis, atrioventricular junctional necrosis).
- Degenerative disease of the conduction system.
- Drug toxicity (especially digitalis).

2. Classifications: AV blocks are classified according to the degree of the block:
   - First-degree AV block.
   - Second-degree AV block type I (Mobitz I, Wenckebach).
   - Second-degree AV block type II (Mobitz II).
   - Third-degree AV block (complete heart block).

First-Degree AV Block

This is not an actual block but a delay in conduction usually at the level of the atrioventricular node. In first-degree heart block, the P-R interval is prolonged more than 0.20 second, and is constant from beat to beat.

1. Etiology:
   - Usually caused by ischemia of the atrioventricular junction.
   - Digitalis preparations.
   - Acute myocardial infarction (though usually transient).
   - Hyperkalemia.
2. Interpretation (using Lead II):
   - The only alteration in the EKG is a P-R interval prolonged greater than 0.20 second.
   - Rate — normal.

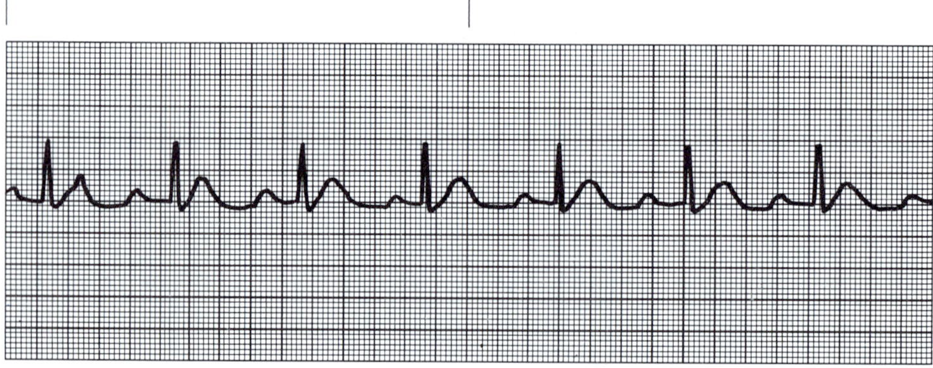

Figure 10-34. First Degree Heart Block.

- Rhythm — regular.
- P wave — normal; each P wave is followed by a QRS complex.
- P-R interval — prolonged beyond 0.20 second, and usually constant.
- QRS complex — normal, unaffected.

3. Clinical significance:
   - No danger in itself because all atrial impulses are conducted to the ventricles, but may represent some other problem.
   - A newly developed first-degree block may be a forerunner of a more advanced block.
4. Treatment: monitor closely; no other treatment is indicated.

Second-Degree AV Block Type I (Mobitz I or Wenckebach Block)

This is an intermittent block usually at the level of the atrioventricular node, where the stimulus from the atria to the ventricles is having progressively more difficulty getting through (seen as an increasing P-R interval), until one P wave is not conducted (blocked) to the ventricles. This results in an absent (dropped) QRS complex. This cycle is repetitive.

The P-P interval is constant, but the R-R interval decreases until a beat is dropped. The ratio of conduction (P waves to QRSs) is commonly 5:4, 4:3, 3:2, 2:1. The pattern may be constant or variable.

1. Etiology:
   - May be caused by increased parasympathetic tone.
   - Drug effects (digitalis toxicity).

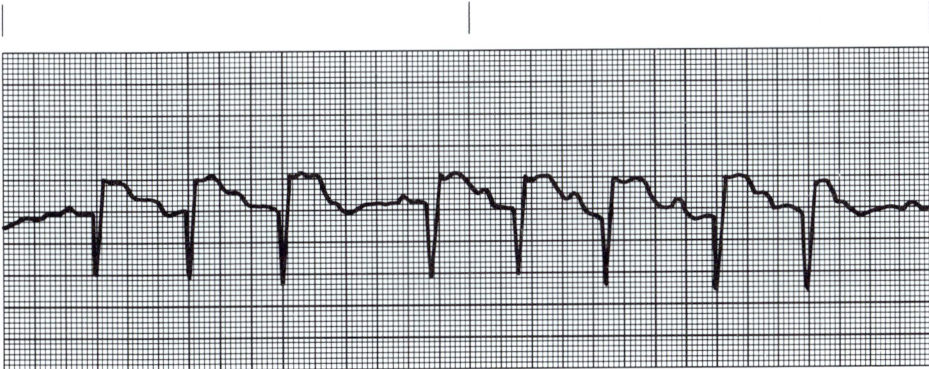

Figure 10-35. Second Degree Heart Block — Mobitz Type I.

- Atrioventricular junctional ischemia.
- Acute inferior wall infarction.

2. Interpretation (using Lead II):
   - Rate — atrial rate is unaffected; ventricular rate will be less than the atrial rate because of the nonconducted beats.
   - Rhythm — atrial, regular; ventricular, may be regular or irregular.
   - P waves — upright and uniform; P waves precede each QRS complex; the blocked P wave produces no QRS complexes.
   - P-R interval — there is a progressive lengthening of the P-R interval until a P wave is blocked (not conducted).
   - QRS complex — may be normal (less than 0.12 second) or wide (0.12 second or greater) and preceded by a P wave.
3. Clinical significance:
   - Frequently, the patient is asymptomatic, unless the heart rate is very slow, possibly causing decreased cardiac output.
   - Often seen in patients with inferior myocardial infarction and may progress to complete heart block.
   - Is often a transient phenomenon.
4. Treatment (see Figure 10-12 on page 237):
   - None if the patient is stable.
   - Atropine by direct physician's order if a slow rate hemodynamically compromises the patient.

Second-Degree AV Block Type II (Mobitz II)

This is an intermittent block characterized by P waves that are not conducted to the ventricles (blocked) but that do not experience a progressive lengthening of the P-R interval prior to the dropped beats. This block is less frequent and more severe than type I.

1. Etiology: usually associated with acute myocardial infarction and septal wall necrosis.
2. Interpretation (using Lead II):
   - Rate — atrial rate unaffected; ventricular rate less than that of the atria and commonly a bradycardia.
   - Rhythm — the atrial is regular; ventricular may be regular or irregular depending on whether the conduction ratio is constant or variable.
   - P waves — upright and uniform; there is more than one P wave for each QRS. The ratio of conduction (P waves to QRSs) is commonly 4:1, 3:1, or 2:1; the ratio block may be constant or variable. 2:1 type II block may not be distinguishable from 2:1 type I block.

Figure 10-36. Second Degree Heart Block — Mobitz Type II.

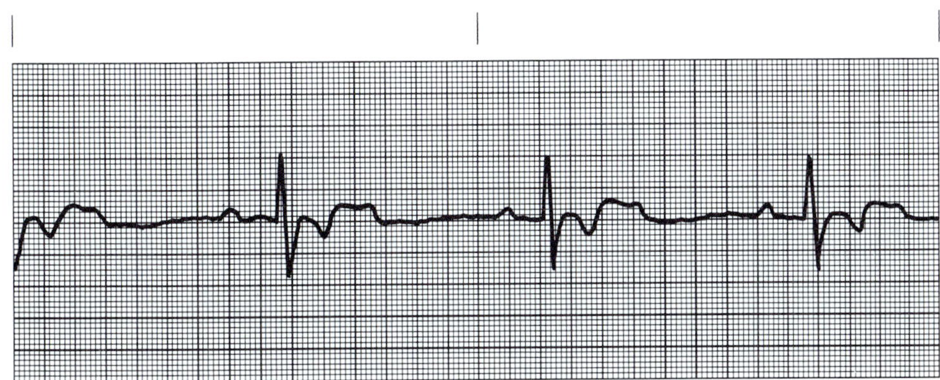

- P-R interval — it may be normal or greater than 0.20 second but will be constant for conducted beats.
- QRS complex — wide (0.12 second or greater) due to an abnormal ventricular depolarization sequence.

3. Clinical significance:
   - Slow rates reduce cardiac output and produce a hemodynamically compromised patient.
   - Frequently progresses to third-degree block.
4. Treatment (see Figure 10-16):
   - If the patient is symptomatic, administer atropine by direct physician's order only.
   - If atropine is unsuccessful, consider administering isoproterenol by direct physician's order only.
   - Generally, these patients need to be treated with a temporary pacemaker; expeditious transport is indicated.

Third-Degree AV Block (Complete Heart Block)

In this type of block there is no transmission of the electrical stimulus between the atria and ventricles. Instead, the atria and ventricles are paced independently, so their respective depolarizations are separate from each other (dissociated). The sinus node (SA node) is the atrial pacemaker and functions normally. The second pacemaker (escape pacemaker) is located below the block in either the junctional tissue or ventricles.

1. Etiology:

- Acute anterior wall myocardial infarction.
- In proximal (high) third-degree blocks, digitalis toxicity.
- Degenerative conduction system disease.

2. Interpretation (using Lead II):
   - Rate — atrial rate is unaffected; ventricular rate is forty to sixty if the escape focus is junctional, or less than forty if the escape focus is ventricular.
   - Rhythm — atrial and ventricular may be regular.
   - P waves — normal configuration with no relationship to the QRS complex.
   - P-R interval — there is no relationship between the P waves and the QRS complex, so there are no P-R intervals.
   - QRS complex — less than 0.12 second if the escape focus is junctional (proximal), and 0.12 second or greater if the escape focus is ventricular (distal).
3. Clinical significance: severe compromise of cardiac output due to slow ventricular rate plus loss of the atrial kick.
4. Treatment (see Figure 10-11):
   - Field treatment is only temporary, since the patient will need a pacemaker insertion.
   - Atropine to try to maintain a rate of sixty per minute, by direct physician's order.
   - If atropine is unsuccessful (note: distal blocks will not respond to atropine), consider isoproterenol at low dosages (two to ten micrograms

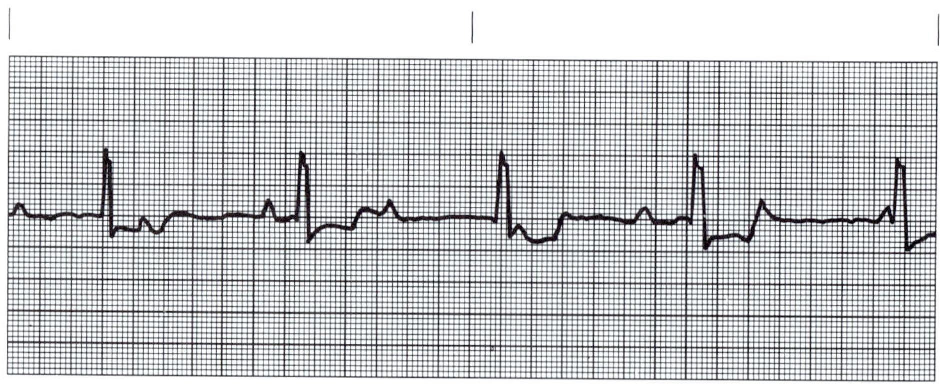

Figure 10-37. Third Degree Heart Block.

per minute), by direct physician's order only, to increase the ventricular rate.

- External pacing.

Disturbance of Ventricular Conduction

The following terms are used to describe impulses that originate above the ventricles only.

1. Aberrant conduction: this terminology is used to describe a single supraventricular beat that is conducted through the ventricles in a delayed manner, usually resulting in a wide QRS complex (0.12 second or greater).
2. Bundle branch block (BBB): this is used to describe a rhythm when all supraventricular beats in that rhythm are conducted through the ventricles in a delayed manner, resulting in wide QRS complexes (0.12 second or greater).

Etiology

1. Ischemia or necrosis of either the right or left bundle branch, making it unable to conduct impulses to the ventricle that it innervates.
2. A premature impulse (PAC or PJC) reaches the ventricles when one of the bundle branches (usually the right) is still refractory and cannot conduct.
3. Commonly seen in atrial fibrillation due to varying speed of repolarization related to irregular rhythm.

ECG Features

1. QRS complex (time): becomes 0.12 second or greater because conduction through myocardial muscle tissue is slower than conduction through the more rapid normal electrical conduction pathway of the heart.
2. QRS morphology (shape): may be notched or slurred; represents rapid depolarization via a normal bundle branch followed by slower depolarization of the branch with a bundle block.

Problems in Rhythm Interpretation

1. It is important to realize that supraventricular beats or rhythms may have abnormally wide QRS complexes.
2. It may be impossible to distinguish between PVCs and aberrantly conducted PACs or PJCs; and between supraventricular tachycardia with BBB or abberant conduction and ventricular tachycardia on a Lead II

rhythm strip.

3. When in doubt, treat all premature beats or rhythms with abnormally wide QRS complexes as ventricular in origin.
   - It is possible for the paramedic to do more harm by not treating the irregularity as ventricular than by treating it as ventricular.
   - For the most accurate interpretation (definitive diagnosis), a twelve-lead ECG is needed.

MANAGEMENT OF DYSRHYTHMIAS

Basic Life Support (CPR)

See current American Heart Association BLS protocols.

Precordial Thump

When to Use

It has been demonstrated that a precordial thump can be effective in converting abnormal rhythms, particularly ventricular tachycardia and possibly bradycardic rhythms where the patient is symptomatic. In the setting of a witnessed cardiac arrest due to ventricular fibrillation, one precordial thump should be administered when a defibrillator is unavailable.

How to Deliver

1. A precordial thump is delivered to the midsternum (center) with a fist (thumb up) from a height no greater than twelve inches.
2. A thump is delivered with the arm parallel to the long axis of the sternum to avoid injuring the ribs.
3. When using a precordial thump on a patient in ventricular tachycardia with a pulse, be sure to have a defibrillator available, since the patient may convert to ventricular fibrillation.
4. A precordial thump is not recommended in pediatric patients.

Defibrillation

Defibrillation is the process of passing an electric current through a fibrillating heart to convert it to organized, coordinated contractions (heartbeats). The ''critical mass'' (not necessarily the entire heart) of the left ventricular myocardium must be depolarized in order to successfully convert the heart to a functioning rhythm. The critical mass is related to heart size but cannot be calculated for a given situation.

The Defibrillator

The defibrillator consists of an adjustable, high-voltage direct-current (DC) power supply; an energy storage capacitor; a current-limiting inductor placed between the capacitor and paddles; and the paddles.

Direct current defibrillators are the most commonly used devices both in the field and in the hospital setting (alternating current [AC] defibrillators are no longer in use). DC defibrillators are more effective, cause less muscular damage, and are more portable than AC defibrillators.

The output of the defibrillator is measured in joules or watt-seconds, which are both measures of energy. Joules equals watts (power) multiplied by seconds (duration). The energy current through the chest lasts between four to twelve milliseconds.

Factors That Influence Delivery of the Current

Several factors influence the delivery of the electrical current to a fibrillating heart:

1. The amount of energy (joules) delivered.
2. Paddle surface area (size).
3. Paddle-to-skin interface.
4. Paddle pressure.
5. Number and time between previous countershocks
6. Respiratory phase at the time of defibrillation.
7. Distance between electrode paddles.

The paramedic has no control over paddle size but does have some control over other factors. If the paddles are placed directly on the skin surface without a conductive gel, the resistance is significantly higher than with the use of some form of conductive substance.

The paddle pressure (paddle-to-skin contact pressure) influences the ease with which the electrical current will flow through the chest wall. It is recommended that twenty-five pounds of pressure (firm pressure) be applied to each paddle on the chest wall. This will reduce the distance between paddles (electrodes) and thereby reduce resistance.

The resistance to the flow of electrical current is reduced after each defibrillation. The resistance is reduced by approximately 8 percent after the second shock.

Factors That Influence the Success of Defibrillation

1. Duration (time) of ventricular fibrillation: a recent study (Eisenberg) indicates that if CPR is initiated in less than four minutes and defibrillation in less than eight minutes, there is a significantly higher rate of successful resuscitation.
2. The condition of the myocardium: it is more difficult to defibrillate in the presence of hypoxia, acidosis, hypothermia, electrolyte imbalance, and drug toxicity. VF secondary to some existing pathology is more difficult to treat than primary VF.
3. Previous countershocks: transthoracic resistance decreases with repeated countershocks, thereby making it possible to deliver more energy to the heart at the same energy setting.
4. Paddle size: the ideal size for adults is not established. It is recommended that circular paddles have a surface area of ten to thirteen centimeters in diameter. Larger paddles are thought to be more effective and to cause less myocardial damage. Four-and-one-half-centimeter-diameter paddles are adequate for infants, and eight-centimeter-diameter paddles for children.
5. Paddle placement:
   - The anteriolateral placement (standard) is recommended for emergency defibrillation; place one paddle to the right of the upper sternum just below the right clavicle, with the other paddle below the left nipple along the midaxillary line. (The paddles may be marked for correct placement; the left — positive electrode, and the right — negative electrode.) Reversing the polarity of the paddles does not affect defibrillation; it only inverts the resulting ECG tracing.
   - The anterior-posterior placement — one paddle is positioned anteriorly over the precordium (to the left of the lower sternal border), and the other is positioned posteriorly behind the heart.
   - There is no evidence to support the superiority of one method over the other.
6. Paddle-skin contact surface: many types of conductive media are available to reduce the resistance of the chest wall. Some are creams, gels, pastes, saline-soaked pads, and prepackaged gelled pads. Exercise care with creams and saline pads to avoid ''bridging'' of the charge due to smearing or running of the conductive medium (which can cause the electrical

charge to run over the chest rather than through it).

7. Paddle contact pressure: the paramedic must use firm, downward pressure equivalent to twenty-five pounds to maximally decrease transthoracic resistance. Do not lean on paddles, however — they may slip.
8. Proper functioning of the defibrillator is, of course, necessary. The defibrillator must actually be delivering the energy indicated by the machine.

Energy Recommendations for Defibrillation

As stated in the AHA ACLS Manual (1987), there are energies that are too low, energies that have a reasonable degree of success, and those that are too high, causing cardiac damage or death. The dosage-to-weight concept plays an important role when differentiating between adult and pediatric defibrillation, but it is not critical in adults. The AHA recommendation for adult defibrillation is as follows:

1. Initial defibrillation: adult should be at 200 joules; if the first shock is unsuccessful, a second shock should be repeated immediately at 200 to 300 joules.
2. If ventricular fibrillation persists after the second shock, the patient should receive a third shock at 360 joules, and all additional shocks should be at 360.
3. Initial defibrillation: pediatric energy dosage recommendations are two joules per kilogram of body weight; if the first shock is unsuccessful, a second shock at four joules per kilogram of body weight should be repeated immediately.
4. After defibrillation, check the algorithms for the correct pharmacologic intervention.

Procedures for Defibrillation

This must be accomplished at the earliest opportunity in ventricular fibrillation. Delegate CPR responsibilities, but monitor effectiveness throughout.

1. Use "quick-look" paddles with a conductive medium to evaluate the rhythm; stop CPR while observing the monitor (five seconds only).
2. If ventricular fibrillation is present, continue CPR while preparing to defibrillate.
3. Turn on defibrillator power, select the proper energy setting (200 joules), and charge the paddles.

4. Place the paddles on the chest in the correct position with a slight twisting motion to distribute the conductive medium.
5. Stop CPR and reverify the presence of V fib or pulseless ventricular tachycardia.
6. The paramedic must "clear" the area and confirm that no personnel (including him/herself) are in direct or indirect contact with the patient.
7. Apply firm pressure on the paddles (do not lean), and deliver the shock by depressing both paddle discharge buttons simultaneously; observe for skeletal muscle contraction (this indicates passage of electrical current).
8. Leave the paddles on the chest and immediately reassess the rhythm.
9. If any kind of organized rhythm appears on the monitor, immediately check for a carotid pulse.
10. If no pulse returns and ventricular fibrillation or pulseless ventricular tachycardia persist, continue CPR and immediately defibrillate a second time at 200 to 300 joules.

Emergency Synchronized Cardioversion

This is the delivery of an electrical shock that is synchronized to the heart's electrical activity so that the shock will not be delivered during the relative refractory period (the vulnerable period on top of the T wave).

The synchronizing circuit in the defibrillator allows for a programmed delivery of a countershock to occur during a specific part of the QRS complex (most often the R wave). Research has shown that synchronization reduces energy requirements and complications due to more powerful forms of electrical cardioversion.

Indications

Synchronized cardioversion is indicated when the hemodynamically unstable patient is experiencing ventricular or supraventricular tachydysrhythmias:

1. Perfusing ventricular tachycardia.
2. Nonperfusing (pulseless) ventricular tachycardia — must be treated as ventricular fibrillation.
3. Paroxysmal supraventricular tachycardias (PSVT).
4. Rapid atrial fibrillation.
5. 2:1 atrial flutter.
6. When the patient is critical (i.e., hypotensive, unconscious, or in pulmonary edema), unsynchronized cardioversion is recommended.

Energy Requirements

1. If the patient is conscious and there is time, anesthesia or analgesia is appropriate, prior to cardioversion.
2. Atrial fibrillation — recommended energy for first shock is 200 joules; second shock is 360 joules.
3. Paroxysmal supraventricular tachycardia — recommended energy for initial shock is 75 to 100 joules. If cardioversion results in a return to NSR, even transiently, a second cardioversion should not be done until additional therapy has been instituted to maintain NSR once it returns.
4. Ventricular tachycardia and atrial flutter will sometimes revert back to NSR with a dosage of only ten joules. The recommended initial shock is fifty joules. Additional shocks for ventricular tachycardia are as follows: 100 joules, 200 joules, 360 joules. Ventricular tachycardia usually converts at the lower energy levels.

Procedure for Synchronized Cardioversion

1. Premedication with valium may be indicated in the conscious patient.
2. Use the lead that provides the maximal R wave height, set the gain high enough to insure sensing, observe the machine for an indication of proper synchronization.
3. Press and hold the discharge buttons until the countershock is delivered (it may take several moments to occur).
4. If the countershock produces ventricular fibrillation:
   - Manually disengage the synchronizer switch.
   - Charge the defibrillator to 200 joules.
   - Defibrillate.

Rotating Tourniquets

A rotating tourniquet decreases venous return to the heart (decreases preload) by pooling venous blood in the peripheral vessels. Rotating tourniquets are not as effective as prompt pharmacologic therapy but may be a useful adjunct until drug intervention is initiated. They are used in the treatment of acute pulmonary edema early in the course and/or when venous access cannot be attained.

Constricting bands or blood pressure cuffs are applied snugly to three extremities as high up on each extremity as possible. Arterial pulses distal to the tourniquets should remain palpable. Rotate the tourniquets every five to ten minutes by releasing one extremity and reapplying them to another extremity.

Carotid Sinus Massage

Carotid sinus massage is used in an attempt to convert paroxysmal supraventricular tachycardias, particularly when they are associated with hypotension or a decreased level of consciousness. By stimulation of the baroreceptors (pressure receptor) found in the carotid sinus, vagal tone can be increased, possibly resulting in a slowing of the heart rate.

Procedures for Carotid Sinus Massage

1. A patient must have ECG monitoring and an IV line prior to starting this procedure.
2. Provide a high flow and high concentration of oxygen.
3. The paramedic must be prepared for a possible cardiac arrest.
   - Have atropine and lidocaine ready, as well as other necessary equipment.
4. The paramedic should be positioned behind the patient, who is lying supine, with neck extended, and head turned away from the side on which the massage is to be performed (if the right carotid is being massaged, the patient's face is to the left).
5. Gently palpate each carotid pulse separately to confirm that equal pulses are present. If the pulses are unequal, if one is absent, or if the patient has a history of stroke, carotid sinus massage is contraindicated. Auscultate the carotids for a bruit; if one is present, do not perform carotid sinus massage.
6. Place the index and middle fingers over the artery on the neck just below the angle of the jaw. Press the artery firmly against the vertebral column while massaging the area. When done properly, carotid sinus massage is painful.
7. Watch the ECG monitor during the massage (obtain a paper tracing), and terminate the massage at the first signs of slowing or heart block.
8. Maintain pressure no longer than fifteen to twenty seconds.
9. May repeat if ineffective, or attempt procedure on the other side after waiting two to three minutes.
10. Never massage both carotids simultaneously.

Complications

1. The production of dysrhythmias: asystole, bradycardia, PVCs, ventricular

tachycardia, and fibrillation.

2. Interference with cerebral circulation, resulting in syncope, seizure, or CVA.
3. Increases parasympathetic tone, resulting in hypotension, nausea, or vomiting.

SUMMARY

It is estimated that approximately 1.5 million people will have heart attacks in 1988. Over 500,000 will die from this event, with more than half dying before reaching the emergency department of a hospital. In addition to these deaths, approximately 30,000 people will die from hypertension, and 250,000 will die from other cardiovascular diseases.

The death rate for cardiovascular disease has been declining steadily since the mid-1960s. Part of this decline is due to an increase in general health awareness and ''fitness'' in the United States, and part is a direct result of medical intervention starting at the prehospital level.

Prehospital care plays a significant role in the delivery of care to the cardiac patient. The paramedic's ability to provide excellent care depends on maintaining a high level of knowledge and skill in assessment of the patient, EKG interpretation, cardiac medications, and general treatment skills (e.g., intubation, IV placement, etc.).

This chapter has presented a great deal of information regarding the assessment and proper treatment of the cardiac patient (and vascular disease patients). The paramedic should review this material often and keep current on new techniques and protocols.

11

Diabetic Emergencies and the Endocrine System

The endocrine system consists of a group of glands that, along with the nervous system, control many bodily functions. It exerts control by secreting hormones (chemical messengers) that are carried throughout the body by the bloodstream.

This system is complex and plays an important role in maintaining homeostasis (balance in bodily fluids and composition). The endocrine system takes longer to affect the body than does the nervous system. It primarily controls widespread processes rather than exerting control over specific organs (e.g., the endocrine system controls growth, development, and metabolism).

This chapter will briefly review the endocrine system. The emphasis will be on the diabetic emergency, because it is the primary endocrine-related problem encountered by paramedics in the field.

ANATOMY AND PHYSIOLOGY

Terminology

1. Hormone: a substance secreted by an endocrine gland that has effects upon other glands, cells, tissues, and systems of the body. It helps in maintaining homeostasis. Stress often stimulates the secretion of hormones.
2. Enzyme: an organic substance that causes an alteration in the rate of chemical reactions and that is not consumed in the reaction.
3. Glycogen: a carbohydrate that is a complex form of glucose. It is stored in the liver and can be converted to glucose when the body has a need for energy.

Glands of the Endocrine System

Pituitary Gland

The pituitary gland is located at the base of the brain and is divided into two distinct portions. Its primary function is regulatory — it is sometimes referred to as the ''master gland'' of the body. Ten hormones are secreted by the pituitary gland that regulate the functions of most of the other endocrine glands.

Thyroid Gland

The thyroid gland has two lobes and is located in the neck, anterior and lateral to the trachea and inferior to the larynx. This gland secretes hormones that regulate the metabolic rate and control the calcium/phosphate levels in the blood.

Parathyroid Glands

The parathyroid glands are four small (pea-sized) glands that are located on the posterior surface of the thyroid gland. They function to control the metabolism of calcium and phosphate in the body.

Adrenal Glands

The adrenal glands are located on the superior portion of each kidney. Each gland is comprised of the medulla and the cortex.

1. The adrenal medulla secretes two hormones: epinephrine and norepinephrine. They both stimulate the sympathetic nervous system.

2. The adrenal cortex produces steroid hormones known as corticoids:
   - Glucocorticoids play a role in the metabolism of carbohydrates and proteins.
   - Mineral corticoids are important in the maintenance of fluid and in electrolyte balance.
   - Cortical sex hormones are not fully understood.

Ovaries

The ovaries are paired organs located in the female pelvic cavity. They have many functions:

1. They play an important role in reproduction (see Chapter 20).
2. They secrete estrogen, which promotes a monthly formation of the inner uterine lining during the menstrual cycle. They also stimulate uterine contraction, cause and maintain the development of accessory sex organs, increase mammary (breast) development, and develop the female secondary sex characteristics.
3. Progesterone, secreted by the ovaries, plays a role in the monthly menstrual cycle, causes milk production, increases sodium/water retention, causes ovulation, and is required for placental formation.

Testes

The testes are located outside the male body cavity in the scrotum. They produce the steroid, testosterone, which is responsible for the development of male secondary sex characteristics, the external genitalia, and the accessory organs of the system.

Pancreas

The pancreas is located inferior to the stomach and adjacent to the duodenum on the right, extending to the spleen on the left. One of its functions is to secrete into the duodenum digestive enzymes that break down all three main foodstuff groups (fats, proteins, and carbohydrates). Its second function is to secrete regulatory hormones, two of which are produced in the Islets of Langerhans.

1. **Insulin.** Insulin is produced and secreted by the beta cells found in the Islets. It is essential for metabolizing glucose (blood sugar) and maintaining a proper glucose level in the blood. Insulin is responsible for glucose transport into the cells. It increases the conversion of glucose to glycogen

in the liver for storage (glycogenesis), and it reduces the blood glucose concentration back to a normal level when high levels of glucose enter the bloodstream. Insulin secretion is dependent on the glucose concentration; increased levels of glucose cause an increase in the secretion of insulin.

2. **Glucagon.** Glucagon is produced and secreted by the alpha cells found in the Islets. When energy production is increased, glucagon causes an increase in the blood glucose level. When there is a moderate decrease in blood glucose, glucagon is secreted. Glucagon also increases liver glycogenolysis, which is the conversion of glycogen into glucose.

PATHOLOGY OF DIABETES

Diabetes Mellitus

Diabetes mellitus is a disease with a complex group of syndromes that disturb the breakdown and utilization of glucose. This is a result of the malfunction of the beta cells in the pancreas, whose function is the production and release of insulin. There are two major types of diabetes mellitus:

1. **Type I:** insulin-dependent diabetes mellitus (IDDM). This type was historically known as juvenile diabetes. It accounts for 5 to 10 percent of all diabetic cases. IDDM usually occurs before the age of thirty, though it sometimes develops later in life. Sufferers of IDDM experience more severe sequelae (serious conditions as a consequence of this type) than do noninsulin-dependent diabetics.
2. **Type II:** noninsulin-dependent diabetes mellitus (NIDDM). The remaining 90 to 95 percent of diabetics fall into this category. Type II is usually caused by either an insufficient quantity of insulin or a delayed response to a glucose load. NIDDM tends to develop later in life than Type I; however, the terms ''juvenile-onset'' and ''maturity-onset'' are misleading, because the very old may develop Type I and the very young may develop Type II.

Diabetes mellitus affects approximately 5 percent of the population of the United States (10 to 12 million people). There is clear evidence that genetic factors play a significant role in the development of this disease. People who have a hereditary predisposition to this disease often exhibit the following precipitating factors:

1. Obesity — there seems to be a strong relationship between obesity and NIDDM.
2. Physiologic or emotional stress.
3. Pregnancy.
4. Recent studies suggest that viral destruction of the insulin-producing beta cells causes IDDM.

Clinical Manifestations of Diabetes Mellitus

This disease may be present with a wide variety of signs and symptoms. In one case, a patient may be asymptomatic, and in another case, a patient may be comatose. When insulin is not available in the body in adequate amounts, sugar is not moved to the cells, where it is normally metabolized.

The following generally occurs in the IDDM patient:

1. A severe upset in carbohydrate metabolism.
2. Osmotic diuresis, resulting from high blood glucose levels (hyperglycemia), which causes passage of large amounts of urine. A high concentration of glucose is found in the urine. This eventually causes dehydration, and more electrodes are excreted than usual.
3. Ketone body formation. Ketones are a product of fat metabolism. They are one of the substances that increases in the blood and urine during the faulty metabolism of fat found in uncontrolled or poorly treated diabetes mellitus.
   - Fat breakdown increases to provide an alternate energy source for cells that can no longer use glucose.
   - The accumulation of acidic ketone bodies in the blood leads to the development of ketoacidosis (a metabolic acidosis).
4. Common signs/symptoms of diabetes mellitus:
   - Polydipsia (excessive thirst).
   - Polyphagia (increased appetite).
   - Polyuria (excessive urine output).
   - Fatigue.

DIABETIC EMERGENCIES

Hypoglycemia

Hypoglycemia is an abnormally low level of glucose in the blood. Normal glucose values are 80 to 120 milligrams per 100 milliliters of blood. Hypoglycemic reactions may occur when the blood glucose level falls below 50 milligrams per 100 milliliters of blood. A reaction may occur as rapidly as five to ten minutes after an insulin dosage.

Hypoglycemia most commonly occurs in the IDDM patient who has injected an excess of insulin, has not had an adequate intake of carbohydrates, and/or has not replenished carbohydrates after exercise. This may cause an inadequate supply of glucose to nourish the brain. In addition, other hormones may cause the critical levels of blood glucose to vary from normal, resulting in hypoglycemia (epinephrine, glycogen, and glucocorticoids tend to cause hypoglycemia by stimulating the breakdown of glycogen or by interfering with the utilization of glucose at the cellular level).

Insulin lowers serum glucose by increasing the transfer of glucose into cells and by stimulating the deposit of glycogen in the liver. With hypoglycemia, glucose stores become depleted, resulting in inadequate nourishment of the brain.

Precipitating Factors

1. Medication error — overdose of insulin (the most common cause). This may be intentional or unintentional.
2. Hypoglycemia can occur after fasting.
3. Increased alcohol consumption without increasing carbohydrate intake.
4. Heavy physical activity without an adequate increase in food intake.
5. Tumor of the pancreas.

Hypoglycemia develops rapidly after glucose depletion — usually within thirty to sixty minutes.

Signs and Symptoms of Hypoglycemia

1. Weak, rapid pulse.
2. Cold, clammy skin (diaphoresis).
3. Weakness, fatigue.
4. Hunger.
5. Tremulousness.
6. Headache.
7. Irritable, nervous, or bizarre behavior.
8. May appear drunk.
9. Seizures.
10. Coma in severe cases.

11. Irreversible brain damage if left untreated (usually more than forty-five to sixty minutes in severe cases).

Hyperglycemia (Ketoacidosis)

Hyperglycemia is an abnormally high glucose level in the blood. It occurs when:

1. The insulin dosage is too low.
2. The patient has not taken his/her insulin dosage. (When the insulin level is low or nonexistent, glucose cannot enter the cells and accumulates in the blood.)
3. A patient is **undiagnosed** for diabetes mellitus.

Diabetic ketoacidosis is a form of metabolic acidosis that is caused by insufficient insulin, resulting in increased ketone bodies and free fatty acids, hyperglycemia, electrolyte imbalance, and hypovolemia. The precipitating factors are:

1. A patient's failure to take a sufficient amount of insulin, or any at all.
2. The presence of infection (e.g., respiratory tract infection, urinary infection, or gastroenteritis).
3. Emotional or physical stress (pregnancy, injury, surgery, anxiety, etc.).

Hyperglycemia progresses gradually over twelve to forty-eight hours.

Signs/Symptoms of Hyperglycemia

1. Polyuria.
2. Polydipsia.
3. Polyphagia.
4. Nausea/vomiting.
5. Tachycardia.
6. Deep, rapid respirations (Kussmaul respirations).
7. Skin is warm, dry, and flushed as a result of dehydration.
8. Fruity odor on the breath — do not confuse with or assume alcohol intoxication.
9. Sometimes fever, abdominal pain, or a falling blood pressure.
10. Decreased level of consciousness occurs gradually.
11. Vital signs are critical. Observe for signs of shock (tachycardia and hypotension).

ASSESSMENT OF THE DIABETIC PATIENT

Primary Survey

1. Airway.
2. Breathing.
3. Circulation.

Secondary Survey

1. Physical assessment.
2. Look for medical alert tag.
3. Vital signs — observe for changes when taking orthostatic vitals in both pulse and blood pressure.
4. History taking:
   - Recent food intake; any dietary changes?
   - Recent exercise?
   - How is the diabetes controlled (recent changes in medications)? Is the patient taking insulin? Other medications? What is the patient's diet?
   - Recent infection (illness)?

MANAGEMENT OF DIABETES

The Conscious Diabetic Patient

1. Airway management, administer oxygen.
2. IV therapy. If unsure whether the condition is hypoglycemia or hyperglycemia, start with volume replacement fluid.
3. If an IV is established, draw blood (red top container) for glucose analysis.
4. Get a glucose reagent strip to measure milligrams of glucose in the blood (reagent strips are not always accurate.) Monitor the patient carefully.
5. Administer oral glucose if necessary, as determined by signs, symptoms, vital signs, and the glucose reagent strip.
6. Monitor the vital signs.
7. Monitor the EKG.

The Unconscious Hypoglycemic Patient

1. Airway management — airway, oxygen, intubate, ventilate as appropriate.
2. Draw blood (red top container) for glucose analysis.

3. Measure the glucose level by using a glucose reagent strip (Dextrostik or Chemstik).
4. Start an IV — D_5W TKO (if an IV cannot be started, place instant glucose in the patient's mouth on the mucous membranes; be sure to protect the patient's airway).
5. If the patient is symptomatic or the reagent strip measures less than 50 milligrams of glucose:
   - Administer 50 milliliters of 50 percent glucose solution IV (D50, 25 grams of glucose). When administering D50, be sure that the IV is properly placed. D50 is very irritating to tissues, so be sure that it does not infiltrate into the surrounding tissue during IV administration. (See Appendix 1 for complete drug information.)
   - If an IV line is unavailable for the hypoglycemic patient, the paramedic may administer glucagon intramuscularly by direct physician's order. (See Appendix 1.)
   - If the patient is alcoholic, thiamine may be indicated to prevent an acute Wernicke's encephalopathy (a condition marked by loss of memory, disorientation, and inappropriate speech).
6. If the cause of unconsciousness is unknown, consider the use of Narcan (see Appendix 1).
7. Monitor the EKG.
8. Monitor the vital signs.

The Unconscious Hyperglycemic Patient

1. Airway management — airway, oxygen, intubate, ventilate as appropriate.
2. Draw blood (red top) for glucose analysis.
3. Measure the glucose level by using a glucose reagent strip (Dextrostik or Chemstick).
4. Start an IV with lactated Ringer's or normal saline solutions.
5. Consider the use of MAST (see Chapter 5), following local protocol.
6. Monitor the vital signs.
7. Monitor the EKG.
8. If the paramedic is unable to determine whether the episode is hyperglycemic or hypoglycemic, administer glucose (D50).

SUMMARY

In spite of the complexities of the endocrine system, the paramedic can play a life-saving role when treating the acutely ill diabetic patient (particularly the hypoglycemic patient). The patient should be evaluated thoroughly, then treated appropriately.

In the hypoglycemic shock (insulin shock) patient, the paramedic will see a rapid return to normal. This may not be so with the hyperglycemic patient, but if treated correctly at the start, a successful outcome is likely.

12

Central Nervous System Emergencies

This chapter presents the anatomy and physiology of the nervous system; assessment of the patient suffering a neurological insult; and specific management of coma, seizures, status epilepticus, and stroke. (Refer to Chapter 7 for head injury due to trauma.) Acute disorders of the central nervous system may have serious sequelae and require rapid assessment, treatment, and frequently emergent transport to the emergency department.

ANATOMY AND PHYSIOLOGY

The nervous system has several divisions or parts that are distinguished on the basis of location and function. It may be classified in the following way:

1. **The Central Nervous System (CNS).** The CNS lies within the skull and vertebral column and consists of two organs: the brain and the spinal cord.
2. **The Peripheral Nervous System (PNS).** The PNS lies outside of the skull and vertebral column and includes the cranial and spinal nerves. Its

divisions include:

- The somatic system (sensory or afferent nerves, which transmit impulses from the body to the brain, and efferent or motor nerves which transmit impulses from the brain to the body). This system supplies the skeletal muscles and skin.
- The autonomic system (both afferent and efferent fibers) supplies smooth muscle (the viscera), cardiac muscle, and glands of the body. Most organs receive nerves from the two divisions of the autonomic system to control their activity. The two divisions are the parasympathetic division, which maintains the normal functioning of bodily proces-

Figure 12-1. Parts of the Brain.

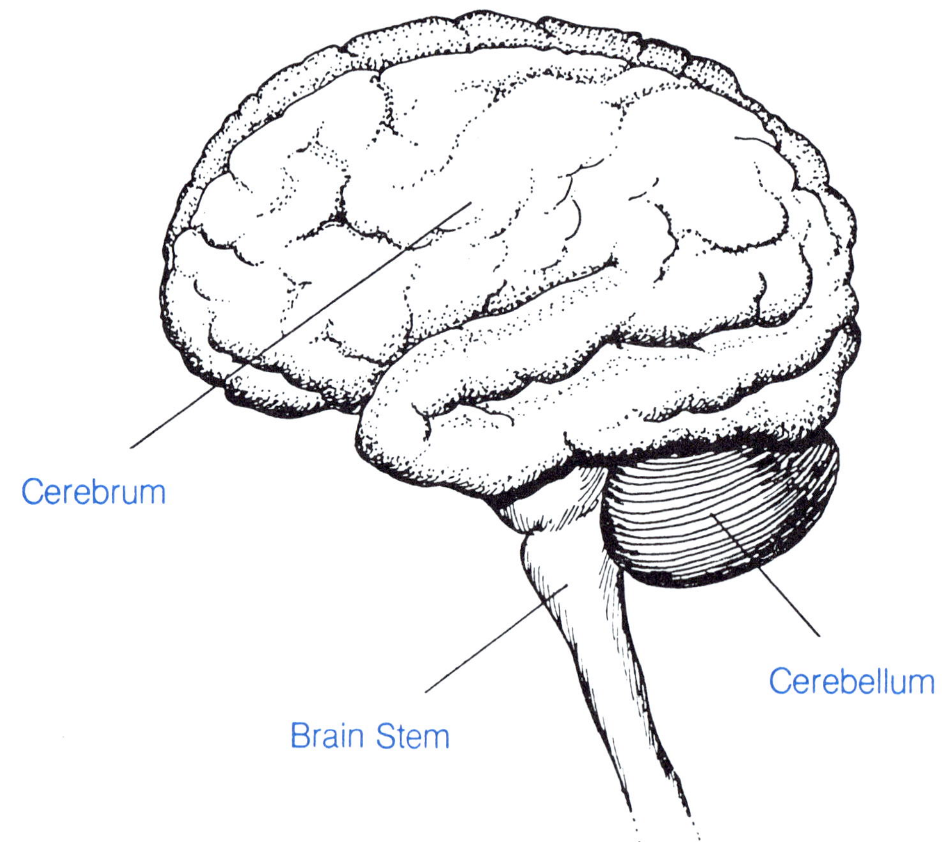

ses and conserves body resources, and the sympathetic division, which accelerates bodily functioning at times of stress.

The Brain

The brain is housed in a snug-fitting space called the cranium (cranial cavity), which is part of the skull. It provides a protective, bony covering for the brain. Problems occur in the brain when swelling develops and the tight-fitting skull does not allow for the brain to expand. When this occurs, pressure is exerted on the brain itself, which may result in serious injury.

The brain is divided into three major parts — the brain stem, the cerebellum, and the cerebrum.

Brain Stem

The brain stem supports the other parts of the brain. From inferior to superior, it consists of:

1. The medulla oblongata (medulla) — contains the vital centers necessary for survival. Among these are cardiac centers, controlling the heart rate; two of the three respiratory centers that initiate and regulate the rate and depth of respirations; and vasomotor centers, which control the diameter of the blood vessels and thus control blood pressure.
2. The pons — inhibits sustained inhalation and deals with the transmission of sensory impulses to the cerebellum and motor impulses from the cerebellum which are concerned with the maintenance of balance and equilibrium.
3. The midbrain — integrates a number of auditory and visual reflexes.
4. The diencephalon — made up of the thalamus and hypothalamus. The thalamus is the major relay station to the cerebral hemispheres for all types of sensory information. It also contributes to the state of wakefulness and alertness of the organism. The hypothalamus is involved in the maintenance of homeostasis (i.e., temperature regulation, regulation of water balance, pituitary function, control of food intake, regulation of gastric secretions, and emotional expression).

Cerebellum

The cerebellum is the second largest portion of the brain and is an important component of the motor system of the body. It operates at a subconscious level. It coordinates and integrates muscular movement and predicts when to stop movements. It also coordinates reflexes that maintain posture and equilibrium.

Cerebrum

The cerebrum — the largest portion of the brain — provides for the higher functions, such as memory, reasoning, feelings, and association. In addition, voluntary movement, coordination of eye and head movements, interpretation of the skin sensations (heat, cold, touch, pressure, and pain), visual interpretation, hearing, speech, and other functions are found in the cerebrum.

There are regions in the cerebral cortex that perform specific functions. These areas have significant overlap of functions. The functions are divided into three areas: motor, sensory, and association. The motor areas handle voluntary movement, the sensory areas interpret impulses that arrive from various sensory receptors, and the association areas function to analyze and interpret sensory experiences that involve memory, reasoning, verbalizing, judgment, and emotional feelings. These areas are located throughout the cerebrum.

1. Frontal lobe. The motor areas control movements of voluntary skeletal muscles. The association areas carry on higher intellectual processes (e.g., complex problem solving, concentration).
2. Parietal lobe. The sensory areas are for the sensations of temperature, touch, pressure, and pain from the skin. The association areas function in the understanding of speech and in using words to express thoughts and feelings.
3. Temporal lobes. The sensory areas are responsible for hearing. The association areas are used in the interpretation of sensory experiences, etc.
4. Occipital lobes. The sensory areas are responsible for vision. The association areas function in combining visual images with other sensory experiences.

Other Anatomical Structures In or Around the Brain

Ventricles

The ventricles are brain cavities that house structures which secrete cerebrospinal fluid. The fluid fills the ventricles and surrounds the brain and spinal cord.

Cerebrospinal Fluid (CSF)

Cerebrospinal fluid is a clear, sticky liquid whose primary function seems to be protective. It protects the brain and spinal cord by absorbing shock and other forces that might othewise jar and damage delicate tissues. Cerebrospinal fluid compensates for changes in blood volume, keeping cranial volume constant. It is also easily removed by spinal puncture for analysis.

Meninges

The brain and spinal cord are surrounded by three membranes collectively called the meninges. They are:

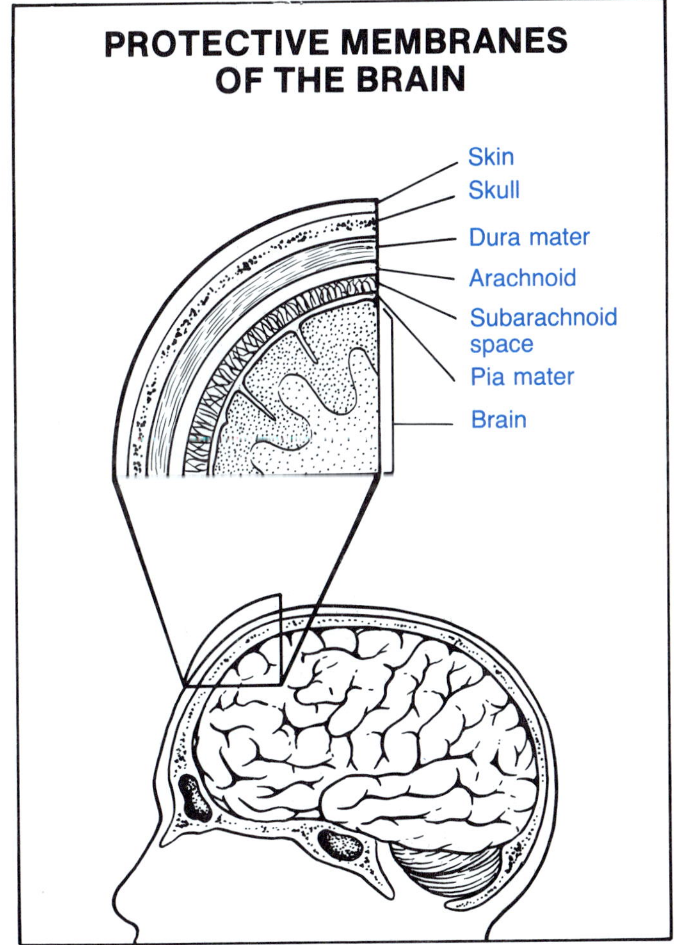

Figure 12-2. Meninges.

1. The dura mater, which is the outermost layer composed primarily of tough, white, fibrous, connective tissue which protects the underlying structures.
2. The arachnoid mater, which is the delicate membrane enclosing a space (subarachnoid space) filled with cerebrospinal fluid.
3. The pia mater, the innermost membrane, is very thin and contains many nerves, as well as blood vessels that aid in nourishing the underlying cells of the brain and spinal cord.
4. "Potential" spaces, which are formed by the meninges. This really means that when injury to the brain or its blood vessels occurs, these potential spaces may become filled with blood. These blood-filled (or fluid-filled) spaces then apply pressure to the brain or cord, which may prove to be life-threatening or fatal to the patient if definitive care is not rapidly available.
   - The epidural space is found between the skull and the dura. This is usually created by arterial bleeding.
   - The subdural space is found beneath the dura and is usually a result of venous bleeding.
   - The subarachnoid space may fill with blood from a rupture of a cerebral aneurysm.

Circulation

More than any other organ of the body, the central nervous system needs a continual supply of blood. As is well known, the delicate tissues of the brain and spinal cord deteriorate rapidly without oxygen.

There are many disorders involving the vessels of the central nervous system. Strokes (cerebral vascular accidents) account for more neurological disorders than any other category of pathological processes. Stroke is the third leading cause of death in the United States.

The following is a brief description of circulation in the brain:

1. A pair of internal carotid arteries that branch off of the common carotid arteries of the neck, and the paired vertebral arteries, arising from the subclavian arteries, form the arterial supply of the brain.
2. The carotids give rise to three pair of cerebral arteries that supply the cerebrum.
3. The vertebral arteries join to form the basilar artery, which supplies the cerebellum and the brain stem.
4. The carotids and basilar arteries are joined by vessels that form the Circle of Willis. The Circle of Willis allows blood from one set of arteries to

flow into an area supplied by the other in case of diminished flow or complete blockage.

5. Venous drainage — the veins in the brain are largely unnamed except for the dural sinuses.

Spinal Cord

The spinal cord is located within the vertebral canal formed by the vertebrae. As with the brain, the cord is surrounded by the meninges and bathed in cerebrospinal fluid. Its length is generally eighteen inches from the foramen magnum (a hole at the base of the cranial vault where the cord merges with the brain stem) to the lower border of the second lumbar vertebra. The diameter of the spinal cord is no more than three-fourths of an inch and is smaller than the spinal canal. The meninges and loose connective tissue fill the rest of the canal.

The spinal cord transmits impulses to and from the brain. Impulses from the body to the brain are called afferent impulses, and impulses from the brain to the body are called efferent impulses. The spinal nerves carry impulses to and from the periphery. The cord also integrates reflex activity.

The spinal cord is divided into the cervical, thoracic, lumbar, and sacral regions.

Spinal Nerves

The cord gives rise to thirty-one pair of spinal nerves that are distributed to the skin and muscles of a particular body region. There is an overlap of approximately 30 percent, so if a given nerve is damaged, all function will not be lost. Each spinal nerve has a dorsal root and a ventral root. The dorsal root conveys impulses to the cord, while the ventral root conveys impulses from the cord to muscles and glands.

Dermatomes

A dermatome is an area of skin supplied with afferent (sensory) nerve fibers from the spinal cord. The higher up the cord an injury occurs, the greater the resultant loss of sensation and movement (see Figure 12-3). Some examples of nerve root control are as follows:

1. Sensation above the shoulder girdle might indicate injury at cervical vertebra 5 (C5).
2. Diaphragmatic breathing (phrenic nerve) may result with injury between

Figure 12-3. Dermatomes.

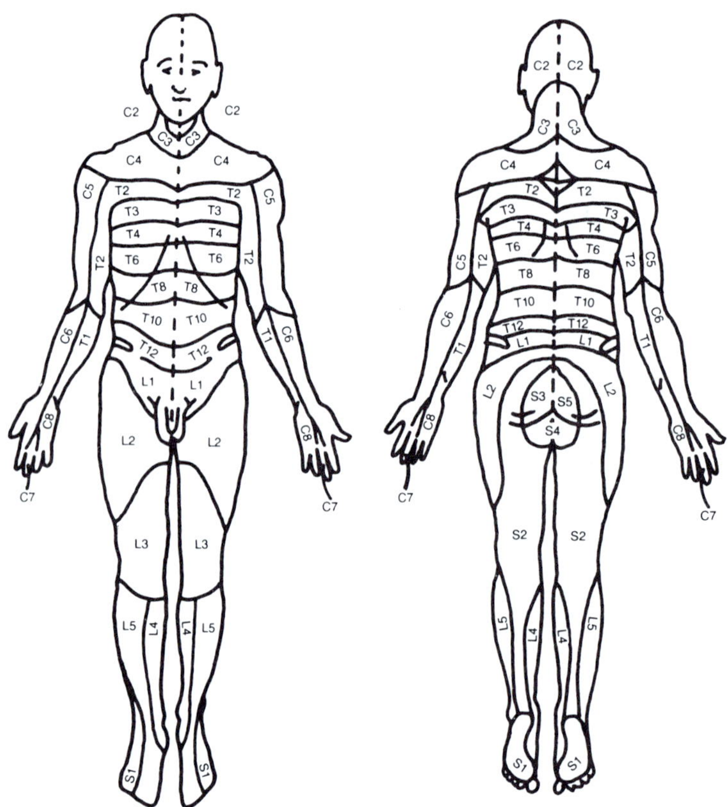

cervical vertebra 3 (C3) and lumbar vertebra 5 (L5).

3. In the thoracic spine, sensation above the nipple level might indicate injury at thoracic vertebra 4 (T4), and sensation above the umbilicus level might indicate injury at thoracic vertebra 10 (T10).
4. If hip extension is lost, it indicates injury at lumbar vertebra 4 and 5.
5. If toe movement is lost, it indicates injury at lumbar vertebra 5 and sacral vertebra 1 and 2.

Vertebral Column

The spinal cord is protected by the vertebral column. The following are the components of a vertebra:

1. Vertebral body.
2. Pedicle.
3. Vertebral foramen.
4. Transverse process.
5. Articulating process.
6. Lamina.
7. Spinous process.

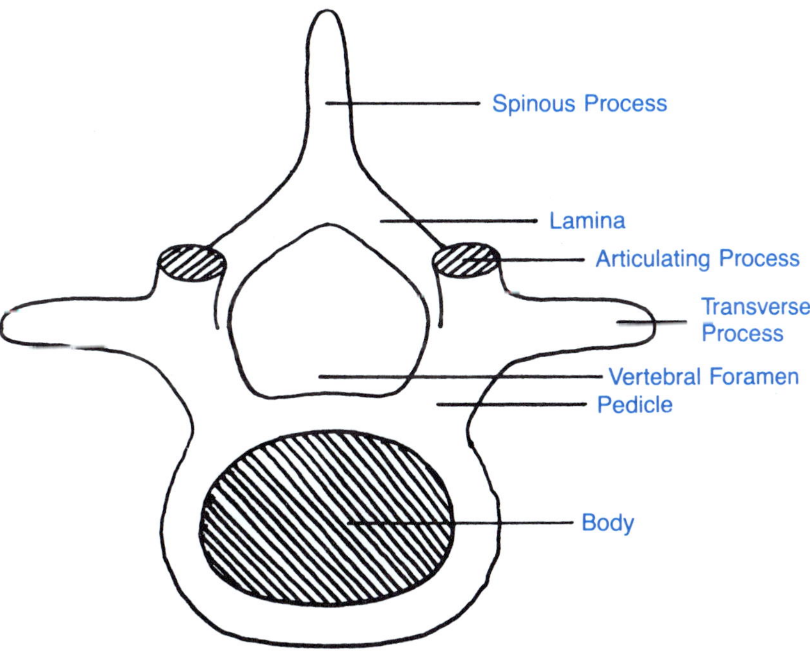

Figure 12-4. Superior View of a Vertebra.

Figure 12-5. The Vertebral Column.

Courtesy Department of Transportation.

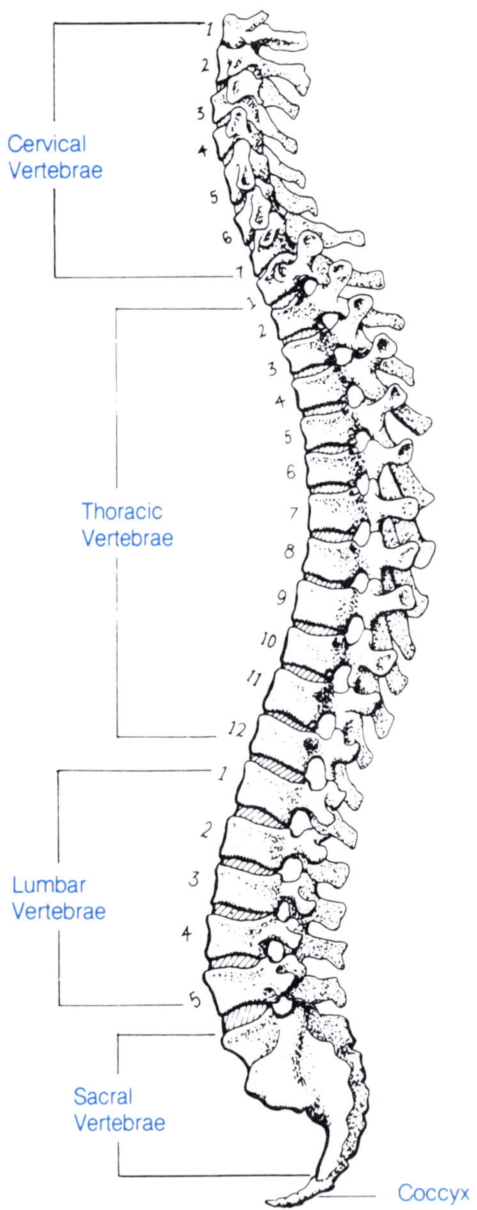

Ligaments and muscle secure the vertebral column in place. The vertebral column is divided into the following:

1. Cervical (seven vertebrae, eight nerves).
2. Thoracic (twelve vertebrae and nerve roots).
3. Lumbar (five vertebrae and nerve roots).
4. Sacral (one made of five fused segments, five nerve roots).
5. Coccygeal (one made of four to five fused segments, one nerve root).

Peripheral Nervous System

Cranial Nerves

The brain gives rise to twelve pair of cranial nerves that supply motor and sensory fibers to the structures in the head, neck, and shoulder regions. The cranial nerves, along with the spinal nerves, make up the peripheral nervous system.

Peripheral Nerves (Spinal Nerves)

These nerves innervate the organs, skin, and muscles. They are categorized into:

1. Somatic sensory, which include sensations of pain, temperature, touch, pressure, position, and muscle sense.
2. Somatic motor (muscle).
3. Visceral sensory, which include the glands and structures of the thoracic and abdominopelvic cavities.
4. Visceral motor.

Both the visceral sensory and motor are part of the autonomic nervous system.

Autonomic Nervous System

The autonomic nervous system works at the reflex level, generally beyond a person's conscious control. It maintains control over the visceral organs, and thus over glandular secretions and smooth and cardiac muscle activity. The autonomic nervous system has two divisions.

Sympathetic (Thoracolumbar) Division

This is called the thoracolumbar division possibly because it is composed of the autonomic fibers of all of the thoracic and lumbar spinal nerves. In this system, norepinephrine is secreted at some nerve endings, giving it the name "adrenergic." Activity in this system tends to increase utilization of body resources and prepares the body for "fight or flight." The sympathetic and parasympathetic innervate all the same organs except the following, which are solely innervated by the sympathetic:

1. Skeletal muscle.
2. Skin.
3. Adrenal medulla.
4. Sweat glands.
5. Spleen.

The effects of the sympathetic are more widespread that those of the parasympathetic. This occurs because the sympathetic supplies a wider body area and because norepinephrine is destroyed more slowly than acetylcholine (the parasympathetic mediator).

When the sympathetic system is stimulated ("fight or flight"), the following effects are noted:

1. Increased heart rate.
2. Increased force of contraction.
3. Increased cardiac output.
4. Increased blood pressure.
5. Blood vessels dilate.
6. Increase in blood sugar.
7. Secretions from sweat glands.
8. Bronchodilation.

The sympathetic nervous system may be affected by certain drugs which are classified by their effects on the body. They may produce either beta effects or alpha effects.

1. Beta effects are: increased heart rate, increased force of cardiac contraction, increased automaticity, vasodilation, and bronchodilation.
2. Alpha effects are: arterial vasoconstriction and mild to no bronchoconstriction; no cardiac effects are produced by alpha drugs.

Parasympathetic (Craniosacral) Division

This is also called the craniosacral division because its nerve outflows come from the cranial and sacral nerves. Some of the nerve fibers secrete acetylcholine, which is why this system is sometimes referred to as the "cholinergic." Activity in the parasympathetic division tends to conserve body resources and preserve normal function.

When the parasympathetic system is stimulated, it tends to affect individual organs rather than have a widespread effect like the sympathetic nervous system. Its effects include:

1. Stimulating the vegetative bodily functions, such as increasing the motility of the digestive tract.
2. Increasing watery saliva secretion.
3. Slowing the heart.
4. Constricting blood vessels.
5. Dilating visceral organs (except heart and lungs).
6. Causing bronchoconstriction.

ASSESSMENT OF THE NERVOUS SYSTEM (NEUROLOGIC EXAM)

History

A good history may be difficult to obtain, because the patient may have impaired mental functioning. The paramedic must identify the mechanism of injury (i.e., traumatic or nontraumatic CNS problems), and obtain information from bystanders in both witnessed and unwitnessed situations.

In traumatic CNS injury (see Chapter 7), ascertain the following:

1. When did the accident occur?
2. How did the accident occur?
3. What was the mechanism of injury?
4. Was there a loss of consciousness (duration)?
5. What is the chief complaint (pain, numbness, tingling, paralysis, etc.)?
6. Complicating factors (i.e., underlying medical problems, alcohol, or drug intoxication).

In nontraumatic CNS illness, ascertain the following:

1. Chief complaints (details of present illness):
   - Gradual onset?
   - Sudden onset?

- Duration of unconsciousness or coma?
- Recent head trauma?
- Complaints of symptoms prior to becoming comatose (i.e., headache, dizziness, nausea, and/or vomiting).

2. Underlying medical problems (heart disease, hypertension, alcoholism, diabetes).
3. Environmental clues:
   - Evidence of current medications?
   - Medic alert tags?
   - Alcohol bottles?
   - Drugs or paraphernalia?
   - Incontinence?

Physical Examination

Primary Survey

During the primary survey, treat life-threatening problems:

1. Maintain the airway (if the patient is unconscious from possible trauma, assume cervical spine injury and treat appropriately — immobilize the head/neck).
2. Provide high-flow, high-concentration oxygen if necessary.
3. Observe for:
   - Level of consciousness.
   - Respiratory distress (anticipate the potential for an arrest due to increased intracranial pressure).
   - Vomiting and aspiration of stomach contents or blood from facial injuries.
   - An absent gag reflex.
   - Position of the patient.
4. **Monitor and record vital signs frequently** — they may change rapidly.

Respiratory Status

1. May be normal.
2. The patient may develop pulmonary edema.
3. Look for Cheyne-Stokes respiration.
4. Look for central neurogenic hyperventilation.
5. Look for ataxic respirations (irregular breathing).
6. Look for apneustic respirations (abnormal respirations marked by sus-

tained inspiration).

7. Observe for evidence of intercostal muscle dysfunction (diaphragmatic breathing).

Blood Pressure/Pulse/Temperature/Pupils

Observe for hypertension, bradycardia, elevation or depression of body temperature, and changes in pupils (e.g., unequal).

1. Early stages of increased intracranial pressure: may not have any vital sign changes. Pupils are normal. The patient may complain of:
   - Nausea.
   - Vomiting.
   - Headache.
2. Later stage:
   - Pulse slows.
   - Blood pressure increases.
   - Temperature may rise.
   - Pupils may be unequal, dilated, constricted, and/or nonreactive to light.
3. Very late stages:
   - Pulse increases.
   - Blood pressure falls.
   - Temperature remains elevated.
   - Pupils may be midpoint, unequal, and/or nonreactive to light.
4. Dysrhythmias are common with increased intracranial pressure, especially with subarachnoid bleeding.

Neurologic Evaluation

Level of Consciousness

The most important sign in evaluation is any change in level of consciousness. Determine the following:

1. Is the patient oriented to person, time (date), and place?
2. Note the patient's recall of recent events.
3. Note speech pattern.
4. Does the patient respond appropriately to questions?
5. Observe the patient's response to commands. Are they rapid or sluggish?
6. If the patient is not alert, note the degree of stimulation required for response: verbal stimulation, light tactile, painful (sternal rub, squeeze

trapezius muscle, or pinprick).

Posturing

Note any abnormal positioning or response to pain, such as:

1. Purposeful versus uncoordinated movements.
2. Abnormal flexion (decorticate) — flexion of any or all of the extremities (due to mid-upper-brain or lower diencephalon injury).
3. Abnormal extension (decerebrate) — the arms and legs extended (due to midbrain and/or upper pons-level injury).
4. Flaccidity (limpness).

Pupils

Determine the following:

1. Are both pupils equal?
2. Do both pupils respond to light? Sluggishly or briskly (normal)?
3. Is there abnormal constriction or dilation?

Glasgow Coma Scale

This is a scale used for evaluating and quantitating the degree of coma by observing for the best eye-opening, motor, and verbal responses to standardized stimuli. Coma may be defined as the absence of eye-opening, verbal, and motor response. A score of 7 or less is classified as coma. Each item is given an individual score, and the scores are then totaled. A total score of 9 or greater means that the patient is not in coma. The lowest score is 3, and the highest is 15. The following is the Glasgow Coma Scale:

Eye Opening:

Spontaneous eye opening . . . . 4 points
Eye opening on command . . . . 3 points
Eye opening to painful stimulus . . . . 2 points
No eye opening . . . . 1 point

Best Motor Response

Follows command . . . . 6 points
Localizes painful stimuli . . . . 5 points
Withdrawal to pain . . . . 4 points
Responds with abnormal flexion to painful stimuli (decorticate) 3 points
Responds with abnormal extension to pain (decerebrate) . . 2 points

Gives no motor response . . . . 1 point

Best verbal response

Answers appropriately (oriented) . . . . 5 points
Gives confused answers . . . . 4 points
Inappropriate response . . . . 3 points
Makes unintelligible noises . . . . 2 points
Makes no verbal response . . . . 1 point

AVPU System of Evaluation

This system allows a quick assessment of the patient's level of consciousness.

A = Is the patient **alert**?
V = Patient responds to **verbal** stimuli.
P = Patient responds to **painful** stimuli.
U = Patient is **unresponsive**.

Head-to-Toe Survey

The paramedic should note the patient's position upon arrival or determine the position from bystanders, if possible. After life-threatening situations are managed, the paramedic may perform a thorough secondary assessment.

1. Normal head-to-toe — the paramedic should take spinal precautions early into the assessment (during the primary survey) of the traumatically injured patient.
2. Eyes:
   - Evaluate pupils.
   - Extraocular movements (do not allow the patient to move his/her head) — have the patient follow the paramedic's finger with his/her eyes to the extreme left, then up and down, then to the extreme right, then up and down.
3. In trauma, evaluate for evidence of vertebral column or cord injury — remember, the mechanism of injury is usually all that is needed to assume and treat as if a spinal injury has occurred:
   - Evaluate for pain and tenderness.
   - Observe for bruises if possible (do not roll the patient just for this observation.
   - Check for deformity (not common).

- Check for sensation and movement in the upper and lower extremities. In trauma, have the patient just wiggle his/her toes and fingers to check movement. In a medical situation, the patient may attempt to move all extremities.
- If the patient is unconscious, pinprick the soles of the feet and the palms of the hands.

4. Observe for the following when assessing the patient:
   - Fruity odor to breath, possible hyperglycemia.
   - Laceration of tongue, possible seizure.
   - Cyanosis, possible respiratory problem.
   - Alcohol on breath, possible intoxication. Be suspicious of other causes in the alcoholic patient.
   - Rigidity of the neck, possible meningitis.
   - Flaccid extremities on one side, possible stroke.
   - Posturing, possible increased intracranial pressure.
   - Needle tracks on arms, a possible drug overdose.
   - Jaundice, possible liver failure.
   - Head trauma, possibly increased intracranial pressure.
   - Incontinence, possible seizure or coma.

PATHOLOGY AND MANAGEMENT OF NONTRAUMATIC CNS DISORDERS

Coma

Coma is an abnormally deep state of unconsciousness from which the patient cannot be aroused by external stimuli.

Causes of Coma

1. Structural — intracranial bleeding, head trauma, stroke, brain tumor, and/or other space-occupying lesions.
2. Metabolic — anoxia, hypoglycemia, thiamine deficiency, diabetic ketoacidosis, kidney or liver failure.
3. Drug use — barbiturates, narcotics, hallucinogens, depressants, or alcohol (occasionally combinations of these are taken).
4. Cardiovascular — hypertensive encephalopathy, shock, hypotension, dysrhythmias, and stroke.
5. Respiratory — pulmonary embolist, COPD, toxic inhalations, and trauma to the chest wall.

6. Infections — meningitis, herpes, etc.
7. The following is a mnemonic for common causes of coma:
   A = Acidosis, alcohol.
   E = Epilepsy.
   I = Infection.
   O = Overdose.
   U = Uremia.
   T = Trauma.
   I = Insulin.
   P = Psychosis.
   S = Stroke.

Assessment

(See Neurological Assessment, pages 303 to 308, this chapter.)

History

1. The paramedic needs information from bystanders and family members.
2. Observe the environment for evidence of possible causes of the coma.
3. Ask specific questions (i.e., length of coma, sudden or gradual onset, etc.).
4. Check for medications — medic alert tag, wallet insert, microfilm.

Physical Examination

(See Neurological Assessment, pages 303 to 308, this chapter.)

1. Perform a primary survey.
2. Perform a neurologic exam.
3. Obtain a complete set of vital signs frequently.
4. Observe for:
   - Hypertension.
   - Bradycardia.
   - Abnormal respiratory patterns.
   - Pupillary changes.
   - Elevation or depression of temperature.
5. Perform a head-to-toe examination.

Treatment

To treat the comatose patient, do the following:

1. Airway:
   - Open the airway.
   - Use an oral/nasal airway as necessary.
   - Perform endotracheal intubation (**with suspected cervical spine trauma, maintain the head in the neutral position. DO NOT flex or extend the neck; use manual stabilization to maintain appropriate positioning**).
2. Support ventilation as needed.
3. Provide cervical immobilization if neck injury is suspected.
4. Start an IV of D_5W TKO (follow local protocol; some agencies recommend normal saline at a keep open rate in place of D_5W).
5. Draw blood for blood glucose determination.
6. Use a reagent strip for blood glucose determination.
7. Administer glucose, twenty-five grams IV (see Appendix 1 for detailed drug description):
   - Be sure to draw one tube for blood glucose determination prior to glucose administration.
   - Inject a 50-cc ampule (1 cc per kilogram of body weight) IV into a secure vein for an adult and child.
8. Administer naloxone (Narcan). (See Appendix 1.)
   - Adult — 0.8 mg IV. If no response is observed, this may be repeated at two- to three-minute intervals for two to three doses. Darvon overdoses may require larger doses.
   - Pediatric — 0.01 mg per kilogram of body weight.
9. Administration of thiamine may be considered in the suspected alcoholic patient.
   - Indications are — for suspected alcoholics before the administration of dextrose and in suspected Wernicke's encephalopathy or Korsakoff's syndrome (Wernicke's encephalopathy is brain dysfunction associated with thiamine deficiency; Korsakoff's syndrome is psychosis with disorientation, muttering, delirium, insomnia, illusions, hallucinations, and painful extremities; this may occur as a sequel to chronic alcoholism).
   - Administration — 100 mg IV (IM if necessary).
10. Constantly monitor the patient.
11. If necessary, protect the eyes by gently taping them shut.
12. Transport the medical patient laterally recumbent.
13. Transport the trauma patient with complete spinal precautions.

Seizures (Convulsions)

A seizure or convulsion is an involuntary contraction or series of contractions of the voluntary muscles. It is usually the result of a massive electrical discharge of one or more groups of neurons in the brain. The following conditions may cause instability or irritability of the brain and possibly lead to seizures:

1. Stroke.
2. Head trauma (recent or past).
3. Toxins, including alcohol and drug withdrawal.
4. Hypoxia.
5. Hypoglycemia and other metabolic abnormalities.
6. Infections.
7. Brain tumors.
8. Vascular disorders.
9. Eclampsia.
10. Idiopathic epilepsy (the most common cause of seizures).

Grand Mal (Major Motor) Seizures

These are generalized motor seizures characterized by loss of consciousness, tonic-clonic movements, and usually tongue biting, incontinence, and mental confusion. Grand mal seizures are followed by a period of sleepiness, where the patient is minimally responsive (postictal state). This phase may last from a few minutes to hours. Grand mal are the most common form of seizure.

The typical progression of a grand mal seizure is as follows:

1. Aura — a sensory perception preceding seizure activity; it may be auditory, visual, olfactory, a taste, or an "odd" feeling in part of the body.
2. A loss of consciousness that may be preceded by a cry and followed by bowel or bladder incontinence.
3. Tonic phase — continuous motor tension that makes the body appear stiff.
4. Hypertonic phase — this involves extreme muscular rigidity and hyperextension of the back.
5. Clonic phase — rigidity that alternates with relaxation, appearing as jerking motions.
6. There may be an autonomic discharge demonstrated by hyperventilation,

salivation, and tachycardia.
7. Postictal state.
8. The patient may experience confusion, fatigue, and headache.

Focal Motor Seizures

These are generally limited to certain muscle groups or to one side of the body. They are characterized by the twitching of one part of the body and may progress to generalized seizures.

Psychomotor Seizures (or Temporal Lobe)

These are characterized by an altered personality state, often preceded by dizziness or a peculiar metallic taste in the mouth. They may cause sudden, involuntary, unexplained attacks of rage or may manifest themselves by gestures resembling catatonic schizophrenic behavior.

Petit Mal Seizures

These occur in children and are characterized by the child staring off into space for a few seconds, then returning to consciousness without demonstrating any motor symptoms. Generally, petit mal seizures do not need to be treated in the field.

Hysterical Seizures

These stem from psychological disorders that may result in sharp, bizarre movements. They typically can be stopped by giving a clear command to discontinue the behavior. The patients rarely injure themselves. Aromatic ammonia may help to differentiate a hysterical seizure from a true seizure.

Assessment

(See Neurological Assessment, pages 303 to 308, this chapter.)

History
1. What is the patient's frequency of seizures?
2. Note any prescribed medications and the patient's compliance in taking them.
3. Try to ascertain a description of the seizure activity, including the length of the seizure, whether the seizure was generalized or focal, if there was an aura, and if the patient experienced incontinence or tongue biting.

Use information provided from bystanders or family members.
4. Is there a recent or past history of head trauma?
5. Is there recent fever, headache, or stiff neck (possible meningitis)?
6. Is there a history of diabetes, heart disease, or stroke?
7. Is there a history of drug or alcohol abuse, including the last time they were used?

Physical Examination

1. Observe for signs of head trauma.
2. Observe for injury to the tongue from tongue biting during a seizure.
3. Check for incontinence.
4. Check for an elevated heart rate.
5. Check for pale or cyanotic skin (during the tonic and clonic phases of a seizure, the respiratory muscles are affected, so breathing ceases).
6. Perform a normal head-to-toe examination.
7. Observe for evidence of alcohol or drug abuse.
8. Evaluate for cardiac dysrhythmias.

Differentiation of a Syncopal Episode from a Seizure

1. Syncope:
   - Usually starts in a standing position.
   - The patient usually remembers a brief warning that he/she was going to faint.
   - The patient usually regains consciousness almost immediately upon becoming supine.
   - Immediately after the syncopal episode, the patient has a slow, weak pulse and is clammy and pale.
2. Seizures:
   - May start in any position.
   - May occur without any warning.
   - Result in tonic/clonic movements during the convulsion.

Treatment of Seizures

To treat a seizure patient, do the following:

1. Primary survey (ABCs):
   - Maintain the airway.
   - **Do not force any objects between the patient's teeth.** (A padded tongue blade or bite block often is unnecessry and may cause vomit-

ing, aspiration, or spasm of the larynx; it should only be used if it can be inserted into the patient's mouth prior to a seizure.)
2. Administer high-flow, high-concentration oxygen.
3. Never attempt to restrain the patient.
4. Protect the patient from objects in the immediate environment.
5. Maintain the patient's body temperature.
6. Position the patient on his/her side after the clonic-tonic phase is over.
7. Suction if necessary.
8. Monitor the cardiac rhythm if indicated.
9. Provide a quiet, reassuring atmosphere.
10. Transport the patient supine or in the laterally recumbent position.

Status Epilepticus

Status epilepticus is defined as two or more seizures without an intervening period of consciousness. Status epilepticus is considered a major emergency that may lead to aspiration, brain damage, fracture of the long bones and of the spine, necrosis of the heart muscle, and severe dehydration. **This is a life-threatening situation.**

The major problem is that in a prolonged seizure, the brain becomes hypoxic. Some of the common causes in adults are withdrawal from prescribed medications (or nonprescribed), toxemia of pregnancy, kidney failure, meningitis, aand encephalitis.

Treatment of Status Epilepticus

1. ABCs.
2. Maintain the airway as necessary.
3. Administer high-flow, high-concentration oxygen.
4. Assist ventilations as necessary.
5. If possible, start an IV of normal saline TKO and secure well. (Dilantin is incompatible with D_5W).
6. Administer glucose, 25 grams IV (only in a secure vein).
7. Diazepam IV:
   - Indicated for status epilepticus in the field.
   - Administer in adults — 5 to 10 mg slow IV push (each 5 mg should be injected over a one-minute period). In infants thirty days of age to children five years — administer 0.2 to 0.5 mg slow IV, every two to five minutes to a maximum of 2.5 mg. Children five years or older — 1 mg IV every two to five minutes to a maximum of 5 mg. Observe

for respiratory depression. This should be administered by direct physician's order or standing orders. (Consult base station for further orders.)

Stroke (Cerebrovascular Accident)

A stroke is a sudden, catastrophic event causing an acute neurologic deficit due to a change in the vascular supply to the brain. Stroke is the third leading cause of death in the United States (preceded by heart disease and cancer) and the frequent cause of disability in the geriatric population. Approximately 200,000 people die each year from stroke.

A stroke may be caused by the occlusion or rupture of a blood vessel, which leads to a reduction of blood flow to the brain and to increased intracranial pressure, or both. The occlusion may be caused by a thrombus or an embolus. Hemorrhage in the brain may be caused by vessel rupture possibly due to hypertension or an aneurysm.

Assessment

(See Neurological Assessment, pages 303 to 308, this chapter.)

History

Stroke usually occurs in the presence of other medical problems that put the patient at risk. Check for the following:

1. Hypertension.
2. Diabetes.
3. High blood lipid levels.
4. Sickle cell disease.
5. Heart disease.
6. Peripheral vascular disease.
7. Previous neurological symptoms; transient ischemic attacks (TIAs).
8. Use of oral contraceptives.
9. When the patient was last noted to be alert.
10. The initial symptoms and if they have progressed.
11. Changes in level of consciousness.
12. Precipitating factors to the event.
13. Dizziness and/or palpitations experienced by the patient.

Physical Examination

The signs and symptoms that develop after a stroke or TIA depend on the area of the brain that is affected or damaged. The areas commonly affected

Figure 12-6. Causes of Stroke.

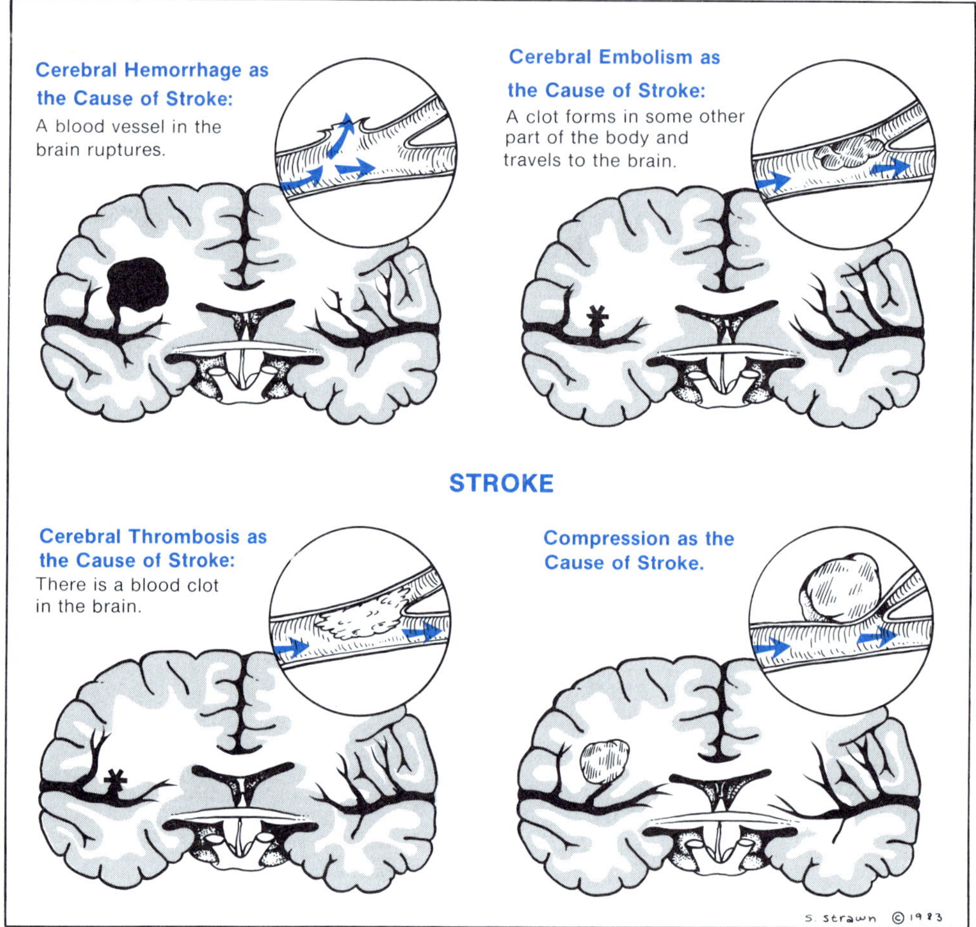

are the motor centers, the speech centers, and the sensory centers.

1. Perform a neurologic exam, especially noting hemiparesis (one-sided weakness) or hemiplegia (one-sided paralysis).
2. Note any speech disturbances, including dysarthria (imperfect articulation of speech due to disturbances of muscular control), motor aphasia (inability to express oneself), and receptive aphasia (inability to understand written, spoken, or tactile speech symbols).

3. Observe for confusion, agitation.
4. Observe for gait disturbances or uncoordination of fine motor movements.
5. Observe for vision disturbances.
6. Note any inappropriate effects, such as excessive laughing or crying.
7. Coma is common in a massive stroke.

Treatment of Stroke

1. ABCs.
2. Establish and maintain an airway (head tilt).
3. Assist ventilations as necessary.
4. Administer high-flow, high-concentration oxygen.
5. Keep the patient supine with the head elevated fifteen degrees.
6. Draw blood for glucose determination.
7. Start an IV with D_5W TKO.
8. Consider glucose, 25 grams IV if hypoglycemia is a possible factor.
9. Monitor for cardiac dysrhythmias.
10. Provide reassurance.
11. Protect the paralyzed extremities.
12. Explain the procedures; even if the patient cannot speak, he/she can probably understand.
13. Be prepared for the development of pulmonary edema in serious cases.
14. Transport the patient safely to the hospital.

Transient Ischemic Attacks (TIAs)

Transient ischemic attacks are episodes of focal cerebral dysfunction that last minutes or occasionally up to an hour, but always less than twenty-four hours. They are caused by insufficient blood flow to the brain. The symptoms are usually the same as in a stroke. TIAs are a common manifestation of carotid artery disease; complete recovery often occurs within twenty-four hours, and they may be a predictor of an eventual full-blown stroke.

Treat the patient of TIAs as if he/she is having a stroke.

Head Trauma

See Chapter 7, page 109.

Spinal Cord Trauma

See Chapter 7, page 115.

SUMMARY

The nervous system is a very complex network. To fully understand its working would take many years of study. What the paramedic can do is perfect his/her assessment and management of the CNS injured or ill patient.

The paramedic must be able to treat these patients efficiently and rapidly in order to insure the patient's survival with a minimum neurologic deficit. The patients that will most commonly be encountered in the field, ill from CNS illness, are the coma, seizure, and stroke patients.

The traumatically injured patient has been omitted from this chapter in order to follow the latest DOT paramedic guidelines.

13

The Acute Abdomen

This chapter reviews the anatomy and physiology of the digestive, genitourinary, and reproductive systems. Patient assessment with specific management is presented for a variety of problems. Evaluation and management of the patient presenting with an acute abdominal emergency must be efficiently and expediently completed. The patient with an acute abdomen is at risk, for his/her condition may rapidly deteriorate unless the problem is quickly identified and appropriately treated.

ANATOMY AND PHYSIOLOGY

Primary Structures of the Digestive System

1. **Mouth.** The oral cavity is made up of the lips, the cheeks, the gums, the teeth, and the tongue. Digestion begins here with the mechanical breakdown of foods and the chemical breakdown of carbohydrates.
2. **Pharynx.** This is the portion of the airway between the nasal cavity and the larynx. It is the common passageway for food and air.
3. **Esophagus.** This is the portion of the digestive tract between the pharynx and the stomach. It is ten inches long and conducts food from the oral cavity to the stomach. There is no digestive function.
4. **Stomach.** This is the hollow digestive organ that receives food from the esophagus, commences the digestion of proteins, and stores food. Both the stomach and the small intestine are where ulcers (lesions in a mucous-membrane-lined organ) may occur.
5. **Small intestines.** This is the portion of the digestive tract between the sto-

mach and the beginning of the large intestine. In the living person, it is ten to twelve feet long. It is divided into three segments — the duodenum (first ten to twelve inches), the jejunum (the next three to four feet), and the ileum (the last six to seven feet). The small intestine receives the secretions of the pancreas and of the liver (bile) and its own glands; digestion of proteins, fats, and carbohydrates is completed here. Nutrients are then absorbed through the lining of the intestinal wall.

6. **Large intestines.** This is the portion of the digestive tract from the ileocecal valve (the end of the small intestine) to the anus. It is about five feet in length and is composed of the cecum, the appendix, the colon, the rectum, and the anal canal. The large intestine has no digestive functions. It absorbs about 400 milliliters of water per day, as well as large quantities of inorganic salt. The production of vitamins K and B and amino acids occurs here. Solid wastes are stored in the intestine until they are evacuated from the body.

Accessory Organs of the Digestive System

1. **Salivary glands.** There are three pair of salivary glands that produce and secrete saliva into the oral cavity via ducts. This substance lubricates the food and starts the digestion of carbohydrates.
2. **Teeth.** The thirty-two teeth found in the oral cavity are used to mechanically break down foodstuffs.
3. **Liver.** This is a large, vascular, solid organ in the right upper quadrant that produces bile (breaks down fats), produces essential proteins, detoxifies many substances, and stores glycogen (a complex form of sugar).
4. **Gallbladder.** This is a sac located beneath the liver that stores and concentrates bile. The bile enters the small intestines to break down fat.
5. **Pancreas.** This gland is found behind the stomach and peritoneal lining. The pancreas secretes digestive enzymes, which break down all three foodstuffs, and insulin, which plays an important role in the transport of glucose to the cells.
6. **Vermiform (wormlike) appendix.** This is a hollow appendage attached to the large intestine that serves no known function (it is a vestigial organ) and may become inflamed, causing appendicitis.

The Urinary System

1. **Kidneys.** There are two kidneys (solid organs) located behind the peritoneum (retroperitoneal space) between the level of the twelfth thoracic

and the third lumbar vertebral bodies. Each kidney receives one major artery off of the descending aorta with a blood flow of approximately 1,300 milliliters of blood per minute. Therefore, injuries to the kidneys may result in significant blood loss in a short period of time. By filtration of the blood, the kidneys eliminate water, salts, and nitrogenous wastes and control the composition of extracellular fluid. They produce urine, help maintain a acid-base balance, maintain electrolyte balance, and play a role in blood pressure regulation.

2. **Ureter.** The ureters are two muscular tubes between eleven and fourteen inches in length which move urine from the kidneys to the urinary bladder by peristalsis (contractions of the tube).
3. **Urinary bladder.** There is one urinary bladder located posterior to the symphysis pubis in the pelvic cavity. It serves as a reservoir for urine until it is excreted.
4. **Urethra.** The urethra carries urine from the bladder to the outside of the body. The female urethra is approximately one and three-fourths inches long and is completely separate from the reproductive system. The male urethra is about eight inches long and serves as the common duct for both the urinary and reproductive systems.

The Male Reproductive System

1. **Testes.** There are two testes located outside the body cavity in the scrotum. They produce male sex cells and secrete the hormone testosterone.
2. **Prostate.** This gland surrounds the upper urethra just below the bladder. The secretions from this gland make up about 40 percent of the ejaculate. It is believed that these secretions activate the sperm to make them motile. The prostate secretions also aid in neutralizing vaginal acidity.
3. **Epididymis.** This is a small organ located behind the testes that serves as a reservoir for sperm cells.
4. **Vas deferens.** This is a small, muscular tube that conducts sperm from the epididymis to the urethra.
5. **Penis.** This structure is part of the male external genitalia and houses structures for the ejaculation of semen and the release of urine from the bladder to outside the body. It is also the male copulary organ.

The Female Reproductive System

1. **Ovary.** This is a small, walnut-sized, glandular organ located on each side of the uterus. The ovaries secrete estrogen and progesterone and produce the ovum (egg).

Figure 13-1. Male Reproductive System.

Figure 13-2. Female Reproductive System.

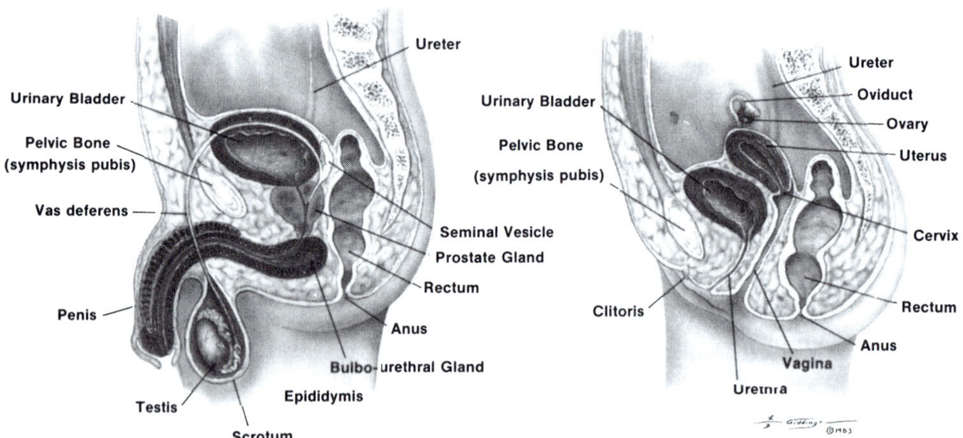

2. **Fallopian tube.** This is a muscular tube whose medial end protrudes into the uterus and whose lateral end is in intimate contact with the ovary but not attached to it. The fallopian tube conducts the ovum from the ovary to the uterus by peristaltic movement and provides a passageway in which sperm may travel to fertilize the egg.
3. **Uterus.** This is a hollow, muscular organ located in the pelvis posterior and superior to the urinary bladder. It is designed to retain the fertilized egg for the duration of pregnancy and to expel both the fetus and the placenta at the end of pregnancy.
4. **Cervix.** This is the inferior portion of the uterus (neck of the uterus) that has the ability to thin out (efface) and dilate to allow for the passage of the fetus and placenta. It leads into the vaginal canal.
5. **Vagina.** This muscular tube extends from the uterus to the vulva and is known as the birth canal. It allows for copulation and the passage of the fetus and placenta.
6. **Vulva.** This is the external genitalia.
7. **Perineum.** This is the area between the vagina and the anus.
8. **Endometrium.** This is the inner lining of the uterus that undergoes cyclical changes (monthly) controlled by hormones.
9. **Labia.** The labia are the folds of skin and underlying fat that extend backward from the mons pubic toward the anus (labia major/libia minor).

External Topography of the Abdominopelvic Cavity

1. The superior border is the diaphragm.
2. The inferior border is the pubis symphysis.
3. The posterior border is the vertebral column and low back musculature.
4. The anterior border is the muscular abdominal wall.

Location of the Abdominopelvic Organs

The abdominopelvic cavity is lined with a serous membrane called the parietal peritoneum. Each organ in this cavity is also covered with a serous membrane called the visceral peritoneum. These coverings hold the organs in place. In addition, the membrane secretes a clear-colored fluid that moistens the surfaces of the organs to allow for a near-frictionless environment when the organs move (during digestion of food, etc.).

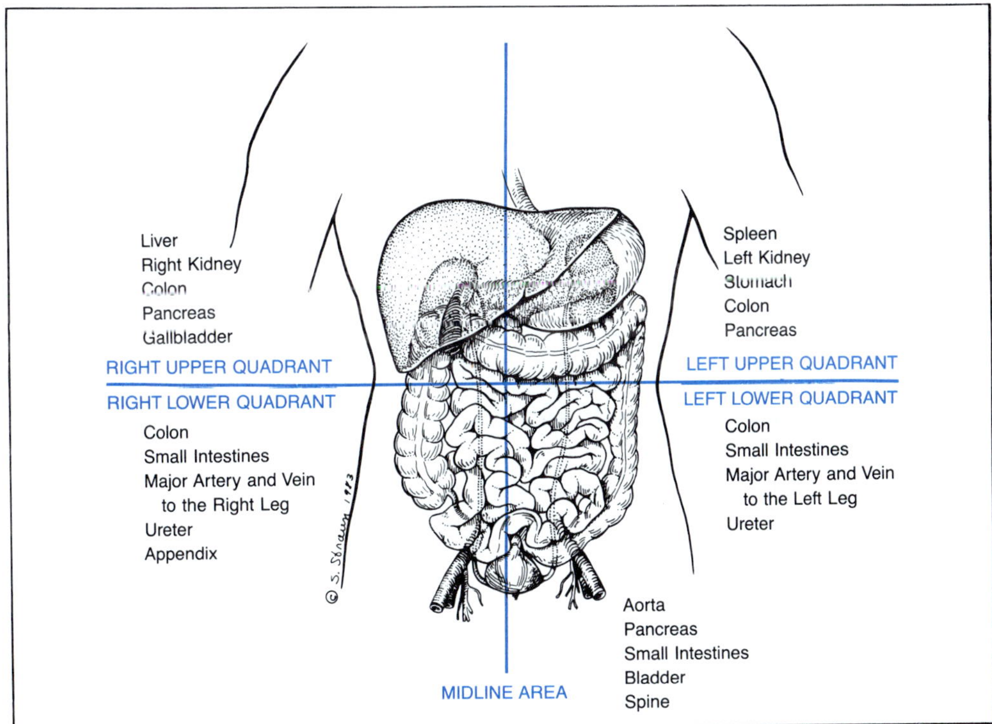

Figure 13-3. The Abdominal Quadrants.

Solid Organs in the Abdominopelvic Cavity

Solid organs are vascular and tend to bleed profusely when injured. It is important that the paramedic recognize the potential for significant bleeding when the abdomen is traumatized. The solid organs are:

1. The liver.
2. The spleen.
3. The pancreas.
4. The kidneys (retroperitoneal).
5. The ovaries.

Hollow Organs in the Abdominopelvic Cavity

Hollow organs do not bleed with the significance that solid organs do, but when they are ruptured, their contents are spilled out, causing significant irritation to the peritoneum. The hollow organs are:

1. The stomach.
2. The small intestine (S.I.).
3. The large intestine.
4. The gallbladder.
5. The urinary bladder.
6. The uterus.

Organs in Right Upper Quadrant

These include:

1. The liver.
2. The gallbladder.
3. The duodenum (first ten to twelve inches of the small intestine).

Organs in Left Upper Quadrant

These include:

1. The stomach.
2. The liver (a small portion).
3. The pancreas.
4. The spleen.

Organs in Right Lower Quadrant

These include:

1. The ascending colon.
2. Part of the transverse colon.
3. The veriform appendix.
4. Part of the small intestine.
5. One of the ovaries.

Organs in Left Lower Quadrant

These include:

1. Part of the transverse colon.
2. The descending colon.
3. Part of the small intestine.
4. One of the ovaries.

THE ACUTE ABDOMEN

Pathology of the Acute Abdomen

Nonhemorrhagic causes of acute abdominal pain include the following:

1. Local organ inflammation due to edema (swelling), obstruction (i.e., kidney stone), trauma, or infection.
2. Peritoneal inflammation due to edema, spilling of hollow organ contents, infection, or trauma.
3. Ectopic pregnancy prior to rupture (see Chapter 20).
4. Distention due to gas.
5. Disease processes related to nonhemorrhagic abdominal pain. A few of the many disorders that may cause abdominal pain are as follows:
   - Peptic ulcer — a lesion occurring at the lower end of the esophagus, in the stomach, or in the duodenum; these may bleed, causing serious hemorrhage.
   - Appendicitis — inflammation of the veriform appendix.
   - Diverticulitis — inflammation of a sac or pouch in the intestines; these may rupture, causing hemorrhage.

- Renal calculus — a stone in the ureter.
- Pelvic inflammatory disease (PID) — an infection that usually starts in the vagina or cervix, and spreads to the uterus, fallopian tubes, and surrounding broad ligaments.
- Pyelonephritis — inflammation of the kidney(s).
- Ovarian cyst — a sac that develops on the ovary; may cause the ovary to twist, or the cyst may rupture, causing pain and hemorrhage.
- Ectopic pregnancy — implantation of the fertilized ovum outside the uterus (this may rupture and cause significant hemorrhage).

Acute abdominal pain may also be caused by disease processes related to hemorrhagic abdominal pain. A few of the many disorders that may cause pain and bleeding are as follows:

1. Esophageal varices — a twisted dilation of veins in the esophagus that are prone to rupture.
2. Peptic/duodenal ulcer (see above).
3. Diverticulitis (see above).
4. Carcinoma of the colon.
5. Ectopic pregnancy (see above).
6. Aortic aneurysm — an abnormal dilation and weakening of the arterial wall that is prone to rupture, leading to life-threatening bleeding.
7. Trauma (see Chapter 7).

Assessment of the Acute Abdomen

Primary Survey

This process consists of the ABCs.

History

Take a history that is related to hemorrhage and nonhemorrhage injury/illness of the patient.

1. Chief complains (usually pain). Questioning for pain might follow this format:
   - P = provocation. What brought ''this'' (pain or episode) on?
   - Q = quality. Description of pain (i.e., sharp, dull, intermittent, constant).

- R = region (location), radiation, referred pain.
- S = severity. The paramedic may use the scale of 1 to 10, with 10 being the most severe.
- T = time.

2. History of present illness (this is a second format for history taking).
   - Type of problem.
   - Character of the pain.
   - Onset of the pain or illness.
   - Location of the pain.
   - Duration of the pain.
   - Alleviation or aggravation (what makes the pain better or worse?).
3. Past pertinent medical history.
4. Medications.
5. Consider the length of time and severity of the case.
6. Determine the fluid loss (if the patient is not in obvious shock) by taking orthostatic vital signs (tilt test) and questioning about vomiting and diarrhea.

Physical Examination

1. Head-to-toe examination (be gentle when examining the abdomen).
2. Signs and symptoms of nonhemorrhagic abdominal pain:
   - Local organ inflammation may result in pain, vomiting, diarrhea, and guarding of the abdomen.
   - Peritoneal inflammation may result in generalized diffuse pain, vomiting, diarrhea, and/or guarding.
   - Vital signs — heart rate which is usually increased, a blood pressure which may be decreased (take orthostatic vital signs as indicated), and respirations which may be normal or increased.
3. Signs and symptoms of hemorrhagic abdominal pain:
   - The upper gastrointestinal (GI) tract may bleed, leading to hematemesis (vomiting of blood). The stomach may accumulate large amounts of blood before the blood is vomited up. The color may be bright red, which indicates that the blood is recent, or dark red (coffee grounds), which means that the blood is old and partially digested.
   - Lower gastrointestinal bleeding. There may be bloody stools that are bright red (from the lower large intestine or rectum), wine-colored (from the colon or from a rapid upper GI bleed), or black and tarry, called melena (from digested blood of an upper GI bleed).
   - Vital signs include a heart rate that is usually increased; a blood pressure

that may be decreased (take orthostatic vital signs); and respirations that may be either normal or increased.

Treatment of the Acute Abdomen

Treatment of the acute abdomen consists of the following:

1. ABCs.
2. Provide oxygen as necessary.
3. Start a large-bore IV with normal saline or Ringer's lactate.
4. Monitor vital signs and cardiac rhythm.
5. Place the patient in a position of comfort.
6. Apply PASG (MAST).
7. Transport the patient.

THE GENITOURINARY SYSTEM

Pathology of the Genitourinary System

General causes of genitourinary disorders include:

1. Inflammation.
2. Infection.
3. Obstruction.
4. Hemorrhage.

Specific diseases are as follows:

Acute Renal Failure

Acute renal failure may be caused by diminished blood flow (due to shock, obstruction, burns, congestive heart failure, dysrhythmias, etc.); damage to the kidneys themselves (due to infection, ischemia, etc.); and bilateral obstruction of urinary outflow (due to kidney stones, tumors, etc.).

Signs and Symptoms

1. Scanty urination.
2. Uremia — retention in the blood of nitrogenous substances normally excreted by the kidneys.
3. As the patient becomes increasingly uremic, the following will be seen — nausea, vomiting, headache, dizziness, convulsions, and/or coma; the pulse will be rapid and blood pressure will be elevated.

Chronic Renal Failure

This is usually the end result of a gradually progressive loss of renal function. Occasionally, it is the result of a rapidly progressive disease of acute onset. Signs and symptoms of chronic renal failure usually do not appear until 75 percent of filtration is lost. A few of the causes are chronic infections, vascular disease, obstructive processes, and any untreated illness that causes acute renal failure.

Signs and Symptoms

Chronic renal failure produces significant changes in all bodily systems. It is similar to acute failure but is more serious because all bodily systems are seriously affected.

Kidney Stones

In the United States, 1 in 1,000 persons develop kidney stones. They are more common in men (particularly between the ages of thirty and fifty) than in women. Predisposing factors are dehydration, infection, and obstruction, along with other metabolic factors.

Signs and Symptoms

The clinical effects will vary with size, location, and cause of the stone.

1. The classical pain radiates from the area around the kidney, along the flank to the suprapubic region.
2. The pain may also be dull and constant and located in the back.

Urinary Tract Infection (UTI)

UTIs are ten times more common in women than in men. They affect about 10 to 20 percent of all women at least once. Most urinary tract infections are caused by bacteria.

Signs and Symptoms

1. Urgency and increased frequency of urination.
2. Cramps or spasm of the bladder, itching, and a feeling of warmth during urination.
3. Low back pain.
4. Malaise.
5. Nausea and/or vomiting.

6. Abdominal pain.
7. Chills.
8. Flank may be present.

Assessment of Genitourinary System Emergencies

(For greater amplification, see pages 328 to 329, this chapter.)

Primary Survey

This process consists of the ABCs.

History

1. The chief complaint is usually pain.
2. The patient has experienced urination problems, with increased frequency, decreased output, pain, and/or possible bleeding.
3. Past medical history — check for the following:
   - Kidney disease.
   - Renal dialysis.
   - Hypertension.
   - Kidney transplant (not common).
4. Determine what medications, if any, the patient is taking.

Physical Examination

1. Vital signs — they may be variable.
2. Inspect/auscultate/palpate the abdomen (as necessary).
3. Palpate for flank tenderness.
4. Conduct a neurological examination.
5. For signs and symptoms of genitourinary emergencies, see each specific disease.

Management of Genitourinary Disorders

Renal Failure

Management of renal failure consists of the following:

1. Primary survey.
2. History.
3. Physical examination.
4. Treat pulmonary edema if present.

5. Treat dysrhythmias if present.
6. Transport the patient to the appropriate facility. The patient may need dialysis.
7. Control shunt bleeding, if present (see hemodialysis).

Renal Calculi (Kidney Stones)

Treatment of renal calculi consists of the following:

1. Transport the patient only (in a position of comfort).
2. Medication may be given depending on the severity of the pain.

Urinary Tract Infections

Urinary track infections generally require no prehospital care.

Renal Dialysis

In dialysis, a semipermeable membrane, along with osmosis and diffusion, imitates normal kidney function to eliminate waste products and poison, maintain acid-base balance and electrolytes, and rid the body of excess fluid.

Types of Dialysis

1. Hemodialysis via an external shunt: the waste products and poisons are removed from the blood after entering a machine external to the body; the patient must have a surgical access made for the machine hookup.
2. Peritonial dialysis — a special solution is infused into the peritoneal cavity and left for several hours; waste products diffuse into the solution, where they remain until the solution is removed from the body.

Complications of Dialysis

1. Hypotension.
2. Chest pain.
3. Disequilibrium syndrome, which may cause lethargy and convulsions.
4. Air embolism.
5. Clotting of the vascular access.
6. Hemorrhaging.

Treatment of the Dialysis Patient

1. Maintain the airway and respirations.
2. Monitor the vital signs.

3. Start an IV with volume-replacement solution (access may be difficult to obtain; administer fluids cautiously).
4. Treat medical emergencies the same as for any patient.
5. Monitor the ECG.
6. To remove the patient from the dialysis machine, turn the machine off and clamp the shunt end.
7. Control shunt bleeding by direct pressure and/or pinching the shunt ends.
8. Follow local protocols.
9. Transport the patient in a position of comfort.

SUMMARY

The nontraumatic abdominal emergency creates a difficult problem for the paramedic. There are many possible disorders that may develop in the abdominopelvic region that are difficult for even the best specialists to identify. The paramedic must be an expert at assessing the patient with an acute abdomen.

Rather than attempting to identify the ailment that the patient is suffering from (it is helpful if it can be identified), the paramedic must recognize the dangers of the problem and manage the patient accordingly.

14

Anaphylaxis

Anaphylaxis is an acute allergic hypersensitivity reaction that may result in respiratory and/or circulatory failure and death, usually from one minute to one hour after its onset. It occurs most commonly after an injection, insect sting, or poisonous bite. It occurs less commonly after ingestion, inhalation, or absorption of the offending material.

It is estimated that less than 100 people a year in the United States die from insect stings. The honey bee and yellow jacket are the most likely insects to cause anaphylactic shock. It is important to note that 75 million people in the United States take an average of two drugs daily, resulting in approximately 300,000 hospitalizations due to adverse drug reactions.

This chapter presents the pathology leading to an anaphylactic shock reaction, as well as the appropriate assessment and management techniques. Rapid assessment and management of the patient experiencing an anaphylactic reaction are crucial to insure the patient's survival.

ANTIBODIES AND ANTIGENS

Antibodies

Antibodies are protein substances developed in response to specific substances (antigens). Antibodies destroy or remove the antigens as threats to the body.

Antigens

Antigens are substances that, when introduced into the body, stimulate the production of antibodies. They are usually proteins, sugars (polysaccharides), or lipid-carbohydrate compounds.

Examples of antigens causing reactions ranging from mild to severe include:

1. Venom (hymenoptera sting — bee, wasp, hornet, fire ant).
2. Antiserum (tetanus and diphtheria antitoxins).
3. Vaccines (tetanus toxoid, measles, influenza, and other egg-containing vaccines).
4. Foods (nuts, fish, shellfish, eggs).
5. Transfusion reactions.

Antigens may be introduced into the body by:

1. Injection of a drug, by an insect sting, or by a bite.
2. Ingestion of an allergen (any substance that causes an untoward reaction).
3. Inhalation of an allergen — not a common occurrence.
4. Absorption of an allergen — not a common occurrence.

When the body is exposed to some antigens, its reaction is incomplete or is not great enough to conifer an immunity to the antigen. The person continues to respond (with hives, runny nose, or edema) to repeated contacts with the antigen. This is an allergy. In some cases, the reaction of antibody to antigen is so severe that it may lead to the person's death due to respiratory obstruction and/or vascular collapse. This is anaphylactic shock.

PATHOLOGY

An antigen enters the body, stimulating antibody production. These antibodies attempt to deactivate the antigen. During sensitization (a condition of being made reactive to a specific substance, an antigen), antibodies specific to the sensitizing antigen attach to certain cells in the body that contain histamine and other substances. The second time the antigen enters the body, the antigen attaches to the antibody on the mast cells, causing the release of these mediators (histamine, etc.). The effects of these mediators may cause:

1. Systemic vasodilation.
2. Increased vascular permeability.
3. Dysrhythmias.
4. Bronchoconstriction.
5. Possible laryngospasm.
6. Possible widespread swelling due to interstitial edema.

ASSESSMENT

Primary Examination

1. Do the ABCs.
2. Treat all life-threatening problems.

Secondary Examination

1. Assess and reassess the airway/respirations.
2. Auscultate breath sounds.
3. Monitor the vital signs (reassess often).
4. Inspect the skin.
5. Monitor the level of consciousness often.

Chief Complaint

1. Depending on the severity of the episode, there may be only itching of the skin to increasing dyspnea over a period of minutes, leading to a complete airway obstruction.
2. The most significant changes caused by the released mediators are vasodilation and smooth muscle contractions, resulting in reduced vascular perfusion.
3. The most common manifestations are flushing, hives, and angioedema (development of edematous areas of skin, mucous membranes, or viscera).

History

1. The patient may have had a recent injection, bite, or sting.
2. The patient may have had a recent ingestion of an offending substance.

Signs and Symptoms

Early General Symptoms

1. Headache of sudden onset.
2. Itching palms and soles.
3. Apprehension.
4. A sensation of warmth.

Skin

The patient may experience:

1. Itching and urticaria (hives).
2. Swelling around the face (angioedema).
3. Flushing (vasodilation).
4. Cyanosis (hypoxia).
5. Pruritus (intense itching of the anal region).

Respiratory System

The patient may experience:

1. Shortness of breath.
2. ''Tightness'' or ''lump'' in the throat due to angioedema of the epiglottis.
3. Stridor, hoarseness, or loss of voice due to laryngeal edema and laryngospasm.
4. Complete occlusion.
5. Chest tightness accompanied by wheezing and dyspnea due to bronchospasm.

   6. Remember that the sequence of these respiratory events may occur very rapidly after the exposure.

Cardiovascular System

The patient may experience:

1. Acute vasodilation and increased vascular permeability, which may result in significant hypotension and vascular collapse (this may occur very rapidly after the exposure).
2. Elevated heart rate.
3. Lightheadedness.
4. Syncope.

5. Cardiac dysrhythmias, which may occur as a result of hypoxia, hypotension, and acidosis secondary to the anaphylactic reaction (a serious complication).

Gastrointestinal System

The patient may experience:

1. Nausea.
2. Vomiting.
3. Abdominal cramping.
4. Diarrhea (may be bloody).
5. Dysphagia (inability to swallow).

Other Signs and Symptoms

In addition to the above, the patient may experience:

1. Convulsions.
2. Incontinence.
3. **Death may occur in minutes as a result of respiratory obstruction and/or vascular collapse.**

MANAGEMENT OF ANAPHYLAXIS

Airway Management

1. Assure an open airway.
2. Provide high-flow, high-concentration oxygen.
3. Use a bag-valve-mask as necessary.
4. Perform endotracheal intubation, cricothyrotomy, or transtracheal ventilation if necessary.

Application of Constricting Band

In the case of insect stings, injections, or bites, apply a constricting band if the exposure occurred on an extremity.

1. Place the band proximal to the injection site.
2. The constricting band should not impede the arterial flow of blood.

Intravenous Therapy

1. Administer a crystalloid volume expander (lactated Ringer's or normal saline). Infuse generously until the systolic blood pressure is above 90 mmHg.
2. Administer epinephrine, 1:1,000; 0.3 ml to 0.5 ml subcutaneously for a mild reaction. (See Appendix 1.)
3. Administer epinephrine IV, 1:10,000; 3.0 ml to 5.0 ml IV slowly (1.0 ml per minute) for a severe reaction.
4. Be cautious in administering epinephrine to patients who have underlying cardiovascular disease or who are over forty years of age.
5. Administer diphenhydramine (Benedryl). (See Appendix 1.)
   - Adults — the usual dosage is 50 mg slow IV push or deep IM.
   - Pediatric patients up to age twelve — 1.0 to 2.0 mg per kilogram of body weight (should not exceed 50 mg per single dosage).
6. Administer aminophylline if symptoms persist — by direct physician's order. (See Appendix 1.)
   - Adults — usual dosage is 6 mg per kilogram added to 100 cc D_5W; titrate to run in fifteen to twenty minutes or to patient response.
   - Pediatric dosage — same as for adults.
   - If infused too rapidly, aminophylline may cause dysrhythmias, ventricular fibrillation, and circulatory collapse. Monitor constantly; IV administration should take at least twenty minutes.

Other Management Techniques

1. Monitor cardiac rhythm.
2. Frequently monitor vital signs.
3. Apply pneumatic antishock garments. The benefit of their use in treating shock is controversial. PSAG (MAST) may be most useful in "warm" shock (anaphylaxis, neurogenic, etc.) and therefore may prove beneficial. In any case, follow local protocol.
4. Provide rapid, safe transport.

SUMMARY

Anaphylaxis is a frightening experience to both victim and rescuers. If the paramedic rapidly assesses the patient and treats him/her appropriately, the chances of patient survival are enhanced.

When anaphylaxis does occur, it often does so unexpectedly. The paramedic must work quickly and efficiently. Consider treating the patient en route to the hospital.

15

Toxicology

This chapter discusses the etiology and treatment of poisoning emergencies. The environment contains a large number of potentially harmful substances, both natural and synthetic, which may accidentally or deliberately be introduced into the human body. These substances include animal and plant toxins, industrial and domestic chemicals, therapeutic pharmaceuticals, and drugs of abuse. Emergency medical personnel play an important role in the management of toxicological problems, since early identification, for prevention of absorption, is crucial to the successful treatment of the patient.

Types of toxic emergencies include:

1. Accidental poisonings (including food-bacterial poisoning).
2. Overdose of drugs.
3. Drug abuse.
4. Alcoholism and abuse.

SCOPE OF THE PROBLEM

Accidental Poisonings

In 1986, the American Association of Poison Control Centers National Data Collection System indicated that 1,098,894 poisonings were reported in the United States, with approximately 65 percent of them in children five years of age and under. Cleaning substances were most frequently involved in human exposures, making up approximately 10 percent of the poisonings.

The overuse of prescribed medications and the inappropriate combination of medications also occasionally result in accidental poisoning. Mixing of medicine and alcohol can end up with serious medical consequences. About 5,000 deaths occur each year from such combinations.

In commercial food preparation, as well as in home food preparation, food may be handled by a number of people, left unrefrigerated too long, or left in the refrigerator too long. It is quite possible for bacteria to be spread in food before it is served. If the handlers have poor sanitary habits, disease may be spread. When the paramedic encounters a patient with abdominal discomfort, it would be wise to keep in mind the possibility of food poisoning. (It may be difficult to distinguish between food poisoning and the flu.)

Overdose of Drugs and Alcohol

Intentional overdose by ingestion of drugs and alcohol accounts for 70 to 90 percent of all suicide attempts.

Drug Abuse

Abuse of therapeutic drugs (e.g., pain medications, sedatives) and greater use of "recreational" drugs (e.g., marijuana, LSD, cocaine) have increased over the past two decades. This abuse and use can lead to a wide range of behavioral and physiological effects.

Alcohol

The use and abuse of alcohol is widespread, not only in the United States, but in most western cultures. It is estimated that at least 50 percent of all traffic fatalities are alcohol-related.

POISON CENTERS

Most large poison centers are based in major medical centers or teaching hospitals that serve a large population (1 to 10 million). Large numbers of people are required to provide a call volume sufficient to maintain the expertise of a staff of medical professionals whose primary duties are toxicological consultations. In addition to the core staff, these centers have access to many resources. It should be noted that some poison centers are located in emergency departments and others are not open twenty-four hours a day. They can provide information on over 450,000 drugs, toxic substances, and other products that include:

1. Drugs (legal, illicit, foreign, veterinary).
2. Chemicals (household, industrial).
3. Plants.
4. Animals, insects, fish, and snakes.
5. Cosmetics.
6. Hazardous materials.

Information and counseling in the large centers are provided twenty-four hours a day, seven days a week. Emergency advice is provided immediately, and followup calls are made by staff members to determine the effectiveness of the suggested treatment and the outcome.

Why Paramedics Use Poison Centers

1. For immediate determination of potential toxicity to a patient of a substance based on type of agent, amount, time of exposure, age/weight/medical condition of the patient, prior to treatment.
2. Identification can be made and definitive treatment initiated in 80 to 85 percent of all poison exposures.
3. A poison center can notify the emergency department of appropriate treatment for a patient while his/her ambulance is en route.
4. The poison center can spot trends through data analysis, notify other centers and/or media about potential public health problems, and evaluate current treatment protocols.

POISON

A poison is a substance that produces harmful physiological or psychological effects.

Routes of Entry

1. Ingestion — the most common manner of poisoning.
2. Inhalation — rapid absorption of toxic agent through the alveoli.
3. Injection — has both immediate and delayed, local and systemic effects.

4. Surface absorption — absorption of poison through the skin or eye, which has both immediate and delayed, local and systemic effects.

Taking Case Histories

1. What was ingested? The paramedic should try to obtain the poison container with a sample of the ingested substance and a sample of the vomitus.
2. When was the substance taken? The time frame may help a paramedic in making an appropriate treatment decision, especially if the patient or bystanders are giving accurate information.
3. How much of the substance was taken? It is important to note that it is difficult to get an accurate answer from the patient. Try to ascertain how much of the substance was originally there and how much was used. This may help to determine a more accurate amount of the substance taken.
4. Was an attempt made to induce vomiting?
5. Was an antidote, activated charcoal, or any other substance administered to the patient?
6. Does the patient have a psychiatric history (helpful information in treating suicide attempts)?

General Assessment

1. Perform a primary survey (ABCs).
2. Perform a secondary survey:
   - Monitor breathing continually.
   - Monitor pulse and blood pressure.
   - Give a physical examination. In particular, the paramedic should observe for:
     — An odor on the patient's breath.
     — Corrosive burns around the lips, mouth, and tongue.
     — Evidence of contamination on clothing.

General Goals and Principles of Management

1. Prevent absorption of the toxin(s).
2. Prevent complications from the toxin(s) by treating the symptoms.
3. Prevent complications by providing specific treatment or antidote.
4. ABCs.
5. Intubate, if indicated (use care if burns are found on the mouth). A sleepy or comatose patient has a high risk of vomiting and aspiration.
6. Decide whether to induce vomiting. More emphasis today is being placed

on binding toxins (i.e., using activated charcoal) than is being placed on inducing emesis. It is important for the paramedic to be completely familiar with local protocols concerning poisoning and emesis.

When and How to Induce Vomiting

Depending on the area protocols, the paramedic may or may not be asked to induce vomiting. In those locales where it is called for, the following are generally accepted guidelines:

1. The Poisondex states that emesis with ipecac is most effective within thirty minutes of exposure.
2. Ipecac is not recommended for all pesticide ingestions. It is contraindicated with organophosphates, carbonates, and camphor-containing products.
3. Emesis may be indicated unless the patient is obtunded, comatose, or convulsing.
4. Some pesticides, heavy metals, halogenated hydrocarbons, camphor-based hydrocarbons, and aromatic hydrocarbons may have a high toxicity. Contact the local poison center for each individual ingestion to determine if ipecac is indicated. Many of these chemicals are easily aspirated, which may result in severe chemical pneumonia. If possible, the airway should be secured prior to emesis. The best protection for the patient's airway is to use a cuffed endotracheal tube. This is a difficult procedure to perform on a conscious patient. In general, it is best not to give syrup of ipecac to these patients in the field. The paramedic should consults his/her local medical control.
5. To induce vomiting, have the patient drink syrup of ipecac.
   - For infants six to twelve months old, 5 to 10 cc followed by water. It is recommended that these patients be "ipecaced" in a health-care facility.
   - For a child one year to twelve years of age, 15 cc followed by water (usually one eight-ounce glass). This dosage may be repeated once if emesis does not occur within thirty minutes.
   - For an adult, 30 cc followed by water (usually two eight-ounce glasses). Repeat ipecac dosage in thirty minutes if vomiting has not occurred.

Use of Activated Charcoal

Activated charcoal is rarely given in the prehospital setting. It is only administered when vomiting is no longer being induced. It should not be administered simultaneously with ipecac (charcoal inactivates ipecac). When appropriate, adults are given 30 to 100 grams and children 1 to 2 grams per kilogram of body weight. A slurry of 240 ml of water per 30 grams of charcoal is administered to the patient.

When Not to Induce Vomiting

Do not induce vomiting in the following circumstances:

1. When the patient is stuporous or comatose.
2. When the patient is having seizures.
3. When the patient is pregnant.
4. When the patient has a possible acute myocardial infarction.
5. When the patient has ingested corrosive substances (strong acids or alkalis).
6. When the patient has ingested certain hydrocarbon substances.
7. Vomiting is rarely indicated for the ingestion of mineral seal oil, signal oil, or furniture polish oils. There is no absorption of these substances in the gastrointestinal tract, and these substances have a high risk for causing aspiration pneumonitis.
8. Vomiting is usually not called for in the ingestion of:
   - Asphalt or tar.
   - Lubricants such as motor oil or transmission oil.
   - Household oils.
   - Mineral oil, baby oil, suntan oil.
   - Fuel oil or diesel oil.

Other Treatment Procedures

1. Start an IV with D_5W or crystalloid (if cardiovascular compromise occurs).
2. Block the effects of the poison by using either a specific antidote or by using Narcan.
3. Contact the poison center if unsure of protocols.

INGESTED POISONS

Commonly ingested poisons include:

1. Household products (petroleum-based products, cleaning agents, and cosmetics.

2. Medications.
3. Toxic plants.
4. Food that contains toxins.

The immediate effects of poisoning by ingestion of corrosive substances (strong acids and alkalis) are burns to the lips, the tongue, the throat, and the upper gastrointestinal tract. Delayed effects may also occur, depending on the rate of absorption from the gastrointestinal tract. Most absorption of poisons occurs in the small intestine. However, poisons may remain in the stomach for several hours.

Strong Acids and Alkalis

Strong acids include toilet bowl cleaners, rust remover, and phenol. Strong alkalis include drain cleaner, ammonia, and bleach.

Signs and Symptoms

These include burns on the lips, mouth, tongue, respiratory tract, and upper gastrointestinal tract.

Treatment

1. Dilute by administering water or milk. The recommendation for dilution in children is **not** to exceed 15 ml per kilogram of body weight. The maximum in a 16-kilogram or larger patient is 250 ml. Vomiting may occur if this amount is exceeded. Do **not** attempt to neutralize. When an acid and alkali are combined, heat is usually generated. It is easy for this combination to create enough heat to cause thermal burns internally.
2. Never induce vomiting.
3. Start an IV of D_5W.

Hydrocarbon Products

These substances account for 7 percent of the accidental poisonings of children under five years of age.

Signs and Symptoms

There is a wide variation of signs and symptoms, depending on the type of material ingested. The following are some of the possible signs and symptoms:

1. Respiratory — cough, dyspnea, tachypnea, cyanosis.
2. Gastrointestinal — mucous membrane irritation, nausea, vomiting.
3. Central nervous system — lethargy, seizures, coma.
4. Systemic — fever, malaise.

Treatment

1. Induction of emesis may be recommended (follow local protocol or check with poison center) for the following conditions:
   - Halogenated hydrocarbons (carbon tetrachloride, trichloroethane, trichlorethylene, methylene chloride).
   - Aromatic hydrocarbons (toluene, xylene, benzene).
   - Turpentine (only if large amounts ingested).
   - Gasoline, kerosene, lighter fluid, petroleum ether, mineral spirits (only if large amounts ingested).
   - Any hydrocarbon with heavy metals, insecticides, nitrobenzene, or aniline.
2. Administer 100 percent oxygen.
3. Start an IV with D_5W.
4. Monitor cardiac rhythm.

Methyl Alcohol and Ethylene Glycol

These substances are present in paints, paint removers, varnishes, and antifreeze. Sometimes these substances are used by destitute alcoholics as a substitute for ethanol. They are sweet flavored and are often attractively colored. Small amounts may produce toxicity. For example, ingestion of as little as 1.5 ml per kilogram of methanol in a ten-kilogram child can produce a potentially toxic blood level.

Signs and Symptoms

Signs and symptoms include:

1. Inebriation without the characteristic odor of ethanol.
2. Hyperpnea.
3. Hypotension.
4. Nausea.
5. Vomiting.
6. Headache.
7. Central nervous system depression.

8. Both of these substances may produce acidosis, methanol blindness, and ethylene glycol renal failure.

Treatment

1. Do the ABCs.
2. Consider inducing vomiting if the patient is conscious.
3. Administer 100 percent oxygen.
4. Monitor cardiac rhythm.
5. Start an IV (D_5W or NS).
6. Administer one ounce of 80-proof ethanol (whiskey) every hour, usually given in a 10 percent solution IV. This inhibits methanol and ethylene glycol metabolism (this is an **in-hospital** procedure).

Cyanide

Cyanide poisoning may occur with the ingestion of cyanide or inhalation of hydrogen cyanide. Ingestion of fruit pits (bitter almonds, cherry, apricot, peach, apple, pear seeds) or laetrile in sufficient quantities may release hydrogen cyanide.

Cyanide poisoning blocks the cellular use of oxygen, causing the rapid development of cellular anoxia (absence of oxygen).

Signs and Symptoms

1. May produce rapid onset of respiratory arrest.
2. Odor of bitter almonds on the breath (not easily detected).
3. Early hyperpnea (increased respiratory rate or deep breathing that is not the norm) and dyspnea, followed by bradypnea (abnormally slow breathing) and gasping.
4. Tachycardia (heart rate over 100 beats per minute) and hypotension.
5. Vomiting.
6. Seizures.
7. Coma.
8. Occasionally bright red skin color or mucous membranes may be noted. Cyanosis is rare except in terminal stages.

Treatment

1. Perform the ABCs.
2. Assist ventilations as needed.
3. Administer 100 percent oxygen.

4. Use commercially available cyanide antidote kit, or break amyl nitrite ampules into a sponge and hold over the patient's nose for twenty to thirty seconds every minute.
5. Treat for shock.
6. Start an IV with crystalloid.
7. Monitor the cardiac rhythm and transport as an emergency.

Food Poisoning (Bacterial)

Food poisoning is most commonly caused by staphylococcus, clostridium, salmonella, streptococcus, shigella, and botulism (a type of clostridium), which is the most severe toxin-producing bacteria.

Signs and Symptoms

1. Nausea, vomiting.
2. Abdominal cramping, diarrhea.
3. Dehydration.
4. Oxygen and respiratory system problems.
5. Botulism — may cause respiratory paralysis; has approximately a 30 percent fatality rate.

Treatment

1. Perform the ABCs.
2. See general principles and goals.
3. Control dehydration with an IV of crystalloid.

Poisonous Plants

Many common household and garden plants are poisonous if ingested (see Appendix 3).

Signs and Symptoms

There are many different signs and symptoms. See Appendix 3 for a more complete listing.

Treatment

1. Depending on which plant was ingested, emesis may be recommended.
2. Bring the plant and vomitus to the emergency department (if possible).
3. Follow general care guidelines for ingested poisons.

INHALED POISONS

Inhaled poisons are toxic gases such as:

1. Carbon monoxide.
2. Ammonia.
3. Chlorine.
4. Freon.
5. Carbon tetrachloride.
6. Methyl chloride.
7. Tear gas.
8. Mustard gas.

General Principles of Assessment and Management

Remove Patient from Poisonous Environment

1. Wear appropriate respiratory protective apparatus.
2. Wear protective clothing to prevent chemical burns (e.g., from ammonia and chlorine).
3. Remove contaminated clothing.

General History

Discover the:

1. Length of exposure.
2. Environment in which the exposure took place (indooors/outdoors).
3. Type of poison inhaled.

Primary and Secondary Surveys

1. Perform the ABCs. (After the respiratory status has been evaluated and stabilized, proceed with the secondary survey.)
2. Take the vital signs.
3. Do a physical examination.

Treatment

1. Perform the ABCs.
2. Provide high-concentration, high-flow oxygen, and provide ventilatory assistance as necessary.

3. Intubate the unconscious patient.

Carbon Monoxide (CO)

Carbon monoxide is a colorless, odorless gas produced during the incomplete burning of organic fuels. More than 2,500 people die each year from carbon monoxide poisoning. The primary sources of carbon monoxide are home heating devices and exhaust fumes from automobiles. Half of all adult suicides occur by carbon monoxide poisoning.

In this type of poisoning, carbon monoxide binds to hemoglobin more strongly than oxygen. This inhibits oxygen delivery to cells and leads to hypoxia at the cellular level.

Signs and Symptoms

1. Headache (low levels of carbon monoxide).
2. Nausea (low levels of carbon monoxide).
3. Tachycardia (higher levels of carbon monoxide).
4. Tachypnea (higher levels of carbon monoxide).
5. Roaring sensation in the ears (higher levels of carbon monoxide).
6. Vomiting (higher levels of carbon monoxide).
7. Confusion (higher levels of carbon monoxide).
8. Seizures (high levels of carbon monoxide).
9. Dilated pupils (high levels of carbon monoxide).
10. Cyanosis (high levels of carbon monoxide).
11. Loss of consciousness (high levels of carbon monoxide).
12. Cherry-red lips (high levels of carbon monoxide); not commonly seen.

Treatment

1. Remove the patient from the exposure site.
2. Perform the ABCs.
3. Administer 100 percent oxygen.
4. Assist respirations (i.e., bag-valve-mask, intubate) if necessary.
5. Monitor the EKG.
6. Start an IV with D_5W.
7. Treat the patient for shock.

Freon

Freon is used as a refrigerant and as a propellant for many aerosols. It is abused by some who inhale it as an intoxicant. The primary danger is cardiotoxicity and the subsequent dysrhythmias caused by the freon.

Treatment

1. Remove the patient from the contaminated environment.
2. Administer 100 percent oxygen.
3. Start an IV with D_5W (or crystalloid for cardiovascular collapse).
4. Monitor the cardiac rhythm.
5. Administer lidocaine for PVCs.

Ammonia

This gas combines with water in the tissues to produce a highly caustic, alkaline compound.

Signs and Symptoms

1. Watering and irritation of the eyes.
2. Irritation of the upper and lower respiratory tracts, producing coughing, choking, and respiratory collapse.
3. Nausea, vomiting, diarrhea, abdominal pain.
4. Provide 100 percent oxygen.

Treatment

1. The paramedic must protect him/herself during rescue.
2. Remove the patient to a well-ventilated space.
3. Maintain an open airway — intubate and use suction as required.
4. Provide 100 percent oxygen.

Chlorinated Hydrocarbons (Carbon Tetrachloride)

These hydrocarbons may cause central nervous system, liver, and kidney damage as a result of an acute high dosage or chronic low dosage exposure.

Signs and Symptoms (Acute Poisoning)

1. Irritation of the eyes and mucous membranes of the respiratory tract.
2. Nausea and vomiting.
3. Headache and mental confusion.

Treatment

1. The paramedic must protect him/herself during rescue.
2. Remove the patient to a well-ventilated space.
3. Remove the patient's contaminated clothing.
4. Maintain the airway — intubate and suction as necessary.
5. Provide 100 percent oxygen.

Methyl Chloride

This is a colorless, combustible gas with an ether-like odor that is easily inhaled by the respiratory tract; some absorption may occur through the skin as well. This may increase the patient's exposure.

Signs and Symptoms

1. Nausea and vomiting.
2. Drowsiness, mental confusion.
3. Seizures and coma.

Treatment

1. Protect self during rescue.
2. Remove the patient from exposure.
3. Avoid sparks, open flames, or use of electrical equipment during rescue.
4. Remove contaminated clothing.
5. Maintain the airway — intubate if necessary.
6. Provide 100 percent oxygen.

INJECTED ANIMAL AND INSECT POISONS

These include poisoning from the following:

1. Insects — bees, hornets, wasps, yellow jackets, spiders (arachnids), fire ants, ticks, and scorpions. Bees, hornets, wasps, and yellow jackets cause more death from allergic reactions than any other venomous animal in the United States.
2. Animal bites — snakebites.
3. Marine animals — jellyfish, Portuguese man-of-war, stingrays, anemones, coral and hydrae, spiny fish.

General Principles of Management

1. Remove the patient from danger of repeated injection (poisoning).
2. Identify the insect or animal; bring it with the patient to the emergency department if possible.
3. Perform the primary and secondary surveys.
4. Watch for anaphylactic reactions.
5. Prevent or delay absorption of poison, if possible.

Insect Stings

These include stings from bees, hornets, wasps, and yellow jackets. The problems encountered are caused by the injection (sting) of a toxin.

The major potential problem is an anaphylactic reaction (see management of anaphylaxis in Chapter 14).

Signs and Symptoms

1. Localized pain, redness, and swelling.
2. Allergic reactions — itchy rash, anaphylaxis.

Treatment

1. Perform the ABCs.
2. Remove the stinger without squeezing the venom sac.
3. Apply ice.
4. Monitor for anaphylaxis and allergic reactions. (Consider the use of epinephrine and benedryl if necessary.)

Brown Recluse Spider Bite (Necrotoxin)

Signs and Symptoms

It is possible to have no initial pain or discomfort after a bite.

1. Localized pain, redness, and swelling usually occur two to eight hours after a bite. Generally, the center of the wound becomes ischemic, and tissue necrosis develops.
2. Systemic reactions include chills, fever, possible nausea, vomiting, and restlessness.

Management

1. Perform the ABCs.
2. Clean the area of the bite.
3. No specific antivenin is available.
4. Definitive care might include: debridement (cleaning of the wound) with an antibiotic and may require surgical excision of the necrotic tissue.

Black Widow Spider Bites (Neurotoxic)

Five percent of these bites result in death. In many cases, the sick, the very young, and the elderly are most susceptible to serious complications and death.

Signs and Symptoms

1. Initially, there may be mild local pain. The patient may describe the bite as a pin-prick-like pain. Severe local pain gradually develops and spreads to the abdomen and extremities.
2. Systemic effects may develop from thirty minutes to two hours after the exposure.
3. Progressive muscular rigidity usually develops in the back, abdomen, and possibly all large muscle groups.
4. Nausea, vomiting, sweating, salivation, cramps, tremors may occur.
5. Later signs and symptoms may consist of bradycardia, weak pulse, restlessness, confusion, and dyspnea.
6. There is a possibility of the patient developing seizures (not common) and paralysis. Weakness and paralysis in children are common.

Treatment

1. Perform the ABCs.
2. Apply ice locally.
3. Start an IV of D_5W.
4. If muscle spasms and pain are severe, administer diazepam, five to ten milligrams, or calcium gluconate, ten milliliters of a 10 percent solution, IV.
5. Transport the patient to the emergency department for possible administration of antivenin.

Scorpion Stings (Neurotoxic)

Scorpions sting primarily when provoked. The stinger is located at the end of a long tail.

Signs and Symptoms

1. Immediate tingling, burning sensation at the point of injection, which may progress to numbness. Most scorpion stings cause just local pain and restlessness.
2. Systemic: restlessness, drooling, dilated pupils, muscular twitching, nausea, vomiting, seizures, possible circulatory and respiratory failure. These are possible but do not occur often in the United States.

Treatment

1. Perform the ABCs.
2. Apply cool packs to the wound.
3. Avoid the use of analgesics — it increases venom toxicity.

Snakebites

Snakebites account for approximately ten to twenty deaths each year from about 5,000 to 6,000 bites each year. The coral snake accounts for approximately 1 to 2 percent of venomous bites, and pit vipers are credited with the rest of the bites in the United States.

Coral Snake

This snake is found primarily in Florida and in the southwestern United States. It is black with adjacent red and yellow or white bands on its body. Coral snakes have small fangs, so the marks left after a bite will be different than those of the pit viper's bite. Snakes with adjacent red and black bands are not poisonous (King snake).

Signs and Symptoms

After envenomation, there may be no local or systemic effects for up to twelve hours.

1. Local effects: weakness, numbness, pain, possible edema, redness.
2. Systemic effects: ptosis (drooping) of the eyelids, nausea, vomiting, dyspnea, weakness, excessive salivation, difficulty in swallowing, euphoria, confusion, seizures, loss of consciousness, respiratory failure, hypotension, weak, irregular pulse and possibly death if left untreated.

3. After initial onset of signs and symptoms, the patient may deteriorate rapidly.

Treatment

Follow the treatment procedures for pit vipers except for the incision/suction method, which is not recommended for coral snake bites.

Pit Vipers

Rattlesnakes, copperheads, and cottonmouth water moccasins are among the pit vipers. They are found almost everywhere in the United States. The rattlesnake is the most common pit viper. The venom of these snakes is complex and produces a combination of cardiotoxic, hemotoxic, neurotoxic, and necrotizing effects.

Signs and Symptoms

1. Local: fang marks, swelling, pain, discoloration, paresthesia around the wound.
2. Systemic: weakness, dizziness, faintness, sweating, nausea, vomiting, tachycardia, hypotension, increased or decreased salivation. Bloody urine and gastrointestinal bleeding (late). Causes the coagulation of blood. Shallow respirations progressing to respiratory failure.

Treatment

1. The primary goal is to slow the absorption of the venom.
2. Make sure that both the patient and the rescuer are safe from receiving additional bites.
3. Keep the patient at rest and reduce anxiety.
4. Use no alcohol or stimulants.
5. Apply a wide (one-inch) constricting band proximal to the bite about three to four inches above it. The band should be loose enough to slip a finger snugly underneath. The purpose of the band is to slow down lymphatic circulation. It should be noted that with envenomation there may be significant and rapid swelling. The paramedic should vigilantly watch the area around the constricting band. It is entirely possible for the swelling to cause a tourniquet (constriction) effect and result in serious additional injury to the patient. Remember — the constricting band is **not** a tourniquet. Deep venous and arterial blood flow are not

to be constricted (restricted).

6. Cleanse the area of the bite if possible.
7. Immobilize the affected limb in the position of function, and position it just below the level of the heart.
8. Start an IV with a crystalloid solution in an uninvolved extremity.
9. Transport the patient to the emergency department for further evaluation and possible administration of antivenin.
10. **Do not** apply ice, cold packs, or freon spray to the wound. This will only make the injury worse.
11. Incision and suction. This is a controversial technique that is generally not recommended. It is definitely not recommended for coral snakebites. The following are guidelines for using this method: If
    - the victim is more than one hour away from a hospital;
    - the bite has occurred less than an hour before the paramedic arrives;
    - swelling quickly developed after the bite;
    - and symptoms appeared within thirty minutes,

    the following procedure may be instituted (**do not delay transport** to perform incision/suction):
    - —Make vertical parallel incisions (one through each fang mark), one-eighth to one-fourth inch long.
    - —Apply suction to these incisions for one hour, preferably using a Sawyer extraction device.
    - —This procedure must be done carefully. There is a risk of causing permanent injury to the extremity.

Marine Animal Poisoning

The marine animals that are poisonous are:

1. Some seasnakes.
2. Octopus.
3. Jellyfish.
4. Portuguese man-of-wars.
5. Corals.
6. Anemones.
7. Sea urchins.
8. Stingrays.
9. Catfish.
10. Scorpion fish.

Signs and Symptoms

There are different signs and symptoms from the stings and bites of the different species of marine animals. But generally the paramedic may see the following:

1. Local effects — intense pain and swelling.
2. Systemic effects — nausea, vomiting, weakness, tachycardia, dyspnea, possible anaphylaxis, respiratory distress, syncope, hypotension, cardiac dysrhythmias.

General Treatment

1. Do the ABCs.
2. Provide symptomatic support.
3. Apply constricting bands when appropriate.
4. Give analgesics for pain.

Specific Treatment

Jellyfish, Man-of-Wars, Corals, and Anemones

1. Inactivate (or remove) nematocysts — the small stingers found in these creatures. This can be done by applying isopropyl alcohol to the wound.
2. A saturated solution of baking soda applied to the wound will neutralize the venom.

Stingray, Scorpion Fish, and Sea Urchins

The venom from these animals may be deactivated by hot water. The wound should be immersed in water as hot as the patient can tolerate (ideally, 110 to 114 degrees Fahrenheit).

SURFACE-ABSORBED POISONS

Organophosphate Chemicals

These are used in insecticides and in some chemical warfare agents. They are very toxic chemicals that can prove fatal if the patient is not treated promptly.

Signs and Symptoms

Most of these stimulate the parasympathetic nervous system, causing:

1. Excessive salivation.
2. Nausea and vomiting.
3. Diarrhea.
4. Sweating.
5. Bradycardia.
6. Hypotension.
7. Blurred vision.
8. Constricted pupils.
9. Abdominal pain.
10. Seizures.

Treatment

1. Remove the patient from continued exposure. Wear adequate protective clothing.
2. Perform the ABCs.
3. Suction the copious bronchial secretions.
4. Flush the patient with large amounts of water.
5. Remove contaminated clothing.
6. Flush the patient with large amounts of water again. Then wash the area with soap and water; then flush the area with rubbing alcohol, followed by washing the area off with soap and water. Do not use rubbing alcohol on children.
7. Start an IV with crystalloid.
8. Monitor the cardiac rhythm.
9. Administer atropine, 2 to 5 mg IV push, and for a child, 0.05 mg per kilogram of body weight; repeat every three to eight minutes as required. Attempt to increase the pulse rate and decrease secretions (until signs of atropinization occur — e.g., dry mouth, increased pulse rate at above sixty with complete clearing of bronchial and pulmonary rales).

Cyanide

Cyanide may also be absorbed through the skin. It gives the same systemic effects as found in ingestion of cyanide, and treatment is the same as for ingestion.

DRUG OVERDOSE

Drug overdose refers to the poisoning or toxic effects caused by a larger dosage of a drug than is customarily taken. The distinction between poisoning and overdose is an arbitrary one, made primarily for convenience. Principles of treatment are the same as for poisoning. Drug overdose (OD) can occur from any of the following causes:

1. Accident.
2. Miscalculation.
3. Changes in drug strength.
4. Suicide attempt.
5. Polydrug abuse.
6. Drug abuse.

Narcotic Overdose

Some common narcotics are heroin, morphine, demerol, codeine, Methadone, Darvon®, Dilaudid®, Lomotil®, and percodan. These drugs are taken orally or nasally or are injected intravenously.

Overdoses on heroin may occur in clusters when an unusually pure supply is available. ''Tracks'' (lines of puncture scars along arm and leg veins) and skin ulcers from infected IV sites are clear indications of a serious drug user. (The paramedic should protect him/herself from contact with the patient's blood. These groups are at high risk for hepatitis and AIDS.)

Signs and Symptoms

1. Early signs: euphoria, ''nodding'' (a state of easily arousable drowsiness), nausea, miosis (abnormal contraction of the pupils) (except with demerol or in combination with other types of drug).
2. Late signs: respiratory depression, apnea, hypotension, shock, central nervous system depression, stupor, and coma.

Treatment

1. Perform the ABCs.
2. Monitor the airway and respirations vigilantly.
3. Provide 100 percent oxygen.
4. Draw a blood sample.
5. Start an IV of D_5W.

6. Administer naloxone (Narcan — see Appendix 1 for full drug description):
   - Indications: respiratory depression, hypotension, and depressed level of consciousness due to narcotics, methadone, propoxyphene (Darvon®), pentazocine (Talwin®).
   - Narcan is used diagnostically in coma of unknown etiology to rule out (or reverse) narcotic depression.
   - Dosage: adult — 2.0 mg IV, IM, or SQ. Darvon® overdoses may require larger dosages. Pediatric — 0.01 mg per kilogram of body weight.
7. Give 50 percent dextrose — 50 cc.
8. It is not recommended to give ipecac with a narcotics overdose if there is any possibility of signs of narcotic overdose and emesis occurring simultaneously.

Sedative Overdose (Hypnotic Overdose)

Sedatives consist of benzodiazepines — Valium and Librium; and barbituates — phenobarbital, amobarbital, and secobarbital. Individually, benzodiazepines are relatively nontoxic but may accentuate the respiratory depression and coma caused by other drugs.

Signs and Symptoms

1. Pupils may initially be constricted and later become fixed and dilated (due to hypercabia).
2. Respiratory depression.
3. Hypotension, which may progress to shock and possibly hypothermia.

Treatment

1. Perform the ABCs.
2. Provide 100 percent oxygen.
3. Draw a blood sample.
4. Start an IV of D_5W.
5. For an unknown cause of unconsciousness, the paramedic should administer naloxone and 50 percent dextrose.
6. If the ingestion is recent, follow ingestion protocols.

Stimulant Overdose

The amphetamine family consists of benzadrine, dexadrine, metaamphetamine, and others. Caffeine and similar mild stimulants act like amphetamines when taken in large dosages.

Cocaine is a commonly used drug of abuse. Approximately 30 million people in the United States have tried cocaine, and approximately 6.2 million people are "users." Cocaine comes from the leaves of an evergreen plant —Erythroxylum coca—which is cultivated extensively in Peru and Bolivia.

Amphetamines are taken orally or injected intravenously. Cocaine is taken orally, intranasally ("snorted"), freebased (a way of treating the drug), in the hard form of crack, and is injected intravenously.

Signs and Symptoms

These will vary depending on the amount of drug taken and the length of time the drug has been used. Signs and symptoms include:

1. Euphoria.
2. Excitement.
3. Decrease in appetite.
4. Reduced need for sleep.
5. Grinding of teeth.
6. Paranoid or suspicious behavior.
7. Palpitations.
8. Chest pain.
9. Elevated pulse and blood pressure.
10. Nausea and vomiting.
11. Chills, sweating, increased temperature.
12. Dilated pupils.
13. General increase in metabolic rate, including cardiac dysrhythmias.
14. Irritability may progress to hallucinations, seizures, or to a violent form of paranoid psychosis.

Treatment

1. Perform the ABCs.
2. If the ingestion is recent, follow the ingestion protocols. It is not recommended to ipecac a stimulated patient because of the possibility of seizures occurring simultaneously.
3. Provide support for the vital functions.
4. Monitor the EKG.

Phencyclidine (PCP) Overdose

PCP is a drug abuse problem. Phencyclidine was originally developed for use as an anesthetic agent but was discontinued because of its adverse effects on the patient. It was reintroduced as an animal tranquilizer in 1969, then was removed when widespread abuse of PCP was recognized. It is presently available by illegal production.

PCP is most commonly sprinkled on marijuana and smoked. It is also ingested, snorted, or injected intravenously.

Signs and Symptoms

These will vary depending on whether a low or high dosage has been taken.

1. Low dosage (when no unconsciousness is present):
   - Mental disturbances.
   - Slowness and dullness or abusive and delusional behavior, with an apparent increase in physical strength of the patient.
   - Insensitivity to pain.
   - Poor coordination.
   - Disorientation.
   - Purposeless talk.
   - Capability of violent and bizarre behavior.
   - Hypertension, hyperpnea, and tachycardia can occur.
2. High dosage (acute — minutes to hours):
   - Hypertension, tachycardia, elevated temperature.
   - Sweating.
   - Salivation.
   - Central nervous system depression or excitation.
   - Convulsions.
   - Coma.
   - Respirations increased (unusual for depression).

Treatment

1. Perform the ABCs.
2. Monitor the EKG.
3. If the ingestion is recent, follow ingestion protocols.
4. Provide a quiet environment if possible.
5. Treat the symptoms (seizures with diazepam).
6. For violent behavior, restrain the patient as appropriate.

Tricyclic Antidepressant (TCA) Overdose

These oral medications, Elavil and Tofranil, are used in the treatment of depression. Frequently, TCAs are the same drugs used in the patient's suicide attempt.

Signs and Symptoms

1. Early: tachycardia, increased temperature, restlessness, and anxiety.
2. Later: convulsions, cardiac dysrhythmias, and coma (the "3 Cs"). A characteristic EKG finding is the widening of the QRS complex.

Treatment

1. Perform the ABCs.
2. Provide oxygen.
3. Monitor the EKG.
4. Even if the ingestion is recent, it is not recommended to ipecac the patient, as signs and symptoms (seizures, coma) can occur rapidly.
5. Administer sodium bicarbonate intravenously for dysrhythmias on direct physician's order. (Alkalizing the serum to pH 7.5 to 7.55 in the treatment of TCA cardiotoxicity is well documented. The mechanism is unknown.)

Salicylate (Aspirin) Overdose

Aspirin tablets are the most commonly found form of aspirin in the home. The substance is also found in many cold preparations, topical ointments, and combinational analgesics.

The three common causes of salicylate poisoning are:

1. Accidental ingestion, primarily found with preschool children.
2. Intentional ingestion (or suicide attempts), primarily found with adults.
3. Chronic ingestion is the most difficult to diagnose.

Signs and Symptoms

1. Increased respiratory rate, resulting in respiratory alkalosis.
2. Faintness.
3. Tinnitus (ringing in the ears).
4. Nausea and vomiting.
5. Fever.
6. Dehydration (possibly leading to hypovolemia).
7. Metabolic acidosis.
8. Disorientation.
9. Convulsions.

10. Coma.

Treatment

1. Perform the ABCs.
2. Maintain the airway and respirations.
3. Administer ipecac to induce emesis.
4. Start an IV of normal saline.
5. Comatose patients should receive sodium bicarbonate to correct acidosis on direct physician's order.

Acetaminophen Overdose

Tylenol, Datril, and Tempra are analgesic, antipyretic agents. As few as thirty standard size (325 mg) acetaminophen tablets will be toxic in an average adult, and 140 mg per kilogram of body weight will be toxic in a child.

Signs and Symptoms

1. First twenty-four hours: malaise, loss of appetite, nausea, and vomiting.
2. Twenty-four to forty-eight hours: onset of upper right quadrant pain, indicating liver damage.
3. Sixty to seventy-two hours: jaundice (sign of liver impairment). In severe overdoses, death may occur due to liver failure.

Treatment

1. Perform the ABCs.
2. Administer ipecac to induce emesis and follow ingestion protocols.
3. Activated charcoal is contraindicated if the overdose involves only acetaminophen, since it will also absorb the antidote (n-acetylcysteine), which must be administered in an emergency department. (These two substances may be given one to two hours apart.)

Hallucinogens Overdose

These include LSD, psilocybin, morning glory seeds, mescaline, peyote, and marijuana.

Signs and Symptoms

1. Hallucinations and distortions of sensory perception (marijuana may lead to perceptual dysfunction and mild anxiety reactions, but seldom true

hallucinations).
2. Possible nausea, vomiting, tachycardia, and rapid respirations.
3. LSD causes dilated pupils.
4. Generally no major medical effects occur.
5. Psychological reactions may lead to unusual behavior.

Treatment

1. Talk-down the patient in a friendly, reassuring voice and in a quiet, secure place that provides contact with reality and security.
2. Manage other physical injuries in an appropriate fashion.

DRUG ABUSE

Drug abuse refers to the use of prescription drugs (e.g., pain medications) for nonprescribed purposes or the use of drugs that have no prescribed medical uses (e.g., PCP).

In the United States, most drugs are used solely for medical reasons (antibiotics); a few are almost solely self-administered for their effects on mood or behavior (cocaine, hallucinogens); and some are used for both medical and nonmedical purposes (narcotics).

Problems from Substance Abuse

Medical Problems

1. Glue sniffing may lead to liver and/or renal damage.
2. Intravenous injection of drugs with unsterile equipment may lead to life-threatening infections and death from overdose and may spread infectious diseases (i.e., hepatitis and AIDS).
3. Drugs cut with talcum powder and other materials may lead to lung or brain infarctions and other problems, depending on the substance with which the drug is mixed.

Psychological Problems

1. **Substance abuse** is defined by three criteria:
   - A pattern of pathological use (i.e., intoxication all day long, continuation of substance use despite the development or exacerbation of a medical problem).

- Impairment of social or work function caused by the pathological use of drugs (or alcohol).
- Duration of more than one month.

2. **Substance dependence** is more severe than substance abuse and almost invariably involves a pattern of pathological use. A substance dependence develops:
   - Tolerance — a decreased response to the regular use of a drug, which leads to a need for increasingly larger dosages for the patient to gain the desired effect.
   - Withdrawal — a group of symptoms that are brought about by an abrupt discontinuation of a drug (e.g., narcotics) to which the person has become addicted.
   - Dependence (psychological or physical) — the need to take a drug either continuously or periodically to experience a feeling of well-being or to avoid the discomfort of the drug's absence.

Common Drugs of Abuse and Dependence

(See the section on overdose in this chapter for signs, symptoms, and management of the following drugs.)

1. Alcohol (see next section).
2. Narcotics: heroin, morphine, Demerol, codeine, Talwin, methadone, Darvon®, Dilaudid, percodan, lomotil.
3. Barbiturates, sedatives, and hypnotics (Valium).
4. Amphetamines or similar central nervous system stimulants.
5. Cannabis (marijuana).
6. Cocaine.
7. Phencyclidine (PCP).
8. Hallucinogens: LSD, mescaline, and similar drugs (these drugs are associated only with abuse, since dependence on them has not been demonstrated).

Guidelines for Dealing with the Drug Abuser or the Drug-Dependent Patient

1. Ask all patients about the use of medications — whether the medications are prescribed by a physician or are self-administered.
2. Recognize that drug abuse is widespread and common among all socioeconomic classes.
3. Recreational drug use is common and should be considered whenever the

EMT-P is confronted by seizures, behavioral changes, stupor, or coma.
4. Patients should be questioned about recreational drug use, not about addiction.
5. Advise a patient that you respond only to medical issues and not to legal issues.
6. The EMT-P's drug box is a potential target for drug addicts. The EMT-P should protect him/herself and the narcotic medications (if they are carried).

ALCOHOL

Alcohol is the most widely used and abused "drug" in the United States and probably in all western cultures. The consequences of alcohol abuse are costly in both human and economic terms. It should be noted that the paramedic will have frequent encounters with the chronic and acute user of alcohol. Approximately one-tenth of the drinking population drinks more than 50 percent of the alcoholic beverages consumed. Alcohol consumption is estimated to be involved in at least 50 percent of all automobile fatalities and plays a significant role in shortening the drinker's life span. It is in the best interests of the patient that the paramedic develop a comprehensive understanding of this national problem.

General Effects of Alcohol

1. Initially a stimulant, then a depressant.
2. Mild dosages depress inhibitions.
3. Impairment of skill performance (e.g., driving).
4. Large dosages may depress consciousness and respiration, leading to death.

Alcoholism

Alcoholism involves the abuse of and dependence on alcohol. Problems that occur from drinking are both immediate and long term for the dependent person. It is estimated that there are at least 8 million alcoholics and many more problem drinkers in the United States. The alcoholic develops drug behaviors similar to other drug abusers and addicts: tolerance, dependence, and withdrawal.

An alcoholic generally:

1. Denies having a drinking problem.

2. Drinks early in the day.
3. Is prone to drink alone or secretly.
4. May have periodic binges of heavy drinking over a period of several days to several weeks.
5. Has a partial or total loss of memory of the heavy drinking period.
6. Has an unexplained history of repeated gastrointestinal problems, especially bleeding.
7. Has the "green tongue syndrome" (comes from chlorophyll-containing compounds used to disguise the odor of alcohol on the breath).
8. May have cigarette burns on clothing caused by falling asleep with lit cigarettes.
9. Has chronically flushed face and palms.
10. Has tremulousness.
11. Has the odor of alcohol on his/her breath even at inappropriate times (at work or early in the morning).

An alcoholic also experiences medical consequences of chronic alcohol ingestion:

1. Poor nutrition due to inadequate food intake.
2. Loss of recent memory.
3. Loss of sensation in the hands and feet.
4. Loss of balance and coordination.
5. Alcoholic hepatitis and liver cirrhosis.
6. Pancreatitis.
7. Hypoglycemia.
8. Upper gastrointestinal bleeding.
9. Subdural hematoma and rib/extremity fractures due to recurrent falls.

Withdrawal Syndrome

Time Factor

Withdrawal comes on several hours after sudden abstinence and lasts for five to seven days.

Signs and Symptoms

1. Coarse tremor of the hands, tongue, and eyelids; nausea/vomiting; weakness; tachycardia; sweating; increased blood pressure; anxiety; depressed mood; irritability; and orthostatic hypotension. Difficulty in sleeping and possibly brief hallucinations.

2. Delirium tremens (DTs). A disorder characterized by anxiety, auditory and visual hallucinations usually occurring during withdrawal from alcohol use. The alcoholic may develop the DTs on the second or third day of withdrawal. The DTs is manifest by hallucinations, excitement, trembling, perspiration, and anxiety (the patient may talk or yell incoherently). The patient may be quiet and paranoid, but this is unusual.
3. Seizures may occur, usually within the first twenty-four to thirty-six hours after the start of abstinence.
4. Seizures or delirium tremens are serious signs. There is a significant mortality from the DTs.

Methanol/Ethylene Glycol Poisoning

Low-income alcoholics may drink methanol (e.g., wood alcohol, sterno) or ethylene glycol (antifreeze), causing blindness or death. Follow poisoning protocols under ingested poison.

General Treatment of Alcohol Overdose

1. Perform the ABCs.
2. Maintain the airway and respirations.
3. For recent ingestion, consider inducing emesis (depending on the patient's age, amount of alcohol consumed, vital signs, and local protocol).
4. Seizures — consider administering Valium per physician's direct order (follow seizure protocols).
5. Local protocols may include the administration of thiamine (see Appendix 1 for complete drug information).

SUMMARY

Managing the poisoned patient whether from accidental poisoning, drug overdose, attempted suicide, or from alcohol abuse can be a difficult task. The paramedic must treat the patient correctly, attempt to identify the toxic substance, deal with potentially violent patients, handle distraught family members and bystanders, and generally be professional and efficient. In addition, it is hoped that the paramedic will be nonjudgmental and handle the patient with sensitivity and understanding. That is much to ask of the rescuer, yet it is expected.

If the paramedic stays current on toxic substance management, uses the available resources (e.g., poison centers), he/she will most often make the correct treatment decisions.

Remember that 65 percent of the reported poisonings in the United States occurred in children under five years of age. Thus, the paramedic will commonly have very upset family members, babysitters, or teachers around. The confidence that the paramedic exhibits at the scene will help in reducing the anxiety levels.

16

Infectious Diseases

Today, the health-care professional must have a clear understanding of the risks that he/she faces from exposure to communicable disease. With the widespread occurrence of AIDS, the paramedic must take appropriate precautions against contact with potential sources of AIDS and other infectious diseases.

This chapter gives a brief presentation of common pathologic organisms that spread disease, and of the human immune system. Attention is also given to the responsibility of the EMT-P for personal care and for cleaning of emergency equipment. It is important for the paramedic to recognize that the risk of contracting a communicable disease is greatly reduced when simple precautions are taken. It should also be recognized that the primary management of the patient with an infectious disease is done in a hospital setting and that only patient stabilization is provided in the field (when necessary).

The Centers for Disease Control's (CDC) Universal Precautions, referred to often in this chapter, are found in Appendix 6. Appendix 5 offers a more complete list of communicable diseases.

COMMON PATHOLOGIC ORGANISMS

Virus

A virus is a minute, infectious organism not visible by the light microscope. It is a parasite dependent upon nutrients inside living cells for metabolic and reproductive needs. Viruses cause a variety of diseases in man, including smallpox, yellow fever, the common cold, most childhood diseases, many upper respiratory infections, and AIDS.

Bacteria

Bacteria are any microorganisms of the class schizomycetes. There are three principal forms:

1. Spherical (ovoid).
2. Rod-shaped.
3. Spiral.

The most commonly known bacteria are staphylococci and streptococci. Many bacteria produce poisonous substances called toxins, like botulism. Bacteria may cause other diseases, like tetanus and diphtheria.

Rickettsia

Rickettsia is a genus of gram-negative bacteria causing many diseases that are usually transmitted by lice, fleas, ticks, and mites.

Fungus

''Fungus'' is a general term for a group of organisms (mushrooms, yeast, mold) marked by the absence of chlorophyll and reproduction by spores. Fungi are present in air, soil, and water, but only a few species can cause disease. Three common fungi are ringworm, athlete's foot, and thrush.

Parasite

A parasite is an organism that lives within, upon, or at the expense of another animal (host). Malaria is a disease caused by a type of parasite whose life cycle takes place in the red blood cells and often causes the death of the host. It is transmitted to other individuals by the anopheles mosquito.

IMMUNE SYSTEM

The immune system is a complex network of specialized organs and cells that has evolved to defend the body against attacks by ''foreign'' invaders. When functioning properly, it fights off infections by agents such as bacteria and viruses. The success of this system in defending the body depends on an elaborate and dynamic regulatory network. Millions and millions of cells, organized into sets and subsets, pass information back and forth like clouds of bees around the hive. The result is a sensitive system of checks and balances that produces a prompt, appropriate, effective, and self-limiting immune response.

Major Components of the Human Immune System

Antibodies

Antibodies are proteins of the class called immunoglobulins. They are natives of the body and are present at birth.

Antigen

An antigen is any substance that can trigger an immune response because the body recognizes it as foreign.

Bone Marrow

Bone marrow is the soft tissue in the hollow shafts of the long bones where lymphocytes are produced.

Leukocytes

Leukocytes are all the white blood cells that protect the body from disease-causing microorganisms.

Lymphocytes

Lymphocytes are a type of leukocyte. They are small, white cells (normally present in the blood and in lymphoid tissue) that bear the major responsibility for carrying out the functions of the immune system.

Lymph Node

A lymph node is a rounded body found at intervals along the lymphatic vessels. It contains lymphocytes, macrophages, and webbed areas that act as filters, keeping particulate matter (e.g., viruses, bacteria) from entering the bloodstream. The lymph nodes bring together many components of the immune system to produce a protective response.

Macrophages and Monocytes

Macrophages and monocytes are cells that ingest microorganisms, other cells, and foreign particles. Macrophages are spread throughout bodily tissues, and monocytes circulate in the blood.

Spleen

The spleen is a dark, ovoid, elongated organ found in the upper left quadrant of the abdomen; it produces and stores blood. Its immunologic function is to filter out particulate matter from the blood.

Thymus

The thymus is an organ located in the mediastinum (the area between the lungs containing the heart, great vessels, trachea, etc.). It plays an important role in the development of the immune system in the newborn and continues to play an immunologic role throughout life. Its functional importance declines with age. T-cells — small- and medium-sized lymphocytes — are produced here. These cells play a valuable role in the body's cellular immune response.

INFECTIOUS DISEASE

An infectious disease occurs when the body is invaded by a microorganism that multiplies, causing local or systemic disturbance due to:

1. The release of toxins.
2. Intracellular replication.
3. Competitive metabolism.
4. Antigen-antibody response.

Modes of Transmission

Airborne

This mode of transmission includes coughing, sneezing, and spitting of pathogens into the air.

Direct Contact

This transmission occurs through contact with contaminated blood, saliva, and semen, and through kissing.

Indirect Contact

Communicable diseases may also be transmitted by inanimate objects, through ingestion of foods, through utensil sharing, and through sharing of bed linens.

Insect Vectors

These include mosquitoes, flies, ticks, and other insects that are capable of hosting and spreading an infectious agent. The anopheles mosquito transmits malaria, and the housefly may transmit typhoid.

Foodborne

Diseases may be spread through improperly prepared or contaminated foods.

Soilborne

Soilborne transmission occurs when spore-forming organisms enter the body through wounds. Tetanus is a common one.

Waterborne

Common waterborne organisms are cholera, dysentery, typhoid, and amoebic infections.

Prenatal

The newborn is infected through the placenta or by contact with infected membranes during birth.

Human/Animal Carriers

Some microorganisms may be carried from animal to man and from man to man. In human carriers, the person may not show any signs or symptoms of the disease being carried. People carrying the AIDS virus may live without signs and symptoms for years. There are many highly communicable diseases transmitted between people: the common cold, herpes, staph/strep infections, pneumonia, and skin fungi. Examples of more serious communicable infections are hepatitis B, AIDS, and tuberculosis.

SPECIFIC INFECTIOUS DISEASES

Hepatitis

Hepatitis is inflammation of the liver. There are several different types: hepatitis A (viral or infectious hepatitis); hepatitis B (serum hepatitis); and hepatitis non-A, non-B. Hepatitis non-A, non-B is the most common post-transfusion hepatitis in the United States.

Signs and Symptoms

1. Fever.
2. Weakness.
3. Loss of appetite.
4. Nausea.
5. Abdominal pain.
6. Jaundice.
7. Dark-colored urine.
8. Light-colored stools.

Incubation Period

1. Hepatitus A — two to six weeks.
2. Hepatitis B — any time up to thirty weeks.
3. Hepatitis non-A, non-B — six to eight weeks after a blood transfusion.

Mode of Transmission

1. Contact with stools, blood, or urine of an infected individual.
2. An inadvertent stick with a contaminated needle.

Paramedic Precautions

Follow the Centers for Disease Control's (CDC) "Universal Precautions."

Followup

If protective measures were not used, or if inadvertent exposure occurred (document the exposure by writing a report), it will be necessary for the paramedic to seek medical examination and probable immunization with ISG (Immune Serum Globulin).

AIDS Virus (Acquired Immunodeficiency Syndrome)

This disease is also known as HIV (human immunodeficiency virus), HTLV-III (human t-lymphotropic virus type III), and LAV (lymphadenopathy-associated virus). The AIDS virus attacks a person's immune system and damages his/her ability to fight other diseases. Without a functioning immune system to ward off microorganisms, the person is vulnerable to infection by bacteria, protozoa, fungi, viruses, and malignancies that cause life-threatening illness, such as pneumonia, meningitis, and cancer. This disease generally proves fatal.

Signs and Symptoms

A person may be carrying the HIV and be asymptomatic. Anyone in a high-risk group may be infected with the disease. The high-risk groups are homosexual and bisexual men, IV drug abusers, prostitutes, and the sex partners of these groups. The risk of getting AIDS from blood transfusions has been reduced to practically zero because of blood testing.

Some signs and symptoms of AIDS may include:

1. Persistent cough and fever associated with shortness of breath or dyspnea.
2. Fever, with profuse night sweats.
3. Unexplained weight loss.
4. Red/purple skin lesions (Kaposi's sarcoma).
5. Pneumocystis carinii pneumonia.

Incubation Period

The incubation period for signs and symptoms of AIDS to develop is two months and possibly as long as five years. Remember — even if there are no signs and symptoms, a person may still carry the AIDS virus and be contagious. It is believed at the present time that there may be as many as 1.5 million people infected with the AIDS virus. It is assumed that all these people are capable of spreading the virus.

Mode of Transmission

AIDS is an infectious disease. It is contagious, but it cannot be spread in the same manner as the common cold or chicken pox. Researchers have clearly shown that HIV cannot be spread by casual contact. There is no evidence of transmission of AIDS virus by everyday contact even in families where members shared food, towels, cups, razors, or toothbrushes. AIDS **is** transmitted via blood, semen, and bodily secretions. Remember to take precautions when dealing with bodily fluids.

Paramedic Precautions

Follow the Centers for Disease Control's "Universal Precautions."

Followup

Document any exposures to the AIDS virus.

Tuberculosis

Tuberculosis is an infectious disease caused by the tubercle bacillus. The disease is chronic and most commonly affects the lungs, although it may occur in almost any part of the body.

Signs and Symptoms

1. Cough.
2. Fever.
3. Night sweats.
4. Weight loss.
5. Fatigue.
6. Hemoptysis.

Incubation Period

The incubation period for tuberculosis is four to twelve weeks.

Mode of Transmission

Tuberculosis develops in the respiratory tract and is transmitted via droplets in the air from sneezing, coughing, and talking.

Paramedic Precautions

Follow the Centers for Disease Control's "Universal Precautions." In addition, avoid prolonged contact with the patient who has an active case of tuberculosis and avoid contact with thick, coughed-up sputum.

Followup

1. Document any exposure to tuberculosis.
2. The paramedic should have a PPD skin test or chest X-ray following contact with an active tuberculosis patient. Repeat the PPD or chest film two to three months after exposure. If the first skin test was negative and the second is positive, then the tuberculosis organism is present but has not yet caused the disease.
3. The paramedic may have a physician prescribe Isoniazid for one year.

Meningitis

Meningitis is an inflammation of the membranes of the spinal cord and/or brain. The term "meningitis" does not refer to a specific pathologic entity, but rather to the inflammatory process itself. The inflammation may be caused by a number of organisms (bacteria, virus, fungi) or by toxins (lead and arsenic).

Symptoms

1. Headache.
2. Nausea and vomiting.
3. Stiff neck.
4. Chills.
5. Fever.
6. Possible confusion and irritability.
7. Seizures occur in approximately 25 percent of the patients.
8. The patient may become comatose.

Incubation Period

An incubation period of two to ten days may vary depending on the initial strain.

Mode of Transmission

Meningitis is transmitted via direct contact with discharges from the nose and throat.

Paramedic Precautions

Use a face mask, or have the patient wear a mask, and follow general handwashing and cleaning procedures.

Followup

Document any exposure to meningitis. A paramedic may need medical care if he/she was involved in resuscitating, intubating, or suctioning a meningitis patient.

Herpes

Herpes is any inflammatory skin disease composed of clusters of vesicles that are caused by one of the herpes viruses.

Types

1. Herpes simplex, Type 1 (cold sore, fever blister).
2. Herpes simplex, Type 2 (genital herpes) — highly contagious.
3. Herpes zoster (shingles), caused by the chicken pox virus.

Signs and Symptoms, Types 1 and 2

1. Burning.
2. Itching.
3. Tingling.
4. Tenderness at the site.
5. Fever.
6. Swollen glands.
7. Thin, white discharge.
8. Lesion may be ulcerated on the penis, vulva, buttocks, and thighs.

Incubation Period

The incubation period for herpes is generally two to twelve days, but this may be variable.

Mode of Transmission

Herpes is transmitted via direct contact with lesions (genital, skin, or oral), where the virus enters through breaks in the skin. The herpes virus is not airborne and cannot be contracted from toilet seats, pools, hot tubs, or sheets.

Paramedic Precautions

Wear gloves and follow general handwashing and cleaning procedures.

Followup

Document any exposure to the herpes virus.

Syphilis

Syphilis is an infectious, chronic venereal disease. It most often manifests itself with lesions that affect both the external and internal organs and tissues of the body. It may exist without producing symptoms for many years.

Signs and Symptoms

Syphilis develops over a long period of time and has three specific stages in which different pathologies develop.

1. Primary stage (two to four weeks after exposure): lesions in the genital area, lymph node enlargement.
2. Secondary stage (approximately six weeks after the development of the primary stage): lesions manifest themselves on the skin and mucous membranes; the patient may experience headache, fever, and malaise.
3. Tertiary stage (this stage may not occur for years): cardiovascular and central nervous system disorders are commonly involved.

Incubation Period

The incubation period for syphilis is two to four weeks after exposure.

Mode of Transmission

1. Direct sexual contact.
2. Blood or plasma transfusions that are contaminated.
3. Contaminated needles or syringes.
4. In utero from mother to fetus.

Paramedic Precautions

Follow the Centers for Disease Control's "Universal Precautions."

Followup

Document any exposure to syphilis.

Gonorrhea

Gonorrhea is a specific, contagious inflammation of the genital mucous membranes which may also affect other organ systems of either males or females.

Signs and Symptoms

1. Male — a yellow, micropurulent discharge from the penis; may affect the prostate; causes painful urination.
2. Female — may be asymptomatic; urethral or vaginal discharge; painful or frequent urination; lower abdominal pain; acute pelvic inflammatory disease.

Incubation Period

The incubation period for gonorrhea is two to seven days.

Mode of Transmission

Gonorrhea is transmitted via direct contact with a contaminated person, with infected towels, or with toilets.

Paramedic Precautions

Follow the Centers for Disease Control's ''Universal Precautions'' and avoid direct contact with infected areas.

Followup

Document any exposure to gonorrhea. Discuss the exposure with a physician if protective measures were not used.

Scabies/Human Lice

Scabies is a highly communicable skin disease caused by an arachnid (itch mite). Lice are small, wingless insects that live as ectoparasites. There are three types of lice: body lice, crab lice, and head lice. Lice are the primary transmitters of epidemic typhus, trench fever, and relapsing fever.

Signs and Symptoms

1. Scabies — papules, pustules, and burrows (where the females lay eggs) cause intense itching, leading to eczema. The parts most commonly affected are the hands, fingers, wrists, axilla, genitalia, and inner aspect of the thighs. Frequently, short, discolored lines will appear in the affected area.
2. Human lice — the area may become sore and infected due to itching and scratching. The lice are grayish and wingless and vary in length from one-sixteenth to one-sixth of an inch.

Incubation Period

The incubation period for scabies and lice is two to six weeks.

Mode of Transmission

Scabies and lice are transmitted via direct contact with an affected person.

Paramedic Precautions

Avoid direct contact with an infected person. Wear gloves and follow general handwashing and cleaning procedures.

Followup

Document any exposure to scabies or lice. Bag used linens and clothing, and wash them in hot water. Dry clothing at a high temperature as well.

Measles

Measles is a highly contagious disease caused by a virus. It is primarily a childhood disease and has two varieties — rubeola, or the red measles, and rubella, also known as the German measles.

Signs and Symptoms

The signs and symptoms for both varieties of the measles are similar. They include:

1. Fever.
2. Dusky or blotchy rash that usually starts on the face and spreads to the rest of the body.

Incubation Period

The incubation period for the measles is eight to thirteen days for rubeola and fourteen to twenty-one days for rubella.

Mode of Transmission

Measles is transmitted by droplet or direct contact and oral/nasal secretions or urine.

Paramedic Precautions

Wear gloves and a mask when in contact with oral/nasal secretions or urine. Follow general handwashing and cleaning procedures.

Followup

Document any exposure to the measles. If the paramedic is not immune, he/she should consider getting an immunization.

Mumps

Mumps is a communicable disease that affects the parotid (salivary) glands. It primarily occurs in children between the ages of five and fifteen.

Signs and Symptoms

1. Fever.
2. Swelling and tenderness of the salivary glands.

Incubation Period

The incubation period for mumps is twelve to twenty-six days.

Mode of Transmission

Mumps is transmitted via direct contact with saliva or with airborne droplets of oral secretions.

Paramedic Precautions

Use disposable gloves and a mask, and follow general handwashing and cleaning procedures.

Followup

Document any exposure to the mı he/she should consider getting an im

Chicken Pox

Chicken pox, or varicella zoster vir is a highly contagious disease.

Signs and Symptoms

1. Fever.
2. Skin eruptions that cover primarily the spread to the arms, legs, and face in se

Incubation Period

The incubation period for chicken pox is t

Mode of Transmission

Chicken pox is transmitted via droplets or airborne secretions from the respiratory tract of infected persons and from lesion secretions.

Paramedic Precautions

Wear a mask and gloves and follow general handwashing and cleaning procedures.

Followup

Document any exposure to chicken pox. If the paramedic is not immune, he/she should consider getting an immunization (varicella-zoster immune globin for the prevention of chicken pox).

CLEANING AND DISINFECTING

The best way to deal with infectious disease is to minimize the paramedic's exposure. This can be accomplished by following the Centers for Disease Control's guidelines and those presented for specific disease entities. The habits that the paramedic develops may prevent a serious exposure. The time that the paramedic takes to clean and disinfect the ambulance will help prevent the spread of infectious disease to other patients, as well as to the paramedic.

Although health-care professionals are at risk of exposure to serious infectious disease, these risks can clearly be reduced. It is the paramedic's responsibility to protect him/herself and others from disease.

When transporting a patient with an infectious disease, the paramedic should report this information to the receiving facility. The hospital personnel will instruct the paramedic on any additional precautions to take and where to deliver the patient. The hospital personnel (infection control practitioner) will recommend followup care for the paramedic.

Handwashing

Handwashing is probably one of the most effective ways of preventing the spread of pathologic organisms. It is clear that washing in the field is difficult, but it should be done as soon as possible.

Handwashing with an antibacterial/antiviral soap is the best solution for removing and killing pathologic material. Handwashing with plain soap may remove most organisms but will not destroy them. Proper handwashing technique requires at least fifteen seconds of scrubbing, turning off the faucet with a paper towel, and drying the hands with a paper towel.

The paramedic should clean uniforms on a regular basis and replace a contaminated uniform immediately (i.e., if blood is absorbed linto a pant leg after starting an IV).

Vehicle Cleaning

Routine cleaning and disinfecting (on a daily basis) of the ambulance is a good investment of time. Cleaning the floors with an appropriate cleaning agent and cleaning the walls will make disinfecting the ambulance after contamination easier. Remember — to truly disinfect, surface areas must be cleaned first, followed by application of a disinfectant. In general, only areas that have been contaminated should be disinfected. When cleaning an infected area, wear disposable gloves. Use an Environmental Protection Agency-approved cleaning agent.

When cleaning a vehicle that has transported a patient with an infectious disease, be sure to bag all contaminated disposable items (wear disposable gloves) and mark them for incineration. Bag all contaminated linens and mark them "contaminated."

Use care when disposing of needles and syringes. The most frequent cause for an inadvertent needle stick is an attempt to replace a needle cover when an ambulance is moving. (A second cause is leaving exposed needles in a drug kit to be disposed of later.) Use a Sharp's container for needle disposal, and use a proper receptacle for syringes.

Equipment Cleaning

Respiratory Equipment

Dispose of respiratory equipment if it is a single-use item, and sterilize it if it is reusable. Sterilization should take place immediately after each use when possible (or at the paramedic's earliest convenience). One form of sterilization is to disassemble the equipment and place it in a cold, liquid sterilization solution for twenty minutes. This should be followed by air drying for at least one hour.

Suction Equipment

Disposable equipment should be bagged for disposal. Tubing and bottles can be cleaned with a liquid sterilization solution.

MAST Equipment

Clean the outer garment and inner bladder as necessary.

SUMMARY

By the nature of his/her work, the paramedic will at times be exposed to infectious disease. When the paramedic takes the appropriate measures during the handling of patients with a known illness and takes the proper precautions when treating unknown patients, the risk of contracting an infectious disease is minimal.

The paramedic should develop the habit of taking protective measures with every patient and performing the "ritual" of handwashing after every patient contact. Naturally, the ambulance should be cleaned daily and disinfected as needed.

17

Environmental Emergencies

This chapter covers the etiology and management of a number of emergencies that result from physical exposure in the external environment. These include hyperthermia, hypothermia, frostbite, near-drowning, underwater diving emergencies, lightning injuries, and exposure to ionizing radiations.

TEMPERATURE-RELATED EMERGENCIES

It is important to recognize that the elderly, the infirm, alcoholics, and the young (less than five years of age) are more susceptible to heat and cold problems. Hypothermia is becoming a common problem in the northern cities of the United States, primarily among the elderly who have problems paying their heating bills and among people who live on the streets (particularly if they drink).

Thermoregulation

The human body maintains a well-regulated state of equilibrium called homeostasis. Normal cellular functions occur within a narrow temperature range, the norm being 98.6 degrees Fahrenheit (37 degrees Centigrade). Slight variations may occur in different individuals. There are situations when environmental (extrinsic) conditions overwhelm thermoregulatory mechanisms, or when internal (intrinsic) thermal stressors (i.e., the breakdown of the sweating mechanism or fever) exceed the ability of the body to compensate for them. In other words, the compensatory mechanisms must be able to cool the body when it is overheated or warm the body when it is too cold. Thermal disorders may occur either in the form of heat-related problems, such heat stroke or heat exhaustion, or cooling problems, such as hypothermia or frostbite.

The following are heat-related disorders:

1. Heat edema.
2. Heat syncope.
3. Heat cramps.
4. Heat exhaustion.
5. Heat stroke.
6. Fever.

The following are cold-related disorders:

1. Hypothermia.
2. Frostbite.

The primary or central thermoregulatory control mechanism is the hypothalamus, found in the brain. In addition to the hypothalamus, temperature receptors in the skin, viscera, and nervous tissues monitor body temperature.

An efficient thermoregulatory system is critical for proper function of the human body. Every movement — be it the heart beating or the eye blinking — produces heat. The body must remove excess heat. If there is a failure of the thermoregulatory system resulting in excessive loss or retention of heat, normal biochemical processes will not be sustained. As previously mentioned, external heat or cold may also disrupt the body's equilibrium.

Heat is produced within the body (intrinsic sources) from the following:

1. Cellular metabolism — the breakdown (change) of chemical substances produces heat.
2. Physical activity — this increases energy production, thereby increasing heat production.
3. Fever — this is commonly caused by the release of pyrogens (any substance that produces fever) from viruses and bacteria or from the destruc-

tion of cells. These pyrogens reset the "thermostat" above the normal 98.6 degrees Fahrenheit.

Heat is also gained from the following environmental (extrinsic) sources:

1. Ambient air temperature — if the ambient air temperature is higher than the skin temperature, heat will flow from the air to the skin.
2. Air humidity — as the humidity rises, the ability of the body to rid itself of heat by radiation and sweating is diminished; when the humidity is greater than 75 percent, the body can no longer dissipate heat — in fact, the body may now absorb heat from the environment.
3. Infrared radiation (sunlight) — heat flows from higher temperature areas to lower temperature areas.

Heat loss and gain may occur in the following ways:

1. Radiation — the process by which energy (heat) is moved through space (heat may be radiated away from the body or toward the body).
2. Conduction — the transfer of heat through a conducting medium.
3. Convection — the transfer of heat via air currents or liquids.
4. Evaporation — the change of a liquid into a vapor (heat is lost when perspiration evaporates off of the body).
5. Respiration — heat is most commonly lost during breathing.

HEAT ILLNESS

Heat illness ranges from mild changes in physiology with few symptoms to heat stroke complete with serious manifestations that occasionally result in death. Approximately 4,000 people die each year in the United States from heat stroke; 80 percent of the victims are over fifty years of age. Heat stroke is the second most common cause of death among high school athletes. It is important for the paramedic to be able to recognize heat illness and manage it appropriately.

Hyperthermia Caused by the External Environment

Heat Edema

Heat edema is the swelling of the feet and ankles. It commonly occurs in the aged who are not acclimatized to a tropical or semitropical environment. The patient may have had long periods of standing or sitting. Heat edema is thought to occur because of vasodilation of the vessels in the lower extremities, along with reduced venous return. This results in accumulation of interstitial fluid (edema) in the feet and ankles.

Heat edema often resolves itself after several days of acclimatization. No treatment is required for this situation. The physician might perform a brief evaluation to rule out thrombophlebitis or congestive heart failure.

Heat Syncope

Heat syncope has numerous causes, some being serious and others being relatively benign. Any individual may experience heat syncope, but it is most commonly seen in the elderly patient. Part of the body's adaptation to a hot environment is the dilation of the cutaneous and muscular vessels, which releases excess heat. People who stand for long periods of time pool blood in their lower extremities. This, in combination with volume loss (perspiration) and vasodilation, may drop cardiac output and reduce cerebral perfusion, resulting in a temporary loss of consciousness.

In heat syncope, the person collapses, but when perfusion to the brain is restored, consciousness is regained. The paramedic needs to evaluate the patient for possible fractures of the skull, face, neck, or hip. The paramedic should transport the patient if there is any doubt as to the cause of the syncopal episode.

Heat Cramps

Heat cramps is the most common and least serious form of heat illness. The condition is often seen in physically active people prior to acclimatization during the summer months. Heat cramps is a result of profuse sweating with an associated loss of sodium (salt), which causes severe muscular cramping.

History

1. There is a history of profuse sweating in a hot environment without sodium replacement.
2. The patient complains of cramps in the extremities and the abdomen.

Signs and Symptoms

1. The patient is mentally alert.
2. The skin is pale, moist, and cool.

3. Profuse sweating occurs.
4. Tachycardia may occur.
5. The patient is normotensive.
6. The core body temperature is normal.
7. The patient may be nauseous, but there is usually no vomiting.

Treatment

1. Remove the patient from the hot environment.
2. Replace the fluid and sodium loss either orally or parenterally (confirm with the base physician).
3. Transport of the patient to the emergency department may not be necessary.

Heat Exhaustion

Heat exhaustion is a more severe form of heat illness resulting from physical activity in a hot environment with a significant loss of water and salt due to sweating. This excess salt/fluid loss causes more severe signs and symptoms.

History

The patient has been physically active with profuse sweating in a hot environment without fluid and salt replacement.

Signs and Symptoms

1. The patient may be anxious, disoriented, or apathetic.
2. The patient may be hypotensive (slight to serious, depending on the severity).
3. Heart rate is increased.
4. Nausea and vomiting may occur.
5. The skin is pale, moist, and cool.
6. Profuse sweating may occur.
7. The patient may be thirsty.
8. Weakness and fainting may occur.
9. The respiratory rate may be elevated.
10. The core temperature may be normal or one to two degrees elevated.

Treatment

1. Move the patient to a cool environment.
2. Provide an IV by administering either normal saline or lactated Ringer's.

3. Transport of the patient to the emergency department is usually required.

Heat Stroke

Heat stroke is the least common and most life-threatening of the heat-related problems. It is a profound disturbance of the heat-regulating system of the body.

Heat stroke often takes place in a hot environment with a relative humidity greater than 75 percent. It results in an increased core body temperature as the heat-dissipating mechanism becomes impaired. This is associated with the shutdown of the sweating mechanism (cooling system) and dehydration. The body temperature may rise to as high as 109 degrees Fahrenheit (43 degrees Centigrade).

As the core body temperature increases, negative effects are seen on the central nervous system, the cardiovascular system, and the respiratory system, as well as on the GI tract, the liver, and the kidneys. Early on, the victim is seen to be confused and may exhibit irrational behavior, with a possible sudden loss of consciousness. If the condition is not corrected, the patient will go into a coma. The patient may develop hypotension (due to volume depletion), peripheral vasodilatation, and cardiac dysfunction. The patient may also develop pulmonary edema.

History

1. There is a history of exposure to a hot, humid environment.
2. The patient may have been physically active and not yet acclimated to the hot environment.
3. There may be a history of illness or poor health.

Signs and Symptoms

1. The patient may experience pyrexia (fever) commonly above 105 degrees Fahrenheit (40.5 degrees Centigrade). This may cause cerebral cellular necrosis and generalized vasodilation leading to cardiovascular collapse.
2. The blood pressure increases initially and later decreases.
3. Respirations decrease in rate and become deep.
4. The heart rate is increased and full (it may become weak later).
5. The skin is flushed and dry.
6. Decreased mentation occurs as the core body temperature increases.
7. Seizures may occur.
8. Coma may occur.

Treatment

1. ABCs — administer oxygen and assist ventilations as necessary.
2. Check the rectal temperature if possible.
3. Start an IV of D_5W; if the patient is hypotensive, use normal saline or lactated Ringer's (TKO or increase flow as needed).
4. Remove the patient's clothing and cool the patient immediately by wrapping him/her in wet sheets. Use ice packs (cold packs) at the neck, the axillae, and the ankles if available. Fanning the patient may also help to reduce his/her core temperature. The paramedic should try to reduce the patient's temperature to 102 degrees Fahrenheit (39 degrees Centigrade).
5. Monitor the ECG, vital signs, and the LOC.

Hyperthermia Caused by the Internal Environment

Fever

Fever is commonly caused by the release of pyrogens from viruses, bacteria, and the destruction of cells. These pyrogens reset the "thermostat" found in the hypothalamus in the brain above the normal 98.6 degrees Fahrenheit (37 degrees Centigrade). Generally, the hypothalmic thermostat eventually resets back to normal levels.

History

1. The patient has a history of illness or an infection associated with fever.
2. The temperature is elevated above 98.6 degrees Fahrenheit orally and 99.6 degrees Fahrenheit rectally.

Signs and Symptoms

1. The pulse may be elevated.
2. The skin may be flushed.
3. The skin may be dry or sweaty.
4. High fever may result in a diminished level of consciousness.
5. There is a possibility of seizures occurring.

Treatment

1. ABCs.
2. The underlying cause must be treated (not part of prehospital care).
3. Fevers above 105 degrees Fahrenheit (40.5 degrees Centigrade) should be actively cooled with tepid water.

COLD INJURIES

Cold injuries historically have been a wartime problem. Today, cold injuries may be found among the elderly in northern urban areas and among construction workers, alcoholics, skiers, and other outdoor enthusiasts.

Human beings are warm-weather, tropical animals that cannot tolerate cold weather or adapt to it very well. Since the development of clothing and shelter, man can now tolerate the most extreme environmental conditions.

Hypothermia

Hypothermia is a cooling of the core body temperature below 95 degrees Fahrenheit (35 degrees Centigrade). Acute systemic hypothermia occurs when heat loss to the environment is greater than the body's heat production, causing a drop in the core body temperature.

The body has compensatory mechanisms that under ordinary circumstances protect the body from a reduction in air temperature. As skin temperature is reduced following cold exposure, peripheral vasoconstriction (sympathetic stimulation) occurs, shunting the flow of blood to the core body (vital organs). This creates an outer insulating shell that helps to maintain core body temperature. The respiratory rate, heart rate, and blood pressure increase. Heat production increases 50 to 100 percent by preshivering muscle tone. If the cold continues, involuntary shivering occurs, increasing heat production (by increasing the metabolism) by 500 percent. As cold exposure continues, the compensatory mechanisms of the body no longer are effective in preventing heat loss.

As core body temperature decreases, specific changes may be seen in the central nervous system, the circulatory system, the heart, the respiratory system, blood sugar levels, and acid-base balance.

Central Nervous System

In the early stages of hypothermia with core temperatures above 90 degrees Fahrenheit (32 degrees Centigrade), the victim becomes withdrawn, apathetic, and lethargic. The victim talks less and is generally less active. As the core body temperature falls below 90 degrees Fahrenheit, the victim becomes more withdrawn, apathetic, and lethargic. There may be moments of complete withdrawal. Eventually, the victim lapses into coma. The victim has a tendency to make serious errors in judgment, increasing the chances of additional mishaps.

Circulatory System

The general effects of hypothermia on this system are to reduce the circulating volume and the flow rate as peripheral resistance and blood viscosity increase. The overall result is poor tissue oxygenation. The victim may develop either metabolic acidosis or alkalosis.

The Heart

In the hypothermic patient, the heart rate, as well as cardiac output and arterial blood pressure, are decreased. Due to pH changes, inadequate oxygenation, electrolyte imbalances, and the cold temperatures, the victim is likely to experience cardiac dysrhythmias. Ventricular fibrillation and asystole are the most common life-threatening dysrhythmias to occur in the hypothermic patient. It appears that ventricular fibrillation most frequently occurs during resuscitation and that asystole occurs most frequently as the presenting rhythm.

The Respiratory System

Initially, the respiratory rate goes up, but as hypothermia continues, the respiratory rate decreases. The cough reflex is depressed, bronchodilation occurs, and there is an increased production of secretions. These increased secretions may be the cause of pulmonary edema that sometimes develops during rewarming of the hypothermic patient.

Moderate Hypothermia

Moderate hypothermia occurs when the core body temperature is between 90 and 95 degrees Fahrenheit (32.2 to 35 degrees Centigrade).

History

1. There is usually exposure to a cold environment.
2. Possible consumption of alcohol by the patient.
3. The patient may be elderly, ill, or very young.
4. Immersion in cold water may have occurred.

Signs and Symptoms

1. A rectal temperature of 90 to 95 degrees Fahrenheit is present (must have a low-reading thermometer).
2. The patient may experience confusion and disorientation.

3. The patient usually experiences uncontrollable shivering.
4. Amnesia may occur.
5. The patient's skin is pale and cool.
6. Cardiac irregularities may occur (the lower the core body temperature, the more likely that serious life-threatening cardiac irregularities will develop).

Treatment

1. Handle the patient gently.
2. Move the patient gently from the cold environment.
3. Provide oxygen and ventilatory support as needed.
4. Start external rewarming by heating the head, the neck, the chest, and the groin with warm packs or hot water bottles. Be sure that the patient's rectal temperature is above 90 degrees Fahrenheit when rewarming with external heat.
5. Warm fluids and sugar sources may be given by mouth to a patient who is awake.
6. Alcohol, coffee, and nicotine are contraindicated.

Severe Hypothermia

Severe hypothermia occurs when the core body temperature is below 90 degrees Fahrenheit (32.2 degrees Centigrade).

History

1. There is usually exposure to a cold environment.
2. Possible consumption of alcohol by the patient.
3. The patient may be elderly, ill, or very young.
4. Immersion in cold water may have occurred.

Signs and Symptoms

1. Cardiac irregularities may be bradycardia, ventricular fibrillation, asystole, or others.
2. The patient is stuporous or in a coma.
3. The patient has cold, pale skin.
4. Muscular rigidity generally occurs.
5. Heart sounds may be inaudible.
6. Respirations are slow or absent.
7. The patient has dilated pupils.
8. Generalized edema may occur.

9. Death usually occurs below 78 degrees Fahrenheit (25.6 degrees Centigrade), and the mortality rate exceeds 50 percent below 86 degrees Fahrenheit (30 degrees Centigrade).

Treatment — Severe Hypothermia with a Pulse

1. Handle the patient gently.
2. Move the patient from the cold environment.
3. Remove wet clothing from the patient.
4. Insulate the patient from the cold.
5. Rewarming — there is controversy over what role, if any, prehospital warming plays when transporting the severely hypothermic patient. One school of thought suggests that the patient not be rewarmed until complete monitoring and control of the patient is established in the hospital setting. The other school of thought suggests that rewarming may carefully be initiated in the field by covering the patient with blankets and **not** overheating the patient compartment. Core rewarming may be started if an oxygen warmer is available. **The paramedic should follow local protocol for rewarming.**
6. Administer oxygen by mask. If the patient is breathing at a rate of less than five per minute, assist ventilations but **do not hyperventilate**; this may initiate ventricular fibrillation. **The use of an ET-tube or other airway adjuncts may cause ventricular fibrillation.** Use an ET-tube only if absolutely necessary. Follow local protocols.
7. Establish an IV of D_5W at a keep-open rate. Some researchers believe that volume expansion with warmed IV fluids, if possible (D_5NS), is quite important for improvement of the cardiovascular system. Give a fluid challenge of 300 to 500 milliliters, then adjust the flow based on the blood pressure and the urinary output in the adult. **Follow local protocol for the administration of fluids to the hypothermic patient.**
8. Attempt to monitor the ECG.
9. Do not administer medications.

Treatment — Severe Hypothermia with No Pulse

1. Move the patient from the cold environment.
2. Assess the pulse and respirations for one to two minutes.
3. If there is no pulse or respiration, start CPR.
4. Observe the ECG rhythm; if the patient is in ventricular fibrillation, defibrillate twice; if it does not convert, continue CPR.
5. Defibrillation does not readily convert until the core body temperature is

more than 88 degrees Fahrenheit (31 degrees Centigrade).
6. If defibrillation is successful, administer a lidocaine bolus IV followed by maintenance infusion (follow local protocols).
7. Warm oxygen and intubation are appropriate for the pulseless/apneic, hypothermic patient.
8. Rewarming — see ''Treatment — Severe Hypothermia with a Pulse,'' above.

Metabolic Factors in Hypothermia

Hypothermia may be precipitated by underlying medical conditions. The following are possible causes of hypothermia:

1. Hypothyroidism, which may depress the metabolic heat-producing mechanisms.
2. A brain tumor or head injury may depress the hypothalmic thermostatic control.
3. Other conditions that may predispose a person to hypothermia are diabetes, hypoglycemia, drugs, undernutrition, old age, and any other factors that contribute to metabolic and circulatory disorders.
4. History:
   - A history that includes precipitating factors.
   - The history may include environmental exposure.
5. Signs and symptoms are similar to those for environmental hypothermia.
6. Treatment is the same as discussed above.

Frostbite (Local Hypothermia or Local Cold Injury)

Frostbite occurs when tissues (epidermis, dermis, subcutaneous fat, blood vessels, nerves, and muscle) are exposed to prolonged cold stress or to extremely low temperatures. It is influenced by several factors, including air temperature, wind chill, moisture, insulation, and contact with super-cooled liquids or metals. If the exposed area is left unprotected, it will eventually freeze, resulting in either superficial or deep frostbite. The most common areas of frostbite are the nose, cheeks, ears, fingers, hands, feet, and toes. Frostbite most commonly occurs without hypothermia and in the lower extremities.

Types of Frostbite

Superficial

Superficial frostbite involves:

1. The epidermis.
2. The dermis.
3. Possibly the shallow subcutaneous layers.

Deep Frostbite

Deep frostbite usually involves:

1. The epidermis.
2. The dermis.
3. The subcutaneous fat.
4. Blood vessels.
5. Nerves.
6. Muscle.
7. Possibly the underlying bone.

Pathology

Tissue goes through four overlapping stages when it freezes.

1. Prior to freezing, vasoconstriction and plasma leakage develop. Vasoconstriction in the exposed body part reduces circulation and causes an accelerated heat loss in the area.
2. Freeze/thaw stage: ice crystals form and melt in the extracellular and intracellular fluid. Tissue damage and dehydration may occur. There may be reduced circulation and cellular oxygenation, along with possible destructive biochemical changes. Rapid freezing and thawing are the most damaging to body tissue.
3. Stagnation stage: this results from changes that take place in the blood vessels (venous dilation and arterial spasm), along with shunting and stagnation of blood with plasma leakage.
4. Ischemia stage (a local and temporary reduction of oxygen supply due to the obstruction of circulation to a part): this results from clotting, shunting of blood away from the injured area, hypoxia, and gangrene. This is not usually seen during prehospital care.

Assessment

History

There is exposure to a freezing environment.

Signs and Symptoms

1. Cold exposure initially causes reddened skin.
2. The skin becomes mottled white or gray with continued cooling.
3. The skin appears white or gray with full freezing.
4. Some compliance may be felt beneath the frozen layer in superficial frostbite. It is difficult to determine superficial from deep frostbite in the field.
5. The frozen part will be hard and noncompliant with deep frostbite.
6. Superficial frostbite is usually painful.
7. Deep frostbite is usually painless.
8. There may be complaints of a burning sensation.
9. Impaired function in the frozen part may occur.

Treatment

1. Move the patient from the cold environment.
2. Do not massage the frozen part or rub it with snow.
3. If the paramedic is close to the hospital:
   - Gently and loosely dress the injured area.
   - Splint for further protection.
   - Do not puncture or drain blisters.
   - Elevate the injured area to reduce swelling.
4. If the paramedic is far from the hospital (several hours):
   - Do not thaw the part if there is any possibility that it might refreeze.
   - Administer an analgesia prior to thawing.
   - Thaw the frozen part by immersion into a 100- to 106-degree-Fahrenheit water bath. Monitor the water temperature constantly, because it will cool rapidly. Maintain the desired temperature by carefully adding hot water. Keep the water circulating. The complete process usually takes thirty to forty minutes. Thawing is considered complete when sensation, color, and softness have returned to the part. Do not use dry heat to thaw.
   - Cover the thawed part with loosely applied, dry, sterile dressings.
   - Elevate the thawed part.
   - Do not puncture or drain blisters.
   - Do not allow the patient to smoke.

DROWNING AND NEAR-DROWNING (Submersion Injury)

Approximately 8,000 people die annually in the United States from drowning, and many more experience a "near-drowning." Drowning is one of the four leading causes of accidental death between the ages of four and forty-four.

The terms "drowning" and "near-drowning" may be confusing. It is recommended that **drowning** refer to the patient who has suffocated (cardiac arrest) while submerged in water and that **near-drowning** refer to the patient who is alive at the scene of the submersion.

Eighty-five percent of near-drowning victims are male, and two-thirds of the victims do not know how to swim. Several factors play a role in near-drownings, the most important being alcohol intoxication. Other factors are medical illness, fatigue, suicide, drug abuse, and trauma. The young are at the greatest risk of drowning. Sixty-four percent of all drowning victims are under thirty years of age, and 26 percent are under the age of five.

Pathology

The factors affecting the outcome of a submersion incident include the following:

1. The length of submersion.
2. The water temperature:
   - As the water gets colder (starting from 70 degrees Fahrenheit), the chance of survival increases and the probability of successful resuscitation is increased. This may occur because of the protective effects of rapid cerebral cooling (hypothermia) and the mammalian diving reflex (a reflex that constricts bloodflow except to the brain, that decreases cardiac output and rate, and that produces a stable arterial blood pressure; it reduces oxygen requirements). This reflex functions most strongly in young people.
   - As water gets warmer, the chance of survival diminishes and the probability of successful resuscitation is reduced.
3. Contaminants present in the water.
4. Age and health of the patient.

Sequence of Events

The following actions are typical of the drowning victim:

1. Panic.
2. Violent struggling.
3. An attempt at breath-holding.

4. Hyperventilation, which is usually uncontrollable, leads to aspiration of water.
5. Swallowing of large amounts of water may occur, resulting in vomiting, followed by aspiration.

Types of Drowning

Dry Drowning

Dry drowning occurs in 10 to 20 percent of victims and is caused by a spasm of the epiglottis and larynx. This prevents aspiration of water, but the person loses consciousness and dies from hypoxia and asphyxia.

Wet Drowning

Wet drowning occurs in 80 to 90 percent of victims and is caused by water entering the lower respiratory tract, preventing oxygenation of the red blood cells. The person loses consciousness and dies from hypoxia.

Freshwater

Fresh water causes surfactant (an agent that lowers surface tension in the lungs) to be washed away, causing atelectasis. This leads to hypoxia. Fresh water is also hypotonic and readily passes out of the alveolus into circulation, causing hemodilution. In freshwater drowning, there are only minor electrolyte changes.

Saltwater

Salt water is hypertonic, causing the movement of fluid into the alveoli and preventing oxygenation (hypoxia) by causing pulmonary edema. As in freshwater drowning, only minor electrolyte changes occur.

Assessment

History

1. Gather as much information as possible from witnesses of the incident.
2. Determine significant facts, if possible (diving, boating accident, etc.).
3. Determine the water temperature, if possible.
4. Attempt to determine the length of submersion.

Signs and Symptoms

1. The patient may be alert and oriented or obtunded.
2. There may be possible cardiac arrest.
3. The skin is pale or cyanotic.
4. A cough and frothy sputum may be present.
5. Rales (crackles), rhonchi (low wheezes), or wheezing may be auscultated.
6. Hypothermia is possible.
7. Examine the patient carefully for fractures, especially of the head and spine.

Treatment

Anyone submerged long enough to be unconscious or to require artificial ventilation should be hospitalized, because patients are likely to have complications in the first twenty-four hours after the near-drowning episode. There is no difference in treatment between freshwater and saltwater near-drownings in the prehospital setting.

1. Remove the victim from the water as soon as possible.
2. If there will be any delay in recovering the victim, a trained rescue swimmer should be used, if available.
   - The rescue swimmer should initiate mouth-to-mouth ventilations (if necessary and possible) **while the victim is still in the water.**
   - In cold water (below 70 degrees Fahrenheit), rescue personnel should wear wetsuits or other thermal protective clothing.
   - A safety line should be attached to the rescue swimmer.
   - Wild-water (white-water) rescue demands that personnel be specifically trained for that environment.
3. Suspect a head or neck injury if there is the slightest suspicion of a fall or diving accident.
   - Slide the patient gently onto a backboard, then remove the patient rapidly from the water.
4. Examine the patient for airway patency, breathing, and pulse.
5. Begin CPR if needed.
6. Airway management is required once the patient is secured.
   - Endotracheal or esophageal intubation should be performed.
   - Be prepared for vomiting.
   - Suction as necessary.
   - Administer 100 percent oxygen by ET-tube, EOA, or nonrebreathing face mask.

- If the patient is hypothermic and transport time is greater than fifteen minutes, use respiratory rewarming if available.
- The efficacy of the Heimlich maneuver is questionable.

7. Insert a large-bore IV with D_5W or D_5 in normal saline.
8. Defibrillation:
   - In the non-hypothermic patient, follow normal AHA-ACLS protocols.
   - In the hypothermic patient, follow protocols for hypothermia.
9. Pharmacotherapy:
   - In the non-hypothermic patient, follow normal AHA-ACLS protocols.
   - In the hypothermic patient, follow protocols for hypothermia.
10. Resuscitation is not indicated when there is evidence of obvious death or when immersion is documented for over one hour in water warmer than 70 degrees Fahrenheit. Follow local protocol.

DIVING EMERGENCIES

Since the development of modern and readily available scuba-diving equipment, more and more people have been getting involved in this underwater sport. In addition, there are both industrial (i.e., oil exploration and bridge building) and scientific (research in pollution control and oceanic food development) applications for scuba diving.

Scuba diving is practiced not only in the oceans and seas, but in most inland parts of the United States where there are lakes and quarries. It behooves the paramedic to be familiar with the most common scuba-diving problems.

The person who is scuba diving is breathing gas under pressure. As the person submerges, a tremendous weight is exerted on the body and on the gases inside of it. When this pressure on the body increases, the gases within the body compress. The body volume decreases, and some of the gases dissolve in the blood. As the person ascends from depth, the pressure on the body decreases and the gases within the body expand and are released from the blood.

General Assessment

1. When did signs and symptoms start?
   - Before surfacing?
   - During surfacing?
   - After surfacing?

2. Identify the type of breathing apparatus that was used.
3. Identify the type of hypothermia protective garment used:
   - Wet suit.
   - Dry suit.
4. Identify the dive parameters:
   - Depth of the dive.
   - Duration of the dive.
   - Number of dives.
   - Type of ascent. Was it controlled or panicked?
5. Determine if there is a significant medical history.
6. Determine if there has been any previous decompression illness.
7. Were there ascents to altitude (aircraft) following the dives?
8. Is the patient taking any medications?

Problems on Descent in the Water

Barotitis (Ear Squeeze)

Barotitis results from a change in pressure between the air in the middle ear and the external ambient water pressure. The tympanic membrane (eardrum) bulges inward. If this is not corrected and the diver continues to descend, the membrane may rupture, causing vertigo along with pain and discomfort.

The diver must curtail diving activities until the membrane has healed. Prehospital care consists of recommending that the patient see an ear specialist immediately or transporting the patient to the emergency department. Assess the patient for any serious problems.

Barosinusitis (Sinus Squeeze)

Barosinusitis occurs when the pressure is less in the paranasal sinus than in the surrounding water, and a relative vacuum develops in the sinus. This produces intense pain with damage to the mucosal lining and bleeding into the sinus cavity.

The diver must curtail his/her activities and seek the advice of a physician. Prehospital care consists of recommending that the patient see a specialist immediately or transporting the patient to the emergency department. Assess the patient for any serious problems.

Decompression Sickness

Decompression sickness is most commonly caused by too rapid of an ascent from depth.

Pathology

Inert gas(es), primarily nitrogen, separates from the bloodstream and tissues as bubbles during the rapid ascent, causing widespread embolization in the body. Both intravascular and extravascular gas bubbles (emboli) will develop.

The effects of the air emboli are:

1. There is decreased blood circulation to bodily tissues and organs.
2. Vital function depression may occur.
3. There may be central nervous system changes (in severe cases), sometimes resulting in permanent disability or death.
4. The surface of the air emboli initiates platelet aggregation and intravascular coagulation.
5. There may be plasma loss, leading to edema and hemoconcentration.

History

The patient or witness will give a history of diving or working in a caisson (a water-tight box in which construction is carried on, usually at some depth).

Signs and Symptoms

Vital signs may be stable in both types I and II. All decompression sickness must be considered serious and treated rapidly.

Type I

1. There is localized musculoskeletal pain, particularly in the joints. There may be swelling in the joints, and the patient may experience difficulty in walking.
2. Skin changes may occur — puritis erythema, spotted pallor or cyanosis, and pitting edema.

Type II

Signs and symptoms for type II include those for type I, plus any of the following:

1. Headache.
2. Dizziness or vertigo.

3. Confusion.
4. Auditory disturbances.
5. Visual disturbances.
6. Paralysis.
7. Paresthesia.
8. Nausea.
9. Dyspnea and chest pain.
10. Loss of consciousness.
11. Hemoptysis (coughing up of blood).

Treatment

1. ABCs.
2. Elevate the hips and feet (Trendelenburg position), and keep the patient in this position en route to the nearest decompression chamber (hyperbaric chamber).
3. Administer oxygen by a nonrebreathing mask at twelve liters per minute.
4. Auscultate breath sounds and observe for pneumothorax.
5. Start a large-bore IV with Ringer's lactate or normal saline at an appropriate rate.
6. Administer medications (under the direction of a physician familiar with diving medicine):
   - An IV of dexamethasone may reduce spinal cord edema in spinal cord decompression.
   - Diazepam (Valium), IV or IM, is used to treat vomiting and vertigo.
7. Do frequent monitoring of vital signs and sequential neurological assessments.
8. Transport the patient to a decompression chamber as soon as possible. If air transportation is used, low-altitude flight must be maintained.

Pulmonary Overpressure Accidents

Pulmonary overpressure accidents most commonly occur during a rapid ascent and/or breath-holding on ascent from depth. This type of injury has resulted from an ascent from as little as six feet of depth with breath-holding.

Pathology

The development of arterial air emboli is the major life-threatening event that occurs from pulmonary overpressure accidents. In addition to this, the following may occur:

1. Rupture of alveolar membranes.
2. Hemorrhage.
3. Reduced oxygen and carbon dioxide transport.
4. Capillary and alveolar inflammation.
5. Pneumothorax and tension pneumothorax.
6. Pneumomediastinum.
7. Subcutaneous emphysema.

History of Air Embolism and Mediastinal-Subcutaneous Emphysema (Air)

The onset is rapid and dramatic, occurring usually within ten minutes after surfacing.

Signs and Symptoms of Air Embolism

1. Seizure activity.
2. Unconsciousness.
3. Confusion.
4. Headache.
5. Visual disturbances.
6. Hemiplegia.

Signs and Symptoms of Mediastinal-Subcutaneous Emphysema

Mediastinal-subcutaneous emphysema is rupture with the release of gas through the visceral pleura into the mediastinum and/or the pericardial sac. This does not occur often. Signs and symptoms are:

1. Substernal pain.
2. Neck swelling.
3. Change in voice.
4. Dyspnea.
5. Bloody sputum.
6. Subcutaneous air (crepitus).
7. Wide pulse pressure with tension pneumothorax.
8. Reduced blood pressure and/or narrow pulse pressure.
9. Possible cyanosis.
10. Abnormal heart sounds.

Treatment

1. ABCs.
2. Place the patient in a left lateral Trendelenburg position.
3. Administer high-flow, high-concentration oxygen by a nonrebreathing mask.
4. Do frequent monitoring of vital signs and sequential neurological assessments.
5. Start a large-bore IV with Ringer's lactate or normal saline at a keep-open rate.
6. Administer Decadron, IV, by physician's order.
7. Transport the patient to a decompression chamber as soon as possible. If air transportation is used, a low altitude must be maintained.
8. Treatment for mediastinal-subcutaneous air ranges from observation to decompression. The paramedic should be conservative and assume the worst.

Pneumothorax and Tension Pneumothorax

See Chapter 7, "Trauma."

LIGHTNING INJURY

Lightning strikes the earth more than 100 times per second during the approximate 2,000 thunderstorms that occur on any given day. The number of people struck by lightning is a small fraction of the number of strikes. It is estimated that between 150 and 300 people die each year from lightning strikes in the United States. The states that have the highest incidence of lightning injuries are those in the South, the Gulf Coast, the Rocky Mountain area, and states along the Ohio, Mississippi, and Hudson rivers.

Lightning may carry an electrical charge of 50 million volts, 500,000 amps, with an initial heat of 8,000 degrees Centigrade that after a few milliseconds falls to 2,000 to 3,000 degrees Centigrade. Lightning is very dangerous for three reasons: high voltage, high heat production, and explosive force. A person may be injured by lightning when hit directly, when lightning hits a building or tree and splashes onto the victim ("splash"), or when lightning hits the ground and spreads out like ripples in the water ("step voltage"). The further a person is located away from the strike, the less the voltage, and the less the damage that may occur from blunt trauma exerted by the force of the lightning.

Assessment

History

1. There may be direct evidence that the victim was struck by lightning (i.e., there may be linear burns and/or clothing exploded off).
2. There may be reports by witnesses.
3. There may be a history of thunderstorms (although this is not necessary for a patient to have been struck by lightning).
4. The patient is found out in the open and may be confused, unconscious, or in cardiac arrest.

Signs and Symptoms — Immediate Manifestations

1. Cardiac asystole (brief or lengthy).
2. Acute myocardial injury.
3. Dysrhythmias.
4. Chest pain.
5. Muscular aches.
6. Central nervous system:
   - Seizures.
   - Coma.
   - Hysteria.
   - Confusion.
   - Amnesia.
   - Deafness.
   - Blindness.
7. Contusions from shock wave.
8. Second- and third-degree burns.
9. Fetal death in a pregnant patient.

Signs and Symptoms — Late Manifestations

1. Hysteria.
2. Hemiplegia.
3. Cataracts.

Treatment

The patient may present in mild, moderate (a comatose patient or one in respiratory arrest), or severe (cardiac arrest) distress. The treatment that the paramedic provides will be dependent on the severity of the injury.

1. The paramedic should ensure his/her own safety.
2. ABCs.
3. For a patient who is alive:
   - Establish and maintain the airway; intubate if necessary.
   - Provide high-flow, high-concentration oxygen; ventilate if necessary.
   - Monitor and document the cardiac rhythm.
   - Treat burns.
   - Assess the patient for other injuries.
4. For a patient who is in respiratory and cardiac arrest:
   - Provide airway management.
   - Follow ACLS protocols (see Chapter 10).

NUCLEAR RADIATION

In this day and age, radioactive substances are found commonly in industry, energy production, and medicine. The likelihood of encountering a nuclear mishap or disaster is more possible than ever before. The notion of a nuclear accident sends shivers through most EMS personnel. The best protection (besides avoidance) is understanding how ionizing radiation acts and knowing the best way to protect oneself from it. The following will outline the different components of ionizing radiation, how it acts on the body, how the paramedic may protect him/herself, and how an exposed patient should be treated.

Ionizing Radiation

Alpha Particle

An alpha particle is the nucleus of an atom that is slow moving with low energy. Alpha particles are a minor hazard when external exposure has occurred. Alpha particles may be stopped by clothing, paper, or even a few inches of air. They become hazardous and harmful to the body when inhaled or ingested.

Beta Particle

A beta particle is an electron and has slightly more penetrating energy than an alpha particle. It can be stopped by heavy clothing and aluminum.

Beta particles become hazardous and harmful to the body when inhaled or ingested.

Gamma Rays and X-Rays

These are rays of energy, not particles, and are highly penetrating. They are capable of causing direct damage to tissues. These rays will not penetrate lead shielding, concrete or earth.

Neutrons

Neutrons are the most penetrating of the four. Neutrons are approximately three to ten times as penetrating as X-rays and gamma rays and can cause significant tissue damage to the body. Neutrons are found primarily near reactor cores in energy-producing facilities.

Units of Measurement

1. Roentgen — this is the unit used to describe the exposure dosage of X-rays and gamma rays.
2. Rads — radiation-absorbed dosage.
3. Rems — radiation equivalent in man. Essentially, rads and rems may be used interchangeably.

Pathology of Ionizing Radiation

1. Radiation damages genetic material; thus, rapidly reproducing tissue is most seriously affected (i.e., sperm and ovum). Cellular reproduction is impaired.
2. Exposure over long periods of time is cumulative:
   - There is a decrease in the number of white cells.
   - Sterility occurs in both males and females.
   - Genetic defects occur in offspring of exposed individuals.
   - There is an increased incidence of cancer.
   - Bone damage occurs.
3. Short-term exposure is dependent upon the dosage:
   - The greater the area of body exposure, the greater the damage to the body.
   - The higher the dosage exposed to the body, the greater the damage to the body.
   - The average exposure during a chest X-ray is measured in millirads.

Signs and Symptoms of Acute Radiation Exposure to the Entire Body

Exposure of this kind usually results from a "dirty" radioactive spill or from the spread of highly radioactive materials.

1. Up to 100 rads — the patient is usually asymptomatic but may experience fatigue, nausea, vomiting, and possible chromosomal damage.
2. 200 to 400 rads — there may be nausea and vomiting, a reduction of white blood cells, loss of hair, and some deaths within sixty days.
3. 500 to 600 rads — the patient develops severe blood disorders, GI damage, and has a 50 percent mortality within thirty days.
4. 600 to 1,500 rads — the patient experiences accelerated GI and blood disorders, and death is within two weeks.
5. 2,000 or more rads — the patient experiences severe central nervous system effects and death occurs within a few hours.

Management of Radiation Emergencies

Paramedic Safety

The paramedic must understand the nature of the radiologic call prior to entering the scene. There are "clean" calls in which no contamination is present in the area. This means that the scene is safe to enter. There are "dirty" calls in which contamination is present in the area. In this situation, the scene is not safe to enter. The paramedic must take safety precautions or allow those with training to deal with the hazardous material. The paramedic has a responsibility to protect him/herself from dangerous exposure. In a "dirty" situation, all contaminated clothing should be removed and bagged at the scene.

1. Time — the shorter the exposure time, the less radiation the body absorbs; the paramedic should keep exposure to a minimum.
2. Distance — the farther away the rescuer is from the source of radiation, the less intense is the radiation; the paramedic should move the patient as far away from the source as reasonably possible.
3. Shield — the paramedic should shield him/herself and the work area from the source of radiation; this may be done by wearing protective clothing and using portable shields and/or earth barriers for protection.

4. Quantity — the greater the quantity, the more intense the exposure; reducing the quantity is important for protection.
5. After the scene is safe, or if proper gear becomes available, the patient should be approached and taken to a safe area for evaluation. If there are life-threatening problems, move the patient to the minimum safe distance.

Emergency Care

Normal principles of emergency care apply if the patient is not contaminated; this means that no radiation is present to harm the rescuers.

If the paramedic is externally contaminated (''dirty''), the paramedic should wear protective garments, a face mask, and gloves when treating the patient.

1. Use normal emergency care procedures.
2. Decontamination of the patient is required.
3. Decontamination of the paramedic is required after emergency care is completed.
4. Avoid cross-contamination of wounds.

SUMMARY

Environmental emergencies consist of temperature-related problems (heat and cold), near-drowning, underwater diving emergencies, lightning injuries, and ionizing radiation exposure. Near-drowning is the most common of the environmental problems that the paramedic will treat in the field. Naturally, the paramedic must be comfortable with handling any of the potential emergencies that he/she may encounter.

A number of situations that the paramedic may face will place him/her in danger. The paramedic must balance the risks and benefits of any actions to be undertaken. It is wise to minimize the risks. If the paramedic is not trained to rescue a victim from an environmental hazard, it is imperative to call for appropriate assistance. There are many documented cases in which paramedics lost their lives or were seriously injured when attempting a rescue that they were not trained to perform. As difficult as it may seem to wait for appropriate help, waiting is better than producing another victim.

18

Geriatrics

This chapter deals specifically with the geriatric patient. Nationwide, over 30 percent of all patients transported by ambulance are over the age of sixty-five, and the geriatric population receives 30 percent of all prescribed medications.

People are living longer than ever before. The percentage of the United States population sixty-five years of age and older has increased from 3 percent in 1900 to 11.7 percent in 1983 (27.4 million people). With the average life expectancy increasing (by the year 2000, 13 percent of the population will be over age sixty-five), birth rates declining, and the absence of major wars and other catastrophes, the fraction of the population over the age of sixty-five will continue to grow each year.

In the United States, life expectancy has increased by an average of 48 percent. The average life span in 1900 was forty-nine years of age. In 1983, the average life expectancy reached almost seventy-five years of age.

The leading causes of death and medical problems in the geriatric population are heart disease, cancer, stroke, fractures, pneumonia, confusion, and misuse of drugs. The functioning of the elderly patient's organs may be markedly altered as a result of normal aging (with or without illness), chronic illness, and symptoms masked by various psychiatric/neurological disorders. As a result of these changes, the geriatric patient's response to illness is changed. In general, the geriatric patient needs to be assessed and treated carefully. Any delay in recognizing health-care needs and providing care may have devastating, irreversible consequences.

ANATOMY AND PHYSIOLOGY OF THE AGING PROCESS

During the aging process, the following alterations in the body may occur:

Thermoregulatory Mechanisms

Thermoregulatory mechanisms may not function optimally. The geriatric patient is prone to heat and cold problems more easily than the younger patient.

Pain Mechanisms

The pain mechanisms of the elderly patient may not function; thus, the patient who would normally present with pain (e.g., AMI) does not (creating the ''silent MI'').

Mental Dysfunction

Mental dysfunction may occur; the elderly patient may develop confusion, loss of memory, regressive behavior, and other mental dysfunction. This makes patient evaluation more difficult.

Respiratory System

Changes in the respiratory system may start occurring at age thirty, and marked changes may appear after age sixty. Pulmonary circulation is reduced by 33 percent, thereby reducing the amount of carbon dioxide and oxygen exchanged at the alveoli. There is also reduced chest wall excursion and loss of muscular flexibility, leading to short inhalations (rapid breathing). There is a decrease in vital capacity (as much as 50 percent), and the maximal breathing capacity may decrease by 60 percent. The maximal work rate and maximal oxygen uptake may also decrease by 70 percent.

Cardiovascular System

Cardiac output may decrease by 50 percent in the elderly (age sixty-five and older). Stroke volume may decline, the force of contractions may decrease, and the heart's conduction system may degenerate. There may be left ventricular hypertrophy up to 25 percent, with loss of arterial flexibility leading to increased peripheral vascular resistance (elevated blood pressure).

Renal System

There is a 30 to 40 percent decrease in the number of functioning nephrons, and renal blood flow may decrease as much as 50 percent. Both of these conditions may lead to a reduced filtration and reabsorption rate. In addition, the bladder size may be reduced by 50 percent.

Nervous System

Confusion, irritability, forgetfulness, and altered sleep patterns may occur because of a decreased flow of blood and oxygen to the brain. There is as much as a 45 percent brain cell loss in certain cortical areas (6 to 7 percent reduction in brain weight), decreased cerebral blood flow as a result of an increase in vascular resistance, and a 15 percent reduction in nerve conduction velocity. The response of the elderly to stimuli is diminished, and they have a slowed reaction time. They also experience a decreased response to pain.

Musculoskeletal System

A decrease in height of two to three inches may occur due to the narrowing of the vertebral disks and to protein loss and changes in posture. Lessening of a person's height may also occur due to slight flexion of the knee and hip joints, and to a reduction in joint flexibility. The elderly may also experience spinal deterioration, a decrease in total skeletal muscle weight, a decrease in muscular strength and function, and demineralization, which leaves bones porous and allows fractures to occur more easily.

Gastrointestinal (GI) System

In the elderly, the volume of saliva is decreased by 33 percent, and gastric secretions may diminish by 20 percent of what was available during youth. Structural changes occur throughout the GI tract, and esophageal motility decreases.

Other Changes

There is a total body water decrease. The person's total body fat decreases by 15 to 30 percent. In addition, a progressive loss of the capacity of homeostatic systems to adjust following illness or injury occurs in the geriatric patient. There is no evidence of decline in the metabolic activity, but a decrease in the total number of body cells occurs.

ASSESSMENT OF THE GERIATRIC PATIENT

Problems in Assessing Elderly Patients

Assessment of the elderly patient may be difficult due to factors that complicate clinical evaluation. These factors include the following:

1. It may be difficult to separate the effects of aging from the consequences of disease.
2. The chief complaint may seem trivial (e.g., constipation).
3. The patient may fail to report important symptoms.
4. The paramedic may fail to note important signs or symptoms.
5. The geriatric patient is likely to suffer from more than one disease (or problem) at a time. Chronic illness may make assessment for acute problems difficult, and signs and symptoms of chronic illness may be confused with signs and symptoms of acute problems.
6. Aging may change the individual's response to illness and injury. Pain may be diminished or absent (e.g., silent myocardial infarction), and the patient or the paramedic may underestimate the severity of the patient's condition.
7. The temperature-regulating mechanism may be depressed, leading to minimal or absent fever with severe infection and making the geriatric patient prone to environmental thermal syndromes.
8. Social and emotional factors may have greater impact on the health of the geriatric patient than on any other age group.
9. Communication problems are common in the older patient. The senses diminish; the patient may have glaucoma, cataracts, blindness, or poor vision. Hearing diminishes, as well as general mental skills. The geriatric patient is much more likely to experience depression than younger patients.

History

The following are common complaints of the geriatric patient that may not be specific to any one disorder: fatigue and weakness, dizziness/vertigo/syncope, falls, headache, insomnia, dysphagia, loss of appetite, inability to void, and constipation/diarrhea.

Significant Symptoms

The paramedic must remember to probe for significant symptoms. The chief complaint may seem trivial, and the patient may not volunteer important information.

Communication Problems

Diminished Sight or Blindness

The paramedic can expect increased patient anxiety because of the patient's inability to see surroundings, coupled with the inability to exert control over the situation. The paramedic must talk calmly and be positioned so that the patient can best see the paramedic.

Diminished Hearing or Deafness

Obtaining a history can be difficult if the patient cannot hear questions. Do not assume that the patient is deaf without first inquiring with the family or with bystanders. Do not shout, as it distorts sounds if the patient has some hearing, and it does not help if the patient is deaf. However, an increase in voice volume may help with the hearing-impaired.

Note writing may help, too. If the patient can lip read, speak slowly and directly toward the patient. Whenever possible, verify the history with a reliable friend or relative, or seek assistance from these individuals in communicating with the patient.

Diminished Mental Status

Remember that many elderly patients have normal mentation. Some may be unable to remember details, while others may be routinely confused. Other elderly patients may have experienced an acute onset of diminished mentation.

Attempt to determine if the patient's mental status is normal for him/her, or if it represents a significant change. Do not assume that the confused, disoriented patient is "just senile." It is the responsibility of the paramedic to provide a complete assessment of the patient, checking for possible underlying physiological abnormalities.

Noise of radios, an ECG, or strange voices may add to the patient's confusion. Attempt to explain or reduce the noise.

Depression

Depression is common and may mimic senility or organic brain syndrome. Depression may be the reason why the patient is acting in an uncooperative manner. In addition, the patient may be malnourished, dehydrated, overdosed, contemplating suicide, or simply imagining physical ailments for attention. Question the patient regarding drug ingestion and possible suicidal thoughts (if appropriate). Suicide is the fourth leading cause of death among the elderly in the United States. Also, alcoholism is more common in the elderly than is generally realized. This may further hamper history taking.

Past Medical History

Past medical history may be complicated — try to determine what is significant. It is important to obtain a history of medications. The geriatric patient is usually on multiple drugs; medication errors and noncompliance are common. If possible, find all current medications and deliver them to the hospital with the patient.

Information from the Environment

Attempt to verify the patient's history with reliable family/neighbors (this is less offensive if done out of the patient's presence). Observe the surroundings for any indication of the patient's ability to care for him/herself, for evidence of drug/alcohol ingestion, and for signs of violence/abuse. Look for medic alert tags, the Vial of Life, and other sources of medical history.

Physical Examination Considerations in the Geriatric Patient

1. The patient may be fatigued easily.
2. The patient commonly wears layers of clothing — this may hamper the physical assessment.
3. The paramedic needs to explain actions clearly before initiating the physical exam of the elderly patient.
4. The patient may minimize or deny symptoms due to fear of being bedridden, institutionalized, or losing his/her sense of self-sufficiency.
5. Peripheral pulses may be difficult to evaluate.
6. The paramedic must distinguish between signs and symptoms of a chronic disease(s) and the acute problems:
   - The geriatric patient may have nonpathological rales.
   - Loss of skin elasticity and mouth breathing may give the false appearance of dehydration.
   - Dependent edema may be secondary to varicose veins, inactivity, and position rather than congestive heart failure.

TRAUMA

Pathology

The elderly are at greater risk for experiencing a traumatic injury (primarily falls), due to the following factors:

1. Elderly people may have slower reflexes, failing eyesight and hearing, arthritis, blood vessels that are less elastic and that are thus more subject to injury, and tissues and bones that are fragile.
2. Elderly people are at high risk for trauma from criminal assault.
3. Elderly people are prone to head injury, even from relatively minor trauma. One cause is that the brain diminishes in size, thus making itself and its blood vessels prone to ripping and tearing. It is important to note that signs and symptoms of brain compression may develop more slowly, sometimes over days or weeks. The patient may have forgotten that he/she was even injured.
4. Elderly people often have a significant degree of cervical spondylosis (a degenerative disease of the cervical vertebrae). Arthritic changes of the vertebrae gradually compress the nerve roots to the arms, or possibly to the spinal cord itself. If injury occurs to the cervical spine, the cord is more likely to be injured. Sudden neck movement, with or without fracture, may cause spinal cord injury.

Management

For more specific treatment, see Chapter 7.

Priorities of care are similar to those for all trauma patients but require consideration of:

1. General organ system decline, particularly of the cardiovascular, pulmonary, and renal systems.
2. The paramedic needs to be aware of concomitant chronic illness.
3. The ease with which bones may be fractured.

Cardiovascular System

1. Recent or past acute myocardial infarction contributes to the risk of dysrhythmias.
2. There may be a decreased response of the heart to hypovolemia in terms of

adjustment of rate and stroke volume (which should increase).

3. The organs may require higher-than-usual arterial pressures for adequate perfusion due to increased peripheral vascular resistance and general hypertension.
4. Care must be taken in IV fluid administration to prevent fluid overload (which may cause pulmonary edema).
5. Hypovolemia and hypotension are poorly tolerated by the elderly patient because the body loses its ability to adequately compensate for volume reduction.
6. The patient's response to drugs may be altered.

Respiratory System

1. Physical changes decrease chest cage movement and vital capacity.
2. Higher PO_2 is required with each passing decade.
3. All organs have less tolerance to anoxia.
4. Chronic obstructive pulmonary disease is common in the elderly patient. Airway management and ventilation must be carefully attuned to provide appropriate oxygenation and carbon dioxide removal.

Renal System

1. In the elderly patient, there is a decrease in the ability of the kidneys to maintain normal acid-base balance and to compensate for fluid changes.
2. Any pre-existing renal disease further decreases the ability of the kidneys to compensate for any changes.
3. Decreased renal function places the injured elderly patient at additional risk for fluid overload and pulmonary edema secondary to IV therapy.

Physical Deformities

Positioning, immobilization, and packaging of the elderly trauma patient may have to be modified to accommodate physical deformities (arthritis, spinal abnormalities, frozen limbs).

RESPIRATORY DISTRESS

Etiologies

1. Pulmonary embolism.

2. In a silent myocardial infarction (one in which the patient does not experience chest pain) — dyspnea may be the only initial symptom.
3. Pulmonary edema.
4. Asthma/COPD.
5. Respiratory infections — classic symptoms may not be present early.
6. Carcinoma (cancer).

Management

For specific treatment, see Chapters 9 and 10.

CARDIOVASCULAR CONDITIONS

For a detailed description and more specific treatment, refer to Chapter 10. Cardiovascular conditions are generally more common in the elderly due to progressive atherosclerotic and arteriosclerotic disease, as well as aging.

Syncope

Syncope, a transient loss of consciousness due to an inadequate flow of blood to the brain, carries a higher incidence of morbidity in patients over sixty years of age. Vasodepressor, orthostatic, vasovagal, and cardiac causes of syncope are the most common.

Cardiac Causes

Syncope is a primary symptom of a silent myocardial infarction, Stokes-Adams syndrome (an altered state of consciousness caused by a decreased flow of blood to the brain), tachydysrhythmias, and the sick sinus syndrome (cardiac abnormalities due to malfunction of the sinoatrial node in the heart).

Myocardial Infarction

Elderly patients are less likely to present with the classic signs and symptoms. The typical presenting signs and symptoms include syncope, dyspnea, abdominal or epigastric pain, and fatigue.

Congestive Heart Failure — Acute and Chronic

Elderly patients may experience left or right heart failure, causing pulmonary edema and/or peripheral edema.

Dysrhythmias

Degeneration of the heart's electrical conduction system predisposes geriatric patients to dysrhythmias. Rate extremes are not well tolerated by the geriatric patient.

Stroke (CVA)

See Chapter 12, "Nervous System Emergencies."

Occlusive strokes are statistically more common in the elderly and are relatively uncommon in younger individuals. The geriatric patient is at higher risk because of atherosclerosis, arteriosclerosis, hypertension, immobility, limb paralysis, congestive heart failure, and atrial fibrillation.

Transient ischemia attacks (TIAs) are also common. One-third of all patients who experience TIAs will have a major, permanent stroke. TIAs are a common cause of syncope in the elderly.

Aortic Dissection

For information on aortic dissection, see Chapter 10, pages 218 to 219.

Abdominal Aortic Aneurysm

For information on aortic aneurysm, see Chapter 10, pages 216 to 217.

Peripheral Arterial and Venous Conditions

For information on peripheral arterial and venous conditions, see Chapter 10, pages 220 to 223.

General Management

1. Management techniques are similar for all age groups (see Chapter 10).
2. Congestive heart failure, renal disease, liver disease, and metabolic problems of the elderly may lead the physician to modify drug therapy and dosages.
3. Use special care in administering IV fluids.

NEUROLOGIC DISORDERS

For detailed description and treatment, see Chapter 12.

Causes

1. Coma.
2. Stroke.
3. Seizures — consider the vast number of causes, including:
   - Seizure disorder.
   - Recent or past head trauma.
   - Brain lesion.
   - Alcoholic withdrawal.
   - Diabetic hypoglycemia.
   - Stroke.
   - Drug overdose.
4. Dizziness — a common complaint of the elderly (the condition may refer to syncope, presyncope, lightheadedness, vertigo, etc.). There are many causes of dizziness:
   - Impairment of the system(s) that orients the body to its environment, including visual impulse impairment, inner ear impairment, peripheral sensory impairment, and central nervous system impairment.
   - Common causes are effects of alcohol and other drugs.
   - Vertigo — a specific sensation of motion perceived by the patient as spinning or whirling as opposed to simple dizziness. Vertigo is accompanied by sweating, pallor, nausea, and vomiting. Meniere's disease (a recurrent and usually progressive group of symptoms including progressive deafness, ringing in the ears, dizziness, and a sensation of fullness behind the ears) causes classic vertigo attacks. Vertigo may be difficult to distinguish from dizziness, syncope, or presyncopal episodes.
5. Senile dementia, organic brain syndromes, and confusional states — the process of mental and physical deterioration that may result from aging and other factors which include organic brain syndromes. Pathologically and clinically, there are similarities with all of these brain dysfunction problems.
   - Causes for these problems may be any of the following: aging, central nervous system disease (e.g., Alzheimer's, subdural hematoma, stroke, head trauma, infection, tumors), cardiovascular disease (e.g., myocardial infarction, congestive heart failure, dysrhythmias, hypotension, hypertension), metabolic disorders (e.g., alcoholism, electrolyte abnormalities, nutritional deficiencies, acidosis, alkalosis, overmedication, drug side effects), and depression.
   - It is important to distinguish between acute and chronic illness.

General Management

1. Make an accurate assessment, treat the underlying cause of the problem, and protect the patient.
2. Distinguish between an acute and chronic event.
3. Historical information may help to determine the type of syncope and/or distinguish it from seizures, Stokes-Adams, etc.
   - Note the position of the patient at the time of the attack.
   - Note any associated symptoms.
   - Note the duration of the attack.
   - Take vital signs, including an evaluation of orthostatic vital signs.

PSYCHIATRIC DISORDERS

Psychiatric problems are common among the elderly. Emotional disorders may be due to isolation, loneliness, loss of self-dependence, loss of strength, and fear of the future. The patient may present with pathological disorders that are a result of the above. In addition, dementia, confusional states, and depression may result.

The following is a simple classification of psychiatric disorders that may occur with old age:

1. Organic brain syndrome.
2. Affective disorders, particularly depression.
3. Neurotic disorders — anxiety, hypochondriasis, phobia.
4. Personality disorders.
5. Paranoid disorders.
6. Alcoholism.

The paramedic should also remember that individuals over sixty-five years of age account for 25 percent of all reported suicides.

For management of psychiatric disorders, see Chapter 21.

ENVIRONMENTAL EMERGENCiES

Constant high or low air temperatures are poorly tolerated by the elderly. Predisposing factors for hypothermia include the following:

1. Accidental exposure.

2. Drugs that interfere with heat production.
3. CNS disorders.
4. Endocrine disorders.
5. Chronic illness, debilitation.
6. Low/fixed income (inability to pay for heat).

Predisposing factors for hyperthermia are:

1. Decreased functioning of the thermoregulatory center.
2. The use of commonly prescribed medications that inhibit sweating (i.e., phenothiazines).
3. Low/fixed income (inability to pay for air-conditioning).

For specific management techniques, see Chapter 17.

GASTROINTESTINAL DISORDERS

Gastrointestinal bleeding is a relatively common problem in the geriatric patient. It is estimated that 50 percent of these cases occur in people over the age of sixty. Gastrointestinal bleeding has a high mortality rate among the elderly.

Causes of Hemorrhage in the Upper Gastrointestinal Tract

1. Peptic ulcer (an ulcer occurring in the lower end of the esophagus, in the stomach, or in the duodenum).
2. Gastritis (inflammation of the stomach).
3. Esophageal varices (enlargement of the veins in the esophagus).
4. Mallory-Weiss syndrome (bleeding from the upper gastrointestinal tract due to a tear in the mucosa of the esophagus or gastroesophageal junction) — this syndrome is associated with chronic alcoholism and is usually preceded by severe vomiting.

Lower Gastrointestinal Hemorrhage

Lower gastrointestinal hemorrhage is less common than upper gastrointestinal hemorrhage and is caused by the following:

1. Diverticulosis (a pouch or sac occurring naturally or created by herniation

of the lining of the mucous membrane or through a defect in the muscular tubular wall of the large intestine) — 70 percent of life-threatening lower gastrointestinal bleeds are caused by diverticulosis.
2. Ischemic colitis (deficiency of tissue oxygenation due to an obstruction in an inflamed colon).
3. Neoplasm (tumor), either benign or malignant.
4. Inflammatory bowel disease.
5. Hemorrhoids.

Signs of Significant Blood Loss

1. "Coffee grounds" emesis or stool.
2. Melena (passage of stools stained with blood).
3. Frank bloody emesis or stool.
4. Orthostatic hypotension.
5. Pulse greater than 100 (unless the patient is on beta blockers).
6. Confusion.
7. Signs of shock.

Complications of Gastrointestinal Bleeding in the Elderly

1. There may be an increase in angina symptoms due to low hemoglobin. This reduces the amount of blood available to oxygenate the heart.
2. Congestive heart failure.
3. Weakness.
4. Dyspnea.
5. Shock syndrome.

Treatment

Hypotension is not well tolerated in the geriatric patient. For general treatment, do the following:

1. Administer high-flow oxygen.
2. Consider application of the pneumatic antishock garment.
3. Administer an IV with crystalloid volume replacement — be careful not to induce pulmonary edema.
4. Do not delay transport if the patient is decompensating (elevated pulse, hypotension).

PHARMACOLOGY

The elderly use 30 percent of all prescribed and over-the-counter drugs sold in the United States. Approximately 30 percent of all hospital admissions are related to drug-induced illnesses; more than 30 percent of these are people sixty years of age or older.

Factors that contribute to adverse drug reactions that commonly occur in the geriatric patient include the following:

1. Absorption, distribution, metabolism, and excretion of drugs in the elderly are altered.
2. Compensatory mechanisms that help to buffer against side effects are less effective as the patient ages.
3. Overdose may be accidental (confusion, vision impairment, self-selection of drugs, forgetfulness) or intentional.
4. Underdose is a common problem:
   - It accounts for about 50 percent of all medication errors.
   - It may be due to forgetfulness.
   - On a limited income, the patient cannot afford to purchase medications and thus reduces the daily dosage to save money.

Drugs that commonly cause toxicity are:

1. Digitalis (the leading cause).
2. Antiparkinsonian drugs.
3. Diuretics.
4. Anticoagulants.
5. Lidocaine:
   - Significant for paramedics.
   - Has a long plasma half-life.
6. Quinidine.
7. Propranolol.
8. Theophylline.
9. Narcotic analgesics and acetaminophen.
10. Sedative and hypnotic drugs.
11. Phenothiazines.
12. Tricyclic antidepressants.

GERIATRIC ABUSE/NEGLECT

Geriatric abuse/neglect refers to a syndrome in which the elderly person has received physical or psychological injury from his/her children or care providers. The abuse may be in the form of forced confinement, denial of rights, neglect of medical needs, and verbal abuse. It is estimated that between 1 and 4 percent of the geriatric population suffers some form of abuse or neglect.

Elderly abuse knows no socioeconomic boundaries and occurs because the elderly person is no longer able to be totally independent or because the family has difficulty upholding the commitment to care for the elder parent (or adult).

The average age of the abused geriatric patient is eighty. The patient may have chronic diseases and/or multiple disorders (congestive heart failure, cancer, incontinence, heart disease). He/she may also be a chronic alcoholic. Regardless of the specific problem, the patient has increasing caretaker needs.

The potential geriatric abuser may display the following characteristics:

1. The potential abuser is stressed.
2. He/she may be experiencing sleep deprivation.
3. Marital discord may be occurring.
4. He/she may be suffering from work-related stress.
5. Alcohol or drug abuse by the caretaker may be occurring.
6. The potential abuser may have a history of criminal or violent behavior.
7. The potential abuser's life may be in disarray; as the patient deteriorates, abuse may be the outcome.

Patient History

1. Obtain a complete patient and family history — note particularly any inconsistencies.
2. Unexplained trauma is a primary finding.
3. History of a fall is inconsistent with the patient's complaint.
4. Some visible signs of abuse or neglect are:
   - Contusions, lacerations, abrasions.
   - Fractures, sprains, dislocations.
   - Burns.
   - Oversedation.
   - Anxiety.
   - Dehydration.

- Poor hygiene.
- Malnutrition.
- Depression.

SUMMARY

As mentioned earlier in this chapter, the geriatric patient makes up approximately 30 percent of the transports by ambulance. This is significant, considering that the geriatric population is approximately 12 percent of the total population. It is obvious that the paramedic will have frequent contact with the elderly patient.

With an increased awareness of the changes in physiology that occur in the elderly person, the paramedic will be better equipped to assess and treat the geriatric patient.

This chapter has discussed the most common medical/psychiatric geriatric problems that the EMT-P will encounter in the field. It is hoped that this chapter will help the paramedic in all aspects of geriatric care.

19

Pediatrics

Pediatrics is generally considered applicable to patients ranging in age from neonate to eighteen years. It is quite evident that this encompasses a whole range of behaviors and difficulties. The ill or injured child presents special problems for health-care providers. This chapter will focus on the special considerations that must be taken into account when treating the pediatric patient.

Few problems encountered by the EMT-P pose the same degree of stress and anxiety as the pediatric emergency. The relatively infrequent number of pediatric cases results in inadequate opportunity to practice assessment and management skills, increasing the paramedic's anxiety. The EMT-P must be especially observant in caring for the pediatric patient. The margin for errors is slight in managing the airway, and the respiratory and circulatory systems, and in medicating these patients. It is important for the EMT-P to frequently review the management, as well as practice the skills essential for rapid and effective intervention with the pediatric patient.

DEVELOPMENTAL STAGES

Neonate (Full-Term)

Normal Growth and Development

1. The gestation age affects early development.
2. There is an initial weight loss (the infant generally recovers in ten days).
3. Normal reflexive behavior is present (rooting, sucking, grasping, motor

response).

4. The infant stares at faces and smiles.
5. Relationship to parents:
   - The infant is close to the mother.
   - The mother, and perhaps the father, can quiet the infant.
   - The infant knows his/her parents and may allow others to hold him/her.

Paramedic Approach

1. The paramedic should take a history from the parents and observe the infant.
2. Keep the infant warm.
3. Observe the skin tone and color and respiratory activity.
4. Auscultate the lung fields early in the exam if necessary.
5. Use a pacifier or a bottle to distract the patient.
6. Have the child lie in the mother's lap.

One to Five Months

Normal Growth and Development

1. Weight gain is usually twice the birth weight.
2. The infant follows the movement of others with his/her eyes.
3. Muscular control develops from head to tail and from the center of the body to the periphery.
4. The infant does not like strangers.
5. The infant is close to the mother and father.

Paramedic Approach

1. The paramedic should take a history from the parents and observe the infant.
2. Keep the infant warm.
3. Observe the skin tone and color and respiratory activity.
4. Use a pacifier or a bottle to distract the patient.
5. Have the child lie in the mother's lap.

Six to Twelve Months

Normal Growth and Development

1. The infant may stand and walk with help.

2. The infant is active.
3. The infant explores the world with his/her mouth.
4. The infant experiences stranger anxiety.
5. The infant is fearful of lying on his/her back.
6. The infant clings and is closer to the mother than to the father.

Paramedic Approach

1. The paramedic should take a history from the parents and observe the infant.
2. Examine the infant on the mother's lap.
3. Conduct the exam in toe-to-head order to reduce patient anxiety.
4. If time and condition permit, allow the infant to become accustomed to the paramedic and equipment (this will encourage cooperation).

Twelve to Thirty-Six Months

Normal Growth and Development

1. Great strides occur in gross motor development.
2. The child explores everything.
3. The child runs and walks and is always moving.
4. The child is becoming more expressive.
5. May cling to the mother or stray.
6. May be brave, curious, and/or stubborn.
7. Into having temper tantrums (this is the ''No'' period).
8. Parent may be able to comfort the child.

Paramedic Approach

1. The paramedic should take the history primarily from the parents and observe the child, asking simple questions.
2. Try to gain the child's confidence — approach slowly, use a doll, and let him/her handle equipment when possible.
3. Conduct the exam in toe-to-head order.
4. The child may be difficult to examine and may resist being touched.
5. Avoid asking questions that allow the child to say no.
6. Tell the child if something will hurt.

Three to Five Years

Normal Growth and Development

1. There is increasing development of fine and gross motor skills.
2. Language usage is improving.
3. The child may know how to talk, but won't.
4. The child may be afraid.
5. The child has a vivid imagination.
6. The child has a temper.
7. The child may view the treatment procedure(s) as hostile.
8. Relationship to parents — the child is close to each one on different occasions, sticks up for parents, is openly loving, and looks to them for support.

Paramedic Approach

1. Elicit a history from the child, but recognize that it may not be accurate and that the child's time frame is off. Request help from the parents.
2. Use a doll to help in the examination of the child.
3. The paramedic must explain what is going to be done.
4. Let the patient sit on a parent's lap.
5. Allow the child to hold onto and use the equipment.
6. Start with the chest and do the head last.
7. Don't trick the patient or lie to him/her.
8. Transport the parent with the patient if possible.

Six to Twelve Years

Normal Growth and Development

1. Six to eight years of age — thin, growing, developing better coordination.
2. Nine to twelve years of age — puberty occurs, with many changes and new fears.
3. This is a time of rapid growth.
4. If injury is sustained doing something forbidden, the child will probably be reluctant to give information.
5. Relationship to parents — the child is usually proud and protective, likes parental attention, and needs both peer and home support.

Paramedic Approach

1. Give the child the responsibility for the history; the mother and father may provide additional information or may interfere.
2. Be honest.
3. The patient is usually modest, so attempt to provide privacy.
4. Tell the patient what is wrong.
5. Explain the function of the ambulance equipment when appropriate. Let the child handle a stethoscope.
6. It may be helpful to have a parent accompany the child in the ambulance.

Twelve to Eighteen Years

Growth and Development

1. There is a wide variation in growth and development in this age range. Some individuals are fully mature, and others are not.
2. They are not necessarily adults yet, but may believe that they are.
3. They want to be liked and included.
4. They are concerned with body image and modesty. Some people of this age are comfortable with their bodies, and others are not. These feelings may be heightened if the paramedic is of the opposite sex.
5. They may have fears of death, body disfigurement, and permanent disability.
6. Relationship to parents — some are attempting separation from parents; the peer group is important, and an interest is developing in the opposite sex.

Paramedic Approach

1. Patients in this age group are good historians; their parents' perception may differ from their own.
2. Be honest.
3. Listen to what they are saying, and read in-between the lines.
4. Provide support and reassurance.
5. Be factual and address the patient's questions and concerns.
6. The paramedic may wish to question the patient without the parents being present.
7. Try to provide privacy.
8. Be understanding of body image and death concerns.

9. Explain to the patient what is happening and what may occur at the hospital.

APPROACHES TO THE PEDIATRIC PATIENT

Age-Group Approach

The paramedic is probably least comfortable when dealing with pediatric patients (primarily up to five years of age). The child is often anxious and fearful. This may be worsened with the surrounding activity, particularly by upset bystanders (parents, friends, babysitter, etc.).

The paramedic must work at establishing a rapport with the patient, which is often a difficult task. If the problem is not life-threatening, the paramedic should take the time to alleviate the child's fear and anxiety. In the brief description of developmental stages, the paramedic is given an idea of what he/she might expect when dealing with different age groups. Using this information, the paramedic will find it easier to deal with pediatric situations.

Management Goals

1. Take an accurate history using the sources available.
2. Perform an accurate patient assessment.
3. Identify the patient's problem(s).
4. Treat the problem(s) correctly.
5. Recognize the situations that require rapid transport to the emergency department.

General Approach

It must be recognized that in patients under five years of age, the majority of information will come from adults. If the child is over five, the paramedic should use the pediatric patient to gain as much information as possible.

1. Patience and understanding are necessary to successfully interact with the pediatric patient.
2. Patient questioning must be specific and direct.
3. When dealing with the patient under the age of five, the focus should be on observed behavior, not solely on what the child or parent says.
4. Approach the patient slowly and gently to encourage cooperation and gain confidence. Be kind and firm.

5. Eye contact is part of the Western cultural trust process. Use eye contact with all pediatric patients.
6. Remember — if the child did something that he/she felt was inappropriate, he/she may not reveal the complete truth.
7. Children may imagine fantasy as real.
8. Visual assessment of the patient is very important.
9. Avoid touching injured or painful areas until the child's confidence has been gained.
10. Begin the examination without instruments.
11. Always be honest with the patient.
12. Children respond to calm reassurance, so talk with the patient.
13. If possible, allow the child to determine the order of the exam.
14. Respect the child's modesty by undressing the patient slowly and keeping the patient warm.
15. Avoid separating the child from the parents unnecessarily.
16. If possible, get on the same physical level as the child (i.e., do not tower above the patient).

General History Assessment

1. Gather information as quickly and accurately as possible.
2. Establish a relationship with the patient and parents.
3. Parents usually are a good source of information.
4. Children may be a good source of information (dependent on the age).
   - Remember — patients under the age of five need to be observed. Do not count on the adult's description only.
   - Children can be accurate in their descriptions.
   - Allow the child to express him/herself.

Physical Examination

Pediatric Vital Signs

1. Be sure that the vital signs correspond to the appropriate age level.
2. Remember to evaluate the total patient, not just the vital signs.
3. Be sure to take several sets of vitals for comparison.
4. Remember that there is wider variation in a pediatric temperature than in an adult temperature.
5. Observe the respiratory rate, depth, regularity, and difficulty before begin-

ning the exam. If the child begins to cry, evaluation becomes much more difficult.

Level of Consciousness

There may be a wide variation in the level of consciousness and in the activity level.

Evaluation of Anterior Fontanelle

Evaluate the anterior fontanelle in patients under one year of age.

1. The normal state of the fontanelle is level with the surface of the skull or slightly sunken when the child is sitting upright. A pulse may be felt.
2. With increased intracranial pressure, the fontanelle will feel tight and may bulge. Pulsations may decrease or disappear altogether.
3. With dehydration, the anterior fontanelle falls below the level of the skull and feels sunken.

Evaluation of Vomiting

1. Gastrointestinal disturbances are common with many childhood illnesses.
2. Vomiting may indicate viral/bacterial infections, intestinal obstruction, increased intracranial pressure, or middle ear infection.
3. The history may be helpful in determining the cause of vomiting.

COMMON CHILDHOOD DISEASES AND INJURIES

Medical Problems

The following are common childhood medical problems:

1. Respiratory distress — may affect children of any age.
2. SIDS (Sudden Infant Death Syndrome) — generally affects one-week to one-year-old infants.
3. Vomiting.
4. Diarrhea.
5. Dehydration.
6. Febrile seizures — most commonly affects children from three months to five years of age.
7. Bronchiolitis — generally affects infants under one year of age.

8. Croup — generally affects pediatric patients from six months to three years of age.
9. Epiglottitis — generally affects children three to seven years of age.
10. Asthma — may affect children of any age.
11. Meningitis.
12. Jaundice.
13. Accidental ingestions — poisoning occurs primarily in children under five years of age.
14. Mononucleosis.
15. Pregnancy.
16. Drug and alcoholic suicidal gestures.

Trauma

Accidents are the leading cause of death in children between the ages of one and fifteen. Trauma in children is caused by any of the following:

1. Child abuse.
2. Accidents.
3. Car accidents.
4. Bicycle accidents.
5. Fractures.
6. Falls.
7. Sports injuries — most frequently high-school-age children.
8. Drowning.
9. Foreign-body obstruction.
10. Sexual abuse.

PEDIATRIC-RELATED PROBLEMS

Sudden Infant Death Syndrome (SIDS)

SIDS is the sudden and unexpected death of an apparently well infant in which a thorough postmortem fails to explain an adequate cause of death.

SIDS is the leading cause of death in the United States of infants between the ages of one week and one year. Approximately 10,000 SIDS deaths occur each year, with two deaths per 1,000 live births. Ninety percent of the deaths occur between one month and six months of age, with the peak incidence occurring between two to four months. SIDS most commonly occurs during sleep and during the winter months.

Infants at the greatest risk are:

1. Premature infants.
2. Males (60 percent of all victims are male).
3. Those with a history of apnea.
4. Those who have a seizure disorder.
5. Those who have a family history of SIDS (siblings).

SIDS is **not** suffocation from a blanket or pillow, the result of aspiration of vomitus, the result of child abuse, or the result of heredity (although SIDS may reoccur in families). It is also **not** caused by allergies.

The factors leading to SIDS still remain a mystery.

Physical Examination

1. The child is usually normally nourished and hydrated.
2. Frothy fluids appear in and around the child's mouth and nostrils.
3. Fluids may be blood-tinged.
4. Vomitus may be present.
5. The infant may be in an unusual position due to muscular spasm at the time of death.
6. Mottling may occur.
7. The child is usually in cardiac arrest.

Management

Provide ABCs (consider starting an intraosseous infusion — see Appendix 7) and AHA advanced cardiac life support protocols found in Chapter 10. Even if it is obvious that the infant is dead, sometimes it may be necessary to provide active care of the patient to assure the parents that everything possible is being done.

The paramedic should expect normal grief reactions from parents and/or the babysitter. Other emotions may include any of the following: disbelief, denial, anger, rage, hostility, blame, guilt, self-reproach, inadequacy as a parent, helplessness, confusion, and/or fear.

The immediate needs of the SIDS family or babysitter should include:

1. Unconditional support from the paramedic.
2. Communication with the family members about procedures, if time permits.

3. Allowing the family to see the infant.

The paramedic should notify the emergency department that the immediate family will be coming so that adequate preparations can be made. SIDS frequently has long-term effects on the family.

Confirmation of SIDS

SIDS is confirmed by ruling out:

1. Pneumonia (by a chest X-ray).
2. CNS hemorrhage (by a lumbar puncture).
3. Septicemia (by a blood culture).

Child Abuse and Neglect

It is estimated that over 1 million children suffer abuse and neglect from parents, foster parents, stepparents, or babysitters. Abuse is physical violence perpetrated against the child. Neglect constitutes the failure to provide food, shelter, clothing, and the emotional needs of the child.

It is important for abuse and neglect to be identified as soon as possible so that a fatal incident may be prevented. If intervention occurs soon enough, the tendency toward abuse may be altered.

Characteristics of the Abuser

The abuser may have any of the following characteristics:

1. Crosses all religious, ethnic, occupational, educational, and socioeconomic boundaries.
2. May resent or reject the child.
3. May have feelings of worthlessness about self or about the child.
4. May have unrealistic expectations of what the child is capable of doing.
5. May be very critical of the child.
6. Oftentimes the abuser is repeating what was learned as a child (i.e., the abuser was more than likely abused as a child).

Characteristics of the Abused Child

The abused child may have any of the following characteristics:

1. If under five years old, is likely to be passive.

2. If over five years old, is likely to be aggressive.
3. Does not look to the parent (the abuser) for support, comfort, or reassurance.
4. May cry without any expectation of receiving help.
5. May be quiet and withdrawn.
6. May be fearful of the parent.

Children at Highest Risk

The following children are at the highest risk of being abused:

1. A handicapped or ill child, or one with special needs.
2. Males are at greater risk than females.
3. Illegitimate children.
4. The uncommunicative child.
5. Children who are not wanted by their parents.

Precipitating Factors

Common crises that may precipitate child abuse include the following:

1. Financial stress.
2. Relationship stress.
3. Work stress.
4. Illness in the parent or child.

Physical Assessment

Suspect abuse when:

1. There are any obvious or suspected fractures in a child under two years of age.
2. There are injuries in various stages of healing, particularly burns and bruises.
3. There are frequent injuries.
4. There are widespread injuries over the body.
5. There are bruises or burns in patterns (e.g., cigarette burns in a ring).
6. There is increased intracranial pressure in an infant.
7. There is suspected intra-abdominal trauma in a young child.
8. There is obvious physical neglect (e.g., malnutrition, lack of cleanliness).

History

Suspect abuse when:

1. The history does not match with the nature or severity of the injury.
2. The parents' account is vague and/or changes.
3. There is an "accident" beyond the developmental capabilities of the child.
4. There is an accusation that the child injured him/herself intentionally.
5. There is a delay in seeking help.
6. The child is dressed inappropriately for the situation.

Treatment

1. Treat injuries as appropriate.
2. Protect the child from further abuse.
3. Obtain information in a nonjudgmental manner.
4. Do not "cross-examine" the patient or the parents.
5. If abuse is suspected, provide ambulance transport rather than allowing the potential abuser to transport the patient.
6. All states have laws requiring the health-care professional to report suspected child abuse/neglect. The paramedic should report any suspicions of abuse to the receiving emergency department staff.
7. Document all factual information on agency trip reports and/or child-abuse report forms.

Seizures (Convulsions)

A seizure is an involuntary contraction or series of contractions of the voluntary muscles. A seizure is symptomatic of some neurologic disorder rather than a disease in and of itself.

The following are possible causes for seizures in the pediatric patient:

1. Fever.
2. Head trauma.
3. Hypoxia.
4. Hypoglycemia.
5. Infection.
6. Toxic ingestions and exposure.
7. Epilepsy (idiopathic).
8. Tumors.
9. Electrolyte abnormalities.
10. Central nervous system malformations.

Febrile Seizures

These are the most common cause of seizures in children between the ages of six months and six years. The paramedic should suspect fever as a cause of the seizure if a high temperature (103 degrees Fahrenheit or higher) is present without other signs and symptoms. (Other causes of seizures must be ruled out.)

Status Epilepticus

Status epilepticus is a prolonged seizure or multiple seizures without a lucid interval between the seizures. This is rarely, if ever, caused by fever. The paramedic must look for another cause.

Present History

1. Identify the type of seizure activity.
2. Establish if more than one seizure has occurred.
3. Identify present medications or the possibility of toxic ingestions.
4. What was the condition of the patient when he/she was first found?
5. Is a fever present?
6. Has there been any recent illness?
7. Has there been a history of headache or stiff neck?
8. Has there been any recent head trauma?
9. Is there a history of irritability or lethargy prior to the seizure (may indicate central nervous system infection)?

Past Medical History

1. Is there a previous history of seizures that were idiopathic?
2. Is there a previous history of seizures that occurred in conjunction with a fever?
3. Is there a history of diabetes or other medical problems?

Physical Examination

1. Evaluate the ABCs.
2. Assess the level of consciousness.
3. Perform a neurologic evaluation.
4. Observe for signs of injury.
5. Observe for dehydration.
6. Evaluate the anterior fontanelle in infants.

Treatment

1. If possible, position the patient on a bed or on the floor to prevent injury during the seizure. Place the patient laterally recumbent after the convulsion if unconscious.
2. Do not restrain the patient.
3. Maintain an airway, but do not force anything between the teeth.
4. Administer oxygen.
5. Monitor the patient's vital signs at regular intervals.
6. If the patient is febrile, cool him/her with tepid water or apply cool, moist towels. Do not delay transport — cool the patient en route to the hospital.
7. If the patient is in status epilepticus:
   - Start an IV with D_5W, D_5NS, or D_5RL. (Consider starting an intraos seous infusion.)
   - IV Diazepam: infants aged thirty days to children five years of age — inject 0.2 to 0.5 milligrams slow IV every two to five minutes up to a maximum of 2.5 milligrams. Children five years or older — 1 milligram every two to five minutes to a maximum of 5 milligrams.
   - Contact the base physician for further orders.
   - Draw a blood tube for glucose determination.
   - Administer glucose 25 percent, 2 cc per kilogram. Glucose (Dextrose) 50 must be dilated 1 to 1 with D_5W (or sterile water) for pediatric administration to reduce osmolarity and corrosiveness to the veins.
   - A trial of 5 percent dextrose IV solution may also be used. Administer 4 cc per kilogram of 5 percent D_5NS or LR.

Dehydration

The most common causes of dehydration are diarrhea and vomiting secondary to a gastrointestinal tract disorder.

History

Note any history of:

1. Diarrhea.
2. Vomiting.
3. Fever.
4. Decreased urination.

Physical Examination, Signs and Symptoms

1. Evaluate the ABCs.
2. Observe for poor skin turgor.
3. Observe for weight loss.
4. Determine if the patient has thick secretions or concentrated urine.
5. Note if the patient's eyes are dull and sunken-looking.
6. An infant may have a depressed fontanelle.

Management

1. Do the ABCs.
2. Monitor the vital signs.
3. Start an IV, D_5NS or D_5LR if the patient is in shock. However, starting an IV in a young child or infant may be difficult; do not delay transport. (Consider starting an intraosseous infusion.)

Meningitis

Meningitis is an inflammation of the meninges that cover the brain and spinal cord. Infants and young children are at higher risk than adults for contracting this infection, which may be either bacterial or viral. Meningitis may be a life-threatening emergency.

History

1. The patient has been ill for one or more days and is usually febrile.
2. The patient may have had a recent ear or respiratory tract infection.
3. The patient may present with a headache and/or a stiff neck.

Physical Examination with Signs and Symptoms

1. The patient appears very ill.
2. The fontanelle may be full or bulging in infants.
3. The patient may be hyperirritable.
4. The patient may be quiet (lethargic).

Treatment

1. Provide supportive care.
2. Monitor the ABCs.
3. Make the child comfortable.
4. Transport.

Septicemia

Septicemia is a generalized infection (pathogenic microorganism) of the bloodstream.

History

1. Infants up to two months with a fever of 100.4 degrees Fahrenheit are suspects for septicemia.
2. Infants three months to one year and a child up to two years of age with no localizing problems and a fever of 102.2 degrees Fahrenheit or higher are suspects for having septicemia.
3. The patient may have been ill for several days.

Physical Examination with Signs and Symptoms

1. Fever is present.
2. The patient is lethargic or irritable.
3. The patient may be in shock.
4. The fontanelle is usually normal in infants.

Treatment

1. Provide supportive care.
2. Transport.
3. Start an IV of D_5NS or D_5LR if the patient is in shock. (Consider starting an intraosseous infusion.)
4. Provide oxygen.

Reye's Syndrome

Reye's syndrome is an acute, potentially fatal disease of childhood. It is characterized by severe edema of the brain, increased intracranial pressure, dysfunction of the liver, and hypoglycemia. Reye's syndrome is one of the ten major causes of death in children over one year of age. It most commonly occurs in school-age children between the ages of five and fifteen years but may occur in any child from two months to nineteen years of age.

Possible Causes

The exact cause of the disease is not known. What is recognized about the disease is the following:

1. It is almost always associated with a previous viral infection.
2. The most frequently reported viral diseases prior to the development of Reye's syndrome are influenza type B and varicella (chicken pox); however, there are many viruses known to have preceded Reye's syndrome.
3. There is an association between the administration of aspirin for acute febrile disease and the subsequent development of Reye's syndrome.

History

1. A recent history of a respiratory tract infection.
2. A recent history of an illness with influenza type B.
3. A recent history of an episode of the chicken pox (found in 10 to 20 percent of the cases).
4. A recent history of an illness with a high fever and use of aspirin.
5. Infants may have a history of gastroenteritis.

Physical Examination with Signs and Symptoms

Signs and symptoms will vary depending on the stage of the disease process. They include the following:

1. Sudden onset of nausea and vomiting often marks the early stages of the disease.
2. Irritability, lethargy, and confusion may occur.
3. Rapid and deep respirations may be present.
4. Possible irregular respirations may occur.
5. The patient may have dilated and sluggish-reacting pupils.
6. There may be signs of increased intracranial pressure.
7. Irrational behavior may be present.
8. Hyperexcitability may occur.
9. Progressive stupor may occur.
10. The patient may appear restless.
11. The patient may develop convulsions.
12. Coma may occur — the patient may demonstrate abnormal extension or abnormal flexion (posturing).

Complications

1. Respiratory failure is common.
2. Cardiac dysrhythmias may develop.
3. Acute pancreatitis may develop.

4. Many patients die of cerebral complications.

Treatment

1. Perform the ABCs.
2. Provide high-flow oxygen.
3. Support ventilations as necessary.
4. Transport rapidly.
5. Attempt insertion of an IV en route to the hospital. (Consider starting an intraosseous infusion.)

Asthma

Asthma is a reversible condition caused by constriction of the bronchial tree and/or swelling of the mucous membranes in the bronchioles. Asthma most frequently occurs in childhood and may be induced by the following conditions: infections, emotional upset, cold air, exercise, and/or allergens.

History

1. The patient may have had prior episodes.
2. There may be a family history of asthma.
3. Illness, emotional stress, exercise, or exposure to allergens may have occurred.

Physical Examination with Signs and Symptoms

1. Rule out other possibilities (pneumonia, foreign body aspiration, pneumothorax, etc.).
2. The patient may complain of dyspnea.
3. Observe for wheezing.
4. The patient generally has an increased respiratory rate (tachypnea).
5. The patient is anxious and restless.
6. Severe distress may include:
   - Nasal flaring.
   - Tracheal tugging.
   - Retractions.
   - Grunting.
   - Cyanosis.

Treatment

1. Perform the ABCs.
2. Administer high-flow oxygen by mask.
3. Start an IV of NS or lactated Ringer's if possible (do not waste time on the scene if difficult). Consider starting an intraosseous infusion.
4. Consider racemic epinephrine by physician's order.
5. Consider epinephrine 1:1,000, 0.1 ml per kilogram of body weight, subcutaneous injection to a maximum of 0.4 ml by physician's order.
6. Consider using aminophylline if epinephrine does not relieve the dyspnea, tachypnea, and wheezing, by direct physician's order only. Refer to Appendix 1 for a detailed description of all medications.

Bronchiolitis

Bronchiolitis is a viral infection of the bronchioles that primarily occurs in infants and children under two years of age. It occurs in the setting of an upper respiratory tract infection and is characterized by prominent expiratory wheezing. Bronchiolitis produces the same symptoms as asthma. Unlike asthma, it is caused by a viral infection resulting in respiratory tract inflammation that is seldom responsive to the same treatment as asthma.

History

1. The patient may have allergies.
2. Possible recent upper respiratory tract infection.
3. A low-grade fever may be present.
4. Bronchiolitis is most common in patients under the age of one, and asthma is uncommon in this age group.

Physical Examination with Signs and Symptoms

1. Observe for evidence of infection and respiratory distress.
2. Note the patient's position.
3. Auscultate the chest for rales (crackles) and wheezes.

Treatment

1. Perform the ABCs.
2. Administer humidified oxygen (if available) by mask.
3. Provide ventilation assistance as needed.
4. Place the patient in a semi-sitting position or in a position of comfort.

5. Consider using racemic epinephrine per physician's order.
6. Administer epinephrine as a subcutaneous injection per physician's order if bronchospasm is severe and if the paramedic cannot rule out asthma (see Appendix 1).

Croup

Croup is an inflammation of the paralaryngeal tissue that is caused by the parainfluenza virus and other viruses. Croup most frequently occurs in infants and children between the ages of six months and three years of age. The typical scenario is that a child has been sick for two to three days with an upper respiratory tract infection and unexpectedly gets worse at night. The child usually presents a noisy cough that sounds like a ''seal bark.'' The infection causes inflammation around the larynx, producing constriction of the airway. Though these patients may present with alarming signs and symptoms, these children do quite well simply by inhaling cool, moist air.

History

1. Possible recent upper respiratory tract infection.
2. The patient is ''comfortable'' during the day.
3. The child develops respiratory distress at night (develops stridorous inspirations and a ''seal bark'' cough).

Physical Examination with Signs and Symptoms

1. Do not visualize the throat (see epiglottitis).
2. The child is usually sitting upright.
3. The patient may have wheezing.
4. The patient may have suprasternal retractions.
5. With severe croup, the child may have nasal flaring, intercostal retractions, and tracheal tugging.
6. The patient may appear anxious and restless.
7. The patient may be cyanotic.
8. The patient may be tachypnic.

Treatment

1. Perform the ABCs.
2. Maintain the airway.
3. Give humidified oxygen by mask.
4. Consider the possibility of epiglottitis and **do not** visualize the throat.

5. Place the patient in a position of comfort.
6. Monitor cardiac rhythm.
7. Consider using racemic epinephrine if the patient finds no relief with cool, moist air or humidified oxygen (in severe cases), by physician's order.
8. Transport.

Epiglottitis

Epiglottitis is a most dangerous condition in children; it can progress from a mild or moderate respiratory distress situation to a fatal respiratory arrest without warning. Epiglottitis is caused by a bacterial infection leading to a swollen, cherry-red epiglottis. It most frequently occurs in children between three and seven years of age.

History

1. It has an abrupt onset.
2. High fever is present.

Physical Examination with Signs and Symptoms

1. **Never attempt to visualize the airway.** Severe laryngospasm and swelling may result, leading to respiratory arrest.
2. The child appears very ill and anxious.
3. The patient sits erect, leaning forward with the head in the sniffing position.
4. The child is tachypnic.
5. The child may be cyanotic.
6. The child is unable to swallow and has obvious drooling.
7. Retractions may occur.
8. The patient may have shallow breathing with possible stridor.

Treatment

1. Perform the ABCs.
2. Administer humidified oxygen by mask if possible. Do not force the child to accept the mask if he/she refuses.
3. Place the patient in a position of comfort.
4. Monitor cardiac rhythm.
5. Provide safe, rapid transport.
6. Intubation is contraindicated unless **total** airway obstruction is present.
7. Transtracheal ventilation may be indicated.

Obstructed Airway in Children

Follow the current AHA guidelines for clearing an obstructed airway in the pediatric patient.

SPECIAL TECHNIQUES FOR THE PEDIATRIC PATIENT

CPR in Children

Refer to the American Heart Association recommendations. (Cardiac arrest in the pediatric patient is usually the result of a primary respiratory problem.)

Defibrillation in Children

1. Dosage: two joules per kilogram.
2. If unsuccessful: double the dosage.
3. If unsuccessful: correct the hypoxia and acid base with ACLS drug guidelines (refer to Chapter 10).

Endotracheal Intubation

1. The technique is similar to that for an adult.
2. Anatomical differences from adults:
   - The tongue is relatively larger.
   - The glottis is higher.
   - The vocal cords slant upward and backward.
3. Equipment:
   - Size of the blades (see Appendix 4).
   - Size of tubes (see Appendix 4).
   - Uncuffed and cuffed endotracheal tubes.
4. Special notes:
   - Precede intubation with oxygenation using 100 percent oxygen by face mask and bag.
   - Monitor the heart rate carefully during intubation for dysrhythmias.
   - Following intubation, auscultate breath sounds bilaterally and the stomach area.

Intravenous Techniques

1. The procedure is the same as for adults.
2. Site selection:
   - May use the neck, arms, hands, feet, or scalp.

- Use the largest accessible vein.
- Secure the extremities with an armboard.
- Limit the use of external jugular veins to life-threatening situations.
- The veins of the hands and feet usually permit a 21- or 23-gauge scalp vein needle.
- Use the veins of the forehead and temporal areas in infants less than one year of age. Use a rubber band for a tourniquet, and point the bore of the needle toward the face or neck.

3. Equipment:
   - Scalp vein needles — use 21- or 23-gauge; flush the needle prior to insertion.
   - Over-the-needle cannulas — 22-gauge needle useful for smaller children.
   - Solutions should contain electrolytes and glucose if possible. Use 5 percent dextrose in normal saline (D_5NS), 5 percent dextrose in lactated Ringer's (D_5LR), D_5, NS, or LR.
   - Volume control — use a microdrip apparatus routinely. If large volumes are needed, use a macrodrip with a volume control chamber if possible. Monitor the infusion rate closely — it is very easy to overload a pediatric patient.
4. Consider intraosseous infusion — see Appendix 7. Follow local protocol.

SUMMARY

Pediatric cases may cause the paramedic undue stress. In addition to the sick or injured child, there is usually a very upset adult (parent, babysitter etc.). This may only add to the crisis at hand.

The paramedic's best defense against the stresses of handling the pediatric case is to be well prepared. Knowledge of pediatric medications and management skills, acting professionally, and considering the needs of the bystanders will all serve to reduce the difficulty of handling these cases.

Division Five

OB/GYN Neonatal

20

Obstetric and Gynecologic Emergencies

This chapter discusses the etiology and treatment of gynecologic emergencies, the normal and abnormal events in pregnancy and childbirth, and the care of the neonate. Female patients with abdominal pain or injury should be evaluated by the paramedic for gynecologic disorders and, in the appropriate age group, for possible pregnancy and its complications. Gynecologic and obstetric emergencies may develop acutely and may prove to be life-threatening.

The first part of this chapter reviews the anatomy and physiology of the female reproductive system, the assessment of the patient presenting with a gynecologic problem, and several gynecologic emergencies that may be encountered by the EMT-P. The second part concerns the obstetric patient. Abdominal complaints in the female patient may be related to medical causes, may be gynecologic in origin, or may be obstetric in nature. This division between gynecologic and obstetric problems may be artificial, but the material is presented in this manner for simplicity.

THE GYNECOLOGIC PATIENT

Anatomy and Physiology of the Female Reproductive System

Location and Physiology

1. Ovary. This is a small, walnut-sized, glandular organ located on each side of the uterus. Each ovary secretes estrogen and progesterone and produces the ovum — the egg.
2. Fallopian tube. This is a muscular tube with the medial end protruding into the uterus and the lateral end being in intimate contact with the ovary but not attached to it. The fallopian tube conducts the egg from the ovary to the uterus by peristaltic movement and provides a passageway for sperm to travel.
3. Uterus. This is a hollow, muscular organ located in the pelvis, posterior and superior to the urinary bladder. It is designed to retain the fertilized egg for the duration of the pregnancy and to expel both the fetus and the placenta at the end of pregnancy.
4. Cervix. This is the inferior portion of the uterus (the neck of the uterus) that has the ability to thin out (efface) and to dilate, allowing for the passage of the fetus and placenta. It leads into the vaginal canal.
5. Vagina. This extends from the uterus to the vulva (the birth canal). It allows for copulation and the passage of the fetus and placenta.
6. Vulva. This is comprised of the external genitalia.
7. Perineum (obstetric). This is the area between the vagina and the anus.
8. Endometrium. This is the inner lining of the uterus that undergoes cyclical changes (monthly) which are controlled by hormones.
9. Labia. These are the folds of skin and underlying fat that extend backward from the mons pubic toward the anus (labia major/libia minor).

The Normal Menstrual Cycle

The onset of menses occurs approximately between the ages of twelve and fourteen and is controlled by the release of female hormones. The "period" generally occurs in a twenty-eight-day cycle, although this may vary widely. Phases of the menstrual cycle are as follow:

1. Proliferative phase — the thickness of the endometrium increases to prepare for implantation of a fertilized ovum.
2. Secretory phase — estrogen and progesterone are secreted to prepare the

endometrium for gestation.
3. Menstrual phase — blood and mucosal tissues are discharged from the nonpregnant uterus through the vagina.
4. Menstrual periods are absent during pregnancy, but scanty bleeding may occur.

Menopause

Menopause is the permanent cessation of ovarian function and menstrual activity. Fifty percent of the time it occurs between the ages of forty-five and fifty.

General Management of the Gynecologic Patient

Primary Survey

This consists of performing the ABCs.

History

The paramedic should determine the following:

1. Is the patient experiencing pain or discomfort:
   - P — provocation.
   - Q — quality.
   - R — region/radiation/referred.
   - S — severity.
   - T — time (frequency, intermittent).
   - Aggravation/alleviation.
2. Note the patient's present health, including any preexisting diseases.
3. Take an obstetric history:
   - Gravida — the number of pregnancies that the patient has had.
   - Para — the number of pregnancies that have produced a viable fetus (twenty gestational weeks or longer).
   - Previous cesarean sections.
4. When the patient had her last menstrual period:
   - Date.
   - Normalcy.
   - Is there bleeding between periods?
   - Regularity of the periods.
5. The possibility of pregnancy — signs of early pregnancy are:

- Breast tenderness.
- Urinary frequency.
- Morning sickness (nausea, vomiting).
- Missed or late period.

6. History of previous gynecologic problems, including:
   - Infections.
   - Bleeding.
   - Miscarriage.
7. Current blood loss (relate the amount of present bleeding to the patient's usual period):
   - Color.
   - Amount (i.e., number of pads/tampons used).
   - Duration of the bleeding.
8. Vaginal discharge:
   - Color.
   - Amount.
   - Odor.
9. Use and type of contraceptive:
   - Birth control pills are a commonly used form of contraceptive. They are usually taken on a daily basis (one pill per day). The following are some of the risks of their use:
     — The development of hypertension.
     — Acute myocardial infarction (the risk is increased four times).
     — Pulmonary embolism (the risk is increased three times).
     — Stroke.
   - An intrauterine device is placed in the uterus to prevent an ovum from implanting in the uterine wall. Risks of use are:
     — Perforation of the uterus.
     — Uterine bleeding.
     — Pain.
     — Possibility of infection.
   - Foams and jellies destroy sperm.
10. History of trauma to the reproductive system.
11. Any associated symptoms:
    - Fever and/or chills.
    - Diaphoresis.
    - Syncope.
    - Diarrhea or constipation.
12. If the patient has any allergies or is taking any medications.
13. The degree of emotional distress.

Physical Examination with Signs and Symptoms

Patients who present with obstetric/gynecologic complaints may be embarrassed, apprehensive, and, if pregnant, concerned for the life of the unborn. Gentleness, understanding, and a caring, supportive environment are important in the management of these patients.

When examining these patients, note the following:

1. The patient's level of consciousness.
2. The patient's general appearance.
3. Skin and mucous membrane color:
   - Cyanosis.
   - Pallor.
   - Flushed.
4. Vital signs, including orthostatic vital signs if blood loss is suspected.
5. Bleeding or discharge, noting color, amount, and evidence of clots and/or tissue.
6. Palpate the abdomen for masses, areas of tenderness, guarding, and distention.

Treatment

The paramedic should do the following:

1. ABCs.
2. Administer oxygen (high-flow, high-concentration as needed).
3. Start an IV with a volume expander (TKO or as vital signs suggest; consider placement of two IVs).
4. Place the patient in a position of comfort.
5. Monitor the patient's cardiac rhythm.
6. In the hypotensive patient, consider the application of the pneumatic antishock garment (in some cases, only the legs will be inflated).
7. Provide emotional support (TLC).
8. Transport the patient emergently if necessary.

Gynecologic Emergencies

Abdominal Pain — Nontraumatic

Pelvic Inflammatory Disease (PID)

This is an acute or chronic infection that may involve the uterus, the tubes, the ovaries, and adjacent structures (the peritoneum and the intestines).

1. Pathology: causative organisms include gonorrhea, staph, strep, other pathogens that enter the vagina and ascend to infect other organs.
2. Assessment:
   - History — 20 percent of the patients will have a history of pelvic inflammatory disease occurring less than one year ago. The onset of pain is often associated with the menstrual period, may follow menses, and is often made worse by sexual intercourse.
   - Signs and symptoms — the patient appears ill, blood pressure is normal, the pulse is elevated, fever may be present, and palpation of the abdomen elicits moderate to extreme pain. The pain may be diffuse lower abdominal pain, moderate to severe; it may localize to one of the lower quadrants; and/or it may radiate to the right shoulder.
   - Associated symptoms — nausea, vomiting, vaginal discharge (may have a strong odor), and erratic menstrual periods.
3. Treatment: see ''General Management'' on pages 465 to 467.

Other Sources of Abdominal Pain

1. Ectopic pregnancy (may be life-threatening).
2. Ruptured ovarian cyst.
3. Appendicitis.
4. Cystitis.
5. Postabortal infection.
6. Mittelschmertz is abdominal pain occurring at the time of ovulation.
7. Endometritis is the inflammation of the lining of the uterine wall.

Vaginal Bleeding from Trauma

Causes

Vaginal bleeding may be caused by the following:

1. Straddle injuries.
2. Blows to the perineum.
3. Foreign bodies inserted into the vagina.
4. Abortion attempts.
5. Soft tissue injury.
6. Sexual assault.

Treatment

1. See "General Management" on pages 465 to 467.
2. For injuries to the external genitalia, the paramedic may apply direct pressure over the wound.
3. For internal bleeding, **do not** pack dressings into the vagina. Start an IV(s) with a crystalloid solution, apply the pneumatic antishock garment (if indicated), and monitor the vital signs.

Sexual Assault

This is one of the fastest growing crimes in the United States. It is estimated that less than 40 percent of rapes in adults are reported; in children, sexual abuse is reported even less frequently. There are no "typical victims."

Rape is a crime of violence and includes any sexual contact without permission. Rapists have many motivations for this behavior, the most common being aggression, humiliation, control, and infliction of pain to the victim.

History

In this sensitive situation, the approach will be different; the victim/patient should not be questioned regarding the details of the event.

1. Do not ask if penetration took place.
2. Do not inquire regarding the patient's sexual history or practices (it is not relevant).
3. Do not ask questions that may lead the patient to have guilt feelings.
4. Reactions may range from anxiety to withdrawal and silence. These behaviors are normal.
5. Other reactions include denial, anger, and fear.

Physical Examination

1. Examine the genitalia only if necessary (i.e., if severe injury is present).
2. Explain all procedures before doing an examination.
3. Avoid touching the patient without her permission.
4. Maintain the patient's privacy.
5. Assess the patient for other physical injury.

Treatment

1. Psychological support is very important to reduce the victim's anxiety and fear. Provide a safe environment.

2. Respond to the victim's wishes to talk or not to talk.
3. Unless injuries are critical, obtain the patient's permission to treat.
4. Do not utilize invasive procedures unless the situation is critical.
5. Preserve any evidence:
   - Handle clothing as little as possible.
   - Do not use plastic bags for blood-stained articles.
   - Bag each item separately.
   - Ask the victim not to change clothes or bathe.
   - Do not disturb the crime scene if possible.
6. **Do not** clean wounds unless absolutely necessary.
7. Maintain a nonjudgmental attitude.
8. If female personnel are available, have them attend to the patient. Either ask the patient directly if she would prefer female personnel, or go on clues from the patient.
9. Confidentiality is very important. The victim may be concerned that others will "find out." Provide reassurance.
10. The paramedic should not allow his/her own feelings and prejudices to get in the way of appropriate communications with and treatment of the patient.

THE OBSTETRIC PATIENT

This section reviews the anatomy and physiology of pregnancy from conception through labor and delivery. The process of fetal development, assessment of the obstetric patient with complications, the normal delivery process, and complications of labor and delivery are discussed. As always, a high index of suspicion by the EMT-P is important in evaluating the pregnant patient to differentiate normal and abnormal occurrences.

Anatomy and Physiology of the Obstetric Patient

Normal Events of Pregnancy

1. Ovulation — the release of an ovum from the ovary.
2. Fertilization — the penetration of the ovum by a sperm; this normally occurs in the distal one-third of the fallopian tube.
3. Implantation — the embedding of a fertilized ovum in the endometrium of the uterus.

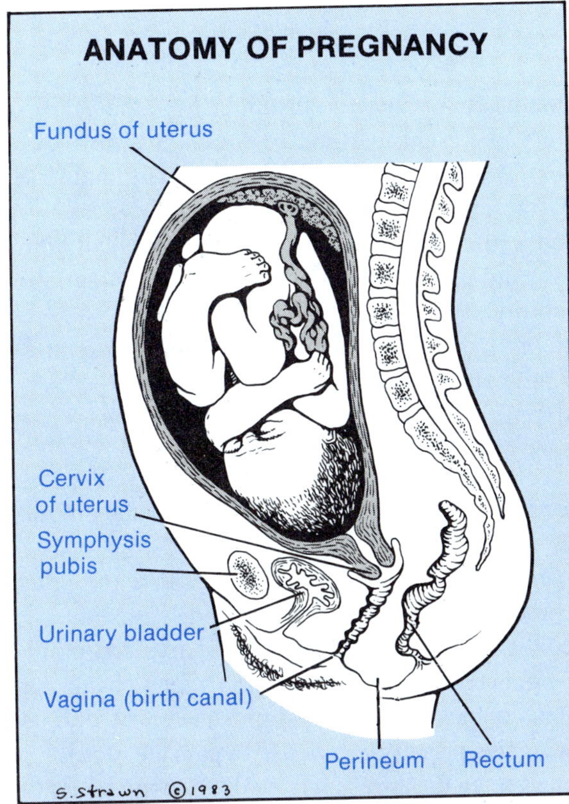

Figure 20-1. Anatomy of Pregnancy.

Accessory Structures of Pregnancy

1. Placenta — the fleshy, disklike organ from which the fetus derives its nourishment. It performs the following functions:
   - Transfer of oxygen and carbon dioxide.
   - Transport of nutrients.
   - Excretion of wastes.
   - Hormone production.
2. Umbilical cord — the cord that develops from the fetus and connects with the placenta. It contains two arteries and one vein.
3. Amniotic sac and fluid — the membranous sac that contains the fetus and the waterlike fluid that protects the fetus. Between 500 and 1,000 cubic centimeters of fluid are present after twenty weeks of gestation.

Fetal Growth Process

Fetal Development

1. By the end of the third month, the sex may be distinguished, the heart is beating, and every structure is present that will be found at birth.
2. By the end of the fifth month, fetal heart tones can be detected, and fetal movement may be felt by the mother.
3. By the end of the sixth month, the fetus may be capable of survival if born prematurely (generally, twenty-eight weeks is considered the earliest period of extrauterine viability).
4. By the end of the seventh month, there is an increased chance of survival of the newborn if delivered prematurely.
5. The middle of the tenth month is term.

Fetal Vital Functions

1. Oxygen and nutritional needs are supplied via the placenta and the umbilical vessels.
2. Fetal circulation differs from extrauterine circulation because the fetus cannot oxygenate its own blood. The umbilical cord is divided into the:
   - Ductus venosus — the shorter, posterior branch of the divided umbilical cord that carries oxygenated blood to the inferior vena cava.
   - Ductus arteriosus — this connects the fetal pulmonary artery with its descending aorta, allowing the majority of blood to bypass the lungs.
   - Foramen ovale — an opening in the atrial septal wall allowing blood to enter the left atrium from the right atrium.

Obstetric Terminology

1. Antepartum — before delivery.
2. Postpartum — the material period following childbirth.
3. Prenatal — existing or occurring before birth.
4. Natal — connected with birth.
5. Primigravida — a woman who is pregnant for the first time.
6. Primipara — a woman who has given birth to her first child.
7. Multigravida — a woman who has been pregnant two or more times.
8. Multipara — a woman who has borne more than one viable fetus.

General Management of the Obstetric Patient

Primary Survey

This consists of performing the ABCs.

History

1. Take an obstetric history:
   - Length of gestation (how many months pregnant is the patient?).
   - Is she a primapara or multigravida?
   - Have there been previous cesarean sections?
   - Is there a history of gynecologic or obstetric complications?
2. Is there pain (P Q R S T)?
3. Is there any vaginal bleeding (note presence, quantity, and character)?
4. Is there a discharge from the vagina?
5. Note the current health of the patient, her prenatal care, and if there have been any complications.
6. Find out if the patient has any allergies or if she is taking any medications.
7. Does the patient state that she is having contractions?
8. Determine if the patient is anticipating multiple births.

Physical Examination with Signs and Symptoms

1. Recognition of pregnancy (early signs and symptoms):
   - Breast tenderness.
   - Urinary frequency.
   - Missed period.
   - Nausea, vomiting (morning sickness).
2. Evaluation of uterine size:
   - Between twelve and sixteen weeks, the uterus is above the symphysis pubis.
   - At twenty-four weeks, the uterus is at the level of the umbilicus.
   - At term, the uterus is near the xiphoid process.
3. Presence of fetal movements (starting approximately at the twentieth week of gestation).
4. Presence of fetal heart sounds (audible at approximately the twentieth week); the normal rate is 120 to 160 beats per minute.
5. Vital signs — take orthostatics if there is potential bleeding (abnormal labor):
   - For orthostatic vital signs, the patient should be in a recumbent position for five minutes.
   - Take the blood pressure and pulse.
   - Sit or stand the patient upright; repeat the vitals.
   - A rise in the pulse rate of greater than fifteen beats per minute or a blood pressure drop of greater than 15 mmHg is considered indicative of a 15 percent loss of circulating blood volume.

  - Be prepared for syncope.
  - Orthostatic vitals are not necessary if the patient is obviously in shock.
6. If indicated, examine for crowning and vaginal bleeding.
7. **Never** perform an internal vaginal exam (the paramedic may visualize the vagina on examination if necessary).

Treatment

The general treatment of the OB patient is the same as for the gynecologic patient with some variations. (Specific treatment modalities are presented later in this chapter.)

1. Perform the ABCs.
2. Administer oxygen (high-flow, high-concentration as needed).
3. Start an IV with a volume expander (TKO or run in as vital signs suggest); consider placement of two IVs.
4. Place the patient in a position of comfort.
5. Monitor the patient's cardiac rhythm.
6. Evaluate the fetus or newborn if possible.
7. In the hypotensive patient, consider application of the PASG (in some cases, only the legs will be inflated).
8. Provide emotional support.
9. Transport the patient emergently, as needed.

Complications of Pregnancy

Trauma

1. Minor injuries are common due to syncopal episodes, diminished coordination, and loosening of the joints.
2. The major trauma patient who is pregnant is more susceptible to a life-threatening episode due to the increased vascularity of the pregnant uterus.
3. With abdominal trauma, the following may occur:
   - Premature separation of the placenta (this does not occur often).
   - Premature labor or abortion.
   - Rupture of the uterus.
   - Fetal death.
4. Death of the fetus may be caused by:
   - Death of the mother.
   - Separation of the placenta.
   - Maternal shock.

- Uterine rupture.
- Fetal head injury.
- Acute appendicitis.
- Acute cholecystitis.
- Infectious disease.
- Drug overdose.

Existing Diseases Worsened by Pregnancy

Pregnancy stresses the female, worsening existing disease entities. These include:

1. Diabetes. It may become unstable during pregnancy, with hypoglycemic or hyperglycemic coma occurring.
2. Essential hypertension. This may be complicated by preeclampsia or eclampsia. In addition, complications may include cerebral hemorrhage, cardiac, or renal failure.
3. Neuromuscular disorders may be aggravated by pregnancy.
4. Cardiac disorders. In general, pregnancy puts additional strain on heart function (i.e., cardiac output is increased) that may already be compromised with cardiac disease.

Bleeding

Abortion

Abortion is the termination of a pregnancy before the fetus has attained viability (twenty weeks). The following are classifications of abortion:

1. Complete. This is when all fetal material is removed from the uterus during an abortion.
2. Incomplete. This is when fetal material is left in the uterus after an abortion.
3. Spontaneous. This is an abortion that starts of its own accord. It is commonly called a miscarriage, and in one out of ten pregnancies, it occurs before the twelfth week of pregnancy. The statistics may be incorrect because many women abort before there is recognition of pregnancy. A woman may abort the fetus if she experiences a severe acute infection, was treated with DES, suffered trauma, or if fetal development is defective.
4. Criminal. This is an abortion performed illegally by medical or non-medical personnel. These abortions may be performed under less-than-desira-

ble conditions.

5. Therapeutic. This is the termination of a pregnancy for the mother's health or by personal choice. It must be performed by trained personnel under the law.

Management of the patient experiencing an abortion is the following:

1. Perform a primary survey (ABCs).
2. Take a patient history:
   - The patient may state that she has recently passed tissue (something unusual) vaginally.
   - The patient complains of abdominal pain and cramping.
3. Perform a physical examination by doing the following:
   - Evaluate the patient for volume depletion by observing for orthostatic vital sign changes (this is a good indicator of early blood loss).
   - Examine for any vaginal bleeding and the amount of it (bleeding may vary from spotting to profuse hemorrhage).
   - Look for the presence of tissue or evidence of infection.
   - The pain may be slight to severe.
4. Treatment:
   - See treatment protocols on pages 465 to 467.
   - Reassure the patient and give psychological support.
   - Transport any passed tissue if possible.

Ectopic Pregnancy

When a fertilized ovum implants anywhere other than in the uterine cavity, such as in the fallopian tube (the most common site), the ovary, the cervix, or the abdominal cavity, ectopic pregnancy occurs. Ectopic pregnancy is a significant cause of death, so the paramedic should suspect the possibility of this condition when examining a female patient in her childbearing years. Approximately 1 of every 200 pregnancies, or 1 percent of all reported pregnancies, is ectopic.

Predisposing factors are:

1. Previous pelvic inflammatory infections (PID).
2. Prior ectopic pregnancies (15 percent chance of recurrence).
3. Tubal adhesions from previous surgery.
4. Tubal ligations.
5. The presence of an IUD.

Management of this situation involves the following:

1. Perform a primary survey (ABCs).
2. Take a history:
   - Observe for any abnormal bleeding, abdominal pain (mild to severe), and hypotension.
   - The pain may be of sudden onset or have developed over a few days.
   - The last normal menstrual period may have been four to six weeks prior, with intermittent spotting.
   - There may be a history of previous ectopic pregnancy or previous PID.
3. Perform a physical examination, noting the following signs and symptoms:
   - Vital signs may deteriorate rapidly. Observe for tachycardia and prepare for hypotension.
   - Abdominal pain is almost always present, either generalized or specific to the area of pregnancy. It may be a sharp, continuous pain.
   - Shoulder pain (radiated) occurs in 25 percent of the ectopic patients.
   - Vaginal bleeding is not always present; possible spotting may occur.
   - The patient may complain of weakness, dizziness, and/or syncope.
4. Treatment of this patient involves the following:
   - See treatment guidelines on pages 465 to 467.
   - Rapid, early transport of the patient is crucial.

Abruptio Placenta

Abruptio placenta is the premature separation of the placenta from its uterine attachment. It occurs one in 200 deliveries, and death of the fetus occurs one in 400 deliveries. This is usually a third trimester complication. An abruptio placenta may be partial or complete.

Management of this patient involves the following:

1. Perform a primary survey (ABCs).
2. Take a history:
   - Twenty-five to 60 percent of all abruptio placenta cases occur in pre-eclamptic mothers.
   - Hypertension of any cause, multiple pregnancies (multiparity), trauma, and a short umbilical cord are all predisposing factors for developing an abruptio placenta.
   - There may be a history of pain with sudden onset that may be constant and severe.

Figure 20-2. Complications of Pregnancy.

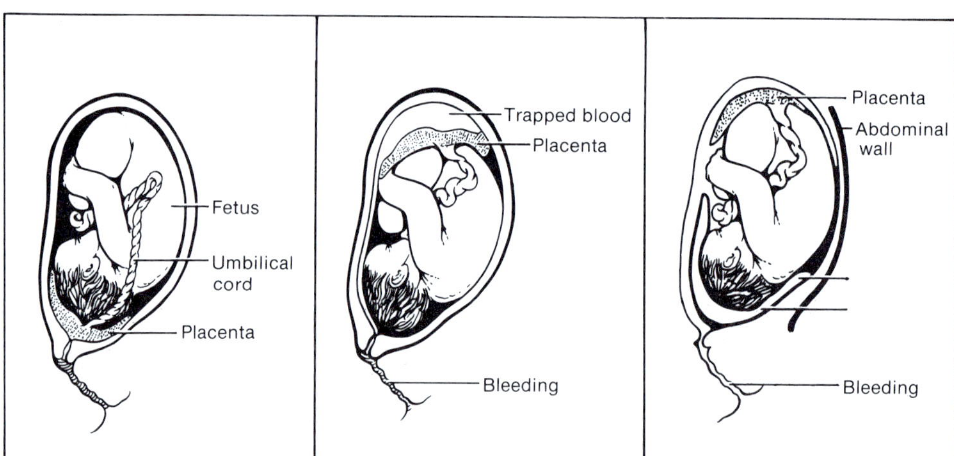

- The patient may have a past history of an abruption.

2. Perform a physical examination, noting the following signs and symptoms:
   - The uterus is tender and may feel tightly contracted.
   - The abdomen is very tender.
   - Vaginal bleeding may be present, and does not predict intrauterine blood loss.
   - The patient may experience contractions.
   - The patient will have a rapid pulse and may be hypotensive.
3. Treatment for this patient is:
   - See treatment guidelines on pages 465 to 467.
   - Carefully monitor the vital signs.
   - Start IV(s), large-bore with volume replacement solution.
   - Consider application of the pneumatic antishock garment.
   - Assess fetal heart tones.
   - Transport the patient early and rapidly.
   - Definitive treatment is a cesarean section if the fetus is viable. Fetal mortality is 100 percent in complete abruption and 30 to 60 percent in partial abruption.

Placenta Previa

In placenta previa, the placenta implants in the lower uterine segment and may partially or completely cover the internal cervical os. This occurs one in 300 deliveries. Previa may be total when the placenta completely covers the os, partial when the placenta partially covers the os, or marginal when the placenta is adjacent to but does not extend beyond the margin of the os. This is usually a third trimester problem occurring when the cervix begins to efface.

The predisposing factors are:

1. Multiple pregnancies (multiparity).
2. A rapid succession of pregnancies.
3. The patient is over thirty-five years old.

Management of this patient involves the following:

1. Perform a primary survey.
2. Take a history:
   - There may be a history of more than two pregnancies.
   - Vaginal bleeding may have occurred during early pregnancy.
   - The patient may have had a previous episode of placenta previa.
3. Do a physical examination, taking signs and symptoms:
   - Painless bleeding late in pregnancy is considered placenta previa until proven otherwise. It may be profuse and bright red.
   - There may be uterine contractions.
   - On palpation, the uterus may be soft with no tenderness, with the fetus in an abnormal position.
4. Treatment of the patient involves the following:
   - See treatment guidelines on pages 465 to 467.
   - Start IV(s), large-bore with volume replacement solution.
   - Consider application of the pneumatic antishock garment.
   - Transport the patient early and rapidly.
   - Definitive treatment is usually a cesarean section.

Medical Complications

Toxemia of Pregnancy (Preeclampsia/ Eclampsia)

Both forms of toxemia occur typically in the last trimester of pregnancy for unknown reasons. Toxemia is associated with preexisting hypertension, renal disease, and diabetes and usually occurs in women who are experiencing their first pregnancy, multiple births, or polyhydramnios (excessive amniotic fluid in their bag of waters). Preeclampsia and eclampsia occur in 5 percent of pregnancies. The mortality rate in eclampsia patients is between 5 and 15 percent. It is the second leading cause of maternal death.

Preeclampsia is the milder form of toxemia. It consists of two out of the following three signs:

1. Hypertension (blood pressure greater than 140/90).
2. Fluid retention with excessive weight gain.
3. Proteinuria (protein in the urine).

Preeclampsia is the nonconvulsive state of toxemia. If left untreated, it may progress to eclampsia.

Eclampsia is a much more serious disorder consisting of hypertension, fluid retention with excessive weight gain, and proteinuria that threatens the life of both the mother and the fetus. In eclampsia, convulsions occur that seriously threaten the life of the fetus by premature placental separation. The complication is also a risk to the mother. Along with convulsions, the mother's life is at risk due to cerebral hemorrhage, liver hemorrhage, or renal shutdown.

Management of toxemia of pregnancy consists of the following:

1. Perform a primary survey (ABCs).
2. Take a history:
   - Is this the patient's first pregnancy?
   - Is the patient anticipating multiple births?
   - Has the patient experienced polyhydramnios?
   - Has the patient had excessive weight gain with edema and/or seizures?
   - Has there been a history of hypertension or headache?
3. Perform a physical examination, noting the following signs and symptoms:
   - Note the presence of headaches and/or epigastric pain (may be a sign of an impending seizure), particularly with eclampsia.
   - The patient may have visual problems.
   - Seizures may occur with eclampsia.
   - The patient may be edematous, pale, hyperreflexic, and hypertensive (blood pressure usually greater than 140/90). However, preeclampsia may exist without high readings.
4. Treatment for the eclamptic patient consists of the following:
   - Follow treatment guidelines on pages 465 to 467.
   - **If a seizure has not occurred:**
     — Keep the patient calm and quiet.

  - Start an IV with D_5W (TKO).
  - Darken the room or ambulance if possible.
  - Position the patient on her side.
  - Transport gently (without lights and sirens).
- **If a seizure has already occurred,** in addition to the preceding:
  - Maintain an open airway.
  - Provide high-flow, high-concentration oxygen.
  - Administer diazepam, 5 to 10 mg IV.
  - Protect the patient from injury, should she have another seizure.
  - Definitive treatment is delivery by cesarean section.

Supine-Hypotensive Syndrome

This occurs near term when the abdominal mass (i.e., the fetus, placenta, and uterus) is largest and compresses the inferior vena cava, reducing venous return to the heart and thereby reducing cardiac output. It may be related to marginal volume in some patients.

Management of this patient consists of the following:

1. Perform a primary survey (ABCs).
2. Take a history:
   - Has the patient had a recent onset of lightheadedness and weakness upon lying supine?
3. Perform a physical examination:
   - Evaluate for volume depletion.
   - Obtain orthostatic vital signs.
   - The patient may be pale, weak, and/or lightheaded.
4. Treatment for this patient is as follows:
   - If volume depletion is not present, place the patient in the left lateral recumbent position and monitor the patient.
   - If volume depletion is suspected, follow general management guidelines, consider placement of two IVs, large-bore with volume replacement solution, and transport.

Braxton-Hicks Sign (Contractions)

This is a benign phenomenon that simulates labor and usually occurs after the third month of pregnancy. Braxton-Hicks contractions are generally painless. This phenonemon accounts for false labor near term. When the paramedic assesses the patient, differentiate these contractions from progressive normal labor. There are no special management techniques for Braxton-Hicks sign.

DELIVERIES

Normal Delivery

Stages of Labor

1. First. This is from the onset of regular contractions to the complete dilation of the cervix; the duration of this stage varies with the number of previous deliveries by the patient.
2. Second. This is from the full dilation of the cervix to the delivery of the baby.
3. Third. This is from the delivery of the baby to the delivery of the placenta.
4. Fourth. This is the immediate postpartum recovery period.

Characteristics of Labor

Signs of True Labor

1. Discomfort in the back and/or the abdomen.
2. Contractions occurring at regular intervals.

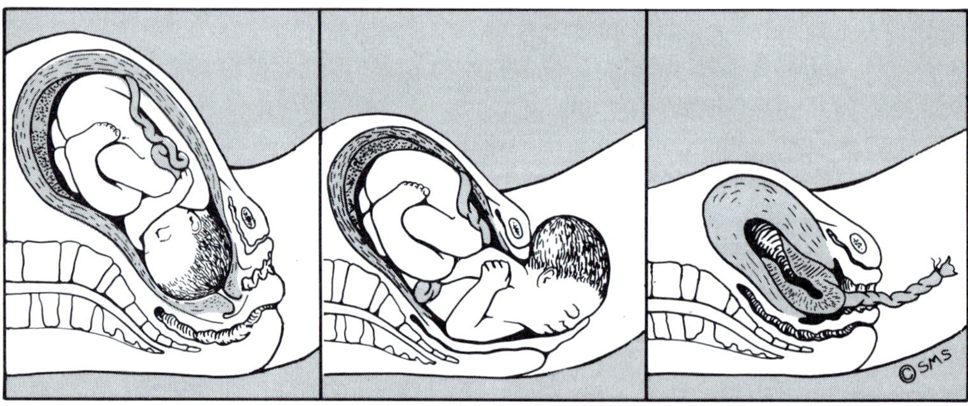

FIRST STAGE: First uterine contraction to dilation of cervix

SECOND STAGE: Delivery of the fetus

THIRD STAGE: Delivery of the placenta

Figure 20-3. Stages of Labor.

3. A progressive increase in the frequency and intensity of contractions. (Contractions are timed from the beginning of one cycle to the beginning of the next.)

Progression of Labor

1. During the first stage of labor, contractions begin short and gently and occur at intervals of ten to fifteen minutes (possibly more).
2. During the second stage of labor, contractions are stronger and longer, lasting fifty to seventy seconds and occurring at intervals of two to three minutes.
3. The amniotic sac (''bag of waters'') frequently ruptures during the second stage.
4. Toward the end of the second stage, the urge to bear down or push becomes very strong.

Physiology of Labor and Delivery

1. Effacement — the thinning and shortening of the cervix during the first stage of labor.
2. Cervical dilation — stretching of the opening of the cervix during the first stage of labor to accommodate the birth of the fetus.
3. Crowning — this occurs during the second stage of labor when the largest part of the fetal head is visible at the vaginal opening.
4. Presenting part — the part of the infant that presents first at the os of the cervix.

Management

When To Transport

1. The decision to expedite transport or remain for delivery is related to the imminence of delivery. Questions to ask:
   - Number of pregnancies? Labor is shortened with multiple pregnancies (multiparity).
   - Frequency of contractions? Contractions less than two minutes apart may signal imminent delivery.
   - Maternal urge to push?
   - Crowning of the presenting part?
2. The decision is also related to the presence of complications.
   - Rupture of the amniotic sac increases the potential for fetal infection, and delivery may be more difficult.

Figure 20-4. Partial Crowning (Left), Crowning (Center), Head Emerging and Turning (Right).

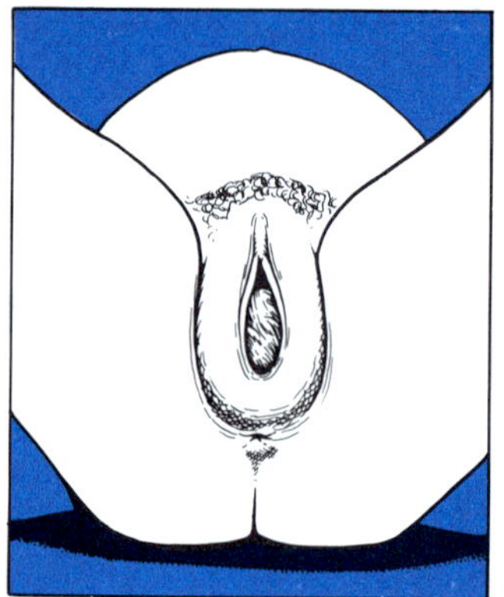 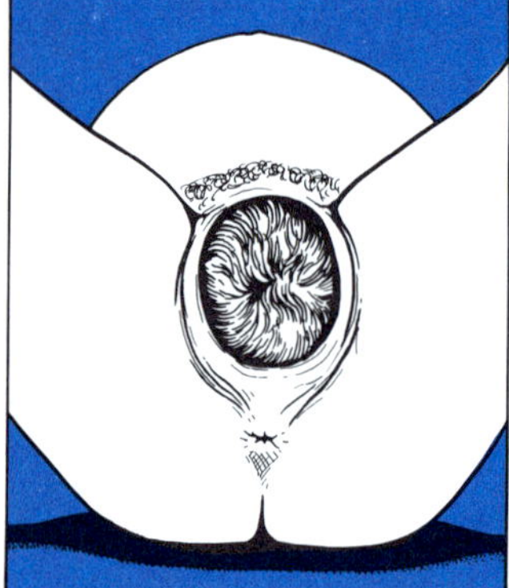 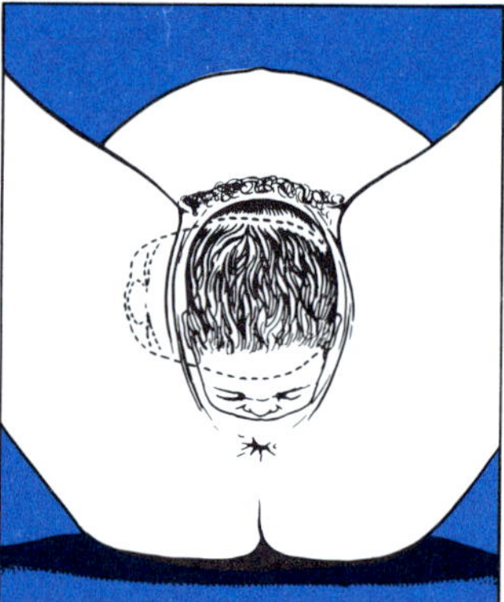

- Abnormal presentations.
- Fetal distress.
- Multiple pregnancies.

Performing the Delivery

1. Prepare a delivery area (clean, adequate space in which to work).
2. Consider providing oxygen to the mother.
3. Establish an IV route for volume expansion (run to keep open).
4. Position the patient on her back and drape appropriately (if possible).
5. Monitor the fetal heart rate (using a stethoscope).
6. Coach the mother in breathing techniques. Panting during contractions helps prevent bearing down and forcing the baby's head out, thus helping to prevent the chances of tearing the perineum. Deep breathing between contractions promotes rest.
7. Encourage the mother to push with contractions.
8. Put on sterile gloves.
9. Control the delivery of the fetal head by applying gentle hand pressure over the head (this prevents an "explosive" delivery).
10. If the amniotic sac (membrane) continues to cover the baby's head as it emerges, the paramedic should tear the sac to permit the escape of amniotic fluid and allow the newborn to start breathing.
11. Examine the infant's neck for the presence of the umbilical cord. If it is wrapped around the neck, slip it over the head or shoulder; if this is

Figure 20-5. Stages of Normal Delivery.

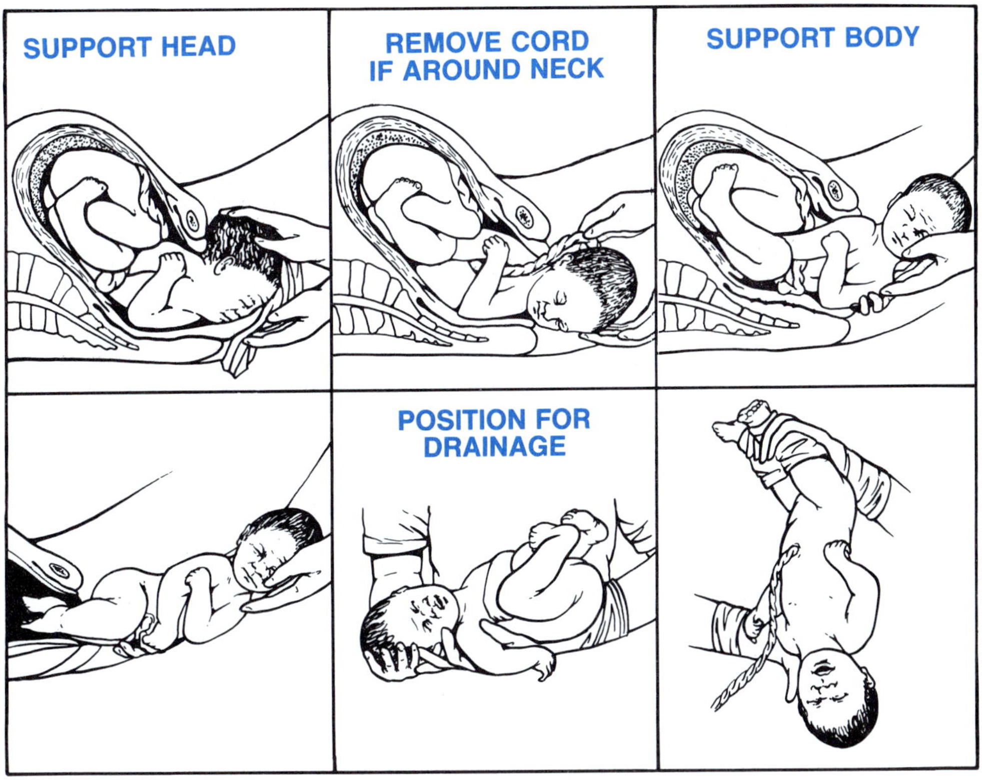

not possible, clamp the cord in two places and cut between the clamps. Avoid excessive tension on the cord.

12. Suction the newborn's mouth and nose with a bulb syringe (squeezing the bulb before placing it in the nose or mouth).
13. Provide support as the head rotates and the shoulders deliver.
14. Delivery of baby — do not lower the baby below the level of the vagina.
15. Clamp the umbilical cord, with the first clamp approximately four inches from the baby and the second clamp six inches from the baby. Cut between the clamps.
16. After the baby is delivered:
    - Resuction the infant.
    - Wipe the baby dry.
    - Inspect the cord.

- Wrap the baby in a dry blanket for warmth.
- Position the baby on its side with his/her head lowered ten to fifteen degrees.

17. Note the time of birth.
18. Evaluate the newborn using the APGAR (see care of neonate).
19. Delivery of the placenta. This usually occurs ten to twenty minutes after the delivery of the newborn. There is no need to delay transport to wait for the delivery of the placenta. If it does deliver, place it in a plastic bag (to keep it intact for later medical examination), and bring it to the hospital.
20. If bleeding is excessive, start fundal massage of the uterus to stimulate contraction. This will help to control bleeding. (Breastfeeding will also stimulate contraction of the uterus, helping to control bleeding.)
21. Manage perineal tears by direct pressure, if applicable.
22. Observe and monitor the mother for signs of hemorrhage and stability of pulse and blood pressure.
23. Monitor the newborn.

Abnormal Deliveries

Breech Presentation

This may be a presentation of either buttocks or feet. There is an increased risk for delivery trauma and anoxia with these fetal presentations.

Treatment

Delivery is best accomplished in the hospital. If field delivery is required:

1. Position the mother with a pillow under her buttocks.
2. Assist the mother in holding her legs in a flexed position.
3. Do not pull on the infant.
4. Deliver the baby's buttocks and legs to the umbilicus.
5. Support the body by draping the newborn's legs over the paramedic's arm.
6. Elevate the feet and legs of the newborn to provide better access to the airway.
7. Push vaginal tissue away from the baby's face to allow for suction of the airway.
8. Deliver the head (if delivery of the head proceeds normally, then continue as with a normal delivery).
9. If the head is not delivered and the baby is breathing spontaneously:

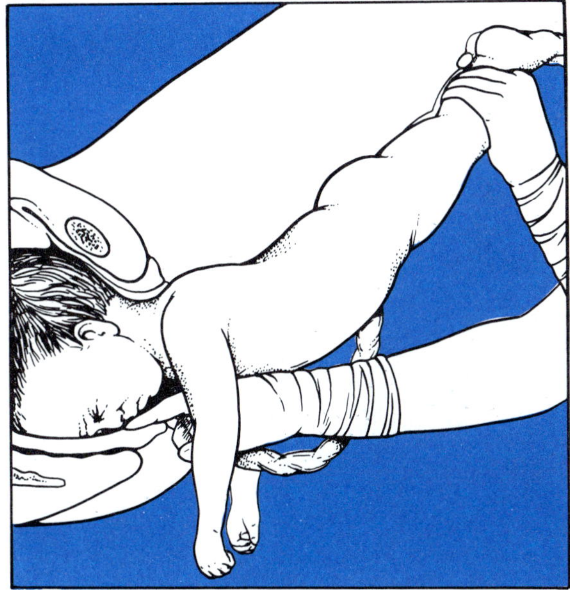

Figure 20-6. Breech Birth.

- Place a gloved hand in the vagina, with the palm facing the infant's face.
- Form a "V" with the fingers on either side of the baby's nose and mouth.
- Push the vaginal wall away from the face.
- Transport the patient emergently to the hospital.

Prolapsed Cord

This occurs one in 300 deliveries when the umbilical cord is the presenting part and is compressed between the baby and the bony pelvis, shutting off fetal circulation.

Predisposing Factors

1. Abnormal presentations.
2. Multiple births.
3. Premature births.
4. Premature rupture of membranes when the baby is not sufficiently engaged.

Treatment

1. If the umbilical cord is seen or felt in the vagina, insert a gloved hand to

Figure 20-7. Prolapsed Cord.

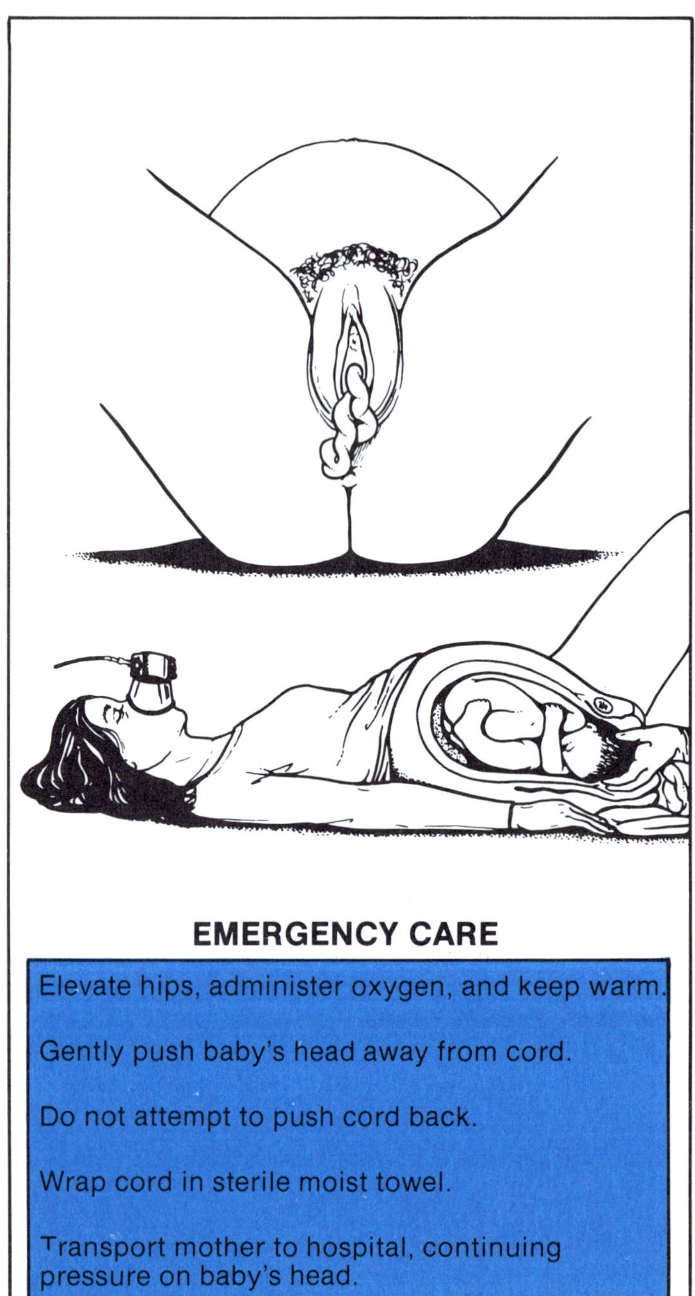

EMERGENCY CARE

Elevate hips, administer oxygen, and keep warm.

Gently push baby's head away from cord.

Do not attempt to push cord back.

Wrap cord in sterile moist towel.

Transport mother to hospital, continuing pressure on baby's head.

elevate the baby (presenting part) off of the cord, and/or push the baby back off of the cord.
2. Check for pulsations of the cord.
3. Position the mother in a knee-to-chest position or the Trendelenberg position.
4. Administer high-flow oxygen to the mother.
5. Transport emergently to the hospital.
6. **Do not** attempt to push the cord back.
7. Definitive treatment is a cesarean section.
8. If possible, the exposed cord should be kept warm and moist with a saline dressing.

Other Abnormal Presentations

1. Occiput posterior presentation — the face looks up instead of down.
2. Face presentation — the face presents rather than the vertex (the incidence is one in 600 deliveries).
3. Brow presentation — the brow presents instead of the vertex (occurs one in 2,000 deliveries).
4. Transverse presentation — the fetus lies across the width of the uterus.
5. Cephalopelvic disproportion — the fetus is too large or the mother's pelvis is too small to allow for a normal delivery.

Treatment

1. Early recognition of the complication.
2. Provide reassurance for the mother.
3. Transport rapidly for definitive management.
4. Frequently, cesarean section is the only definitive management.

Multiple Births

The incidence of multiple births is one in ninety deliveries.

Assessment

1. The mother may suspect or know that she is carrying multiple fetuses.
2. The abdomen remains large after delivery of the first baby.

Treatment

1. Follow the normal delivery guidelines.
2. There may be more than one placenta.
3. Tie the cord as each baby is delivered.

4. Infants in multiple births are generally smaller than normal newborns and need special attention to maintain body heat.
5. There is a high risk of prematurity with this group.

Maternal Complications of Labor and Delivery

Postpartum Hemorrhage

Postpartum hemorrhage is loss of more than 500 cubic centimeters of blood in the twenty-four hours after delivery. It is normal for all postpartum patients to experience some blood loss for up to three weeks after delivery.

Pathology

1. Lack of uterine tone.
2. Vaginal or cervical tears.
3. Retained pieces of the placenta.
4. Clotting disorders.
5. The uterus fails to return to normal size following delivery (usually requires five to six weeks) and may result in late postpartum hemorrhage.

Primary Survey

Conduct a primary survey of this patient.

History and Predisposing Factors

1. The infant is large.
2. Multiple births have occurred.
3. Multiple pregnancies have occurred.
4. The patient has had placenta previa.
5. The patient has had abruptio placenta.
6. The patient has had a prolonged labor.

Physical Examination

Perform a physical exam, noting the following signs and symptoms:

1. The paramedic must rely on the patient's clinical appearance and vital signs.
2. The uterus feels soft on palpation.
3. Inspect the vagina for signs of external bleeding.
4. Look for signs of hypovolemic shock.

Treatment

1. Perform the ABCs.
2. Provide high-flow, high-concentration oxygen as needed.
3. Place the infant at the mother's breast if just delivered.
4. Provide uterine massage (after delivery).
5. Start an IV(s), large-bore with volume replacement.
6. Apply pneumatic antishock garment.
7. Administer oxytocin per physician's order:
   - Indications: to stimulate immediate postpartum contraction of the uterus and to control postpartum uterine bleeding, especially if uterine massage is ineffective or the patient is in shock.
   - Administration: injectable oxytocin (Pitocin) contains 10 USP units (20 mg) per milliliter.
     — Intravenous dosage: Ten to twenty USP units in 1,000 ml crystalloid. Flow rate of twenty to thirty drops per minute, titrated to the severity of hemorrhage and uterine response.
     — Intramuscular dosage: Ten USP units (1 ml) IM only if unable to start an IV.
8. Do not attempt to force delivery of the placenta.
9. Do not pack the vagina.
10. Transport the patient immediately.

Uterine Rupture

Uterine rupture is a rare complication, but it carries a high mortality rate for both mother and infant. It most frequently occurs after the onset of labor. Any of the following may be predisposing factors: trauma, previous cesarean section, prolonged or obstructed labor, and/or abnormal presentations.

For management of this patient, do the following:

1. Perform a primary examination (ABCs).
2. History:
   - Complaints of abdominal pain that is continuous and becoming progressively worse.
   - The patient may start with normal labor, then contractions cease as the uterus ruptures.
3. Perform a physical examination, noting the following signs and symptoms:
   - Profound shock.
   - External blood loss may be minimal (concealed hemorrhage).

- Fetal heart tones are absent.
- Abdominal tenderness.

4. Treatment:
   - See general management for the obstetric patient.
   - Start an IV(s), large-bore with volume replacement solution. (Run wide open if the patient is in profound shock.)
   - Monitor vital signs and cardiac rhythm.
   - Apply pneumatic antishock garment, leg compartments.
   - Transport the patient early and rapidly.
   - Definitive treatment is cesarean section with repair or removal of the uterus.

Uterine Inversion (Prolapse of the Uterus)

This occurs when, after the birth of the infant, the uterus turns inside out and produces profound shock. It may result from pulling on the umbilical cord or attempting to speed the delivery of the placenta when the uterus is relaxed.

Treatment

1. Follow general management guidelines.
2. **Do not** attempt to detach the placenta or pull on the cord.
3. Try once to replace the uterus manually, exerting pressure on the area surrounding the cervix. If this does not work, cover all protruding tissue with sterile, moist dressings.
4. Transport rapidly and early.

Pulmonary Embolism

This is an obstruction of the pulmonary artery or one of its branches. It is usually a venous thromboembolism that occurs most commonly after cesarean section, but it may occur anytime during pregnancy, labor, or the postpartum period. It is one of the most common causes of maternal death.

Management of this patient involves doing the following:

1. Perform a primary examination.
2. Take a history:
   - Sudden onset of dyspnea.
   - Sudden onset of sharp, focal chest pain.
3. Perform a physical examination, noting the following signs and symptoms:

- Tachycardia.
- Tachypnea.
- Hypotension.

4. Treatment:
   - ABCs.
   - Provide high-flow, high-concentration oxygen.
   - Start an IV of D_5W TKO.
   - Monitor the vital signs and cardiac rhythm.
   - Transport the patient rapidly and early.

Care of the Neonate

This section reviews the routine care of the newborn infant, including those with special needs, care of the distressed infant, and neonatal transport. Care of the neonate is made more difficult by the fact that the EMT-P has two patients — the mother and the infant. The paramedic should be aware that this is a very important time psychologically for both mother and newborn, and the paramedic must provide a supportive environment.

Routine Care of the Newborn

Clamping the Cord

1. Do not strip or milk the cord; it may result in the following:
   - Increases red blood cell destruction, leading to hyperbilirubinemia.
   - Polycythemia increases blood viscosity, leading to cardiopulmonary problems.
2. Hold the infant at the level of the vagina following delivery.
3. The cord may be clamped thirty to forty-five seconds after birth.
4. Inspect the cord at intervals for blood loss.

Positioning of the Head

Position the infant's head to the side and slightly lower than the body to facilitate drainage of fluid and prevent aspiration.

Airway Management

1. Suction:
   - Use a bulb syringe or a DeLee suction unit.
   - Suction the nose, then the mouth (squeeze the bulb prior to insertion).
   - Take care not to oversuction.
2. Stimulation:

- If the infant does not cry and stimulation is needed, gentle rubbing along the back will usually be sufficient.
- Avoid vigorous spanking or rubbing.

Heat Loss

Heat loss occurs normally in all newborns and can endanger the infant. Management is aimed at minimizing such loss. Heat loss occurs by:

1. Evaporation — the most extensive form of heat loss.
2. Convection — this is dependent on room temperature and movement of room air.
3. Conduction — this occurs between the infant and the surfaces that he/she contacts.
4. Radiation — infants lose heat to colder surfaces or objects.

General management of heat loss is accomplished by:

1. Rapid drying of the infant.
2. Keeping the environmental temperature at seventy-four to seventy-six degrees Fahrenheit.
3. Preventing drafts.
4. Keeping warm, dry blankets on the infant.
5. Do not wrap the infant with the same moist towel used to dry him/her.
6. Use well-insulated hot water bottles or rubber gloves filled with warm water (take care not to burn the newborn).

Evaluation of the Newborn

Vital Signs

1. The pulse is 150 to 180 at birth and slows to 130 to 140 per minute.
2. Crying indicates a good respiratory effort.
3. The respiratory rate is forty to sixty per minute.
4. APGAR scoring chart. The purpose of this system is to identify and differentiate infants who require routine care and those who need further assistance. The APGAR scoring is performed at one minute following birth and five minutes following birth. The two scores help to identify infants who need intervention and observe whether or not intervention has the desired effect. The parameters for APGAR and scoring are listed in Table 20-1.

Table 20-1

Parameter	0 points	1 point	2 points
A Appearance	Blue, pale	Body pink, extremities blue	Completely pink
P Pulse rate	Absent	Below 100	Over 100
G Grimace	No response	Grimaces	Cries
A Activity	Limp	Some flexion of extremities	Active motion
R Respiratory effort	Absent	Slow, irregular	Good strong cry

The scoring ranges for the APGAR scale are:

1. 7-10: Active, vigorous infant, routine care.
2. 4-6: Moderately depressed infant, requires stimulation to breathe and oxygen.
3. 0-3: Severely depressed infant, immediate ventilatory assistance required.

Premature Infants

These infants weight less than 5.5 pounds (2,500 grams) and are born before the thirty-sixth week of gestation. They are at risk for developing hypothermia, volume depletion, respiratory problems, and cardiovascular problems related to hypoxia.

Treatment

1. Keep the newborn warm.
2. Keep the airway clear and open.
3. Prevent bleeding from the umbilical cord.
4. Prevent contamination of the newborn.

Care of the Distressed Infant

1. Resuscitation is addressed primarily toward adequate ventilation and oxygenation.
2. IVs, drugs, and cardiac care are generally not indicated.
3. Suctioning, drying, and keeping the infant warm are especially important in the distressed neonate.
4. Stimulation:
   - Gentle rubbing along the back.
   - Gently tapping the soles of the feet.
5. Oxygen administration:
   - Four to five minutes from tubing or from a mask held near the face; if the infant is pale or cyanotic, give oxygen until the patient is pink.
   - Toxicity in the field is unlikely, since administration time is short.
6. Ventilatory assistance;
   - Mouth-to-mouth and nose.
   - Bag, valve, mask — use only infant resuscitation bag and monitor chest expansion closely. **Do not** use adult equipment.
   - Avoid the use of oral airways because they are difficult to keep in place.
   - Use clear infant-size masks (allows visualization of nose and mouth).
   - Bagging techniques: maintain the newborn's head in the sniffing position (avoid hyperextension), pull the chin upward, and avoid hyperinflation.
   - **Do not** use mechanical resuscitators; they can overinflate and damage the newborn's lungs.
   - Endotracheal intubation is possible, but usually not necessary.
   - Ventilatory rate is thirty to forty breaths per minute; observe for decreased respiratory drive with hyperventilation.
7. CPR if necessary.
8. Observe for meconium staining (normal with breech delivery, but otherwise indicates a hypoxic condition of the fetus).
   - The presence of meconium in the amniotic fluid may indicate distress due to placental insufficiency and obstruction of the cord.
   - If inhaled, it may cause severe lung inflammation.
   - Treatment: frequent and vigorous suctioning before the first breath with DeLee, administering oxygen, and constantly monitoring the patient; report the presence of meconium staining to the physician.

Neonatal Transport

Major Problems

Major problems during transport are:

1. The maintenance of body temperature.
2. The controlled administration of oxygen.
3. Ventilatory assistance.

Heat Sources

1. Ambulance heater (keep the ambulance warm).
2. Hot water bottles or rubber gloves (the temperature of the water should not exceed 104 degrees Fahrenheit [40 degrees Centigrade]); protect the infant from burns.
3. Commercial heat sources are radiant heating units and heated mattresses.
4. **Do not** use chemical heat packs.
5. A space blanket (aluminum foil wrap) helps to maintain body heat.

SUMMARY

This chapter has been separated into three sections: gynecological problems, obstetric problems, and the newborn. The information is presented this way with the belief that learning will be simplified.

The paramedic will have noticed that the treatment of some obstetric emergencies is similar to many of the gynecologic problems. It is hoped that the repetition will be of help by reinforcing the important points.

The delivery of a newborn is one of the joyful events in which the paramedic may have an opportunity to participate. It might also be noted that it is not a common prehospital event (it is most common in large urban areas). With regular review and observation (if the paramedic is fortunate enough to observe child delivery at a hospital), the paramedic can have an incredible experience when the opportunity does occur.

Division Six

Behavioral

21

Behavioral Emergencies

The psychiatric emergency is a situation that causes great concern to the paramedic because it is difficult to provide adequate training for the diversity of behavioral problems. The EMT-P is often confronted by feelings of uncertainty and helplessness commonly due to:

1. The difficulty in determining the cause of the crisis.
2. Lack of scientific tools to assess the situation.
3. Few protocols developed for the prehospital care provider
4. Protocol approach to care does not ensure a positive outcome.
5. The final outcome is not as predictable as in a trauma or medical case.
6. A wish to avoid all psychiatric situations.
7. An uncertainty whether intervention can affect an outcome positively.
8. Reluctance to learn more about crisis intervention.
9. General lack of confidence in the ability to deal with behavioral emergencies.

The purpose of this chapter is to assist the paramedic in recognizing that:

1. Intervention is possible.
2. Intervention is essential, or the crisis may get worse.

3. The paramedic can make a positive contribution to the outcome of a patient in crisis.
4. Psychiatric situations can be evaluated in an organized manner.

UNDERSTANDING BEHAVIORAL EMERGENCIES

Behavioral emergencies are changes in a person caused by intrapsychic, environmental, situational, or organic alterations resulting in behavior that cannot be tolerated by the person or others and that requires immediate attention.

Key elements that the paramedic must attend to include:

1. Changes in the behavior of a patient.
2. The inability of a patient to handle an alteration in circumstances.
3. The patient's inability to deal with loss.
4. Immediate intervention may be required.

Intrapsychic Causes for Behavioral Emergencies

Behavioral changes that occur from within the person may lead to a wide range of behavior. The behavioral crisis may be due to an acute episode of an underlying psychotic condition. The patient's crisis may result in any of the following behaviors:

1. Catatonic state — characterized by periods of physical rigidity, negativism, excitement, and stupor.
2. Depression — a morbid sadness, dejection, or melancholy.
3. Disorientation — loss of patient's familiarity with his/her surroundings.
4. Homicidal acts — the actual or attempted killing of a human being by another.
5. Hysterical conversion — psychic transformation of anxiety into physical signs or symptoms. This is most commonly manifest as psychic blindness, deafness, or paralysis.
6. Paranoia — a mental disorder characterized by the presence of systematized delusions. Excessive or irrational suspicions or distrustfulness are usually apparent.
7. Phobia — an unfounded, exaggerated, and morbid dread or fear.
8. Regression — a return to childlike behavior due to an inability or refusal to function at a more adult level.

9. Suicide — the actual or attempted act of taking one's life.
10. Violent acts — exertion of abusive physical force which may cause injury.
11. Withdrawal — a pathological retreat from reality.

Interpersonal/Environmental Causes for Behavioral Emergencies

These usually result from reactions to stimuli outside the patient, often described as ''overwhelming incidents.'' The following are possible causes of a crisis:

1. Death of a loved one.
2. Rape.
3. Loss of a job.
4. Career change.
5. Natural disaster (flood).
6. Manmade disaster (war).

A change in behavior can frequently be linked to a specific incident or to a series of incidents. The range of behaviors is broad, depending on the type of incident experienced by the patient.

Organic and Chemical Causes for Behavioral Emergencies

Disturbances in the physical/biochemical state of a patient may cause significant changes in behavior. It is important for the paramedic to consider organic damage as a possible cause for behavioral abnormalities. A physical assessment should be routine with all patients. The following is a list of possible causes of organic and chemical reasons for a behavioral crisis:

1. Drugs.
2. Alcohol.
3. Trauma.
4. Illness (diabetes — electrolyte imbalance).
5. Dementia (organic brain syndrome).

Substance abuse plays an important role in causing behavioral problems.

It is defined as a pathological use of a substance(s) that significantly interferes with normal activities.

Alcohol is the most abused substance in western culture and can cause serious behavioral problems. It can often complicate underlying problems (either psychological, traumatic, or medical) and acts as a central nervous system depressant. The paramedic may assess the patient for alcohol use by:

1. The odor of the patient's breath.
2. Slurred speech.
3. Unsteady gait (ataxia).
4. The slowness with which the patient responds to questions.

Frequently there is evidence of alcohol consumption in the patient's environment from empty bottles, reports from bystanders, etc.

Drug abuse from either prescription or street drugs is also common in western culture. It is much more difficult to evaluate drug abuse than alcohol abuse due to the variety of drugs available. The paramedic's assessment should include:

1. Taking the patient's vital signs.
2. Observing pupillary reaction.
3. Observing the scene for evidence of drugs taken.
4. Examining the patient for the route of drug administration (IV use, ingested orally, inhaled nasally, or smoked).
5. Behavior due to a specific substance is unpredictable from one patient to another. The following are some serious behaviors that the paramedic may encounter in the field:
   - Withdrawal.
   - Suicidal attempts or success.
   - Violence.
   - Homicide or attempts.
   - Hysteria.

Dementia, or organic brain syndrome, is a result of damaged brain cells caused by poor circulation or an insufficient supply of oxygen. This is often associated with the aging process. Patients experience a loss of recent memory, impaired judgment, and a lack of mental clarity. The onset of this process is usually slow and gradually takes place over a long period of time.

Trauma as a Cause of Behavioral Changes

Injuries to the head or body may play a role in causing behavioral problems. When a patient has experienced trauma to the head or body with resultant increased intracranial pressure, decreased circulation to the brain, or hypoxia due to hypoperfusion, he/she may become uncooperative or combative. This occurs because the patient's brain is not getting needed oxygen.

Naturally, these uncooperative or combative patients cannot be treated by normal psychiatric management. They must have immediate and definitive care, which might include surgery. Field care includes administering high-flow, high-concentration oxygen, IV fluid therapy, and expeditious transport; i.e., normal trauma management.

Patients who are injured may have a variety of emotional responses related to their injury or to the injury of a nearby person. Some of the patient's responses may be normal, realistic, and expected. The paramedic must know what is and what is not appropriate. Usually, if his/her behavior does not interfere with the treatment, the patient's response is "acceptable." The following are several possible feelings that a patient may experience:

1. Anxiety — which may be related to pain, disability, economic hardship, and to fear of death. These are all realistic fears.
2. Denial — the patient is ignoring the problem.
3. Anger — which may be directed at the paramedic as well as at bystanders.
4. Confusion — which may be a common event in the elderly.
5. Regression — this is a return to childlike behavior, commonly due to stress.
6. Depression — normal response to loss (though not an emotion that the pre-hospital care provider will normally encounter).

Medical Illness as a Cause of Behavioral Emergencies

A physiological imbalance may result in changes of behavior. For example, diabetes can cause behavioral abnormalities primarily due to hypoglycemia. The following are a few signs that a paramedic should note (this may alert the paramedic to the fact that the patient's problem may be related to physical illness rather than psychological factors):

1. Confusion.

2. Slurred speech.
3. Unsteady gait.
4. Uncooperative or combative behavior.

SCENE EVALUATION

Since there is a high incidence of EMT-Ps being injured in the field, evaluation of the scene for possible dangers is and must be the highest priority for emergency personnel. The paramedic must realize that he/she cannot provide medical care if injured.

The following are situations that the paramedic should not enter unless appropriate backup (i.e., police or fire) has secured the area:

1. A patient with weapons.
2. Riot scenes.
3. Fire scenes.
4. Hostage situations.
5. Hazardous material situations.

If the potential for danger is minimal, the scene should be observed for:

1. Evidence of acts of violence.
2. Evidence of substance abuse.
3. Evidence of suicidal attempt.

TECHNIQUES AND GUIDELINES FOR OBTAINING A HISTORY

The paramedic should first gather pertinent information necessary for the immediate management of life-threatening conditions and then should obtain a more complete set of information through:

1. Observations made by the paramedic.
2. Patient history.
3. Information received from family, bystanders, and/or first responders.

The paramedic must use a systematic approach in gathering information, as with all patient history taking. The following areas should be explored by the paramedic when questioning a patient in a behavioral crisis:

1. Precipitating situation/problem.
2. Current life situations.
3. Recent history.
4. Past history.
5. Mental status.
6. Physical signs.
7. Patient behavior.

If possible, remove the person from the crisis situation and exclude disturbing persons. The paramedic should be confident, honest, firm, and reasonable. Much of the required information can be gained through direct questioning. The paramedic should be positioned so as not to intimidate the patient (do not tower over the patient — eye level may be best).

Patients should be encouraged to sit, relax, and speak freely at their own pace. Do not interrupt the patient once he/she begins talking. If the patient begins to cry, do not interfere by talking. Encourage the patient by using an occasional phrase such as "I see," or "tell me more," or by simply using a nod of the head. Provide structure and support for the patient who views the situation as chaotic or overwhelming. Do not argue with or yell at a patient. Touching a patient should only be done when permission is granted. A patient should be allowed to talk during the history taking unless the patient is depressed, minimally responsive, or suicidal. If the patient is reluctant to respond or leaves long periods of silence, the paramedic should remain relaxed and attentive, and not press the person to talk, because this may cause the patient to completely withdraw.

The EMT-P should not be judgmental toward the patient. The situation will dictate the scope of the interview. Only information critical to the field management and transportation of the patient should be requested unless offered voluntarily by the patient. A patient's emotional condition will affect the information obtained. Essential information must be gathered immediately (i.e., "What did you take?").

The EMT-P should be prepared to spend whatever time is necessary to manage a patient (the paramedic should not rush), unless the patient's condition is serious or the patient is in imminent danger to him/herself or to someone else.

PSYCHIATRIC DISORDERS

Depression

Depression may be caused by both external and internal causes. Grief reactions and situational reactions are classified as external causes. Anger and guilt may be classified as internal causes.

Symptoms

The patient may:

1. Seem sad most of the time.
2. Exhibit persistent pessimism — "It'll never get better."
3. Exhibit a tendency to cry easily.
4. Exhibit feelings of hopelessness, worthlessness, and isolation.
5. Exhibit withdrawal from social relationships.
6. Be agitated and overly active, or may be very lethargic and slow.
7. Exhibit a loss of appetite.

Suicide

Changes in the Patient

Several changes may take place in a suicidal person that may lead a paramedic to suspect suicidal tendencies, allowing the paramedic to take proper precautions.

1. The patient loses the ability to communicate effectively and has feelings of hopelessness.
2. The patient may attempt to communicate directly ("I don't want to live") or indirectly by expressing anger ("I'm angry with you").
3. The person may manipulate his/her relationships by arousing sympathy or anxiety in others.
4. Ambivalence. A patient may not be able to decide whether to live or die. The suicide drive ebbs and flows. (In management of this type of patient, the EMT-P should make use of the patient's desire to live.)

Patient Profile

Men are more successful at committing suicide than women and tend to use more violent means (guns, knives). Women use pills or carbon monoxide most often.

The Suicide Plan

The paramedic should:

1. Assess how relatively lethal the method selected is (i.e., gun, pills, etc.).
2. Assess how available the method selected is (i.e., is the gun in the patient's hand or possession? A paramedic should not be near a patient with a lethal weapon).
3. Assess how specific the plan is — the more specific and detailed, the greater the suicide potential.
4. Have prior attempts at suicide been made?

Stress

Stress precipitates suicidal behavior. If stress symptoms are high, the suicide potential is high. If symptoms are severe and stress is low, either the paramedic is not aware of all the pertinent details of the case or the patient is chronically unstable.

Symptoms

1. Most symptoms relate to depression.
2. Agitation is exhibited through tension, guilt, feelings of anger, or revenge.
3. Agitation may occur in alcoholics and drug addicts.
4. Agitation may occur in patients in psychotic states.

Resources

1. Inquire as to what people resources are available to help lend support in the suicidal crisis (e.g., family, close friends, physicians, or clergy).
2. Consider aspects of the patient's life that may provide a lift from depression (e.g., job or other areas that may boost self-esteem).
3. Remember that when no support is available or all attempts of help have been exhausted, the suicide potential increases.

Lifestyle

1. A patient with a previously stable lifestyle and no history of suicidal behavior may turn suicidal because of a precipitating event, such as loss

of a job, a death, divorce, etc.

2. A patient with an unstable life with a history of poor adjustment to repeated difficulties in major situations may turn suicidal.

Management of a Suicidal Crisis

1. The paramedic's safety comes first.
2. Consider armed individuals as potentially homicidal as well as suicidal. Law enforcement officers should handle such a situation. Once a patient has been disarmed, the paramedic may intervene.
3. Give emergency care, if required, first.
4. Conduct a brief interview to assess the situation.
5. Remember — every attempted suicide must be evaluated by a physician, and in most states a patient who attempts suicide gives up his/her rights.

Rage, Hostility, Violence, and Uncooperative Behavior

These are not necessarily called psychiatric emergencies. However, they may be symptoms of an underlying psychiatric or medical problem. A patient's abnormal behavior may be a response to an illness (insulin shock), or it may be a patient's way of dealing with feelings of helplessness.

If possible, a paramedic should not respond with anger or defensiveness. A one-to-one discussion should be conducted in a private room, if conditions permit (i.e., the paramedic is not going to be in danger). The patient should be told:

1. What the patient can expect from the paramedic.
2. What is expected of the patient; the patient should be given an opportunity to comply.
3. That the paramedic is there to help the patient.

If the patient is angry, ask why. If hostility and violent behavior cannot be calmed through verbal persuasion, restraining the patient may become necessary. Threats should not be made without intention to follow through. It is best to have a law enforcement agent(s) at the scene to assist with patient restraint. Be sure to follow local guidelines when handling this type of situation.

If the situation cannot be controlled by the paramedic, appropriate law enforcement personnel must be notified quickly. (It is a good idea to have law enforcement personnel on the scene when handling any potentially violent patient.)

Paranoid Reactions

Paranoid reactions may be displayed by a patient only in a few, limited circumstances. Acute anxiety may cause the emergence of paranoia, while disabling paranoid reactions may be noticeable in psychotic patients. It is important to check the validity of a patient's observations if possible. A paramedic's assessment of the situation may help calm a patient's fears.

There are several ways in which paranoia may become apparent:

1. It may appear suddenly and dramatically. An internal or external crisis may overwhelm adaptive and defensive systems, or a prolonged period of increasing stress may suddenly cause an obvious paranoid reaction.
2. It may be preceded by a well-marked incubation period. The patient's first reactions to confusion may be marked by a partial or complete withdrawal. Suddenly, a paranoid explanation seems to clarify the situation for the patient.
3. It may develop gradually and insidiously. In this case, there is no sharp delineation of the paranoid behavior.

Management

In the management of paranoid reactions, the paramedic should do the following:

1. Clearly identify him/herself and explain what he/she is trying to do.
2. Act in a friendly, businesslike, neutral fashion. Showing kindness or warmth may be interpreted by the paranoid patient as an attempt to gain the patient's confidence in order to ''get'' him/her.
3. Do not respond to a patient's anger.
4. Do not speak with bystanders in hushed, secretive tones. This would reinforce paranoid delusions.
5. Use tact and firmness in persuading the patient to go to a hospital.
6. Do not lie to the patient. A paramedic should never lie to a patient except to avert bodily injury or in the case of hysterical, uncontrollable patients.

Hysterical Conversion Reaction

This is psychological transformation of anxiety into physical symptoms, most commonly seen as psychic blindness, deafness, or paralysis.

Management

Do not try to convince a patient that the problem is "all in his/her head." Treat the signs and symptoms as if they were real. Inform the receiving institution staff of any evidence that the patient may be experiencing a conversion reaction.

The Disorganized and Disoriented Patient

A patient in such a state may display uncontrolled and disconnected thoughts. The patient is usually incoherent or has rambling speech. The patient may have been discovered wandering aimlessly and inappropriately dressed.

Frequently, disoriented patients do not know where they are, what day it is, or what their name is. This type of situation is most common among the elderly and is usually complicated by regressive behavior. It is important to remember that head injury, drug ingestion, and metabolic disorders may cause disorientation.

Management

1. The disorganized patient requires structure. The paramedic should identify him/herself and clearly describe what he/she plans to do.
2. The paramedic should explain what the patient can do to help.
3. The patient should be properly oriented to time, place, and person at the scene.
4. The paramedic should be sure to repeat him/herself as many times as is necessary to help the patient understand the situation.

GENERAL MANAGEMENT AND INTERVENTION TECHNIQUES FOR BEHAVIORAL EMERGENCIES

1. A professional attitude must be maintained, and the paramedic should be warm, sensitive, and compassionate.
2. The EMT-P must first assess the risk to his/her own safety. Injury restricts a paramedic from performing his/her responsibilities.
3. Remember — life-threatening injuries receive first priority.
4. The paramedic should intervene in a behavioral situation only to the ex-

tent that he/she feels capable.

5. The paramedic should be aware of his/her own professional limitations.
6. If the paramedic does not feel capable of administering aid, the patient should be transported rapidly to an appropriate facility where such care can be provided.
7. Do not overreact to the patient's behavior or emotional attacks.
8. Assess the patient's needs and try to meet them.
9. Take command of the situation.
10. Do not attempt to suppress a patient's reactions or feelings as long as they do not endanger anyone.
11. Be calm and reassuring when possible.
12. Anxiety may be avoided among family, friends, and bystanders by good scene management (i.e., removal of unnecessary persons from disturbing situations — unfamiliar bystanders may magnify the problems in a situation).
13. The patient may require support from familiar persons.
14. A physical examination may heighten anxieties in the patient. It is important to develop a rapport with the patient prior to the examination if possible.
15. Remember — with an anxious or confused patient, meticulous explanations of procedures may be necessary.

LOCAL RESOURCES

It is important for the paramedic to be familiar with the available personnel resources when handling the psychiatric patient.

Field Crisis Workers

These individuals may be available in some communities (professionals and paraprofessionals). They are specially trained in field management of emotional crises and generally may be summoned to the scene (or receiving facility) with a rapid response time.

The EMT-P should be familiar with the crisis workers' training, availability, situations in which they should be contacted, procedures for contacting them, and their responsibilities at the scene.

Bureaus of Mental Health

Most states have established bureaus of mental health.

Mental Health Centers

Most localities have mental health centers that provide referral services for patients and may be responsible for administering involuntary commitment procedures. Their personnel may be consulted for specific training requests.

Local Law Enforcement Personnel

Law enforcement agents are often helpful and important in the management of emotionally disturbed patients. Frequently, these patients are transported while under arrest. It is important to note that the paramedic often acts under the auspices of a law enforcement officer and/or a court. Under these circumstances, it is often best to have a police officer ride in the ambulance with the patient.

Good communication links are critical for rapid response by law enforcement personnel. It is best for the police to arrive at the scene prior to an EMT-P's arrival.

BEHAVIORAL CRISIS IN THE PEDIATRIC PATIENT

In a pediatric crisis, the paramedic should try to determine a patient's developmental stage. This will enable the paramedic to better determine the child's response.

1. Children under six years of age become concerned when separated from their parents, they generally fear pain and disapproval, and they usually do not understand descriptions of treatment that a paramedic may provide.
2. Children seven to twelve years of age will tolerate limited separation from parents, may cooperate and understand simple instructions, and have begun to develop defenses for coping.
3. Children twelve to eighteen years of age are striving for and achieving independence. They usually place great importance on body image.

Management

1. Avoid separating the younger child from his/her mother.
2. Try to prevent the child from seeing things that will increase emotional upset.

3. Identify yourself to the patient by giving your name and title.
4. Be calm and speak slowly.
5. Touching is important and reassuring. Simply holding the patient's hand may help calm him/her down.
6. Explanations should be brief, simple, and repeated as often as necessary.
7. Telling a child the truth will develop trust (i.e., if a procedure is going to hurt, tell the child).
8. Encourage a child to help with the procedure when possible.
9. Do not discourage a child from crying.
10. Allow a child to take a favorite blanket or toy.
11. Be sure to formally introduce to a child any other person who may be treating him/her.
12. Do not leave the child alone.

BEHAVIORAL CRISIS IN THE ELDERLY PATIENT

See Chapter 17 for greater detail.

Chronological age is not an adequate indication of the patient's physical or mental status. The paramedic should avoid categorizing according to age and should remember that many elderly people function quite well on their own.

Problems associated with aging may be physical in nature. These may include organic brain syndrome, chronic illness, failing eyesight and hearing, and other maladies. Some problems may be emotional in nature, such as depression, the death of a close friend, retirement, and/or loneliness. It is important to note that these may arise from a combination of physical and emotional problems.

Management

1. Assess the patient's ability to communicate.
2. Continual reassurance is important.
3. Physical contact is reassuring, particularly with patients who have sight and hearing impairment.
4. Treat the patient with respect. Call the patient by his/her name and proper title. Do not use "Dear" or "Honey."
5. Avoid administering medication. If this is absolutely necessary, do so only by direct order of a physician.
6. A description of the intended procedure should be given to the patient.

7. Act with restraint to reduce the ''hurry up'' feelings.
8. Allow family and friends to remain with the patient if possible.

CONTROLLING THE VIOLENT SITUATION

Severely disturbed patients who pose a threat to themselves or others may be hospitalized against their will (with **legal authorization only**). Every state government has a different statute covering the criteria for involuntary commitment. The paramedic must have a clear understanding of all applicable laws in his/her state.

A standard set of procedures should be developed by any organization providing ambulance service. The premise upon which most state laws are based is that one person may restrain another to protect life or prevent injury.

If in the EMT-P's assessment the patient may be homicidal, the EMT-P should:

1. Not enter the area or should carefully try to remove him/herself from the situation.
2. Contact law enforcement personnel immediately.
3. Stand by until the scene is secured by the police.
4. Avoid heroic efforts.

Containment of Violent Behavior

1. If possible, seek police assistance and authorization before proceeding with restraint.
2. Plan restraining actions.
3. Use only reasonable force sufficient to restrain the patient (do not be overly zealous).
4. The paramedic should be sure that adequate manpower is available for restraining patients.

Methods for Restraining a Patient

The more familiar a paramedic can be with the potential range of motion of a patient's extremities and the methods for restraint, the more effective he/she can be in immobilizing a patient.

Range of Motion of the Joints

Know the range of motion of the joints:

1. Arms cannot flail backward.
2. Legs cannot kick backward.
3. The spinal column does not allow the patient to double over backward.

Muscle Groups

Consider the muscle groups involved in the extremity to be controlled and in what direction the extremity may be moved with the least amount of force (i.e., flexing an arm is easier than straightening an arm).

Position of Patient

Whenever possible, position a patient in such a way that the effectiveness of his/her strength and range of his/her motion can be restricted.

Restraining Devices

The paramedic must be familiar with the restraining devices used in his/her system.

1. Commercially manufactured restraints.
2. Improvised restraints:
   - Small towels or face cloths wrapped around wrists or ankles with strong tape over the cloth, which is secured to the stretcher.
   - Use of cravats and a secure knot.
   - Use of roller bandages.
   - Simple blanket roll.

The paramedic should not attempt to simply hold a patient for long periods, because:

1. Either the patient or paramedic may end up being injured.
2. This may set up a confrontation and aggravate the situation.
3. This does not allow the paramedic the freedom to deal with other matters.
4. Continuous physical restraint requires more than one paramedic or assistant per patient.

Unarmed Patients

When handling an unarmed patient who requires restraints:

1. The paramedic should be familiar with the restraining techniques.

2. The paramedic should have adequate assistance. This will reduce the likelihood of injury to the patient and the paramedic.
3. A final request to the patient for cooperation should be made. If the patient does not respond to this offer, a minimum of two EMT-Ps should move swiftly toward the patient.
   - The patient cannot focus on both individuals.
   - Swiftness minimizes the accuracy of a potential kick or blow.
   - One paramedic should continue talking with the patient.
4. Both personnel should move close to and slightly behind the patient.
5. The paramedic must be cautious and should never assume that he/she has complete control unless the patient is fully restrained. The patient may still kick, bend forward, bite, or spit and jerk.
6. If the patient does in fact calm down, the paramedic may decide to transport the patient without restraints; however, continued restraint is suggested for maximum safety.
   - Continued reassurance is called for.
   - Keep the patient on the stretcher with the normal straps on.
   - The paramedic should always position him/herself between the patient and the doors (or, if the paramedic suspects that the patient may try to bolt out of the ambulance, the patient should be restrained).
   - If the patient becomes dangerous to him/herself or to others, use restraints en route. This is a difficult task. The ambulance must be stopped and the driver must come to the back of the ambulance to assist.

Resistant Patient

The sequence of actions when handling resistant patients requiring restraint is as follows:

1. The paramedics should position one leg forward in front of the patient's leg and force the patient forward into the prone position.
   - The prone position prevents the patient from using strong abdominal muscles to sit up.
   - Arms are more easily restrained on a patient in the prone position.
   - The legs are less effective in kicking in this position.
   - Biting and spitting are effectively controlled this way.
2. Continued reassurance of the patient is necessary.
3. Each paramedic should maintain his/her grip on the patient's outstretched arm while leaning his/her weight on the patient's back.

Positioning a Patient on a Stretcher

Positioning and restraining a patient on the stretcher for transport involves the following steps:

1. Position the patient either prone or laterally recumbent.
   - Continually assess and maintain the airway.
   - This position dramatically reduces effective resistance.
2. Adjust the stretcher to its lowest position. This improves stability and reduces the distance a patient can fall.
3. Restrain one of the patient's arms by the side and the other over the head.
4. Place the webbed strap directly across the lumbar region — do not overtighten.
5. After applying restraints to the ankles, secure the restraints to the stretcher or to one another underneath the stretcher.
6. Do not remove the restraints until there are sufficient emergency medical or law enforcement personnel present to maintain proper control of the situation.

Methods for Avoiding Injury

Methods that may be used to avoid injury are as follows:

1. When in a room with a hostile patient, the paramedic should:
   - Remain at a safe distance.
   - Do not allow the patient to block the exit.
   - Keep furniture between the paramedic and the patient.
   - Avoid making threatening statements.
   - Two paramedics should stay separated at an adequate distance.
2. The paramedic may protect him/herself from thrown objects by holding one edge of a blanket in the hand and the bottom of the blanket under the foot. The blanket must be held away from the body, since the blanket may absorb the impact of thrown objects. The blanket may also be used to wrap a violent patient.

SUMMARY

In the medical or trauma patient, the paramedic must attend to their physical and emotional needs. Generally, most paramedics believe they are capable of meeting their patients' needs. The behavioral emergency presents an entirely different set of circumstances, making these cases more difficult to manage.

Nonmedical psychiatric patients is probably the group least encountered by rescue personnel. Because of the low number of cases handled, the paramedic should remember the following points to help make managing these patients easier:

1. The ability of the paramedic to initiate good communications with his/her patient (as well as with bystanders) will establish a mood which may increase the likelihood of patient cooperation. This will allow treatment and transport to occur with less stress to all involved.
2. Observe the patient's appearance and behavior, speech (fast, slow, loud, or soft), mood, perceptions (acute or illusional), and ability to reason. This information will help the paramedic in determining the patient's mental status and the best way to manage the situation.
3. When interviewing the patient, ask questions that are relevant to the present situation and that will help in treating the patient appropriately. The paramedic should be supportive during this process, which will improve patient rapport.

These situations may be trying to all persons involved. With patience, sensitivity, understanding, and compassion, the paramedic will have greater success in managing the psychiatric patient.

Appendices

A-1

Paramedic Field Drugs

ALUPENT

Actions

1. Rapid onset.
2. Decreases reversible brochospasm.
3. Relieves associated dyspnea.

Indications

1. Bronchial asthma.
2. Reversible bronchospasm which may occur in association with bronchitis and empysema.

Precautions

1. Is contraindicated with cardiac dysrhythmias associated with tachycardia.
2. Patients with hypertension, coronary artery disease, congestive heart failure, and diabetes.
3. Safety and effectiveness of the inhalant solution in children below the age of twelve has not been established.

How Supplied

Inhalant solution (5 percent, 6 percent)

Administration

Administered by oral inhalation with the aid of a hand-held nebulizer or on an intermittent, positive-pressure breathing apparatur (IPPB). Should begin with the lowest effective dosage and tritate the dosage according to the individual patient's requirements. Not recommended for use in children under the age of twelve years.

Side Effects

1. Nervousness.
2. Tachycardia.
3. Tremor.

AMINOPHYLLINE (Theophylline)

Actions

1. Acts mainly as a bronchodilator by relaxing the smooth muscles of bronchial airways.
2. Increases heart rate and cardiac output.
3. Causes mild diuresis.
4. CNS stimulation.

Indications

(Relieves bronchospasm/constriction.)

1. To bronchodilate in episodes of acute asthmatic attacks and decompensating COPD.
2. To relieve bronchoconstriction in anaphylaxis.
3. To reduce respiratory distress in pulmonary edema.

Precautions

1. Use with caution in patients with severe cardiac or hepatic disease — decrease dosage.
2. Must be administered slowly to avoid toxic and side effects — usually given as an IV drip.
3. Monitor ECG during administration.
4. If patient is already taking oral theophylline preparations, determine how much and when last taken (reduce dosage appropriately).

How Supplied

Ampules of 250 mg or 500 mg.

Administration

1. Initial adult dosage: 250-500 mg (5-6 mg/kg) added to 50-100 ml of D_5W with microdrip and administered IV over 20 minutes (a reduced dosage may be ordered history dependent — CHF or recent theophylline usage).
2. Pediatric dosage: 6 mg/kg (generally not used with children in the field).

Side Effects

1. Cardiac irritability and dysrhythmias.
2. Hypotension.
3. Nausea and vomiting.
4. Headache, nervousness, dizziness, lightheadedness.

ATROPINE SULFATE (Parasympathetic Blocking Agent)

Action

1. Blocks parasympathetic impulses responsible for brady dysrhythmias.
2. Accelerates sinus node discharge rate.
3. Improves AV conduction.
4. By increasing sinus rate, may reduce chances of ectopic escape ventricular activity.
5. May restore cardiac rhythm in asystole.

Indications

1. **Any** bradycardia accompanied by **significant hypotension and/or ventricular ectopic beats.** (Less likely to be effective than beta stimulators in complete block, but should be tried first to increase AV conduction.)
2. May be indicated for **ventricular asystole**.
3. An antidote for **organophosphate poisoning.**

Precautions

1. Should not be used for bradycardia unless signs of poor perfusion or ventricular ectopy are present.
2. Atrial flutter or atrial fibrillation with a rapid ventricular rate.
3. Use with caution when patients have glaucoma.

4. Use with caution in patient having a myocardian infarction.

How Supplied

Prefilled syringes 1 mg/1 ml or multidosage vials with a concentration of 1 mg/1 ml.

Administration

1. Initial adult dosage: **0.5 mg IV push** repeated at 5-minute intervals until desired heart rate is reached, **not to exceed a total dosage of 2.0 mg.**
2. **1.0 mg** can be given as initial dosage for asystole.
3. Pediatric dosage: **0.01-0.03 mg/kg (0.1 mg minimum).**
4. May be administered through endotracheal.
5. Should not be pushed slowly or in smaller than recommended dosages; might slow rate further.
6. Organophosphate poisoning: **2 mg IM and 1 mg IV.** IV dosage may be repeated every 5 to 10 minutes until secretions decrease.

Side Effects

1. Decreased GI motility, urinary retention, blurred vision, pupil dilation, flushed, dry, warm skin, dry mouth.
2. Possible rapid pulse.
3. Possible ventricular tachycardia or fibrillation.

BRETYLIUM TOSYLATE (Bretylol)
Antiarrhythmic

Actions

(Actions are complex and not completely understood.)

1. Elevates ventricular fibrillation threshold.
2. May convert ventricular fibrillation to an effective rhythm.
3. Sometimes an initial increase in rate and arterial pressure followed by a modest decrease.
4. Conductivity and contractility not affected.

Indications

1. Ventricular fibrillation that has not been converted by defibrillation and lidocaine.
2. Ventricular fibrillation that has recurred despite lidocaine.
3. Refractory ventricular tachycardia, unresponsive to standard therapy measures.

Precautions

1. There are no contraindications to use in the treatment of life-threatening dysrhythmias.
2. Use with extreme caution if digitalis toxicity suspected.

How Supplied

10 ml ampules containing 500 mg (50 mg/ml).

Administration

1. Refractory ventricular fibrillation: Initial: **5 mg/kg bolus IV (350-500 mg) followed by defibrillation.** If ventricular fibrillation persists, **subsequent dosage: 10 mg/kg** — may be repeated at 15- to 30-minute intervals. Do not exceed a maximum dosage of 30 mg/kg. Onset of action, 2 to 4 minutes.
2. Refractory or recurrent ventricular tachycardia: Initial: **dilute 500 mg of bretylium tosylate in 50 ml D_5W (concentration of 10 mg/ml); give 10 mg/ml by IV infusion over 8 to 10 minutes.** Subsequent: May be given as a constant infusion at 1 to 2 mg/minute. Onset of action, 20 minutes or more with ventricular tachycardia.

Side Effects

1. Hypotension.
2. Postural hypotension.
3. Nausea and vomiting.
4. Transient hypertension.

CALCIUM PREPARATIONS

Actions

1. Reverses overdose with magnesium sulfate or calcium channel blockers (verapamil).
2. Relieves specific muscle spasms.

Indications

1. **No longer recommended for use in asystole or electromechanical dissociation.**
2. Antidote to verapamil overdose.
3. Antidote to magnesium sulfate.

4. Calcium gluconate may relieve pain and muscle spasms due to black widow spider bite.

Precautions

1. Do not give in the same infusion with sodium bicarbonate.
2. Give with extreme caution and reduced dosage in patients taking digitalis.

How Supplied

1. Calcium chloride: 10 ml in a 10 percent solution in a prefilled syringe.
2. Calcium gluconate: 10 ml of a 10 percent solution in a prefilled syringe.

Administration

(Calcium preparations are given slow IV.)

1. Verapamil toxicity, **10 ml of 10 percent calcium gluconate slow IV.**
2. Magnesium sulfate overdose, **10 ml of 10 percent solution clacium gluconate slow IV.**
3. Black widow spider bite with severe pain and muscle spasms, **10 ml of a 10 percent solution of clacium gluconate.**

Side Effects

1. May increase cardiac irritability in presence of digitalis.
2. Precipitates when mixed wtih sodium bicarbonate.
3. Rapid injection may slow heart; administer over 2 to 3 minutes.
4. Causes tissue irritation and necrosis if infiltrated at IV site.

DEXAMETHASONE (Decadron)

Actions

1. Inhibits inflammatory response of tissues due to mechanical, chemical, infectious, inflammatory, or other causes.
2. Preserves the integrity of small blood vessels in shock.
3. Increases cardiac output.
4. Stabilizes cellular membranes.
5. Any improvement will occur 4 to 6 **hours**, not minutes, after administration.

Indications

1. Cerebral edema caused by trauma, cerebrovascular accident, or tumors, to prevent immediate death and allow time for diagnostic procedures (chemical decompression of the brain).
2. Spinal trauma.
3. Anaphylactic shock.
4. Status asthmaticus.

Precautions

1. Allergy to sulfites.
2. Systemic fungal infections.

How Supplied

Various size vials that contain a solution of 4 mg/ml (1 ml, 5 ml, and 25 ml size vials).

Administration

1. 12 to 100 mg dexamethasone IV push (depending on area protocol, physician choice).
2. Administer only by physician order and with approval of the receiving hospital.

Side Effects

1. Dexamethasone is not an emergency drug. Therefore, it is generally not used unless the transport time is prolonged and only by physician order.
2. Documentation of neurological status is essential prior to administering the drug. Remember that subsequent neurologic evaluation is made more difficult when you add another variable by administering Decadron.

DEXTROSE 50%

Actions

1. Increases circulating blood sugar levels when used in hypoglycemic conditions.
2. Short-acting osmotic diuretic.

Indications

1. Coma due to hypoglycemia.
2. Unknown cause of coma.

3. Seizures of unknown cause.
4. Patients with a reagent strip (Dextrostix) reading less than 45 mg with an altered state of consciousness.
5. A medical cardiac arrest.

Precautions

Intracranial hemorrhage.

How Supplied

Prefilled syringe containing 50 ml of a 50 percent dextrose (25 grams of dextrose).

Administration

1. Draw one tube of blood for glucose determination prior to administration of Dextrose 50%.
2. Make sure that it is being administered in a secure IV.
3. Dosage: **50 ml of 50 percent dextrose IV push.**

Side Effects

1. Tissue necrosis if it infiltrates.
2. May precipitate severe neurologic symptoms in the alcoholic patient. Give thamine (50 mg IV) along with Dextrose 50%.

DIAZEPAM (Valium)

Actions

1. Tranquilizes, calms patient.
2. Terminates seizure activity.
3. Relaxes skeletal muscle.

Indications

1. Treat status epilepticus.
2. Given prior to cardioversion in the conscious patient.
3. To sedate possible AMI patients who have little pain, but high anxiety level.
4. Reduce anxiety in selected patients.

Precautions

1. Respiratory depression (monitor respiratory status closely).
2. Hypotensive patients.
3. Pregnant patients.
4. Patients who have taken alcohol or sedative drugs.

How Supplied

Prefilled syringes of 2 ml concentration of 5 mg/ml.

Administration

1. Should not be mixed with other drugs or IV solutions — pinch tubing well and administer right at IV site rather than higher up tubing.
2. Status epilepticus: **Initial dosage, 2.5 mg-5.0 mg slow IV push.** Monitor blood pressure if stable and, if necessary, give second dosage of 2.5 mg-5.0 mg slow IV push. Do not exceed a total dosage of 10 mg in the field.
3. Sedation or cardioversion: **2.0-5 mg slow IV push** (5 mg/minute) until desired degree of sedation obtained.

Side Effects

1. Respiratory depression/arrest.
2. Dizziness, ataxia.
3. Transient hypotension.

DIPHENHYDRAMINE (Benedryl)

Actions

1. Blocks histamine effects that are caused by an allergic reaction.
2. Reverses the side effects of phenothiazine antipsychotic medications.
3. Reduces or prevents motion sickness.

Indications

1. A second line drug after epinephrine in anaphylactic shock and severe allergic reactions.
2. To counter the extrapyramidal effects of using phenothiazine medications (e.g., an oculogyric crisis).

Precautions

1. Pregnancy.
2. Asthma.
3. Glaucoma.
4. Prostate problems.
5. Alcohol/depressants intoxication.

How Supplied

1. Prefilled syringes containing 50 mg in 1 ml.
2. Ampules of 1 ml containing 50 mg/ml.

Administration

1. Adults: **50 mg slow IV push or deep IM.**
2. Pediatrics (to age 12): **1-2 mg/kg body weight, not to exceed 50 mg in a single dosage.**

Side Effects

1. Drowsiness, confusion.
2. Pediatric may cause excitation.
3. Blurred vision.
4. Dry mouth.
5. Wheezing.

DOPAMINE (Intropin) Beta Sympathetic Drug

Actions

1. Chemical precursor of epinephrine, naturally occurring in man.
2. Stimulates alpha, beta, and dopamine receptor sites.
3. Actions of this drug are dependent on the dosage level.
4. Dilate renal and mesenteric arteries.
5. Increase the force and rate of cardiac contractions.
6. Low dosages, beta effects predominate.
7. High dosages, alpha effects are developed, causing vasoconstriction.
8. Causes less increase in cardiac O_2 usage than isoproterenol.

Indications

1. Cardiogenic shock while maintaining good renal blood flow.
2. May be useful in treating other hypotension except that secondary to hypovolemia.

Precautions

1. May by inactivated if mixed with sodium bicarbonate.
2. Contraindicated for hypovolemic shock.
3. In the presence of uncontrolled tachydysrhythmias or ventricular fibrillation.
4. Infusion rate must be regulated carefully to obtain desired effects — may be hazardous in the field.
5. Tissue necrosis and sloughing can occur from IV infiltration (like Levophed).
6. Potentiated by drugs such as Parnate, Marplan, and Nardil. Dosage may need to be decreased.
7. Serious acute hypertension may develop in patients with pheochromocytoma.

How Supplied

5 ml ampules containing 40 mg/ml.

Administration

1. Adult dosage: **by IV drip only.** Mix 200 mg dopamine in 250 ml D_5W with microdrip for a concentration of 800 mcg/ml. The following are effects at specific dosages:

   Begin infusion at **2 to 5 mcg/kg/minute** — adjust according to clinical response (e.g., increase as necessary to attain an adequate blood pressure and level of consciousness).

   At a dosage of 1 to 2 mcg/kg/minute — dilates renal and mesenteric blood vessels with no effect on heart rate or blood pressure.

   At a dosage of 2 to 10 mcg/kg/minute — increased cardiac output due to beta effects on heart.

   At a dosage of 10 to 20 mcg/kg/minute — peripheral vasoconstriction (alpha effect) and increased blood pressure may begin to cause renal vasoconstriction.

   At a dosage above 20 mcg/kg/minute — alpha effect reverses dilation of renal and mesenteric vessels and decreases flow through these vessels.

2. Pediatric dosage: **2 to 10 mcg/kg/minute.**

Side Effects

1. Tachydysrhythmias/ectopy.
2. Nausea, vomiting.
3. Dyspnea, angina.
4. Headache.
5. Excessive vasoconstriction at high dosages.

EPINEPHRINE (Adrenalin)

Actions

1. Both alpha and beta effects.
2. Increased heart rate.
3. Increased force of contractions.
4. Increased arterial blood pressure.
5. Increased systemic vascular resistance.
6. Increased myocardial oxygen demand.
7. Stimulates cardiac contractions in asystole.
8. May restore electrical activity in asystole.
9. Converts fine ventricular fibrillation to coarse.
10. Bronchodilation.

Indications

1. First-line drug in cardiac arrest: to enhance defibrillation in ventricular fibrillation, in asystole, and electromechanical dissociation (EMD).
2. To increase systemic vascular resistance, improving perfusion during resuscitation.
3. To treat life-threatening anaphylaxis.
4. To treat acute asthmatic attacks.

Precautions

1. Avoid mixing with bicarbonate; it may inactivate epinephrine.
2. **No contraindications in cardiac arrest or anaphylactic shock.**
3. Use with caution in patients who have hypertension, angine, hyperthyroidism, or are over 40 years of age.

How Supplied

Prefilled syringes containing 1 mg of epinephrine in 10 ml (1:10,000 solution).
Ampules containing 1 mg epinephrine in 1 ml (1:1,000 solution).

Administration

1. In **cardiac arrest: adults** 0.5 to 1.0 mg of 1:10,000 solution IV push repeated at 5-minute intervals as needed.

   May be given through endotracheal tube if IV line placement delayed — 1 mg (10 ml) 1:10,000 solution.

   Avoid intracardiac injection (optional skill) due to numerous complications.

   May be given by drip to increase and sustain blood pressure and heart rate — 1 mg epinephrine in 250 ml 5 percent dextrose in water to infuse at 1 to 4 mcg/minute.

   Pediatric dosage: 0.1 ml/kg of 1:10,000 IV bolus.

2. In **anaphylactic shock:**
   Mild: May be given subcutaneously at 0.5 mg (0.5 ml of a 1:1,000 solution). If the reaction was caused by an injection or insect sting on the extremity, a constricting band should be placed proximal to the site of the injection (sting). Then, 0.5 ml of 1:1,000 solution may be injected subcutaneously to delay absorption. Do not inject in fingers or toes. Give the initial dosage in the other extremity.
   Severe: With shock, give 0.5 mg (5 ml of a 1:10,000 solution) slow IV push.

3. **Mild to moderate asthmatic attack:** Subcutaneously, 0.5 ml to 0.5 ml of a 1:1,000 solution.

Side Effects

1. In the conscious patient: Palpitations, hypertension, dysrhythmias.
2. Remember that the use of epinephrine increases myocardial oxygen demand, so provide high-flow/high-concentration oxygen to the patient.

FUROSEMIDE (Lasix)

Actions

This is a potent diuretic.

1. Inhibits sodium reabsorption in the kidneys, promoting diuresis; also causes increased potassium excretion.
2. Thought to cause venous dilation, decreasing venous return (preload).
3. Rapid onset of action (5 minutes), peaking in 30 to 60 minutes, with short duration of effect (2 hours).

Indications

1. To reduce fluid overload associated with congestive heart failure and acute pulmonary edema.
2. May be used with increasing intracranial pressure in systems that do not use mannitol.

Precautions

1. Can cause profound diuresis — monitor blood pressure closely.
2. Should not be administered to pregnant women.
3. In hypovolemic states.
4. In hypokalemic patients.

How Supplied

Ampules of 2 ml and 10 ml containing a concentration of 10 mg/ml.

Administration

1. **Adult initial dosage:** 0.5 to 2.0 mg/kg IV bolus (40 mg) administered over 2 minutes.

2. **Pediatric dosage:** 1 mg/kg IV bolus.

Side Effects

1. Immediate: Nausea and vomiting.
2. Later: Volume depletion and dehydration.
3. Potassium depletion with dysrhythmias.

GLUCAGON (Hormone Excreted by the Pancreas)

Actions

1. Elevates blood sugar by stimulating release of glycogen from the liver.
2. Return to consciousness should be within 20 minutes of intramuscular injection.
3. Increases heart rate and force of contractions.

Indications

Insulin shock when patient is unconscious, combative, and IV line cannot be started. When a 50 percent dextrose solution is not available.

Precautions

Glucagon is a protein; hypersensitivity is a possibility.

How Supplied

1 mg vial with 1 ml vial of dilutant.

Administration

1. Adult: **0.5 mg to 1.0 mg.** May be given subcutaneously, intramuscularly, or by IV. **In the field, give intramuscularly or subcutaneously.**
2. Generally requires direct physician order.
3. Use of glucagon is restricted to patients who are seizing, combative, or with collapsed veins and in whom an IV cannot be started.

Side Effects

1. Nausea and vomiting may occur.
2. **May be no response if patient has no stores of glycogen.**
3. IV glucose or dextrose is the treatment of choice for insulin shock.

ISOPROTERENOL (Isuprel)

Actions

(Pure beta stimulator.)
1. Increased heart rate.

2. Increased force of contractions.
3. Increased myocardial oxygen consumption.
4. Decreased peripheral vascular resistance.
5. Bronchodilation.

Indications

Hemodynamically significant bradycardia and bradycardia due to heart block refractory to atropine.

Precautions

1. This drug increases O_2 requirement of the myocardium. It should not be used with AMI patients.
2. Use with extreme caution in presence of ventricular dysrhythmias — watch for development of new dysrhythmias.

How Supplied

Ampules of 1 ml (0.2 mg) and 5 ml (1 mg).

Administration

1. **Adult dosage: Given by IV drip only.** Mix **1 mg isoproterenol in 250 D_5W** with microdrip for **concentration of 4 mcg/ml.** Infuse at 2 to 20 mcg/minute, titrated to heart rate and blood pressure response.
2. **Pediatric dosage:** Start drip at **0.1 mcg/kg/mlinute;** usual effect at 0.1 to 1.0 mcg/kg/minute.

Side Effects

1. Ventricular dysrhythmias — slow or stop infusion.
2. Tachycardia.
3. Infarct extension: Secondary to increased oxygen consumption and decreased coronary artery perfusion if diastolic pressure drops.
4. Blood pressure may decrease due to vasodilation — monitor closely.
5. Sweating, flushing, headache, palpitations, dyspnea, angina.

LIDOCAINE HYDROCHLORIDE

Actions

1. Suppresses dysrhythmias of ectopic ventricular origin.

2. In ischemic tissue, thought to further depress conduction and interrupt re-entry pathways.
3. Does not significantly alter conduction or contractility on healthy tissue.
4. Elevates ventricular fibrillation threshold.
5. Little effect with normal dosages on atrial muscle.

Indications

1. PVCs, especially in the setting of myocardial ischemia when they are frequent, occur two or more in a row, multifocal, fall on the T-wave.
2. Ventricular tachycardia.
3. Refractory or recurrent ventricular fibrillation.
4. Prophylactic administration in the setting of acute MI.
5. Following successful defibrillation.

Precautions

1. Known allergy to ''caine'' medications (novacaine given at the dentist.
2. Use with caution with conduction system disorders and/or bradycardia. (Second- or third-degree heart block, sinus bradycardia, or sinus arrest.)
3. Reduce dosage to one-half in presence of reduced cardiac output (CHF, shock) or liver disease to prevent toxicity.

How Supplied

Ampules and prefilled syringes containing 100 mg in 5 ml for bolus injection.
Vials of 1 or 2 grams for infusion solution.

Administration

1. Administer **IV bolus slowly** by 50 mg/minute.
2. **Adult dosage** options: Initial bolus **1 mg/kg** followed by IV drip at 1 to 4 mg/minute; additional half-dosage boluses if ectopy continues; or, initial bolus of 75 mg and IV drip at 2 mg/minute; then if ectopy persists, additional 50 mg boluses every 5 minutes to total of 225 mg; drip increased 1 mg/minute with each bolus to maximum of 4 mg/minute.
3. For prophylaxis: Similar bolusing and drip.
4. **Pediatric dosage:** Bolus of 1 mg/kg of body weight to a maximum of 50 mg.
5. May be administered through ET tube.
6. **Bolus administration must precede a drip. The drip by itself takes 30 to 60 minutes to obtain desired effect.**

Side Effects

1. Hypotension.
2. Numbness, alter state of consciousness, drowsiness.
3. When given in high dosages, may cause seizures.

MANNITOL (Osmitrol)

Actions

1. Osmotic diuretic.
2. Draws fluid out of the cells and promotes excretion of fluid from the body.

Indications

1. Treatment of cerebral edema.
2. Promote diuresis in certain drug overdoses.

Precautions

1. Patient unable to urinate.
2. Pulmonary edema and congestive heart failure.
3. Pregnancy.
4. Intracranial bleeding.
5. Hypotension.

How Supplied

1. 5 to 10 percent solution in 1,000 ml.
2. 10 to 15 percent solution in 500 ml.

Administration

1. IV infusion over 20 minutes.
2. **1 gm/kg** (include pediatrics) using an administration set that has an **in-line filter.**
3. 500 ml 20 percent solution equals 100 grams (1 gm/5 ml).
4. Generally by physician order only.
5. Should have a Foley catheter inserted, particularly for long transport times.

Side Effects

1. May cause congestive heart failure in the borderline patient.
2. Headache and nausea in the conscious patient.

3. Documentation of patient status important.
4. Should be used when transport time is prolonged.

MEPERIDINE (Demerol)

Actions

1. Relief of moderate pain.
2. More rapid onset and shorter duration than morphine sulfate.
3. Less effective than morphine sulfate for AMI.

Indications

1. Relief of pain from: Traumatic injuries, orthopedic injuries, severe lacerations.
2. Burns.

Precautions

1. Hypersensitivity.
2. Head injury/increased intracranial pressure.
3. COPD and asthmatic patients.
4. If patient hypotensive.
5. Acute abdominal problems.

How Supplied

Prefilled syringe (Tubex) 2 ml containing 200 mgs (a solution of 100 mg/ml).

Administration

1. **Adult:** 500 to 100 mg IM; 30 to 50 mg slow IV push.
2. **Pediatric:** 1.0 to 1.8 mgs/kg body weight, IM to a **maximum** of 50 mg.
3. IM or SQ the preferred route. May be given IV.

Side Effects

1. Use cautiously in patients with atrial flutter or other supraventricular tachycardias.
2. May increase the risk of seizures in a patient who has a seizure disorder.
3. Respiratory depression (may be reversed with naloxone).

METARAMINOL (Aramine)

Actions

1. Its effects are in between epinephrine and norepinephrine.
2. Increases heart rate and force of contractions (beta effects).
3. Produces vasoconstriction (alpha effect).
4. Increases blood pressure.
5. Improves cerebral, coronary, and renal blood flow.

Indications

1. Cardiogenic shock.
2. Neurogenic shock.

Precautions

1. Head injury.
2. Hypertension.
3. Hypotension. This drug should not be used as a first line drug in treating hypotension due to hypovolemia. **Fluid replacement first.**

How Supplied

1 ml ampules and 10 ml vials in a concentration of 10 mg/ml.

Administration

(Given by drip only.)
Dilute 100 mgs. in 250 ml D_5W to yield a concentration of **4 mg/ml.** Start drip at about **0.2 mg/minute (0.5 ml/minute).** Titrate to patient's response a blood pressure of 90 systolic.

Side Effects

1. Tissue necrosis if infiltrates tissue surrounding IV.
2. Sweating.
3. Headache.
4. Dysrhythmias.

MORPHINE SULFATE

Actions

1. Potent narcotic analgesic.
2. Dilates peripheral vasculature (arterial and venous), causing reduction of preload and afterload, thus reducing cardiac workload and oxygen consumption.
3. Reduces pulmonary edema.
4. Reduces respiratory rate and tidal volume.
5. Constricts pupils.
6. Reduces anxiety/apprehension.

Indications

1. Acute pulmonary edema.
2. Acute myocardial infarction.
3. To reduce pain in selected situations.

Precautions

1. Hypotension.
2. COPD or asthma (may reduce drive to breathe).
3. Respiratory depression except that caused by pulmonary edema.
4. Head injury.
5. If other depressant drugs have been taken (including alcohol).

How Supplied

Prefilled syringe (Tubex) containing 10 to 15 mg.

Administration

(May be given IV or IM.)
1. Must be administered slowly (IV — 2 mg/minute).
2. **2 to 5 mg increments IV titrated to pain relief or desired hemodynamic effect.**
3. Monitor blood pressure closely before and after administration.
4. May be repeated every 5 to 30 minutes as needed.
5. **Do not exceed 15 mg in the field.**

Side Effects

1. Respiratory depression — be prepared to assist ventilations (reversed with naloxone).

2. Hypotension — most often in hypovolemic patient.
3. Nausea and vomiting.
4. Decreased level of consciousness.
5. Side effects reduced by administering small dosages and administering slowly.

NALOXONE (Narcan)

Actions

1. Is a narcotic antagonist which competitively binds to narcotic sites and exhibits almost no pharmacologic activity of its own.
2. Will reverse stupor, coma, respiratory depression when due to a narcotic overdose.
3. Duration of action is 1 to 4 hours.

Indications

1. Known narcotic overdose; coma, respiratory depression due to a narcotic overdose (Demerol, heroin, Dilaudid, Darvon, percodan, codeine, Lomotil, Talwin, morphine, and methadone).
2. Diagnostically in coma of unknown etiology if drugs are suspected (or to rule them out).
3. Possible role in the treatment of shock, spinal cord injury, and stroke.

Precautions

None.

How Supplied

Vials of 1 ml containing 0.4 mg and 1 ml containing 2.0 mg.

Administration

1. Adult: **0.8 mg SLOW IV push** (may be given IM or SQ). Watch for increased respirations. If no response, may be repeated at 2- to 3-minute intervals for 2 to 3 dosages.
2. Pediatric: **0.01 mg/kg.**

Side Effects

1. Rapid administration may cause vomiting and ventricular dysrhythmias.
2. May cause acute withdrawal with the narcotic-dependent patient.

3. Duration of naloxone is shorter than most narcotics. **Monitor patient closely.** Patients who have been roused may fall back into coma and/or respiratory depression.

NITROGLYCERINE

Actions

1. Relaxes smooth muscle, particularly vascular smooth muscle.
2. May increase coronary blood flow by coronary artery dilation.
3. Relieves coronary artery spasm.
4. May decrease left ventricular work and oxygen demand by dilation of peripheral vascular bed and reduction of preload and afterload.

Indications

1. To relieve pain of angina pectoris.
2. May be used for pulmonary edema due to left heart failure.

Precautions

1. Patients with early (recent) AMI.
2. Increased intracranial pressure.
3. Contraindicated in hypotension/shock.
4. Glaucoma.

How Supplied

In the field, generally 0.3 mg tablets (1/200th grain) or 0.4 mg tablets (1/150th grain).

Administration

(Given sublingually.)

1. **0.3 mg (grains 1/200) or 0.4 mg (grains 1/150) sublingually.**
2. May be repeated at 5-minute intervals up to 3 dosages.
3. Must be dissolved under tongue.
4. Best to have patient sitting or semi-reclined.

Side Effects

1. Transient throbbing headache.
2. Hypotension.

3. Dizziness, weakness.
4. Drug is unstable and deterioration hastened by exposure to air, light, and temperature extremes. Store in dark glass bottles and limit opening and closing.
5. Monitor blood pressure closely before and after administration.

NITROUS OXIDE (Nitronox)

(Combination of nitrous oxide and oxygen in a 50:50 ratio)

Actions

1. A reversible, easily used medication to reduce pain.
2. Produces CNS depression and decreases sensitivity to most pain.
3. Effects dissipate within 2 to 5 minutes after cessation of administration.

Indications

For pain of any etiology, including:
1. Myocardial infarction.
2. Burns.
3. Pain from other causes (kidney stone, fractures).

Precautions

1. Decreased or impaired level of consciousness.
2. Alcohol or drug intoxication.
3. Chest trauma.
4. Pulmonary edema.
5. Abdominal distention or trauma.
6. COPD.
7. Cyanosis with nitronox administration.
8. Inability to comply with instructions (senility, mental retardation).
9. Pregnancy.
10. Shock.

How Supplied

Comes in two compressed gas cylinders; one is 100 percent O_2 and the other is nitrous oxide joined together by a valve where they are combined at a 50:50 ratio.

Administration

1. **Must always be self-administered by the patient to prevent an overdose.**
2. Intermittently inhaled through a demand valve via mask or mouthpiece as needed for pain relief or until drowsiness occurs.
3. Patient must be given oxygen during intervals that nitronox is not being used.

Side Effects

1. Drowsiness (common).
2. Possible nausea and vomiting.
3. Lightheadedness.
4. Numbness, tingling.
5. The ventilation fan in the ambulance must be running during nitronox administration to avoid inhalation by the EMT-P; use of an exhalation scavenger also recommended.
6. Patients with myocardial pain should always be given oxygen by face mask during intervals that nitronox is not being used and at termination of administration.

NOREPINEPHRINE (Levophed)

Actions

(Primarily alpha and has beta properties):
1. Raises blood pressure promptly — more rapid response than other catecholamines.
2. Potent peripheral vasoconstriction.
3. Renal and mesenteric constriction.
4. Increased myocardial contractility (beta 1).

Indications

1. Hemodynamically significant hypotension due to cardiogenic shock, neurogenic shock, and possibly anaphylactic shock.
2. To support blood pressure after CPR.

Precautions

1. Not indicated in cases of hypovolemia or hypotension secondary to bradycardia — treat the bradycardia first.
2. Hypotension when fluid replacement is required first (norepinephrine is not a first line drug in this situation).

3. In patients with severe hypoxia or hypercarbia.
4. Use with extreme caution with AMI patients; norepinephrine increases myocardial O_2 requirements.

How Supplied

Ampules of 4 ml containing 4 mg (1 mg/ml).

Administration

(Blood pressure must be monitored closely while titrating drip):
1. **Adult dosage: Given by IV drip only.** Mix 4 mg Levophed in 250 ml D_5W with microdrip to make a solution of **16 mcg/ml. Initial dosage** of 2 to 3 ml/minute, adjusted to maintain blood pressure at 90 to 100 systolic.
2. **Pediatric dosage:** Start drip at 0.1 mcg/kg/minute.

Side Effects

1. Local tissue necrosis; check for IV patency before and during administration; IV infiltration causes tissue necrosis and sloughing. If infiltration occurs, dilute 5 to 10 mg of phentolamine in 10 to 15 ml of normal saline, then infiltrate into the area where the norepine-phrine extravasation took place.
2. With the therapeutic dosage, there are few side effects.
3. If the drip is inadvertently sped up, the following is possible: Nausea, vomiting, hypertension, dysrhythmias.
4. **Monitor drip rate carefully and often!**

OXYGEN

Actions

1. An odorless, tasteless, colorless gas necessary to sustain all cellular life and proper cellular metabolism.
2. Adding oxygen to inspired air raises the amount of oxygen in the blood and, therefore, the amount delivered to tissues.
3. Helps to reverse hypoxemia.

Indications

Any hypoxic patient or situation where it appears hypoxia might soon ensue, including:

1. Cardiac arrest.
2. Respiratory arrest.
3. Dyspnea.
4. Pain from myocardial ischemia/necrosis.
5. Congestive heart failure, pulmonary edema.
6. Shock (of any etiology).
7. Head injury, stroke.
8. Pulmonary edema.
9. Toxic inhalations.
10. Near-drowning.
11. Asthmatic attack.
12. Any patient in serious condition.

Precautions

None. In some cases of COPD, high concentrations of oxygen will reduce their respiratory drive. Carefully monitor these patients. This is **not** a reason to withhold oxygen from these patients. Be prepared to assist ventilations.

How Supplied

As a compressed gas stored in different size tanks.

Administration

(By inhalation):

1. May be administered by nasal cannula, simple face, partial or non-rebreathing face mask. The patient must have a patent airway and be breathing.
2. Various kinds of positive pressure ventilation devices may be used for the non-breathing patient.
3. In cardiac arrest and the critical patient, administer 100 percent O_2 as soon as possible.

Side Effects

1. There is no danger of oxygen toxicity from short-term administration in emergencies (under 24 hours in adults).
2. Non-humidified oxygen may be drying and irritating to mucous membranes.
3. Reassure patients who are anxious about face mask but are in need of high

concentrations of oxygen before reverting to lower flow nasal cannula.

OXYTOCIN (Pitocin)

Actions

1. Hormone that acts directly on uterine smooth muscle to produce contractions to reduce postpartum bleeding.
2. Stimulates the flow of milk from the mammary glands postpartum.
3. Onset within one minute.

Indications

1. To control postpartum uterine bleeding, especially if uterine massage ineffective or patient is hypotensive.
2. To be used only after delivery of the newborn. In a multiple birth situation, be sure that all babies are delivered before use of oxytocin.

Precautions

In a patient with cardiovascular disease.

How Supplied

Ampules and prefilled syringes containing 10 units in 1 ml.

Administration

(**Given as an infusion only**):
Inject 10 units of oxytocin into 1,000 ml bag of normal saline and titrate to physician orders or patient's response.

Side Effects

1. Generally none, if used correctly.
2. Possible side effects include nausea, vomiting, cardiac dysrhythmias, uterine rupture.

PROPRANOLOL (Inderal)

Actions

(Beta 1 and beta 2 blocker):

1. Decreased automaticity throughout the heart.
2. Decreased conductivity; decreases sinus rate; slows atrial conduction; delays conduction through the AV node.
3. Decreased ventricular contractility (decreased stroke volume).
4. Decreased cardiac work and oxygen consumption.
5. Causes bronchoconstriction.

Indications

1. Treatment (control) of supraventricular tachycardias and other supraventricular dysrhythmias.
2. Prevention of recurrent ventricular tachycardia.
3. Long-term management of angina pectoris.
4. Ventricular control in atrial fibrillation and flutter when digitalis cannot be used.
5. Management of hypertension long-term not acute.

Precautions

1. Cardiogenic shock, impaired cardiac function.
2. Sinus bradycardia greater than first-degree block.
3. Asthma and COPD.
4. Congestive heart failure.

How Supplied

Ampules of 1 ml containing 1 mg.

Administration

1. In the field, **1 mg injected IV over 5 minutes.** No response, second dosage of 0.5 mg slow IV push 5 to 10 minutes after first dosage.
2. May be used IV for refractory ventricular tachycardia and fibrillation not controlled by other antidysrhythmics, but generally not used prehospital.
3. Most frequently encountered as an oral medication taken by patient at home.

Side Effects

1. May precipitate acute heart failure.
2. Toxic levels may cause severe sinus bradycardia and various degrees of AV block.

RACEMIC EPINEPHRINE (Vaponephrin)

Actions

Racemic epinephrine is an epinephrine preparation in a 1:100 dilution for use by oral inhalation **only**. Effects are those of epinephrine. Inhalation causes local effects on the upper airway as well as sytemic effects from absorption. Vasoconstriction may reduce swelling in the upper airway, and beta effects on bronchial smooth muscle may relieve bronchospasm.

Indications

1. Life-threatening airway obstruction due to croup.
2. Asthma in patients under 40 (as alternate to SQ epinephrine).

Precautions

1. Mask and noise may be frightening to small children. Agitation will aggravate symptoms of respiratory obstruction. Try to enlist the support of parents and child for administration.
2. Try to differentiate croup from epiglottitis by history. **Do not** use a tongue blade to examine the back of the throat. The diagnosis is frequently difficult in the field, but a critical patient deserves a trial of racemic epinephrine. Although it is **specific therapy for croup,** it may also buy some time in patients with epiglottitis.
3. In the less-than-critical patient, saline alone via nebulizer may bring marked symptomatic relief from croup.
4. Racemic epinephrine is heat and light sensitive. It should be stored in a dark, cool place. Discoloration is an indication for discarding it.

How Supplied

0.5 fluid ounces 2 percent solution of racemic epinephrine.

Administration

1. 0.5 ml racemic epinephrine, diluted with 2 ml saline, via nebulizer driven by O_2 (5 to 8 l/minute) to create fine mist.
2. Nebulizer treatment may cause blanching of the skin in the mask area due to local epinephrine absorption. Reassure parents.
3. Clinical improvement in croup can be dramatic after administration of racemic epinephrine, and presentation in the emergency department may be markedly altered. Rebound worsening of airway obstruction can occur, however, in 2 to 4

hours. For this reason, many physicians admit any patient whom they treat with racemic epinephrine. **Field administration should be limited to those critically ill patients who are in danger of imminent respiratory arrest.**

4. If respiratory arrest occurs, it is usually due to patient fatigue or laryngeal spasm. Complete obstruction is not usually present; ventilate the patient, administer O_2 and transport rapidly. If you can ventilate and oxygenate the patient adequately, intubation is best left to a specialist in a controlled setting. Cricothyrotomy is a last resort.

Side Effects

Similar to epinephrine.

SODIUM BICARBONATE ($NaHCO_3$)

Actions

1. An alkalinizing agent used to neutralize excess acid (treatment of acidosis).
2. Increases response to epinephrine.

Indications

1. Cardiac arrest after the first 10 minutes, i.e., all first line therapeutic modalities used.
2. Treat acidosis of other causes: Poisonings (ethylene glycol, barbituate OD).
3. Treat hyperkalemia.

Precautions

1. Hypokalemia.
2. Congestive heart failure where the patient cannot tolerate salt loading.
3. Not indicated in cardiac arrest of less than 10-minute duration or respiratory arrest without cardiac arrest.

How Supplied

Prefilled syringes of 50 ml containing 1mEq/ml.

Administration

1. For cardiac arrest, adult dosage: **1 mEq/kg after the first 10 minutes of the arrest.**
2. Pediatric dosage: 1 to 2 mEq/kg after the first 10 minutes of the arrest.

3. In other cases, as physician ordered.
4. Good ventilation must occur along with administration of bicarbonate to correct acidosis.

Side Effects

1. Metabolic alkalosis.
2. Acute hypokalemia.
3. Carbon dioxide retention if patient not well ventilated.
4. Salt and water overload with high dosages.
5. Should not be allowed to mix or be given in too rapid succession with catecholamines (inactivates) or calcium (precipitates).
6. Overcorrection of pH (alkalosis) with too much bicarbonate more difficult to treat than acidosis.

SYRUP OF IPECAC

Actions

Induces vomiting in the hopes of emptying the stomach of ingested poisons or an overdose of drugs. This may only be effective if given within the first twenty to thirty minutes after ingestion.

Indications

To induce vomiting in poisonings and drug overdose.

Precautions

1. Acute MI.
2. Pregnancy.
3. Stupor, coma, or seizures.
4. Ingestion of corrosives (strong acids/alkalis) or petroleum products.
5. Strychnine or iodides.
6. Do not give charcoal after ipecac.

How Supplied

In 16-ounce bottle containing 70 mg/ml.

Administration

1. Give orally only.
2. Adults: 1 to 2 **tablespoons** (15 to 30 ml) followed by 2 to 3 glasses of water.
3. Pediatrics: 3 to 5 **teaspoons** (15 to 25 ml) followed by 1 to 2 glasses of warm water.
4. Walking should be encouraged.
5. Check with medical control prior to administration. Many systems are moving away from Ipecacing in the field.

Side Effects

The possibility of aspiration. **Protect** the patient.

THIAMINE

Actions

Replace this missing B-vitamin in the alcoholic patient prior to administration of D_5O. In alcoholics, this deficiency causes Wernicke's syndrome, an acute and reversible encephalopathy characterized by ataxia, eye muscle weakness, and mental derangements. More seriously is Korsakoff's psychosis, a memory disorder which may be irreversible once it becomes established. For this reason, treatment with thiamine is indicated if Wernicke's or Korsakoff's syndrome is recognized. Since thiamine is utilized in carbohydrate metabolism, the syndromes may be precipitated by the administration of dextrose to the alcoholic.

Indications

1. In alcoholics with the administration of dextrose.
2. In suspected Wernicke's or Korsakoff's syndrome.

Precautions

Possible allergic reactions.

How Supplied

Prefilled syringe 100 mg in 10 ml.

Administration

100 mg IV push (IM if necessary).

Side Effects

With correct dosage, none.

VERAPAMIL (Isoptin, Calan)

Actions

1. Inhibits slow-channel calcium activity in cardiac and vascular smooth muscle.
2. Reduces contractility and myocardial oxygen consumption.
3. Dilates coronary and peripheral blood vessels, reducing systemic vascular resistance.
4. Slows conduction and prolongs refractory period in AV node.

Indications

1. To treat supraventricular tachycardias.
2. To reduce ventricular rate in atrial fibrillation and flutter.
3. May be of use in cerebral ischemia.

Precautions

1. Patients with **AV block, sick sinus syndrome.**
2. Cardiac failure.
3. Hypotension not due to the dysrhythmia.
4. Patients taking beta-blockers.
5. Caution with digitalized patients.
6. Patients with known WPW with atrial fibrillation or flutter.

How Supplied

Ampules of 10 mg in 2 ml (5 mg/ml).

Administration

1. **Adult dosage:** 0.075 to 0.15 mg/kg; may be repeated in 30 minutes in 0.15 mg/kg dosage; 10 mg maximum single dosage.
2. **Pediatric dosage:** 0.1 to 0.2 mg/kg; total single dosage: 0.75 to 2.0 mg.
3. Administer over one minute.
4. Peak effect occurs within 3 to 5 minutes.

Side Effects

1. Hypotension.
2. Bradycardia.
3. AV block.
4. Cardiac arrest.

DIGITALIS (Digoxin, Lanoxin)

This is an important cardiac drug not used in the prehospital setting.

Actions

1. Increases force of ventricular contraction.
2. Slows impulse conduction through AV node.
3. Decreases ventricular response to certain supraventricular tachycardias; slows cardiac rate.
4. Increased cardiac output.

Indications

1. Treatment of congestive heart failure.
2. Treatment of rapid supraventricular dysrhythmias such as atrial fibrillation, atrial flutter, and paroxysmal supraventricular tachycardias.

Administration

1. Patients take daily oral dosage at home.
2. May be given IV, but the indications in the emergency care setting are limited due to the problems of digitalis toxicity.

Side Effects

1. Most adverse effects are a reflection of toxicity.
2. Anorexia, nausea, and vomiting; diarrhea.
3. Yellow vision, blurred vision.

A-2

Common Drugs Used at Home

This listing is not complete but gives some of the most common names of the medications used.

DIGITALIS MEDICATIONS

1. Increases the force of contractions.
2. Slows down conduction through the AV node.
3. Names: Lanoxin, Digitoxin, Digoxin.

NITROGLYCERIN MEDICATIONS

1. Vasodilator.
2. May decrease the workload of the heart.
3. Names: Isordil, Nitroglycerin, Nitrostat, Sorbitrate.

DIURETICS

1. Used to reduce fluid overload primarily found in CHF patients.

2. Names: Commonly called ''water pills'' by the patient, Aldactazide, Diruil, Dyazide, Hydrochlorothiazide, Lasix.

ANTIARRHYTHMIC MEDICATIONS

1. To control or prevent certain cardiac dysrhythmias.
2. Names: Dilantin; Inderal, Lanoxin, Pronestyl, Quinidine.

ANTIHYPERTENSIVE MEDICATIONS

1. To control, reduce, or prevent hypertension.
2. Names: Aldomet, Inderal, Lopressor, Minipress, Tenormin.

ANTIPSYCHOTIC MEDICATIONS

1. To control negative behaviors in the mentally ill or disturbed patient. To enable them to lead more normal lives.
2. Names: Haldol, Lithane, Mellaril, Stelazine, Thorazine, Trilafon.

ANTIDEPRESSANT MEDICATIONS

1. To reduce and alleviate depression.
2. Names: Adapin, Elavil, Sinequan, Tofranil, Triavil.

TRANQUILIZER MEDICATIONS

1. To relieve anxiety.
2. Names: Librax, Librium, Miltown, Valium, Vistaril.

ANTICONVULSANT MEDICATIONS

1. To control chronic seizures.
2. Names: Dilantin, Mesantoin, Nembutal, Phelantin, Tegretol.

A-3

Common Poisonous Plants

HOUSE PLANTS

Hyacinth Narcissus

Toxic Part: Bulbs.

Symptoms: Nausea, vomiting, diarrhea. May be fatal.

Oleander

Toxic Part: Leaves, branches.

Symptoms: Extremely poisonous. Produces severe digestive upset and has caused death.

Poinsettia

Toxic Part: Leaves.

Symptoms: Fata. One leaf can kill a child.

Dieffenbachia (Dumb Cane), Elephant Ear

Toxic Part: All parts.

Symptoms: Intense burning (Dumb Cane) and irritation of the mouth and tongue. Death can occur if base of the tongue swells enough to block the air passage of the throat.

Rosary Pea, Castor Bean

Toxic Part: Seeds.

Symptoms: Fatal. A single rosary pea seed has caused death. One or two castor bean seeds are near the lethal dose for adults if crushed or chewed.

Mistletoe

Toxic Part: Berries.

Symptoms: Fatal. Both children and adults have died from eating the berries.

FLOWER GARDEN PLANTS

Larkspur

Toxic Part: Young plant, seeds.

Symptoms: Digestive upset, seeds cause nervous excitement, depression. May be fatal.

Monkshood

Toxic Part: Fleshy roots.

Symptoms: Digestive upset and nervous excitement.

Autumn Crocus, Star of Bethlehem

Toxic Part: Bulbs.

Symptoms: Vomiting and nervous excitement.

Lily of the Valley

Toxic Part: Leaves, flowers.

Symptoms: Irregular heart beat and pulse, usually accompanied by digestive upset and mental condition.

Iris

Toxic Part: Underground stem.

Symptoms: Severe, but not usually serious; digestive upset.

Foxglove

Toxic Part: Leaves.

Symptoms: One of the sources of the drug digitalis, used to stimulate the heart. In large amounts, the active principles cause dangerously irregular heartbeat and pulse, usually digestive upset, and mental confusion. May be fatal.

Bleeding Heart (Dutchman's Breeches)

Toxic Part: Foliage.

Symptoms: May be poisonous to the heart in large amounts. Has proven fatal to catal.

VEGETABLE GARDEN PLANTS

Rhubarb

Toxic Part: Leaf blade.

Symptoms: Fatal. Large amounts of raw or cooked leaves can cause convulsions and coma, followed rapidly by death.

ORNAMENTAL PLANTS

Daphne

Toxic Part: Berries.

Symptoms: Fatal. A few berries can kill a child.

Wisteria

Toxic Part: Seeds, pods.

Symptoms: Mild to severe digestive upset. Many children are poisoned by this plant.

Golden Chain

Toxic Part: Bean-like capsules in which the seeds are suspended.

Symptoms: Severe poisoning. Excitement, staggering, convulsions, and coma. May be fatal.

Laurels, Rhododendron, Azaleas

Toxic Part: All parts.

Symptoms: Fatal. Produces nausea and vomiting, depression, difficult breathing, prostration, and coma.

Jessamine

Toxic Part: Berries.

Symptoms: Fatal. Digestive disturbance and nervous symptoms.

Lantana Camara (Red Sage)

Toxic Part: Green berries.

Symptoms: Fatal. Affects lungs, kidneys, heart, and nervous system. Grows in the southern United States and in moderate climates.

Yew

Toxic Part: Berries, foliage.

Symptoms: Fatal. Foliage more toxic than berries. Death is usually sudden without warning symptoms.

TREES AND SHRUBS

Wild and Cultivated Cherries

Toxic Part: Twigs, foliage.

Symptoms: Fatal. Contains a compound that releases cyanidc when eaten. Gasping, excitement, and prostration are common symptoms that often appear within minutes.

Oaks

Toxic Part: Foliage, acorns.

Symptoms: Affects kidneys gradually. Symptoms appear only after several days or weeks. Takes a large amount for poisoning. Children should not be allowed to chew on acorns.

Elderberry

Toxic Part: Shoots, leaves, bark.

Symptoms: Children have been poisoned by using pieces of the pithy stems for blowguns. Nausea and digestive upset.

Black Locust

Toxic Part: Bark, sprouts, foliage.

Symptoms: Children have suffered nausea, weakness, and depression after chewing the bark and seeds.

PLANTS IN WOODED AREAS

Jack-in-the-Pulpit

Toxic Part: All parts, especially roots.

Symptoms: Like dumb cane, pulpit contains small, needle-like crystals of calcium oxalate that cause intense irritation and burning of the mouth and tongue.

Moonseed

Toxic Part: Berries.

Symptoms: Blue, purple color, resembling wild grapes. Contains a single seed (true wild grapes contain several small seeds). May be fatal.

Mayapple

Toxic Part: Apple, foliage, roots.

Symptoms: Contains at least 16 active toxic principles, primarily in the roots. Children often eat the apple with no ill effects, but several apples may cause diarrhea.

PLANTS IN SWAMPY OR MOIST AREAS

Water Hemlock

Toxic Part: All parts.

Symptoms: Fatal. Violent and painful convulsions. A number of people have died from hemlock poisoning.

PLANTS IN FIELDS

Buttercups

Toxic Part: All parts.

Symptoms: Irritant juices may severely injure the digestive system.

Nightshade

Toxic Part: All parts, especially the unripe berry.

Symptoms: Fatal. Intense digestive disturbances and nervous symptoms.

Poison Hemlock

Toxic Part: All parts.

Symptoms: Fatal. Resembles a large wild carrot. Used in ancient Greece to kill condemned prisoners.

Jimson Weed (Thorn Apple)

Toxic Part: All parts.

Symptoms: Abnormal thirst, distorted sight, delirium, incoherence, and coma. Common cause of poisoning. Has proven fatal.

A-4

Pediatric Measurements

DRUG DOSAGES

Aminophylline: 5.0 mg/kg diluted with 50 to 100 cc D_5W over 15 minutes.

Atropine: .01 to .03 mg/kg IV slow push.

Benadryl: 2 mg/kg IV slowly.

Bicarb: 1 to 2 mEq/kg IV (see ACLS protocols). Dilute 1:1 D_5W or sterile water.

Decadron: .25 mg/kg IV.

Defibrillation: 2 to 4 watt sec/kg.

Dextrose: (50 percent) 0.5 to 1.0 gram/kg IV. Dilute 1:1 D_5W or sterile water.

Dopamine: 5 to 20 mg/kg/min IV infusion (6 mg x wt [kg] in 100 ml D_5W; 1 ml/hr = 1 mg/kg/min).

Epinephrine: 1:10,000, 0.1 cc/kg/dosage IV or down ETT.

Isuprel: 0.05 to 1.5 mg/kg/min IV infusion (0.6 mg x wt [kg] in 100 ml D_5W; 1 ml/hr = 0.1 mg/kg/min).

Morphine: 0.1-0.2 mg/kg IV or IM.

Narcan: 0.4 to 0.8 mg/dosage IV or IM — no maximum.

Valium: 0.2-0.3 mg/kg IV slowly.

Vaponephrine: 0.25-0.5 ml in 2.5 ml of sterile water or saline through nebulizer.

MAINTENANCE IV FLUID RATES

1st 10 kg: 100 cc/kg/24°
2nd 10 kg: 50 cc/kg/24°
20 kg: 20 cc/kg/24°

Example: Child weighing 22 kg:
10 kg at 100 cc/kg = 1,000 cc
10 kg at 50 cc/kg = 500 cc
2 kg at 20 cc/kg = 40 cc
Total: 1540 cc/24° = 64 cc/hr.

FLUIDS

(Shock): 20 cc/kg/dose IV LR or NS (repeated once if needed).

AVERAGE WEIGHT

AGE	WEIGHT	
	Kg.	Lbs.
Birth	3.4	7.4
3 months	5.7	12.5
6 months	7.4	16
1 year	10.0	22
2 years	12.4	27
3 years	14.5	31
4 years	16.5	36
5 years	19.0	41
6 years	21.5	47
7 years	24.1	53
8 years	26.8	59
9 years	29.4	65

10 years	32.3	71
11 years	35.5	78
12 years	39.0	86

AVERAGE SYSTOLIC BLOOD PRESSURE

AGE (years)	BOYS	GIRLS
2	96	96
4	96	96
6	96-98	96
8	104	104
10	110	110
12	115	115
14	120	118
16	124	120

AVERAGE PULSE RATES

AGE	PULSE	
	GIRLS	BOYS
Newborn	125	125
1 to 11 months	120	120
2 years	110	110
4 years	100	100
6 years	100	100
8 years	90	90
10 years	90	90
12 years	90	85
14 years	85	80
16 years	80	75
18 years	75	70

AVERAGE RESPIRATORY RATES

AGE (Years)	RATE (awake)
½ - 1	64
1 - 2	35
2 - 4	31
4 - 6	26
6 - 8	23
8 - 10	21
10 - 12	21
12 - 14	22

BLOOD PRESSURE

2 (age in years) + 80 = Systole.

⅔ Systole = Diastole.

INTUBATION TUBE SIZE

Age	Weight (Kg)	ET-Tube (mm)
Newborn	1	2.5 mm
Newborn	2-3	3.0 mm
1 month	4	3.5 mm
6 months	7	3.5 mm
1 year	10	4.0 mm
2-3 years	12-14	4.5 mm
4-5 years	16-18	6.0 mm
6-8 years	20-26	6.5 mm
10-12 years	32-42	7.0 mm
greater than 14 years	greater than 50	7.5-8.5 mm

A-5

Common Communicable Diseases with Mode of Transmission

DIPHTHERIA

Entry into Body

Through mouth to throat or nose to throat.

How Pathogen Exits Body

1. Sputum and discharges from nose and throat.
2. Skin lesions.

Ways Pathogen Transmitted

1. Direct contact.
2. Droplet infection from patient coughing.
3. Hands of nurse.
4. Articles used by and about patient.

Period of Incubation

Two to five days.

GONOCOCCAL DISEASE

Entry into Body

1. Directly onto mucous membrane.
2. Through breaks in membrane.

How Pathogen Exits Body

1. Lesions.
2. Discharges from infected mucous membranes.

Ways Pathogen Transmitted

1. Direct contact as in sexual intercourse.
2. Towels, bathtubs, toilets, etc.
3. Hands of infected persons soiled with their own discharges.
4. Hands of attendant.

Period of Incubation

Three to six days.

HEPATITIS, Infectious viral or serum

Entry into Body

1. Oral route.
2. By innoculation when viral-contaminated equipment such as needles and syringes is used.

How Pathogen Exits Body

Extreta from intestinal tract or from blood or serum.

Ways Pathogen Transmitted

1. Direct contact with feces of patient.

2. Direct contact with equipment contaminated by blood from the patient.

Period of Incubation

1. Type A: Fifteen to forty-five days.
2. Type B: Forty to 180 days.
3. Type Non-A, Non-B: Fifteen to 160 days.

INFLUENZA

Entry into Body

Through mouth and nose to lungs.

How Pathogen Exits Body

Sputum and discharges from nose and throat.

Ways Pathogen Transmitted

1. Direct contact.
2. Hands of nurse.
3. Articles used by and about patient.

Period of Incubation

Dependent on infecting organism.

MEASLES (Rubella)

Entry into Body

Through mouth and nose.

How Pathogen Exits Body

1. Discharges from nose and throat.
2. Skin lesions.

Ways Pathogen Transmitted

1. Direct contact.

2. Hands of nurse.
3. Articles used by and about patient.

Period of Incubation

Eight to thirteen days.

MENINGITIS, MENINGOCOCCAL

Entry into Body

Mouth and nose.

How Pathogen Exits Body

Discharges from nose and throat.

Ways Pathogen Transmitted

1. Direct contact.
2. Hands of nurse or attendant.
3. Articles used by and about patient.
4. Flies.

Period of Incubation

Dependent on infecting organism.

MUMPS

Entry into Body

Mouth and nose.

How Pathogen Exits Body

Discharges from infected glands and mouth.

Ways Pathogen Transmitted

Direct contact with persons afflicted.

Period of Incubation

Twelve to twenty-six days.

PNEUMONIA

Entry into Body

Through mouth and nose to lungs.

How Pathogen Exits Body

1. Sputum.
2. Discharge from nose and throat.

Ways Pathogen Transmitted

1. Direct contact.
2. Hands of nurse.
3. Articles used by and about patient.

Period of Incubation

Dependent on infecting organism.

POLIOMYELITIS

Entry into Body

Through mouth and nose.

How Pathogen Exits Body

1. Discharges from nose and throat.
2. Via feces.

Ways Pathogen Transmitted

1. Direct contact.
2. Hands of nurse or attendant.
3. Rarely in milk.

Period of Incubation

Five to thirty-five days.

RUBEOLA

Entry into Body

Through mouth and nose.

How Pathogen Exits Body

Secretions from nose and throat.

Ways Pathogen Transmitted

1. Droplet spread from nose or throat by direct contact with nasal or throat secretions.
2. Airborne spread is possible.

Period of Incubation

Sixteen to eighteen days.

SMALLPOX

Entry into Body

Thought to be through mucous membrane of respiratory tract.

How Pathogen Exits Body

1. Discharges from nose and throat.
2. Skin lesions.

Ways Pathogen Transmitted

1. Direct contact.
2. Hands of nurse.
3. Articles used by and about patient.

Period of Incubation

Eight to seventeen days.

STREPTOCOCCAL SORE THROAT

Entry into Body

Mouth and nose.

How Pathogen Exits Body

1. Discharges from nose and throat.
2. Skin lesions.

Ways Pathogen Transmitted

1. Direct contact.
2. Hands of nurse or attendant.
3. Articles used by and about patient.

Period of Incubation

One to five days.

SYPHILIS

Entry into Body

1. Directly into blood and tissues through breaks in skin or membrane.
2. Contaminated needles and syringes.

TETANUS

Entry into Body

Directly into bloodstream through wounds (organism is an anaerobe and prefers deep, incised wound).

How Pathogen Exits Body

Excreta from infected herbivorous animals and man.

Ways Pathogen Transmitted

1. Soil, especially that with manure or feces in it.

2. Dust, etc.
3. Articles used about stables.

Period of Incubation

Three to four weeks, mild; two days, severe.

TUBERCULOSIS, HUMAN

Entry into Body

1. Through mouth to lungs and intestines.
2. From intestines via lymph channels to lymph vessels and to tissues.

How Pathogen Exits Body

1. Sputum.
2. Lesions.
3. Feces.

Ways Pathogen Transmitted

1. Direct contact, such as kissing.
2. Droplet infection from person coughing with mouth uncovered.
3. Sputum from mouth to fingers, thence to food and other things.
4. Soiled dressings.

Period of Incubation

Four to eight weeks.

TYPHOID FEVER

Entry into Body

Through mouth in infected food or water and thence to intestinal tract.

How Pathogen Exits Body

Through feces and urine.

Ways Pathogen Transmitted

1. Direct contact.
2. Hands of nurse or attendant.
3. Linen and all articles used by and about patient.
4. Hands of carriers soiled by their own feces.
5. Water polluted by excreta.
6. Food grown in or washed with such water.
7. Milk diluted with contaminated water.
8. Flies.

Period of Incubation

Seven to twenty-one days.

WHOOPING COUGH

Entry into Body

Mouth and nose.

How Pathogen Exits Body

Discharges from respiratory tract.

Ways Pathogen Transmitted

Direct contact with person affected.

Period of Incubation

Seven days.

A-6

Universal Precautions from the Centers for Disease Control

Since medical history and examination cannot reliably identify all patients infected with HIV or other blood-borne pathogens, blood and body-fluid precausions should be consistently used for *all* patients. This approach, referred to as "universal blood and body-fluid precautions" or "universal precautions," should be used in the care of *all* patients, *especially* including those in *emergency care settings* in which the risk of blood exposure is increased and the infection status of the patient is usually unknown.

1. All health-care workers should routinely use appropriate barrier precautions to prevent skin and mucous membrane exposure when contact with blood or other body fluids of any patient is anticipated. Gloves should be worn for touching blood and body fluids, mucous membranes, or non-intact skin of all patients, for handling items or surfaces soiled with blood or body fluids, and for performing venipuncture and other vascular access procedures. Gloves should be changed after contact with each patient. Masks and protective eyewear or face shields

should be worn during procedures that are likely to generate droplets of blood or other body fluids to prevent exposure of mucous membranes of the mouth, nose, and eyes. Gowns or aprons should be worn during procedures that are likely to generate splashes of blood or other body fluids.

2. Hands and other skin surfaces should be washed immediately and thoroughly if contaminated with blood or other body fluids. Hands should be washed immediately after gloves are removed.

3. All health-care workers should take precautions to prevent injuries caused by needles, scalpels, and other sharp instruments or devices during procedures; when cleaning used instruments; during disposal of used needles; and when handling sharp instruments after procedures. To prevent needlestick injuries, needles should not be recapped, purposely bent or broken by hand, removed from disposable syringes, or otherwise manipulated by hand. After they are used, disposable syringes and needles, scalpel blades, and other sharp items should be placed in puncture-resistant containers for disposal; the puncture-resistant containers should be located as close as practical to the use area. Large-bore resuable needles should be placed in a puncture-resistant container for transport to the reprocessing area.

4. Although saliva has not been implicated in HIV transmission, to minimize the need for emergency mouth-to-mouth resuscitation, mouthpieces, resuscitation bags, or other ventilation devices should be available for use in areas in which the need for resuscitation is predictable.

5. Health-care workers who have exudative lesions or weeping dermatitis should refrain from all direct patient care and from handling patient-care equipment until the condition resolves.

6. Pregnant health-care workers are not known to be at greater risk of contracting HIV infection than health-care workers who are not pregnant; however, if a health-care worker develops HIV infection during pregnancy, the infant is at risk of infection resulting from perinatal transmission. Because of this risk, pregnant health-care workers should be especially familiar with and strictly adhere to precautions to minimize the risk of HIV transmission.

Implementation of universal blood and body-fluid precautions for *all* patients eliminates the need fo ruse of the isolation category of ''Blood and Body Fluid Precautions'' previously recommended by the Centers for Disease Control for patients known or suspected to be infected with blood-borne pathogens. Isolation precautions (e.g., enteric, "AFB") should be used as necessary if associated conditions, such as infectious diarrhea or tuberculosis, are diagnosed or suspected.

PRECAUTIONS FOR INVASIVE PROCEDURES

An invasive procedure is defined as surgical entry into tissues, cavities, or organs or repair of major traumatic injuries (1) in an operating or delivery room, emergency department, or outpatient setting, including both physicians' and dentists' offices; (2) cardiac catheterization and angiographic procedures; (3) a vaginal or cesarean delivery or other invasive obstetric procedure during which bleeding may occur; or (4) the manipulation, cutting, or removal of any oral or perioral tissues, including tooth structure, during which bleeding occurs or the potential for bleeding exists. The universal blood and body-fluid precautions listed above, combined with the precautions listed below, should be the minimum precautions for *all* such invasive procedures.

1. All health-care workers who participate in invasive procedures must routinely use appropriate barrier precautions to prevent skin and mucous membrane contact with blood and other body fluids of all patients. Gloves and surgical masks must be worn for all invasive procedures. Protective eyewear or face shields should be worn for procedures that commonly result in the generation of droplets, splashing of blood or other body fluids, or the generation of bone chips. Gowns or aprons made of materials that provide an effective barrier should be worn during invasive procedures that are likely to result in the splashing of blood or body fluids. All health-care workers who perform or assist in vaginal or cesarean deliveries should wear gloves and gowns when handling the placenta or the infant until blood and amniotic fluid have been removed from the infant's skin and should wear gloves during post-delivery care of the umbilical cord.

2. If a glove is torn or a needlestick or other injury occurs, the glove should be removed and a new glove used as promptly as patient safety permits; the needle or instrument involved in the incident should also be removed form the sterile field.

MANAGEMENT OF EXPOSURES

If a health-care worker has a parenteral (e.g., needlestick or cut) or mucous membrane (e.g., splash to the eye or mouth) exposure to blood or other body fluids or has a cutaneous exposure involving large amounts of blood or prolonged contact with blood — especially when the exposed skin is chapped, abraded, or afflicted with dermatitis — the source patient should be informed of the incident and tested for serologic evidence of HIV infection after consent is obtained. Policies should be developed for testing source patients in situations in which consent cannot be obtained (e.g., an unconscious patient).

If the source patient has AIDS, is positive for HIV antibody, or refuses the test, the health-care worker should be counseled regardiffng the risk of infection and evaluated clinically and serologically for evidence of HIV infection as soon as possible after the exposure. The health-care worker should be advised to report and seek medical evaluation for any acute febrile illness that occurs within 12 weeks after the exposure. such an illness — particularly one characterized by fever, rash, or lymphadenopathy — may be indicative of recent HIV infection. Seronegative health-care workers should be retested 6 weeks post-exposure and on a periodic basis thereafter (e.g., 12 weeks and 6 months after exposure) to determine whether transmission has occurred. During this follow-up period — especially the first 6 to 12 weeks after exposure, when most infected persons are expected to seroconvert — exposed health-care workers shoudl follow U.S. Public Health Service (PHS) recommendations for preventing transmission of HIV.

No further follow-up of a health-care worker exposed to infection as described above is necessary if the source patient is seronegative unless the source patient is at high risk of HIV infection. In the latter case, a subsequent specimen (e.g., 12 weeks following exposure) may be obtained from the health-care worker for antibody testing. If the source patient cannot be identified, decisions regarding appropriate follow-up should be individualized. Serologic testing should be available to all health-care workers who are concerned that they may have been infected with HIV.

If a patient has a parenteral or mucous membrane exposure to blood or other body fluid of a health-care worker, the patient should be informed of the incident, and the same procedure outlined above for management of exposures should be followed for both the source health-care worker and the exposed patient.

A-7

Intraosseous Infusion

Intraosseous infusion means to introduce a liquid substance within the bone. In specific medical or trauma cases when normal IV routes cannot be established in the pediatric patient under five years of age (follow local protocol for age limits), an infusion may be started directly into the bone.

Serious study of intraosseous infusions was initiated in 1915. Yet, as far back as the late 1860s there was literature documenting the study of this type of infusion. The 1940s and 1950s saw regular use of intraosseous infusions. By the late 1950s and early 1960s, this technique fell into disuse.

Again, in the early 1980s, interest in the use of intraosseous infusion was renewed. Presently, the use of this procedure continues to grow, with many advanced life-support prehospital agencies and emergency departments routinely inserting them in the pediatric patient as needed.

The following is a recommended procedure guideline for intraosseous infusions:

INTRODUCTION

1. Venous access in children can be extremely difficult. Central lines run a high risk for pneumothorax (i.e., from internal jugular, subclavian) and septic hip (i.e., from femoral). Intraosseous infusion provides quick and reliable access to the venous circulation. Infused substances pass from the marrow cavity into sinusoids, to large medullary venous channels, to nutrient and emissary veins,

and finally into the systemic venous circulation.
2. Fluids which can be infused intraosseously include normal saline, D_5W, Ringer's lactate, plasma, and blood. Up to 200 cc per minute of crystalloid can be given with manual pressure.
3. ACLS drugs which can be infused intraosseously include epinephrine, atropine sulfate, sodium bicarbonate, lidocaine HCl, dopamine HCl, and dobutamine. Injecting bretylium tosylate into the bone marrow has not been reported. However, only sodium bicarbonate has been scientifically studied intraosseously.
4. Anticonvulsant drugs which can be infused intraosseously include Diazepam, Dilantin, and Phenobarbital. Phenobarbital has not been scientifically studied intraosseously.

INDICATIONS

Intraosseous infusion is only indicated when all of the following criteria are met:

1. The patient is less than five years of age.
2. There is confirmed existence of shock or cardia arrest (including SIDS).
3. Two peripheral IV attempts have been unsuccessful.
4. The patient is comatose.

TECHNIQUE

1. Confirm approval from the base station physician prior to establishing an intraosseous infusion, except in cardiac arrest situations.
2. The site preferences for intraosseous infusions are:
   - First choice — the tibia; one finger breadth below the tibial tuberosity on the anteromedial surface.
   - Second choice — the femur; two finger breadths above the patella.
3. Clean the skin with Povodine iodine.
4. Place an 18-gauge or larger spinal needle or a bone marrow needle either perpendicular to the bone or forty-five degrees from the nearest growth plate.
5. Hold the needle shaft with the left hand and apply firm downward pressure on the needle; entrance into the bone marrow is heralded by a sudden loss of resistance.
6. Visible aspiration of marrow contents (i.e., dark blood) will confirm proper needle placement, although it may not always be appreciated. Easy flow of IV solution alone does not confirm correct placement (i.e., needle only in the perios-

teum, needle completely through bone, etc.). The best indicator of proper placement is the absence of tissue swelling around the site during fluid infusion.

7. If properly placed, the needle needs no securing; it will be solidly lodged in the bone. The IV tubing should be taped. Only a dressing is needed at the needle site.
8. Only one intraosseous attempt is permissible on each bone (i.e., 2 tibias plus 2 femurs equals 4 attempts, maximum) since successful placement on the second try in the same bone will result in all fluids or drugs draining out the first hole instead of into the venous circulation.

COMPLICATIONS AND SPECIAL CONSIDERATIONS

The complications of intraosseous infusion include:

1. Compartment syndrome.
2. Bone fracture.
3. Osteomyelitis (5 percent incidence) occurs in septic patients, use of intraossoeus lines beyond twenty-four hours, and infusion of hypertonic solutions (i.e., sodium bicarbonate).
4. Needle broken off in the bone (one reported case; needle left in bone without subsequent complications).
5. Growth plate and marrow damage from intraosseous infusions are largely unstudied.

Taken from *Prehospital Care Protocol Manual*, City and County of Denver Department of Health and Hospitals, EMS/Paramedic Division, November 1987.

Glossary

a-, an-, ano-: Prefix meaning without.

abandonment: A termination of a paramedic-patient relationship by the paramedic without consent of the patient and without care to the patient by qualified medical providers.

abdominal: Pertaining to the abdomen.

abduct: To draw away from the midline.

abduction: The act of abducting; the state of being abducted.

abortion: The premature expulsion of the products of conception from the uterus; miscarriage.
- **incomplete:** The expulsion of part of the fetus, or of other parts of the products of conception, from the uterus before term.
- **missed:** Retention of the contents of the uterus after the fetus dies.
- **spontaneous:** An abortion occurring naturally.
- **therapeutic:** An induced abortion, usually accomplished by qualified medical personnel under ideal conditions; the purpose is usually to preserve the life of the mother.
- **threatened:** The appearance of signs and symptoms of possible loss of the fetus; characterized by bleeding and cramps.

abrasion: An injury consisting of the loss of a partial thickness of skin from rubbing or scraping on a hard, rough surface; also called a brush burn, friction burn.

abruptio placentae: A premature separation of a normally implanted placenta from the uterine wall usually occurring during the third trimester of pregnancy and accompanied by pain and bleeding.

abscess: A localized collection of pus in any part of the body; formed by disintegration of tissues and accumulation of white blood cells.

absolute refractory period: The period during which the cardiac muscle fiber depolarization process when no stimulus can cause the fiber to depolarize again; occurs during the QRS interval to the beginning of the T wave.

accelerated nodal rhythm: The name given for a heart rhythm that is stimulated by the AV node, but is faster than the nodal intrinsic rate of 40 to 60 beats per minute.

acetabulum: The cup-shaped cavity on the external surface of the innominate bone in which the rounded head of the femur fits.

acetone: A chemical compound found normally in small amounts in the urine; diabetic patients are said to produce a "fruity odor" when larger amounts are produced in blood and urine.

acetylcholine: A reversible acetic acid ester of choline; found in the synapses of the autonomic system, especially at the end plates of the parasympathetic system; parasympathomimetic agent; medication for patients with myasthenia gravis.

acid: Sour; a substance that forms hydrogen ions in solution and from which hydrogen may be displaced by a metal when a salt is formed.

acidosis: An abnormal state of the body in which the pH falls below 7.35; excessive amounts of carbon dioxide (respiratory acidosis) and lactic acid and organic acids (metabolic acidosis) produce the acidotic state.

acromioclavicular joint: The point of the shoulder; the junction (union) between clavicle and scapula plus the supporting ligaments.

acromion: The lateral, triangular, bony projection of the scapular spine forming the point of the shoulder with the lateral part of the clavicle.

activated charcoal: Powdered charcoal that has been treated to increase its powers of absorption; used in a slurry to absorb ingested poison.

acute: Having rapid onset, severe symptoms, and a relatively short duration.

acute abdomen: A serious intra-abdominal condition causing irritation or inflammation of the peritoneum, attended by pain, tenderness, and muscular rigidity (board-like abdomen).

acute myocardial infarction: The acute phase of a heart attack, wherein a spasm or blockage of a coronary artery produces a spectrum of signs and symptoms, commonly including chest pain, nausea, diaphoresis, anxiety, pallor, lassitude.

Adam's apple: The projection on the anterior surface of the neck, formed by the thyroid cartilage of the larynx.

addiction: The state of being

strongly dependent upon some agent; drugs, tobacco, for example.

adduct: To move toward the center of the body, particularly a limb or head.

adipose: Fatty tissue.

adjunct: An accessory or auxiliary agent or measure; an oropharyngeal airway is an airway management adjunct.

adrenal gland: The small gland on the superior aspect of the kidney; produces corticosteroids, catecholamines, and other hormones.

Adrenalin: The proprietary name for epinephrine.

adrenergic: Activated by, characteristic of, or secreting epinephrine or other substances with similar activities (catecholaminic).

advanced life support: Basic life support plus invasive techniques leading to definitive therapy to save the patient's life.

afferent: Bearing or conducting inward.

affinity: Attraction.

afterbirth: The placenta and membranes expelled after the birth of a child.

agglutination: Clumping together of blood cells.

agonal: Pertaining to death or dying.

air: The gaseous mixture which composes the Earth's atmosphere; composed of approximately 21 percent oxygen, 79 percent nitrogen, plus trace gases.

air embolism: The presence of air bubbles in the heart or blood vessels, causing an obstruction.

air hunger: A term for labored breathing.,

air passage: Any of several tubes that normally transmit air into the lungs.

air splint: A double-walled plastic tube that immobilizes a limb when sufficient air is blown into the space between the walls of the tube, to cause it to become almost rigid.

airway: An air passage.
artificial airway: A device used to assure free passage of air through the nose, mouth, and pharynx into the trachea.
lower airway: The air passage from the larynx to the pulmonary alveoli.
upper airway: The air passage from the nose and mouth to the larynx.

albumin: A protein substance found in human tissues as well as in other animals and in plants.

alcohol: A transparent, colorless, volatile fluid produced by fermentation of carbohydrates with yeast.

alcoholic: Pertaining to or containing alcohol; also a person who becomes habituated, dependent, or addicted to alcoholic consumption.

alimentary tract: The digestive tube from the mouth to the anus.

alkali: Any compound of electropositive element (usually a metal such as sodium) in combination with an electronegative hydroxyl ion or similar ion.

alkaline: Having a pH greater than 7.0; in human physiology, having a pH greater than 7.35.

alkalosis: An abnormal state of the body in which the pH rises above 7.45; loss of too much carbon dioxide by hyperventilation (respiratory alkalosis) or too much acid by vomiting or by an overdose of alkalizing agents (metabolic alkalosis).

allergen: A substance capable of inducing an allergy or specific hypersensitivity.

allergic reaction: A local or general reaction to an allergen, usually characterized by hives or tissue swelling or dyspnea.

allergy: Hypersensitivity to a substance, causing an abnormal reaction.

alpha particle: A positively charged nuclear particle consisting of two neutrons and two protons; ejected from the nucleus of a radioactive atom.

alpha receptor: A center that reacts only to those compounds called alpha adrenergic, or alpha blockers.

alpha stimulator: A substance that activates the alpha receptors; also alpha adrenergic.

alveolus: A cavity; specifically, the socket holding a tooth; or a terminal air sac of the lung.

amenorrhea: Absence of the menstrual flow.

AMI: Abbreviation for acute myocardial infarction.

amino acid: An organic acid in which one of the hydrogen atoms has been replaced by a molecular amine group; the chief component of protein.

aminophylline: A drug of the theophylline family, helpful in the treatment of asthma, chronic obstructive pulmonary disease, and pulmonary edema.

amnesia: Loss or impairment of

memory.

amniotic fluid: The fluid surrounding the fetus in the uterus, contained in the amniotic sac.

amniotic sac: A thick, transparent sac that holds the fetus suspended in the amniotic fluid.

amobarbital: A drug of the barbiturate class, with hypnotic/sedative action; a controlled substance drug.

amphetamine: A class of drugs that produces potent central nervous system stimulation; an "upper."

amplitude: The height of an EKG wave or complex, measured in millimeters; also, volume of the audio portion of the radio transmission.

ampule: A sealed glass container for medication.

amputation: Complete removal of an appendage.

anaerobic: Life without oxygen.

anaerobic metabolism: Metalism without air, caused by a lack of gas exchange at the cellular level; product of cardiac arrest mechanism, where no oxygen reaches the cells.

anal canal: The terminal portion of the alimentary canal extending from the rectum to the anus.

analgesic: A pain-relieving drug; a class of drugs used to reduce pain.

anaphylaxis: An exaggerated allergic reaction, usually caused by foreign proteins.

anasarca: A severe, generalized edema.

anastomosis: A joining together of blood or lymph vessels by an anatomical, natural arrangement or by accessory channels around a joint, whereby if a chief arterial supply is interrupted, a constant blood flow will be achieved; also a surgical joining of two hollow organs, or of part of the same organ, or between blood vessels.

anatomic position: The presumed body position when referring to anatomical landmarks; upright, facing the observer, with hands and arms at sides, thumbs pointing away from the body, legs and feet pointing straight ahead.

anatomy: The structure of the body, or the study of body structure.

anemia: The condition in which the blood is deficient in hemoglobin, red blood cells, or in total volume.

anesthesia: A partial or complete loss of sensation with or without loss of consciousness; can result from drug administration or from injury or disease.

aneurysm: A permanent blood-filled dilation of a blood vessel resulting from disease or injury of the blood vessel wall.

angina pectoris: A spasmodic pain in the chest, characterized by a sensation of severe constriction or pressure on the anterior chest; associated with insufficient blood supply to the heart; aggravated by exercise or tension and relieved by rest or medication.

stable angina: A condition characterized by a recurrent pain in the chest with predictable and similar patterns.

unstable angina: A condition characterized by a changing pattern of pain in the chest more easily precipitated, more frequent, greater in intensity, longer in duration, or less responsive to rest or nitrate therapy than the pain previously experienced by the patient; can occur during rest and often precedes an acute myocardial infarction; preinfarctional angina.

Angiocath: The Deseret trade name for an intravenous cannula with a Teflon catheter over the metallic needle; has become a generic name for such a device.

angiogram: A radiographic depiction of blood vessels through the use of an injected contrast medium.

angioneurotic edema: A condition characterized by a sudden appearance of temporary edematous areas of the skin and mucous membranes, often associated with hives, and may be an allergic reaction involving the larynx, face, and other areas of the body; may be a manifestation of anaphylaxis.

angulation: The formation of an angle; an abnormal angle in an extremity or organ.

anion: An element that in electrolysis passes to the positive pole; an ion that has a negative charge.

anisocoria: A condition in which two ocular pupils are not equal in size.

anorexia: A lack of appetite for food.

anorexia nervosa: A serious nervous condition in which the patient loses his/her appetite and systematically refuses to take adequate nutrition.

anoxia: Without oxygen; a reductin of oxygen in body tissues below required physiology levels.

antagonism: An opposite or contrary action, such as that between muscles or medications.

antagonist: Opponent; commonly used as description of a drug that directly counteracts another drug; naloxone is an opiate antagonist.

ante-: A prefix meaning before in time or place.

antecubital: In front of the elbow.

antenatal: Before birth.

antepartum: Before delivery.

anterior: Situated in front of, or in the forward part of; in anatomy, used in reference to the ventral or belly surface of the body.

anti-: A prefix that shows a negative or reversal of the word root placed after it.

antiarrhythmic drug: A class of drugs that prevent or terminate cardiac arrhythmias.

antibiotic: A chemical compound produced by and obtained from certain living cells, especially lower plant cells, which is antagonistic to some other form of life, especially pathogenic or noxious organisms.

antibody: A substance produced in the body in response to an antigen that destroys or inactivates the antigen.

anticholinergic: An agent that blocks passage of impulses through the parasympathetic nerve; parasympatholytic.

anticoagulant: A class of drugs that prevents clotting of blood.

anticonvulsant: A class of drugs that prevents or terminates convulsions.

antidote: A substance to counteract or combat the effect of poison.

antiemetic: A remedy used to control nausea and vomiting.

antigen: A substance that causes the formation of antibodies.

antihistamine: A substance capable of counteracting the pharmacologic effects of histamine by a mechanism other than the production of exactly opposite effects.

antihypertensive: A class of drugs that is used to lower blood pressure.

antipyretic: A class of drugs that reduces fever.

antiseptic: Any preparation that prevents the growth of bacteria.

antiserum: A serum that contains antibodies against a specific disease-producing organism, such as rabies antiserum.

antivenin: An antiserum containing antibodies against reptile or insect venom.

anus: The outlet of the rectum lying in the fold between the buttocks.

anxiety: A feeling of apprehension, uncertainty, and fear.

aorta: The largest artery in the body, originates at the left ventricle and terminates at the bifurcation of the iliac arteries.

aortic arch: The portion of the aorta as it leaves the aortic sinus and begins its posterior descent through the chest.

aortic sinus: The small swelling of the aorta just above the aortic valve; point of origin of the coronary arteries.

aortic valve: The valve at the outlet of the left ventricle into the aorta; prevents blood return to the heart from the aorta.

apathy: Lack of emotion or feeling; indifference.

apex of the heart: In normal adults, the pointed end of the ventricle located at the midclavicular line in the fifth intercostal space.

apex of the lung: The upper part of the lung, lying above the clavicle.

APGAR score: A method developed by Dr. Virginia Apgar for assessing the newborn infant at 1 minute of age by designating a score of 0, 1, or 2 for the following: A = appearance; P = pulse rate; G = grimace; A = activity; and R = respiration.

aphasia: Loss of power of expression or comprehension of speech, writing, or signs, due to injury or disease.

motor aphasia: An inability to coordinate muscles controlling speech.

sensory aphasia: Inability to understand spoken, written, or tactile speech symbols, due to disease of appropriate centers.

aphonia: Loss of voice.

apical: Pertaining to an apex.

apnea: Absence of respiration.

aponeurosis: A flat, fibrous sheet of connective tissue that serves to connect a muscle with the part that it moves.

apoplexy: Stroke, cerebrovascular accident, caused by blockage or rupture of an artery.

apothecary system: System of weights and measures using pounds and ounces, yards and inches, gallons and pints.

appendicitis: Inflammation of the vermiform appendix.

appendix: Vermiform appendix, a wormlike diverticulum, or pouch from the cecum.

aqueous humor: Fluid circulating in the anterior and posterior chambers of the eye.

arachnoid: Resembling a spider's web; the membrane interposed between the dura mater and pia mater; one of the meninges.

arrest: Sudden cessation or stoppage.

arrhythmia: Any disturbance in the rhythm of the heart.

arterial blood: Oxygenated blood.

arteriole: A small artery that at its distal end leads into a capillary.

arteriosclerosis: A generic name for several conditions that cause the walls of the arteries to become thickened, hard, and inelastic.

artery: A blood vessel consisting of three layers of tissue and smooth muscle that carries blood away from the heart.

arthritis: Inflammatory disease of the joints.

articulation: Joining of bones, a joint; touching of one part with another.

artifact: That which is artificial, out of place, introduced by human interference.

artificial ventilation: Movement of air into and out of the lungs by artificial means.

ascending aorta: That portion of the aorta beyond the aortic sinus and before its arch posteriorly.

ascites: An excessive accumulation of fluid in the abdominal cavity.

asphyxia: Suffocation.

aspirate: To inhale foreign material into the lungs; to remove fluid or foreign material from the lungs or elsewhere by mechanical suction.

aspirin: Salicylic acid acetate; a drug known for its analgesic, fever reducing, and antirheumatic properties.

asthma: A condition marked by recurrent attacks of dyspnea with wheezing due to spasmodic constriction of the bronchi, often as a response to allergens, or by mucous plugs in the bronchioles.

asymptomatic: Without symptoms.

asystole: Having no contraction of the heart's ventricles.

ataxia: Failure of muscular coordination; often used to describe a staggering gait.

atelectasis: Collapse of the pulmonary alveoli.

atherosclerosis: A common form of arteriosclerosis caused by fat deposits in arterial walls.

atlas: The first cervical vertebra.

atrial: Pertaining to one of the atria of the heart.

atrial arrhythmias: Disturbances of the heart's rhythm caused by malfunction of the sinoatrial node or ectopic focal activity in atrial tissue.

atrial depolarization: The electrical discharging of resting atrial muscles, produces the P wave of the EKG and produces atrial contraction.

atrial fibrillation: An arrhythmia characterized by discharge of the individual atrial muscle fibers, producing no distinct P wave, and a grossly irregular ventricular rhythm having no pattern; the QRS is narrow, within .12 second.

atrial flutter: An arrhythmia characterized by a persistent stimulus arising from a focus of atrial origin, or a circus movement within the atrium, producing atrial contractions 100 to 400 times per minute; ventricular response is regulated by the degree of refractory block in the AV node.

atrial repolarization: The electrical process of recharging the depolarized atrial muscle following contraction; represented on EKG by the atrial T wave, usually not seen because of the overwhelming electrical activity of the concurrent ventricular depolarization.

atrial systole: The period of atrial contraction that occurs before ventricular contraction.

atrioventricular block: A condition in which the passage of stimuli from the atrium through the AV node is hindered or prevented.

atrioventricular node: A cluster of specialized cells that retard the passage of the atrial stimulus toward the ventricles, allowing the atria to complete their contraction; located near the junction of the atrial septum with the ventricular septum, next to the septal leaflet of the tricuspid valve.

atrium: A thin-walled chamber of the heart; the right atrium receives venous blood from the venae cavae; the left atrium receives oxygenated blood from the pulmonary veins.

atropine: A drug of the parasympathetic blocker class; used to increase the heart rate in sinus bradycardia or in AV blocks by reducing the block.

auditory nerve: The eighth cranial nerve, mediates hearing and balance.

aura: A premonitory sensation of impending illness, usually used in connection with an epileptic attack.

auricle: The external ear; also

atrium.

auscultation: The technique of listening for and interpreting sounds that occur within the body, usually done with a stethoscope.

automatic reaction: An action performed without conscious thought.

automaticity: The ability of pacemaker sites within the cardiac conduction fibers to initiate stimuli spontaneously.

autonomic nervous system: Part of the nervous system concerned with the regulation of bodily functions not controlled by conscious thought; composed of the sympathetic and parasympathetic systems.

autotransfusion: A transfusion effected by redirecting the patient's own blood from one part of the body to another.

AV: Abbreviation for atrioventricular.

avulsion: An injury that leaves a piece of skin or other tissue either partially or completely torn away from the body.

axilla: The armpit.

axillary temperature: A measured body temperature obtained by placing a thermometer in the axilla while holding the arm close to the body for a period of ten minutes.

axis: The second cervical vertebra; a line around which a revolving body turns or about which a structure would turn if it did revolve.

Babinski reflex: A reflex response of movement of the big toe; positive reflex is determined when, on stroking the sole, the toe turns upward; negative is determined by a downward or no movement of the toe.

bag of waters: The amniotic sac and its contained amniotic fluid.

bag-valve-mask: A portable artificial ventilation unit consisting of a face mask, one-way valve, and an inflatable bag; producing positive pressure ventilation.

balanced salt solution: A solution of water and salts formulated to match the composition of normal blood; sodium, potassium, and calcium should be in correct proportion as that of blood.

ball-and-socket joint: A joint wherein the distal bone has a rounded head (ball) that fits into the proximal bone's cuplike socket; the hip and shoulder joints, for example.

band: A term applied to a group of radio wave frequencies.

bandage: A material used to hold a dressing in place.

barbiturates: A class of drugs that produces a calming, sedative effect.

basal cell: The early keratocyte; a cell present in the basal layer of the epidermis.

basal skull fracture: A fracture involving the base of the cranium.

base: Alkaline: a compound that dissociates with formation of a hydroxyl ion; a solution having a pH greater than 7.0.

basic life support: Maintenance of the ABCs (airway, breathing, and circulation) without adjunctive equipment.

bile ducts: Any of the ducts that convey bile between the liver and the intestines, including hepatic, cystic, and common bile ducts.

biliary system: A ductal system consisting of the gallbladder and the bile dicts connecting the liver to the intestine.

bilious: Characterized by bile, or excess of bile; an archaic term for a syndrome of nausea, anorexia, vomiting, and lethargy, usually remedied by a "dose of salts."

biological death: A condition present when irreversible brain damage has occurred usually from 3 to 10 minutes after cardiac arrest.

biomedical telemetry: The transmission of biological data from a living subject to a monitoring point by means of radio or wire circuits.

biopsy: The removal of a small piece of tissue for microscopic examination.

birth canal: Uteral cervix and vagina.

bivalent: Having two like charges.

bladder: A membranous sac; commonly referring to the muscular membranous sac that stores urine.

blanch: To become white or pale.

bleb: A large flaccid blister, at least 1 centimeter in diameter.

blister: A collection of fluid under or within the epidermis.

blocker: A drug that counteracts or inhibits the action of another drug or agent; atropine as a parasympathetic blocker.

blood: The fluid that circulates through the heart, arteries, capillaries, and veins, carrying nutriment and oxygen to the body cells, removing waste products such as carbon dioxide and various metabolic products for excretion.

blood clot: A soft, coherent, jellylike mass resulting from the conversion of fibrinogen to fibrin, thereby entrapping the red blood cells and other formed elements within the fibrinic web.

Battle's sign: A contusion on the mastoid process of either ear; sign of a basilar skull fracture.

Benadryl: Trade name for diphenhydramine hydrochloride, an antihistamine.

bends: Pain in the limbs and abdomen occurring as a result of bubbles of nitrogen in the blood; caused by too rapid decompression; caisson disease, decompression sickness.

benign: Not dangerous; noncancerous; nonmalignant.

beta particle: An electron, either positively charged (positron) or negatively charged (negatron), that is emitted during beta decay of a radionuclide.

beta receptor: A nerve center that reacts only to those compounds with molecules to fit the receptor cells; beta adrenergic receptors.

beta stimulator: Any agent that activates the beta receptors of the body; isoproterenol, for example; beta adrenergic compounds.

bevel: The slanting edges of the point of a needle.

Benzadrine: Brand name for amphetamine sulfate, a central nervous system stimulant.

bicarbonate: Any salt having two parts carbonic acid to one of any basic substance; often used as an abbreviated form of sodium bicarbonate; also bicarb.

biceps: The large muscle of the front part of the arm that bends the forearm at the elbow; also, one of the hamstring muscles located on the back of the thigh that flexes and rotates the knee.

bifurcation: A division into two branches; the point of such division.

bigeminy: A pattern of cardiac arrhythmias wherein there are two beats, one normal and one premature, commonly means ventricular bigeminy, one normal beat and one ventricular premature contraction.

bile: A fluid secreted by the liver that is concentrated and stored in the gallbladder and then discharged into the intestine where it aids in digestion of fats.

blood pressure: The pressure exerted by the pulsatile flow of blood against the arterial walls.
  diastolic: The blood pressure measured during ventricular diastole.
  systolic: The blood pressure measured during ventricular systole.

blood type: One of the several groups into which human blood is divided according to its antigens.

blood volume: The total amount of blood in the heart and blood vessels; represents 8 to 9 percent of body weight in kilograms.

blood volumne expander: The synthetic solution administered intravenously to expand blood volume in the treatment of shock.

bloody show: The mucous and bloody discharge signaling beginning of labor.

bolus: A single, large, loading dose of a drug that provides an initial high therapeutic level in the blood.

bone: The hard form of connective tissue that constitutes most of the skeleton in a majority of vertebrates.

bone suture: The type of fibrous joint in which the close bony surfaces are so closely united by a very thin film of connective tissue that no movement can occur.

bowel: See intestine.

BP: Abbreviation for blood pressure.

brachial artery: The artery of the arm that is the continuation of the axillary artery, that in turn branches at the elbow into the radial and ulnar arteries.

bradycardia: An abnormally slow heart rate, usually any rate less than 60 beats per minute.

brain: A soft, large mass of nerve tissue that is contained within the cranium.

brain contusion: See cerebral contusion.

brain stem: The stemlike portion of the brain that connects the brain with the spinal cord; includes the pons, medulla, and mesencephalon.

breech birth (breech delivery): The delivery during which the presenting part of the fetus is the buttocks or foot instead of the head.

bronchial asthma: The common form of asthma.

bronchiole: Any of the smaller bronchi leading into the alveoli of the lung.

bronchiolitis: A condition seen in children under 2 years of age characterized by dyspnea and wheezing, a viral infection often confused with asthma.

bronchitis: Inflammation of the bronchi.

bronchoconstriction: A narrowing of the bronchial tubes.

bronchodilation: A widening of the bronchial tubes.

bronchodilator: An agent that causes the dilation of the bronchi and bronchioles.

bronchospasm: A severe constriction of the bronchial tree.

bronchus: One of the two main branches of the trachea that lead to the right and left lungs; any of the larger air passages of the lungs.

bruise: An injury that does not break the skin but causes rupture of small underlying blood vessels with resulting tissue discoloration; a contusion.

buccal: Pertaining to the cheek or mouth.

buffer: A substance in a fluid that tends to minimize changes in pH that would otherwise result from adding an acid or base to the fluid; the system of the body that corrects most acid-base imbalances, consists of the carbonate system, which eliminates hydrogen from carbonic acid, converting into bicarbonate anions.

bundle branch block: A disturbance in the conduction of the excitation stimulus through the right or left bundle branch from the AV bundle, or Bundle of His.

Bundle of His: The atrioventricular bundle; that portion of the Purkinje system leading out of the atrioventricular node and into the septum of the ventricles.

burn: An injury caused by heat, electrical current, and chemicals of extreme acidity or alkalinity.

burn center: A medical facility especially designed, equipped, and staffed to treat severely burned patients.

buttock: The prominence formed by the gluteal muscles on the posterior of both sides of the body.

c: Abbreviation for *cum*; with.

caisson disease: See bends.

calcium: A mineral substance necessary for life functioning; plays a vital role in heart contraction, nerve conduction, and muscle contractions; cation with double valence.

calcium chloride: $CaCl_2$; used to restore electrolyte balance; used in severe cardiac dysfunction as a positive inotropic agent.

cancer: A malignant tumor; commonly any form of malignancy, including leukemia.

cannula: A tube, often fitted with a trocar, used to enter a duct or cavity.

capillary: Any one of the small blood vessels that connect arteriole and venule, and through whose walls various substances pass into and out of the interstitial tissues, and thence on to the cells.

capsule: A cylindrical gelatin container enclosing a dose of medication, usually in powdered form.

carbohydrate: A compound represented by the sugars, starches, and celluloses; contains carbon, hydrogen, and oxygen.

carbon dioxide: CO_2; a colorless and odorless gas that neither supports combustion nor burns; a waste product of aerobic metabolism; in combination with water, forms carbonic acid.

carbon monoxide: CO; a colorless, odorless, and dangerous gas formed by the incomplete combustion of carbon; it combines four times as quickly with hemoglobin than oxygen; when in the presence of heme, replaces oxygen and reduces oxygen uptake in the lungs.

cardiac: Pertaining to the heart.

cardiac arrest: The sudden cessation of cardiac function with no pulse, no blood pressure, unresponsiveness.

cardiac asthma: A condition characterized by left heart failure and pulmonary edema with wheezing respirations; not related to bronchial asthma.

cardiac compression: A technique of external heart massage to restore the pumping action of the heart.

cardiac cycle: The interval from the beginning of one heartbeat to the succeeding beat; each cardiac cycle includes ventricular contraction (systole) and relaxation (diastole).

cardiac output: The amount of blood pumped out by the heart per minute, computed by the following equation: Cardiac output = stroke volume times heart rate.

cardiac standstill: The absence of cardiac contraction or electrical activity.

cardiac tamponade: A condition resulting from excess fluid accumulation in the pericardium.

cardiogenic: Of cardiac origin.

cardiogenic shock: The inability of the heart to pump adequate amounts of blood to perfuse the vital organs.

cardiopulmonary arrest: The cessation of cardiac and respiratory activity.

cardiopulmonary resuscitation (CPR): Application of artificial ventilation and external cardiac compression in patients with cardiac arrest to provide an adequate circulation to suppport life.

cardiotonic drugs: A class of drugs that improves and strengthens myocardial contraction.

cardiovascular: Pertaining to the heart and blood vessels.

cardiovascular collapse: Failure of the heart and blood vessels; shock.

cardioversion: An application of synchronized direct current shock to the chest wall to convert ineffective arrhythmias to an effective rhythm.

carina: The point where the trachea bifurcates into the right and left mainstem bronchi.

carotid artery: The principal artery of the neck, palpated easily on either side of the thyroid cartilage.

carotid sinus: A dilated area in the internal carotid artery, usually found just superior to the bifurcation of the common carotid artery; contains baroreceptors and chemoreceptors.

carotid sinus massage: The application of fingertip pressure to the carotid sinus to convert various supraventricular tachyarrhythmias to a more effective rhythm; pressure causes parasympathetic stimulation to the heart, causing it to slow, or to stop, in some instances.

carpals: The eight small bones of the wrist.

carpopedal spasm: A muscular spasm of the hands and feet.

cartilage: A tough, elastic, connective tissue that covers opposite surfaces of movable joints and also forms parts of the skeleton, such as ear and nose.

cartilaginous: Relating to or consisting of cartilage.

cataract: The partial or complete opacity of the crystalline lens of the eye or its capsule.

catecholamine: A biologically active amine, such as epinephrine, norepinephrine and dopamine, which exerts a strong sympathetic action on the heart and peripheral blood vessels, thereby increasing cardiac output and blood pressure.

catheter: A tube used for withdrawing or infusing fluids into various structures of the body.

catheter embolism: The loss of a catheter fragment in a vein from shearing of an indwelling IV catheter.

cation: A positively charged ion, such as sodium.

caudad: Toward the tail.

caustic: Corrosive, destructive to living tissue.

cavity: A hollow or space, especially a space within the body or one of its organs.

abdominal cavity: The space bounded by the abdominal walls, the diaphragm, and the pelvis; contains most of the organs of digestion.

cecum: The pouchlike portion of the large intestine just inferior to the junction of the ileum and ascending colon; the vermiform appendix is attached on the inferior surface.

cell: A small cavity or compartment.

Celsius scale: See centigrade scale.

centigrade scale: The temperature scale in which the freezing point of water is zero degrees and the boiling point at sea level is 100 degrees; Celsius scale.

ment of the metric system, one one-hundredth of a meter; approximately two-fifths of an inch.

central nervous system: The portion of the nervous system consisting of the brain and spinal cord.

central neurogenic hyperventilation: An abnormal pattern of ventilation seen in severe illness or injury involving the brain; characterized by marked tachypnea and hyperpnea.

central venous pressure: The pressure of the blood in veins that aids in the return of blood to the heart; the pressure is much less than that of the blood in arteries; controlled by the blood volume and capacity of the veins.

cephalic: Pertaining to the head.

cephalic delivery: A delivery in which the head is the presenting part of the fetus; generally considered to be the normal mode of birth.

cerebellum: That portion of the brain behind and below the cerebrum; coordination is the general function.

cerebral: Pertaining to the brain.

cerebral contusion: A bruise of the brain, causing a characteristic symptomatic response.

cerebral hemorrhage: Bleeding into the cerebrum; one form of stroke or cerebrovascular accident.

cerebrospinal fluid: The fluid contained in the four ventricles of the brain and the subarachnoid space around the brain and spinal cord.

cerebrovascular accident (CVA): The sudden cessation of circulation to a region of the brain, due to thrombus, embolism, or hemorrhage; also, a stroke or apo-

centimeter: A unit of measure-plexy.

cerebrum: The portion of the brain controlling major functions of the body, including movement, sensation, thinking, and emotions.

cervical: Pertaining to the neck.

cervical collar: A device used to immobilize and support the neck.

cervical spine: The superior seven bones of the vertebral column, located in the neck.

cervix: The lower portion, or neck, of the uterus.

cesarean section: The delivery of a fetus by means of an incision into the uterus, usually through the abdominal wall.

cheek: The side of the face forming the lateral wall of the mouth.

cheekbone: The quadrilateral bone that forms the prominence of the cheek; the zygomatic or malar bone.

chemotherapy: The treatment of disease by drugs; particularly the treatment of malignancy by drugs.

Cheyne-Stokes respiration: An abnormal breathing pattern characterized by rhythmic increase and decrease in depth of ventilations, with regularly recurring periods of apnea; seen in association with central nervous system dysfunction.

CHF: Abbreviation for congestive heart failure.

chief complaint: The problem for which a patient seeks help, stated in a word or short phrase.

chills: A sensation of cold, with convulsive shaking of the body.

cholesterol: A fatty substance found in animal tissue, egg yolks, and in various oils and fats; thought to contribute to arteriosclerosis.

cholinergic: Pertaining to the type of chemical activity that is characteristic of acetylcholine.

chordae tendineae: Tendons that attach to the free edges of the leaflets of the mitral and tricuspid valves and to the papillary muscles.

chronic: Of long duration, or recurring over a period of time.

chronic obstructive pulmonary disease (COPD): A term comprising chronic bronchitis, emphysema, and asthma; an illness that causes obstructive problems in the airways.

chronotropic: Affecting the time or rate; applied especially to drugs whose administration affects the contraction rate of the heart.

circulatory: Pertaining to the heart and blood vessels.

circulatory collapse: The failure of the cardiac and peripheral circulation.

circulatory system: The body system consisting of the heart and blood vessels.

cirrhosis: Chronic progressive fibrosis of the liver, often associated with heavy alcohol ingestion.

clammy: Damp and usually cool.

clavicle: The collarbone; attached to the uppermost part of the sternum at a right angle, and joins the scapular spine to form the point of the shoulder.

clinical: Pertaining to the patient.

clinical death: A term that refers to the lack of signs of life, when there is no pulse and no blood pressure; occurs immediately after the onset of cardiac arrest.

clonic: Pertaining to a spasm in which rigidity and relaxation succeed each other.

closed fracture: A fracture in which there is no laceration in the overlying skin.

clot: A semisolid mass of fibrin and cells.

clubbing: Proliferation of soft tissue about the terminal phalanges of fingers and toes, without osseous change.

CNS: Abbreviation for central nervous system.

coagulation: The process of changing a liquid into a thickened or solid state; the formation of a clot.

cocaine: A crystalline alkaloid obtained from *Erythoxylon coca* (coca leaves) used as a topical anesthetic, but now used more often as a central nervous system stimulant; often abused.

coccyx: The lowest part of the backbone; composed of three to five small, fused vertebrae; also called the tailbone.

coffee grounds vomitus: A vomitus having the appearance and consistency of coffee grounds; indicates slow bleeding in the stomach and represents the vomiting of partially digested blood.

coke: Street name for cocaine; also colloquial for Coca-Cola, a popular soda drink, nonalcoholic and nonaddictive.

colic: Acute abdominal pain characterized by intermittent cramps; common in infants and young children; also, pertaining to the colon.

Colles' fracture: A fracture at the distal end of the radius; can be accompanied by a fracture of a small fragment of the ulnar styloid process.

colloid: An intravenous solution containing protein.

colostomy: The creation of an opening between the colon and the surface of the body to provide bowel drainage.

coma: A state of unconsciousness from which the patient cannot be aroused even by powerful stimulation.

comatose: In a state of coma.

comminuted fracture: A fracture in which the bone ends are broken into many fragments.

common bile duct: The duct formed by the union of the common hepatic ducts and the cystic duct; empties into the duodenum.

communicable disease: A disease that is transmissible from one person to another.

compensatory pause: The longer than normal R-R interval occurring after a premature ventricular contraction; caused by the failure of the ventricle to contract after the atrial contraction which occurred during the PVC.

complete heart block: A third-degree AV block; the stimulus that stimulates the atrial contraction does not cause the ventricles to contract because the AV node will not allow the stimulus to pass through; ectopic focus causes ventricular contraction.

compliance: The quality of yielding to pressure or force without disruption, or an expression of the measure of ability to do so; the ability of the lung to distend with air as it is forced into the airways.

compound fracture: An open fracture; a fracture in which there is an open wound of the skin and soft tissues leading down to the location of the fracture.

compress: A folded cloth or pad used for applying pressure to stop hemorrhage or as a wet dressing.

concave: Rounded and somewhat depressed or hollowed out.

concussion: A violent jar or shock; the central nervous system injury results from the impact.

conductivity: The ability of muscle, including cardiac muscle, to conduct a stimulus from one muscle fiber to another.

conductor: Any substance capable of transmitting a stimulus.

condyle: Rounded projection on a bone, may be covered by cartilage at the joining with another bone.

confrontation: The technique of mentioning to patients significant points in their conversation or behavior of which they may not have been aware; used in interviews with emotionally disturbed patients.

congenital: Referring to any condition that is present at birth.

congestive heart failure: Excessive fluid in the lungs or tissues caused by the failure of the ventricles to effectively pump blood.

conjunctiva: The delicate membrane that lines the eyelids and covers the exposed surface of the eyeball.

connective tissue: The tissue that binds together and supports the various structures of the body.

conscious: Capable of responding to sensory stimuli and having subjective experiences.

consent: An agreement by patients to accept treatment offered as explained by medical personnel.

implied consent: An assumed consent given by an unconscious adult when emergency lifesaving treatment is required.
informed consent: A consent given for treatment by a mentally competent adult who understands what the treatment will involve; can also be given by parent or guardian of a child, as defined by the state, or for a mentally incompetent adult.

constrict: To be made smaller by drawing together or squeezing.

constricting band: A band used to restrict the lymphatic flow of blood back to the heart.

contagious disease: An infectious disease transmissible by direct or indirect contact; now synonymous with communicable disease.

contaminated: A term used in reference to a wound or other surface that has been infected with bacteria; may also refer to polluted water, food, or drugs.

contraction: A shortening of muscle fiber.

contractility: The ability of any muscle fiber to contract when it is depolarized by a stimulus.

contraindication: Not indicated; a situation that prohibits the use of a drug or technique.

contralateral: On the opposite side.

contusion: A bruise; an injury that causes a hemorrhage in or beneath the skin but does not break the skin.

convection: The conveyance of heat in liquid or gaseous form by movement of heated particles (as when the warm air of a room ascends to the ceiling); the loss of body heat to the atmosphere when air passes over the body.

conversion hysteria: A condition in which psychic energy from a repressed idea is converted into physical symptoms.

convex: Rounded and somewhat elevated.

convulsion: A violent involuntary contraction or series of contractions of the voluntary muscles; a fit or seizure.

COPD: Abbreviation for chronic obstructive pulmonary disease.

core temperature: A body temperature measured centrally, from within the esophagus or rectum.

cornea: The transparent structure covering the pupil.

cornified: Converted into tough tissue; keratinized; used to describe the outermost layer of skin.

coronary: A term applied to the cardiac blood vessels that supply blood to the walls of the heart.

coronary artery: One of the two arteries arising from the aortic sinus to supply the heart muscle with blood.

coronary artery disease: A progressive narrowing and eventual obstruction of the coronary arteries by the atherosclerotic process.

coronary bypass: The surgical procedure whereby a graft of part of the external saphenous vein is used to pass by a blocked coronary artery.

coronary occlusion: An obstruction in the coronary artery that hinders the flow of blood to some part of the heart; may be caused by narrowing of the vessel by atheromatous plaque or by a clot or by spasm of the vessel itself.

coronary thrombosis: The blockage of a coronary artery by a clot.

corticosteroid: A class of drugs, similar to the naturally occurring steroid hormones, sometimes used to counteract inflammation.

costal: Pertaining to the ribs.

costochondral: Pertaining to a rib and its cartilaginous portion attached to the sternum.

costovertebral angle: The angle formed by the spinal column and the 12th ribs; the general anatomic location of the kidneys.

countershock: The application of direct current to the patient in order to counteract some dysrhythmia of the heart.

CPR: Abbreviation for cardiopulmonary resuscitation.

cramp: A painful spasm, usually of a muscle; a gripping pain in the abdominal area; colic.

craniad: Toward the head.

cranial nerves: The 12 pair of nerves connected directly with the brain.

cranium: Skull.

cravat: A special type of bandage made from a large triangular piece of cloth and folded to form a band; used as a temporary dressing for a fracture or wound.

crepitus: A grating sound heard and the sensation felt when the fractured ends of a bone rub together.

crib death: See sudden infant death syndrome.

cricoid cartilage: The thick ring-shaped cartilage inferior to the thyroid cartilage of the larynx.

cricothyroid membrane: The fibrous tissue between the superior thyroid cartilage and the inferior cricoid cartilage.

cricothyrotomy: An incision into the lower airway through the cricothyroid membrane.

cricothyrotome: A surgical instrument used to make an opening into the trachea through the cricothyroid membrane.

crisis: A critical turning point or juncture; applied to both medical and psychiatric problems.

croup: A common viral disease of children; characterized by spasm of the larynx and resulting upper airway obstruction.

crowning: The stage of birth when the presenting part of the baby is visible at the vaginal orifice.

crystalloid: A substance capable of crystallization that, in solution, may be diffused through animal membranes; does not contain protein molecules.

CSF: Abbreviation for cerebrospinal fluid.

cumulative action: Action of increased intensity evidenced after several portions of the drug are taken.

cutaneous: Pertaining to the skin.

CVA: Abbreviation for cerebrovascular accident.

cyanosis: A blueness of the skin due to insufficient oxygen in the blood.

cyclic: Occurring periodically.

cystic: Pertaining to cysts; also to the urinary bladder.

D_5W: Abbreviation for dextrose 5 % in water; a solution of 50 grams in 1,000 milliliters of water.

$D_{50}W$: Abbreviation for a solution of dextrose 50% in water; 500 grams in 1,000 milliliters water.

Darvon: A trade name for propoxyphene, a narcotic.

decerebrate posture: A posture assumed by a patient with severe brain dysfunction; characterized by extension and internal rotation of the arms and extension of the legs.

decimal: A system of expressing fractions based on the number 10.

decompensation: Failure of the heart to maintain sufficient circulation of the blood.

decompression: Removal of compression or pressure.

decompression chamber: A chamber of compressed air into which a person may be introduced to treat decompression sickness by recompressing the person and gradually lowering the pressure in the chamber to match the local atmosphere; also, hyperbaric chamber.

decompression sickness: Bends; a condition caused by nitrogen bubbles that have returned to a gaseous state becoming lodged in blood or body tissues; characterized by pain in joints and chest, itching of skin, pulmonary edema.

decontaminate: Remove foreign substance that could cause harm; frequently used to describe removal of radioactive material from person, clothing, or area.

decorticate posture: The posture assumed by patients with a lesion at the brainstem level or above; characterized by tightly flexed arms, clenched fists, and slightly extended legs.

defibrillation: Removal of fibrillation; applying unsynchronized direct current electrical shock to terminate fibrillation.

defibrillator: Any agent or measure that causes fibrillation to cease.

definitive care: Care given that will actually reverse, or act as a medium to reverse, a pathologic condition.

dehydration: Loss of water and electrolytes; excessive loss of body water.

delirium: A mental disturbance characterized by illusions, hallucinations, excitement, physical restlessness, having a short duration.

delirium tremens: DT's, a form of insanity, often temporary, caused by alcohol poisoning; characterized by sweating, tremor, great excitement, precordial pain, anxiety, and mental distress; occurs usually following heavy alcohol intake.

delusion: A belief or feeling that has no basis in fact; seen in several types of mental illness.

demand pacer: An implanted or temporary electronic pacer that stimulates the heart only if the normal heart stimulus is absent.

demand valve unit: An intermittent, positive pressure breathing unit used to assist or control ventilation; with a manual control, it is acceptable emergency equipment.

Demerol: A trade name for meperidine hydrochloride, a synthetic narcotic.

dementia: Progressive mental deterioration due to organic disease of the brain.

denial: The psychic defense mechanism of dealing with unwanted information or feelings by ignoring their existence.

dependency: The condition of requiring help or support from another.

depolarization: The first step in activating a muscle or nerve cell; the membrane changes polarity from an exterior positivity to negativity, caused by influx of sodium and calcium ions into the cell, expelling potassium; contraction or conduction, or both, occurs as a result of the change.

depolarization wave: A stimulus causing depolarization.

depressant: An agent that lowers functional activity; a sedative.

depressed fracture: A skull fracture with impaction, depression, or a sinking in of the fragments.

depression: A mental state characterized by feelings of dejection, psychomotor retardation, insomnia, or weight loss, often of delusional proportion.

derm-: Prefix meaning having to do with skin.

dermis: The inner layer of skin; contains the skin appendages, hair follicles, sweat glands, nerves, and blood vessels.

dextran: A water-soluble polysaccharide used as a synthetic plasma volume expander in infusions.

dextrose: A preparation obtained by the hydrolysis of starch; used as an intravenous nutrient; a sugar.

diabetes: A general term referring to disorders characterized by excessive urine excretion, excessive thirst, and excessive hunger.

diabetes mellitus: A systemic disease marked by lack of production of insulin, which causes an inability to metabolize carbohydrates, resulting in an increase in blood sugar.

diabetic coma: Loss of consciousness due to severe diabetes mellitus which has not been treated or to treatment which has not been adequately regulated.

diagnosis: The determination of the nature of a pathological condition.

diagnostic signs: The indications of a patient's physiologic state and the determining factors for treatment.

dialysis: The passage of substances through a membrane; the process of removing undesirable factors from a fluid through a selectively permeable membrane.

diaphoresis: Profuse perspiration.

diaphragm: The flat group of muscles and tendons that separate the abdominal and thoracic cavities.

diaphysis: The shaft of a long bone.

diarrhea: The passage of frequent watery or loose stools.

diastole: The period of cardiac cycle in which the heart relaxes and the ventricles fill with blood.

diazepam: A tranquilizer and muscle relaxant drug sometimes used for treatment of seizures; trade name is Valium.

diffusion: The process of spreading out without use of energy, as through a membrane as in dialysis.

digestion: The process by which food is converted into simple chemical substances that can be absorbed by the intestines.

digestive tract: The passage of tubes leading from the mouth and pharynx to the anus; the alimentary tract; mouth, pharynx, esophagus, stomach, small intestine, large intestine, rectum, and anus.

digitalis: A drug used in the treatment of heart disease, especially heart failure and some atrial arrhythmias; a cardiac glycoside from *digitalis purpura*, or purple foxglove, a common herb.

digitalis toxicity: A state caused by an overdose of digitalis marked by anorexia, nausea, vomiting, yellow or green vision, and by increasing AV block, premature contractions, bradycardia.

dilatation: The act of widening an orifice beyond its normal dimensions.

dilated pupil: An ocular pupil enlarged beyond its normal size.

dilation: The process of expanding or enlarging.

Dilaudid: The trade name for dihydromorphinone, a drug with analgesia of the narcotic variety, and a respiratory depressant.

diplopia: Double vision.

direct current electric shock: Electric shock derived from storage batteries, as opposed to electric shock derived from alternating current; preferred method of defibrillation.

disc: The cartilaginous pad between the vertebrae that separates and cushions them.

discharge: Setting free or liberation; release the electrical charge in defibrillation.

dislocation: The state of being misaligned; the displacement of the ends of two bones at their joint so that the joint surfaces are no longer in proper contact.

disorganization: A disturbed mental state characterized by the inability to estimate direction or location or to be aware of time or other people.

distal: Farthest from any point on the center or median line; in extremities, farthest from the point of junction of the trunk of the body.

distention: The state of being inflated or enlarged, particularly of the abdomen.

diuresis: Increased secretion of urine.

diuretic: An agent used to increase the secretion of urine by the kidneys.

diverticulitis: Inflammation of a diverticulum of the colon.

diverticulosis: The presence of diverticula of the colon; having a small blind pouch off the lumen of the colon.

DOA: Abbreviation for dead on arrival.

dominant pacemaker: That part of the cardiac conduction system that has control of the heart stimulus; normally the sinoatrial node.

dorsal: Toward the back.

dorsalis pedis: The artery whose pulse is palpated on the dorsal part of the foot (the instep).

DOS: Abbreviation for dead at the scene.

dressing: A protective covering for a wound; used to stop bleeding and to prevent contamination of the wound.

dromotropic: Affecting the conductivity of a nerve fiber, especially the cardiac conduction system; positive dromotropic describes a faster conduction than normal.

droplet contract: A means of transmitting a communicable disease indirectly by spray droplets from an infected person's coughing or sneezing.

D.T.s: See delirium tremens.

duodenum: The segment of the small intestines that lies just distal to the stomach, said to be about twelve fingerbreadths in length.

duplex: A radiocommunications system employing more than one frequency.

dura mater: The outermost and strongest of the three meninges.

dying heart: A heart with feeble, ineffectual ventricular contractions; evidenced on EKG by greatly widened QRS complexes with electromechanical dissociation; asystole.

dys-: Prefix meaning bad, or difficult.

dysarthria: Imperfect articulation due to disturbance of muscular control caused by damage to central or peripheral nervous system.

dysconjugate vision: A condition in which the two eyes are not aligned, but stare in different directions.

dysfunction: Abnormal function of an organ or body part.

dysmenorrhea: Painful or difficult menstruation; menstrual cramps.

dysphagia: An inability to swallow or difficulty in swallowing.

dyspnea: Painful or difficult breathing; usually used to mean rapid, shallow respirations.

dysrhythmia: A disturbance in the cardiac rhythm.

eardrum: A flexible membrane that forms most of the outer wall of the tympanic cavity and separates it from the external auditory canal; the tympanum.

ecchymosis: Blood under the skin causing a black and blue mark; bruise.

ECF: Abbreviation for extracellular fluid.

ECG: Abbreviation for electrocardiogram; also EKG.

eclampsia: A toxic condition of pregnancy, causing convulsions and coma, associated with hypertension, edema, and proteinuria.

-ectomy: Suffix meaning surgical removal, as in appendectomy.

ectopic: Out of place; located away from the normal position.

ectopic focus: A stimulus initiated away from the sinoatrial node.

ectopic pregnancy: A pregnancy in which the fetus is implanted elsewhere than in the uterus, e.g., in the fallopian tube or in the abdominal cavity; produces abdom inal pain, bleeding.

edema: A condition in which fluid escapes into the body tissues from the vascular or lymphatic spaces and causes local or generalized swelling.

EEG: Abbreviation for electroencephalograph.

EENT: Abbreviation for eye, ear, nose, and throat.

efferent: Conducting or progressing away from a center or specific site of reference.

effusion: A leakage of fluid from tissues into a cavity, such as into the pleural cavity.

EKG: Abbreviation for electrocardiogram.

electrocardiogram: A graphic tracing of the electrical currents generated by the process of depolarization and repolarization of the myocardial tissues.

electrocution: Death caused by passage of electrical current through the body.

electrode: A probe used to sense electrical activity.

electroencephalogram: A recording of the electrical potentials on the skull generated by currents emanating spontaneously from nerve cells in the brain.

electrolyte: A substance whose molecules dissociate when put into solution.

electrolyte imbalance: A deviation from the normal concentrations of serum electrolytes due to excessive intake or loss of various electrolytes.

electromechanical dissociation: The state in which the electrical currents in the heart are active but the mechanical (contracting) action is not effectively pumping blood; the EKG complexes may be present, but there is no pulse.

electron: One of the subatomic particles, usually found negatively charged, circling the positively charged nucleus.

elixir: A liquid oral medication containing flavorings, sweetening, and alcohol.

emboli: Plural of embolus.

embolism: The sudden blocking of an artery or vein by a clot or foreign material which has been brought to the site of lodgement by the blood current.

embolus: A clot or another plug brought by the blood from another vessel and forced into a smaller one, thus obstructing the circulation.

embryo: In animals, the derivatives of the fertilized egg, that eventually become offspring, during their period of most rapid development, in man, from about 2 weeks after fertilization to the end of the seventh or eighth week.

emesis: Vomiting.

emetic: An agent that causes vomiting.

emphysema: A chronic lung disease caused by distention of the alveoli and/or destruction of their walls; a pathological accumulation of air in tissues, or organs, as in subcutaneous emphysema.

emulsion: A preparation of one liquid distributed in small globules throughout the body of a second liquid; used as a lubricant.

encephalitis: Inflammation of the brain.

encephalopathy: Any disorder of the brain.

endobronchial: Within the bronchus or bronchi.

endocardium: The membrane lining the inside of the heart.

endocrine: Secreting internally.

endoscope: An instrument for the examination of the interior of a hollow organ, such as the stomach or bladder.

endothelium: The layer of epithelial cells that lines the cavities of the heart and the blood and lymph vessels, and the serum-producing lining of the cavities of the body.

endotracheal: Within or through the trachea, an endotracheal tube.

endotracheal intubation: The insertion of a tube through the mouth or nose and into the trachea.

endotracheal tube: One of a series of graduated tubes, with or without inflatable cuffs, to be inserted in the trachea for the purpose of maintaining an airway and/or delivery of oxygen.

enteritis: An inflammation of the small intestine, usually accompanied by diarrhea.

envenomation: The poisonous effects caused by the bites, stings, or deposits of insects, spiders, snakes, or other poison-carrying animals.

enzyme: A protein substance capable of accelerating or producing by catalytic action some change in another substance for which it is often specific.

EOA: Abbreviation for esophageal obturator airway.

epi-: Prefix meaning on top of or above.

epicardium: The serous layer of pericardium covering the outside of the heart.

epidemic: An occurrence of a disease among many people over a given area.

epidermis: The outermost and nonvascular layer of the skin.

epidural: Located outside or above the dura, the outermost membrane that covers the brain.

epigastrium: The upper and middle regions of the abdomen within the costal angle.

epiglottis: The lidlike cartilaginous structure overhanging the superior entrance to the larynx and serving to prevent food from entering the larynx and trachea while swallowing.

epiglottitis: A bacterial infection occurring in children, marked by swelling of the epiglottis, high fever, pain on swallowing, and drooling; airway obstruction can result with great rapidity.

epilepsy: A chronic brain disorder marked by paroxysmal attacks of brain dysfunction, usually associated with some alteration of consciousness, abnormal motor behavior, psychic or sensory disturbances; may be preceded by an aura.

epinephrine: A hormone released by the adrenal medulla which stimulates the sympathetic nervous system, producing vasoconstriction, increased heart rate, and bronchodilation.

epiphyseal injury: An injury that results in a break of a bone at the cartilaginous epiphysis, a growth center, at the end of a long bone, producing possible deformity or stunting of that bone.

epiphyseal plate: The disc of cartilage between the shaft and the epiphysis of a long bone that exists during the growth of the bone.

epiphysis: Either end of a long bone.

epitaxis: Nosebleed.

epithelium: The purely cellular, avascular layer covering all the free surface of the body; cutaneous, mucous, and serous functions.

erythema: A redness of the skin produced by congestion of the capillaries.

erythrocyte: A red blood cell.

esophageal obturator airway: A

device used to provide an adequate airway by blocking off the esophageal opening with a cuffed obturator and providing ventilation through a series of side holes located at the level of the epiglottis.

esophagus: The portion of the digestive tract that lies between the pharynx and the stomach.

estrogen: One of the classes of female sex hormones.

ethanol: Ethyl alcohol, the type of alcohol present in alcoholic beverages.

etiology: The study of the factors that cause disease.

euphoria: A feeling of well-being and happiness.

eustachian tube: The tube leading from the back of the throat to the middle ear; serves to equalize pressure in the middle ear.

evaporation: Conversion of a liquid or solid to a gas.

eviscerate: To remove or expose the intestines.

exacerbation: A relapse or worsening of a disease condition.

excitability: The capability of any cell to be stimulated to act.

excitation stimulus: An electrical stimulus that arises through the physiologic capability of the heart's conduction system and that causes the depolarization and consequent contraction of the fibers.

excretion: The process whereby the residue of food and waste products of metabolism are eliminated.

exhalation: The act of breathing out; expiration.

exsanguinate: To bleed to death.

extension: The process of straightening; the movement by which the two ends of any joined part are drawn away from each other.

external cardiac compression: The method by which mechanical depression of the lower half of the sternum compresses the ventricles and forces blood into the systemic and pulmonary circulation.

extracellular fluid: The portion of the total body water outside the cells, composed of the interstitial and intravascular fluid.

extract: A concentrated preparation of a drug prepared by dissolving the drug in alcohol or water and evaporating off the excess solvent to a prescribed standard.

extraocular motions: The movement of the eyes.

extrasystole: An extra heartbeat, often a premature contraction.

extravasation: A discharge or escape, as of blood from a vessel into the tissues.

extremity: A limb, an arm, or a leg.

extrication: Disentanglement; freeing from entrapment.

extruded: Pushed out of normal position.

exudate: Material, such as cells, fluids, deposited in tissues or on tissue surfaces, usually as a result of inflammation.

eyelid: Either of the two movable conjunctival-cutaneous folds that protect the anterior surface of the eyeball.

facemask: A device used for the administration of gases, particularly oxygen, or for the redirection of room air, as in the esophageal obturator airway.

facilitation: The technique of encouraging patients to communicate by small positive responses, such as nodding the head or saying, "I see."

Fahrenheit scale: The temperature scale in which the freezing point is 32 degrees and the boiling point at sea level is 212 degrees.

fainting: A momentary loss of consciousness caused by insufficient blood supply to the brain; syncope.

fallopian tube: The bilateral tubes extending from the ovaries to the uterus.

false motion: A motion of an extremity or a part of the body where ordinarily there should be none, indicative of a fracture or dislocation.

fatigue fracture: A fracture in which the bone breaks as a result of repeated stress that cannot be tolerated by that particular bone; most likely involving bones of feet or legs.

febrile: Pertaining to fever.

feces: The product expelled by the bowels; semisoft waste products of digestion.

femoral: Pertaining to the femur or thigh bone.

femoral artery: The principal artery of the thigh, a continuation of the iliac artery; supplies blood to the lower abdominal wall, the external genitalia, and the lower body extremities; pulse may be palpated in the groin area.

femoral head: The rounded protuberance at the proximal end of the femur; fits into the acetabulum of the innominate bone to make the hip joint.

femoral pulse: Located approximately two finger-breadths inferior to the midpoint of a line between the anterior superior iliac spine and the pubic symphysis.

femur: The bone that extends from the pelvis to the knee; the longest and largest bone of the body; the thigh bone.

fetus: The unborn offspring in the postembryonic period after major structures have been outlined; in man, from 7 or 8 weeks after fertilization until birth.

fever: An elevation of body temperature beyond normal.

fibrillation: Asynchronous, uncoordinated contraction of individual muscle fibers, producing no effective contraction.

fibrillatory waves: On the EKG, the waves that appear as numerous, dissimilar, and irregularly shaped, rounded waves caused by chaotically firing multiple ectopic foci or multiple circus movements in muscle bundles.

fibula: The smaller of the two bones of the lower leg; the most lateral bone of the lower leg.

first responder: A person who arrives first at the scene of a medical emergency, usually police or firefighters.

fistula: A deep, sinuous passage or tract, often leading to an internal hollow organ.

flaccid: A term meaning soft, limp, without any muscular tone.

flail chest: A condition in which several ribs are broken, each in at least two places; or a sternal fracture or separation of the ribs from the sternum producing a free-floating segment of the chest wall that moves paradoxically on respiration.

flail segment: That segment of the chest wall, in a flail chest injury, lying between the rib fractures and moving paradoxically with respiration.

flexion: The act of bending, or the condition of being bent.

flowmeter: A device used to measure the rate of any agent introduced into a patient; specifically, used in connection with the use of oxygen.

flow rate: The rate at which oxygen flows from a cylinder; the rate at which an intravenous infusion is administered.

flutter waves: Sawtooth waves, as atrial depolarizations, on EKG, indicative of atrial flutter.

fontanelle: One of the membrane-covered spaces remaining at the junction of the sutures in an incompletely ossified skull; a baby's soft spot on the skull.

foramen: Any natural opening through a bone or other structure of the body; plural, foramina.

forearm: The part of the upper extremity between the elbow and the wrist.

foreskin: The free fold of skin that covers the glans penis more or less completely.

Fowler's position: The head of the patient is raised 18 to 20 inches above level, with the knees of the patient raised also.

fracture: A break or rupture in a bone.

fracture-dislocation: A fracture of a bone near an articular with a concomitant dislocation at that joint.

fracture of the hip: A fracture that occurs at the upper end of the femur, most often at the neck of the femur.

frontal: Pertaining to the forehead region, of the frontal bone; the position of facing straight ahead; the plane that divides the body into front and back parts.

frontal lobe: The portion of the brain under the frontal bone.

frost nip: The superficial local tissue destruction caused by freezing; limited in scope and does not destroy the full thickness of skin.

frostbite: The damage to tissues as a result of prolonged exposure to extreme cold.

fungus: Any vegetable organism of the class to which mushrooms and molds belong, many classes being pathogenic for man.

furosemide: A potent diuretic agent used in the treatment of congestive heart failure and hypertension; trade name is Lasix.

fuse: To unite or join together.

fused joint: A joining of bones to form a rigid structure, as in the skull or sacrum.

gait: The manner in which a person walks.

gallbladder: The sac located just beneath the liver that concentrates and stores bile.

gamma rays: An electromagnetic radiation emitted from radioactive substances analogous to X-rays.

ganglion: A knot or mass; a group of nerve cell bodies located outside the central nervous system.

gangrene: Local tissue death as the result of an injury or inadequate blood supply.

gas gangrene: A disease originating in a wound infected with *Clostridium perfringens*; results in rapid tissue destruction.

gastric: Pertaining to the stomach.

gastric juice: The digestive fluids secreted by the stomach; a thin, colorless liquid that has an acid reaction; contains mainly hydrochloric acid, pepsin, and mucous.

gastrointestinal: Pertaining to the stomach and intestine.

gastrointestinal tract: The digestive tract, including stomach, small intestine, large intestine, rectum, and anus.

gauge: A term that refers to the diameter of a needle or a needle cannula.

Geiger counter: An instrument consisting of a Geiger-Muller tube and the electronic equipment used in conjunction with it; records the current pulsations produced by the passage of radioactive particles within the tube gas.

generic name: The name given to a drug by the company that first manufactures it; usually a simplified version of the chemical name.

genital system: The system including all the reproductive organs.

genitalia: The external sex organs.

genitourinary system: The system including all the organs involved in reproduction and in the formation and voiding of urine.

geriatric: A term that refers to the elderly.

germicidal: Destructive to germs (microbes).

gestation: The period of development of the young; pregnancy.

gland: An organ or any cell group that produces a secretion not related to its ordinary needs.

Glasgow Coma Scale: A method of quantifying a patient's state of consciousness.

glaucoma: A disease that produces increased pressure within the eyeball; can lead to blindness.

glenohumeral joint: The shoulder joint; the joint between the upper end of the humerus and the scapula.

globulin: One of a class of simple proteins that are insoluble in water, soluble in dilute salt solution, and precipitated by ammonium sulfate; found in human serum and tissue and in seeds and nuts.

glomerulus: A small tuft or cluster, as of blood vessels or nerve fibers; specifically, the cluster of blood vessels projecting into the capsule of each of the urine-producing tubules of the kidney.

glottis: The vocal apparatus of the larynx, consisting of the true vocal cords and the opening between them.

glucose: A simple sugar.

glycogen: The form in which carbohydrates are stored in animal and human tissue.

glycolysis: The breaking down of sugars into simpler compounds.

gonad: An ovary or testis.

gonorrhea: A contagious inflammation of the genital mucous membrane; the most common venereal disease.

gram: The unit of weight of the metric system.

grand mal: A type of epileptic attack; characterized by a short-term, generalized, convulsive seizure.

gravid: Pregnant.

groin: The inguinal region; junction of the abdomen and the thigh.

gtt: Abbreviation for drops.

habituation: A situation in which a patient produces a tolerance to a drug and becomes psychologically dependent on the drug.

half-ring splint: A traction splint with a hinged half-ring at the upper end that allows the splint to be used on either right or left leg.

hallucination: A sensory perception not founded on objective reality; may involve smell, touch, taste, sight, and hearing.

hallucinogen: A drug or agent that has the capacity to induce hallucinations.

Hgb: Abbreviation for hemoglobin.

HCT: Abbreviation for hematocrit.

head-tilt maneuver: A procedure for opening the airway to relieve obstruction caused by the tongue; with one hand beneath the patient's neck and one hand on the patient's forehead, the neck is lifted and the head is tilted backward as far as possible; not recommended in patients with possible neck injury.

heart: A hollow, muscular organ that receives the blood from the veins, sends it through the lungs to be oxygenated, then pumps it to the arteries.

heart attack: A layman's term for a condition resulting from blockage of a coronary artery and subsequent death of part of the heart muscle; an acute myocardial infarction; a coronary.

heat cramps: A painful muscle cramp resulting from excessive loss of salt and water through sweating.

heat exhaustion: A prostration caused by excessive loss of water and salt through sweating; characterized by clammy skin and a weak, rapid pulse.

hematemesis: A condition in which the patient vomits blood.

hematochezia: The passage of grossly bloody stools or bright red blood from the rectum.

hematocrit: The percentage of red blood cells in the total blood volume.

hematoma: A localized collection of blood in an organ, tissue, or space as a result of injury or a broken blood vessel.

hematuria: Blood in the urine.

hemiparesis: A weakness on one side of the body.

hemiplegia: Paralysis of one side of the body.

hemithorax: Refers to one side of the chest.

hemodialysis: The process of removing certain noxious agents from the blood by diffusion through a semipermeable membrane.

hemoglobin: The oxygen-carrying substance of the red blood cells; when it has absorbed oxygen in the lungs, it is bright red and called oxyhemoglobin; after it has given up its oxygen to the tissues, it is purple in color and is called carboxyhemoglobin.

hemolysis: The distintegration of the red blood cells due to an adverse factor, such as transfusion reaction or snakebite.

hemophilia: An inherited blood disease occurring mostly in males, characterized by the inability of the blood to clot.

hemopneumothorax: The accumulation of air and blood in the pleural cavity.

hemoptysis: Coughing up blood from the lungs.

hemorrhage: Abnormally large amount of bleeding.

hemorrhagic shock: A state of inadequate tissue perfusion due to blood loss.

hemostasis: The stopping or slowing of a hemorrhage; the method of stopping hemorrhage.

hemostat: An instrument for stopping hemorrhage by compressing the bleeding vessel; a type of clamp.

hemothorax: Bleeding into the thoracic cavity.

heparin: A mucopolysaccaride acid, occurring naturally in tissues, but most abundant in liver and lung; a drug to prevent clotting, used in embolism and other clotting problems.

hepatitis: Inflammation of the liver.

hernia: The abnormal protrusion of any organ through an opening into another body cavity; most common is the inguinal hernia where a loop of intestine descends into the inguinal canal in the groin.

heroin: An alkaloid prepared from morphine by acetylization; formerly used for relief of coughs; because of the great danger of addiction following use of the drug, its manufacture and importation into the United States is prohibited.

Hg: Chemical symbol for mercury.

hiatus hernia: A protrusion of the stomach into the mediastinum through an opening in the diaphragm; can cause chest pain similar to angina pectoris or that of acute myocardial infarction.

hinge joint: A specialized joint found in the elbow, knee.

hip: The lateral prominence of the pelvis from the waist to the thigh; more strictly, the hip joint.

hip joint: The ball-and-socket joint formed by the articulation of the head of the femur and the acetabular fossa.

histamine: A decomposition product of histidine, formed in the intestines and found in most body tissues or produced synthetically; it causes dilation and increased permeability of capillaries and stimulates gastric secretion and visceral muscle contraction.

history: Information about the patient's chief complaint, symptoms, data leading up to the acute episode, previous illnesses, family history, and surgical history.

hives: Red or white raised patches on the skin, often attended by severe itching; a characteristic reaction in allergic responses.

homeostasis: A tendency toward stability in the body's internal environment; a return to normal after any deviation.

homocide: The act of deliberately taking another person's life.

hormone: A substance secreted by an endocrine gland that has effects upon other glands or systems of the body.

host: The organism upon which or within which a parasite lives.

hostility: A strong dislike, anger, or resistance toward an individual, group, or idea.

humerus: The bone of the upper arm.

humidifier: A device used with an oxygen supply to moisten the oxygen and to prevent its drying effect on the mucous membranes of the patient.

humor: The extracellular fluids of the body; also, mirth.

hydration: The state of water balance in the body.

hydrochloric acid: The acid in gastric juice.

hydrothorax: Fluid in the chest cavity.

hyper-: Prefix meaning excessive, or increased.

hyperactive: A term meaning excessively or pathologically active.

hypercapnia: Excess of carbon dioxide in the blood.

hypercarbia: An excessive amount of carbon dioxide in the blood; a carbon dioxide pressure greater than 45 to 50 torr.

hyperextend: An overextension of a limb, or other part of the body.

hyperflexia: An overactive reflex.

hyperglycemia: An abnormally increased concentration of sugar in the blood.

hyperkalemia: An excessive amount of potassium in the blood.

hypernatremia: Excess of sodium (Na) in the blood.

hyperpnea: An increased depth of respiration.

hyperpyrexia: An abnormally high fever; hyperthermia.

hypersensitivity: A reaction to contact with certain substances; allergy.

hypertension: High blood pressure, usually in reference to a diastolic pressure greater than 90-95 mmHg.

hyperthermia: An abnormally increased body temperature; hyperpyrexia.

hypertonic: A solution having an osmotic pressure greater than a solution to which it is being compared (usually the intracellular fluid, or plasma).

hypertrophy: The morbid enlargement or overgrowth of any organ or part due to an increase in the size of its constituent cells.

hyperventilation: An increased rate and depth of breathing resulting in an abnormal lowering of arterial carbon dioxide, causing alkalosis.

hyphema: Hemorrhage within the anterior chamber of the eye.

hypnotic: A medication causing sleep.

hypo-: A prefix meaning less than, lack of, a deficiency.

hypocarbia: An abnormally low carbon dioxide tension in the blood.

hypoglycemia: An abnormally diminished concentration of sugar in the blood; insulin shock.

hypokalemia: A low concentration of potassium in the blood.

hyponatremia: Too little sodium in the blood.

hypopharynx: The lowest part of the pharynx leading to the larynx and esophagus.

hypopnea: Abnormal decrease in depth and rate of breathing.

hyposensitive: Less sensitive than normal.

hypotension: Low blood pressure.

hypothalamus: The portion of the brainstem that activates, controls, and integrates peripheral autonomic mechanisms, endocrine activity, water balance, and automatic functions, such as sleep.

hypothermia: Decreased body temperature.

hypotonic: A solution having an osmotic pressure less than a solution to which it is being compared (usually the intracellular fluid, or plasma).

hypoventilation: A reduced rate and depth of breathing resulting in a rise in arterial carbon dioxide pressure, acidosis.

hypovolemia: A decreased amount of blood in the body.

hypovolemic shock: Shock caused by a reduction in blood volume, such as caused by hemorrhage.

hypoxemia: A term that refers to inadequate oxygen in the blood; an arterial oxygen pressure of less than 60 torr.

hypoxia: A low oxygen content in the blood; lack of oxygen in inspired air.

ICF: Abbreviation for intracellular fluid.

idopathic: Of unknown cause.

idiosyncrasy: Anything that is peculiar to the individual; an unusual reaction to a drug, food, idea, action, or substance that is peculiar to the individual.

idioventricular: Of, or relating to, or affecting the cardiac ventricle only; an idioventricular rhythm is one that arises in the ventricle.

ileocecal valve: The protrusion of the terminal ileum into the large intestine at the ileocolic junction; protects the terminal ileum from feces forced back from the cecum.

ileum: The most distal portion of the small intestine lying between the jejunum and the colon.

ileus: An intestinal obstruction commonly caused by paralysis of bowel motility caused by peritonitis or other inflammatory processes.

ilium: Either of the two broad uppermost portions of the hip bone.

IM: Abbreviation for intramuscular.

immersion feet: A disorder of the feet following prolonged immersion in water; when first removed from the water, the patient's feet are swollen, cold, waxy white with cyanotic areas, and anesthetic; a short time later the parts become red and hot and the swelling increases.

immobilization: To hold a part firmly in place, as with a splint.

immobilize: To make incapable of moving.

immune: Resistant to an infectious disease.

immunization: The process or procedure by which resistance is produced in a living organism; vaccination.

impaled object: An object that has caused a puncture wound and remains embedded in the wound.

incision: A wound usually made deliberately in connection with surgery; a clean cut as opposed to a laceration.

incompatibility: In blood typing, the situation in which donor and recipient blood cannot be mixed without clumping or other adverse reactions.

incomplete AV block: A delay or intermittent disturbance in the conduction of the stimulus from the atria to the ventricles, occurring in the AV junction, AV node, bundle of His, or bundle branches; causes prolongation of the P-R interval or absent QRS complexes, in the presence of regularly appearing P waves; first or second degree block.

incontinence: An inability to prevent the release of urine or feces.

incubation: The time period between exposure to an infection and the appearance of the first symptoms.

incubator: A device that provides protection and temperature control for a newborn infant or a high-risk infant of any age.

indication: The circumstances in which a drug or other treatment is of value in the care of a patient.

indirect contact: A means of transmitting a communicable disease through the use of a vector, a third item that acts as a mediary.

indwelling catheter: A hollow tube that has been inserted into the lumen of a vessel, or in a hollow organ, for the purpose of transferring some liquid either into or out of that structure.

infarction: The death (necrosis) of a localized area of tissue by cutting off its blood supply.

infect: To contaminate an organism with a disease-inducing substance.

infection: An invasion of a body by disease-producing organisms.

infectious: Capable of being transmitted by infection.

inferior: Anatomically, situated below, or directed downward, or the lower surface or part of a structure.

inferior vena cava: One of the two largest veins in the body that empties venous blood into the right atrium receiving blood from the lower extremities and abdominal organs.

infiltration: Leakage of fluid into the interstitial compartment, usually as a result of improper cannulation of a vein, or by design, to render insensitive the area of surgical procedures, such as suturing.

inflammation: A tissue reaction to disease, irritation, or infection, characterized by pain, heat, redness, and swelling.

infusion: Induction by gravity of a therapeutic fluid other than blood into a vein.

ingestion: Intaking of food or other substances through the mouth.

inhalation: The drawing of air or other substances into the lungs.

injection: The forcing of a liquid through a needle or other tube into subcutaneous tissues, the blood vessel, a muscle mass, or an organ.

innervation: Nerve supply to an area; distribution of the nerves.

innocuous: Not harmful.

innominate: Not named; having no name.

innominate artery: The brachiocephalic artery; arising at the aortic arch; it supplies head and arm on the right side, dividing into the right subclavian and right common carotid arteries.

innominate bone: One of two bones forming the pelvic girdle; made up of the fusion of the ilium, ischium, and pubis.

inotropic: Tending to increase the force of cardiac contraction.

insertion: The point at which a muscle is attached to the bone or fascia that it moves.

inspection: A careful visual examination of the patient, for the purpose of identifying any abnormality.

inspiration: Inhalation.

insufficiency: The condition of being inadequate.

insufflate: To blow a powder, vapor, or gas into a cavity.

insulin: A hormone secreted by the islets of Langerhans in the pancreas; essential for the proper metabolism of blood sugar.

insulin shock: Not a true form of shock; hypoglycemia caused by excessive insulin dosage, characterized by sweating, tremor, anxiety, unusual behavior, vertigo, and diplopia; may cause death of brain cells.

integument: A covering or sheath; the skin.

intercostal: Between the ribs.

intercostal muscles: Muscles between the ribs.

intercostal space (ICS): The space between the ribs; identified by the number of the rib above that space, e.g., the first intercostal space is the space below the first rib, directly above the second rib.

intermittent positive pressure ventilation: Assisted or controlled ventilation; most often supplied by bag-valve-mask or by demand valve; mouth-to-mouth ventilation.

internodal conduction pathways: The cardiac conduction system in the atria; characterized by specialized conductive tissue paths from the SA node to the left atrium and through both atrial musculature, terminating at the AV junction.

interstitial fluid: The fluid bathing the cells; part of the extracellular fluid; continuous with the lympathic fluid.

interventricular septum: The membranous-muscular wall dividing the right and left ventricles of the heart.

intervertebral disc: The pad of fibrocartilage between the bodies of adjacent vertebrae.

intestine: The portion of the alimentary canal extending from the pylorus to the anus.

large intestine: The portion of the digestive tube extending from the ileocecal valve to the anus, composed of cecum, colon, and rectum; the large bowel.

small intestine: The portion of the digestive tube between the stomach and the cecum; composed of the duodenum, the jejunum, and the ileum; the small bowel.

intima: The tunica intima, the innermost layer of tissue forming the wall of an artery, capillary, or vein.

intoxicate: To poison; commonly, to cause diminished mental control by means of drugs, alcohol.

intracardiac injection: An injection of medication directly into the heart chamber through the thoracic and ventricular walls.

intracellular fluid: The portion of total body water contained within the cells.

intracerebral: Within the cerebrum.

intracerebral hematoma: An extravasation of blood within the brain.

intracranial: Within the skull.

intramuscular: Within the muscle.

intravascular fluid: The portion of the total body water contained within the blood vessels.

intravenous: Within or into a vein.

intravenous fluid: Sterile water containing additives such as electrolytes and/or sugar in various combinations and concentrations for the purpose of administering to patients per venous infusion.

intubation: An insertion of a tube into an organ that is connected to the outside of the body by means of a hollow tube; commonly, the insertion of a tube into the trachea or esophagus.

involuntary action: An act performed independent of the will; not voluntary.

involuntary commitment: The commitment of a patient to a hospital for treatment or observation against the patient's will.

involuntary muscle: The muscles that act without voluntary control; smooth muscle.

ion: An atom or group of atoms carrying a positive (cation) or negative (anion) charge of electricity.

ionization: Dissociation of matter into ions; such as salt, when added to water, breaks down into sodium (Na) and chlorine (Cl) ions.

ionizing radiation: Any radiation resulting when a stable, neutral atom is disrupted, releasing individual ions that bear either positive or negative charges.

ipecac syrup: A medication used to induce vomiting.

IPPV: Abbreviation for intermittent positive pressure ventilation.

iris: The colored portion of the eye that surrounds the pupil.

irritation: The act of stimulating; undue sensitivity; slight or temporary disruption of tissues.

ischemia: A reduced blood flow into a portion of tissue due to narrowing or occlusion of the artery for that area, thereby producing tissue anoxia.

ischial tuberosity: A protuberance on the inferior surface of the ischium lateral to the anus and bearing weight when the person is seated.

ischium: Either of the two lowermost portions of the innominate bone.

islets of Langerhans: The cluster of cells in the pancreas that produce insulin.

isoelectric line: The baseline of an EKG.

isoproterenol: A drug that stimulates the beta receptors of the body; beta adrenergic, trade name: Isuprel.

isotonic: Having the same osmotic pressure as a reference solution; usually the intracellular fluid, or the red blood cell.

-itis: A suffix meaning inflammation.

IV: Abbreviation for intravenous.

jaundice: The presence of excessive bile pigments in the bloodstream that give the skin, mucous membranes, and eyes a distinct yellow color.

jaw thrust maneuver: A procedure for opening the airway, wherein the jaw is lifted and pulled forward to keep the tongue from falling back into the airway.

jejunum: The second portion of the small intestine, between the duodenum and ileum.

joint: The point at which two or more bones articulate; commonly, portion of marijuana.

joint capsule: A fibrous sac that, with its synovial lining, encloses a joint.

jugular: Pertaining to the neck; large vein on either side of the neck, draining the head via its portion named external jugular, or draining the brain via the internal jugular.

junctional rhythm: An arrhythmia arising from ectopic foci located in the atrioventricular (AV) junction, characterized by absence of positive P wave, short P-R (far point of visual accommodation) interval, and a rate in the range of 40 to 60 beats per minute.

K^+: The chemical symbol for potassium ion.

kalemia: The presence of potassium (K) in the blood; potassium is normally present in the blood.

kaliuresis: Abnormal excretion of potassium in the urine.

keep open rate: A very slow rate of IV infusion designed to keep the route open and not permit the line to clot; a rate of 25 milliliters per hour (American Heart Association).

ketoacidosis: A condition arising in diabetics where their insulin dose is insufficient to their needs; fat is metabolized, instead of sugar, to ketones; characterized by excessive thirst, urination, vomiting, and hyperventilation of the Kussmaul type.

ketone: A compound that is organic and derived by oxidation from a secondary alcohol; produced by metabolism without sugar.

kidneys: The paired organs located in the retroperitoneal cavities that filter blood and produce urine; also act as adjuncts to keep a proper acid-base balance.

kilogram: A unit of measurement in the metric system, equal to 1,000 grams or 2.2 pounds.

knee: A hinge joint between the femur and the tibia.

KVO: Abbreviation for keep open, or keep vein open, a slow drip rate.

Kussmaul's respiration: A deep, rapid respiration characteristic of hyperglycemia, or diabetic coma, caused by acidosis and the necessity of the body to blow off carbon dioxide as a compensatory mechanism.

labia: The lips; the folds of skin and mucous membranes that comprise the vulva.

labor: The muscular contractions of the uterus designed to expel the fetus from the mother.

lacerate: To tear or cut roughly.

laceration: A wound made by tearing or cutting of body tissues.

lacrimal system: The system that produces and secretes tears; includes the lacrimal gland and its extretory ducts, lacrimal canaliculi, the lacrimal sac, and the nasolacrimal duct.

lactated Ringer's solution: A frequently used sterile intravenous solution containing sodium, potassium, calcium, and chloride ions in approximately isotonic concentrations; lactate is added as a buffer for acidotic conditions.

lactic acid: An organic acid normally present in tissue and produced in carbohydrate matter by bacterial fermentation; one of the acids produced by anaerobic metabolism, contributing to the acidosis produced in cardiac arrest.

lactic acidosis: An excessive amount of lactic acid in the blood causing a low blood pH.

ladder splint: A flexible splint consisting of two stout parallel wires and finer crosswires; resembles a ladder.

landline: A telephone line.

laparotomy: Incision in the abdominal wall; usually for the purpose of inspection of viscera for abnormalities.

laryngectomee: A person who has undergone a total or partial surgical removal of the larynx.

laryngectomy: The surgical removal of the larynx.

laryngoscope: An instrument used for directly visualizing the larynx and its related structures.

laryngospasm: A severe constriction of the vocal cords, often in response to allergy or noxious stimuli.

laryngotracheobronchitis: Croup; inflammation of the larynx, trachea, and bronchi.

larynx: The organ of voice production.

lateral: Of or toward the side; away from the midline of the body.

lateral malleolus: The rounded projection on the lateral side of the ankle joint.

lavage: A washing-out of a hollow organ, such as the stomach.

lead: A recording on electrocardiogram that reflects the flow of electrical current produced by the heart's depolarization from a certain position of the body.

left heart: Comprised of the left atrium and left ventricle.

left heart failure: Failure of the left ventricle to effectively pump blood, causing excessive backup of blood into the lungs as well as causing poor perfusion of brain, kidneys, and other parts of the body; pump failure; cardiogenic shock may be the outcome.

lens: The portion of the eye that focuses light rays onto the retina.

lesion: A distinct area of pathologically altered tissue; an injury or wound.

lethal: Fatal.

lethargy: A lack of activity; drowsiness; indifference.

leukemia: A disease of the blood-forming organs, characterized by proliferation of white blood cells and pathological changes in the bone marrow and other lymphoid tissue; cancer of the blood.

leukocyte: White blood cell.

lidocaine: A drug used to prevent or terminate life-threatening ventricular dysrhythmias by suppressing ventricular ectopic activity; trade name: Xylocaine.

life-threatening arrhythmia: Any arrhythmia that causes compromise of the cardiac output, usually ventricular in origin but may be of atrial origin especially if the rate is either extremely slow or extremely rapid (less than 40 or more than 160 per minute).

ligament: A tough band of fibrous tissue that connects bone to bone or that supports any organ.

ligate: To tie or bind with a ligature.

ligature: Any substance, such as catgut, cotton, silk, wire, or artificial fabric, used to tie a vessel or strangulate a part.

limb presentation: A delivery in which the presenting part of a fetus is an arm or a leg.

linear fracture: A fracture running parallel to the long axis of the bone.

linear skull fracture: A skull fracture that runs in a straight line.

lipid: Fat; any one of a group of fats that is insoluble in water but soluble in fat solvents.

listless: A condition characterized by a lack of inclination toward exertion.

liter: A unit of volume measure of the metric standard; equal to 1,000 milliliters and 1.04 quarts.

liver: The large organ in the right upper quadrant of the abdomen that secretes bile, produces many essential proteins, detoxifies many substances, and stores glycogen.

loading dose: A single large dose of a drug that produces the high blood level necessary to achieve the drug's therapeutic effect.

log roll: A method for placing a patient on a carrying device, usually a long spineboard or a flat litter; the patient is rolled on his side, then back on the litter.

LSD: Lysergic acid diethylamide; a serotonic antagonist that induces schizophrenic-like states in humans, with hallucinations that are visual rather than auditory; may produce psychosis; used in the treatment of chronic alcoholism and psychotic disorders.

lumbar: Refers to the five vertebrae between the thoracic and sacral vertebrae; also to the region of the trunk between the costal margin and brim of the pelvis.

lumbar spine: The five vertebrae between the superiorly placed thoracic and inferiorly oriented sacral vertebrae.

lumbosacral plexus: The network of nerves formed by the union of the anterior primary division of the lumbar, sacral, and coccygeal nerves.

lumen: The cavity or channel within a tube.

lungs: The paired organs in the thorax that affect ventilation and oxygenation.

lye: A solution of alkaline salts obtained by the leaching of wood ashes.

lymph: A straw-colored fluid that circulates in the lymphatic vessels and interstitial space.

lymph node: Any one of the round, oval, or bean-shaped bodies located along the course of the lymphatic vessels; producing lymphocytes and acting as filters for lymphatic system; when there is infection present, the lymph nodes in the area swell and are detected more easily in the neck and groin.

lymphoid tissues: A three-dimensional network of tissue found in the lymph nodes, spleen, thymus, adenoids, and tonsils that intercept and destroy pathogenic substances.

Magill forceps: An instrument, similar to scissors, but without sharp points or blades, to remove foreign objects in the upper airway, must be used with a laryngoscope.

malaise: A general feeling of vague bodily discomfort.

malignant: Cancerous; tending to become progressively worse and resulting in death.

malingering: Willful, deliberate, and fraudulent feigning or exaggeration of the symptoms of illness or injury to attain a consciously desired end.

malleolus: The large, rounded bony protuberance on either side of the ankle joint.

malnutrition: Any disorder of nutrition; usually taken to mean too little nourishment.

mandible: The lower jawbone.

mania: Disordered mental state of extreme excitement.

manic depressive: Marked by alternating periods of elation and depression.

manubrium: The upper portion of the sternum to which the clavicles and first two pairs of ribs are attached.

marrow cavity: The central cavity in the shaft of the long bone where yellow marrow is contained.

MAST: Abbreviation for medical antishock trousers, or military antishock trousers.

mastoid: A portion of the temporal bone that lies behind the ear, contains spongy bone tissue.

maxilla: The bone of the face that contains the alveoli of the upper teeth.

maxillary artery: The artery on both sides of the face that supplies blood to the face; palpable in front of the ear.

mean arterial pressure: The pressure measurement midway between the systolic and diastolic pressures.

meconium: A dark green, mucilaginous substance in the intestine of a full-term fetus, being a mixture of the secretions of the intestinal glands and some amniotic fluid.

medial: Toward the midline of the body.

medial malleolus: The rounded projection on the medial side of the ankle joint.

mediastinum: The space within the thorax that contains the heart, pericardium, large blood vessels, vagus nerve, trachea, and esophagus; located between the left and right pleural spaces.

medulla oblongata: The portion of the brain between the cerebellum and spinal cord that contains the centers for control of respiration, heartbeat, and other major control centers.

melena: The passage of dark stools stained with blood pigment and digested blood; characteristically the stools are black and of a sticky, tarry consistency.

membrane: A thin sheet or layer of pliable tissue that serves as a covering or envelope of a part, or the lining of a cavity.

meninges: The three membranes

covering the spinal cord and brain; the dura mater (external), arachnoid (middle), and pia mater (internal).

meningitis: An inflammation of the meninges; characterized by a stiff neck, fever, and delirium.

menopause: The point that marks the permanent cessation of menstrual activity.

menorrhagia: An excessive flow during a menstrual period.

menses: The normal periodic discharge of blood fluid from the uterus; menstruation.

menstrual flow: The regular discharge during menses consisting of blood and the shed endometrium (mucous membrane lining of the uterus).

menstrual period: The time period of the menstrual flow; usually from 3 to 7 days.

mescaline: The most active alkaloid present in the mescal cactus; produces effects similar to those produced by LSD, such as an alteration in mood, changes in perception, visual hallucinations, and an increase in body temperature and blood pressure.

mesentary: The tissues by which the intestines are connected to the back surfaces of the abdominal cavity.

metabolism: The conversion of food into energy and waste products.

metacarpal bones: The five cylindrical bones of the hand extending from the wrist to the fingers.

metaraminal bitartrate: A drug that stimulates release of epinephrine and thus stimulates both alpha and beta receptors; increases constriction of the arterioles and venules, but does not significantly increase heart rate.

metatarsal bones: The five cylindrical bones of the foot extending from the ankles to the toes.

meter: A unit of linear measurement in the metric system; 1 meter equals 1,000 millimeters, equals 39.37 inches.

Mg: Chemical symbol for magnesium, cation with double valence.

methanol: Methyl alcohol; wood alcohol; poisonous if ingested, causing extreme metabolic acidosis.

metric system: A system of weights and measurements based on decimal units.

microdrop fluid administration set: A plastic device used to deliver intravenous fluids and medications at a very slow, accurate rate; approximately 60 drops per milliliter, but may vary among various manufacturers.

midclavicular line: An imaginary line beginning in the middle of the clavicle and running parallel to the sternum, passing medially to the male nipple line.

microgram (mcg): A unit of weight measurement in the metric system; equal to 0.001 milligrams.

middle ear: The tympanic cavity and its ossicles.

Military Anti-Shock Trousers: See MAST.

milk: In pharmacology, an aqueous suspension of the insoluble drugs.

milliequivalent (mEg): A unit of measurement for electrolytes based on a chemical combining power; defined as the weight of a substance present in 1 milliliter of normal solution.

milligram (mg): A metric weight measurement, equal to 0.001 gram.

milliliter (ml): A metric volume measurement, equal to 0.001 liter.

millimeter (mm): A metric linear measurement, equal to 0.001 meter.

millimeter of mercury (mmHg): A metric measurement used in the determination of blood pressure; commonly referred to as torr (Torricelli Unit) when used to designate gas tensions in the blood.

milliroentgen: A unit of measure of radiation, equal to 0.001 roentgens.

millivolt: A unit of electrical energy, equal to 0.001 volts.

mineral acid: A strong acid, such as sulfuric, nitric, or hydrochloric.

minute volume: The volume of air inhaled and exhaled during 1 minute; calculated by multiplying tidal volume by respiratory rate.

miosis: An abnormal contraction of a pupil.

miscarriage: A lay term for the abortion or the premature expulsion of a nonliving fetus from the uterus.

mitral valve: A valve located between the left atrium and left ventricle.

Mobitz Type I: A type of second degree heart block caused by a disturbance in conduction of the stimulus in the upper part of the AV junction; the P-R interval widens progressively in each of the succeeding complexes until the last P wave is not followed by a QRS complex, the cycles repeating; also known as the Wenckebach phenomenon.

Mobitz Type II: A type of second degree heart block, usually caused by a disturbance in conduction of the stimulus through the bundle of His or through both bundle branches (trifascicular block): P-R interval does not vary, but every second, third, or fourth P wave is not conducted.

varying Mobitz II: Heart block that may have a 1:1 atrial:ventricular conduction, with occasional runs of 2:1, 3:1, etc., conduction; the P-R interval remains constant.

molestation: A meddling or interference, often of a sexual nature.

monitor: To watch or listen to some transmission; the instrument that enables a person to watch or listen, such as a cardiac monitor.

morbidity: A synonym for illness; generally used to refer to an untoward effect of an illness or injury.

morphine: A narcotic analgesic used to relieve pain and anxiety; helpful in pulmonary edema because of its peripheral dilating effects.

mortality: Refers to death from a given disease or injury; generally thought of as a statistic to state the ratio of death to recovery.

motion sickness: A sensation induced by repetitive motion, characterized by nausea and lightheadedness.

motor nerves: The nerves that transport messages from the brain to various organs and muscles to stimulate involuntary and voluntary actions.

mottled: Characterized by a patchy, discolored appearance.

mouth-to-mouth ventilation: The preferred emergency method of artificial ventilation when adjuncts are not available.

mouth-to-nose ventilation: An emergency method of artificial ventilation when mouth-to-mouth cannot be used.

mucosa: Any mucous membrane.

mucous membrane: A membrane that lines many organs of the body and contains mucous-secreting glands.

mucus: A viscid, slippery secretion that lubricates and protects various body structures.

multifocal: Arising from or pertaining to many foci or locations.

multipara: A woman who has previously given birth.

murmur: A sound that may be detected in the heart when one of the valves is leaking or partially closed off.

muscle: A tissue composed of elongated cells that have the ability to contract when stimulated, thus causing bone and joints to move, or other anatomical structures to be drawn together.

muscle avulsion fracture: A tearing away of a part of bone, usually by a tendon, ligament, or capsule.

muscle tremor artifact: The numerous extraneous spikes and waves in the EKG caused by voluntary or involuntary muscle movement or shivering.

musculature: The muscular system of the body, or a part of the system.

musculoskeletal system: All the collective bones, joints, muscles, and tendons of the body.

myalgia: A tenderness or pain in the muscles.

mydriasis: A pronounced abnormal dilation of the pupil.

myocardial: Pertaining to the musculature of the heart.

myocardial contusion: A bruise of the muscular tissue of the heart.

myocardial infarction: The damaging or death of an area of heart muscle resulting from a lack of blood supplying the area.

myocardial rupture: The breaking apart of a damaged portion of the myocardium, usually several days after the onset of acute myocardial infarction; causes bleeding into the pericardial space, cardiac tamponade, and death if untreated.

myocardium: The cardiac muscle.

myoglobin: The oxygen-transporting protein of muscle, resembling hemoglobin in function.

Na^+: The chemical symbol for sodium ion.

$NaHCO_3$: The chemical formula for sodium bicarbonate.

nailbed: The area of the corium on which the nail rests.

naloxone: A narcotic antagonist drug used in the treatment of narcotic overdose; trade name: Narcan.

narcosis: An unconscious state produced by narcotics or accumulation of carbon dioxide in the blood, often accompanied by depression of the respiratory system and apnea.

narcotic: A drug used to depress the central nervous system, thereby relieving pain and producing sleep.

nasal bone: Either of the two small oblong bones that together form the bridge of the nose.

nasal cannula: A small tubular prong that fits into the patient's nostril to provide supplemental oxygen; usually there are two, one for each nostril.

nasopharyngeal: Relating to the pharynx at the body of the nose.

nasopharynx: The upper part of the pharynx above the level of the palate.

nausea: An unpleasant sensation, vaguely referred to the epigastrium and abdomen, often culminating in vomiting.

nebulizer: An apparatus for distributing liquid in the form of a fine spray or vapor.

neck: The supporting structure of the head, formed by the seven cervical vertebrae, and lying between the head and shoulders.

necrosis: A death of an area of tissue, usually caused by the cessation of blood supply.

necrotic: Pertaining to dead tissue.

neonate: Newborn, up to age of 1 month.

nerve: A cordlike structure composed of a collection of fibers that convey impulses between a part of the central nervous system and some other region.

nerve root: One of two bundles of nerve fibers emerging from the spinal cord at each vertebra to join and form a spinal nerve.

nervous system: The brain, spinal cord, and nerve branches from the central, peripheral, and autonomic systems.

neural: Relating to any part of the nervous system.

neural canal: The canal formed by the vertebrae that houses the spinal cord.

neurogenic: Of or originating in the nervous system.

neurogenic shock: A shock caused by massive vasodilation and pooling of blood in the peripheral vessels to a degree that adequate perfusion cannot be maintained.

neurological: Of or relating to the branch of medical science dealing with the nervous system and its disorders.

neuron: A nerve cell.

neurotic: A term that refers to a person suffering disorders in thought processes that are not due to demonstrable disease of the central nervous system.

neurotoxic: Poisonous to nervous tissue.

neurotransmitter: The substance secreted by the axons of nerves to bridge the synapse in order to stimulate the adjoining neuron.

neutralize: To render neutral; specifically, the chemical combinations of hydrogen and hydroxyl ions to form water, rendering each ion harmless.

nitrogen: An element (N) making up about 80 percent of the atmosphere; present in the tissues of all plants and animals.

nitrogen narcosis: A drugged condition created when the nitrogen in the body is exposed to great pressure, as in a deep dive; similar to alcoholic intoxication; the condition can cause divers to remove their breathing equipment while underwater; also called "rapture of the deep."

nitroglycerin: A drug used in the treatment of angina pectoris, usually taken under the tongue.

nocturia: The necessity to get up at night to urinate.

nodal: Usually pertaining to the AV node.

noise: Any extraneous spikes, waves, and complexes in the EKG signal caused by various conditions such as muscle tremor, 60 cycle alternating current interference, improperly attached electrodes, and out of range transmission.

nonconductor: Anything that does not transmit an electrical impulse or other source of energy.

nondirecting question: An interview technique in which the paramedic asks open-ended questions in an attempt to calm the patient and gather information on the patient's problem.

norepinephrine: A hormone and drug used in the treatment of shock primarily for its alpha stimulating properties; causes vasoconstriction; trade name Levophed.

normal saline: An intravenous solution containing 0.9 percent sodium chloride in water; used when volume replacement is desired.

normal sinus rhythm: The normal rhythm of the heart in which the rate is between 60 to 100 beats per minute, the rhythm is regular, the QRS interval is less than 0.12 second, the P-R interval is between 0.12 and 0.20 second, and there is only one P wave per QRS.

noxious: injurious.

nucleus: Specifically, the central portion of an atom where most of the mass and all of the positive charges are concentrated; the largest centriole of a cell, containing the genes.

nystagmus: Continuous rolling movement of the eyeball.

obese: Fat.

oblique fracture: A fracture that runs diagonally to the long axis of the bone.

obstruction: Blockage.

occipital: Pertaining to the back of the head.

occiput: The back of the skull.

occlude: To close off or stop up; obstruct.

occlusion: The act of closure or closing off; an obstruction.

occlusive dressing: A watertight dressing for a wound.

ocular: Pertaining to the eye.

oculomotor nerve: Cranial nerve number three; carries impulses to cause the pupil to react to light by constricting; cerebral edema presses this nerve against the tentorium, causing it to cease functioning, thus indicating the "blown pupil."

odontoid process: The toothlike structure projecting from the second cervical vertebra.

ointment: A semisolid preparation for external application to the body usually containing a medicinal substance.

olfactory nerve: Cranial nerve number one; the nerve that transmits smell impulses to the brain; passes through the cribiform plate of the ethmoid bone.

oliguria: Secretion of a diminished amount of urine in relation to the fluid intake.

open fracture or dislocation: A fracture or dislocation exposed to the exterior; an open wound lies over the fracture or dislocation.

open pneumothorax: A pneumothorax caused by an opening in the chest wall; a sucking chest wound.

open wound: A wound in which the affected tissues are exposed by an external opening.

opiate: Technically, one of several alkaloids derived from the opium poppy plant.

opisthotonos: A convulsive, rigid arching of the back that is seen in tetanus, severe meningitis, epilepsy, strychnine poisoning, and hysteria.

optic nerve: Cranial nerve number two; the nerve that transmits visual impulses from the eye to the brain.

oral: Pertaining to the mouth.

orbits: The bony, pyramid-shaped cavities in the skull that hold the eyeballs.

organic chemical: A substance obtained by a chemical process, prepared for use in chemical manufacture or for producing a chemical effect.

organic compound: A compound composed of atoms held together by shared electron bonds; an acid made up of molecules containing organic radicals.

organism: Any living thing.

orifice: The entrance to, or outlet of, any body cavity.

oropharyngeal airway: The respiratory adjunct placed in the patient's upper airway so that the distal part lies behind the base of the tongue and holds the tongue forward, preventing occlusion of the airway.

oropharynx: The area behind the base of the tongue that lies between the soft palate and upper portion of the epiglottis.

orthopnea: A severe shortness of breathing or difficulty in breathing when lying down; relieved by placing the patient in a sitting position.

oscilloscope: A display device with a screen for viewing an EKG or other physiologic data.

osmolality: The concentration of the solute in a solution per unit of solvent.

osmosis: The passage of pure solvent from a solution of lower solute concentration to one of higher solute concentration across a semipermeable membrane.

osmotic pressure: The pressure exerted by a solution of greater solute concentration upon water in a solution of lower solute concentration.

ossicle: A small bone; specifically, one of the three bones of the middle ear, malleus, incas, or stapes.

-otomy: A suffix meaning surgical incision into an organ, as in tracheotomy.

ovary: The female gonad in which eggs and female hormones are produced.

overhydration: A condition that results from excessive retention of fluids; circulatory overload.

overreaction: Overly intense reaction or response to a stimulus.

ovum: Egg.

oxygen: A colorless, odorless, tasteless gas essential to life and comprising 21 percent of the atmosphere; chemical formula: O_2.

oxygen drive: The stimulus to

breathe when the arterial level of oxygen in the blood is low.

oxygen mask: A device that fits over a patient's nose and mouth to permit breathing of oxygen which is fed into it.

oxygen toxicity: An unusual condition caused by excessive concentration of oxygen in inspired air, resulting in damage to lung tissue; it is very seldom seen in emergency work.

oxytocin: A drug used to promote uterine contractions; trade name: Pitocin.

PAC: Abbreviation for premature atrial contraction.

pacemaker: The specialized tissue within the heart that initiates stimuli; also an artificial device used to stimulate the heart to beat when the electrical conduction system of the heart is malfunctioning.

pacemaker site: The site of origin of the excitation impulse in the SA node or an ectopic focus in any of the electrical conduction system of the heart.

palate: The roof of the mouth.

pallor: A paleness of the skin.

palpate: To examine by feeling and pressing with the palms and the fingers.

palpation: The act of palpating; the act of feeling with the hands for the purpose of determining the consistency of the part beneath.

palpitation: A sensation felt under the left breast when the heart "skips a beat" caused by premature ventricular contractions.

palsy: A paralysis.

pancreas: An intra-abdominal gland that secretes insulin and important digestive juices.

pancreatitis: An inflammation of the pancreas.

papillary muscle: The muscular protrusions of the myocardium into the ventricular cavities to which the chorae tendineae are attached; purpose is to hold the mitral and tricuspid valves in place (closed) while the ventricles contract.

papule: A small, circumscribed, solid elevation of the skin.

paracentesis: A draining of fluid from the abdominal cavity by means of a needle or catheter introduced into the cavity through the abdominal wall.

paradoxical movement: The motion of an injured section of a flail chest; opposite to the normal movement of the chest wall.

paralysis: Loss of impairment of motor function of a part due to a lesion of the neural or muscular mechanism.

paranoia: A mental disorder characterized by abnormal suspicions or other delusions, often of persecution or grandeur.

paraplegia: The loss of both sensation and motion in the legs and lower parts of the body; most commonly due to damage of the spinal cord.

parasite: An animal or vegetable organism that lives on or in another organism.

parasympathetic nervous system: A subdivision of the autonomic nervous system involved in control of the involuntary functions; restores the body to normality after stimulus.

parasympatholytic: A term used to describe any agent that blocks the effects of stimulation of the parasympathetic system.

parasympathomimetic: A term used to describe any agent that mimicks the effects of stimulation of the parasympathetic nervous system.

parenchyma: The essential or specialized part of an organ as distinguished from its supporting connective tissue.

parenteral: The administration of a medication or fluid by a means other than the digestive tract; intramuscularly or intravenously.

paresis: Incomplete or partial paralysis.

paresthesia: An abnormal skin sensation, often of the pins-and-needles variety, indicating a disturbance in nerve function.

parietal area: Pertaining to or forming any wall of a cavity.

parietal lobe: The upper control lobe of the cerebrum; pertaining to or located near the parietal bone of the skull.

parietal pleura: A serous membrane that lines the inside of the chest wall and the pericardium.

paroxysm: A spasm; a sudden, intense periodic attack, or recurr ence of symptoms.

paroxysmal atrial tachycardia (PAT): A sudden onset of tachycardia which originates in the atrial conduction system, ending abruptly through some stimulation of the parasympathetic system.

paroxysmal nocturnal dyspnea (PND): A severe shortness of breath that occurs at night after several hours of recumbency and forces the patient to sit upright to breathe; caused by left heart failure.

patella: A small, flat bone that protects the knee joint; the kneecap.

patent: Open; unobstructed; obvious.

pathogenic: Capable of causing a disease process.

pathologic: Indicative or caused by disease.

pathological fracture: A fracture in which a specific weakness or destruction of the bone, caused by a certain process, such as cancer, is the reason for the break.

pathophysiology: The study of the changes in normal body function in the presence of disease.

pediatrics: The medical specialty devoted to the diagnosis and treatment of diseases of children.

pelvic cavity: The lowermost portion of the abdominal cavity containing the rectum, urinary bladder, and, in the female, the internal sex organs.

pelvic girdle: The large, bony structure supporting the abdominal and pelvic organs; made up of two ossa innominata.

pelvis: See pelvic girdle.

penetrate: To pierce; to pass into the deeper tissues or into a cavity.

Penrose drain: A surgical instrument made by drawing a strip of gauze through a tube of thin rubber; also the tube of thin rubber itself; sometimes the latter is used as a tourniquet.

peptic ulcer: An ulcer produced by the action of acid, pepsin, gastric juice in the stomach, lower esophagus, and proximal duodenum.

percussion: The act of tapping a part of the body; used as an aid in diagnosing the condition of the underlying body structures by the sound obtained by tapping with the fingers.

percutaneous: Through the skin.

perfusion: The act of pouring through or into; the blood getting to the cells in order to exchange gases, nutrients, etc., with the cells.

pericardial cavity: The space or sac formed by the two layers of the pericardium, the outer parietal pericardium, and the inner visceral pericardium.

pericardial fluid: The small amount of fluid secreted by the inner, serous, visceral pericardium.

pericardial effusion: The fluid within the pericardial sac.

pericardial tamponade: The accumulation of excess fluid or blood in the pericardial sac; interferes with heart action.

pericardium: The double-layered sac holding the heart and the origins of the superior vena cava and pulmonary artery.

perineum: The region between the genitals and the anus.

periosteum: The dense, fibrous tissue covering the bone.

peripheral: Pertaining to the outside; that which is situated away from the center part.

peripheral nervous system: The portion of the nervous system consisting of the nerves and ganglia outside the brain and the spinal cord.

peripheral vascular resistance: The resistance to blood flow in the systemic circulation; depends on the degree of constriction or dilation of the small arteries, arterioles, venules, and veins making up the peripheral vascular system.

peripheral vasoconstriction: The constriction of blood vessels causing an increase in blood pressure.

peripheral vasodilation: The dilation of blood vessels causing a decrease in blood pressure.

peristalsis: The successive waves of muscular contraction and relaxation proceeding uniformly along a hollow tube, such as the esophagus or intestine; this motion propels the contents of the tube forward.

peritoneal cavity: The abdominal cavity.

peritoneum: The serous membrane lining the abdominal cavity.

peritonitis: An inflammation of the peritoneum.

petechia: A minute red spot due to escape of a small amount of blood within the skin.

petit mal seizure: A type of epileptic attack, characterized by a momentary loss of awareness but not accompanied by loss of motor tone.

pH: A symbol used to indicate the acidity or alkalinity of a substance; the negative log of the concentration of hydrogen ions in a substance.

-phagia: Suffix meaning to swallow, to eat, to ingest.

phalanx: Any bone of the finger or toe.

pharmacology: The study of drugs and their origin, nature, properties, and effects.

pharyngeal: Pertaining to the pharynx.

pharynx: The portion of the airway between the nasal cavity and the larynx.

phenobarbital: One of the barbiturates; a hypnotic-sedative.

phlebitis: An inflammation of the wall of a vein manifested by tenderness, redness, and a slight edema along part of the length of the vein.

phobia: An abnormal and persistent fear of a specific object or situation.

phrenic nerve: The motor nerve of the diaphragm.

physical dependence: Habituation or use of a drug, or other maneuver, because of its physiologic support, and because of the undesirable effects of withdrawal.

physiologic action: The action caused by a drug when given in the concentrations normally present in the body; applies only to drugs that are derived from normal body chemicals.

physiology: The study of body functions.

pia mater: The innermost and most delicate of the three membranes covering the brain and spinal cord.

PID: Abbreviation for pelvic inflammatory disease.

piggyback: Used to describe the process of adding another solution to an infusion set by inserting a needle connected to a second infusion set into the first set.

pill: A small ball or oval that has been molded or compressed from a powdered drug; often coated to disguise an unpleasant taste, or to delay absorption.

pin index: A safety attachment on the outlet valve of a gas-filled cylinder.

pinna: The outer portion of the ear that leads to the ear canal.

pitting edema: A severe edema of the extremities in which pressure on the tissue with the fingers causes an indentation that persists after release of pressure.

placenta: A vascular organ attached to the uterine wall that supplies oxygen and nutrients to the fetus; also called the afterbirth.

placenta previa: A delivery in which the placenta is the presenting part; may result in exsanguinating hemorrhage.

plasma: The fluid portion of the blood; retains the clotting factors but has no red or white cells.

platelet: A small cellular element in the blood that assists in blood clotting.

pleura: A continuous serous membrane that lines the outer surfaces of the lungs and the internal surface of the thoracic cavity.

pleural cavity: The potential space between the parietal and visceral pleura.

pleuritic pain: A sharp chest pain that is made worse by deep breathing, coughing, or laughing; characteristic of pleuritis.

pleuritis: Inflammation of the pleura.

plexus: A network or tangle of nerves, blood, or lymphatic vessels.

brachial plexus: A network of nerves containing the motor and sensory innervation of the arm.

lumbosacral plexus: A network of nerves containing the motor and sensory innervation of the leg.

PND: Abbreviation for paroxysmal noctural dyspnea.

-pnea: Suffix for respiration, breathing.

pneumo-: Prefix for air or gas; lung.

pneumonia: An acute infectious disease of the lungs; causes an effusion.

pneumothorax: An accumulation of air in the pleural cavity, usually entering after a wound or injury that causes a penetration of the chest wall or laceration of the lung.

p.o.: Abbreviation for *per os*, by mouth.

point of maximal impulse (PMI): A palpable thrust of the apex of the heart against the thoracic cage during ventricular contraction; normally palpated in the fifth left intercostal space in the midclavicular line.

point tenderness: An area of tenderness limited to 2 or 3 centimeters in diameter; point tenderness can be located in any area of the body; usually associated with acute inflammation, as in peritonitis (abdominal point tenderness).

poly-: Prefix meaning many or much.

polydipsia: A condition of excessive thirst.

polyphagia: A condition of excessive hunger.

polyuria: A condition of excessive urination.

popliteal: The area or space behind the knee joint.

popliteal artery: The continuation of the femoral artery in the area behind the knee joint; used to auscultate pulse when taking a femoral blood pressure.

posterior: Situated in the back of or behind a surface.

posterior tibial artery: The artery located posterior to the medial malleolus; supplies blood to the foot.

postictal: Refers to the period after the convulsive stage of a seizure.

postmortem: After death; commonly, the detailed examination of a body after death to determine the cause of death.

postpartum: After childbirth.

potassium: A mineral substance necessary for the proper functioning of the heart and other tissues.

potentiation: The enhancement of the effect of one drug by another.

powder: A drug that has been ground into powder form.

P-QRS-T: One heartbeat on EKG, representing the atrial depolarization (P), ventricular depolarization (QRS), and ventricular repolarization (T).

precordial: A term that refers to the general area overlying the heart and lower thorax.

precordial thump: A sharp blow delivered to the midsternum for the purpose of terminating ventricular tachycardia or stimulating the heart to beat in systole. No longer recognized by the American Heart Association as an effective maneuver.

precursor: Something in a stage of a process that precedes a later stage.

pre-eclampsia: The condition that precedes eclampsia, or toxemia of pregnancy, characterized by hypertension, edema, and seizures.

preinfarction angina: An unstable angina.

premature atrial contraction (PAC): An extra atrial and ventricular contraction with normal QRS complexes; occurring early in the cardiac cycle; caused by excitation impulses arising in single or multiple foci in the internodal pathways.

premature junctional contraction (PJC): Also called premature nodal contractions (PNC); extra ventricular contractions with normal or abnormal QRS complexes arising in single or multiple ectopic foci in the AV junction.

prenatal: Before birth.

presenting part: The part of the baby that emerges first during delivery.

pressure dressing: A dressing with which enough pressure is applied over a wound site to stop bleeding.

pressure point: One of several places on the body where the blood flow of a given artery can be restricted by pressing the artery against an underlying bone.

pressure splints: An inflatable plastic circumferential splint that can be applied to an extremity and inflated to achieve stability after a fracture.

priapism: A persistent erection of the penis, especially when due to disease, injury, or excessive quantities of androgens.

primipara: A woman who is about to give birth to a baby for the first time.

P-R interval (PRI): The period of time between the beginning of the atrial depolarization and the beginning of the ventricular depolarization, signifying the time of conduction of a stimulus.

prn: Abbreviation for *pro re nata*; as needed.

prognosis: A probable outcome of a disease based on assumptive knowledge.

prolapse: To fall out or slip down; usually refers to an organ or other body part.

prolapsed cord: A delivery in which the umbilical cord appears at the vaginal opening before the head of the infant.

prone: A position of lying face down.

prophylaxis: A method for taking measure to prevent the occurrence of a given disease or abnormal state.

propranolol: A drug used to prevent or terminate life-threatening arrhythmias; also used to reduce tachycardias, to suppress the beta receptors of the sympathetic system; trade name: Inderal.

prostate: A gland at the base of the male bladder that often becomes enlarged later in life and causes an obstruction of urine flow.

prosthesis: An artificial part made to replace a natural one.

prostration: A collapse.

proteinuria: Protein in the urine.

proximal: Closer to any point of reference; usually refers to closeness to the midline of the body.

psilocybin: A hallucinogenic agent obtained from the mushroom *Psilocybe mexicana*.

psychiatry: The medical study

dealing with mental disorders.

psychogenic shock: A fainting spell as a result of transient generalized cerebral ischemia; not a true shock condition.

psychological dependence: Dependence of a drug, or other therapeutic maneuvers, because of its support to the patient's psyche, rather than to his physiological function.

psychosis: A mental disorder characterized by a disintegration of personality and loss of contact with reality.

psychosomatic: An indication of an illness in which some part of the cause is related to emotional factors.

pubic symphysis: The joint formed by union of the bodies of the pubic bones in the midsagittal plane; characterized by a thick mass of fibrocartilage.

pulmonary: Pertaining to the lungs or related structures.

pulmonary alveoli: The air sacs of the lungs.

pulmonary artery: The major artery leading from the right ventricle to the lungs.

pulmonary circulation: The passage of blood from the right ventricle through the pulmonary artery and all of its branches and capillaries in the lungs, and then back to the left atrium through the pulmonary veins.

pulmonary contusion: A bruise of the pulmonary tissue.

pulmonary edema: The condition of the lungs when the pulmonary alveoli are filled with exudate and foam, usually secondary to left heart failure.

pulmonary embolism: Obstruction of the pulmonary arteries by emboli of any foreign material in the venous system.

pulmonary resuscitation: A technique providing artificial ventilation, through mouth to mouth, mouth to nose, or using any of the airway adjuncts.

pulmonary valve: The valve between the right ventricle and the pulmonary artery.

pulmonary veins: The veins that carry oxygenated blood from the lungs to the left atrium.

pulsatile: A term that refers to a pulsating or throbbing action.

pulse: The rhythmic expansion and contraction of an arterial wall caused by ventricular systole and diastole.

pulse deficit: The difference in heart rate between apical rate and the rate obtained by palpating a peripheral artery.

pulse pressure: The difference between the systolic and diastolic pressures.

pulse rate: The heart rate determined by counting the number of pulsations occurring in any superficial artery.

pump failure: A partial or total failure of the heart to pump blood effectively; causes cardiogenic shock.

pupil: The small opening in the center of the iris.

Purkinje network: The portion of the electrical conduction system in the ventricles that conducts the electrical impulses causing depolarization of the myocardium.

PVC: Abbreviation for premature ventricular contractions.

P wave: The wave on EKG that represents depolarization of the atria.

q.d.: Abbreviation for *quaque die*; every day.

q.h.: Abbreviation for *quaque hora*; every hour.

q. 2 h.: Abbreviation for *quaque seconda hora*; every 2 hours.

q.i.d.: Abbreviation for *quater in die*; four times a day.

QRS complex: The deflections of the EKG produced during ventricular depolarizations; Q is the first negative deflection before the first positive deflection; R is the first positive deflection; and S is a negative deflection occurring after the R.

Q-T interval: The period between the onset of ventricular depolarization and the end of repolarization of the ventricle; measured from the beginning of the QRS complex to the end of the T wave; the length of time it takes for the ventricles to depolarize and repolarize.

quadrant: One of the four quarters of the abdomen.

quadriplegia: A paralysis of both arms and legs.

quinidine: A drug used to treat various atrial and ventricular arrhythmias.

Q wave: The first negative deflection of the QRS complex; not preceded by an R wave.

raccoon sign: Bilateral symmetrical periorbital ecchymoses seen with basal skull fractures; also called coon's eyes.

rad: A measure of the dose absorbed from ionizing radiation; equivalent to 100 ergs of energy per gram.

radial: Pertaining to the radial bone of the arm.

radial artery: One of the major arteries of the forearm; the pulse is palpable at the base of the thumb.

radial nerve: One of the three major nerves of the arm; descending at the back of the arm closely applied to the humerus and then into the forearm; it is ultimately distributed to the skin at the back of the arm, forearm, and hand.

radiant energy: Any energy that is radiated from any source.

radiation: The process of emitting energy in a particulate or wave form.

radiation sickness: The condition that follows excessive irradiation from any source.

radioactivity: The property of spontaneously emitting rays or subatomic particles of matter accompanied by the release of large amounts of energy.

radius: The bone on the thumb side of the forearm.

rales: An abnormal breath sound produced by the flow of air through bronchi and bronchioles when they are constricted by spasm or filled by secretions.

rape: Sexual intercourse by force.

rash: An eruption of the skin, either localized or generalized.

receptor: A specialized area in a tissue that initiates a certain action upon specific stimulation.

recompression: The repressurization of divers who have been decompressed too soon.

rectal temperature: The core body temperature obtained by insertion of a thermometer into the rectum and retaining it for a minute; normally 1 degree Fahrenheit higher than oral temperature.

rectum: The distal portion of the large intestine.

red blood cell: An erythrocyte; the cell that carries oxygen from alveoli to cell.

reduce: To restore a part to its normal position.

reflex: An involuntary muscular action in response to stimulation.

reflex action: An automatic reaction to a stimulus such as pulling one's hand away from something hot.

reflex arc: The nervous root utilized in a reflex action, consisting of an afferent (sensory) nerve, internuncial (connecting) nerve, and an efferent (motor) nerve.

regression: In psychiatry, a return to an earlier or former developmental state.

regurgitation: A backward flowing, as the casting up of undigested food from the stomach to the mouth.

relative refractory period: The period of repolarization of the heart muscle and conduction systems during which another stimulus may cause a premature contraction.

renal: Pertaining to the kidney.

repolarization: The electrical process of recharging depolarized muscle fibers back to the resting state.

reproductive system: The body system that includes all the organs necessary for reproduction.

rescue: The freeing of persons from threatening or dangerous situations by prompt and vigorous action.

respiration: The act of breathing; the exchange of oxygen and carbon dioxide in the tissues, lungs.

- **internal respiration:** The exchange of oxygen and carbon dioxide at the cellular level.
- **external respiration:** The exchange of oxygen and carbon dioxide between the alveoli and blood in the lungs.

respiratory arrest: The cessation of breathing.

respiratory failure: A failure of the respiratory system to maintain an oxygen pressure greater than 60 torr and a carbon dioxide pressure of less than 50 torr.

respiratory system: A system of organs that controls the inspiration of oxygen and the expiration of carbon dioxide.

response time: The length of time required for the emergency medical services team to arrive at the scene of an emergency after receiving a call for help.

resting potential: The electrical charge of the muscle fibers during the resting polarized state.

resuscitation: The act of reviving an unconscious patient.

retention: The inability to void.

retina: The lining of the back of the eye that receives visual images and transmits them via the optic nerve to the brain.

retractions: The drawing in of the intercostal muscles above the clavicles; seen in respiratory arrest.

retro-: The prefix meaning located behind.

retrograde amnesia: An amnesia for events that occurred before a traumatic event or before the disease that caused the condition.

retroperitoneal: Pertaining to a location behind the peritoneum.

retrosternal: Situated or occurring behind the sternum.

Rh factor: An antigen present in the blood cells of some individuals; when present, the individual is said to be Rh positive; when not present, to be Rh negative.

rhonchi: Coarse rattling sounds somewhat like snoring, usually caused by secretions in the bronchial tubes.

rib: One of the 24 bones forming the thoracic cavity wall.

rib cage: The skeletal framework of the chest; composed of the sternum, the ribs, and the thoracic vertebrae.

right atrium: The upper chamber of the right heart that is continuous with the venae cavae and channels blood into the right ventricle.

right heart: The right atrium and the right ventricle.

right heart failure: The failure of the right ventricle to pump blood effectively, causing backup of blood into the systemic veins, with consequent edema of body tissues.

right ventricle: The lower right chamber of the heart that receives blood from the right atrium and pumps blood out through the pulmonary valve into the pulmonary artery.

rigid splint: A splint made of a firm material that can be applied to an injured extremity to prevent motion at the site of a fracture or dislocation.

risk factor: A variable that contributes to the initiation and continuation of a disease process.

Robinson stretcher: Split frame stretcher.

roentgen: The international unit of X-ray or gamma radiation.

roller dressing: A strip of rolled-up material used for dressings.

R-on-T phenomenon: An ominous premature ventricular contraction that occurs very near the vulnerable period of the relative refractory period; may produce ventricular fibrillation.

rotation: The turning or movement of a body around its axis.

R-R interval: The interval of the EKG between the onset of the ventricular depolarization of one complex and the onset of the subsequent ventricular depolarization.

rupture: A tear or dissolution of continuity; a break of any organ or tissue.

R wave: The initial positive wave or deflection of the QRS complex on EKG.

s: Abbreviation for *sine*; without.

sacral: Pertaining to the sacrum, which is the fused bone of the five sacral vertebrae, part of the pelvic girdle.

sacral spine: The five fused vertebrae which make up the sacrum.

sacroiliac joint: Left and right joining of the sacrum and ilia.

sacrum: The part of the lower spine made up of the five fused sacral vertebrae.

saddle joint: A joint formed where a portin of one bone hangs over another, as in the thumb.

safe residual: The pressure reading at which an oxygen cylinder should be replaced to avoid totally depleting its contents; the standard safe residual is 100 psi.

saline: Containing salt.

saline solution: A solution of any salt, but usually refers to a solution of sodium chloride.

saliva: The clear, alkaline fluid secreted by the salivary glands.

salivary glands: The glands that produce and secrete saliva, connected to the mouth by ducts.

salivation: An excess secretion of saliva.

scab: A crust formed by the coagulation of blood, pus, serum, or any combination of these on the surface of an ulcer, erosion, abrasion, or any other type of wound.

scalp vein set: An intravenous needle and tube set with butterfly wings; used for initiating an IV line in the veins of a child's scalp.

scapula: The shoulder blade.

scapular spine: The prominent triangular ridge on the dorsal aspect of the scapula.

sciatic nerve: A major collection of nerve fibers arising from the lumbosacral plexus and subserving most sensation of the lower extremity and motion of the leg and foot.

sclera: The white, opaque, outer layer of the eyeball.

scrotum: A pouch of thickened skin hanging at the base of the penis in the midline; contains the testes and their accessory ducts and vessels.

SCUBA: Abbreviation for self-contained underwater breathing apparatus.

seal bark: A characteristic hoarse, barking cough heard in croup.

sebaceous gland: A gland in the dermis that secretes sebum.

sebum: The secretion of the sebaceous gland; a thick, oily, semifluid substance composed of fat and epithelial debris from the cells of the skin.

secondary infection: An infection occurring in a patient already suffering from a wound or disease.

second-degree burn: A burn penetrating beneath the superficial skin layers, producing edema and blisters.

sedative: A drug that depresses the activity of the central nervous system; has a calming effect.

seizure: A sudden attack or recurrence of a disease; a convulsion; an attack of epilepsy.

self-contained air mask: A mask used for delivery of air to a rescuer when entering contaminated areas filled with smoke or poisonous gases; consists of a tight-fitting mask, controls, and an air supply.

semicircular canals: The small structures in the inner ear that maintain one's equilibrium.

semiconscious: Stuporous; partially conscious.

seminal duct: The duct through which sperm pass into the seminal vesicles.

seminal vesicles: Either of the paired, sacculated pouches attached to the posterior past of the urinary bladder in the male; the duct of each joins the ductus deferens of the same side to form the ejaculatory duct.

senile: Pertaining to old age; implies loss of mental ability.

sense: Any one of the faculties by which the conditions or properties of things are perceived.

sensory nerves: The nerves that conduct impulses from various sense modalities through the spinal cord to the brain.

sepsis: The presence in the blood or other tissues of pathogenic microorganisms or their toxins.

septum: A dividing wall or partition, usually separating two cavities.

sequelae: Any lesion or affection following or caused by an attack of disease.

serum: The liquid portion of the blood containing all of the dissolved constituents except those used for clotting.

shivering: A trembling from cold or fear; produces heat by muscular contractions.

shock: A state of inadequate tissue perfusion that may be a result of pump failure (cardiogenic shock), volume loss or sequestration (hypovolemic shock), vasodilation (neurogenic shock), or any combination of these.

anaphylactic shock: A rapidly occurring state of collapse caused by hypersensitivity to drugs or other foreign material (insect venom, certain foods, inhaled allergenic); symptoms may include hives, wheezing, tissue edema, bronchospasm, vascular collapse.

septic shock: A shock developing in the presence of, and as a result of, severe infection.

shoulder girdle: The encircling bony structure supporting the upper limbs; comprised of the scapulae, clavicles, and their central attachment.

shoulder joint: A ball-and-socket joint between the head of the humerus and the glenoid fossa of the scapula.

shunt: A situation in which a portion of the output of the right heart reaches the left heart without being oxygenated in the lungs; may be due to atelectasis, pulmonary edema, or a variety of other factors.

dialysis shunt: The surgically produced shunt between the radial artery and cephalic vein between the wrist and elbow of the dialysis patient; used to transfer blood to and from the dialysis machine.

sickle cell anemia: A hereditary, genetically determined hemolytic anemia occurring in the black population; characterized by joint pain, acute attacks of abdominal pain, and recurrent embolic episodes.

SIDS: Abbreviation for sudden infant death syndrome.

sigmoid colon: The terminal division of the large intestine that makes several turns, roughly resembling the letter sigma, and terminates at the rectum.

sign: Any objective evidence of physical manifestation of a disease.

silent acute myocardial infarction: An acute myocardial infarction not accompanied by pain.

simple fracture: A fracture that is not compound; the skin is not broken over the break in the bone.

sinoatrial node (SA node): The physiological pacemaker of the heart; a group of specialized fibers that rhythmically initiate stimuli at the rate of approximately 72 beats per minute that in turn traverse the heart's conduction system to cause the atria and then the ventricles to contract; can develop stimuli at the lower rate of 40 per minute to an upper limit of approximately 160 per minute.

sinus: A general term for a hollow space, such as a channel for venous blood in the cranium or an air cavity in one of the facial bones.

sinus arrhythmia: A common and usually innocuous dysrhythmia characterized by an irregular rhythm with an otherwise normal sinus rhythm; caused by breathing rhythms.

sinus bradycardia: A sinus rhythm with a heart rate of greater than 100 beats per minute.

skeletal muscle: A striated muscle usually attached to, and moving, the bones, sometimes fascia; generally under voluntary control.

skeleton: The hard, bony structure that forms the main support of the body.

skin: The outer integument or covering of the body, consisting of the dermis and the epidermis; the largest organ of the body; contains various sensory and regulatory mechanisms.

skull: The bony structure surrounding the brain; consists of the cranial bones, the facial bones, and the teeth.

slough: To cast off tissue, usually necrotic, separating from living tissue.

small intestine: The portion of the intestine between the stomach and the colon.

smooth muscle: A nonstriated muscle found in the walls of the internal organs and blood vessels; generally not under voluntary control.

sniffing position: The position for endotracheal intubation with the neck flexed and the head extended.

socket: A hollow in a joint or other part into which a corresponding organ or part fits.

sodium bicarbonate: A drug with alkaline properties used to raise the pH of the body when acidosis is present.

soft tissue: The nonbony and noncartilaginous tissue of the body.

solution: A liquid consisting of two or more substances that are molecularly dispersed through one another in a homogeneous manner.

source: The object, person, or substance from which an infectious agent passes to a host.

spasm: A sudden, violent, involuntary contraction of a muscle, or group of muscles, attended by pain and interference with function; a sudden but transitory constriction of a passage, canal, or orifice.

sphincter: A muscle that encircles a duct, tube, or opening in such a way that its contraction constricts the opening.

sphygmomanometer: A device for measuring blood pressure.

spinal canal: The tunnel through which the spinal cord passes.

spineboard: A wooden or metal device used primarily for extrication and transportation of patients with actual or suspected spinal injuries.

spiral fracture: A fracture in which the line of break runs diagonally around the long axis of the bone.

spirits: A preparation of volatile substances dissolved in alcohol.

spleen: The largest lymphatic organ of the body; located in the left upper quadrant of the abdomen.

splint: Any support used to immobilize a fracture or to restrict movement of a part.

spontaneous pneumothorax: A rupture of the lung parenchyma, resulting in the accumulation of air in the pleural space without trauma.

sprain: A trauma to a joint, causing injury to the ligaments.

sputum: Expectorated matter, especially mucus or matter resulting from diseases of the air passages.

squelch: A system for removing unwanted background noise in a radio frequency.

S-T segment: The interval of the EKG between the end of the QRS complex and the beginning of the T wave; often elevated, reflecting current of injury in that part of the heart scanned by the particular lead, or depressed, reflecting ischemia of the same area.

stat: Abbreviation for statim, immediately.

status asthmaticus: A severe, prolonged asthmatic attack that cannot be broken with epinephrine.

status epilepticus: The occurrence of two or more seizures without a period of complete consciousness between them.

stenosis: The narrowing or stricture of a duct or canal.

sterilize: To render sterile or free from bacterial contamination; to make an organism unable to reproduce.

sternoclavicular joint: The articulation of the clavicle, the sternum, and the cartilage of the first rib with an articular disc; subdivides the joint into two cavities.

sternum: The long, flat bone located in the midline in the anterior part of the thoracic cage; articulates above with the clavicles and along the sides with the cartilages of the first seven ribs.

sternocleidomastoid muscle: The large muscle on either side of the neck that flexes the head.

stethoscope: An instrument for performing auscultation.

stillbirth: The birth of a dead fetus.

stimulant: Any agent that increases the level of bodily activity.

stoma: A small opening, especially an artificially created opening.

stomach: The hollow digestive organ in the epigastrium that receives food from the esophagus.

stool: Feces; the matter discharged at defecation.

strain: An injury to a muscle caused by a violent contraction or an excessive forceable stretching.

stress: Any chemical, physical, or emotional factor that causes mental or bodily tension; may be a cause of disease.

stretcher: A carrying device that enables two or more persons to lift and carry a patient who is lying down.

stridor: A harsh, high-pitched respiratory sound associated with severe upper airway obstruction.

stroke: A cerebrovascular accident of sudden onset.

stroke volume: The amount of blood pumped forward by the heart each time the ventricles contract.

stupor: A state of reduced sensitivity; mental confusion.

subclavian vein: The large vein located beneath the clavicle and joining the internal jugular vein.

subcutaneous: Beneath the skin.

subcutaneous emphysema: A condition in which trauma to the lung or airway results in the escape of air into body tissues, especially the chest wall, neck, and face; a crackling sensation will be felt on palpation of the skin.

subdural: Refers to any lesion in the brain that occurs beneath the dura.

subdural hematoma: A collection of blood or clot between the dura mater and the arachnoid usually caused by a laceration or rupture of a meningeal blood vessel.

sublingual: Under the tongue.

substernal: Beneath the sternum; retrosternal.

sucking chest wound: An open pneumothorax.

suction catheter: A hollow, semirigid tube of various diameters that is used to aspirate material from within the pharynx, trachea, and upper bronchi.

sudden infant death syndrome (SIDS): A sudden, unexplained death of an infant within the first six months of life; crib death.

suffocate: To impede respiration; to asphyxiate.

suicide: The act of deliberately taking one's own life.

superficial: Confined to or pertaining to the surface.

superior: In anatomy, used to refer to an organ or part that is located above another organ or part.

superior vena cava: One of the two largest veins in the body that empty venous blood into the right atrium; receives blood from the upper extremities, head, and neck.

supinate: To turn the forearm so that the palm faces upward.

supine: Lying horizontally in a face-upward position.

suppository: A drug mixed in a firm base that melts at body temperature, shaped to fit various body orifices, such as the rectum, urethra, and vagina.

supraventricular arrhythmia: An arrhythmia arising from any portion of the electrical conduction system that is above the ventricles.

supraventricular tachycardia: A rapid regular tachycardia with the ectopic pacemaker originating above the ventricles.

surgery: The branch of medicine that deals with trauma and diseases that require operative intervention.

suspension: A dispersin of a finely divided drug in a suitable liquid medium.

suture: A type of fibrous joint in which the opposed surfaces are closely united; also, the material used in closing a surgical wound, or repairing a gaping wound.

swathe: A cravat tied around the body to decrease movement of a part.

S wave: The negative deflection of the ventricular depolarization complex following the R deflection (positive) on EKG.

sweat gland: A gland that secretes water and electrolytes through the skin.

sympathetic nervous system: A subdivision of the autonomic nervous system that governs the body's reaction to stresses by stimulating the heart, bronchodilation, and other reactions.

sympatholytic: A term that describes any agent that blocks any action of the sympathetic nervous system.

sympathomimetic: A mimicking of the effects of the impulses conveyed by the sympathetic nervous system; relating to an agent that produces effects similar to those of impulses conveyed by the sympathetic nervous system, hence an alpha or beta sympathomimetic drug.

symphysis pubis: The midline articulation of the pubic bones.

symptom: A subjective sensation or awareness of disturbance of bodily function.

syncope: Fainting; a brief period of unconsciousness.

syndrome: A complex of symptoms and signs characteristic of a condition.

synergism: The joint action of agents such that their combined effect is greater than the sum of their individual effects.

synovial fluid: A clear, viscid fluid that lubricates joints; secreted by the synovial membrane.

synovium: The lining membrane of a joint cavity.

syrup: A drug suspended in sugar and water to improve its taste.

systemic: Refers to anything that affects the body as a whole.

systemic circulation: The passage of blood from the left ventricle through the aorta and all of its branches and capillaries and back to the right atrium through the venules, veins, and venae cavae.

systole: The period during which the ventricles contract.

systolic: Relating to, or occurring during cardiac systole.

systolic blood pressure: The highest peak pressure exerted on the arterial walls during ventricular contraction.

tablet: A small disc that has been molded or compressed from a powdered drug.

tachyarrhythmia: A rapid heart rate, over 120 to 160 per minute.

tachycardia: Abnormally rapid heart rate, over 100 beats per minute.

tachypnea: Excessively rapid rate of respiration, over 25 per minute in adults.

talus: The ankle bone that articulates with the tibia, fibula, calcaneous, and navicular bone.

tamponade: A condition resulting from excess fluid accumulation in the pericardium; may result from pericarditis or injuries to the heart, with an accumulation of blood; also the act of plugging with a tampon.

tarsal: Pertaining to the tarsus, the ankle.

TBW: Abbreviation for total body water.

telemetry: The measurement of diagnostic signs by electrical instruments and the transmission of them, especially by radio, to a distant place for recording; used for EKG signals.

temperature: The degree of heat of a living body; varies in cold-blooded animals with environmental temperature and is constant, within a narrow range, for warm-blooded animals; 98.6 degrees Fahrenheit oral temperature and 99.6 degrees rectal are considered normal for humans.

temple: The portion of the head above and anterior to the ears and above the zygomatic arch.

temporal artery: The artery located on either side of the face above and in front of the upper portion of the ear; supplies blood to the scalp.

temporal lobe: A region of the cerebral hemisphere below and lateral to the frontal and occipital lobes; contains the control center for speech.

temporomandibular joint (TM joint): Mandibular joint, the articulation between the head of the mandible and the mandibular fossa and articular tubercle of the temporal bone.

tendon: A tough band of dense, fibrous, connective tissue that attaches muscles to bone and other parts.

tension pneumothorax: A situation in which air enters the pleural space through a defective one-way valve in the lung, causing progressive increase in intrapleural pressure, with lung collapse and impairment of circulation.

testes: The male reproductive glands that produce spermatozoa.

tetanus: An infectious disease caused by an exotoxin of a bacteria, *Clostridium tetani*, that is usually introduced through a wound, characterized by extreme body rigidity and spasms, trismus, or opisthotonus, of voluntary body muscles.

thalamus: Either one of two grey matter masses situated on either side of the third ventricle near the brainstem; all sensory stimuli except olfactory, are received, synthesized, associated, and relayed to specific cortical areas of the brain.

thermal: Pertaining to heat.

thigh: The portion of the lower extremity between the hip and knee.

third-degree burn: A full-thickness burn destroying all skin layers and underlying tissue; has a charred or white, leathery appearance; insensitive.

Thomas splint: A rigid metal or plastic splint that provides support for and a steady longitudinal pull on the lower extremity.

thoracic cage: The rib cage.

thoracic cavity: The space within the chest walls between the diaphragm and the base of the neck.

thoracic spine: The vertebrae, usually 12 in number, between the cervical spine and the lumbar spine.

thorax: The portion of the trunk between the neck and the diaphragm, encased by the ribs; chest.

thready pulse: A pulse that is weak or scarcely audible, characteristic of a person in shock.

thrombophlebitis: A condition in which inflammation of a vein leads to the formation of a clot in the vein.

thrombosis: Formation of a blood clot or thrombus.

thyroid cartilage: The largest of the laryngeal cartilages, the Adam's apple.

thyroid gland: A ductless endocrine gland lying in front of the trachea; produces hormones involved in metabolism regulation.

tibia: The larger of the two bones in the leg; the shin bone.

t.i.d.: Abbreviation for *ter in die*; three times a day.

tidal volume: The amount of air inhaled or exhaled during any level of activity; the volume of one breath at rest approximates 500 milliliters.

tincture: A diluted alcoholic extract of a drug.

tinnitus: A ringing, tinkling, buzzing, or roaring noise in the ears.

tissue: An aggregation of similarly specialized cells and their intercellular substance united in the performance of a particular function.

tolerance: The state of enduring, or of less susceptability to the effects of a drug or poison after repeated doses.

tonic-clonic: Refers to the muscular spasms in which tonic and a clonic phase exist.

torr: The Torricelli unit; a measurement of pressure; one torr is the pressure needed to support 1 millimeter of mercury at 0 degrees Centigrade.

torsion: Twisting.

total body water: The total fluid content of the body; equivalent to about 60 percent of body weight in the adult male.

tourniquet: A constrictive device used on the extremities to impede venous blood return to the heart or obstruct arterial blood flow to the extremities.

toxemia: A condition wherein the blood contains poisonous products manufactured by body cells or microorganisms.

toxemia of pregnancy: A condition sometimes occurring during the second half of pregnancy manifested by symptoms of eclampsia.

toxin: Any poison manufactured by plant or animal life.

toxoid: A chemically modified toxin that, when injected, stimulates the development of immunity to a specific disease.

trachea: The cartilaginous tube extending from the larynx to its division into the primary bronchi; windpipe.

tracheostomy tube: A tube inserted into an opening made by a tracheotomy.

traction: The act of exerting a pulling force.

trade name: The name under which a drug is marketed by a given manufacturer; also referred to as the brand or proprietary name.

transfusion: An injection of blood, saline solution, or other liquid into a vein.

transfusion reaction: Any adverse reaction, allergic, febrile, or hemolytic produced in a patient due to a blood transfusion.

transient ischemic attack (TIA): A temporary condition wherein the blood supply to the brain is interfered with; usually an indication of an impending stroke.

transmission: The conveyance of disease from one person to another.

transverse colon: The division of the large intestine that crosses the abdomen, located between the ascending colon and the descending colon.

transverse fracture: A fracture in which the line of break forms a right angle to the axis of the bone.

trauma: Surgical definition: physical injury; psychiatric definition: emotional distress, relating to a specific incident.

traumatic asphyxia: A syndrome resulting from a very severe compression injury of the chest; cyanosis of the face and neck, bulging of the eyes, and a flail chest are external results.

tremor: An involuntary trembling or quivering of voluntary muscles.

triage: A system used for sorting patients to determine the order in which they will receive medical attention.

triangular bandage: A piece of cloth cut in the shape of a right-angled triangle; used as a sling, or folded for a cravat bandage.

tricuspid: The AV valve between the right atrium and right ventricle.

trunk: The body, excluding the head and limbs; torso.

turgor: The normal state of tension in living cells.

T wave: The wave following the QRS on the EKG, representing ventricular repolarization; under certain conditions, or in different leads, it may be positive, biphasic, flat, or inverted.

tympanic cavity: The cavity just behind the eardrum; the cavity of the middle ear.

tympanic membrane: The eardrum.

UHG: Abbreviation for ultra-high frequency band; refers to that part of the radio frequency spectrum between 300 and 3,000 megaHertz.

ulcer: An open lesion of the skin or mucous membrane.

ulna: The larger bone of the forearm, on the side opposite that of the thumb.

ulnar artery: A major artery of the forearm; pulse is palpable on the medial wrist at the base of the fifth finger.

umbilical clamp: A device, usually made of plastic, used to compress the umbilical cord that allows the cord to be cut without endangering the mother or baby from blood loss; proper cord cutting requires two clamps, one to prevent bleeding from the stump attached to the baby and one attached to the mother.

umbilical cord: A flexible structure connecting the fetus to the placenta.

umbilicus: The navel.

unconscious: Without awareness, the state of being comatose.

universal dressing: A large (9 by 36 inches) dressing of multilayered material that can be used open, folded, or rolled to cover most wounds, to pad splints, or to form a cervical collar.

uremia: A toxic condition caused by the inability of the kidneys to remove waste products from the blood.

ureter: Either of the tubes that convey urine from the kidneys to the bladder.

urethra: The canal that leads urine from the bladder to the urethral orifice.

urinary bladder: A musculomembranous bag serving as a storage place for urine until the urine is discharged from the body.

urinary system: The organs concerned with the formation and voiding of urine; consists of the kidneys, ureters, bladder, and urethra.

urine: The fluid secreted from the blood by the kidneys, stored in the bladder, and discharged through the kidneys.

urticaria: Hives.

uterus: The muscular organ that holds and nourishes the fetus, opening into the vagina through the cervix; the womb.

uvula: The small conical appendix attached to the free edge of the soft palate containing the uvular muscle.

vagina: The canal in the female extending from the uterus to the vulva; the birth canal.

vagus: The tenth cranial nerve; chief mediator of the parasympathetic system.

vas deferens: The spermatic duct of a testicle.

vascular: Relating to, or containing blood vessels.

vasoconstriction: The narrowing of the diameter of a blood vessel.

vasoconstrictor: A drug, nerve, hormone, or other agent that narrows the diameter of blood vessels.

vasodilator: A drug, nerve, hormone, or other substance that dilates or widens the diameter of blood vessels.

vasopressor: Any agent that raises the blood pressure by causing vasoconstriction.

vasovagal: Pertaining to the vagus nerve and blood vessels; a reflex caused by stimulation of the vagus nerve that slows the heart rate.

vasovagal attack: A syndrome consisting of hypertension, sweating, anxiety, nausea, and occasionally, syncope.

VD: Abbreviation for venereal disease.

vein: Any blood vessel that carries blood from the tissues to the heart.

venae cavae: The two largest veins of the body returning blood to the right atrium.
inferior vena cava: Principal vein returning blood from the lower portion of the body.
superior vena cava: Principal vein returning blood from the upper portion of the body.

venereal disease: A disease generally acquired through sexual intercourse with an infected partner; syphilis, gonorrhea, and chancroid are common ones; herpes II has become epidemic.

venipuncture: A surgical puncture of a vein for any purpose.

venom: A poison, usually derived from reptiles or insects.

venous blood: Unoxygenated blood, containing hemoglobin in the carboxyhemoglobin state.

ventilation: Breathing; supplying fresh air to the lungs.

ventilatory assistance: A means of providing or improving ventilation during respiratory failure.

ventricles: The thick-walled, muscular chambers in the heart that receive blood from the atrium and force blood into the arteries; also any small cavities; cerebral chambers containing cerebrospinal fluid.

ventricular aneurysm: A localized dilation or ballooning of the wall of the ventricle, usually the left.

ventricular fibrillation: A rapid, tremulous, and ineffectual contraction of the cardiac myofibrils, producing no cardiac output; cardiac arrest.

ventricular standstill: Asystole; no muscular contraction of the ventricles.

ventricular tachycardia: A serious cardiac arrhythmia with rapid, regular, or slight irregular, ventricular contractions; AV dissociation is present, and often there is no cardiac output.

Venturi mask: A brand of breathing unit that has a graduated valve for setting a specific concentration of oxygen delivered through the mask.

venule: A very small vein.

vertebra: Any one of the 33 bones of the spinal column.
cervical vertebrae: The upper 7 vertebrae, forming the skeleton of the neck.
coccygeal vertebrae: The 3 to 5 lower rudimentary vertebrae of the vertebral column that form the coccyx or tail bone.
lumbar vertebrae: The 5 vertebrae of the vertebral column between the thoracic and sacrum.
sacral vertebrae: The 5 fused vertebrae of the vertebral column that form the sacrum, a part of the pelvic girdle.
thoracic vertebrae: The 12 vertebrae of the vertebral column between the cervical vertebrae and the lumbar vertebrae.

vertebral: Pertaining to the vertebrae.

vertebral arch: The posterior projection of each vertebra through which the spinal cord passes.

vertebral body: The round solid bone forming the front part of the vertebra; articulates with the cartilagenous pads between the vertebrae.

vertebral spine: The bony projection dorsal to the arch; the spinous process of the vertebra.

vertigo: A dizziness; an hallucination of movement; a sensation as if the external world is spinning; may be right or left, upward to downward.

viable: Living; capable of living.

vial: A small glass container.

virus: A group of minute structures of living proteins capable of infecting most animal and plant kingdoms, characterized by a lack of independent metabolism and by a complete dependence on live cells to reproduce.

viscera: The internal organs of the body.

visceral pleura: The serous membrane covering the lungs; produces the pleural fluid.

vital capacity: The volume of air that can be forcefully expelled from the lungs following a full inspiration.

vital signs: The indication of life through values that reflect mental status, blood pressure, pulse rate, and respiration rate and depth.

vitreous fluid: A jellylike, transparent substance filling the inside of the eyeball.

vocal cords: Either of two pairs of folds of mucous membrane in the larynx that project into the cavity of the larynx; activated by the passing of air over the folds, causing vibration; source of the voice sound.

voice box: The larynx.

volume expander: The intravenous fluid that stays in the vascular space, usually a colloid, but can be an isotonic fluid with electrolytes.

voluntary: Of, relating to, or acting under obedience to the will.

voluntary commitment: The commitment of a patient to a hospital for treatment or observation with the patient's consent.

voluntary muscle: Any muscle that functions under the control of the will.

vomiting: A forceful, active expulsion of stomach contents through the mouth, as opposed to regurgitation, which is passive.

vomitus: The matter ejected from the stomach by vomiting.

vulnerable period: The interval during the relative refractory period of the ventricular repolarization corresponding to the downcurve of the ventricular repolarization wave, the T wave, in which ventricular fibrillation is produced by an ectopic impulse or other strong stimulus.

vulva: The external parts of the female genitalia.

watt: A unit of electrical energy obtained by multiplying amperes by volts.

watt-seconds: A unit of electrical energy expressed as watts per second delivered.

wheeze: A high-pitched, whistling sound characterizing an obstruction or spasm of the lower airways.

wheezing: Breathing noisily and with difficulty.

wind-chill factor: The relationship of wind velocity and temperature in determining the effect of the factor on a living organism.

windpipe: The trachea.

white blood cell: Leukocyte; cellular element of the blood that produces antibodies and participates in the inflammatory responses.

withdrawal: A symptom produced by abstinence from a drug to which one is addicted, or has been taking.

womb: The uterus.

wrist: The joint or the region of the joint between the forearm and the hand.

xiphoid process: A sword-shaped cartilaginous process at the lowest portion of the sternum that ossifies in the aged and has no ribs attached to it.

X-ray: Electromagnetic radiation; roentgen ray.

zygomatic bone: The cheekbone; the malar bone.

zygomatic process of the frontal bone: The massive projection from the supraorbital margin of the frontal bone that articulates with the zygomatic bone.

Index